TRANSFORMATIVE APPLIED RESEARCH IN COMPUTING, ENGINEERING, SCIENCE AND TECHNOLOGY

TRANSFORMATIVE APPLIED RESEARCH IN COMPUTING, ENGINEERING, SCIENCE AND TECHNOLOGY

Proceedings of International Conference on Transformative Applied Research

Editors
Dr. Damayanthi Dahanayake
Editor in Chief
Dr. Miruna Rabindrakumar
Associate Editor

CRC Press
Taylor & Francis Group
Boca Raton London New York

CRC Press is an imprint of the
Taylor & Francis Group, an **informa** business

First edition published 2024
by CRC Press
4 Park Square, Milton Park, Abingdon, Oxon, OX14 4RN

and by CRC Press
2385 NW Executive Center Drive, Suite 320, Boca Raton FL 33431

CRC Press is an imprint of Informa UK Limited

British Library Cataloguing-in-Publication Data
A catalogue record for this book is available from the British Library

ISBN: 978-1-041-01781-3 (hbk)
ISBN: 978-1-041-01782-0 (pbk)
ISBN: 978-1-003-61636-8 (ebk)

DOI: 10.1201/9781003616368

Typeset in Times LT Std
by Aditiinfosystems

Contents

Transformative Applied Research in Computing, Engineering, Science and Technology – Dr. Damayanthi Dahanayake et al. (eds)
© 2024 Taylor & Francis Group, London, ISBN 978-1-041-01782-0

List of Figures

Transformative Applied Research in Computing, Engineering, Science and Technology – Dr. Damayanthi Dahanayake et al. (eds)
© 2024 Taylor & Francis Group, London, ISBN 978-1-041-01782-0

List of Tables

Transformative Applied Research in Computing, Engineering, Science and Technology – Dr. Damayanthi Dahanayake et al. (eds)
© 2024 Taylor & Francis Group, London, ISBN 978-1-041-01782-0

Preface

On behalf of the Organizing Committee of the 1st International Conference on Transformative Applied Research (ICTAR) 2024, it is our great pleasure to welcome all the authors and delegates to this pioneering event hosted by the Research Council of NSBM Green University, Sri Lanka. This conference is a culmination of international collaboration and academic excellence, dedicated to addressing pressing global challenges through applied research and innovation.

Under the theme of "**Breaking Boundaries: Pioneering Solutions for Global Challenges**," the conference provides a dynamic platform for academics, researchers, and professionals to present and exchange their ideas, and discuss cutting-edge research that spans a wide range of disciplines to reshape communities and industries. Over the course of the event, we aim to foster dialogue and explore innovative solutions on a variety of themes that drive progress in the modern world.

The papers included in these proceedings underwent a rigorous double-blind review process, ensuring that the contribution reflect the highest standards of scholarship and innovation.

We are also pleased to highlight that the highest-scoring papers will be published in a special issue by Taylor & Francis, further amplifying the impactful research presented at the conference. These efforts demonstrate the conference's commitment to academic integrity.

We extend our heartfelt gratitude to our chief guest, keynote speaker, panelists, and participants whose insights and experiences have greatly enriched our discussions. We also wish to acknowledge the tireless efforts of the organizing committee, the reviewers, and the volunteers who made this conference a success. We are confident that the research shared here will inspire new ideas and collaborations that will pave the way for a more sustainable and innovative future.

We wish all participants a stimulating and rewarding conference experience.

The conference organizing committee
ICTAR 2024

Transformative Applied Research in Computing, Engineering, Science and Technology – Dr. Damayanthi Dahanayake et al. (eds)
© 2024 Taylor & Francis Group, London, ISBN 978-1-041-01782-0

Message From Vice-Chancellor

PROF. E.A. WEERASINGHE,
VICE-CHANCELLOR,
NSBM GREEN UNIVERSITY, HOMAGAMA, SRI LANKA.

In today's era defined by rapid advancements and unprecedented global challenges, fostering a scientific culture is fundamental in driving innovation, shaping policy, and providing solutions to complexities that impede progress. In this transformative process, universities act as epicentres of knowledge generation and innovation, fostering inquiry and collaboration that ultimately influences global growth trajectories.

To contribute to this goal, the Research Council at NSBM Green University has taken the initiative to host its inaugural International Conference on Transformative Applied Research (ICTAR). This conference provides a valuable platform for exchanging ideas, building collaborations, and shaping the future of applied research.

ICTAR 2024 is unfolding in an era world as a whole faces shared challenges that are increasingly interconnected and demand urgent solutions. Within this context, ICTAR 2024, themed "Breaking Boundaries; Pioneering Solutions for Global Challenges" emphasizes the need for collaborative and innovative approaches that transcend national and disciplinary lines to facilitate knowledge exchange and develop effective solutions for the benefit of humanity. Consequently, I believe this international conference is timely, bringing together a diverse community of scholars to explore innovative methods and breakthroughs in applied research across various fields.

I am confident that ICTAR 2024 will benefit the university's research culture through significant enhancement and contribute to the development of our nation. Hence, I would like to make this an opportunity to extend my heartiest congratulations to the organizing committee for establishing this platform for experts in different fields to gather.

Most importantly, I express my sincere appreciation to all the presenters and delegates for enriching ICTAR 2024 with their insightful presentations, engaging discussions, and collegial relationships. I wish you all a highly informative and productive conference and genuinely hope that you create many fond memories during your time with us, as this conference is poised to continue for many years to come.

Thank You..!

Transformative Applied Research in Computing, Engineering, Science and Technology – Dr. Damayanthi Dahanayake et al. (eds)
© 2024 Taylor & Francis Group, London, ISBN 978-1-041-01782-0

Message From Deputy Vice-Chancellor

PROF. CHAMINDA RATHNAYAKE,
DEPUTY VICE- CHANCELLOR,
NSBM GREEN UNIVERSITY, HOMAGAMA, SRI LANKA.

It is with great pleasure that I share this message for the first-ever International Conference on Transformative Applied Research (ICTAR) 2024, organized by the Research Council at NSBM Green University. This conference signifies an important milestone not only for the university but also for the broader academic community and society at large.

We are undeniably living in an era that calls for concerted efforts and innovative solutions from scholars, researchers, and practitioners alike to address significant challenges and build a sustainable foundation for future generations.

As a premier academic hub in the region, NSBM Green University is always dedicated to inspiring current and future generations of leaders, foster an environment that encourages the creation of new knowledge through cutting-edge research and innovation, and contribute Mactively to shaping the direction of a sustainable world.

With the theme "Breaking Boundaries; Pioneering Solutions for Global Challenges," ICTAR 2024 represents a new chapter for NSBM and encapsulates our commitment to exploring novelty and innovation across a wide range of disciplines. By providing such a vital knowledge platform, we aim to cultivate and share profound, thought-provoking ideas and discussions among a wide array of local and international scholars.

As we embark on this exciting journey together, I eagerly anticipate a fruitful conference of timely and informatively essential. I extend my warmest wishes to the organizing committee for their hard work and dedication, as well as to all attendees of ICTAR 2024. I sincerely hope this inaugural endeavour marks a significant milestone in NSBM's history and lays the groundwork for many more successful conferences in the years to come.

Thank you..!

Message from the Head of Academic Development and Quality Assurance

PROF. J. BARATHA DODANKOTUWA,
CHIEF ADVISOR, ICTAR-2024,
HEAD- ACADEMIC DEVELOPMENT AND QUALITY ASSURANCE,
NSBM GREEN UNIVERSITY, HOMAGAMA, SRI LANKA.

It is with great pleasure and immense pride that I extend my warmest greetings to the International Conference on Transformative Applied Research (ICTAR) 2024 at NSBM Green University. Building on the success achieved through numerous international conferences hosted by NSBM over the years, I sincerely hope that this inaugural initiative, organized by the Research Council, will leave a lasting impact by fostering new knowledge and developing strategies that inspire decisive actions.

At the core of NSBM's ethos is a robust research culture that is both impactful and socially relevant. Since its inception, the university has dedicated itself to addressing pressing issues faced by communities by nurturing both new and existing knowledge across a variety of disciplines. ICTAR 2024 stands to play a crucial role in these ongoing efforts, bringing together local and international experts eager to engage in meaningful discussions on transformative actions that can positively impact society and contribute to a more sustainable future.

Embracing the responsibility of steering development through sustainable solutions, ICTAR 2024 has been organized under the theme "Breaking Boundaries; Pioneering Solutions for Global Challenges." This theme aims to foster scientific solutions that effectively tackle pressing challenges while delivering measurable real-world benefits.

I express my heartfelt appreciation to the Organizing Committee for their tireless efforts in bringing this significant event to fruition. As I congratulate all participants of ICTAR 2024, I genuinely hope that this conference will be another rewarding endeavour that brings us closer to addressing some of the complex challenges facing humanity today. Together, let us seize this opportunity to collaborate, innovate, and inspire one another in our quest for a brighter future for all.

Thank You..!

Transformative Applied Research in Computing, Engineering, Science and Technology – Dr. Damayanthi Dahanayake et al. (eds)
© *2024 Taylor & Francis Group, London, ISBN 978-1-041-01782-0*

Message from the Conference Chair

DR. RASIKA RANAWEERA,
CONFERENCE CHAIR, ICTAR-2024
NSBM GREEN UNIVERSITY, HOMAGAMA, SRI LANKA.

It is with great honor and pleasure that I welcome you to the inaugural International Conference on Transformative Applied Research (ICTAR) 2024, hosted at NSBM Green University. This event represents a significant step forward in our collective commitment to advancing applied research and fostering collaboration among scholars, practitioners, and industry leaders.

We are excited to showcase a diverse array of articles submitted by both local and international researchers. Following a rigorous double-blind review process, we look forward to presenting the best works, which will be published in Taylor and Francis. This not only highlights the quality of research being conducted but also positions our conference as a vital platform for sharing innovative ideas and findings.

The theme of this year's conference, "Breaking Boundaries: Pioneering Solutions for Global Challenges," is designed to inspire meaningful discussions that bridge gaps across multidisciplinary research areas. In these challenging times, it is essential that we come together to share insights and develop solutions that drive progress and innovation.

I would like to express my heartfelt gratitude to several key individuals who have played an instrumental role in making this conference possible. My sincere thanks go to our Vice Chancellor, Prof. E. A. Weerasinghe; Deputy Vice Chancellor, Prof. Chaminda Rathnayaka; and Prof. J. Baratha Dodankotuwa, Head of Academic Development and Quality Assurance. Their unwavering support and vision for enhancing research capabilities at our university have been invaluable. My sincere gratitude goes to our chief guest, Prof. Sivalingam Sivananthan and keynote speaker, Prof. G. Neelika Malavige. I also want to acknowledge the hard work of the organizing committee members and the research council of NSBM Green University whose dedication has ensured that every detail of the conference has been meticulously planned. Your efforts are truly appreciated.

Finally, I extend my gratitude to all participants for contributing to the success of ICTAR 2024. I hope you find the sessions enriching and leave with lasting memories of your time with us. We look forward to seeing you at NSBM Green University in the near future.

Thank You..!

Transformative Applied Research in Computing, Engineering, Science and Technology – Dr. Damayanthi Dahanayake et al. (eds)
© 2024 Taylor & Francis Group, London, ISBN 978-1-041-01782-0

Message from the Editor-in-Chief

DR. DAMAYANTHI DAHANAYAKE,
EDITOR-IN-CHIEF, ICTAR-2024
HEAD- RESEARCH COUNCIL,
NSBM GREEN UNIVERSITY, HOMAGAMA, SRI LANKA.

It is with great enthusiasm that I welcome you to the 1st International Conference on Transformative Applied Research (ICTAR) 2024, hosted by the Research Council of NSBM Green University, Sri Lanka. This event marks a significant milestone in our university's academic calendar, focusing on international collaboration and innovation under the theme "Breaking Boundaries: Pioneering Solutions for Global Challenges."

ICTAR 2024 has received an impressive 150 full paper submissions across ten tracks, representing fields like Computer Science, Engineering, Science, and Management. Through a rigorous double-blind review process, the top papers have been selected for publication by Taylor and Francis, a testament to our commitment to academic excellence. This process highlights the hard work of our national and international reviewers, ensuring the high standard of the conference proceedings.

As Editor-In-Chief, I am honored to lead this conference, bringing together esteemed academics and forward-thinkers from around the world. I extend my heartfelt gratitude to our leadership team, including the Vice-Chancellor, Deputy-Vice Chancellor, Head of Academic Development and Quality Assurance, Deans of the faculties, and the Conference Chair, for their unwavering support. I also extend my heartfelt gratitude to our chief guest, keynote speaker, the organizing committee, and everyone involved in making this event a success. A special thanks to our Associate Editor, reviewers, and co-chairs for their meticulous efforts in ensuring the quality of the review process.

I proudly present the top-selected proceedings of ICTAR 2024, which reflect cutting-edge research and spirited discussions. I hope these inspire further collaboration and innovation, propelling us toward a sustainable and brighter future in applied research.

Thank You..!

Transformative Applied Research in Computing, Engineering, Science and Technology – Dr. Damayanthi Dahanayake et al. (eds)
© 2024 Taylor & Francis Group, London, ISBN 978-1-041-01782-0

Organizing Committee

Advisory Board

Prof. E.A. Weerasinghe - Vice Chancellor
Prof. Chaminda Rathnayake - Deputy Vice Chancellor
Prof. J. Baratha Dodankotuwa - Head, Academic Development & Quality Assurance

Conference Committee

Prof. J. Baratha Dodankotuwa - Conference Chief Advisor
Dr. Rasika Ranaweera - Conference Chair/ Dean, Faculty of Postgraduate Studies & Professional Advancement
Dr. Damayanthi Dahanayake - Conference Editor-in-Chief
Dr. Miruna Rabindrakumar - Conference Associate Editor
Dr. Bhagya Deepachandi - Conference Co-chair
Dr. Malsha Mendis - Conference Co-chair
Mr. Chamara Disanayaka - Conference Co-chair
Ms. Piyumi Wickramasinghe - Conference Co-chair
Ms. Kaumadee Samarakoon - Conference Secretary
Ms. Sachini Malsha Thennakoon - Conference Secretary
Ms. Thilini De Silva - Dean, Faculty of Business
Prof. Chaminda Wijesinghe - Dean, Faculty of Computing
Dr. Chandana Perera - Dean, Faculty of Engineering
Dr. Nuwanthi Katuwavila - Dean, Faculty of Science

Editorial Committee

Dr. Rasika Ranaweera
Dr. Damayanthi Dahanayake
Dr. Miruna Rabindrakumar
Dr. Bhagya Deepachandi
Dr. Samindi Jayawickrama

Dr. Malsha Mendis
Dr. Nadeesha Hettiarachchi
Mr. Chamara Disanayaka
Mr. W.M. Dinuka Nuwan
Ms. Sachini Malsha Thennakoon

Designed By:

Mr. Ashika K. Witiwalarachchi
Ms. Semini Siriwardana
Mr. Osanda Sandaruwan
Ms. Savindri Weerakoon

Transformative Applied Research in Computing, Engineering, Science and Technology – Dr. Damayanthi Dahanayake et al. (eds)
© 2024 Taylor & Francis Group, London, ISBN 978-1-041-01782-0

Review Board

Dr. Malithi Fonseka, *Intel Corporation, USA*

Dr. Malsha Mendis, *NSBM Green University, Sri Lanka*

Dr. Manori Perera, *University of Sri Jayewardenepura, Sri Lanka*

Dr. Manuja Gunawardana, *University of Moratuwa, Sri Lanka*

Dr. Medha Gunarathna, *University of Kelaniya, Sri Lanka*

Dr. Mohamed Shafraz, *NSBM Green University, Sri Lanka*

Dr. Mohamed Fazil Mohamed Firdhous, *University of Moratuwa, Sri Lanka*

Dr. Nadeeka Jayaweera, *University of Moratuwa, Sri Lanka*

Dr. Vikum Premalal, *University of Sri Jayewardenepura, Sri Lanka*

Dr. Vindya Udalamaththa, *Spectrum Institute of Science and Technology, Sri Lanka*

Dr. Vishal Mahale, *Sandip Institute of Engineering and Management, India*

Dr. Wijendra Gunathilaka, *Kothalawala Defence University, Sri Lanka*

Dr. Thamali Perera, *University of Sri Jayewardenepura, Sri Lanka*

Dr. Tharindunee Jayakody, *University of Colombo, Sri Lanka*

Dr. Thilina Thanthriwatta, *University of Moratuwa, Sri Lanka*

Dr. Tilani Gunawardena, *University of Peradeniya, Sri Lanka*

Dr. Udeshika Bandara, *NSBM Green University, Sri Lanka*

Dr. Umayal Branavan, *University of Colombo, Sri Lanka*

Dr. Upamali Peiris, *Wayamba University of Sri Lanka, Sri Lanka*

Dr. Upul Jayasinghe, *University of Peradeniya, Sri Lanka*

Dr. Sulochana Sooriyaarachchi, *University of Moratuwa, Sri Lanka*

Ms. Kalaimani Rabindrakuamar Lakshmi Lashini, *Uptime SL (PVT) Ltd, Sri Lanka*

Ms. Kaumadee Samarakoon, *NSBM Green University, Sri Lanka*

Ms. Kumara Vidanalage Jeeva Ekanayake, *The Open University of Sri Lanka, Sri Lanka*

Ms. Lahiruni Ranasinghe, *University of New South Wales, Australia*

Ms. Maheshika Maduwanthi Ranige, *University of Sri Jayewardenepura, Sri Lanka*

Ms. Neranga Hettiwatta, *Sabaragamuwa University of Sri Lanka, Sri Lanka*

Ms. Nimasha Arambepola, *University of Kelaniya, Sri Lanka*

Ms. Niwanthika Ranasinghe, *University of Moratuwa, Sri Lanka*

Dr. Thelma Abeysinghe, *The Open University of Sri Lanka, Sri Lanka*

Dr. Chamila Kadigamuwa, *University of Kelaniya, Sri Lanka*

Dr. Chitraka Wickramarachchi, *University of Sri Jayewardenepura, Sri Lanka*

Dr. Dilanka Fernando, *Monash University, Australia*

Dr. Jayalath Ekanayake, *Uva Wellassa University, Sri Lanka*

Dr. Ranjith Perera, *Uva Wellassa University, Sri Lanka*

Dr. Thilina Gunathilaka, *University of Colombo, Sri Lanka*

Dr. Kushani De Silva, *University of Colombo, Sri Lanka*

Dr. Duleepa Pathiraja, *University of Colombo, Sri Lanka*

Dr. G.G.W. Chamali Wijesekara, *The Open University of Sri Lanka, Sri Lanka*

Dr. Gayan Priyadarshana, *University of Sri Jayewardenepura, Sri Lanka*

Dr. Himalshi Rupasinghe, *Kothalawala Defence University, Sri Lanka*

Dr. Induni Siriwardane, *University of Kelaniya, Sri Lanka*

Dr. Kalpa Samarakoon, *Kothalawala Defence University, Sri Lanka*

Dr. Kachchakaduge Deshani Fernando, *Mid-America Christian University, USA*

Dr. Kaneeka Vidanage, *Kothalawala Defence University, Sri Lanka*

Dr. Kanishka Senarath, *Augusta University, Medical College of Georgia, Georgia*

Dr. Kanishka Senathilake, *University of Colombo, Sri Lanka*

Dr. Kasun Amarasinghe, *Carnegie Mellon University, USA*

Dr. Kasun Thambugala, *University of Sri Jayewardenepura, Sri Lanka*

Dr. Kaveesha Wijesinghe, *University of Colombo, Sri Lanka*

Transformative Applied Research in Computing, Engineering, Science and Technology – Dr. Damayanthi Dahanayake et al. (eds)
© 2024 Taylor & Francis Group, London, ISBN 978-1-041-01782-0

Keynote Address

PROF. G. NEELIKA MALAVIGE
DEPARTMENT OF IMMUNOLOGY & MOLECULAR MEDICINE,
FACULTY OF MEDICAL SCIENCES,
UNIVERSITY OF SRI JAYEWARDENEPURA, SRI LANKA

Many lower middle-income countries (LMICs) such as Sri Lanka, face significant challenges due to non-communicable diseases and infectious diseases. Climate change and rapid urbanization worsen the burden of vector borne infections such as dengue, zika and chikungunya, while changes in lifestyle are significantly increasing the burden due to cardiovascular disease, diabetes, dementia and taking a toll on mental health. To navigate these existing and emerging challenges globally, it is crucial that all countries should carry out research and innovations to overcome these challenges.

Unfortunately, very limited investments are being made for research and development (R and D) in Sri Lanka, as seen in many low-income and LMICs. Limited investments in R and D leads to limited funds for research, poor infrastructure, limited access to technology, which subsequently leads to lack of innovations, limited career progress for scientists, brain drain and the existing problems getting worse each day. The situation is further worsened by highly bureaucratic procurement processes, limited supply chains, high taxation of research reagents and again the lengthy process and multiple permissions required in grant approvals, and clearing of research reagents. All these setbacks make countries like Sri Lanka, less competitive in the global research market. Furthermore, inequalities in research collaborations, colonial science, biases towards scientists by policy makers in their own countries, further complicate the existing challenges. The solutions to these problems cannot happen overnight.

While multiple challenges exist to limit progress, this does not mean that it is impossible to carry out impactful research in countries like ours. It is important to find our strengths and weaknesses and where we have a strategic advantage. We should encourage international collaboration are done in a manner where there is true capacity building, technology transfer and led or co-led by our scientists. Most importantly, we must have a culture of nurturing each other and especially younger scientists, who find it extremely difficult to obtain funds and establish themselves in the modern highly competitive world. It is a culture of collaboration and not unhealthy competition, that will help us to face the existing and evolving challenges.

Thank You..!

Transformative Applied Research in Computing, Engineering, Science and Technology – Dr. Damayanthi Dahanayake et al. (eds)
© 2024 Taylor & Francis Group, London, ISBN 978-1-041-01782-0

1

A Review on the Effects of Adverse Childhood Experiences on Young Adults' Self-Esteem and Anxiety

BLDKP Thilakawardana
Department of Life Sciences, NSBM Green University,
Sri Lanka

Lakshani Jayasinha*
Department of Health Sciences, NSBM Green University,
Sri Lanka

Abstract

Adverse Childhood Experiences (ACEs) are stressful circumstances children encounter up to the age of 18 years. These adverse experiences can have a toll on mental and physical well-being in later stages. Recent research suggests that negative childhood experiences relate to a greater risk of poor self-esteem, and this relationship can be mediated by challenges with emotional regulation and a diminished sense of self-identity. Thus, the present review aims to synthesize existing research to explore the relationship between ACEs and mental health outcomes such as self-esteem and anxiety. Adverse experiences such as physical abuse, emotional abuse, sexual abuse, neglect, and dysfunction in the family can lead to anxiety in young adulthood and beyond. These traumatic experiences can result in persistent stress and changes in brain function, raising the likelihood of anxiety disorders and several other mental health issues. Negative views of oneself can lead to constant self-doubt and concern. This highlights the link between low self-esteem to anxiety. Individuals with low self-esteem may view events as more dangerous, leading to anxiety and avoidance behaviors. Healthcare providers and families could take action to avoid and lessen the harmful consequences on young adults' mental health by detecting the association between adverse childhood experiences, anxiety, and self-esteem.

Keywords

Adverse childhood experiences, Anxiety, Low self-esteem, Maltreatment, Negative self-image

1. Introduction

Adverse childhood experiences are uncomfortable situations that children face, involving safety, stability, and bonding. The CDC-Kaiser Adverse Childhood Experience study proclaims that over 60% of the respondents reported at least one ACE and a total of 12.5% had more than four ACEs [1]. The prevalence of adverse childhood

---

*Corresponding author: lakshani.j@nsbm.ac.lk

DOI: 10.1201/9781003616368-1

experiences is more common in South Asian countries than in other parts of the world, due to limited child protective services, cultural differences, and gender inequalities [2]. The World Health Organization states that three in four children between the ages of 2 and 4 years constantly experience physical or psychological maltreatment from their parents or caregivers, and more girls than boys have suffered from sexual abuse before the age of 17 years [3]. Adverse childhood experiences can affect negatively later in life [4]. Recent research has focused on how emotional and physical trauma have negatively influenced distress symptoms (low self-esteem, depression, and anxiety) and behavioral issues. The leading outcomes of adverse childhood experiences include mental health problems and substance abuse [5]. Individuals who have had many adverse experiences feel less focused in life [6]. A study found that each category of adverse experience in childhood was associated with some form of violence in adulthood [7]. Since childhood is a critical development period that influences adult health and wellness, reliable adverse childhood experience evaluations are critical to improve clinical diagnosis [8]. Adverse childhood experiences can cause low self-esteem in later stages of life, and this review focuses mainly on how traumatic events in childhood can lead to low self-esteem and anxiety in young adults.

Self-esteem can be defined as an individual's favorable or negative impressions of themselves [9]. Self-esteem can have an impact on healthy relationships and mental well-being. Adverse childhood experiences cause emotions of guilt, shame and worthlessness which have a negative impact on one's ability to retain healthy self-esteem. The Self-Regulation Shift Theory states that a stress factor that exceeds the threshold can result in low self-esteem in an individual who has previously experienced adversities [10]. Findings suggest childhood neglect is related to dysfunctional patterns of emotions leading to low self-esteem in later years [11]. A study done in the UAE indicate that participants who have experienced childhood maltreatment show signs of poor self-esteem, and depressive symptoms. It also states that physical maltreatment can be high in uneducated households [12]. A study indicates that the most common adverse childhood experience is family dysfunction. It also shows that female adults who have experienced adversities in their childhood are at a higher risk of developing low self-esteem in later years than males [13]. Another study suggests that adult females who have experienced childhood maltreatment have more issues in their adult love relationships than those with no negative childhood experiences which leads to low self-esteem [14].

Anxiety is a normal reaction to stress or danger, and it may help individuals to deal with potentially dangerous circumstances. However, when anxiety becomes extreme, it can disrupt daily activities and lead to anxiety disorders. Different types of anxiety disorders include generalized anxiety, phobias, separation anxiety, social anxiety, and panic disorder etc. Young adults who were psychologically or physically abused as children are more prone to acquire anxiety disorders, and data shows that even individuals with remitted anxiety disorders can relapse [15]. Adverse childhood experiences contribute equally to all the above-mentioned types of anxiety disorders. [16]. Understanding the effect of adversity in childhood on anxiety is critical, as is providing appropriate therapies and support to help them cope with the lasting effects of their trauma.

2. Methodology

This systematic review adhered to the Preferred Reporting Items for Systematic Reviews and Meta-Analyses (PRISMA) guidelines to ensure a comprehensive approach to synthesizing the literature. The present review focused on understanding the relationships between Adverse Childhood Experiences (ACEs) and self-esteem, ACEs and anxiety, self-esteem and anxiety, as well as any other factors associated with ACEs.

To conduct this review, a thorough search of electronic databases, including PubMed, PsycINFO, and Scopus, was performed. The search utilized combinations of keywords such as "Adverse Childhood Experiences," "Childhood Trauma," "Self-Esteem," "Anxiety," and "Young Adults" to locate relevant peer-reviewed articles. Studies assessing the impact of ACEs on self-esteem and/or anxiety, published in peer-reviewed journals and focusing on young adults aged 18-30, were included in this systematic review. Studies from any of the paradigms—quantitative, qualitative, and mixed-methods—were considered.

Studies that did not specifically address ACEs or their effects on self-esteem and anxiety, as well as those focusing on populations outside the specified age range, were excluded from the review. Selected articles (titles and abstracts) were independently reviewed twice to screen for eligibility based on the inclusion and exclusion criteria. The studies selected for this review were assessed based on their relevance to the research question, the quality of evidence, and their alignment with the review's focus on the psychological impact of ACEs. Discrepancies between reviewers were resolved through discussion. Data were synthesized to summarize the findings from the included studies.

3. Results

3.1 Adverse Childhood Experiences

Adverse childhood experiences are negative events like physical or sexual abuse, abandonment, being raised in a family of domestic abusers, parent separation, and drug misuse encountered in childhood that cause negative effects in adult life [17]. Recent studies have demonstrated that adverse experiences in childhood can result in a variety of undesirable outcomes in early adulthood [18]. Some of the effects include mental health problems, physical health problems (heart disease, diabetes, and obesity), various relationship issues, academic problems, and financial difficulties [19]. According to research, negative childhood events can have a long-term influence on the brain, particularly in regions connected to emotion regulation and stress response [20]. Multiple studies have found that having poor socioeconomic or caregiving situations as a child increases the probability of developing chronic health problems as an adult, which can lead to sickness and death [21]. According to the cognitive model, negative comments play a significant role in posttraumatic stress disorder (PTSD) in children and adults in Sri Lanka [22]. Over three out of every four students in high school in the United States were found to suffer from at least one type of adverse childhood experience, with one in 13 suffering from four or more adverse experiences [23]. Gender and degrees of emotional abuse showed substantial interaction effects. Girls showed worse mental health and well-being due to emotional abuse than boys [24]. Emotional abuse such as verbal insults, threats, and neglect is much more common in girls than boys. Supporting children who have been ill-treated in their upbringing is crucial to their academic and personal development. Schools must develop a safe and supportive learning environment for children suffering from ACEs, which includes offering trauma-informed care, counseling services, and specialized assistance [25].

3.2 Association between Adverse Childhood Experiences and Self-Esteem

It is proven that adverse childhood experiences can eventually result in low self-esteem in later stages of life. Self-esteem develops during childhood and is impacted by diverse experiences and relationships such as cultural diversity, educational diversity, and socioeconomic diversity [26]. For example, a child who is subjected to physical abuse may believe that they are incapable of defending themselves or that they are deserving of punishment. This view can lead to feelings of inferiority and inadequacy, which emerge as poor self-esteem in young adulthood. If the child's experiences are not acknowledged, or if they are blamed for the abuse or neglect, they have suffered, they may believe that their feelings and experiences are invalid. This lack of affirmation can lead to a lack of confidence in others and a continuous sense of worthlessness. Lack of support and affirmation from parents or caregivers may increase the effects of negative childhood experiences on self-esteem. Children who suffered parental rejection and neglect were inclined to have poor self-esteem in adulthood, even after other forms of ACEs were controlled for [27]. Low self-esteem caused because of childhood adversities is a frequent issue that may afflict young adults and harm their personal and professional lives. Individuals with poor self-esteem seek negative comments from their life partners to validate their bad self-esteem concept [28]. People who engage in negative self-talk have lower self-esteem than those who engage in positive self-talk. Criticizing oneself for earlier errors, concentrating on personal weaknesses, and comparing oneself to others are all examples of negative self-talk [29]. Individuals who had been ill-treated as children show high levels of depression, which led to lower self-esteem. Addressing depressive symptoms in young adults who had negative childhood experiences may assist in improving self-esteem. According to a Chinese study, the influence of adversities in childhood on low self-esteem is higher on males than the effect on females [30]. In contrast, another Chinese research stated that male college students who have suffered from adverse childhood experiences have lower self-esteem than female students, due to different coping mechanisms, emotional expressions, social support, societal expectations and gender norms [31]. Supportive relationships with family, friends, and peers tend to cause higher self-esteem in individuals than those who do not, because supportive relationships provide a sense of connection and affirmation in those who have suffered from childhood trauma. It can assist individuals feel more confident in themselves and their abilities [32]. Based on the available evidence, three conclusions can be drawn on the influence of adverse childhood experiences on self-esteem. Firstly, self-esteem tends to increase drastically up to adulthood, reach its peak at middle adulthood, and decline rapidly as a person enters old age. Furthermore, the development of self-esteem does not seem to alter considerably among different generations. Secondly, while self-esteem is a relatively stable characteristic, it is not entirely fixed; at some point in life, individuals are likely to maintain the level of self-esteem. Finally, having high self-esteem can improve a person's achievements and wellness in areas such as work, relationships, and health [33].

3.3 Association between Adverse Childhood Experiences and Anxiety

Individuals suffering from anxiety are on high alert until the situation is handled, stimulating mental defense systems which results in profoundly anxious, negative emotional states [34]. Young adults with extremely high levels of anxiety may express symptoms such as abdominal pain, dizziness, headache, throat ache, weakness in legs, raised heart rate, and shortness of breath. Adverse experiences in childhood and anxiety share a strong relationship that can progress into adulthood. According to a survey done on college students, those suffering from four or more adverse childhood experiences are more likely to acquire anxiety and depression [35]. Individuals who had experienced adversity in childhood, such as neglect or assault, showed alterations in the Hypothalamic- Pituitary- Adrenal (HPA) axis, which increased their vulnerability to stress and anxiety in later stages. The HPA axis is a neuroendocrine system involved in the stress response, as an individual experiences a stressful situation the HPA axis activates to help cope with the situation [36]. A study discovered that negative cognitive evaluations, such as a poor self-image and a pessimistic vision of the future, were mediated by childhood trauma and anxiety [37]. Adults who had suffered childhood trauma had impaired connection between the prefrontal cortex and the amygdala, which are important in regulating emotional response. This decreased connection gives rise to anxiety and depressive symptoms in adulthood [38]. Some people may use alcohol to temporarily reduce anxiety symptoms caused due to adverse childhood experiences. Yet it is proven that alcohol can actually worsen anxiety with time. Research states that the frequency of self-medication with alcohol and narcotics among individuals suffering from anxiety disorders due to childhood maltreatment varies from 21.9% to 24.1% [39]. Social support can be used to eliminate anxiety caused by adverse childhood experiences [40]. Supportive family and friends operate as a protective barrier, which helps to reduce the occurrence of anxiety disorders. Anxiety can be generated by a mix of hereditary, environmental, and psychological factors. Understanding the mechanism behind the association allows the creation of more effective therapies and support networks for individuals who have experienced childhood trauma.

3.4 Relationship between Anxiety and Self-Esteem

There is a proven relationship between anxiety and self-esteem. Individuals with poor self-esteem are more prone to suffer from anxiety [41]. Poor self-esteem can cause individuals to be doubtful about themselves, and their talents, and concern about how others view them, which can add to feelings of anxiety. Anxiety can also lead to poor self-esteem because people may believe their anxiety symptoms make them weaker or less capable than others. Social media may worsen feelings of anxiety, depression, and poor self-esteem, especially when people compare their lives to the idealized images of others that are frequently displayed on social media [42]. This might result in a poor self-image and feelings of inadequacy. A study done on Vietnamese secondary school students proves that the level of self-esteem in students have been found to have a strong correlation with adverse psychological results such as anxiety, depression, and academic stress, which can have a detrimental impact on their overall well-being and even lead to suicidal thoughts [43]. Adults who have low self-esteem are more inclined to engage in risk-aversion activities such as avoiding social settings or not taking chances. These anxiety-relieving actions may bring momentary relief, but they can also reinforce negative thoughts and lead to additional decreases in self-esteem. Individuals with high self-esteem, on the other hand, are more likely to use positive coping techniques, such as seeking social support or applying problem-solving abilities, which can help reduce anxiety. Psychological therapy, pharmacotherapy, or combined therapy is used to help individuals to develop coping mechanisms for anxiety which may lead to the building of self-esteem [44]. Cognitive-behavioral therapy (CBT) is a proven strategy for ending the vicious cycle of anxiety and low self-esteem [45].

3.5 Association between Adverse Childhood Experiences and Other Variables

Individuals suffering from adverse childhood experiences frequently feel isolated and lonely, which can harm their self-esteem [46]. Although research indicates a substantial link between poor self-esteem and emotions of loneliness, it is unclear why low self-esteem leads to loneliness [47]. According to studies, people with low self-esteem often rely on parasocial relationships as a means of achieving personal growth that they may not attain through real-life relationships [48]. Self-esteem and depression are closely related. Yet there is not enough evidence on the nature of the relationship between low self-esteem may give rise to depressive symptoms according to the vulnerability model. It is a psychological framework used to understand the development of adverse outcomes [49]. Although low confidence can contribute to feelings of hopelessness, helplessness, and worthlessness, which are frequent symptoms of depression, it is not the only factor involved [50]. People experiencing depression may struggle to retain healthy self-esteem. According to a study, poor self-esteem leads to low psychological and physical health, aggressive conduct, and harmful real-world consequences [51]. Adverse childhood experiences can have an impact on attachment patterns, interpersonal connections, and cognitive performance, making people more susceptible to anxiety. Psychopathy is a group of behaviors that includes impulsive, antisocial behavior, and emotional qualities. According to previous research, adverse childhood experiences may play a role in the formation of psychopathic characteristics [52]. Specific adverse childhood experiences have been linked to a higher frequency of poor psychological health and suicidal behavior than others [53].

4. Conclusion

The above information demonstrated that adverse experiences during childhood can have a major influence on the onset of anxiety and low self-esteem in young adults. Adverse experiences like physical or psychological abuse, abandonment, and household dysfunction in childhood can lead to poor self-beliefs and poor self-esteem, which might result in the development of anxiety disorders. According to the findings, the relationship between anxiety and self-esteem is complicated. Anxiety can result in low self-esteem and poor self-esteem also contributes to anxiety. Individuals with low self-esteem usually talk negatively about themselves, which can lead to anxiety about social interactions or performances, whereas those with high self-esteem are more confident and are capable of managing anxiety well.

Effective interventions that address both anxiety and low self-esteem are important for improving mental health outcomes in young adults who have been ill-treated in their childhood. To help people identify and overcome negative self-talk, it is important to develop coping mechanisms for anxiety and boost their self-esteem. Cognitive behavioral therapy is one type of an effective coping mechanism that employs positive reinforcement and self-compassion. Early diagnosis and intervention are also crucial in addressing the long-term impacts of adverse childhood experiences on psychological outcomes. Young adults can be guided to overcome the negative consequences of unfavorable events and enhance their overall quality of life by providing them with the appropriate skills and support.

5. Future Directions

While there is a substantial body of research on how adverse childhood experiences can negatively affect self-esteem and anxiety, there are still gaps in the understanding of this relationship. A few gaps include the lack of diversity in samples or not much research done in South Asian countries, not all studies have covered the different types of adverse childhood experiences and how they affect self-esteem and anxiety, and less attention is given to resilience. Furthermore, focus must be given to understanding the influence of adverse childhood experiences on the rise of specific anxiety disorders. Addressing these gaps can help to understand the complex effects of adverse childhood experiences on self-esteem and anxiety.

REFERENCES

1. Y. Kim, H. Lee, and A. Park, "Patterns of adverse childhood experiences and depressive symptoms: self-esteem as a mediating mechanism," *Soc Psychiatry Psychiatr Epidemiol*, vol. 57, no. 2, pp. 331–341, 2022, doi: 10.1007/s00127-021-02129-2.
2. Arnab Roy, "Influence of Childhood Adverse Experiences and Resilience on Self-esteem in Early Adulthood," *International Journal of Indian Psychology*, vol. 6, no. 4, 2018, doi: 10.25215/0604.122.
3. "Child maltreatment," 2022.
4. S. Weber, A. Jud, and M. A. Landolt, "Quality of life in maltreated children and adult survivors of child maltreatment: a systematic review," *Qual Life Res*, vol. 25, no. 2, pp. 237–255, Feb. 2016, doi: 10.1007/S11136-015-1085-5.
5. E. Park, J. Lee, and J. Han, "The association betwee adverse childhood experiences and young adult outcomes: A scoping study," *Child Youth Serv Rev*, vol. 123, p. 105916, Apr. 2021, doi: 10.1016/J.CHILDYOUTH.2020.105916.
6. J. P. Davis, T. M. Dumas, and B. W. Roberts, "Adverse Childhood Experiences and Development in Emerging Adulthood," *Emerging Adulthood*, vol. 6, no. 4, pp. 223–234, Aug. 2018, doi: 10.1177/2167696817725608.
7. N. N. Duke, S. L. Pettingell, B. J. McMorris, and I. W. Borowsky, "Adolescent Violence Perpetration: Associations with Multiple Types of Adverse Childhood Experiences," *Pediatrics*, vol. 125, no. 4, pp. e778–e786, Apr. 2010, doi: 10.1542/PEDS.2009-0597.
8. D. Moreira *et al.*, "Relationship between adverse childhood experiences and psychopathy: A systematic review," *Aggress Violent Behav*, vol. 53, p. 101452, Jul. 2020, doi: 10.1016/J.AVB.2020.101452.
9. "Enhancement of Self-Image."
10. C. C. Benight, K. Shoji, and D. L. Delahanty, "Self-Regulation Shift Theory: A Dynamic Systems Approach to Traumatic Stress," *J Trauma Stress*, vol. 30, no. 4, pp. 333–342, Aug. 2017, doi: 10.1002/JTS.22208.
11. C. Yumbul, S. Cavusoglu, and B. Geyimcia, "The effect of childhood trauma on adult attachment styles, infidelity tendency, romantic jealousy and self-esteem," *Procedia Soc Behav Sci*, vol. 5, no. 2, pp. 1741–1745, 2010, doi: 10.1016/j.sbspro.2010.07.357.
12. S. M. Shah *et al.*, "Child maltreatment and neglect in the United Arab Emirates and relationship with low self-esteem and symptoms of depression," *International Review*

of Psychiatry, vol. 33, no. 3, pp. 326–336, 2021, doi: 10.1080/09540261.2021.1895086.

13. F. Khodabandeh, M. Khalilzadeh, and Z. Hemati, "Novelty in Biomedicine NBM The Impact of Adverse Childhood Experiences on Adulthood Aggression and Self-Esteem-A Study on Male Forensic Clients," *Novelty in Biomedicine*, vol. 2, pp. 85–91, 2018.

14. G. McCarthy and B. Maughan, "Negative childhood experiences and adult love relationships: The role of internal working models of attachment," *http://dx.doi.org/10.1080/14616734.2010.501968*, vol. 12, no. 5, pp. 445–461, 2010, doi: 10.1080/14616734.2010.501968.

15. E. Seidl *et al.*, "How current and past anxiety disorders affect daily life in adolescents and young adults from the general population—An epidemiological study with ecological momentary assessment," *Depress Anxiety*, vol. 38, no. 3, pp. 272–285, 2021, doi: 10.1002/da.23133.

16. A. K. Vallance and V. Fernandez, "anxiety disorders in children and adolescents: aetiology, diagnosis and treatment," *BJPsych Adv*, vol. 22, no. 5, pp. 335–344, 2016, doi: 10.1192/apt.bp.114.014183.

17. S. Lester, M. Khatwa, and K. Sutcliffe, "Service needs of young people affected by adverse childhood experiences (ACEs): A systematic review of UK qualitative evidence," *Child Youth Serv Rev*, vol. 118, no. June, p. 105429, 2020, doi: 10.1016/j.childyouth.2020.105429.

18. R. S. O'Neill, M. Boullier, and M. Blair, "Adverse childhood experiences," *Clinics in Integrated Care*, vol. 7, p. 100062, Aug. 2021, doi: 10.1016/J.INTCAR.2021.100062.

19. M. T. Merrick, K. A. Ports, D. C. Ford, T. O. Afifi, E. T. Gershoff, and A. Grogan-Kaylor, "Unpacking the impact of adverse childhood experiences on adult mental health," *Child Abuse Negl*, vol. 69, pp. 10–19, Jul. 2017, doi: 10.1016/J.CHIABU.2017.03.016.

20. C. P. Navalta, L. McGee, and J. Underwood, "Adverse Childhood Experiences, Brain Development, and Mental Health: A Call for Neurocounseling," *J Ment Health Couns*, vol. 40, no. 3, pp. 266–278, Jul. 2018, doi: 10.17744/MEHC.40.3.07.

21. G. Morris, M. Berk, M. Maes, A. F. Carvalho, and B. K. Puri, "Socioeconomic Deprivation, Adverse Childhood Experiences and Medical Disorders in Adulthood: Mechanisms and Associations," *Mol Neurobiol*, vol. 56, no. 8, pp. 5866–5890, 2019, doi: 10.1007/s12035-019-1498-1.

22. T. Ponnamperuma and N. A. Nicolson, "Negative Trauma Appraisals and PTSD Symptoms in Sri Lankan Adolescents," *J Abnorm Child Psychol*, vol. 44, no. 2, pp. 245–255, 2016, doi: 10.1007/s10802-015-9985-y.

23. K. N. Anderson *et al.*, "Adverse Childhood Experiences During the COVID-19 Pandemic and Associations with Poor Mental Health and Suicidal Behaviors Among High School Students — Adolescent Behaviors and Experiences Survey, United States, January–June 2021," *MMWR Morb Mortal Wkly Rep*, vol. 71, no. 41, pp. 1301–1305, Oct. 2022, doi: 10.15585/MMWR.MM7141A2.

24. J. M. Hagborg, I. Tidefors, and C. Fahlke, "Gender differences in the association between emotional maltreatment with mental, emotional, and behavioral problems in Swedish adolescents," *Child Abuse Negl*, vol. 67, pp. 249–259, 2017, doi: 10.1016/j.chiabu.2017.02.033.

25. J. Eccard, "Supporting Students with Adverse Childhood Experiences Within the Classroom," pp. 8–12, 2021.

26. Y. Kim, H. Lee, and A. Park, "Patterns of adverse childhood experiences and depressive symptoms: self-esteem as a mediating mechanism," *Soc Psychiatry Psychiatr Epidemiol*, vol. 57, no. 2, pp. 331–341, 2022, doi: 10.1007/s00127-021-02129-2.

27. Y. Lim and O. Lee, "Relationships between Parental Maltreatment and Adolescents' School Adjustment: Mediating Roles of Self-Esteem and Peer Attachment," *J Child Fam Stud*, vol. 26, no. 2, pp. 393–404, Feb. 2017, doi: 10.1007/S10826-016-0573-8/METRICS.

28. J. F. Sowislo and U. Orth, "Does low self-esteem predict depression and anxiety? A meta-analysis of longitudinal studies," *Psychol Bull*, vol. 139, no. 1, pp. 213–240, 2013, doi: 10.1037/A0028931.

29. F. Sánchez, F. Carvajal, and C. Saggiomo, "Self-talk and academic performance in undergraduate students," *Anales de Psicologia*, vol. 32, no. 1, pp. 139–147, 2016.

30. X. Zhang, C. Li, and W. Ma, "The Direct and Indirect Effects of Adverse Childhood Experiences on Depressive Symptoms and Self-esteem of Children: Does Gender Make a Difference?," *International Journal of Mental Health and Addiction 2022*, pp. 1–25, Jul. 2022, doi: 10.1007/S11469-022-00871-5.

31. J. Zhao, F. Kong, and Y. Wang, "The role of social support and self-esteem in the relationship between shyness and loneliness," *Pers Individ Dif*, vol. 54, no. 5, pp. 577–581, Apr. 2013, doi: 10.1016/J.PAID.2012.11.003.

32. R. Matos *et al.*, "At the 'risky' end of things: labelling, self-concept and the role of supportive relationships in young lives," *https://doi.org/10.1080/13676261.2023.2174007*, 2023, doi: 10.1080/13676261.2023.2174007.

33. U. Orth and R. W. Robins, "The Development of Self-Esteem," *https://doi.org/10.1177/0963721414547414*, vol. 23, no. 5, pp. 381–387, Oct. 2014, doi: 10.1177/0963721414547414.

34. A. N. Abdivalievna and B. X. R. Qizi, "Psychological characteristics of anxiety in medical studnets," *British Journal of Global Ecology and Sustainable Development*, vol. 13, pp. 71–75, Feb. 2023.

35. T. Watt, N. Ceballos, S. Kim, X. Pan, and S. Sharma, "The Unique Nature of Depression and Anxiety among College Students with Adverse Childhood Experiences," *J Child Adolesc Trauma*, vol. 13, no. 2, pp. 163–172, Jun. 2020, doi: 10.1007/S40653-019-00270-4/METRICS.

36. K. S. Dempster, D. D. O'Leary, A. J. MacNeil, G. J. Hodges, and T. J. Wade, "Linking the hemodynamic consequences of adverse childhood experiences to an altered HPA axis and acute stress response," *Brain Behav Immun*, vol. 93, pp. 254–263, Mar. 2021, doi: 10.1016/J.BBI.2020.12.018.

37. H. J. Huh, K. H. Kim, H. K. Lee, and J. H. Chae, "The relationship between childhood trauma and the severity of adulthood depression and anxiety symptoms in a clinical

sample: The mediating role of cognitive emotion regulation strategies," *J Affect Disord*, vol. 213, pp. 44–50, Apr. 2017, doi: 10.1016/J.JAD.2017.02.009.

38. M. H. Teicher and A. Khan, "Childhood Maltreatment, Cortical and Amygdala Morphometry, Functional Connectivity, Laterality, and Psychopathology," *https://doi.org/10.1177/1077559519870845*, vol. 24, no. 4, pp. 458–465, Sep. 2019, doi: 10.1177/1077559519870845.

39. S. Turner, N. Mota, J. Bolton, and J. Sareen, "Self-medication with alcohol or drugs for mood and anxiety disorders: A narrative review of the epidemiological literature," no. April, pp. 851–860, 2018, doi: 10.1002/da.22771.

40. R. Brunton, T. Wood, and R. Dryer, "Childhood abuse, pregnancy-related anxiety and the mediating role of resilience and social support," *https://doi.org/10.1177/1359105320968140*, vol. 27, no. 4, pp. 868–878, Nov. 2020, doi: 10.1177/1359105320968140.

41. A. Al Nima, P. Rosenberg, T. Archer, and D. Garcia, "Anxiety, Affect, Self-Esteem, and Stress: Mediation and Moderation Effects on Depression," *PLoS One*, vol. 8, no. 9, p. e73265, Sep. 2013, doi: 10.1371/JOURNAL.PONE.0073265.

42. B. Schivinski, M. Brzozowska-Woś, E. Stansbury, J. Satel, C. Montag, and H. M. Pontes, "Exploring the Role of Social Media Use Motives, Psychological Well-Being, Self-Esteem, and Affect in Problematic Social Media Use," *Front Psychol*, vol. 11, no. December, pp. 1–10, 2020, doi: 10.3389/fpsyg.2020.617140.

43. D. T. Nguyen, E. P. Wright, C. Dedding, T. T. Pham, and J. Bunders, "Low self-esteem and its association with anxiety, depression, and suicidal ideation in vietnamese secondary school students: A cross-sectional study," *Front Psychiatry*, vol. 10, no. SEP, pp. 1–7, 2019, doi: 10.3389/fpsyt.2019.00698.

44. D. S. Riggs, "Treatment of Anxiety Disorders," *Living and Surviving in Harm's Way: A Psychological Treatment Handbook for Pre- and Post-Deployment of Military Personnel*, no. 2017, pp. 211–237, 2009, doi: 10.4324/9780203893906-21.

45. C. Otte, "Cognitive behavioral therapy in anxiety disorders: Current state of the evidence," *Dialogues Clin Neurosci*, vol. 13, no. 4, pp. 413–421, 2011, doi: 10.31887/dcns.2011.13.4/cotte.

46. H. Du, X. Li, P. Chi, S. Zhao, and J. Zhao, "Loneliness and Self-Esteem in Children and Adolescents Affected by Parental HIV: A 3-Year Longitudinal Study," *Appl Psychol Health Well Being*, vol. 11, no. 1, pp. 3–19, Mar. 2019, doi: 10.1111/APHW.12139.

47. J. Vanhalst, K. Luyckx, R. H. J. Scholte, R. C. M. E. Engels, and L. Goossens, "Low self-esteem as a risk factor for loneliness in adolescence: Perceived - But not actual - Social acceptance as an underlying mechanism," *J Abnorm Child Psychol*, vol. 41, no. 7, pp. 1067–1081, Oct. 2013, doi: 10.1007/S10802-013-9751-Y/METRICS.

48. J. L. Derrick, S. Gabriel, and B. Tippin, "Parasocial relationships and self-discrepancies: Faux relationships have benefits for low self-esteem individuals," *Pers Relatsh*, vol. 15, no. 2, pp. 261–280, Jun. 2008, doi: 10.1111/J.1475-6811.2008.00197.X.

49. J. F. Sowislo and U. Orth, "Does low self-esteem predict depression and anxiety? A meta-analysis of longitudinal studies," *Psychol Bull*, vol. 139, no. 1, pp. 213–240, 2013, doi: 10.1037/A0028931.

50. J. O. K. Chung *et al.*, "Relationships among resilience, self-esteem, and depressive symptoms in Chinese adolescents," *J Health Psychol*, vol. 25, no. 13–14, pp. 2396–2405, Nov. 2020, doi: 10.1177/1359105318800159.

51. K. H. Trzesniewski, M. B. Donnellan, T. E. Moffitt, R. W. Robins, R. Poulton, and A. Caspi, "Low self-esteem during adolescence predicts poor health, criminal behavior, and limited economic prospects during adulthood," *Dev Psychol*, vol. 42, no. 2, pp. 381–390, 2006, doi: 10.1037/0012-1649.42.2.381.

52. D. Moreira *et al.*, "Relationship between adverse childhood experiences and psychopathy: A systematic review," *Aggress Violent Behav*, vol. 53, p. 101452, Jul. 2020, doi: 10.1016/J.AVB.2020.101452.

53. K. N. Anderson *et al.*, "Adverse Childhood Experiences During the COVID-19 Pandemic and Associations with Poor Mental Health and Suicidal Behaviors Among High School Students — Adolescent Behaviors and Experiences Survey, United States, January–June 2021," *MMWR Morb Mortal Wkly Rep*, vol. 71, no. 41, pp. 1301–1305, Oct. 2022, doi: 10.15585/MMWR.MM7141A2.

Transformative Applied Research in Computing, Engineering, Science and Technology – Dr. Damayanthi Dahanayake et al. (eds)
© 2024 Taylor & Francis Group, London, ISBN 978-1-041-01782-0

2

Application of Activated Charcoal-Chitosan Composite Material for the Pre-Esterification of Palm Oil Fatty Acid Distillate for the Production of Biodiesel

H. M. S. D. Herath
Department of Chemical Sciences,
South Eastern University of
Sri Lanka

T. M. M. Marso*
Department of Chemical Sciences,
South Eastern University of
Sri Lanka
Postgraduate Institute of Science,
University of Peradeniya,
Sri Lanka

Abstract

Biodiesel production from waste oil feedstocks with high free fatty acid (FFA) content, such as Palm Oil Fatty Acid Distillate (POFAD) often encounters issues with saponification, rendering the entire oil unusable. Reducing the FFA level via acid-catalyzed pre-esterification followed by base-catalyzed transesterification is the most effective solution to address this. Heterogeneous acids are preferred over homogeneous acids due to their greener approach. This study explores the use of an Activated Charcoal–Chitosan Composite (AC-Chitosan Composite) material for the pre-esterification of POFAD with methanol, enabling biodiesel production through a soap-free pathway. Catalyst characterization was performed using FTIR spectroscopy and Scanning electron microscopy. The catalytic study revealed a 97.14% reduction in the acid value of POFAD, from 128.58 to 3.65 mg KOH g^{-1} over four catalytic cycles (2 hours) under mild reaction conditions (45 °C, 400 rpm, 5% catalyst by oil weight, 50% methanol by oil weight). Additionally, the catalyst demonstrated easy recovery and reusability, confirming its heterogeneous nature. More importantly, this pre-esterification method effectively prevents saponification issues typically associated with biodiesel conversion from waste POFAD, achieving a high biodiesel yield of 84.6% and meeting international standards for practical application.

Keywords

AC-Chitosan composite, Biodiesel, POFAD, Pre-esterification

*Corresponding author: marso@seu.ac.lk

DOI: 10.1201/9781003616368-2

1. Introduction

The exploration of renewable, sustainable, and clean energy sources has intensified in response to the pressing issues associated with traditional energy sources. Biodiesel has emerged as a promising alternative, offering a potential solution to mitigate environmental concerns [1] and reduce dependency on petroleum-based diesel fuels [2]. Moreover, biodiesel presents a viable option for powering engines currently reliant on conventional diesel, addressing a critical need for sustainable transportation solutions [3].

The utilization of waste feedstocks for biodiesel production has gained traction due to economic viability, with feedstock accounting for approximately 70% of the total production cost [4]. Among the various potential waste feedstocks for biodiesel production, Palm Oil Fatty Acid Distillate (POFAD) stands out as a promising candidate. It is a by-product of the palm oil refining process, offering accessibility, affordability, and avoiding competition with food sources [5]. Like other waste and non-edible feedstocks, POFAD poses challenges, notably high acidity (primarily in the form of free fatty acids (FFA)), moisture, and other solid impurity levels [5].

Direct conversion of such feedstocks into biodiesel via base-catalyzed transesterification is hindered by irreversible saponification reactions, leading to reduced biodiesel yields [6]. While acid-catalyzed transesterification offers an alternative to prevent saponification, it requires higher energy input and extended reaction times, increasing production costs [7]. To overcome these challenges, a two-step approach involving acid-catalyzed pre-esterification followed by base-catalyzed transesterification has emerged as the most suitable pathway for feedstocks with high acidity levels [8]. The pre-esterification step aims to reduce acid levels to a desired threshold, thereby minimizing soap formation during subsequent transesterification.

Traditionally, sulfuric acid has been used as the homogeneous acid catalyst in the pre-esterification process due to its availability and efficiency. However, it has several drawbacks, including corrosiveness, non-reusability, the need for special systems to recover methanol and water, difficulties in the separation and purification of biodiesel, the necessity of neutralizing sulfuric acid at high temperatures, and requiring a large amount of base during the transesterification process [9,10]. These issues can be resolved by substituting a heterogeneous base catalyst for the homogeneous acid catalyst. Heterogeneous catalysts offer several advantages, such as easy separation from the reaction mixture, reusability, and stability under reaction conditions, thus preventing undesirable reactions [11].

This work primarily aims to investigate the potential of Activated Charcoal-Chitosan Composite materials for POFAD pre-esterification to produce biodiesel via a soap-free pathway. Additionally, it assesses the physicochemical properties of the produced biodiesel to evaluate its quality.

2. Methodology

2.1 Materials

POFAD was obtained from the waste oil pit of a local palm oil production facility. To purify the POFAD, it underwent centrifugation to separate the upper oil layer from the heavy sludge deposit, followed by filtration (Whatman® qualitative filter paper, Grade 1). Prawn shells and coconut shell-based activated charcoal (BET surface area: 1219 m^2 g^{-1}, Extractable pH: 10, particle size distribution (% by vol.) +325 mesh - 1.7%, -325 mesh - 98.3%, ash (% by wt.) 2.9%, moisture (% by wt.) 3.3%) were acquired from local seafood processing plants and activated charcoal manufacturers, respectively. All chemicals used for chemical analysis and material synthesis were of analytical-grade quality.

2.2 Synthesis and Characterization of the Materials

Chitosan Extraction

The collected prawn shell samples were thoroughly washed with fresh water and dried under sunlight for 12 hours. The dried samples were then ground into a fine powder and sieved through 60-120 μm mesh. Chitosan extraction was carried out according to the modified procedure from the work reported by Rashmi et al. [12] and Poeloengasih et al. [13] involving deproteinization, demineralization, decolorization, and finally deacetylation. *Deproteinization:* The sample was treated with a 4% NaOH solution (1:10 m/v) at room temperature for 24 hours with constant stirring. The resultant sample was washed with distilled water until the pH of the washings became neutral. *Demineralization:* The deproteinized sample was then treated with a 4% HCl solution (1:10 m/v) at ambient conditions. The solution was stirred for 16 hours to remove minerals, and the pH was adjusted to neutral by washing the demineralized sample with distilled water to obtain raw chitin. This raw chitin was then dried at room temperature. *Purification:* The dried raw chitin was further purified by treating it with 2% NaOH and 1% HCl solutions, followed by washing with distilled water for about 2 hours to obtain pure chitin. *Decolorization:* The chitin was treated with acetone with stirring. *Deacetylation:* The pure chitin samples were then subjected to deacetylation by treating them with a 65% NaOH solution (1:5 m/v) at ambient conditions with stirring for 36 hours. The alkali-treated samples were washed with distilled water until the pH reached neutral. Finally, the chitosan samples were dried at room temperature.

Preparation of Oxidized Activated Charcoal

In a glass container, 2.5 g of activated charcoal was mixed with 50 mL of a 0.5 M, H_2SO_4(aq) solution and continuously stirred. A 0.5 M, $KMnO_4$(aq) solution was then added dropwise to the mixture, with stirring maintained until the externally added $KMnO_4$ was fully decolorized. The temperature of the reaction mixture was kept at 50 °C using a hot water bath. After oxidation, the charcoal sample was thoroughly washed with distilled water while stirring until the washings reached a neutral pH. Finally, the oxidized charcoal was dried in an oven at 110 °C to remove any adsorbed moisture.

Preparation of Activated Charcoal-Chitosan Composite (AC-Chitosan Composite)

Initially, 2.5 g of oxidized activated charcoal was added to 7.5 mL of a 3% gel chitosan solution (prepared by dissolving 3 g of chitosan in 100 mL of 10% acetic acid). The mixture was agitated using a shaker for 24 hours. Following this, the mixture was filtered, washed with distilled water, and dried. This process of treating the material with the gel chitosan solution was repeated three times to further develop the composite. After the three successive treatments, the resulting solid material was immersed in 0.5% NaOH for 3 hours to neutralize it, then filtered and washed with distilled water to achieve a neutral substrate. The final composite was dried at 110 °C until a constant weight was achieved.

Characterization of Solid Catalyst

FTIR Spectroscopic (Thermo Fisher Scientific, NicoletTM iG50) and scanning electronic microscopic (ZEISS EVO LS15) characterizations were conducted for solid samples.

2.3 Pre-esterification of POFAD

Procedure

A 100 mL portion of purified POFAD was placed into a 500 mL round-bottom flask equipped with a reflux condenser. The flask was submerged in a constant-temperature water bath and connected to a magnetic stirrer. The mixture was stirred continuously at 400 rpm until the desired temperature of 45 °C was reached. Next, 50% (v/v oil) methanol was added, and the stirring speed was adjusted to ensure a thorough blending of the oil and methanol phases. Then, 5% (by oil wt.) of the prepared composite was added to the reaction mixture while maintaining the designated temperature. The reaction was allowed to proceed for 2 hours. Upon completion, the reaction mixture was

separated from the deposited solid catalyst and transferred to a separation funnel. The resultant liquid was left to stand for 1 hour to allow the unreacted methanol to separate into the upper layer.

Four cycles were conducted on the resultant oil product under the same reaction conditions and using the same recovered catalyst until the desired acid value (4 mg KOH g^{-1}) suitable for the transesterification reaction was achieved. Similarly, three trials were conducted following the aforementioned procedure to validate the accuracy of the results obtained. Additionally, the same reaction was conducted without a catalyst and with 1% (oil wt.) H_2SO_4 serves as a homogeneous catalyst for comparative analysis.

Solid Catalyst Recovery

Utilized solid catalysts were washed five times with a solvent mixture containing toluene, isopropyl alcohol (IPA), and water in a 100:99:1 volume ratio. After the final wash, the catalysts were heated at 160 °C for 15 minutes to completely remove any adsorbed solvent molecules.

Evaluate the Reaction Progress

The percentage reduction of acid value ($\Delta AV\%$) was used to evaluate the progress of the pre-esterification reaction and determined as per Equation (1) shown below.

$$\Delta AV\% = \{(AV_i - AV_f)/AV_i\} \times 100\% \qquad (1)$$

Where, AV_i and AV_f are acid values of initial and final products, respectively.

The acid value of the oil product was assessed using the titrimetric method as per the ASTM D974-2014 procedure [14].

2.4 Transesterification

Transesterification was conducted using the same reactor setup as the pre-esterification process. The esterified oil was transferred to the reaction container and gradually heated to 45 °C while continuously stirring at 400 rpm. A solution consisting of 1% (w/w oil) KOH pellets (>97%) dissolved in 25% (v/v oil) methanol was introduced dropwise into the esterified oil, maintaining the temperature at 45 °C. The stirring speed was adjusted to ensure thorough blending of the oil and methanol phases for 2 hours.

2.5 Separation and Purification of Crude Biodiesel

The trans-esterified reaction mixture was transferred to a separatory funnel and allowed to undergo gravity-based separation for 24 hours. This process yielded an upper layer (crude biodiesel) and a lower layer (crude glycerine). The separated crude biodiesel was then subjected to three rounds of washing with hot water (in a ratio of 1 part oil to

3 parts water by volume) until the resulting washing water reached a neutral state. Subsequently, the biodiesel sample was left to stand for an additional 24 hours to facilitate the removal of any separated water. The resulting refined biodiesel sample was then analyzed for its fuel quality parameters.

2.6 Physicochemical Characterization

The purified biodiesel (B100) was evaluated for selected physicochemical parameters using ASTM test methods, and the results were compared with ASTM 6751 specifications. Additionally, FTIR (Thermo Fisher Scientific, NicoletTM iG50) analysis of the purified biodiesel was performed.

3. Discussion

3.1 Synthesis and Characterization of the Materials

According to the results, 25% of chitosan was successfully extracted from the selected prawn shell sample, aligning with values reported in the literature [15]. Additionally, the extracted chitosan was observed to be an off-white, lightweight, finely powdered substance, consistent with descriptions in previous studies [16]. The physical appearance of the product obtained after each step of the chitosan production process, removing colour impurities is shown in Fig. 2.1.

The chemical structures can be further verified using FTIR data (Fig. 2.2) obtained from the product at each stage of the extraction process. The FTIR peak appearing at 1633 cm^{-1}, corresponding to carbonyl bond vibrations, is observed until the development of the chitin structure and then disappears in chitosan. This confirms the removal of the acetyl group from its main structure (chitin deacetylation).

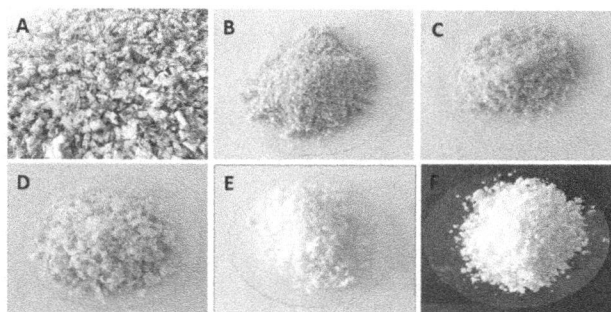

Fig. 2.1 The physical appearance of the product obtained after each step of the chitosan extraction process: A. washing of prawn shells, B. deproteinization, C. demineralization, D. purification, E. decolorization, and F. deacetylation

Additionally, during the conversion from chitin to chitosan, the peak at 1539 cm^{-1} disappears, and a broad, strong peak around 1423 cm^{-1} appears. These changes are due to the in-plane bending of the N-H bonds (scissoring). During deacetylation, the amide group converts into an amine, causing a change in the chemical environment and a shift of the peak towards lower wavenumbers. This indicates the structural changes during the conversion from chitin to chitosan [17].

Activated charcoal, also known as activated carbon, has a highly porous structure characterized by a large surface area. Its chemical structure is complex and consists of a network of carbon atoms with various functional groups, including hydroxyl, carbonyl, ester, lactone, epoxide, and carboxylic groups [18, 19]. During the preparation of the composite structure, activated charcoal was oxidized using a strong oxidizing agent (H_2SO_4/$KMnO_4$) to convert functional groups with lower oxidation states, such as

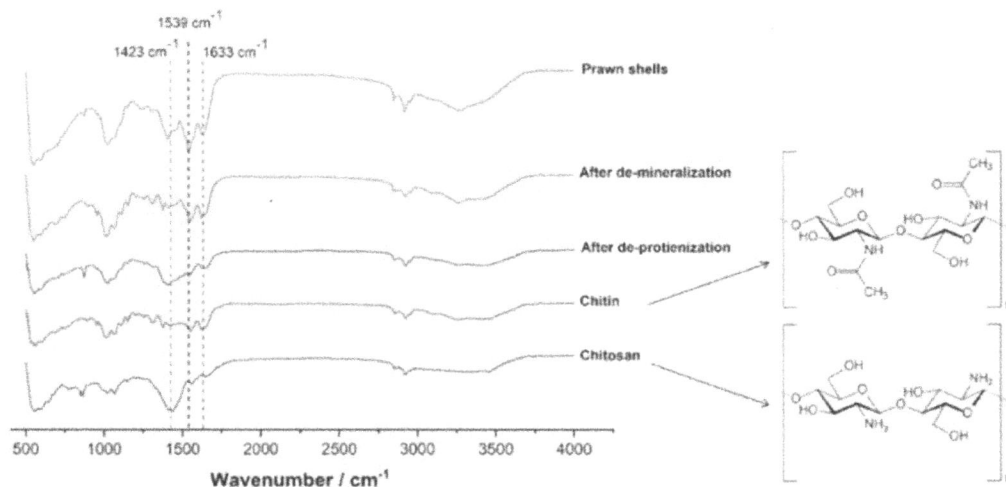

Fig. 2.2 FTIR spectra of initial, intermediate, and final products obtained during Chitosan production

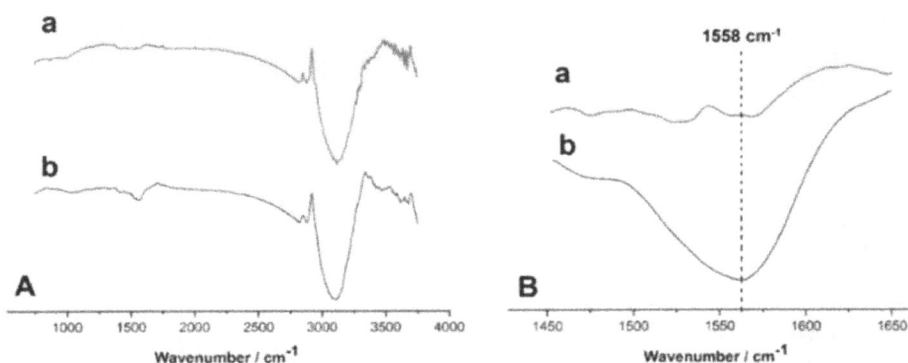

Fig. 2.3   FTIR spectra of a. activated charcoal and b. chemically oxidized activated charcoal in A. 400-3750 cm^{-1} and B. 1450-1650 cm^{-1} wavenumber region

hydroxyl and aldehyde groups, into carboxylic groups. The FTIR spectrum of chemically oxidized activated charcoal (Fig. 2.3) reveals the appearance of a new peak at 1558 cm^{-1}. This peak is indicative of carboxylate ions (R-COO$^-$), which exhibit an asymmetric stretching vibration in this region. This observation provides evidence confirming the occurrence of further oxidation [20].

Additionally, during the chemical oxidation process, when acidic KMnO$_4$ (Purple) is added to activated charcoal with continuous stirring at 50 °C, a sudden decolorization occurs, indicating the reduction of KMnO$_4$ to Mn^{2+}. During the subsequent washing process, the medium is made basic to remove excess acidity. In this basic medium,

Mn^{2+} is oxidized in the presence of dissolved oxygen as per Equation (2) [21];

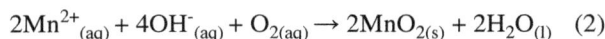

$$2Mn^{2+}_{(aq)} + 4OH^-_{(aq)} + O_{2(aq)} \rightarrow 2MnO_{2(s)} + 2H_2O_{(l)} \quad (2)$$

This reaction is confirmed by the observation of a brown, gelatinous solid forming during the washing step of the composite.

In the composite formation, it is expected that the oxidized activated charcoal and chitosan link via amide and ester bond formation, as illustrated in Fig. 2.4. The formation of amide bonds is confirmed by the FTIR spectrum, which shows a strong and broad peak at 3334 cm^{-1}, corresponding to N-H stretching vibrations (Fig. 2.5). Additionally, a

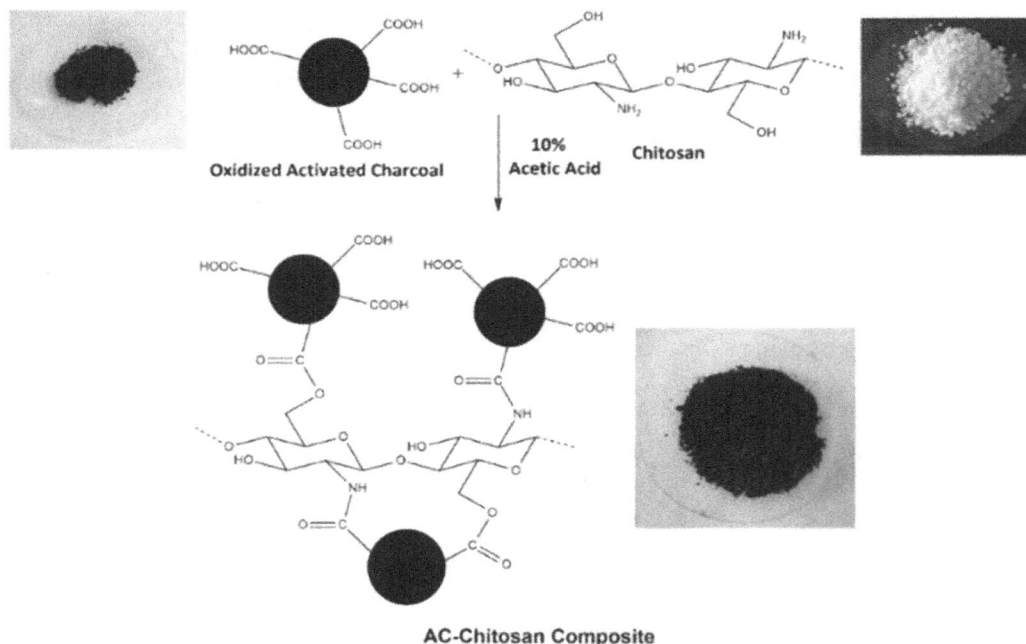

Fig. 2.4   A suggested mechanism for the formation of AC-Chitosan composite and the appearance of the solid products obtained during the process

broad, strong peak at 1427 cm^{-1}, attributed to the in-plane bending (scissoring) of the N-H bonds in the amine group [17] of the extracted chitosan, has disappeared. This confirms the successful esterification through the amine end during the composite formation.

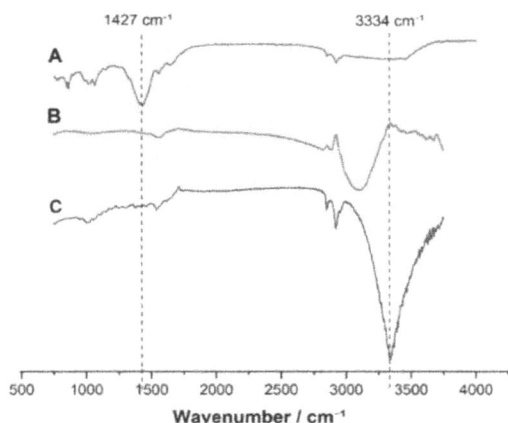

Fig. 2.5 FTIR spectrum of: A. oxidized activated charcoal, B. chitosan, and C. AC-chitosan composite

As shown in Fig. 2.4, during the formation of the composite, its appearance, colour, and shape become distinct from the original materials. The dark black colour of activated charcoal lightens, and the powdered form transforms into spherical bead-like structures.

The surface morphological changes during the material's development were further validated using scanning electronic microscopic (SEM) techniques. SEM images (Fig. 2.6) confirm the alterations in surface morphology, particularly the formation of a porous structure in the composite material. This suggests an increase in specific surface area compared to the original raw material.

This morphological change results from the incorporation of chitosan and the agglomeration of charcoal particles into rounded shapes. These modifications make the composite easier to handle for the esterification reaction. Unlike chitosan and activated charcoal, which remain suspended in the oily product, the composite settles to the bottom when agitation stops. This allows for easy separation from the final product and improves recoverability.

3.2 Conversion of POFAD into Biodiesel

During the pre-esterification reaction, FFAs are expected to esterify with methanol. In addition to that, the highly polar fragments present in the POFAD are anticipated to extract the unreacted methanol layer, which then separates and forms a layer on top of the oil (Fig. 2.7. B, C, and D). Consequently, a reduction in the available acidic components, which can react with alcoholic KOH during AV determination titration, is expected. This reduction, used to measure the progress of the reaction, is illustrated in Fig. 2.8. Observations from Fig. 2.8. A and B indicate the effect of the catalyst on the pre-esterification

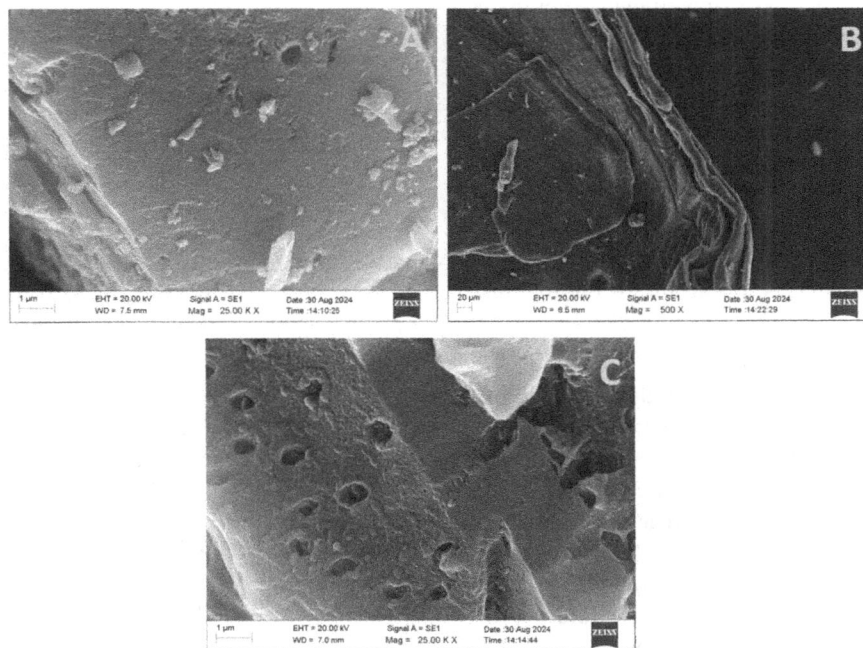

Fig. 2.6 SEM images of A. Activated charcoal, B. Synthesized chitosan, and C. AC-Chitosan composite

Fig. 2.7 The physical appearance of: A. POFAD, B. pre-esterified mixture without catalyst, C. pre-esterified mixture with H_2SO_4 acid, D. pre-esterified mixture composite, E. product obtained direct transesterification, product obtained after transesterification when oil is pre-esterified in the presence of F. H_2SO_4 acid and G. composite

reaction, showing a significant difference in performance with and without the catalyst. Although the H_2SO_4 acid-catalyzed pathway is considered less environmentally friendly, it achieves higher conversion efficiency compared to the heterogeneously catalyzed pathway. H_2SO_4 (1% by oil wt.) and the composite catalyst (5% by oil wt.) required 3 and 4 reaction cycles, respectively, to achieve the desired acid value (less than 4 mg KOH g^{-1}) for safe soap-free transesterification. This observation arises because a homogeneous catalyst interacts effectively with the reactants throughout the reaction. In contrast, a heterogeneous catalyst can have its surface saturated by reactants and other impurities during the reaction, which inhibits the active sites of the catalyst and reduces its efficiency.

The yield of pure biodiesel obtained through different pre-esterification pathways is mentioned in Table 2.1. Direct alkaline-catalyzed transesterification (no pre-esterification step) of POFAD oil faces issues like saponification (Fig. 2.7. E), leading to reaction retardation, separation challenges, and ultimately significant reduction in biodiesel yield. The pre-esterified mixture without any catalyst also does not reduce the acid value to the desired level and hence faces saponification during the transesterification step. In contrast, the introduction of

Table 2.1 Yield of purified biodiesel obtain via different pre-esterification methods

Pre-esterification method	Average Biodiesel Yield ± SD/ %
Without pre-esterification	7.67 ± 2.52
Without any catalyst	54.01 ± 5.30
Presence of H_2SO_4 catalyst	91.33 ± 0.58
Presence of composite catalyst	84.66 ± 3.06

a catalyst during pre-esterification lowers the acidity of POFAD to a negligible level, making the oil suitable for base-catalyzed transesterification. This pre-esterified oil experiences minimal saponification during base-catalyzed transesterification, preventing the negative effects seen with direct alkaline-catalyzed transesterification (Fig. 2.7. F and G). The product obtained from the composite-catalyzed pathway (Fig. 2.7. F) is purer compared to that from the H_2SO_4-catalyzed pathway (Fig. 2.7. G). In the H_2SO_4-catalyzed process, impurities such as oxidized and reduced fragments from the H_2SO_4 acid, salts formed by reactions between H_2SO_4 and KOH, and other polar components present in POFAD accumulate in the final product. This accumulation complicates the post-washing procedure.

This saponification of POFAD primarily occurs due to the high FFA content of the feedstock (128.58 mg KOH

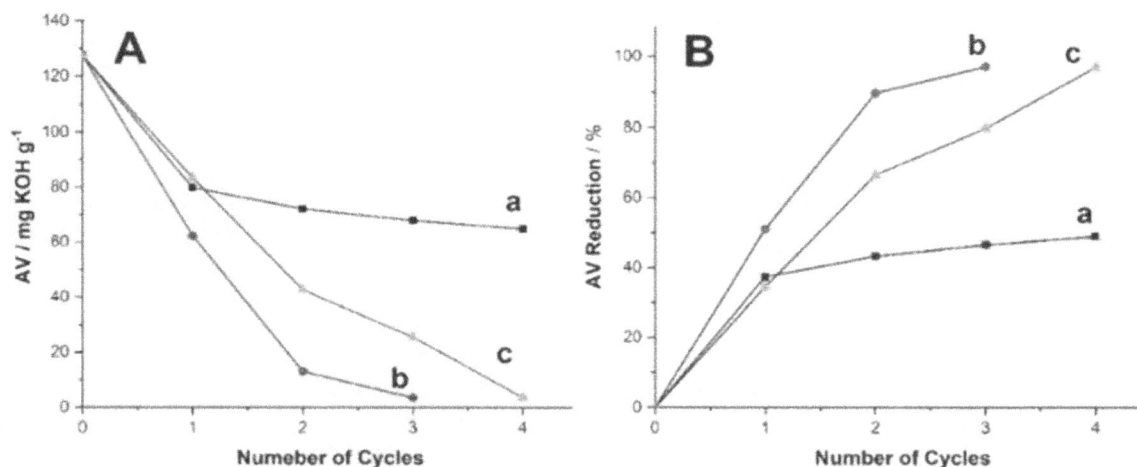

Fig. 2.8   A. Acid value variation and B. % acid value reduction after each cycle of pre-esterification a. without any catalyst, b. with H_2SO_4 catalyst, and c. AC-Chitosan catalyst

g^{-1}). During base-catalyzed transesterification, FFA reacts with the base to form soap (Equation 3), which is a highly favorable and irreversible reaction [22]. The soap produced, being a polar product, is washed away during the washing step, reducing the yield. Additionally, the water generated during the reaction accelerates the base-catalyzed hydrolysis of triglycerides (TG) and fatty acid methyl esters (FAME), producing more FFA, which can further react to form soap [23].

$$RCOOH + NaOH \rightarrow RCOO^-Na^+ + H_2O \qquad (3)$$

3.3 Separation and Purification of Crude Biodiesel

Crude biodiesel was purified using a water-washing technique to remove polar components from the crude sample. During the washing process, a color reduction from ASTM color 3.5 to 2.0 was observed, indicating improved clarity and the removal of impurities (Fig. 2.9). These polar impurities can cause emulsions and gum formation when used in engines, leading to fuel injector blockages, reactions with engine components, and potential engine

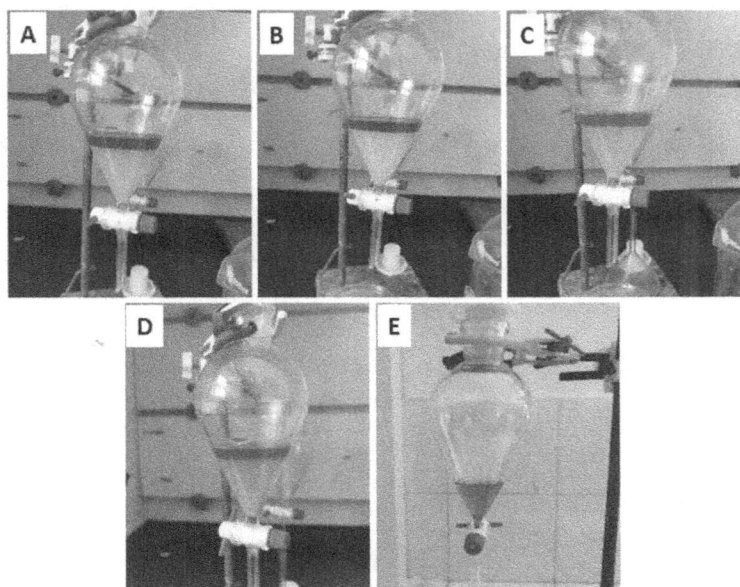

Fig. 2.9   The appearance of the product after the A. 1st washing, B. 2nd washing, C. 3rd washing, D. 4th washing, and E. final purified sample

malfunctions [24]. Furthermore, storing biodiesel with such polar components may result in undesirable reactions, such as ester hydrolysis and double bond oxidation, which can cause suspensions and deposits in the biodiesel sample [25]. Therefore, proper post-purification of raw biodiesel is essential to improve the quality and durability of produced biodiesel.

3.4 Physiochemical Characterization Of Biodiesel

The fuel quality parameters of the refined biodiesel, obtained through the AC-Chitosan composite-catalyzed pre-esterification pathway, were assessed. All parameters met ASTM standards. The values are presented in Table 2.2.

Table 2.2 Values of physicochemical parameters of biodiesel (B100)

No.	Property	Test Method	B100 Requirement as per ASTM 6751 Specifications	Observed Value
1	Flashpoint (^{0}C)	ASTM D93	Min 130	145
2	Kinematic Viscosity at 40 ^{0}C (mm^2 sec^{-1})	ASTM D445	1.9 - 6.0	5.3835
3	Density at 15 ^{0}C (kg m^{-3})	ASTM D1298	860 - 900	862.5
4	Cu Strip corrosion	ASTM D130	Max No. 3	No.1
5	Color	ASTM D 1500	N/A	2.5
6	Calorific value (kJ kg^{-1})		N/A	40.23

The FTIR spectral analysis (Fig. 2.10) of the oily product at each stage of biodiesel production elucidates the purity of the product. The peak observed at 1743 cm^{-1} in the FTIR spectrum corresponds to the stretching vibration of the carbonyl group (C=O) [26], signifying the presence of ester functional groups within the molecule. Peak broadening may occur due to the association of various functional groups with the ester molecule, contributing to a diverse chemical environment [27]. In the raw oil and esterified oil, a broad peak is evident due to the presence of different esters. Such compounds may be present in minor quantities as impurities. However, during transesterification, these impurities may be separated, potentially accumulating in a glycerine phase. Consequently, the sharpening of this peak indicates an improvement in the oil's purity, serving as an additional indicator of biodiesel quality.

4. Conclusion

The Activated Charcoal-Chitosan Composite (AC-Chitosan Composite) produced from work reported herein demonstrates efficient catalytic activity for the pre-esterification of Palm Oil Fatty Acid Distillate (POFAD) with methanol, achieving a 97.14% acid value reduction from 128.58 to 3.65 mg KOH g^{-1} over four catalytic cycles (2 h) under mild reaction conditions (45°C, 400 rpm, 5% catalyst by oil wt., 50% methanol by oil wt.). The catalyst could be easily recovered and reused, confirming its heterogeneous nature. More importantly, pre-esterified oil from this method avoids the saponification issues typically associated with converting biodiesel from waste POFAD, resulting in a high biodiesel yield of 84.6% and meets international standard requirements ensuring its practical applicability.

Acknowledgment

The authors gratefully acknowledge the financial support provided by the South Eastern University of Sri Lanka through the research grant SEU/ASA/RG/2023/04.

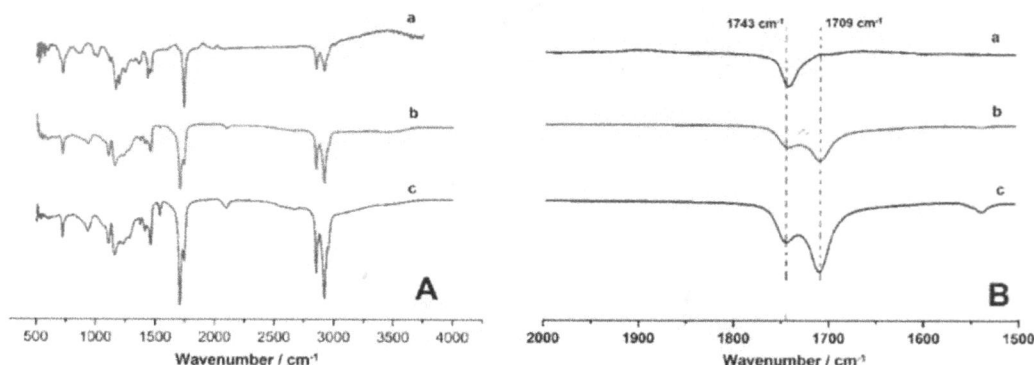

Fig. 2.10 FTIR spectra of a. biodiesel, b. esterified oil, and c. POFAD in A. 500- 4000 cm^{-1} and B.1500- 2000 cm^{-1} wavenumber region

References

1. Atabani, A. (2013). Biodiesel: a promising alternative energy resource. Researchgate.Net, January 2013, 15–18.
2. Ajala, O. E., Aberuagba, F., Odetoye, T. E., & Ajala, A. M. (2015). Biodiesel: Sustainable Energy Replacement to Petroleum-Based Diesel Fuel – A Review. ChemBioEng Reviews, 2(3), 145–156.
3. Ogunkunle, O., & Ahmed, N. A. (2019). A review of global current scenario of biodiesel adoption and combustion in vehicular diesel engines. Energy Reports, 5, 1560–1579.
4. Behzadi S., M. M. Farid. (2007). Review: examining the use of different feedstock for the production of biodiesel. Technology, 7(17), 743–753.
5. Abdul Kapor, N. Z., Maniam, G. P., Rahim, M. H. A., & Yusoff, M. M. (2017). Palm fatty acid distillate as a potential source for biodiesel production - A review. Journal of Cleaner Production, 143, 1–9.
6. Alsultan, A. G., Asikin-Mijan, N., Ibrahim, Z., Yunus, R., Razali, S. Z., Mansir, N., Islam, A., Seenivasagam, S., & Taufiq-Yap, Y. H. (2021). Current State and Challenges on Biodiesel Production. Catalysts, 11(11), 1–36.
7. Wang, B., Wang, B., Shukla, S. K., & Wang, R. (2023). Enabling Catalysts for Biodiesel Production via Transesterification. Catalysts, 13(4).
8. Haq, I. ul, Akram, A., Nawaz, A., Zohu, X., Abbas, S. Z., Xu, Y., & Rafatullah, M. (2021). Comparative analysis of various waste cooking oils for esterification and transesterification processes to produce biodiesel. Green Chemistry Letters and Reviews, 14(3), 461–472.
9. Marso, T. M. M., Kalpage, C. S., & Udugala-Ganehenege, M. Y. (2020). Application of Chromium and Cobalt Terephthalate Metal-Organic Frameworks as Catalysts for the Production of Biodiesel from Calophyllum inophyllum Oil in High Yield Under Mild Conditions. Journal of Inorganic and Organometallic Polymers and Materials, 30(4), 1243–1265.
10. Jothiramalingam, R., & Wang, M. K. (2009). Review of recent developments in solid acid, base, and enzyme catalysts (heterogeneous) for biodiesel production via transesterification. Industrial and Engineering Chemistry Research, 48(13), 6162–6172.
11. Deutschmann, O., Knözinger, H., Kochloefl, K., & Turek, T. (2011). Heterogeneous Catalysis and Solid Catalysts, 3. Industrial Applications. Ullmann's Encyclopedia of Industrial Chemistry.
12. Rashmi S. H., Mahendra, Basavaraj Biradar, Krishnaji Maladkar, and Kittur A. A. (2016). Extraction of chitin from prawn shell and preparation of chitosan. Research Journal of Chemical and Environmental Sciences (Vol. 4), 70-73
13. Poeloengasih, C. D., Hernawan, H., & Angwar, M. (2010). Isolation and Characterization of Chitin and Chitosan Prepared Under Various Processing Times. Indonesian Journal of Chemistry, 8(2), 189–192.
14. ASTM. (2016). Designation: D974 – 14´214´2 Standard Test Method for Acid and Base Number by Color-Indicator Titration 1. Standard Test Method for Acid and Base Number by Color-Indicator Titration 1, 5(1), 1–7.
15. Mohammed, M. H., Williams, P. A., & Tverezovskaya, O. (2013). Extraction of chitin from prawn shells and conversion to low molecular mass chitosan. Food Hydrocolloids, 31(2), 166–171.
16. Ewais, A., Saber, R. A., Ghany, A. A., Sharaf, A., Sitohy, M., (2023). High quality, low molecular weight shrimp and crab chitosans obtained by short-time holistic high-power microwave technology. SN Applied Sciences. 5, 365.
17. Kumirska, J., Czerwicka, M., Kaczyński, Z., Bychowska, A., Brzozowski, K., Thöming, J., & Stepnowski, P. (2010). Application of spectroscopic methods for structural analysis of chitin and chitosan. Marine Drugs, 8(5), 1567–1636.
18. Sarathchandran, C., Devika, M. R., Prakash, S., Sujatha, S., & Ilangovan, S. A. (2021). Activated carbon: Synthesis, properties, and applications. Handbook of Carbon-Based Nanomaterials, September, 783–827.
19. Díaz-Terán, J., Nevskaia, D. M., López-Peinado, A. J., & Jerez, A. (2001). Porosity and adsorption properties of an activated charcoal. Colloids and Surfaces A: Physicochemical and Engineering Aspects, 187–188, 167–175.
20. Syamsu, K.S., Fahma, F. and Gustan P. (2020). Characterization of Ball-Milled Bamboo-Based Activated Carbon Treated with $KMnO_4$ and KOH as Activating Agents. BioResources 15(4), 8303-8322.
21. Clesceri, L. S., Greenberg, A. E., & Trussell, R. R. (1990). Standard methods for the examination of water and wastewater: Washington DC, American Public Health Association. In Standard Methods for the Examination of Water and Wastewater, American Public Health Association.
22. Leung, D. Y. C., Wu, X., & Leung, M. K. H. (2010). A review on biodiesel production using catalyzed transesterification. Applied Energy, 87(4), 1083–1095.
23. Georgogianni, K. G., Kontominas, M. G., Tegou, E., Avlonitis, D., & Gergis, V. (2007). Biodiesel production: Reaction and process parameters of alkali-catalyzed transesterification of waste frying oils. Energy and Fuels, 21(5), 3023–3027.
24. Mishra, V. K., & Goswami, R. (2018). A review of production, properties, and advantages of biodiesel. Biofuels, 9(2), 273–289.
25. Bharathiraja, B., Chakravarthy, M., Kumar, R. R., Yuvaraj, D., Jayamuthunagai, J., Kumar, R. P., & Palani, S. (2014). Biodiesel production using chemical and biological methods - A review of process, catalyst, acyl acceptor, source, and process variables. Renewable and Sustainable Energy Reviews, 38, 368–382.
26. Chien, Y. C., Lu, M., Chai, M., & Boreo, F. J. (2009). Characterization of biodiesel and biodiesel particulate matter by TG, TG-MS, and FTIR. Energy and Fuels, 23(1), 202–206.
27. Nautiyal, P., Subramanian, K. A., & Dastidar, M. G. (2014). Production and characterization of biodiesel from algae. Fuel Processing Technology, 120(June), 79–88.

Note: All the figures and tables in this chapter were made by the authors.

Transformative Applied Research in Computing, Engineering, Science and Technology – Dr. Damayanthi Dahanayake et al. (eds)
© 2024 Taylor & Francis Group, London, ISBN 978-1-041-01782-0

3

MalDitectist: An Ensemble Approach for Malware Detection using Machine Learning and Deep Learning

Nimna Niwarthana*
Department of Computer Security and Network Systems,
NSBM Green University,
Sri Lanka

Dilhara Batanarachchige
School of Computing, Macquarie University,
Australia

Chamara Disanayake
Department of Computer Security and Network Systems,
NSBM Green University,
Sri Lanka

Abstract

Malware poses a significant threat to personal and organizational computer systems and information. This research aimed to develop reliable and efficient Machine Learning and Deep Learning-based malware detection models to enhance the performance of existing malware detection methods. The proposed approach employed regression, classification, and neural network model architectures for model training. The use of the three machine-learning models was also considered and assessed for its efficiency in enhancing the detection process of malware. The results indicated that the Random Forest Classifier achieved a validation accuracy of 98.85%, with a precision of 98.94, F1 score of 98.98, and R2 score of 95.30. The Neural Network model attained an accuracy of 96.32%, with a precision of 96.64, F1 score of 96.76, and R2 score of 85.02. The Logistic Regression models performed less effectively, with validation accuracies of 85.54% and 86.1%. The first Logistic Regression model had a precision of 83.53, F1 score of 87.93, and R2 score of 41.09, while the second model had a precision of 84.09, F1 score of 88.37, and R2 score of 43.35. Therefore, the Random Forest Classifier and Neural Network models were selected as the top models for classifying malware due to their high accuracy in identifying such threats. The following methodology in this research successfully trained accurate machine-learning models for malware classification. The final ensemble approach was developed by combining random forest and neural network models. This research offers a comprehensive solution to the increasing malware threats, ensuring the security of computer systems.

Keywords

Malware, Malware detection, Machine learning, Deep learning

*Corresponding author: gvnngalpola@students.nsbm.ac.lk

DOI: 10.1201/9781003616368-3

1. Introduction

Malicious software or Malware has become a serious threat to computer systems and information security in recent years. With the rapid advancement of technology, this issue of malware activity has risen significantly. These malware activities are responsible for many major data breaches and IT operation interruptions. Malware comes in various forms, including viruses, worms, Trojan viruses, spyware, adware, and ransomware. This can be categorized into main groups: Replicators, Remotely Attackers, Differenter, Autonomous, and Direct Stealers. These malware programs are designed to exploit vulnerabilities in computer systems and networks, granting unauthorized access to steal information and gain control of infected devices. It is essential to have a tool for malware detection since malware criminals mostly target personal devices. According to "statcounter.com", data Windows has taken around 30% and Android has taken over 40% of the operating system market share worldwide [1]. This makes them prime targets for cybercriminals.

In recent years, Machine Learning and Deep Learning have emerged as potent defenses against cyber threats. These technologies, through automated malware detection, enable quicker and more accurate malware identification, reducing potential damage and enhancing security. This study developed MalDitectist, a high-accuracy Machine Learning and Deep Learning-based application that identifies known and unknown malware, thereby helping to enhance the efficiency of existing malware detection methods. Although anti-virus software exists, the rapid evolution of malware necessitates the development of new tools for more efficient detection. This study primarily aims to develop machine learning and deep learning models for malware detection, which can later be used to create an application that works with these models.

2. Literature Review

This literature review aims to review the recent studies conducted about machine learning for malware detection with emphasis on the datasets used for malware detection, feature engineering and feature selection, and static and dynamic analysis methods.

A recent study [2] presents a comprehensive review of various malware detection techniques, focusing on behavior-based malware detection and neural network-based malware detection. In this review, a new method for malware detection is introduced, using CNNs to reduce the data and time needed for machine learning systems [3]. Their method includes the process of encoding the malware code into images and employing CNN-based autoencoders as well as unsupervised learning. Using multilayered CNNs to improve image reconstruction, their system does so, surpassing traditional methods with a diminished amount of training data.

In their paper, authors discuss the different categories of malware, the roles of these malicious programs in society, and the problems associated with identifying and classifying malware [4]. Malware is a general term that refers to viruses, worms, Trojan horses, key loggers and more, with the primary intention of causing harm to the computing devices and its users. Some of the issues that the authors have addressed include the fact that different commercial AV vendors use different names in labeling malware. To this end, they employ the CARO (Computer Anti-virus Researchers Organization) malware naming standard, with backing from major players such as Microsoft, Trend Micro and Symantec. The paper also points out that advanced malware may include programs belonging to different classes and may involve the use of several programs to work as a single entity, for instance the trojan horses and worms [4].

The authors worked on a machine learning method for Windows malware detection, paying much attention to the Portable Executable (PE) file headers for feature extraction of clean and malicious files [5]. This system is able to detect the 0-day malware in the executable files, which would be a major concern for Windows users especially with the presence of many PE files on Virus Total. The model employs a static analysis approach divided into four layers: data acquisition, pre-processing, prediction, and performance evaluation [5]. The system employs supervised machine learning for binary classification where the program detects clean and malicious files. Thus, F1-score, precision, recall, accuracy, and support were employed to evaluate the system. The Random Forest algorithm achieved a 99.44% accuracy in malware detection, outperforming other methods [5].

In this research the authors explored the possibility of using the Windows operating system to detect malware in PE files using machine learning [6]. They focused on the standardized structure of information in PE headers, suggesting that deviations indicate malware. A large dataset of 140,297 PE header samples, including 44,214 malware samples and 96,083 benign samples, was used for evaluation [6]. The research studied various machine learning algorithms, such as AdaBoost, Gradient Boosting, Decision Tree, Extra Tree, and Random Forest, to classify PE files. The goal was to find a model with a desirable accuracy and reasonable time of training. The authors also managed to filter out fields that were not as useful in the dataset, thus reducing the size of the dataset and the resources needed for the model training, which enhanced effectiveness. The results suggested a possible improvement in the identification of malware in PE files through machine learning.

This research illustrates the architecture of Portable Executable (PE) files used in Windows for executable files [9]. PE files which are based on the UNIX Common Object File Format, determine the loading of code and the required libraries to the Windows dynamic linker. The authors describe PE files as comprising two main parts: the PE header and PE sections. The PE sections include critical components such as the .text section (file's code), the .data section (initialized data), the .rdata section (read-only data), and the .bss section (uninitialized data). The PE header which contains section headers, DOS Header, and the Optional Headers contains information on how the code contained in the file can be loaded into memory. The Optional Header is particularly important because it may contain Data Directories, Import tables, and Export tables [9]. The analysis of the PE files is crucial when it comes to detecting malware since attackers may manipulate the PE files to hide the code. The authors emphasize that anomalies in the PE sections or the PE header, especially the Optional Header, can indicate the presence of malware. This knowledge is essential for machine learning-based malware detection, enabling analysts to identify and investigate irregularities in PE files that may signal compromise.

In another study, researchers explored the use of logistic regression in polymorphic malware identification by using the ANOVA F-test with an accuracy of 97.7% [7]. They conducted their safeguard system on Windows XP and Kali Linux environment, and this shows that there is a need to experiment on other operating systems. The study's methodology selected class names and method names as features, suggesting that future research should validate the effectiveness of their approach on larger datasets. The increasing number of malware attacks requires efficient preventive measures. A comprehensive analysis of the literature reveals that machine learning algorithms can efficiently detect and analyze malware on different platforms, including the Android platform. Specifically, logistic regression has been deemed more effective for detecting malware in big data sets because it is probabilistic. The authors emphasized that logistic regression classifiers outperformed other methods, demonstrating enhanced performance in identifying malware [7].

In this study, the authors discuss the major issues associated with modern malware detection approaches and focus on the problem of signature-based detection methods [8]. They note that malware developers often enhance and manipulate publicly available malicious code, employing obfuscation techniques like polymorphism, metamorphism, and encryption, which traditional methods struggle to detect. The primary drawback of signature-based detection is that it requires the use of a set of pre-defined signatures and cannot detect new or mutated forms of malware. The authors classify malware analysis into two categories and find that 18% of studies used both supervised and unsupervised learning methods. Detection methods often utilized opcodes, byte sequences, and API/system call-based techniques, with opcodes achieving a 91.7% detection accuracy [8]. They emphasize the need for a benchmark dataset and recommend machine-learning techniques to predict future malware variants. However, they also acknowledge a trade-off in machine learning: larger feature sets increase time complexity, while reduced feature sets may decrease detection accuracy, necessitating a balance to address the evolving malware landscape.

In this research the authors analyzed the impact of PE header features on the effectiveness of the malware detection model with an emphasis on the aspect of feature selection [10]. Their study aimed to identify critical data that maximize detection accuracy while minimizing superfluous information. They conducted four trials per case study, using labels such as NN_MLPC_0.3_10 and NN_MLPC_0.15_3 to denote test size and random states in the Neural Network Multi-Layer Perceptron (NN-MLP) [10]. They established accuracy standards: 0.97 as maximum precision, 0.95 - 0.96 as satisfactory, and 0.94 or below as minimal precision, with similar benchmarks for the Decision Tree model. To improve the study efficiency, they decided to use only some features from the total of 29 taking into consideration some findings [10]. This process was called subgrouping, and it included defining accuracy ranges, selecting the minimum number of features that ensured high accuracy, and constructing new feature sets. The NN-MLP model showed that adding more features beyond the optimal number led to a decrease in accuracy. The careful selection and strategic replacement of features were pivotal in maintaining high detection accuracy. Their approach highlights the critical role of feature selection in enhancing the precision of neural network-based malware detection.

From the reviewed literature, the authors provide a good understanding of the current approaches to malware detection and highlight the importance of feature selection, dataset quality, and machine learning models. The authors of the research pointed out the need for improvements in neural network-based approaches, stating that CNNs are effective in the utilization of less data and time in processing,

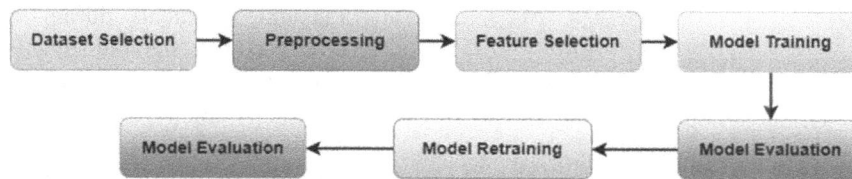

Fig. 3.1 Proposed methodology

which increases the chances of detection [2, 3]. Another study provides a more general view of the classification issues arising from different types of Malware, including the call for common classification names and effective approaches [4]. The authors of the next two research studies demonstrated that PE file headers can be used in malware detection with models such as Random Forest [5,6]. It can achieve high accuracy, particularly for Windows-based systems. Reference [7] states that logistic regression is quite effective with polymorphic malware detection augmented by the ANOVA F-test for feature identification. Some authors have criticized traditional signature-based methods and have advocated for using a machine-learning approach to detect new generations of malware variants, with a particular focus on opcode-based detection [8]. Reference [9] analyzes the structure of PE files to show how these files are vital to studying and detecting malware. The authors of another paper point out the significance of feature selection in enhancing the accuracy of the neural network model [10]. Based on this literature, this research focuses on a PE file dataset and utilizes models such as Random Forest, Logistic Regression, and Neural Networks. The reliability and effectiveness of these models suggest that integrating them into malware detection methods will likely improve the overall reliability of the detection.

3. Methodology

3.1 Dataset Selection

A critical part of this study involved the use of the PE Malware Machine Learning Dataset curated by Michael Lester [11]. This dataset was instrumental in developing MalDitectist. It provides raw labeled portable executables, offering researchers the opportunity to explore beyond pre-extracted metadata. This flexibility was a defining factor in choosing the dataset for this study. All files in the dataset, totaling 201,549 samples, are Portable Executables (PE) with the .exe extension, split between 86,812 legitimate and 114,737 malicious files. Malicious files were mainly sourced from VirusShare, MalShare, and TheZoo, while most of the legitimate files came from Windows 7 and subsequent versions or were false positives from the mentioned sources.

3.2 Preprocessing

After choosing the dataset, a Linux-based environment, specifically Ubuntu, was used to safely handle the files. This environment offered a secure platform and aided in extracting and organizing data for further analysis. The process entailed downloading the dataset, extracting PE files from the zip file, and creating a custom CSV dataset. The selected dataset underwent a preprocessing phase, primarily carried out using Python scripts, aimed at refining the data for Machine Learning models. In this phase, ensure that the executable file names and the provided metadata are correctly compatible. After verifying that, proceeded to feature selection and create the final dataset.

3.3 Feature Selection

In this phase, the purpose was to extract valuable features from Portable Executable (PE) files. Initially, a script was created to extract PE features using the pefile library. Based on the literature review, the availability of the library, and the commonly available features in executable files, 37 features were selected for this research. These features included machine_type, number_of_sections, timestamp, pointer_to_symbol_table, number_of_symbols, size_of_optional_header, characteristics, iat_rva, major_version, minor_version, check_sum, compile_date, datadir_IMAGE_DIRECTORY_ENTRY_BASERELOC_size, datadir_IMAGE_DIRECTORY_ENTRY_EXPORT_size, datadir_IMAGE_DIRECTORY_ENTRY_IAT_size, datadir_IMAGE_DIRECTORY_ENTRY_IMPORT_size, debug_size, export_size, size_of_code, size_of_initialized_data, size_of_uninitialized_data, size_of_image, size_of_headers, subsystem, major_operating_system_version, minor_operating_system_version, number_of_rva_and_sizes, base_of_code, entry_point_rva, resource_size, size_of_heap_commit, size_of_heap_reserve, size_of_stack_commit, size_of_stack_reserve, status, file_length, and entropy. These were collected in a dictionary and consolidated in a list. Due to the dataset's volume, features were saved in separate CSV files in batches and eventually combined into a single file. This process resulted in the exclusion of some files due to errors, leading to a minor decrease in the dataset size from 201,549 to 201,362 samples. After this process, a final dataset was prepared to train the selected model algorithms.

3.4 Model Training

Based on the literature previously reviewed, this research has selected the following 3 model architectures for training.

(a) *Random Forest model:* The study utilized the Random Forest model, renowned for its robustness, accuracy, and capacity to manage large, high-dimensional datasets. It operates on the principle of ensemble learning, generating multiple decision trees and amalgamating them for a more accurate, stable prediction. The model's effectiveness relies heavily on the dataset's quality, which underwent thorough preprocessing. The data was partitioned into independent variables (PE file features) and dependent variables (classification list, with Blacklist as 1 and Whitelist as 0), then split into a training set for model training and a test set for performance validation. The division adhered to a 70:30 ratio, resulting in a training set of 140,953 samples and a test set of 60,409 samples. The RandomForestClassifier function from the sklearn.ensemble library was used to train the Random Forest model with a 32 maximum depth. In this training process, the model learned to predict by discerning the relationship between the PE file features and the target binary classification indicating a file's malware status.

(b) *Logistic Regression models:* The study incorporated Logistic Regression, a machine learning classification algorithm known for predicting the likelihood of a categorical dependent variable, typically binary. Two different Logistic Regression models were deployed, each using a unique solver. The first model used the 'lbfgs' solver, optimized for smaller datasets, created with the LogisticRegression function from the sklearn.linear_model library. The second employed the 'saga' solver, suitable for larger datasets, with an 'L2' penalty for regularization and a maximum of 10,000 iterations. The use of two distinct models sought to compare their performance, offering insights into the robustness of different machine learning models in varied data scenarios.

(c) *Neural Network model:* The study's final model is a Neural Network designed for malware detection. Capable of interpreting sensory data and categorizing raw input, these algorithms are particularly effective for pattern recognition tasks. The chosen model configuration comprised three hidden layers with 16, 8, and 4 neurons respectively, and a single neuron in the output layer. The Rectified Linear Unit (ReLU) activation function was utilized in the hidden layers, known for its simplicity and efficiency in mitigating vanishing gradients during training. The output layer used the 'sigmoid' function, which effectively transforms the input into a value between 0 and 1, suitable for binary classification problems. In the retraining, a larger model with up to 1024 neurons was tested and showed improved performance, illustrating the benefits of added complexity. The optimal model was trained over 30 epochs and selected based on the key performance indicators.

4. Results and Discussion

After the text edit has been completed, the paper is ready for the template. Duplicate the template file by using the Save As command, and use the naming convention prescribed by your conference for the name of your paper. In this newly created file, highlight all of the contents and import your prepared text file. You are now ready to style your paper; use the scroll down window on the left of the MS Word Formatting toolbar.

4.1 Random Forest Model

Once the model was trained, it was evaluated to ascertain its performance. This was done with the use of the test set to establish the actual labels against which the model's prediction was made. The training accuracy of the model was 100%, which pointed to a high capability of the model in learning from the data set. However, to prevent overfitting, it was crucial to evaluate the model on unseen data, which was the purpose of the test set. The model performed exceptionally well on the test data, with a validation accuracy of 98.8462%. This indicated that the model could correctly classify malware and legitimate files with a high degree of certainty. Other performance metrics such as precision, F1 score, and R2 score were also high, further attesting to the model's effectiveness (Fig. 3.8).

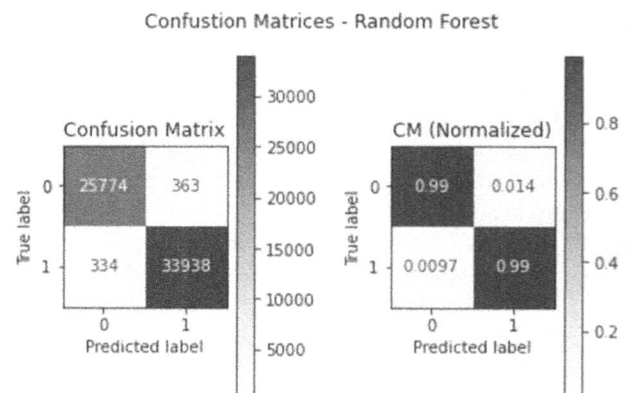

Fig. 3.2 Confusion matrix of random forest

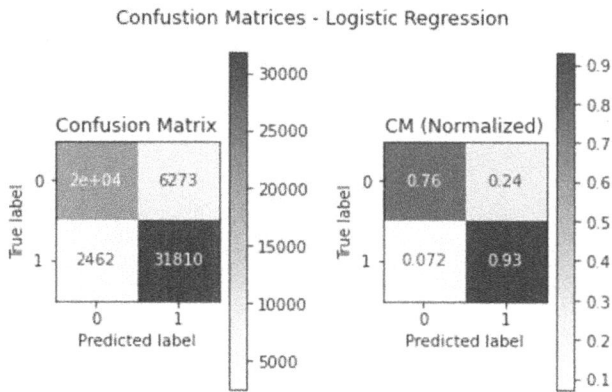

Fig. 3.3 Logistic regression - default: lbfgs

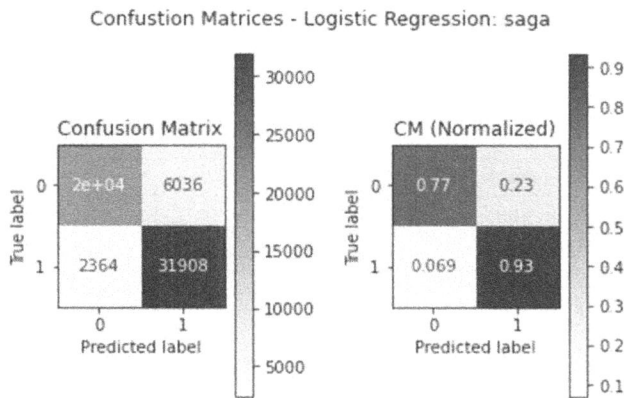

Fig. 3.4 Logistic regression - solver: saga

To gain a more detailed understanding of the model's performance, a confusion matrix was created. The model demonstrated to be proficient in detecting malware and legitimate files while keeping the rate of misclassifications low (Fig. 3.2).

4.2 Logistic Regression Models

The performance of the Logistic Regression model was evaluated using two solvers: lbfgs and saga (Fig. 3.3 and Fig. 3.4). The choice between 'lbfgs' and 'saga' solvers depends on the dataset's complexity. The 'lbfgs' solver is suited for smaller datasets, while 'saga' is preferable for large, high-dimensional datasets. For the saga solver, the model's training accuracy was 86.24% and validation accuracy was 86.09%. The validation loss was 13.91%. Precision was 84.09%, and the F1 score was 88.37%. The R2 score was 43.35%. True positive and true negative rates were 93.10% and 76.91%, while the false positive and false negative rates were 23.09% and 6.90% (Fig. 3.8).

4.3 Neural Network Model

The model development began with a 16-neuron configuration, yielding strong performance metrics. A more complex model with up to 1024 neurons across multiple hidden layers was then tested, resulting in improved accuracy (Fig. 3.5). This demonstrated the benefit of increasing model complexity for enhanced predictive capabilities, though this relationship may vary with different datasets. Experiments were conducted to determine the optimal number of epochs for the 1024-neuron configuration, ranging from 5 to 100 epochs (Table 3.1). Various architectures were tested, including the introduction of a dropout layer in the 10 and 30 epoch runs (Table 3.2 and Table 3.3). Metrics such as accuracy, validation loss, precision, F1 score, and error rates were used for evaluation. The 30-epoch configuration emerged as the most effective, achieving the highest training accuracy of 97.04% and validation accuracy of 96.59%. It also recorded the peak precision and F1 scores, along with the lowest mean squared error and mean absolute error. This configuration balanced true positives and true negatives optimally, with controlled false positive and false negative rates. Compared to other epoch configurations,

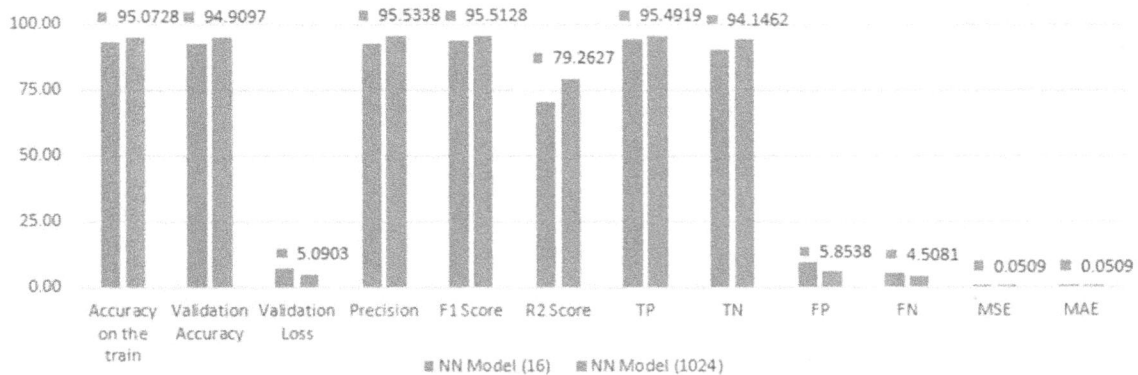

Fig. 3.5 Neurons comparison of 16 & 1024

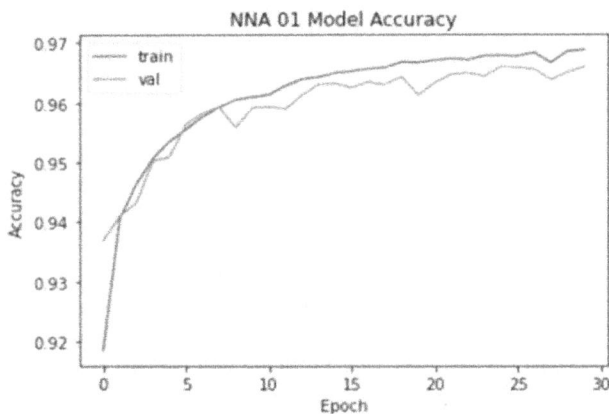

Fig. 3.6 Neural network model validation accuracy

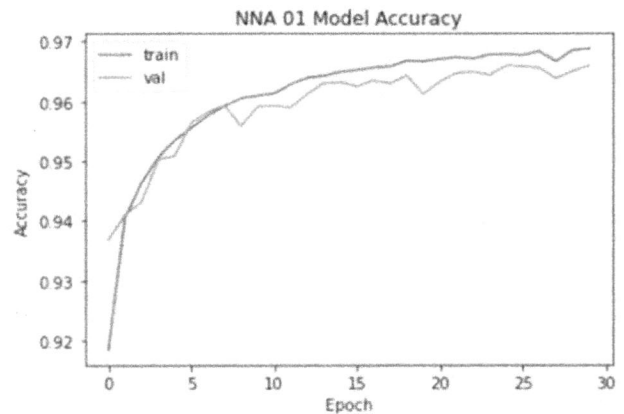

Fig. 3.7 Neural network model validation loss

Table 3.1 Epochs comparison

Model (1024 Neurons)	5 Epochs	10 Epochs	20 Epochs	30 Epochs	40 Epochs	50 Epochs	100 Epochs
Train Accuracy	95.0728	96.0391	96.5116	97.0444	96.7691	96.0121	96.4492
Validation Accuracy	94.9097	95.6463	96.2406	96.5932	96.2506	95.7192	96.1132
Validation Loss	5.0903	4.3537	3.7594	3.4068	3.7494	4.2808	3.8868
Precision	95.5338	96.5187	96.1842	96.9921	95.7360	95.2916	98.1828
F1 Score	95.5128	96.1483	96.7047	96.9977	96.7299	96.2658	96.5163
R2 Score	79.2627	82.2637	84.6848	86.1212	84.7252	82.5605	84.1655
Tp	95.4919	95.7808	97.2310	97.0034	97.7445	97.2602	94.9055
Tn	94.1462	95.4700	94.9420	96.0554	94.2916	97.2602	97.6968
Fp	5.8538	4.5300	5.0580	3.9446	5.7084	6.3014	2.3032
Fn	4.5081	4.2192	2.7690	2.9966	2.2555	2.7398	5.0945
Mse	0.0509	0.0435	0.0376	0.0341	0.0375	0.0428	0.0389
Mae	0.0509	0.0435	0.0376	0.0341	0.0375	0.0428	0.0389

Table 3.2 Comparison of 10 epochs - (remove & dropout layers)

Model (1024 Neurons)	10 Epochs	10 Epochs (Remove 8,4 Layers)	10 Epochs (One Dropout Layer)
Train accuracy	96.0391	96.1980	95.2232
Validation accuracy	95.6463	95.8450	95.0819
Validation loss	4.3537	4.1550	4.9181
Precision	96.5187	95.9334	93.4097
F1 score	96.1483	96.3542	95.7753
R2 score	82.2637	83.0730	79.9641
TP	95.7808	96.7787	98.2639
TN	95.4700	94.6207	90.9094
FP	4.5300	5.3793	9.0906
FN	4.2192	3.2213	1.7361
MSE	0.0435	0.0416	0.0492
MAE	0.0435	0.0416	0.0492

Table 3.3 Comparison of 30 epochs - (remove & dropout layers)

Model (1024 Neurons)	30 Epochs	30 Epochs (Remove 8,4 Layers)	30 Epochs (One Dropout Layer)
Train accuracy	97.0444	96.8316	96.2910
Validation accuracy	96.5932	96.4889	96.0436
Validation loss	3.4068	3.5111	3.9564
Precision	96.9921	96.9426	95.6265
F1 score	96.9977	96.9044	96.5467
R2 score	86.1212	85.6963	83.8823
TP	97.0034	96.8662	97.4848
TN	96.0554	95.9942	94.1539
FP	3.9446	4.0058	5.8461
FN	2.9966	3.1338	2.5152
MSE	0.0341	0.0351	0.0396
MAE	0.0341	0.0351	0.0396

	Train Accuracy	Validation Accuracy	Validation Loss	Precision	F1 Score	R2 Score	TP	TN	FP	FN
■ RF Model	100.0000	98.8462	1.1538	98.9417	98.9836	95.2996	99.0254	98.6112	1.3888	0.9746
■ LR Model 01 (lbfgs)	85.7236	85.5402	14.4598	83.5281	87.9276	41.0927	92.8163	75.9995	24.0005	7.1837
▨ LR Model 02 (saga)	86.2429	86.0948	13.9052	84.0923	88.3682	43.3518	93.1022	76.9063	23.0937	6.8978
▨ NN Model	96.7205	96.3221	3.6779	96.6373	96.7631	85.0166	96.8931	95.5733	4.4267	3.1069

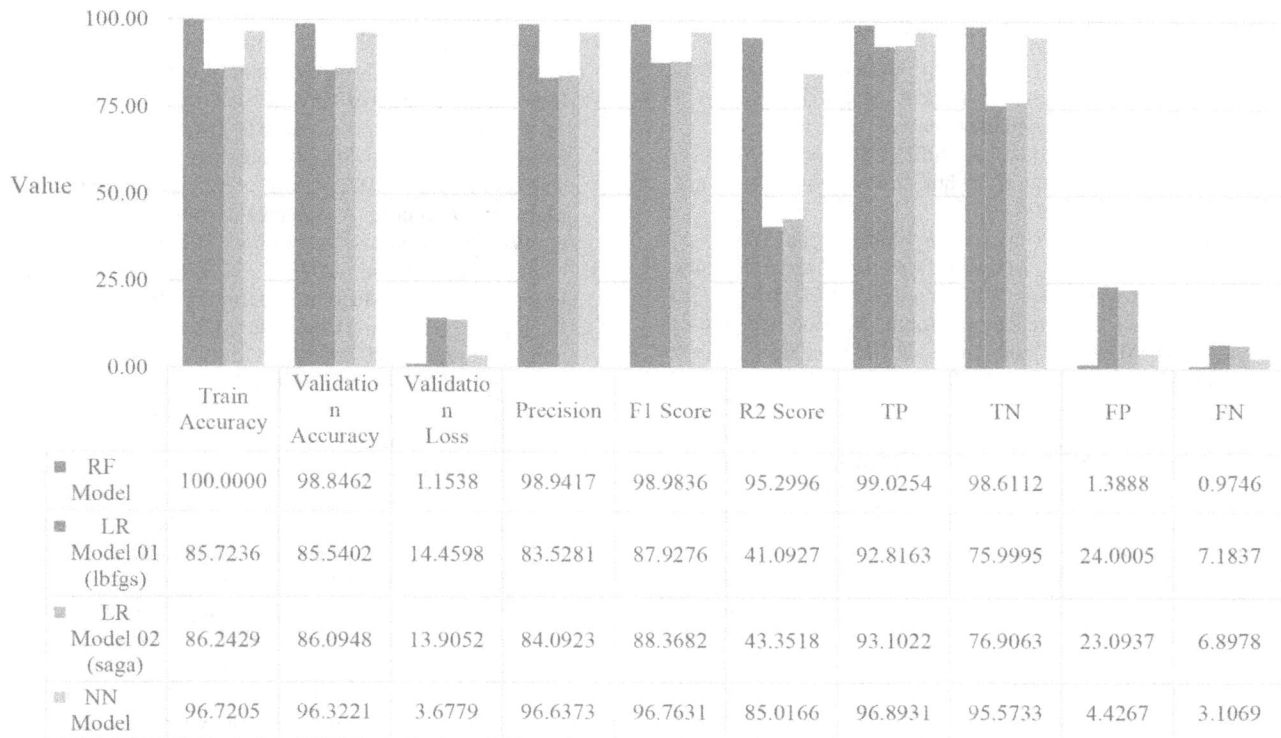

Fig. 3.8 Performance overview of final models

the 30-epoch setup provided superior performance across key indicators, making it the optimal choice for the neural network model.

5. Model Overview

Following an extensive evaluation process, two models were selected for the development of the back-end machine learning program: the Random Forest (RF) model and the Neural Network (NN) model. These models were selected because they provided better results for training accuracy, validation accuracy, validation loss, precision, F1 score, and R2 score. As we can see, both models had a good ratio of True Positives (TP) against True Negatives (TN) with minimum False Positives (FP) and False Negatives (FN). It was also observed that the Random Forest model had a high level of accuracy in both the training and validation set with high values of precision and F1 score that shows its ability to classify instances with high accuracy and balance between precision and recall. The R2 score proved that there was a very high level of fit between the actual and the predicted values. Likewise, the accuracy of training and validation, precision, and F1 scores of the Neural Network model were high, and for this reason, the model was accurate in classification and prediction (Fig. 3.8).

6. Conclusion

This research successfully developed high-accuracy Machine Learning and Deep Learning models for malware detection, demonstrating their potential to enhance existing methods. The Random Forest Classifier achieved a validation accuracy of 98.85%, while the Neural Network achieved 96.32%. However, combining these models using an ensemble approach provides a more stable and reliable solution compared to using the models individually. This addresses the concern of a slightly higher accuracy reported by a researcher, where a 99.44% accuracy was achieved [5]. The Random Forest Classifier also achieved a precision of 98.94, F1 score of 98.98, and R2 score of 95.30, while the Neural Network model achieved a precision of 96.64, F1 score of 96.76, and R2 score of 85.02. These models were integrated into the ensemble approach, combining their strengths for malware identification. Additionally, the ensemble approach was deployed in a web application to demonstrate its practical applicability [12]. This study underscores the importance of advanced machine learning techniques in addressing the evolving threat landscape, offering a robust solution for securing computer systems against malware.

REFERENCES

1. StatCounter. 2023. "Operating System Market Share Worldwide." StatCounter Global Stats. 2023. https://gs.statcounter.com/os-market-share.

2. Haq, Muhammad Ijaz Ul. 2021. "Survey of Malware Detection Techniques." https://www.researchgate.net/publication/356781806.

3. Jin, Xiang, Xiaofei Xing, Haroon Elahi, Guojun Wang, and Hai Jiang. 2020. "A Malware Detection Approach Using Malware Images and Autoencoders." 2020 IEEE 17th International Conference on Mobile Ad Hoc and Sensor Systems (MASS), Delhi, India, 2020, December. https://doi.org/10.1109/mass50613.2020.00009.

4. Vijayanand. C. D, and Arunlal. K. S. 2019. "Impact of Malware in Modern Society Efficient Algorithm for MIMO System View Project A Focus on Wearable Electronics View Project Impact of Malware in Modern Society." International Journal of Scientific Research and Engineering Development 2. www.ijsred.com.

5. Hussain, Abrar, Muhammad Asif, Maaz Bin Ahmad, Toqeer Mahmood, and M. Arslan Raza. 2022. "Malware Detection Using Machine Learning Algorithms for Windows Platform." In Lecture Notes in Networks and Systems, 350:619–32. Springer Science and Business Media Deutschland GmbH. https://doi.org/10.1007/978-981-16-7618-5_53.

6. Kim, Tuan Nguyen, Ha Nguyen Hoang, and Nguyen Tran Truong Thien. 2022. "Detecting Malware in Portable Executable Files Using Machine Learning Approach." International Journal of Network Security & Its Applications 14 (3): 11–17. https://doi.org/10.5121/ijnsa.2022.14302.

7. Farooq, Muhammad Shoaib, Zeeshan Akram, Atif Alvi, and Uzma Omer. 2022. "Role of Logistic Regression in Malware Detection: A Systematic Literature Review." http://vfast.org/journals/index.php/VTSE@.

8. Namita, and Prachi. 2021. "PE File-Based Malware Detection Using Machine Learning." In Advances in Intelligent Systems and Computing, 1164:113–23. Springer. https://doi.org/10.1007/978-981-15-4992-2_12.

9. Connors, Collin, and Dilip Sarkar. 2022. "Machine Learning for Detecting Malware in PE Files," December. http://arxiv.org/abs/2212.13988.

10. Al-Khshali, Hasan H., and Muhammad Ilyas. 2023. "Impact of Portable Executable Header Features on Malware Detection Accuracy." Computers, Materials and Continua 74 (1): 153–78. https://doi.org/10.32604/cmc.2023.032182.

11. Pracsec. 2024. "PE Malware Machine Learning Dataset." Practical Security Analytics LLC. May 5, 2024. Accessed December 12, 2022. https://practicalsecurityanalytics.com/pe-malware-machine-learning-dataset/.

12. nimna29. 2022. "GitHub - Nimna29/MalDitectist: AI and Machine Learning-Based Malware Detection and Prevention Application." GitHub. 2022. https://github.com/nimna29/MalDitectist.

Note: All the figures and tables in this chapter were made by the authors.

Transformative Applied Research in Computing, Engineering, Science and Technology – Dr. Damayanthi Dahanayake et al. (eds)
© 2024 Taylor & Francis Group, London, ISBN 978-1-041-01782-0

4

Impact of Serum Vitamin D Levels in Semen Quality—An Updated Systematic Review

Umayal Branavan*

Department of Obstetrics & Gynaecology,
Faculty of Medicine, University of Colombo,
Sri Lanka

Abstract

Infertility is a physical as well as psychological issue affecting millions of people worldwide. Its prevalence is estimated to be 10 to 15%. Male factor infertility is the major problem in about one-third (approximately 40%) of infertile couples. Men's reproductive potential is deteriorating in recent years. However, no clear etiologic factors have been identified for the decline in sperm count and concentration. In recent years, vitamin D has been known to play a role in male fertility. However, the underlying mechanism between serum vitamin D levels and semen quality is unclear. This review aims to analyze the latest research to examine the relationship between serum vitamin D levels and semen parameters such as sperm concentration/motility/morphology in men. The study was conducted as per PRISMA guidelines and MEDLINE, Cochrane, and Web of Science databases were used for literature search. An increasing number of observational studies proved a significant correlation between serum vitamin D levels and sperm parameters, with a particular emphasis on sperm motility. However, the majority of the interventional studies failed to find any association. Although the majority of the observational studies confirmed the association of serum vitamin D levels with semen quality, there is still no solid evidence to support the use of vitamin D supplementation to improve the outcomes of patients with poor semen quality. Larger randomized clinical trials may be warranted to draw conclusions and guide future research.

Keywords

Vitamin D, Sperm concentration, Sperm motility, Sperm morphology, Semen quality

1. Introduction

Infertility is known as a psychological as well as physical condition and its prevalence is estimated to be 10 to 15%. Infertility is considered a multifactorial condition, resulting in devastating consequences [1]. In about 30-40% of couples, a male factor is the primary problem causing the infertility [2]. Recent reports suggest an increase in male factor infertility, but the underlying cause for sperm dysfunction is unknown [3-5]. Studies have shown that sperm counts around the world have halved over the past 50 years [3,6,7]. However, the reason for the decline is

*Corresponding author: umayal@obg.cmb.ac.lk

DOI: 10.1201/9781003616368-4

not clearly understood. Evidence showed pollutants from the environment, unhealthy lifestyle patterns, and exposure to toxic agents may have contributed to the decline in sperm count [8-10].

These environmental toxins/pollutants stimulate the production of reactive oxygen species (ROS) which can damage the cells by producing oxidative stress. Oxidative stress affects cellular structures, such as cell membranes, lipids, proteins, lipoproteins, and DNA [11-16]. Recent research shows that oxidative stress is one of the major mechanisms that result in the dysfunction of sperm by causing sperm DNA damage [17-20] and sperm DNA fragmentation (SDF). Sperm with higher levels of DNA damage results in male infertility issues poorer pregnancy outcomes and increased risk of miscarriage [21]. In addition, studies on infertile males have shown that oxidative stress negatively correlates with semen parameters [22,23] and impairs sperm motility and the ability of the sperm to fuse with oocytes [24,25]. Various studies have also shown that vitamin D enhances the strength of the antioxidant defense system by increasing antioxidant capacity and controlling ROS. The antioxidant property of vitamin D has created more interest worldwide in investigating the role of vitamin D in improving male reproductive potential.

Vitamin D receptor (VDR) and vitamin D metabolizing enzymes (VDME) are expressed in the male reproductive tract and human sperm demonstrate that vitamin D may have a role in male reproduction [26]. Additionally, VDR and metabolizing enzymes are expressed in germ cells of adult testes suggesting a role of vitamin D in spermatogenesis and sperm function [26,27].

Vitamin D has been shown to have antioxidant properties and many studies reports that it can reduce oxidative stress (OS) by upregulating cellular GSH and antioxidant systems such as glutathione peroxidase and superoxide dismutase and inhibiting ROS secretion [28]. Further, evidence demonstrated that vitamin D supplementation decreases oxidative stress [29,30]. Therefore, many studies were carried out to identify the role of vitamin D in male infertility and its underlying mechanism in modulating semen quality.

Sri Lanka's climate gives warmth and sunshine throughout the year, which indicate Sri Lankan men may get good source of vitamin D from sunlight. On the other hand, agricultural pesticide uses in Sri Lanka has increased to 43% from 1991 to 2018 [31]. Additionally, an increasing trend in smoking and substance abuse among adolescents has been reported worldwide [32]. These environmental toxins and unhealthy lifestyle choices stimulate the production of excessive amounts of ROS which can damage the cells by producing oxidative stress. Importantly, the damage caused by oxidative stress can be eliminated either by reducing oxidative stress in the body or increasing the body's ability to scavenge ROS by introducing antioxidants. Since vitamin D has a proven antioxidant property, it can eliminate the ROS and prevent the cells from oxidative stress. Although, importance of serum vitamin D in male fertility has earned considerable interest, no similar studies have been carried out in Sri Lankan men. Due to the limited studies on vitamin D levels and their association with semen quality in Sri Lanka, many clinicians may not be aware of how vitamins D improve male reproductive potential. As a result, male factor sub-fertility/infertility due to Vitamin D deficiencies are ignored during infertility treatment. Notably, vitamin D deficiency which is neglected during infertility treatment may result in poor pregnancy outcomes and increased risk of miscarriage.

Due to the expanding vitamin D research and the need for further evidence to guide clinical applications, a comprehensive systematic review was conducted. Hence, this review aimed to provide an update comprehensive review of the existing literature regarding the experimental and clinical evidence of the effects of serum vitamin D levels in male infertility.

2. Methodology

MEDLINE, Cochrane, and Web of Science databases were used for literature search. Keywords used in the search were: vitamin D, cholecalciferol, ergocalciferol, male fertility/infertility, sperm and semen parameters and male reproductive potential. The literature search covered English scientific papers published from January 2013 to June 2024.

Randomized clinical trials, retrospective, prospective, observational, and comparative human studies were included for the study.

Case reports, comments/letters to the editor, reviews and in vitro investigations were excluded.

3. Results

The database search found 94 studies. After screening and including the inclusion criteria a total of 40 articles were selected for the review. Method of selection is shown in the PRISMA chart (Fig. 4.1).

Data collected from the search are summarized in Table 4.1. This review included patients from 19 different countries: Argentina, Bangladesh, Brazil, China, Denmark, Egypt, India, Iran, Iraq, Ireland, Italy, Jordan, Nigeria, Pakistan, Poland, Slovakia, Spain, Turkey, and the USA. The age of participants ranged from 18 to 60 years. Majority of the

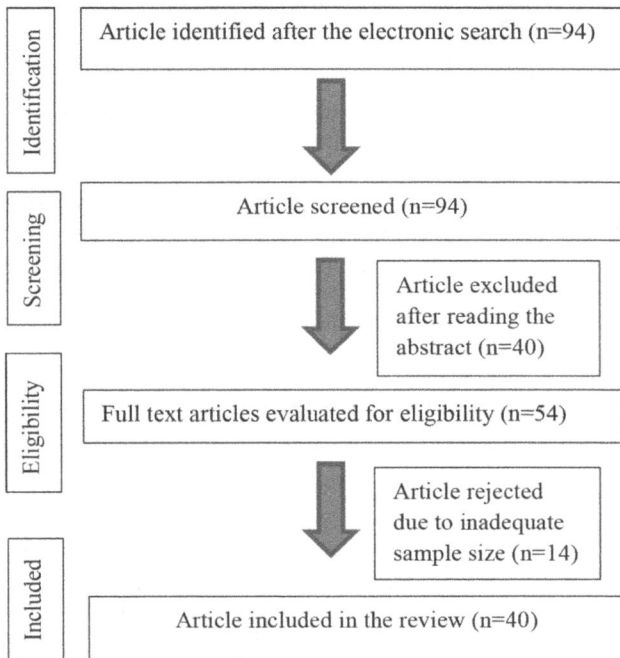

Fig. 4.1 PRISMA flow chart of the literature search

studies focused on middle aged men and only few studies focused on young age group (Age between 20 – 25).

This review included 35 observational studies and 5 interventional studies. Serum vitamin D level was assessed by various techniques which include chemiluminescence immunoassay (n = 8), electrochemiluminescence (n = 5), enzyme-linked immunosorbent assay (n = 12), isotope dilution liquid chromatography tandem mass spectrometry (n = 2), enzyme linked fluorescent assay (n = 1), high performance liquid chromatography (n = 3), competitive protein-binding assay (n = 1), competitive immuno-luminometric assay (n=5) chemiluminescent microparticle immunoassay (n = 1). Two studies did not report the method used for vitamin D measurement.

3.1 Association of Serum Vitamin D Levels with Semen Quality

Majority of the observational studies showed that vitamin D has a beneficial effect on semen quality. In addition, many studies confirmed that vitamin D has positive correlation with total/progressive sperm motility [33, 35, 38, 39, 41-43, 45, 48, 49, 51, 53, 55, 59-63, 66-68,71].

Table 4.1 Summary of studies on vitamin D and semen quality

Study	Country	Study Design	Number of Patients	Age	Vitamin D Measurement method	Conclusion
Aşır F et al, 2024 [33]	Turkey	prospective cohort study	306	20 - 48	Immunoassay commercial kits	Vitamin D demonstrated significant positive correlations with type A and B sperm motility. Significant negative correlations with type C and D sperm motility.
Akinajo et al, 2024 [34]	Nigeria	cross-sectional study	132	Mean age 40	ELISA	There was no significant association between vitamin D levels, male infertility, and seminal fluid parameters.
Güngör et al, 2022 [35]	Turkey	cross-sectional study	58	Mean age is 33	Electrochemilumi-nescence immuno-assay (ECL)	Serum vit D levels were significantly lower in men with unexplained infertility. Positive correlation was found between vit D and the number, motility, and morphology of sperm
Holzer et al, 2022 [36]	Argentina	cross-sectional study	56	20-45	chemilumines-cence immuno-assay	Vit.D concentrations were lower in patients than in controls. The sperm concentration was significantly lower in the patient group than in the control group.
Kamal et al, 2022 [37]	Egypt	cross-sectional study	100	20 - 50	ELISA	No significant relationship was found on the role of Vit. D in semen parameters or male fertility status
Rezayat et al, 2022 [38]	Iran	cross-sectional study	114	20 - 59	ELISA	Positive correlation was observed between serum vitamin D with sperm motility, sperm count, and serum testosterone level in fertile males compared to infertile men
Horsanali et al, 2022 [39]	Turkey	cross-sectional, observational, retrospective study	297	Mean age 32	chemilumines-cence assay	Positive correlation was observed between serum 25(OH)D levels, total sperm motility, progressive sperm motility and negative association with impaired sperm morphology.

Study	Country	Study Design	Number of Patients	Age	Vitamin D Measurement method	Conclusion
Maghsoumi-Norouzabad, et al, 2022 [40]	Iran	Cross-sectional study	119	20 - 50	Not mentioned	Positive relationship was found between serum vitamin D levels, and seminal parameters and sex hormones in Iranian infertile males.
Aded et al, 2022 [41]	Iraq	Cross-sectional study	112	Mean age 35/36	Competitive immunoluminometric assay	Vitamin D3 supplementation improves sperm quality especially the motility and sperm abnormalities.
Santra et al, 2022 [42]	India	Cross-sectional study	52	25 - 40	Competitive immunoassay	Reduced Vitamin D levels in infertile men disturb normal physiological mechanisms. A significant association was found between sperm motility and Vitamin D level
Kumari et al, 2021 [43]	India	Cross sectional study	224	18-45	Competitive immunoassay	Semen parameters – sperm concentration, total motility, progressive motility, and morphology positively correlated with serum vitamin D levels
Shahid et al, 2021 [44]	Pakistan	cross-sectional (pilot) study	88	25–55	ELISA	Vitamin D serum concentration showed a significant positive correlation with sperm count and morphology
Bartl et al, 2021 [45]	Slovakia	A prospective single-center study	34	Mean age 36.6	High-performance liquid chromatography (HPLC)	This study proved that supplementation of vitamin D improves sperm mobility, concentration, and morphology
Ciccone et al, 2021 [46]	Brazil	cross-sectional study	508	18 - 60	ECLIA/ HPLC	Serum vitamin D level was associated with overall semen quality, male reproductive potential, and testosterone levels.
Banks et al, 2021 [47]	USA	Double-blind, randomized, controlled trial	154	30 - 36	ELISA	Vitamin D deficiency does not appear to negatively impact semen parameters or DNA fragmentation
Hajianfar et al, 2021 [48]	Iran	Cross sectional study	350	20 - 50	ECLIA	Higher serum vitamin D levels are positively associated with higher semen volume, sperm count, percentage of sperm total motility, and normal morphology rate
Hussein et al, 2021 [49]	Egypt	Cross-sectional study	100	18 - 50	Enzyme-linked fluorescent assay technique	Serum levels of 25OHD were significantly lower in patients compared to controls. Positive correlation was found between serum level of 25OHD and sperm concentration in patients' group and progressive motility in total studied group.
Nasreen et al, 2021 [50]	Bangladesh	Observational (cross-sectional comparative) study	112	20 - 40	Immulite chemiluminescence immunoassay	Serum vitamin D (25OHD) levels are not significantly different among fertile and infertile men. Men with vitamin D insufficiency are more likely to be infertile than men with vitamin D sufficiency.
Begum et al, 2021 [51]	Bangladesh	prospective observational study	110	25 – 45	CLIA	Supplementation of Vitamin D in deficient asthenozoospermic infertile male improves the sperm quality, mainly sperm motility.
Gheflati et al, 2021 [52]	Iran	Double-Blind Clinical Trial	44	18 -45	ELISA	Vitamin D supplementation did not improve semen quality markers
Maghsoumi-Norouzabad et al, 2021 [53]	Iran	Triple-masking, clinical trial	86	Mean age 35/34	ELISA	VD3 supplementation may affect sperm motility in men with asthenozoospermia and serum 25(OH)VD3 < 30 ng/ml.
Amini et al, 2020 [54]	Iran	Triple-blind randomized controlled trial	62	35-39	ELISA	The intake of vitamin D3 did not change the quality and quantity of spermograms

Study	Country	Study Design	Number of Patients	Age	Vitamin D Measurement method	Conclusion
Derakhshan, et al, 2020 [55]	Iran	Cross-sectional study	70	18 - 60	HPLC	Positive significant correlation was found between sperm concentration, vitality, progressive motility, and total motility with serum levels of vitamin D
Hassan et al, 2020 [56]	Egypt	cross-sectional cohort study	301	30 - 45	Solid-phase competitive ELISA kits	Decreased Vit.D3 could play a role in male infertility by affecting semen parameters
Chen et al, 2020 [57]	China	cross-sectional study	1308	25-40	chemiluminescent immunoassay	Infertile males with higher serum 25OHD levels exhibit better sperm morphology, and serum 25OHD levels may contribute to total sperm number in participants with impaired semen quality
Rudnicka et al, 2020 [58]	Spain	Cross sectional study	198	18–23	CLIA	No associations were found between vitamin D status and reproductive outcomes. Vitamin D is not associated with poor semen quality
Wadhwa et al, 2020 [59]	India	Longitudinal observation study	60	23 - 40	Not mentioned	Vitamin D supplement improves sperm concentration and progressive motility in infertile males
Jueraitetibaike et al, 2019 [60]	China	Cross sectional study	222	20 - 40	ECLIA	Seminal plasma vitamin D may be involved in regulating sperm motility. The active form of vitamin D may enhance sperm motility
Jamali et al, 2018 [61]	Pakistan	cross-sectional study	243	20 - 45	Automated Immunoassay	Vitamin D3 levels are low in infertile males and are associated with abnormal semen parameter (count/morphology/motility) and significantly affecting the male fertility
Rehman et al, 2018 [62]	Pakistan	cross-sectional study	313	25 - 55	ELISA	Significantly lower levels of 25OHD were observed in infertile men who had "altered sperm parameter/s" stated in terms of reduced total sperm count, motility, and/or normal morphology.
Azizi et al, 2018 [63]	Iran	Cross-Sectional	62	Mean age 33 and 34	CLIA	Vitamin D may affect motility and morphology of spermatozoa. Lower content of serum vitamin D may affect fertility of men
Józ'ków et al, 2018 [64]	Poland	Cross sectional study	177	20 - 35	ECLIA	Serum concentration of 25(OH)D3 was not correlated with semen quality
Jensen et al, 2018 [65]	Denmark	Ttriple-blinded, randomized clinical trial	330	Mean age 34/35	Isotope-dilution liquid chromatography–tandem mass spectrometry	High-dose vitamin D supplementation did not improve semen quality in vitamin D–insufficient infertile men
Alzoubi et al, 2017 [66]	Jordan	Case-Control study	117	20-45	ELISA	Vitamin D supplementation improves sperm motility in idiopathic male infertility patients with low vitamin D.
Abbasihormozi et al, 2017 [67]	Iran	Cross sectional study	278	20 - 50	ECLIA	Vitamin D deficiency probably has a direct effect on sperm motility in OAT men
Tirabassi et al, 2017 [68]	Italy	Retrospective study	104	Mean age 33	Chemiluminescence assay	Vitamin D levels were found to be positively associated with progressive and total sperm motility
Jensen et al, 2016 [69]	Denmark	Cross sectional study	1189	28 - 38	Isotope dilution liquid chromatography tandem mass spectrometry (LC–MS/MS)	Vitamin D deficiency and ionized calcium may influence sex steroid bioavailability and semen quality in infertile men.
Neville et al, 2016 [70]	Ireland	Cross sectional study	73	Mean age 37	Total automated competitive binding protein assay	No correlation was found between fertility variables or pregnancy outcomes and male or female vitamin D status.
Zhu et al, 2016 [71]	China	Case-Control study	265	Mean age 27/28	ELISA	Lower vitamin D could be a risk factor for poor semen quality in infertile men.

However, few observational studies failed to find any significant association between serum vitamin D levels and semen parameters [34, 37, 50, 58, 64, 70]. In contrast, this review postulated that the association between serum vitamin D levels and sperm count, and sperm morphology is contradictory. Some studies have found a significant association between serum vitamin D levels and sperm concentration/morphology [35, 39, 43, 44, 45, 48, 57, 61, 62]. However, majority of the studies failed to find any association between vitamin D and sperm morphology/concentration.

Importantly, out of 5 clinical trial studies, only one study has found Vitamin D3 supplementation may affect sperm motility in men with asthenozoospermia [53] and reaming 4 studies failed to find any significant association between vitamin D supplementation with semen parameters [47, 52, 54, 55].

Nevertheless, a study by Azizi et al (2018) found a relationship between serum vitamin D levels and sperm DNA fragmentation. This study demonstrated that there may be corelation between serum 25-hydroxyvitamin D [25-OHD] and reactive oxygen species (ROS) in semen and sperm DNA fragmentation [63].

4. Discussion

Studies on male infertility is increasing and concentrating mainly on declining sperm count and increasing male reproductive system abnormalities [3,4]. Recent literatures support that vitamin D plays an important role in male reproductive function, spermatogenesis and maturation of human spermatozoa [72]. Role of vitamin D in male infertility and semen abnormalities has been examined in various studies. However, the results of these studies were conflicting. Although majority of the studies found a positive and statistically significant correlation between vitamin D levels and semen quality, there are few studies that failed to find such association. This may be due to the heterogeneity in the study design. Sample size, environmental factors (e.g exposure to sunlight, toxins, etc), lifestyle, eating habits, ethnicity and age may have played a role in the interpretation of the results.

Interestingly, many studies demonstrated a positive association of serum vitamin D levels with sperm motility. Additionally, interventional studies confirmed that vitamin D supplementation has a positive effect on sperm motility, especially progressive motility. Sperm motility is one of the key elements affecting successful fertilization. However, underlying mechanism of increasing sperm motility by vitamin D is not well studied. A study by Jueraitetibaike et al. demonstrated sperm kinetic parameters increased after incubation with 25-hydroxyvitamin D [25(OH)D] and suggesting the effect of vitamin D on sperm motility [60].

It is noteworthy, there is a discrepancy regarding the relationship between vitamin D levels and other sperm parameters. In this review, only few studies postulated positive correlation of vitamin D with sperm concentration and/or morphology. The association between vitamin D and improvement in sperm morphology/concentration has not been explained yet. Demanding a proper invitro study to identify the underlying mechanism of vitamin D in improving sperm morphology and concentration in future. Identifying the mechanism and influence of vitamin D in other semen parameters will shed a light in the primary prevention method for male infertility.

In addition, some studies reported a positive correlation between vitamin D and male reproductive hormones such as sex hormone-binding globulin [73,74] and total or free testosterone [75, 76, 77]. Hence, vitamin D may indirectly influence male reproductive potential via modulating male reproductive hormones. Further, recent evidence proved that sperm DNA fragmentation index (DFI) and Reactive Oxygen Species (ROS) are one of the important factors that contribute to semen quality [78, 79]. However, a majority of the selected literature included in this analysis did not analyse these factors. Hence, more studies on the correlation between serum vitamin D levels and DFI/ROS are needed in the future.

Nevertheless, this review included only 5 clinical trials and majority of the clinical trials failed to find any improvement in semen parameters after vitamin D supplementation. Since the number of clinical trials included in the review is less, more clinical trial studies are needed to draw a conclusion.

Importantly, no studies have been carried out to identify the semen quality of Sri Lankan men and their association with serum vitamin D levels. Hence, the effect of vitamin D in semen quality in Sri Lankan men is unknown and highlighting the importance of semen quality studies in Sri Lanka.

5. Conclusions

The studies in this review showed that vitamin D exerts beneficial effect on semen quality, mainly sperm motility. However, the role of vitamin D and its effect on male sex hormones were not analysed in this review. Sex hormones mainly testosterone plays a major role in spermatogenesis and may affect the semen quality. Further, vitamin D prevent oxidative stress by eliminating the ROS from the body and prevent sperm damage. Hence it is evident that vitamin D improves the semen quality by acting through various pathways.

However, there is still no absolute data to support the use of vitamin D supplementation to improve the semen parameters in men. Larger scale studies are warranted to clarify the relationship between vitamin D levels and semen abnormalities in men. In addition, future studies can be focussed on genetic and epigenetic factors involved with vitamin D receptor. This will give a clear idea of the mechanism behind vitamin D metabolism and action in male infertility.

REFERENCES

1. R. J. Aitken, "Impact of oxidative stress on male and female germ cells: Implications for fertility," Reproduction, vol. 159, no. 4, Apr. 2020. doi:10.1530/rep-19-0452

2. T. Alahmar, "Role of Oxidative Stress in Male Infertility: An Updated Review," Journal of Human Reproductive Sciences, vol. 12, no. 1, pp. 4–18, Jan. 2019, doi: 10.4103/JHRS.JHRS_150_18.

3. H. Levine et al., "Temporal trends in sperm count: a systematic review and meta-regression analysis.," Human Reproduction Update, vol. 23, no. 6, pp. 646–659, Nov. 2017, doi: 10.1093/HUMUPD/DMX022.

4. C. M. K. Nelson and R. G. Bunge, "Semen Analysis: Evidence for Changing Parameters of Male Fertility Potential," Fertility and Sterility, vol. 25, no. 6, pp. 503–507, Jun. 1974, doi: 10.1016/S0015-0282(16)40454-1.

5. MacLeod and R. Z. Gold, "The male factor in fertility and infertility. iii. an analysis of motile activity in the spermatozoa of 1000 fertile men and 1000 men in infertile marriage," Obstetrical & Gynecological Survey, vol. 6, no. 6, p. 897, Dec. 1951, doi: 10.1097/00006254-195112000-00067

6. C. Huang et al., "Decline in semen quality among 30,636 young Chinese men from 2001 to 2015.," Fertility and Sterility, vol. 107, no. 1, pp. 83–88, Jan. 2017, doi: 10.1016/J.FERTNSTERT.2016.09.035.

7. C. De Jonge and C. L. R. Barratt, "The present crisis in male reproductive health: an urgent need for a political, social, and research roadmap.," Journal of Andrology, vol. 7, no. 6, pp. 762–768, Jun. 2019, doi: 10.1111/ANDR.12673.

8. U. Schagdarsurengin and K. Steger, "Epigenetics in male reproduction: effect of paternal diet on sperm quality and offspring health.," Nature Reviews Urology, vol. 13, no. 10, pp. 584–595, Oct. 2016, doi: 10.1038/NRUROL.2016.157.

9. M. A. Beal, C. L. Yauk, and F. Marchetti, "From sperm to offspring: Assessing the heritable genetic consequences of paternal smoking and potential public health impacts.," Mutation Research-reviews in Mutation Research, vol. 773, pp. 26–50, Jul. 2017, doi: 10.1016/J.MRREV.2017.04.001.

10. A. Soubry, C. Hoyo, R. L. Jirtle, and S. K. Murphy, "A paternal environmental legacy: Evidence for epigenetic inheritance through the male germ line," BioEssays, vol. 36, no. 4, pp. 359–371, Apr. 2014, doi: 10.1002/BIES.201300113.

11. W. Dröge, "Free Radicals in the Physiological Control of Cell Function," Physiological Reviews, vol. 82, no. 1, pp. 47–95, Jan. 2002, doi: 10.1152/PHYSREV.00018.2001.

12. J. K. Willcox, S. L. Ash, and G. L. Catignani, "Antioxidants and Prevention of Chronic Disease," Critical Reviews in Food Science and Nutrition, vol. 44, no. 4, pp. 275–295, Jan. 2004, doi: 10.1080/10408690490468489.

13. P. Pacher, J. S. Beckman, and L. Liaudet, "Nitric Oxide and Peroxynitrite in Health and Disease," Physiological Reviews, vol. 87, no. 1, pp. 315–424, Jan. 2007, doi: 10.1152/PHYSREV.00029.2006.

14. M. Genestra, "Oxyl radicals, redox-sensitive signalling cascades and antioxidants," Cellular Signalling, vol. 19, no. 9, pp. 1807–1819, May 2007, doi: 10.1016/j.cellsig.2007.04.009.

15. B. Halliwell, "Biochemistry of oxidative stress." Biochemical Society Transactions, vol. 35, no. 5, pp. 1147-1150, 2007, doi: 10.1042/bst0351147.

16. I. S. Young, "Antioxidants in health and disease." Journal of Clinical Pathology, vol. 54, no. 3, pp. 176-186, 2001, doi: 10.1136/jcp.54.3.176.

17. R. K. Sharma and A. Agarwal, "Role of reactive oxygen species in male infertility." Urology, vol. 48, no. 6, pp. 835-850, 1996, doi: 10.1016/s0090-4295(96)00313-5.

18. F. F. Pasqualotto, R.K. Sharma, H.Kobayashi, D.R. Nelson, A.J.T.JR, and A.Agarwal, "Oxidative Stress in Normospermic Men Undergoing Infertility Evaluation." Journal of Andrology, vol. 22, no. 2, pp. 316-322, 2001, doi: 10.1002/j.1939-4640.2001.tb02185.x.

19. S. Loft, "Oxidative DNA damage in human sperm influences time to pregnancy." Human Reproduction, vol. 18, no. 6, pp. 1265-1272, 2003, doi: 10.1093/humrep/deg202..

20. J. Tesarik, R. Mendoza-Tesarik, and C. Mendoza, "Sperm nuclear DNA damage: update on the mechanism, diagnosis and treatment." Reproductive BioMedicine Online, vol. 12, no. 6, pp. 715-721, 2006, doi: 10.1016/s1472-6483(10)61083-8.

21. A. Borini, "Sperm DNA fragmentation: paternal effect on early post-implantation embryo development in ART." Human Reproduction, vol. 21, no. 11, pp. 2876-2881, 2006, doi: 10.1093/humrep/del251.

22. A. Agarwal and S. M. Wang, "Clinical Relevance of Oxidation-Reduction Potential in the Evaluation of Male Infertility." Urology, vol. 104, pp. 84-89, 2017, doi: 10.1016/j.urology.2017.02.016.

23. A. Agarwal, S. Roychoudhury, R. Sharma, S. Gupta, A. Majzoub, and E. Sabanegh, "Diagnostic application of oxidation-reduction potential assay for measurement of oxidative stress: clinical utility in male factor infertility." Reproductive BioMedicine Online, vol. 34, no. 1, pp. 48-57, 2017, doi: 10.1016/j.rbmo.2016.10.008.

24. K. Tremellen, "Oxidative stress and male infertility—a clinical perspective." Human Reproduction Update, vol. 14, no. 3, pp. 243-258, 2008, doi: 10.1093/humupd/dmn004.

25. R. J. Aitken, M. A. Baker, G. N. De Iuliis, and B. Nixon, "New Insights into Sperm Physiology and Pathology." Handbook of Experimental Pharmacology, pp. 99-115, 2010, doi: 10.1007/978-3-642-02062-9_7.

26. M. Blomberg Jensen, "Vitamin D Metabolism and Effects on Pluripotency Genes and Cell Differentiation in Testicular

Germ Cell Tumors In Vitro and In Vivo." Neoplasia, vol. 14, no. 10, p. 952, 2012, doi: 10.1593/neo.121164.

27. S. T. Corbett, O. Hill, and A. K. Nangia, "Vitamin D receptor found in human sperm." Urology, vol. 68, no. 6, pp. 1345-1349, 2006, doi: 10.1016/j.urology.2006.09.011.

28. X. Yao et al., "Vitamin D receptor expression and potential role of vitamin D on cell proliferation and steroidogenesis in goat ovarian granulosa cells," Theriogenology, vol. 102, pp. 162–173, 2017..

29. S. K. Jain and D. Micinski, "Vitamin D upregulates glutamate cysteine ligase and glutathione reductase, and GSH formation, and decreases ROS and MCP-1 and IL-8 secretion in high-glucose exposed U937 monocytes," Biochem. Biophys. Res. Commun., vol. 437, no. 1, pp. 7–11, 2013.

30. Z. Asemi, H. Teibeh, K. Maryam, S. Mansooreh and E. Ahmad. "Retraction of Effects of vitamin D supplementation on glucose metabolism, lipid concentrations, inflammation, and oxidative stress in gestational diabetes: a double-blind randomized controlled clinical trial. Am J Clin Nutr 2013;98(6):1425-32," Am. J. Clin. Nutr., vol. 113, no. 5, p. 1382, 2021..

31. Faostat, F. A. O., & Production, A. C. (2016). Food and agriculture organization of the united nations, 2010. Roma, Italy.

32. World Health Organisation, Global Youth Tobacco Survey Guyana Report, World Health Organisation, 2000

33. H. Abid, K. Mehmood, A. Abid, and E. Abid, "Comment on Aşır et al. Investigation of Vitamin D Levels in Men with Suspected Infertility. Life 2024, 14, 273," Life (Basel), vol. 14, no. 7, p. 913, 2024..

34. O. R. Akinajo, G. Olorunfemi, P. O. Oshun, M. A. Ogunjimi, and A. A. Oluwole, "Serum vitamin D deficiency and male infertility: A relationship?," Cureus, vol. 16, no. 3, p. e56070, 2024.

35. 1. K. Güngör, N. D. Güngör, M. M. Başar, F. Cengiz, S. S. Erşahin, and K. Çil, "Relationship between serum vitamin D levels semen parameters and sperm DNA damage in men with unexplained infertility," Eur. Rev. Med. Pharmacol. Sci., vol. 26, no. 2, pp. 499–505, 2022.

36. M. Holzer, E. Massa, and S. Ghersevich, "Relationship between serum vitamin D concentration and parameters of gonadal function in infertile male patients," Curr. Urol., vol. 18, no. 3, pp. 237–243, 2024.

37. E. E. Kamal, R. M. Bakry, M. Y. Danyail, and A. Y. Badran, "Nonsignificant relation of seminal and serum vitamin D levels and semen parameters of males in Upper Egypt," Egypt. J. Dermatol. Venerol., vol. 42, no. 1, pp. 27–33, 2022.

38. A. A. Rezayat, A. A. Asadpour, A. Yarahmadi, H. Ahmadnia, A. M. Hakkak, and S. Soltani, "Association between serum vitamin D concentration with spermiogram parameters and reproductive hormones among infertile Iranian males: A cross-sectional study," Reprod. Sci., vol. 29, no. 1, pp. 270–276, 2022.

39. M. O. Horsanalı, H. Eren, A. Caglayan, and Y. Issi, "Is serum vitamin D level a risk factor for idiopathic male fertility?," J. Mens Health, vol. 18, no. 4, p. 86, 2022.

40. L. Maghsoumi-Norouzabad, L. Maryam, Z.J.Ahmad, A.H. Seyed, A.K. Gholam, and D. Maryam. "Association of Vitamin D, Seminal Fluid Parameters and Reproductive Hormones with Male Infertility: A Cross-Sectional Study on Iranian Men." International Journal of Reproductive BioMedicine 20, no. 4, pp. 331-338, 2022.ʃ

41. H. H. Abed, A. M. Ali, and Z. S. Mahdi, "Effect of vitamin D3 supplement on the semen quality in human patients with vitamin D deficiency," Hayati, vol. 29, no. 5, pp. 562–569, 2022.

42. P.S Santra, D. Bandyopadhyay, R.K. Biswas, and J.R. Choudhury, "Evaluation of Serum Vitamin B12 and Vitamin D Levels in Infertile Males with Suboptimal Semen Parameters-A Pilot Study from Eastern India" Journal of Clinical and Diagnostic Research. 2022 Dec, Vol-16(12): BC19-BC22

43. S. Kumari, K. Singh, S. Kumari, H. Nishat, and B. Tiwary, "Association of vitamin D and reproductive hormones with semen parameters in infertile men," Cureus, vol. 13, no. 4, p. e14511, 2021.

44. M. Shahid, S. Khan, M. Ashraf, H. Akram Mudassir, and R. Rehman, "Male infertility: Role of vitamin D and oxidative stress markers," Andrologia, vol. 53, no. 8, p. e14147, 2021.

45. I. Bartl et al., "Treatment with cholecalciferol leads to increase of selected semen parameters in young infertile males: Results of a 6-month interventional study," Physiol. Res., vol. 70, no. Suppl 1, pp. S99–S107, 2021.

46. I. M. Ciccone et al., "Serum vitamin D content is associated with semen parameters and serum testosterone levels in men," Asian J. Androl., vol. 23, no. 1, pp. 52–58, 2021.

47. N. Banks et al., "Male vitamin D status and male factor infertility," Fertil. Steril., vol. 116, no. 4, pp. 973–979, 2021.

48. H. Hajianfar, E. Karimi, N. Mollaghasemi, S. Rezaei, and A. Arab, "Is there a relationship between serum vitamin D and semen parameters? A cross-sectional sample of the Iranian infertile men," Basic Clin. Androl., vol. 31, no. 1, p. 29, 2021.

49. T. M. Hussein, N. Eldabah, H. A. Zayed, and R. M. Genedy, "Assessment of serum vitamin D level and seminal vitamin D receptor gene methylation in a sample of Egyptian men with idiopathic infertility," Andrologia, vol. 53, no. 9, p. e14172, 2021.

50. K. Nasreen et al., "Comparison of vitamin D (25OHD) status between fertile and infertile men," Int. J. Reprod. Contracept. Obstet. Gynecol., vol. 10, no. 4, p. 1303, 2021.

51. M.A. Begum, S. Ishrat, M. Rani Saha, F. Parveen, M. Shah Alam, F. Deeba, and P. Fatima, "Vitamin D Supplementation Improves Sperm Motility in Infertile Males with Asthenozoospermia: A Prospective Observational Study." Obstetrics and Gynecology., vol. 4, no. 8, p. 331-336, 2021.

52. A. Gheflati, S. A. M. Mirjalili, M. Kaviani, A. Salehi-Abargouei, E. Hosseini-Marnani, and A. Nadjarzade`h, "Effects of vitamin D supplementation on semen quality and reproductive hormones in patients with Asthenozoospermia: A randomized double-blind placebo-controlled clinical trial," J. Nutr. Food Secur., 2021.

53. L. Maghsoumi-Norouzabad, A. Zare Javid, A. Mansoori, M. Dadfar, and A. Serajian, "The effects of Vitamin D3 supplementation on Spermatogram and endocrine factors in asthenozoospermia infertile men: a randomized, triple blind, placebo-controlled clinical trial," Reprod. Biol. Endocrinol., vol. 19, no. 1, p. 102, 2021.

54. L. Amini et al., "Evaluation of the effect of vitamin D3 supplementation on quantitative and qualitative parameters of spermograms and hormones in infertile men: A Randomized controlled trial," Complement. Ther. Med., vol. 53, no. 102529, p. 102529, 2020.

55. M. Derakhshan, M. Derakhshan, E. Omidi, and M. Heidarpour, "The association between serum vitamin D level and sperm parameters; A pilot study in a subset of Iranian infertile males," Immunopathol. Persa, vol. 6, no. 2, pp. e30–e30, 2020.

56. M. H. Hassan, H. M. Ibrahim, and M. A. El-Taieb, "25-Hydroxy cholecalciferol, anti-Müllerian hormone, and thyroid profiles among infertile men," Aging Male, vol. 23, no. 5, pp. 513–519, 2020.

57. Y. Chen et al., "Effect of serum 25-hydroxyvitamin D levels on sperm quality and assisted reproductive technology outcomes for men of infertile Chinese couples," Andrology, vol. 8, no. 5, pp. 1277–1286, 2020.

58. A. Rudnicka et al., "Vitamin D status is not associated with reproductive parameters in young Spanish men," Andrology, vol. 8, no. 2, pp. 323–331, 2020.

59. L. Wadhwa, S. Priyadarshini, A. Fauzdar, S. N. Wadhwa, and S. Arora, "Impact of vitamin D supplementation on semen quality in vitamin D-deficient infertile males with oligoasthenozoospermia," J. Obstet. Gynaecol. India, vol. 70, no. 1, pp. 44–49, 2020.

60. K. Jueraitetibaike et al., "The effect of vitamin D on sperm motility and the underlying mechanism," Asian J. Androl., vol. 21, no. 4, pp. 400–407, 2019.

61. A. A. Jamali et al., "Vitamin D3: Association of low vitamin D3 levels with semen abnormalities in infertile males," Adv. Sex. Med., vol. 08, no. 04, pp. 39–59, 2018.

62. R. Rehman, S. Lalani, M. Baig, I. Nizami, Z. Rana, and Z. J. Gazzaz, "Association between vitamin D, reproductive hormones and sperm parameters in infertile male subjects," Front. Endocrinol. (Lausanne), vol. 9, 2018.

63. E. Azizi, M. Naji, M. Shabani-Nashtaei, A. Aligholi, A. Najafi, and F. Amidi, "Association of serum content of 25-hydroxy vitamin D with semen quality in normozoospermic and oligoasthenoteratozoospermic men," Int. J. Reprod. Biomed. (Yazd), vol. 16, no. 11, pp. 689–696, 2018.

64. P. Jóźków, M. Słowińska-Lisowska, A. Zagrodna, M. Mędraś, and F. Lwow, "Vitamin d and semen quality in urban, young, healthy men (androls)," J. Mens Health, vol. 14, no. 2, p. 1, 2018.

65. M. Blomberg Jensen, J. G. Lawaetz, J. H. Petersen, A. Juul, and N. Jørgensen, "Effects of vitamin D supplementation on semen quality, reproductive hormones, and live birth rate: A randomized clinical trial," J. Clin. Endocrinol. Metab., vol. 103, no. 3, pp. 870–881, 2018.

66. A. Alzoubi et al., "Normalization of serum vitamin d improves semen motility parameters in patients with idiopathic male infertility," Acta Endocrinol. (Buchar.), vol. 13, no. 2, pp. 180–187, 2017.

67. S. Abbasihormozi et al., "Association of vitamin D status with semen quality and reproductive hormones in Iranian subfertile men," Andrology, vol. 5, no. 1, pp. 113–118, 2017.

68. G. Tirabassi et al., "Association between vitamin D and sperm parameters: Clinical evidence," Endocrine, vol. 58, no. 1, pp. 194–198, 2017.

69. M. Blomberg Jensen et al., "Vitamin D deficiency and low ionized calcium are linked with semen quality and sex steroid levels in infertile men," Hum. Reprod., vol. 31, no. 8, pp. 1875–1885, 2016.

70. G. Neville et al., "Vitamin D status and fertility outcomes during winter among couples undergoing in vitro fertilization/intracytoplasmic sperm injection," Int. J. Gynaecol. Obstet., vol. 135, no. 2, pp. 172–176, 2016.

71. C.-L. Zhu et al., "Investigation of serum vitamin D levels in Chinese infertile men," Andrologia, vol. 48, no. 10, pp. 1261–1266, 2016.

72. L. Zanatta, et al., "Effect of 1α, 25-dihydroxyvitamin D3 in plasma membrane targets in immature rat testis: ionic channels and gamma-glutamyl transpeptidase activity," Archives of biochemistry and biophysics, vol. 515, no. 1-2 pp. 46–53, 2011.

73. K.-Y. Chin, S. Ima-Nirwana, and W. Z. Wan Ngah, "Vitamin D is significantly associated with total testosterone and sex hormone-binding globulin in Malaysian men," Aging Male, vol. 18, no. 3, pp. 175–179, 2015.

74. 2. V.-V. Välimäki et al., "Serum estradiol, testosterone, and sex hormone-binding globulin as regulators of peak bone mass and bone turnover rate in young Finnish men," J. Clin. Endocrinol. Metab., vol. 89, no. 8, pp. 3785–3789, 2004.

75. A. C. Heijboer et al., "Vitamin D supplementation and testosterone concentrations in male human subjects," Clin. Endocrinol. (Oxf.), vol. 83, no. 1, pp. 105–110, 2015.

76. R. Rafiq et al., "Associations of vitamin D status and vitamin D-related polymorphisms with sex hormones in older men," J. Steroid Biochem. Mol. Biol., vol. 164, pp. 11–17, 2016.

77. J. Lee et al., "Serum 25-hydroxyvitamin D levels and testosterone deficiency in middle-aged Korean men: a cross-sectional study," Asian J. Androl., vol. 17, no. 2, p. 324, 2015.

78. L. G. A. Campos, L. C. Requejo, C. A. R. Miñano, J. D. Orrego, E. C. Loyaga, and L. G. Cornejo, "Correlation between sperm DNA fragmentation index and semen parameters in 418 men seen at a fertility center," JBRA Assist. Reprod., vol. 25, no. 3, pp. 349–357, 2021.

79. P. E. Castleton, J. C. Deluao, D. J. Sharkey, and N. O. McPherson, "Measuring reactive oxygen species in semen for male preconception care: A scientist perspective," Antioxidants (Basel), vol. 11, no. 2, p. 264, 2022.

Note: The figure and the table in this chapter were made by the authors.

Transformative Applied Research in Computing, Engineering, Science and Technology – Dr. Damayanthi Dahanayake et al. (eds)
© 2024 Taylor & Francis Group, London, ISBN 978-1-041-01782-0

5

Biomedical Advances in High-Throughput Screening of Marine-Derived Drugs in Cancer Therapy

H. S. Kumarasinghe
Department of Interdisciplinary
Graduate Program in Advanced Convergence Technology and Science,
Jeju National University, Jeju, South Korea

M. P. Theja Virajini
Institute for Combinatorial Advanced Research and Education (KDU-CARE),
General Sir John Kotelawala Defence University,
Ratmalana, Sri Lanka

M. D. T. L. Gunathilaka*
Department of Basic Science and Social Science for Nursing,
Faculty of Nursing, University of Colombo,
Colombo, Sri Lanka

Abstract

Cancer remains a leading cause of death globally, with nearly 10 million fatalities in 2023. The search for new cancer therapies is critical, and marine ecosystems, rich in biodiversity and unique chemical environments, offer promising sources of novel bioactive compounds. These marine-derived compounds possess unique structures and potent biological activities, distinguishing them from terrestrial sources. Notable examples, such as trabectedin and eribulin mesylate, have shown significant efficacy in treating cancers like soft tissue sarcoma and metastatic breast cancer. High-throughput screening (HTS) has transformed drug discovery by enabling rapid and efficient assessment of large libraries of compounds. Recent advancements in HTS technology, including automation, miniaturization, and computational methods, have increased throughput and cost-effectiveness. In marine-derived drug discovery, HTS is essential for identifying potential anticancer compounds. The integration of HTS with genomics, proteomics, and metabolomics enhances the understanding of the pharmacological properties of these compounds and their mechanisms of action. This comprehensive approach accelerates the identification and optimization of lead candidates for clinical development. The synergy between marine-derived compounds and advanced HTS technologies holds substantial promise for developing innovative and effective cancer therapies.

Keywords

Bioactive compounds, Cancer therapy, Drug discovery, High-throughput screening (HTS), Marine-derived drugs

*Corresponding author: thilina@dss.cmb.ac.lk

DOI: 10.1201/9781003616368-5

1. Introduction

Cancer remains one of the most significant global health challenges, prompting an ongoing quest for new and effective therapeutic agents. According to the World Health Organization (WHO), cancer was responsible for nearly 10 million deaths in 2023, making it one of the leading causes of death worldwide. The most common cancers include breast, lung, colon, and prostate cancer, with lung cancer being the deadliest, accounting for approximately 1.8 million deaths annually (WHO 2023). This alarming statistic underscores the urgent need for innovative cancer therapies [1]. Marine ecosystems, with their vast biodiversity and unique chemical environments, have emerged as a rich source of novel bioactive compounds including fucoxanthins, eckol, dieckol, gallic acids and quercetin [2]. These marine-derived compounds offer promising avenues for the development of new cancer therapies. This article explores the current landscape of marine-derived compounds in cancer therapy and highlights the importance and evolution of high-throughput screening (HTS) in advancing these compounds from discovery to clinical application.

1.1 Current Landscape of Marine-Derived Compounds in Cancer Therapy

Marine-derived compounds have gained considerable attention in oncology due to their unique structures and potent biological activities [3]. The marine environment, encompassing diverse habitats such as coral reefs, deep-sea vents, and polar regions, harbors organisms that produce a wide array of bioactive molecules. These compounds often possess novel mechanisms of action that are distinct from terrestrial sources, making them valuable candidates for cancer drug development [3].

Several marine-derived drugs have made significant strides in clinical oncology. For instance, trabectedin, originally isolated from the sea squirt *Ecteinascidia turbinata*, has been approved for the treatment of soft tissue sarcoma and ovarian cancer. Another example is eribulin mesylate, a synthetic derivative of halichondrin B, a compound found in the marine sponge *Halichondria okadai*, which is used to treat metastatic breast cancer [4]. These success stories underscore the potential of marine-derived compounds to fill critical gaps in cancer therapy [5].

1.2 Importance and Evolution of High-Throughput Screening (HTS) in Drug Discovery

High-throughput screening (HTS) has revolutionized drug discovery by enabling the rapid assessment of vast libraries of compounds for biological activity. The development and refinement of HTS technologies have been pivotal in addressing the bottlenecks traditionally associated with natural product drug discovery, including the identification of bioactive compounds from complex mixtures [6]. The evolution of HTS is marked by significant technological advancements. Early HTS efforts were hampered by limitations such as low throughput, high costs, and labor-intensive processes. However, recent innovations have transformed HTS into a highly efficient and cost-effective approach [6]. Automation, miniaturization, and advances in robotics have increased the throughput of screening assays, allowing for the simultaneous testing of thousands to millions of compounds. Additionally, the integration of computational methods, such as virtual screening and machine learning, has enhanced the ability to predict and identify potential drug candidates [7].

In the context of marine-derived drug discovery, HTS plays a crucial role in identifying compounds with anticancer potential. Marine natural product libraries, which consist of extracts and isolated compounds from various marine organisms, can be systematically screened using HTS to uncover bioactive molecules. This approach not only accelerates the discovery process but also enables the identification of compounds with specific mechanisms of action [8]. The integration of HTS with other omics technologies, such as genomics, proteomics, and metabolomics, further enhances its effectiveness. For instance, combining HTS with transcriptomic and proteomic analyses can provide insights into the molecular targets and pathways affected by marine-derived compounds. This holistic approach facilitates a deeper understanding of the pharmacological properties of these compounds and aids in the optimization of lead candidates for clinical development [7], [8].

2. High-Content Screening (HCS) and Advanced Imaging

2.1 Recent Developments in High-Content Screening Technologies in Oncology

Recent advancements in HCS technologies have significantly enhanced the ability to analyze complex biological systems. Modern HCS platforms incorporate high-resolution imaging, sophisticated software for data analysis, and the capability to handle large-scale screens efficiently. Key developments include improvements in automation, the introduction of 3D cell culture models, and the use of advanced fluorescent markers [8].

Advanced fluorescent markers and biosensors have also expanded the capabilities of HCS. These markers enable the real-time monitoring of various cellular processes,

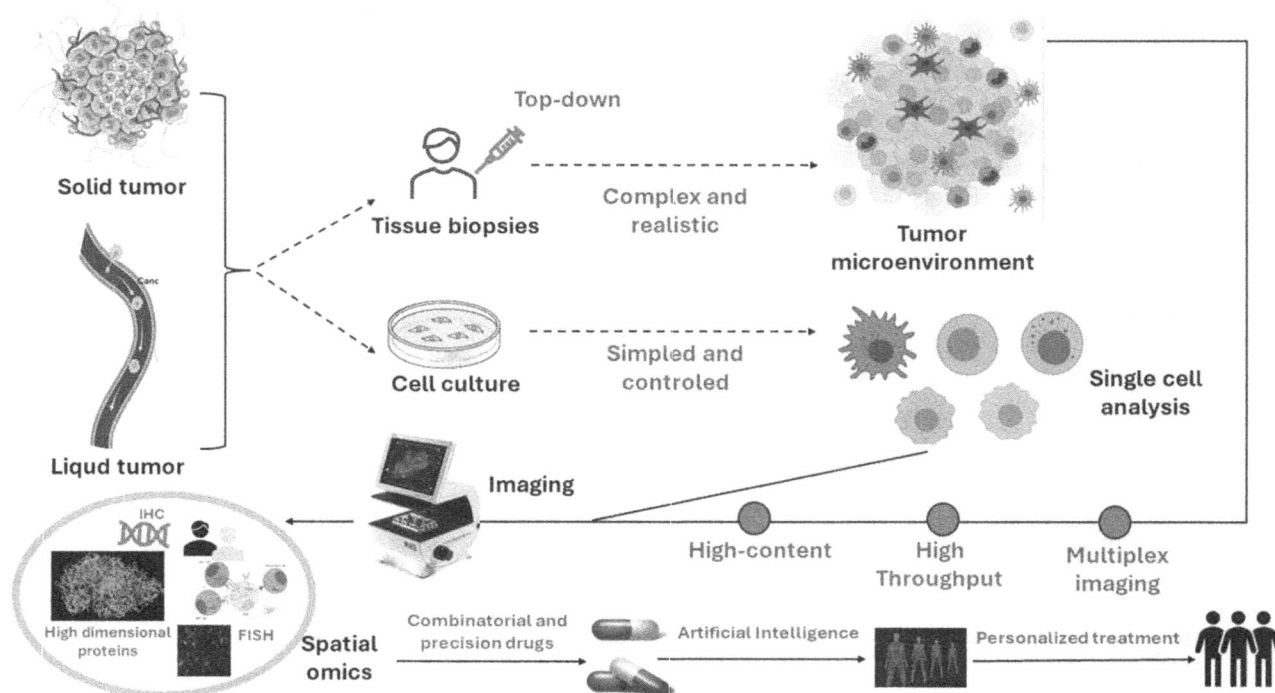

Fig. 5.1 Biomedical Advances in High-Throughput Screening of drugs

Source: Authors

such as apoptosis, cell cycle progression, and signal transduction pathways. For instance, genetically encoded fluorescent reporters can be used to visualize specific protein-protein interactions or the activation of signalling cascades, providing detailed insights into the mechanisms of action of potential anticancer compounds [9].Integration of AI and Machine Learning in Image Analysis

The integration of AI and machine learning in image analysis has revolutionized HCS by enabling the extraction of more complex and detailed information from high-contentimages. Machine learning algorithms, particularly deep learning techniques, are adept at recognizing patterns and features in large datasets, making them ideal for the analysis of high-dimensional HCS data [10].

AI-driven image analysis can automate the identification and classification of cellular phenotypes, significantly reducing the time and effort required for manual annotation. These algorithms can be trained to recognize subtle changes in cell morphology, intensity, and texture that may indicate a compound's biological activity. Furthermore, AI can integrate multi-parametric data from various imaging channels to provide a holistic view of cellular responses [11].

One notable application of AI in HCS is the prediction of compound toxicity and efficacy. By analyzing historical HCS data, machine learning models can predict the potential toxicity of new compounds based on their phenotypic profiles. This predictive capability not only accelerates the drug discovery process but also improves the safety and effectiveness of lead compounds [12].

HCS has been instrumental in identifying the anti-cancer properties of marine-derived compounds. The ability to conduct high-throughput and high-content analyses makes HCS an ideal platform for screening complex natural product libraries. One example is the use of HCS to evaluate the anticancer potential of marine-derived compounds from sponges and algae [12]. Researchers have utilized HCS to screen extracts from the marine sponge *Haliclona simulans*, identifying compounds that induce apoptosis in cancer cells through mitochondrial disruption. Similarly, extracts from marine algae have been screened for their ability to inhibit cancer cell proliferation and migration, leading to the discovery of compounds with novel mechanisms of action [13]. Another application involves the screening of marine microbial metabolites. For instance, salinosporamide A, a potent proteasome inhibitor derived from the marine bacterium *Salinispora tropica*, was identified using HCS. This compound exhibits strong anticancer activity, particularly against multiple myeloma, by inducing apoptosis through proteasome inhibition. HCS enabled the detailed characterization of its cytotoxic effects and helped in elucidating its mechanism of action [14].

3. Omics in Screening Marine-Derived Drugs

Genomics is a multidisciplinary scientific field focused on the comprehensive study of the entire genome. In contrast to genetics, which investigates specific gene traits, genomics seeks to understand the interactions among genes and their collective effects, as well as the interplay between genes and environmental factors [33][34].

The transcriptome encompasses all RNA transcripts present in a cell or tissue, including various alternative splice variants. Studying the transcriptome is crucial because most human genes undergo alternative splicing [35]. Transcriptomics involves studying the transcriptome, which pertains to the RNA molecules present in cells, tissues, or organisms under various biological conditions [36][37].

3.1 Genomics in Marine-Derived Drug Research

Genomic analysis has greatly improved the discovery and development of cancer-fighting compounds derived from marine sources. Utilizing next-generation sequencing (NGS), researchers can thoroughly examine the genetic material of marine organisms to identify the genes responsible for producing bioactive substances. An illustrative case is the cyanobacterium Moorea producens. Genomic research on M. producens uncovered the gene cluster responsible for creating curacin A, a powerful anti-cancer compound. By decoding the organism's genetic blueprint, scientists were able to pinpoint the specific genes involved in the production of curacin A. This genomic strategy not only aids in the discovery of new drugs but also improves the efficiency of their development. By identifying and understanding the biosynthetic pathways responsible for these compounds, researchers can manipulate and enhance these pathways to boost yield and effectiveness, potentially resulting in more potent cancer treatments [38].

Finding secondary metabolites with anticancer qualities is made easier with the use of high-throughput genomic screening. Methods like CRISPR-Cas9-mediated gene editing allow these metabolites to be functionally validated. Researchers can link genetic information to bioactivity by observing changes in the production of bioactive chemicals caused by specific gene disruptions. Using this technique, the gene cluster responsible for the manufacture of the cytotoxic chemical theopalauamide was discovered and functionally described in the study of the marine sponge *Theonella swinhoei* [39]. Pheophytins sourced from brown algae like Laminaria and Sargassum exhibit antioxidant properties and induce apoptosis in cancer cells. Dictyopterenes found in red algae such as Laurencia demonstrate cytotoxicity against various cancer cell lines by disrupting cellular integrity. Halogenated compounds like bromophenols from Rhodomela and Odonthalia inhibit cancer cell proliferation through metabolic enzyme interference [39]. Additionally, meroterpenoids from brown algae like Sargassum mitigate cancer cell migration and invasion by targeting metastasis-related pathways [38]. Bisindole alkaloids derived from green algae Caulerpa hinder cancer cell proliferation by interfering with DNA synthesis and cell cycle progression. These discoveries are facilitated by metagenomic studies identifying biosynthetic gene clusters (BGCs), transcriptomic analyses revealing biosynthetic pathways, and bioinformatics tools predicting novel bioactive compounds. As genomic technologies advance, they promise to unlock further therapeutic potential from marine ecosystems, paving the way for innovative anticancer treatments derived from natural marine sources [39].

Furthermore, comparative genomics can help to forecast and discover potential anti-cancer drugs by identifying conserved biosynthetic pathways among various marine species. For instance, the identification of several polyketide-derived anticancer medicines, such as the powerful antitumor drug halichondrin B from the marine sponge *Halichondria okadai*, has been made possible by the conserved polyketide synthase (PKS) genes in marine microbes [40].

3.2 Transcriptomics in Marine-Derived Drug Research

By offering insights into gene expression profiles and regulatory networks in response to chemicals obtained from marine sources, transcriptomic analysis enhances genomic methods. High-throughput transcriptome analysis made possible by RNA sequencing (RNA-Seq) makes it possible to identify differentially expressed genes (DEGs) in response to therapy with medications originating from marine sources [41][42]. Transcriptome profiling of cancer cells treated with trabectedin, a marine-derived chemical, for example, showed notable alterations in the expression of genes related to apoptosis, DNA repair, and the cell cycle. Such information is essential for deciphering the molecular pathways that underlie the anticancer effects of medications obtained from marine sources and for locating putative biomarkers for therapeutic response [43]. The comprehension of the intricate biological impacts of medications obtained from marine sources is further improved by integrating transcriptome data with other omics datasets, such as proteomics and metabolomics. This multi-omics method offers a thorough understanding of the molecular alterations brought about by these substances, which makes it easier to find new therapeutic targets and create combination treatments [44].

3.3 Proteomics and Metabolomics of Marine-Derived Drug Research

The study of compounds derived from marine sources has shown that these natural products can be rich sources of novel therapeutics with strong anticancer properties. Since these natural products often have distinct mechanisms of action, they are very useful in the continuous fight against cancer. The identification and development of these drugs has been greatly aided by high-throughput screening (HTS) techniques. Among these HTS approaches, the combination of proteomics and metabolomics has proven to be an effective way to fully understand the molecular mechanisms and therapeutic potential of these compounds [45][46].

Understanding the physiological effects of medications obtained from marine sources requires a thorough understanding of proteins, their structures, and functions of a field known as proteomics. Researchers can find changes in protein expression, modifications, and interactions by comparing the complete protein complement of cancer cells before and after treatment with marine-derived compounds. This data is essential for identifying the networks and pathways that the medications impact, as well as for gaining understanding of their modes of action and possible treatment targets. Proteomic investigations, for example, have proved useful in clarifying the mechanism of action of trabectedin, an anticancer drug produced from the sea squirt *Ecteinascidia turbinata*. Research has demonstrated that trabectedin affects the production of proteins involved in the cell cycle, apoptosis, and DNA repair all of which are vital processes in the development of cancer.

Similarly, bioactive compounds derived from algae such as fucoxanthin from the brown seaweed *Undaria pinnatifida*, phlorotannins from the brown algae Ecklonia cava, caulerpin from the green algae *Caulerpa racemosa*, scytonemin from the cyanobacterium *Scytonema* species, gracilariopsis extract from the red algae *Gracilariopsis chorda*, and *halomon* from the red algae *Portieria hornemannii* have been investigated for their anticancer properties. Fucoxanthin has been shown to induce apoptosis and cell cycle arrest in various cancer cell lines, while phlorotannins have exhibited strong antioxidant properties and potential to inhibit cancer cell proliferation. Caulerpin has demonstrated the ability to suppress tumor growth and induce apoptosis. *Scytonemin* has shown potential

anticancer activity by inhibiting cancer cell proliferation and inducing cell cycle arrest. *Gracilariopsis* extract has demonstrated anticancer effects by inducing apoptosis and inhibiting angiogenesis. *Halomon* has shown cytotoxic activity against various cancer cell lines.

Transcriptomic data complement these proteomic findings, offering a more complete picture of the drug's effects on cancer cells. Integrating such multi-omics data provides a comprehensive understanding of the molecular mechanisms underlying the therapeutic effects of marine-derived compounds and helps in identifying novel targets for cancer treatment [47].

The study of metabolites and cell metabolism, or "metabolomics," adds another level of understanding to the impacts of medications originating from marine sources. By revealing changes in cellular metabolism induced by drug therapy, metabolomic profiling can identify potential biomarkers for therapeutic response and resistance mechanisms [47]. Integrating metabolomics data with other omics datasets, such as transcriptomics and proteomics, provides a comprehensive picture of cellular reactions to medications derived from marine sources.

This multi-omics approach has been instrumental in elucidating the metabolic alterations brought about by compounds from marine algae. Similarly, phlorotannins from brown algae (*Ecklonia cava, Ascophyllum nodosum*) have been investigated through metabolomics to understand their antioxidant and anticancer activities by elucidating their impact on cellular metabolic processes. These metabolomic studies contribute crucial insights into how algae-derived compounds modulate cellular metabolism, potentially influencing their therapeutic applications in cancer and other diseases. This integrated approach not only enhances our understanding of marine-derived drugs at a molecular level but also guides the development of targeted therapies and personalized medicine strategies. By leveraging multi-omics methodologies, researchers can uncover the intricate metabolic pathways and mechanisms underlying the efficacy of algae-derived compounds, paving the way for innovative drug discoveries and advancements in biotechnology.

Compiling transcriptome data with proteomics, metabolomics, and transcriptomics offers a thorough understanding of the molecular actions of medications derived from marine algae. This multi-omics approach is pivotal for identifying new therapeutic targets and unraveling the complex biological responses elicited by these compounds. For example, integrating proteome and transcriptome data has provided crucial insights into the roles of microbial communities and their interactions with bioactive compounds from algae, as observed in studies on marine microbiomes [48]. Additionally, genome mining tools have been instrumental in elucidating the biosynthetic pathways of algae-derived bioactive substances, thereby enhancing drug discovery efforts [47].

Recent advancements in multi-omics data integration have significantly enhanced our ability to analyze complex datasets from marine algae. These methodologies facilitate the identification of key regulatory networks and pathways affected by algae-derived medications, aiding in the development of more effective combination therapies for cancer treatment. By integrating data from proteomics, metabolomics, transcriptomics, and genomes, researchers gain a comprehensive understanding of the molecular changes induced by compounds from marine algae. For instance, fucoidan, a complex polysaccharide from brown algae (*Fucus vesiculosus* and *Undaria pinnatifida*), has been studied using transcriptomics to uncover its immunomodulatory effects and metabolomics to identify targets in inflammation-related pathways, thereby bolstering its therapeutic potential. Similarly, salinosporamide A from marine actinomycetes has benefited from multi-omics analyses to reveal its anticancer mechanisms, including interactions with cell cycle regulators and apoptosis pathways. Dolastatin 10, isolated from marine cyanobacteria (*Dolabella auricularia*), has also been subjected to multi-omics approaches to characterize its biosynthetic pathway and develop analogs with enhanced pharmacological properties.

By employing systems genomics techniques to decipher interconnections across different molecular layers, researchers can uncover intricate biological mechanisms and potential targets for treatment. This comprehensive analysis is essential for tailoring personalized medicine strategies and maximizing the therapeutic benefits of algae-derived medications [49]. This integrated approach not only enhances our understanding of the mechanisms of algae-derived compounds but also accelerates the discovery of novel treatments for cancer and other diseases.

4. Single-Cell Technologies

4.1 Single-Cell RNA Sequencing (scRNA-seq)

The technique known as single-cell RNA sequencing, or scrRNA-seq, offers comprehensive transcriptome profiling at the single-cell level, exposing cellular heterogeneity and varying gene expression in reaction to medications obtained from marine sources. Plitidepsin is a chemical produced from marine sources; one example of its application is the research of its effects on multiple myeloma cells using scRNA-seq. This study provided insights into putative modes of action and resistance routes by identifying unique

cell subpopulations that were either highly sensitive to the drug or resistant to it [50]. The discovery process in HTS can be greatly improved by using scRNA-seq. Through simultaneous transcriptome analysis of thousands of individual cells, scientists can pinpoint distinct indicators linked to both therapeutic effectiveness and toxicity. This method makes it easier to find biomarkers for medication response and to optimize treatment plans [51].

4.2 Mass Cytometry (CyTOF)

Several protein indicators can be measured at the single-cell level using mass cytometry, also known as CyTOF, which combines flow cytometry and mass spectrometry. This method provides a comprehensive perspective of the phenotypic and functional states of cells by enabling the simultaneous measurement of dozens of cellular proteins [52]. CyTOF can be utilized in the context of marine-derived drug screening to examine how chemicals affect immune cell contacts and cancer cell signaling pathways. For instance, ecteinascidin 743 (ET-743), an anticancer medication produced from marine sources, was evaluated using CyTOF for its effect on the immunological microenvironment of malignancies. This investigation showed that ET-743 promoted an immune-suppressive phenotype that may affect treatment results by regulating the activity of tumor-associated macrophages [53].

There are various benefits to combining single-cell technologies with HTS platforms in the discovery of cancer therapies derived from marine sources. First, it makes it possible to map drug reactions in detail across a variety of cell populations, which makes it possible to identify uncommon but important cell subtypes that may be in charge of sensitivity or resistance. Furthermore, it offers a more profound comprehension of the molecular processes that underlie the effects of drugs, which makes it easier to formulate logical combination treatments and discover new targets for medical therapy.

5. Organoids and 3D Cell Culture Models

5.1 Development of Advanced Organoid and 3D Cell Culture Technologies

Advanced organoid and 3D cell culture technologies significantly enhance the relevance of high-content screening (HCS) by providing more complex and physiologically accurate models that mimic human tissues and organ function. Unlike traditional 2D cultures, these 3D models allow for a deeper understanding of disease mechanisms and drug responses in a more realistic context. By integrating HCS, researchers can analyze these complex models in a high-throughput, quantitative manner, improving the accuracy of drug screening, disease modeling, and personalized medicine approaches [15].

The development of organoid and 3D cell culture technologies has revolutionized in vitro modelling in biomedical research, providing more accurate models for studying cancer biology and testing therapeutic agents. These advanced technologies aim to replicate the complex architecture and functionality of tissues and organs, allowing for more precise and relevant experimental outcomes [16].

Organoids are three-dimensional structures derived from stem cells or organ progenitors that self-organize into miniaturized and simplified versions of organs. They can mimic key structural and functional characteristics of their tissue of origin, making them invaluable for studying disease mechanisms and drug responses. The use of patient-derived organoids (PDOs) has become particularly prominent in cancer research, enabling the study of tumor heterogeneity and personalized medicine approaches. Organoids can be derived from various cancer types, including colorectal, pancreatic, breast, and liver cancers, providing a versatile platform for high-throughput drug screening and mechanistic studies [17].

3D Cell Culture Models offer a more accurate representation of the in vivo environment compared to 2D cultures. These models include spheroids, scaffolds, and hydrogels, each providing different advantages for mimicking the extracellular matrix and cellular interactions. Spheroids, for instance, can be generated from cancer cells to form multicellular aggregates that exhibit gradients of nutrients, oxygen, and drugs, more closely mimicking the tumor microenvironment. Scaffold-based cultures, on the other hand, provide a structural framework that supports tissue-specific architecture and function [18]. Bioprinting involves the use of 3D bioprinting technologies to precisely fabricate complex tissue structures by depositing cells and biomaterials layer by layer. This technology enables the creation of tissue models with high spatial resolution and structural complexity, facilitating the study of cancer biology and drug responses in a more controlled environment [19].

Microfluidics integrates microfluidic devices with 3D cell cultures, leading to the development of "organ-on-a-chip" systems. These microfluidic platforms provide precise control over the cellular microenvironment, including fluid flow, nutrient supply, and mechanical forces, allowing for the study of dynamic processes in real-time. Organs-on-chips can be used to model various physiological and pathological conditions, offering a powerful tool for drug screening and toxicity testing [20]. The integration of these advanced technologies into organoid and 3D cell culture platforms has significantly expanded their applications in cancer research. For instance, bioactive compounds derived from marine algae have been incorporated into these models to explore their therapeutic potential [20].

Fucoxanthin from the brown seaweed *Undaria pinnatifida* has been studied for its ability to induce apoptosis and cell cycle arrest in cancer cells [21]. Similarly, phlorotannins from the brown algae *Ecklonia cava* have exhibited strong antioxidant properties and potential to inhibit cancer cell proliferation [22]. For example, *Gracilaria lemaneiformis* extracts have been incorporated into 3D culture models to assess their effects on colorectal cancer spheroids, demonstrating reduced cell viability and enhanced apoptosis [23]. Similarly, fucoidan from *Fucus vesiculosus* has been used in hydrogel-based 3D cultures to study its impact on breast cancer cells, showing inhibition of cell proliferation and metastasis [24].

Organoid models have been used to study the response of colorectal cancer to targeted therapies, revealing insights into resistance mechanisms and potential combination strategies. Similarly, 3D cultures have been employed to investigate the invasion and metastasis of breast cancer cells, shedding light on the interactions between cancer cells and the surrounding stromal tissue [18]. These technologies provide a comprehensive toolset for researchers to explore the complexities of cancer biology and the efficacy of potential therapies. By enabling more accurate modeling of human tissues and their responses to treatments, organoid and 3D cell culture technologies hold great promise for advancing personalized medicine and improving therapeutic outcomes.

6. Nanotechnology and Drug Delivery Systems in Cancer Biology

6.1 Innovations in Nanotechnology for Enhanced Drug Delivery and Screening

Recent innovations in nanotechnology have significantly enhanced drug delivery systems, offering improved efficacy and specificity through the use of nanoparticles, liposomes, dendrimers, and other nanomaterials. These advancements provide unique advantages such as enhanced permeability and retention (EPR) effect, targeted delivery, and the ability to bypass biological barriers. Engineered nanoparticles, such as gold and magnetic nanoparticles, are designed for targeted drug delivery to tumor cells, minimizing systemic toxicity, and they also serve dual functions in drug delivery and imaging [25]. Liposomes and dendrimers enhance the effectiveness of anticancer drugs and reduce side effects by encapsulating and protecting both hydrophilic and hydrophobic drugs and allowing for the attachment of multiple drug molecules or targeting ligands, respectively [26]. Polymeric nanoparticles, made from biodegradable polymers like PLGA and PEG, offer controlled drug release and respond to specific stimuli in the tumor microenvironment [27]. Additionally, innovative delivery mechanisms such as stimuli-responsive nanocarriers release drugs in response to tumor-specific conditions, and multifunctional nanocarriers can deliver multiple drugs simultaneously, addressing drug resistance [28]. Nanoarrays rapidly identify potential therapeutic agents by screening drug-target interactions, while nanosensors detect biological interactions with high sensitivity, aiding in real-time monitoring of cellular responses to drugs and identifying marine-derived anticancer compounds [28]. Furthermore, microfluidic systems integrated with nanomaterials allow precise control of fluid flow and efficient manipulation of small volumes, making them ideal for screening complex natural product libraries and assessing the efficacy of marine-derived nanoparticles [27], [28].

6.2 Nanotechnology Applications in Marine-Derived Cancer Drug Research

Marine-derived alkaloids, such as those isolated from sponges and tunicates, have shown potent anticancer activity. Nanoparticles have been used to enhance the solubility and bioavailability of these alkaloids, improving their delivery to tumor sites. For example, nanoparticle formulations of ecteinascidin-743 (ET-743) have demonstrated enhanced cytotoxicity against cancer cells compared to the free drug [29].

Peptides derived from marine organisms, such as fish and mollusks, possess anticancer properties but often suffer from poor stability and rapid degradation. For instance, peptides such as piscidin, derived from fish (Morone saxatilis), and hemocyanin, derived from mollusks (Conus magus), have shown significant anticancer activities. Dendrimers have been employed to encapsulate and protect these peptides, facilitating their sustained release and targeted delivery to cancer cells. This approach has shown promise in preclinical models, enhancing therapeutic potential of marine peptides [30].

Marine polysaccharides, such as fucoidan and carrageenan, from Fucus vesiculosus, and Chondrus crispus exhibit anticancer activities by modulating immune responses and inhibiting tumor growth. Liposomal formulations of these polysaccharides have been developed to improve their stability and bioavailability. These liposomal formulations have shown enhanced anticancer effects in vitro and in vivo, highlighting the potential of marine

polysaccharides in cancer therapy [31]. Another example is phloroglucinol, a polyphenol derived from the brown alga Ecklonia cava, which exhibits anticancer effects through its antioxidant and anti-inflammatory properties. Encapsulation of phloroglucinol in nanoparticles has been shown to enhance its delivery to cancer cells, improving its therapeutic outcomes [22]. Moreover, ulvan, a sulfated polysaccharide extracted from the green alga *Ulva lactuca*, has demonstrated anticancer potential by inhibiting tumor cell proliferation and metastasis. Liposomal formulations of ulvan have been developed to increase its bioavailability and targeted delivery, showing promising results in cancer treatment [32].

7. Conclusion

In conclusion, the exploration of marine ecosystems for novel bioactive compounds represents a vital frontier in the ongoing battle against cancer. The distinct chemical structures and potent biological activities of marine-derived compounds, exemplified by drugs underscore the therapeutic potential harbored within the ocean's depths. The advent of high-throughput screening (HTS) technologies has revolutionized drug discovery, enabling the efficient and rapid evaluation of vast compound libraries. The advancements in HTS, coupled with the integration of genomics, proteomics, and metabolomics, facilitate a deeper understanding of the pharmacological profiles and mechanisms of action of marine-derived compounds. This comprehensive and synergistic approach not only accelerates the identification and optimization of promising anticancer agents but also paves the way for the development of innovative and effective cancer therapies. As such, the confluence of marine biotechnology and advanced HTS methodologies offers a promising avenue for addressing the global challenge of cancer.

REFERENCES

1. R. L. Siegel, K. D. Miller, N. S. Wagle, and A. Jemal, "Cancer statistics, 2023," *CA Cancer J Clin*, vol. 73, no. 1, pp. 17–48, Jan. 2023, doi: 10.3322/caac.21763.

2. P. P. Bhuyan, R. Nayak, S. Patra, H. S. Abdulabbas, M. Jena, and B. Pradhan, "Seaweed-Derived Sulfated Polysaccharides; The New Age Chemopreventives: A Comprehensive Review," Feb. 01, 2023, *MDPI*. doi: 10.3390/cancers15030715.

3. D. Matulja, F. Vranješević, M. K. Markovic, S. K. Pavelić, and D. Marković, "Anticancer Activities of Marine-Derived Phenolic Compounds and Their Derivatives," Feb. 01, 2022, *MDPI*. doi: 10.3390/molecules27041449.

4. K. N. Ganjoo and S. R. Patel, "Trabectedin: An anticancer drug from the sea," 2009. doi: 10.1517/14656560903277236.

5. A. Mcbride and S. K. Butler, "Eribulin mesylate: A novel halichondrin B analogue for the treatment of metastatic breast cancer," May 01, 2012, *American Society of Health-Systems Pharmacy*. doi: 10.2146/ajhp110237.

6. P. Szymański, M. Markowicz, and E. Mikiciuk-Olasik, "Adaptation of high-throughput screening in drug discovery-toxicological screening tests," 2012, *MDPI AG*. doi: 10.3390/ijms13010427.

7. H. Aldewachi, R. N. Al-Zidan, M. T. Conner, and M. M. Salman, "High-throughput screening platforms in the discovery of novel drugs for neurodegenerative diseases," Feb. 01, 2021, *MDPI AG*. doi: 10.3390/bioengineering8020030.

8. N. J. Ayon, "High-Throughput Screening of Natural Product and Synthetic Molecule Libraries for Antibacterial Drug Discovery," May 01, 2023, *MDPI*. doi: 10.3390/metabo13050625.

9. V. S. Ovechkina, S. M. Zakian, S. P. Medvedev, and K. R. Valetdinova, "Genetically encoded fluorescent biosensors for biomedical applications," Nov. 01, 2021, *MDPI*. doi: 10.3390/biomedicines9111528.

10. L. Pinto-Coelho, "How Artificial Intelligence Is Shaping Medical Imaging Technology: A Survey of Innovations and Applications," Dec. 01, 2023, *Multidisciplinary Digital Publishing Institute (MDPI)*. doi: 10.3390/bioengineering10121435.

11. M. S. Durkee, R. Abraham, M. R. Clark, and M. L. Giger, "Artificial Intelligence and Cellular Segmentation in Tissue Microscopy Images," Oct. 01, 2021, *Elsevier Inc*. doi: 10.1016/j.ajpath.2021.05.022.

12. S. Guan and G. Wang, "Drug discovery and development in the era of artificial intelligence: From machine learning to large language models," *Artificial Intelligence Chemistry*, vol. 2, no. 1, p. 100070, Jun. 2024, doi: 10.1016/j.aichem.2024.100070.

13. W. Bae *et al.*, "Apoptosis-Inducing Activity of Marine Sponge Haliclona sp. Extracts Collected from Kosrae in Nonsmall Cell Lung Cancer A549 Cells," *Evidence-based Complementary and Alternative Medicine*, vol. 2015, 2015, doi: 10.1155/2015/717959.

14. H. S. Lee and G. S. Jeong, "Salinosporamide A, a Marine-Derived Proteasome Inhibitor, Inhibits T Cell Activation through Regulating Proliferation and the Cell Cycle," *Molecules*, vol. 25, no. 21, Nov. 2020, doi: 10.3390/molecules25215031.

15. S. Y. Lee, I. S. Koo, H. J. Hwang, and D. W. Lee, "In Vitro three-dimensional (3D) cell culture tools for spheroid and organoid models," Jun. 01, 2023, *Society for Laboratory Automation and Screening (SLAS)*. doi: 10.1016/j.slasd.2023.03.006.

16. W. H. Abuwatfa, W. G. Pitt, and G. A. Husseini, "Scaffold-based 3D cell culture models in cancer research," Dec. 01, 2024, *BioMed Central Ltd*. doi: 10.1186/s12929-024-00994-y.

17. S. Yang *et al.*, "Organoids: The current status and biomedical applications," Jun. 01, 2023, *John Wiley and Sons Inc*. doi: 10.1002/mco2.274.

18. M. Kapałczyńska *et al.*, "2D and 3D cell cultures – a comparison of different types of cancer cell cultures," *Archives of Medical Science*, vol. 14, no. 4, pp. 910–919, 2018, doi: 10.5114/aoms.2016.63743.

19. S. Tripathi, S. S. Mandal, S. Bauri, and P. Maiti, "3D bioprinting and its innovative approach for biomedical applications," Feb. 01, 2023, *John Wiley and Sons Inc*. doi: 10.1002/mco2.194.

20. G. Saorin, I. Caligiuri, and F. Rizzolio, "Microfluidic organoids-on-a-chip: The future of human models," Jul. 30, 2023, *Elsevier Ltd*. doi: 10.1016/j.semcdb.2022.10.001.

21. M. Hosokawa, M. Kudo, H. Maeda, H. Kohno, T. Tanaka, and K. Miyashita, "Fucoxanthin induces apoptosis and enhances the antiproliferative effect of the PPARγ ligand, troglitazone, on colon cancer cells," *Biochim Biophys Acta Gen Subj*, vol. 1675, no. 1–3, pp. 113–119, Nov. 2004, doi: 10.1016/j.bbagen.2004.08.012.

22. H. Zheng, Y. Zhao, and L. Guo, "A Bioactive Substance Derived from Brown Seaweeds: Phlorotannins," Dec. 01, 2022, *MDPI*. doi: 10.3390/md20120742.

23. X. Long *et al.*, "Insights on preparation, structure and activities of Gracilaria lemaneiformis polysaccharide," *Food Chem X*, vol. 12, Dec. 2021, doi: 10.1016/j.fochx.2021.100153.

24. H. Lee, J. S. Kim, and E. Kim, "Fucoidan from Seaweed Fucus vesiculosus Inhibits Migration and Invasion of Human Lung Cancer Cell via PI3K-Akt-mTOR Pathways," *PLoS One*, vol. 7, no. 11, Nov. 2012, doi: 10.1371/journal.pone.0050624.

25. X. Cheng, Q. Xie, and Y. Sun, "Advances in nanomaterial-based targeted drug delivery systems," 2023, *Frontiers Media S.A.* doi: 10.3389/fbioe.2023.1177151.

26. M. Chehelgerdi *et al.*, "Progressing nanotechnology to improve targeted cancer treatment: overcoming hurdles in its clinical implementation," Dec. 01, 2023, *BioMed Central Ltd*. doi: 10.1186/s12943-023-01865-0.

27. A. Gagliardi *et al.*, "Biodegradable Polymeric Nanoparticles for Drug Delivery to Solid Tumors," Feb. 03, 2021, *Frontiers Media S.A.* doi: 10.3389/fphar.2021.601626.

28. G. C. N. B. Lôbo *et al.*, "pharmaceutics Nanocarriers Used in Drug Delivery to Enhance Immune System in Cancer Therapy," 2021, doi: 10.3390/pharmaceutics.

29. E. Wang, M. A. Sorolla, P. D. G. Krishnan, and A. Sorolla, "From seabed to bedside: A review on promising marine anticancer compounds," Feb. 01, 2020, *MDPI AG*. doi: 10.3390/biom10020248.

30. M. Librizzi *et al.*, "Natural Anticancer Peptides from Marine Animal Species: Evidence from In Vitro Cell Model Systems," Jan. 01, 2024, *Multidisciplinary Digital Publishing Institute (MDPI)*. doi: 10.3390/cancers16010036.

31. A. I. Barbosa, A. J. Coutinho, S. A. Costa Lima, and S. Reis, "Marine polysaccharides in pharmaceutical applications: Fucoidan and chitosan as key players in the drug delivery match field," *Mar Drugs*, vol. 17, no. 12, Nov. 2019, doi: 10.3390/md17120654.

32. V. H. N. Tran *et al.*, "Structural Characterization and Cytotoxic Activity Evaluation of Ulvan Polysaccharides Extracted from the Green Algae Ulva papenfussii," *Mar Drugs*, vol. 21, no. 11, Nov. 2023, doi: 10.3390/md21110556.

33. S. C. Roth, "What is genomic medicine?," *J. Med. Libr. Assoc.*, vol. 107, no. 3, pp. 442–448, 2019, doi: 10.5195/jmla.2019.604.

34. A. Khodadadian *et al.*, "Genomics and transcriptomics: The powerful technologies in precision medicine," *Int. J. Gen. Med.*, vol. 13, pp. 627–640, 2020, doi: 10.2147/IJGM.S249970.

35. R. Lowe, N. Shirley, M. Bleackley, S. Dolan, and T. Shafee, "Transcriptomics technologies," *PLoS Comput. Biol.*, vol. 13, no. 5, pp. 1–23, 2017, doi: 10.1371/journal.pcbi.1005457.

36. S. Moein, M. Vaghari-Tabari, D. Qujeq, M. Majidinia, S. M. Nabavi, and B. Yousefi, "MiRNAs and inflammatory bowel disease: An interesting new story," *J. Cell. Physiol.*, vol. 234, no. 4, pp. 3277–3293, 2019, doi: 10.1002/jcp.27173.

37. A. Anvarnia, F. Mohaddes-Gharamaleki, M. Asadi, M. Akbari, B. Yousefi, and D. Shanehbandi, "Dysregulated microRNAs in colorectal carcinogenesis: New insight to cell survival and apoptosis regulation," *J. Cell. Physiol.*, vol. 234, no. 12, pp. 21683–21693, 2019, doi: 10.1002/jcp.28872.

38. P. D. Boudreau *et al.*, "Expanding the described metabolome of the marine cyanobacterium moorea producens jhb through orthogonal natural products workflows," *PLoS One*, vol. 10, no. 7, 2015, doi: 10.1371/journal.pone.0133297.

39. C. Jiang *et al.*, "Applications of CRISPR/Cas9 in the Synthesis of Secondary Metabolites in Filamentous Fungi," *Front. Microbiol.*, vol. 12, no. February, pp. 1–15, 2021, doi: 10.3389/fmicb.2021.638096.

40. J. Selvin, G. Sathiyanarayanan, A. N. Lipton, N. A. Al-Dhabi, M. V. Arasu, and G. S. Kiran, "Ketide Synthase (KS) domain prediction and analysis of iterative type II PKS gene in marine sponge-associated actinobacteria producing biosurfactants and antimicrobial agents," *Front. Microbiol.*, vol. 7, no. FEB, pp. 1–12, 2016, doi: 10.3389/fmicb.2016.00063.

41. C. Song *et al.*, "A Comparative Transcriptome Analysis Unveils the Mechanisms of Response in Feather Degradation by Pseudomonas aeruginosa Gxun-7," *Microorganisms*, vol. 12, no. 4, 2024, doi: 10.3390/microorganisms12040841.

42. L. Beaulieu, "Insights into the regulation of algal proteins and bioactive peptides using proteomic and transcriptomic approaches," *Molecules*, vol. 24, no. 9, 2019, doi: 10.3390/molecules24091708.

43. M. D'Incalci, N. Badri, C. M. Galmarini, and P. Allavena, "Trabectedin, a drug acting on both cancer cells and the tumour microenvironment," *Br. J. Cancer*, vol. 111, no. 4, pp. 646–650, 2014, doi: 10.1038/bjc.2014.149.

44. Y. J. Heo, C. Hwa, G. H. Lee, J. M. Park, and J. Y. An, "Integrative multi-omics approaches in cancer research: From biological networks to clinical subtypes," *Mol. Cells*, vol. 44, no. 7, pp. 433–443, 2021, doi: 10.14348/molcells.2021.0042.

45. D. Martins-de-Souza, "Proteomics, metabolomics, and protein interactomics in the characterization of the molecular features of major depressive disorder," *Dialogues Clin. Neurosci.*, vol. 16, no. 1, pp. 63–73, 2014, doi: 10.31887/dcns.2014.16.1/dmartins.

46. D. Martins-de-Souza, "Proteomics and metabolomics in psychiatry," *Proteomics and Metabolomics in Psychiatry*, vol. 29, pp. 1–142, 2014, doi: 10.1159/isbn.978-3-318-02600-9.

47. N. Rosic, "Genome Mining as an Alternative Way for Screening the Marine Organisms for Their Potential to Produce UV-Absorbing Mycosporine-like Amino Acid," *Mar. Drugs*, vol. 20, no. 8, 2022, doi: 10.3390/md20080478.

48. L. F. Messer, C. E. Lee, R. Wattiez, and S. Matallana-Surget, "Novel functional insights into the microbiome inhabiting marine plastic debris: critical considerations to counteract the challenges of thin biofilms using multi-omics and comparative metaproteomics," *Microbiome*, vol. 12, no. 1, pp. 1–19, 2024, doi: 10.1186/s40168-024-01751-x.

49. S. Graw *et al.*, "Multi-omics data integration considerations and study design for biological systems and disease," *Mol. Omi.*, vol. 17, no. 2, pp. 170–185, 2021, doi: 10.1039/d0mo00041h.

50. A. Anloague and J. Delgado-Calle, "Osteocytes: New Kids on the Block for Cancer in Bone Therapy," *Cancers (Basel).*, vol. 15, no. 9, pp. 1–19, 2023, doi: 10.3390/cancers15092645.

51. Q. Jia, H. Chu, Z. Jin, H. Long, and B. Zhu, "High-throughput single-cell sequencing in cancer research," *Signal Transduct. Target. Ther.*, vol. 7, no. 1, 2022, doi: 10.1038/s41392-022-00990-4.

52. A. W. Kay, D. M. Strauss-Albee, and C. A. Blish, "Application of mass cytometry (CyTOF) for functional and phenotypic analysis of natural killer cells," *Methods Mol. Biol.*, vol. 1441, pp. 13–26, 2016, doi: 10.1007/978-1-4939-3684-7_2.

53. P. Allavena, C. Belgiovine, E. Digifico, R. Frapolli, and M. D'Incalci, "Effects of the Anti-Tumor Agents Trabectedin and Lurbinectedin on Immune Cells of the Tumor Microenvironment," *Front. Oncol.*, vol. 12, no. March, pp. 1–8, 2022, doi: 10.3389/fonc.2022.851790.

Transformative Applied Research in Computing, Engineering, Science and Technology – Dr. Damayanthi Dahanayake et al. (eds)
© 2024 Taylor & Francis Group, London, ISBN 978-1-041-01782-0

6

Mirror on the Wall or Camera on the Phone? Role of Augmented Reality Applications in Spreading Brand Related Electronic Word of Mouth: A Conceptual Model

W.D.H De Mel*
Faculty of Postgraduate Studies and
Professional Advancement,
NSBM Green University,
Sri Lanka

G.D. Samarasinghe
Faculty of Business,
University of Moratuwa, Sri Lanka

B.A.N. Eranda
Faculty of Management,
University of Peradeniya, Sri Lanka

Abstract

Augmented reality, with its unmatched capability to overlay virtual details onto the real world, has become a leading interactive technology. Its swift advancement has revolutionized the shopping experience for consumers, with numerous brands effectively incorporating augmented reality into e-commerce across various industries. Fashion retail is no exception, as augmented reality technology allows for virtual try-ons, providing customers with a distinctive and innovative experience. Despite the technology's potential, limited studies focus on why people use augmented reality applications and how it would lead to brand related electronic word of mouth on social media platforms. This paper aims to bridge the gap in the literature by proposing a conceptual model to explore the uses and gratifications of augmented reality applications and their effect on brand-related electronic word of mouth. Stimulus-Organism-Response model is employed as the broader theoretical framework. Additionally, the model includes technology readiness as a moderator to understand consumer perceptions of adopting augmented reality. The paper also discusses the managerial implications of empirically testing the proposed model in the online fashion retail context. Finally, it outlines a research agenda for further investigation into the impact of augmented reality applications on consumer behavior in online fashion retail.

Keywords

Augmented reality, Consumer engagement, Electronic word of mouth, Fashion retail, Social media, Uses and gratifications

*Corresponding author: wdhdemel@students.nsbm.ac.lk

DOI: 10.1201/9781003616368-6

1. Introduction

The emergence of e-commerce has transformed the retail industry, reshaping how consumers interact with brands and purchase goods and services. The developments in e-commerce rooted in internet has encompassed various platforms including websites in the dot-com era, mobile applications on e-commerce and social media platforms. Today organizations are focusing on immersive technologies in terms of Augmented Reality (AR) and Virtual Reality (VR) to enrich shopping experience [1]. AR modifies the actual world by overlaying digital objects into it, giving users a greater sense of realism than VR. On the contrary, VR immerses the viewer in a completely virtual environment. However, AR connects the real and digital worlds by adding virtual aspects to the real environment [2].

AR in gaming gained quick popularity along with the release of "Pokemon Go" mobile gaming application. This facilitated players to catch virtual Pokemon characters on the actual environment using smartphone devices [3]. Going beyond gaming, AR has gained significant attention across many industries. However, based on a global survey of key technological trends in the retail sector, fashion retail is identified as top ranked, where AR is the most popular technology in fashion retail [4]. The challenge encountered by online fashion retailers is that customers are likely to abandon their e-carts and are skeptical of the selection of clothing [5]. This often results in product returns, which is a tedious procedure for both businesses and consumers, resulting in additional cost, time and dissatisfied customers [6]. Therefore, AR facilitates fashion brands to come with applications embedding "try before you buy" facility. Hence, consumers could direct the cameras of the smartphones towards themselves and virtually try on the fashion items to get some insights [7]. Accordingly, properly integrated AR features within online stores would enhance better customer experience while improving their purchase decisions [8].

Prior empirical research revolving around AR in fashion retail has unveiled that AR applications positively impact on purchase intention [9, 10]. Consumer-to-consumer interactions are also becoming increasingly important due to advances in social media platforms [11]. However, this has not been extensively studied in light of fashion retail with AR applications. Given the nature of AR applications, which facilitates virtual try on, customers are unlikely to be restricted to mere purchasing of the selected products. Rather, customers are enticed to take pictures of themselves virtually wearing various fashion items and even post them on social media platforms [12]. Owing to limited studies focusing on this phenomenon, the present

study aims to develop a conceptual model which examines the influence of AR applications in fashion retail on brand related electronic word of mouth (e-WOM) behavior of the consumers.

The remaining sections of the paper are organized as follows. First, the study undertakes literature review that summarizes the extant literature pertaining to AR applications and consumers' behavioral outcomes. Subsequently, the conceptual model is presented along with the propositions, followed by directions for future research.

2. Literature Review

AR allows organizations to enhance digital information to customers [13]. Among the many definitions of AR, Zhou et al. [14, p. 193] defined AR as, "a technology which allows computer generated virtual imagery to exactly overlay physical objects in real time. Unlike virtual reality (VR), where the user is completely immersed in a virtual environment, AR allows the user to interact with the virtual images using real objects in a seamless way". Hence, AR utilizes the actual environment as the background [15] whereas such actual environmental components could be surroundings, items or even people [16].

Numerous brands have taken notice of AR as a means of improving consumer experience. One of the well-known furniture brands, IKEA, has released a smartphone app that incorporates AR, allowing users to realistically arrange furniture in their real environment [17]. Similar experiences have been extended to fashion retail consumers by various fashion brands as well. Few examples in the fashion retail context was summarized by [9]. Accordingly, Rimmel's "Get The Look" app uses AR technology, where users may experiment on various makeup looks from celebrities by superimposing scanned images of their faces on users' faces. The app facilitates the makeup to remain on consumers' mirrored face even when moving their head. Burberry introduced "Digital run-away nail bar" facilitated through AR technology, which allows customers to virtually try on different manicure colors, through virtual mirrors being set up in the stores. Topshop fashion brands allowed their customers to virtually try-on clothing items. Topology brand enabled similar experience to their customers in virtually trying out eyewear. Widyani [18] highlighted that Gucci's AR applications with virtual try-on facilities enhance brand loyalty.

2.1 Effects of AR Applications on Consumer Behavior

AR significantly impacts consumer behavior in various ways. Studies have shown that AR features such as technology anxiety, virtuality and background influence the attitudes of consumers, behavioral intentions, and purchasing decisions [19], [20]. Compared to traditional websites, AR improves the buying experience by offering vivid and immersive experience, enhancing customer engagement, and favorably impacting purchase intentions [21]. When designing AR applications, it is vital in balancing vividness, novelty and interactivity to enhance consumer flow and experience [22]. Virtual dressing rooms with AR technology reduce perceived risks in shopping clothing items online, enhance the confidence of customers, and improve customer-brand relationships. Hence, virtual dressing rooms ultimately impact e-shopping behavior of the consumers positively [12]. Moreover, AR allows customers to interact with the product via resizing and rotating at their discretion [8]. This would enhance customer experience leading to purchase decisions, customer satisfaction and even reduction in product returns. Need for touch which is deprived via AR applications was studied by Gatter et al. [23]. The findings revealed that AR material is generally rated even higher by customers with a strong autotelic demand for touch than by those with a low need for touch, suggesting that AR can replace in-store experience.

Differences in the user adoption of technology have been a persistent phenomenon in several new technologies, and augmented reality is no exception. Customers' adoption of AR technology is not always ensured by its integration into websites or mobile applications [24]. Moreover, Chung et al. [25] provided more confirmation of this, stating that although augmented reality technology is accessible in the tourism sector, user adoption has not reached anticipated results. Romano et al. [26] claimed that certain consumers have varying views regarding the adoption of AR. Accordingly, not all customers are willing to embrace this technology with open arms and consumers were categorized into four categories based on their eagerness in adopting this technology. The four types were named as, AR enthusiasts, AR open, AR hesitant, AR averse. Hence, as AR studies are fragmented, there is a growing need for future research in this field.

2.2 Reserarch Gap

Extant studies relating to AR have been based on a variety of theories in explaining its relationship with various dimensions of consumer behavior. A systematic review conducted by Jayaswal and Parida [27] summarized some of these theories as, Technology Acceptance Model (TAM), Self-Referencing Theory, Psychological Reactance Theory, Habituation Tedium theory, Stimulus Organism Response (SOR) model, Uses and Gratifications Theory, Situated Cognition Theory, Equity Theory, Psychological

Ownership Theory and Cue Utilization Theory. In addition, Flow Theory [28], Process Theory [29], Unified Theory of Acceptance and Use of Technology (UTAUT) [30], UTAUT2 [31] were also employed as theoretical underpinning in AR related literature.

Owing to the novelty of AR, scholarly literature is paying more and more attention to this phenomenon, despite the fact that earlier research has empirically evaluated this in connection to many elements of consumer behavior. The Stimulus-Organism-Response (SOR) model developed by Mehrabian and Russell [32] is a popular model for analyzing how experiential online retail elements impact customer behavior [9]. As per the SOR model, stimulus are the outside factors that influence people, organisms stand for internal psychological processes and responses are the behavioral outcomes.

Integrating SOR model, prior research has studied how AR based stimulus affects consumers' behavioral outcomes. Accordingly, Watson et al. [9] studied how AR stimuli affects consumers' affective states and purchase intention which were the response variables. Moreover, Wang et al. [33] studied AR app use in beauty product industry integrating SOR model. Consumers' perception of mobile AR services was incorporated as stimulus, which shapes the organism in terms of spatial presence, flow experience and decision comfort leading to behavioral response of purchase intention. In order to identify how mobile AR applications can influence consumers shopping behavior, Qin et al [34] theorized on SOR model. AR app characteristics were identified as stimulus, particularly focusing on interactivity and virtuality. Study involved hedonic, utilitarian, informativeness and ease of use as organism whereas response variables were attitude and behavioral intentions. Furthermore, Daassi and Debbabi [35] employed SOR model explaining perceived augmentation as the stimulus, AR based experience (perceived realism, sense of product presence, sense of immersion) as the organism which affects the outcomes in terms of attitudes and intention to reuse.

Accordingly, most of the prior studies have extensively focused on AR characteristics as stimulus. It is argued that technological affordances of novel media might shape user requirements to generate unique gratifications. As a result, Uses and Gratifications (U&G) Theory should be extended to novel media settings [36]. Hence, the present study integrates U&G theory with SOR model. Extant literature extensively included attitudes or behavioral intentions as response. Prior studies have also shown that future studies pertaining to augmented reality should take into account other behavioral outcomes as customer happiness, loyalty, and consumer-to-consumer interactions [9], [38]. In today's context, consumers' behavioral outcomes are not simply restricted to purchase intentions, such that social media allows users to share brand related experience with many others [38]. On this backdrop, what gratifications of AR applications drive people to use these applications and how such gratifications would affect consumer to consumer interactions have seldom been explored. The present study continues that line of research and aims to bridge this gap by integrating U&G theory with SOR model. U&G provides explanation on what stimulus as per the SOR model can be influential in media context [39], hence this is linked to the context of AR as well, since it is virtual medium [9]. Accordingly, what gratifications of AR drive people to use AR applications and how this would result in consumer-to-consumer interactions on social media platforms will be studied by considering SOR model as the broader theoretical framework.

While technology applications in the retail sector can offer better experience to customers [40], such favorable outcomes may not always be guaranteed. Accordingly, technology may enhance as well as harm consumer experience along the customer journey [26]. The investigation of Romano et al. [17] sentiments across different customer categories about the adoption and application of AR in retail revealed notable disparities. Thus, it is not sufficient for retailers to merely implement AR technology in their retail setting, rather they also need to take into account how ready their customers are in adopting this technology. In light of this, determining customers' technology readiness for embracing AR technology is imperative.

There is a dearth of studies on the moderating influence of technology readiness on consumer behavior [41]. SOR model alone is not adequate to bridge this gap, as it does not explain under what conditions or contingencies SOR framework operates and predicts responses in an online media context. Accordingly, the present study integrates technology readiness as a moderating variable. Additionally, brand engagement explains how organism would be shaped in the online context [42] and hence is presented as a mediator leading to e-WOM behavior as responses of consumers.

2.3 Theoritical Framework

The present study employs the SOR model as the broader theoretical framework. Uses and gratifications pertaining to numerous media have been considered as stimuli of SOR model in prior consumer behavior studies [44], [45]. On this notion, the present study also integrates U&G of AR applications as the stimulus. As for the organism in SOR model, the present study aims to integrate how individual characteristics in terms of emotions would take place

on online platforms. Hence, the study would look into consumer engagement which is integrated as organism. Since the present study aims to identify why people use AR applications and how it would lead to consumer-to-consumer interactions, the study integrates brand related e-WOM behavior as the response component in the SOR model.

3. Methodology

A concept paper provides integration of literature, which leads to development of a framework and thereby highlight the future research directions [45]. Accordingly, a concept paper requires proposing novel relationships among identified constructs, rather than empirical testing of data. In line with this, the present concept paper also follows a similar approach which studied prior literature pertaining to AR in consumer behavior and taking the identified research gap into consideration, research propositions and research design are proposed.

4. Research Propositions

e-WOM content comprises vital information exchanged in online discussions, hence it is essential in influencing consumer decisions [46]. e-WOM is defined as "any positive or negative statement made by potential, actual or former customers about a product or company, which is made available to a multitude of people and institutions via the Internet" [48, p. 39]. According to Ruggiero [48] the U&G Theory explains why individuals decide to utilize particular media. People now select media for a variety of reasons other than just wanting to make a purchase; as a result, social media is becoming increasingly vital in consumer-to-consumer interactions. Therefore, individuals use e-WOM and select channels according to what makes them happy [49].

U&G factors in terms of social enhancement, information seeking and hedonic value develop user satisfaction and would result in positive e-WOM on Facebook [50]. Moreover, Ibáñez-Sánchez et al. [51] studied U&G of AR filters on social media and their impact on e-WOM. Accordingly, authors found that gratifications of AR filters would lead to satisfactory experience which compel uses to share the experience with others. Kamboj [52] stated that uses and gratifications obtained in social media affects word of mouth behavior within social media related brand communities. Recent developments in the e-WOM literature has encompassed various forms of brand related e-WOM behavior such as brand evangelism [53] and online brand advocacy [54]. On this notion, Sohaib et al. [55] mentioned that as per the U&G theory, social media interactions may elevate perceived values, resulting in heightened satisfaction and the emergence of brand evangelists.

Proposition 1: U&G of AR applications impact on brand related e-WOM behavior.

Brand engagement on social media by consumers is receiving more attention in marketing. Novel media technologies have further enabled consumers to transition from being passive receivers of information to becoming active producers of it [56]. Social-media users share their thoughts to connect and interact with like-minded individuals about particular products or brands on social-media platforms [57]. Brand related content on social media was given much prominence in the past where consumers could interact with such context through "likes" and "comments". Hence, this interaction with brands constituted consumer engagement which was largely facilitated by social media platforms [58]. Brand created content was subsequently overridden by user-generated content where customers started creating content. These were deemed more authentic and credible [59].

In relation to social media, information gratifications of social media lead to user generated content where users strive to share information among others on various online platforms [60]. Over the years, user-generated content on social media has grown quickly and is reportedly changing the face of traditional media [61]. As far as AR technologies are concerned, they provide unique interactivity via augmentation which is facilitated by the nature of the technology [16]. When consumers can virtually try on items via AR, it enables them to take snapshots of them and create posts which they would ultimately share online by engaging with brands [12]. Such engagement has transformed into novel ways such as creation of posts with hashtags further enhancing customer engagement [62]. Hence it is proposed;

Proposition 2: U&G of AR applications impact on consumer engagement.

Consumer actions toward sharing content pertaining to brands on social media are strategically important in the area of digital marketing [63]. This is especially noticeable in a time when customers are more prone to believe one another than content posted by brands [64]. Moreover, brand awareness and purchase intention are likely improve when customers interact with companies on social media platforms voluntarily [65]. Furthermore, e-WOM is considered a crucial behavioral consequence of customers interacting with companies on digital platforms [66].

Proposition 3: Consumer engagement impacts on brand related e-WOM behavior.

Customers who are deeply engaged with businesses are compelled to write, publish, and share messages on social media platforms that express their thoughts and views about those brands [66]. AR applications in particular provide whole new immersive experience to customers with virtual try on facilities specially in fashion retail context [9]. Hence, the consumers are able to envisage possibilities and novel ideas owing to AR applications experience which enhances engagement and subsequent behavioral outcomes [67]. These special features possessed by AR applications would induce consumers to engage more with the brands through novel experience being offered to customers [68].

Moreover, AR filters on social media encourage consumers to spread the word about such filters through online platforms [51]. Social media platforms are fostering e-WOM interaction in a variety of ways and brands are constantly striving to get consumers involved and engaged with brands while sharing the positive feedback with others [69]. Therefore, when people start acting as brand advocates, such shared material may benefit the organizations [70].

Proposition 4: Consumer engagement mediates the relationship between U&G of AR and brand related e-WOM behavior.

Prior research reported positive relationship between technology utilizations and technology readiness, meaning that consumers who are more tech-ready are more inclined to embrace a certain technology. Moreover, personal factors of users increase the likelihood of them utilizing technology [71]. Technology acceptance affects participants' enthusiasm towards AR applications usage. Accordingly, perceived usefulness is the most influencing technology acceptance factor towards AR applications while perceived ease of use affect consumers' intention to use virtual mirrors powered by AR technology established in stores [72]. In terms of VR, technology readiness towards VR moderates the relationship between VR based brand engagement and brand cocreation [73]. Therefore, a crucial component of consumer behavior in an interactive digital environment is customer brand engagement [74].

Proposition 5: Technology readiness moderates the relationship between U&G of AR and consumer engagement.

5. The Proposed Conceptual Framework

Based on the review of literature and propositions, the conceptual framework has been developed and is depicted in Figure 1. Considering the broader theoretical framework of SOR model, stimulus is identified as the Uses and

Gratifications of AR applications which is the independent construct. The organism is the consumer engagement, the mediator. The said stimulus and organisms lead to brand related e-WOM which is the dependent construct. In addition, addressing the theoretical gap, technology readiness is included as the moderator.

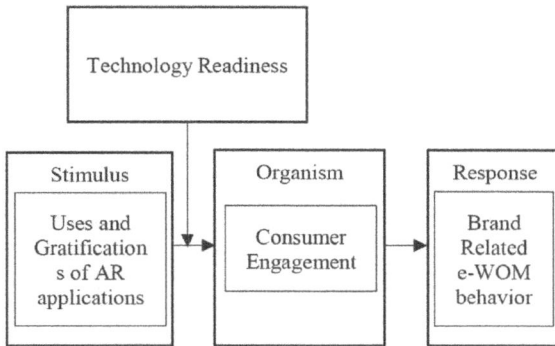

Fig. 6.1 Conceptual framework

Source: Authors

6. Theoritical Implications

Based on the SOR model as the broader theoretical framework, the present study integrates U&G theory as stimulus and consumer engagement as the organism which leads to the response of brand related e-WOM. The present study also responds to the advanced SOR model suggested by Fiore and Kim [75], that highlighted the need to integrate the appropriate moderators in consumer shopping experience related studies. Authors suggested such moderators to be individual characteristics or shopping situations which would strengthen the nexus between stimulus and response. Hence, this present concept paper proposes the technological readiness to be incorporated in the SOR model as the moderator given the importance of technological know-how of consumers in AR related consumer behavior studies.

The importance of technology readiness of consumers in AR shopping context was also highlighted in Romano et al. [17] findings that stated four different consumer segments pertaining to embracing AR technology in terms of AR enthusiast, AR open, AR hesitant and AR averse.

7. Managerial Implications

Empirically testing the proposed conceptual framework, the future studies would have implications on fashion retailers. Having identified what gratifications of AR apps in fashion retail would drive consumers to embrace the technology enable the organizations to better integrate such factors when designing AR applications.

Moreover, the present study may also provide insights to marketers in designing their social media marketing strategies revolving around AR applications. Additionally, AR can foster deeper customer engagement by creating interactive brand stories and exclusive content for loyal customers, enhancing their sense of connection to the brand. Moreover, by providing a clearer understanding of products and reducing purchase uncertainty, AR can significantly improve customer trust in online fashion retail.

8. Conclusion and Directions for Future Research

The current study has presented a conceptual framework, that can be utilized in future research revolving around AR applications. The paper has provided new insights on AR applications related gratifications and consumer behavior. Theorizing on SOR model, the framework proposes to study what gratifications of AR drive people to use these applications and how consumers would engage on social media leading to e-WOM behavior. Hence, the study proposes brand related e-WOM to be integrated as consumers' behavioral outcome without having limited to purchase intention. Accordingly, future research may include more precise brand related e-WOM behavioral aspects such as brand evangelism [53] or online brand advocacy [76]. In addition, the study integrates technology readiness as a moderating variable, given the fragmented research which studies this phenomenon, yet been identified as a crucial factor when introducing new technologies in the retail setting. This conceptual model may be applied in future studies to examine these relationships in different contexts.

REFERENCES

1. C. Ntumba, S. Aguayo, and K. Maina, "Revolutionizing Retail: A Mini Review of E-commerce Evolution," J. Digit. Mark. Commun., vol. 3, no. 2, pp. 100–110, 2023, doi: 10.53623/jdmc.v3i2.365.
2. A. M. Al-Ansi, M. Jaboob, A. Garad, and A. Al-Ansi, "Analyzing augmented reality (AR) and virtual reality (VR) recent development in education," Soc. Sci. Humanit. Open, vol. 8, no. 1, 2023, doi: 10.1016/j.ssaho.2023.100532.
3. A. Aluri, "Mobile augmented reality (MAR) game as a travel guide : insights from Pokémon GO," J. Hosp. Tour. Technol., vol. 8, no. 1, pp. 55–72, 2017, doi: 10.1108/JHTT-12-2016-0087.
4. R. M. Wickramarathne, D. W. A. Gooneratne, and R. K. H. S. Wimalasiri, "Factors affecting the adoption of augmented reality (AR) technology as a marketing strategy in the fashion retailing sector of Sri Lanka," in 13th International Conference on Business & Information (ICBI), 2022, pp. 532–554.

5. R. Namboodiri, K. Singla, and V. Kulkarni, "GAN Based Try-On System: Improving CAGAN Towards Commercial Viability," in 12th International Conference on Computing Communication and Networking Technologies (ICCCNT), 2021, pp. 1–6, doi: 10.1109/ICCCNT51525.2021.9579703.

6. B. Stöcker, D. Baier, and B. M. Brand, New insights in online fashion retail returns from a customers' perspective and their dynamics, vol. 91, no. 8. 2021.

7. V. Lavoye, J. Mero, and A. Tarkiainen, "Consumer behavior with augmented reality in retail: a review and research agenda," Int. Rev. Retail. Distrib. Consum. Res., vol. 31, no. 3, pp. 299–329, 2021, doi: 10.1080/09593969.2021.1901765.

8. H. Dethe and E. Joy, "Revolutionizing E-commerce with 3D Visualization: An Experimental Assessment of Behavioural Shopper Responses to Augmented Reality in Online Shopping," in 4th International Conference for Emerging Technology (INCET), 2023, pp. 1–6, doi: 10.1109/INCET57972.2023.10170472.

9. A. Watson, B. Alexander, and L. Salavati, "The impact of experiential augmented reality applications on fashion purchase intention," Int. J. Retail Distrib. Manag., vol. 48, no. 5, pp. 433–451, 2020, doi: 10.1108/IJRDM-06-2017-0117.

10. S. H. A. Kazmi, R. R. Ahmed, K. A. Soomro, A. R. Hashem E, H. Akhtar, and V. Parmar, "Role of augmented reality in changing consumer behavior and decision making: Case of Pakistan," Sustain., vol. 13, no. 24, pp. 1–28, 2021, doi: 10.3390/su132414064.

11. L. C. Hsu, "Investigating the brand evangelism effect of community fans on social networking sites: Perspectives on value congruity," Online Inf. Rev., vol. 43, no. 5, pp. 842–866, 2019, doi: 10.1108/OIR-06-2017-0187.

12. G. Yaoyuneyong, J. Foster, and L. Flynn, "Factors impacting the efficacy of augmented reality virtual dressing room technology as a tool for online visual merchandising," J. Glob. Fash. Mark., vol. 5, no. 4, pp. 283–296, 2014, doi: 10.1080/20932685.2014.926129.

13. P. van Esch, D. Arli, M. H. Gheshlaghi, T. Andonopoulos, Vicki. von der Heidt, and G. Northey, "Anthropomorphism and augmented reality in the retail environment," J. Retail. Consum. Serv., vol. 49, no. C, pp. 35–42, 2019, doi: 10.1016/j.jretconser.2019.03.002.

14. F. Zhou, H. Duh, and M. Billinghurst, "Trends in Augmented Reality Tracking, Interaction and Display: A Review of Ten Years of ISMAR," in IEEE International Symposium on Mixed and Augmented Reality, 2008, pp. 193–201, doi: 10.1109/ISMAR.2008.4637362.

15. D. Fonseca, N. Martí, E. Redondo, I. Navarro, and A. Sánchez, "Relationship between student profile, tool use, participation, and academic performance with the use of Augmented Reality technology for visualized architecture models," Comput. Human Behav., vol. 31, pp. 434–445, 2014, doi: 10.1016/J.CHB.2013.03.006.

16. A. Javornik, "Augmented reality: Research agenda for studying the impact of its media characteristics on consumer behaviour," J. Retail. Consum. Serv., vol. 30, pp. 252–261, 2016, doi: 10.1016/j.jretconser.2016.02.004.

17. B. Romano, S. Sands, and J. Pallant, "Virtual shopping: segmenting consumer attitudes towards augmented reality as a shopping tool," Int. J. Retail Distrib. Manag., vol. 50, no. 10, pp. 1221–1237, 2022, doi: 10.1108/IJRDM-10-2021-0493.

18. D. Widyani, "Brand Loyalty in Gucci Mobile Application," Sch. J. Econ. Bus. Manag., vol. 8, no. 9, pp. 364–367, 2021, doi: 10.36347/sjebm.2021.v08i09.001.

19. P. Dogra, K. A. Kumar, K. Prateek, and A. Kaushal, "Influence of augmented reality on shopping behavior," Manag. Decis., vol. 61, no. 7, pp. 2073–2098, 2023, doi: https://doi.org/10.1108/MD-02-2022-0136.

20. N. Hilal, "The Impact of the Use of Augmented Reality on Online Purchasing Behavior Sustainability: The Saudi Consumer as a Model," Sustain., vol. 15, no. 6, 2023, doi: 10.3390/su15065448.

21. S. Qadari, M. Mir, and M. Khan, "Exploring the Impact of Augmented Reality on Customer Experiences and Attitudes: A Comparative Analysis with Websites," Int. J. Manag. Res. Emerg. Sci., vol. 13, no. 2, pp. 168–192, 2023, doi: 10.56536/ijmres.v13i2.421.

22. J. Barhorst, G. McLean, E. Shah, and R. Mack, "Blending the real world and the virtual world: Exploring the role of flow in augmented reality experiences," J. Bus. Res., vol. 122, pp. 423–436, 2021, doi: 10.1016/j.jbusres.2020.08.041.

23. S. Gatter, V. Hüttl-Maack, and P. Rauschnabel, "Can augmented reality satisfy consumers' need for touch?," Psychol. Mark., vol. 39, no. 3, pp. 508–523, 2022, doi: 10.1002/mar.21618.

24. T. Jung, N. Chung, and M. C. Leue, "The Determinants of Recommendations to use Augmented Reality Technologies: The Case of Korean Theme Park," Tour. Manag., vol. 49, pp. 75–86, 2015.

25. N. Chung, H. Han, and Y. Joun, "Tourists' intention to visit a destination: The role of augmented reality (AR) application for a heritage site," Comput. Human Behav., vol. 50, pp. 588–599, 2015.

26. B. Romano, S. Sands, and J. Pallant, "Augmented reality and the customer journey: An exploratory study," Australas. Mark. J., vol. 29, no. 4, pp. 354–363, 2021, doi: 10.1016/j.ausmj.2020.06.010.

27. P. Jayaswal and B. Parida, "The role of augmented reality in redefining e-tailing: A review and research agenda," J. Bus. Res., vol. 160, p. 113765, 2023, doi: 10.1016/j.jbusres.2023.113765.

28. T. L. Huang and S. Liao, "A model of acceptance of augmented-reality interactive technology: the moderating role of cognitive innovativeness," Electron. Commer. Res., vol. 15, no. 2, pp. 269–295, 2015, doi: 10.1007/s10660-014-9163-2.

29. A. Javornik, B. Marder, M. Pizzetti, and L. Warlop, "Augmented self - The effects of virtual face augmentation on consumers' self-concept," J. Bus. Res., vol. 130, pp. 170–187, 2021, doi: 10.1016/J.JBUSRES.2021.03.026.

30. M. Akçayır and G. Akçayır, "Advantages and challenges associated with augmented reality for education: A systematic review of the literature," Educ. Res. Rev., vol. 20, pp. 1–11, 2017, doi: 10.1016/j.edurev.2016.11.002.

31. M. A. Khashan, M. Elsotouhy, T. H. Alasker, and M. A. Ghonim, "Investigating retailing customers' adoption of augmented reality apps: integrating the unified theory of acceptance and use of technology (UTAUT2) and task-technology fit (TTF). Marketing Intelligence & Planning," Mark. Intell. Plan., vol. 41, no. 5, pp. 613–629, 2023, doi: 10.1108/mip-03-2023-0112.

32. A. Mehrabian and J. A. Russell, An Approach to Environmental Psychology. Cambridge, MA: MIT Press, 1974.

33. Y. Wang, E. Ko, and H. Wang, "Augmented reality (AR) app use in the beauty product industry and consumer purchase intention," Asia Pacific J. Mark. Logist., vol. 34, no. 1, pp. 110–131, 2022, doi: 10.1108/APJML-11-2019-0684.

34. H. Qin, D. A. Peak, and V. Prybutok, "A virtual market in your pocket: How does mobile augmented reality (MAR) influence consumer decision making?," J. Retail. Consum. Serv., vol. 58, p. 102337, Jan. 2021, doi: 10.1016/J.JRETCONSER.2020.102337.

35. M. Daassi and S. Debbabi, "Intention to reuse AR-based apps: The combined role of the sense of immersion, product presence and perceived realism," Inf. Manag., vol. 58, no. 4, 2021, doi: 10.1016/j.im.2021.103453.

36. S. S. Sundar and A. M. Limperos, "Uses and Grats 2.0: New Gratifications for New Media," J. Broadcast. Electron. Media, vol. 57, no. 4, pp. 504–525, 2013, doi: 10.1080/08838151.2013.845827.

37. A. M. Fiore and J. Kim, "An integrative frameworkcapturing experiential andutilitarian shopping experience," Int. J. Retail &Distribution Manag., vol. 35, no. 6, pp. 421–442, 2007, doi: 10.1108/09590550710750313.

38. M. L. Cheung, G. D. Pires, and P. J. Rosenberger, "Developing a conceptual model for examining social media marketing effects on brand awareness and brand image," Int. J. Econ. Bus. Res., vol. 17, no. 3, pp. 243–261, 2019, doi: 10.1504/IJEBR.2019.098874.

39. B. Sampat and S. Raj, "Fake or real news? Understanding the gratifications and personality traits of individuals sharing fake news on social media platforms," Aslib J. Inf. Manag., vol. 74, no. 5, pp. 840–876, 2022, doi: 10.1108/AJIM-08-2021-0232.

40. K. A. Theeb, A. M. Mansour, A. S. D. Khaled, A. A. Syed, and A. M. M. Saeed, "The impact of information technology on retail industry: an empirical study," Int. J. Procure. Manag., vol. 16, no. 4, pp. 549–568, 2023, doi: 10.1504/IJPM.2023.129553.

41. H. A. D. M. Arachchi and G. D. Samarasinghe, "Intention to Adopt Intelligent Clothing in the Fashion Retail Industry: Extending the HISAM Model with Technology Readiness," Int. J. Hum. Comput. Interact., 2023, doi: 10.1080/10447318.2023.2254622.

42. Y. Chen, C. Prentice, S. Weaven, and A. Hisao, "The influence of customer trust and artificial intelligence on customer engagement and loyalty – The case of the home-sharing industry," Front. Psychol., vol. 13, no. August, pp. 1–15, 2022, doi: 10.3389/fpsyg.2022.912339.

43. I. C. Gogan, Z. Zhang, and E. D. Matemba, "Impacts of gratifications on consumers' emotions and continuance use intention: An empirical study of Weibo in China," Sustainability, vol. 10, no. 9, pp. 1–20, 2018, doi: 10.3390/su10093162.

44. S. Jung, S. Lee, and S. Leitch, "Examining the effect of gamification mobile app on conference engagement: an integration of S-O-R framework and UGT," Int. J. Event Festiv. Manag., pp. 1758–2954, 2024, doi: 10.1108/IJEFM-08-2023-0070.

45. L. L. Gilson and C. B. Goldberg, "Editors' Comment: So, What Is a Conceptual Paper?," Gr. Organ. Manag., vol. 40, no. 2, pp. 127–130, 2015, doi: 10.1177/1059601115576425.

46. T. P. Erhan, P. Purnamaningsih, and N. Rizkalla, "Brand's Cool Dimension Effect on Customer Satisfaction and Its Implication to Visual E-WoM," Int. J. NEW MEDIA Technol., vol. 6, no. 2, 2019, doi: 10.31937/IJNMT.V6I2.1224.

47. T. Hennig-Thurau, K. P. Gwinner, G. Walsh, and D. D. Gremler, "Electronic word-of-mouth via consumer-opinion platforms: What motivates consumers to articulate themselves on the Internet?," J. Interact. Mark., vol. 18, no. 1, pp. 38–52, 2004, doi: 10.1002/dir.10073.

48. T. E. Ruggiero, "Uses and Gratifications Theory in the 21st Century," Mass Commun. Soc., vol. 3, no. 1, pp. 3–37, 2000, doi: https://doi.org/10.1207/S15327825MCS0301_02.

49. H. Kreis and S. A. Gottschalk, "Relating EWOM Motives To EWOM Channel Choice - Why Do We Post Where We Do?," Schmalenbach Bus. Rev., vol. 67, pp. 406–429, 2015, doi: https://doi.org/10.1007/BF03396927.

50. P. R. Pintrich, "The Role of Goal Orientation in Self-Regulated Learning," Handb. Self-Regulation, pp. 451–502, 2000, doi: 10.1016/b978-012109890-2/50043-3.

51. S. Ibáñez-Sánchez, C. Orús, and C. Flavián, "Augmented reality filters on social media. Analyzing the drivers of playability based on uses and gratifications theory," Psychol. Mark., vol. 39, no. 3, pp. 559–578, 2022, doi: 10.1002/mar.21639.

52. S. Kamboj, "Applying uses and gratifications theory to understand customer participation in social media brand communities: Perspective of media technology," Asia Pacific J. Mark. Logist., vol. 32, no. 1, pp. 205–231, 2019, doi: 10.1108/APJML-11-2017-0289.

53. E. P. Becerra and V. Badrinarayanan, "The influence of brand trust and brand identification on brand evangelism," J. Prod. Brand Manag., vol. 22, no. 5, pp. 371–383, 2013, doi: 10.1108/JPBM-09-2013-0394.

54. V. Wilk, P. Harrigan, and G. N. Soutar, "Navigating online brand advocacy (OBA): an exploratory analysis," J. Mark. Theory Pract., vol. 26, no. 1–2, pp. 99–116, 2018, doi: 10.1080/10696679.2017.1389246.

55. M. Sohaib, A. A. Safeer, and A. Majeed, "Does firm-created social media communication develop brand evangelists? Role of perceived values and customer experience," Mark. Intell. Plan., 2024, doi: 10.1108/MIP-09-2023-0465.

56. D. W. Stewart and P. A. Pavlou, "From consumer response to active consumer: Measuring the effectiveness of interactive media," J. Acad. Mark. Sci., vol. 30, no. 4, pp. 376–396, 2002, doi: 10.1177/009207002236912/METRICS.

57. E. A. Ryu and E. K. Han, "Social media influencer's reputation: Developing and validating a multidimensional scale," Sustain., vol. 13, no. 2, pp. 1–18, 2021, doi: 10.3390/su13020631.

58. W. Tafesse and B. P. Wood, "Followers' engagement with instagram influencers: The role of influencers' content and engagement strategy," J. Retail. Consum. Serv., vol. 58, 2021, doi: 10.1016/j.jretconser.2020.102303.

59. R. A. Raji, S. M. Rashid, and S. M. Ishak, "Consumer-based brand equity (CBBE) and the role of social media communications: Qualitative findings from the Malaysian automotive industry," J. Mark. Commun., vol. 25, no. 5, pp. 511–534, 2019, doi: 10.1080/13527266.2018.1455066.

60. L. Chavez, C. Ruiz, R. Curras, and B. Hernandez, "The role of travel motivations and social media use in consumer interactive behaviour: A uses and gratifications perspective," Sustain., vol. 12, no. 21, pp. 1–22, 2020, doi: 10.3390/su12218789.

61. G. Shao, "Understanding the appeal of user-generated media: a uses and gratification perspective," Internet Res., vol. 19, no. 1, pp. 7–25, 2009, doi: 10.1108/10662240910927795.

62. P. A. Rauschnabel, P. Sheldon, and E. Herzfeldt, "What motivates users to hashtag on social media?," Psychol. Mark., vol. 36, no. 5, pp. 473–488, 2019, doi: 10.1002/mar.21191.

63. B. Schivinski, "Eliciting brand-related social media engagement: A conditional inference tree framework," J. Bus. Res., vol. 130, pp. 594–602, 2021, doi: https://doi.org/10.1016/j.jbusres.2019.08.045.

64. B. Schivinski, D. G. Muntinga, H. M. Pontes, and P. Lukasik, "Influencing COBRAs: the effects of brand equity on the consumer's propensity to engage with brand-related content on social media," J. Strateg. Mark., vol. 29, no. 1, pp. 1–23, 2021, doi: https://doi.org/10.1080/0965254X.2019.1572641.

65. B. Schivinski, D. G. Muntinga, H. M. Pontes, and P. Lukasik, "Influencing COBRAs: the effects of brand equity on the consumer's propensity to engage with brand-related content on social media," J. Strateg. Mark., vol. 29, no. 1, pp. 1–23, 2021, doi: 10.1080/0965254X.2019.1572641.

66. X. Liu, H. Shin, and A. C. Burns, "Examining the impact of luxury brand's social media marketing on customer engagement: Using big data analytics and natural language processing," J. Bus. Res., vol. 125, pp. 815–826, 2021, doi: https://doi.org/10.1016/j.jbusres.2019.04.042.

67. J. M. Kang, J. Kim, J. Lee, and S. Lin, "How mobile augmented reality digitally transforms the retail sector: examining trust in augmented reality apps and online/offline store patronage intention," J. Fash. Mark. Manag. An Int. J., vol. 27, no. 1, pp. 161–181, 2023, doi: 10.1108/JFMM-12-2020-0273.

68. I. Khan and M. Fatma, "AR app-based brand engagement and outcomes: A moderated mediation approach," J. Retail. Consum. Serv., vol. 76, no. November 2023, p. 103618, 2024, doi: 10.1016/j.jretconser.2023.103618.

69. P. Kotler and K. L. Keller, Marketing Management, 14th ed. Pearson Education, 2012.

70. V. Wilk, G. N. Soutar, and P. Harrigan, "Online brand advocacy and brand loyalty: a reciprocal relationship?," Asia Pacific J. Mark. Logist., vol. 33, no. 10, pp. 1977–1993, 2021, doi: 10.1108/APJML-05-2020-0303.

71. M. Blut and C. Wang, "Technology readiness: a meta-analysis of conceptualizations of the construct and its impact on technology usage," J. Acad. Mark. Sci., vol. 48, pp. 649–669, 2020, doi: 10.1007/s11747-019-00680-8 J.

72. L. Xue, C. J. Parker, and C. A. Hart, "How augmented reality can enhance fashion retail: a UX design perspective," Int. J. Retail Distrib. Manag., vol. 51, no. 1, pp. 59–80, 2023, doi: 10.1108/IJRDM-09-2021-0435.

73. R. A. Rather, L. D. Hollebeek, S. M. C. Loureiro, I. Khan, and R. Hasan, "Exploring Tourists' Virtual Reality-Based Brand Engagement: A Uses-and-Gratifications Perspective," J. Travel Res., 2023, doi: 10.1177/00472875231166598.

74. D. Gligor, B. Siddik, and R. Ivan, "Achieving customer engagement with social media: A qualitative comparative analysis approach," J. Bus. Res., vol. 101, no. C, pp. 56–69, 2019, doi: 10.1016/j.jbusres.2019.04.006.

75. A. M. Fiore and J. Kim, "An integrative framework capturing experiential and utilitarian shopping experience," Int. J. Retail Distrib. Manag., vol. 35, no. 6, pp. 421–442, 2007, doi: 10.1108/09590550710750313.

76. V. Wilk, G. N. Soutar, and P. Harrigan, "Online brand advocacy (OBA): the development of a multiple item scale," J. Prod. Brand Manag., vol. 29, no. 4, pp. 415–429, 2020, doi: 10.1108/JPBM-10-2018-2090/FULL/XML.

Transformative Applied Research in Computing, Engineering, Science and Technology – Dr. Damayanthi Dahanayake et al. (eds)
© 2024 Taylor & Francis Group, London, ISBN 978-1-041-01782-0

7

Designing an Automated Vehicle Fitness Evaluation System by Integrating Machine Learning to Achieve Unbiased Results in Warrant of Fitness Assessments

D.G.T.L Geethmal
Department of Information and Systems Sciences,
NSBM Green University,
Sri Lanka

Mohamed Sapraz*
Department of Software Engineering and Information Systems,
NSBM Green University,
Sri Lanka

Abstract

This research focuses on enhancing road safety in Sri Lanka by developing an automated Warrant of Fitness (WOF) inspection result evaluation system using machine learning. The current vehicle inspection process relies heavily on manual result evaluation and human judgment, leading to potential biases and inconsistencies. By integrating machine learning, this study proposes a result evaluation system that automates the evaluation of vehicle inspection parameters, reducing human involvement in score calculation and result prediction. The research follows the Design Science Research Methodology (DSRM) framework, which guided the systematic design, development, and evaluation of the proposed solution. Although no primary data was collected from public sources a quantitative approach was utilized by employing historical WOF parameters from the New Zealand Transport Agency (NZTA) website and developing a synthetic dataset based on the parameters originating from the NZTA and enhanced the dataset to ensure the data-driven predictions on vehicle roadworthiness. The Random Forest model, tested against logistic regression, demonstrated superior performance with 99% accuracy, ensuring reliable identification of roadworthy and unfit vehicles. This automated approach not only streamlines the inspection process but also contributes to improving road safety by ensuring roadworthy vehicles only have access to public roads. The research findings highlight the potential benefits of adopting machine learning-based automation in vehicle inspections and highlight its scalability and adaptability for Sri Lanka's transportation network.

Keywords

Decision-making, Machine learning, Road safety, Vehicle inspection, Warrant of fitness

*Corresponding author: shafraz@nsbm.ac.lk

DOI: 10.1201/9781003616368-7

1. Introduction

1.1 Research Background

Sri Lanka, renowned for its natural beauty and rich cultural heritage, is currently grappling with a significant road safety crisis. This challenge stems from the lack of a systematic approach to assess vehicle roadworthiness before their operation on public roads. Although the country boasts a well-developed transportation network, the absence of standardized checks has contributed to a troubling increase in road accidents and safety risks associated with inadequately maintained vehicles [1].

The consequences of this issue are severe, resulting in numerous fatalities, extensive property damage, and disruptions to traffic flow. Alarming statistics indicate that road traffic accidents have surged, highlighting the urgent need for effective interventions to protect road users. A study titled "An Analysis of the Enduring Factors of Road Traffic Accidents in Sri Lanka" reveals that the frequency and severity of road accidents have escalated over recent decades, leading to significant loss of life and injuries. This research, conducted over two decades, identifies a strong correlation between the number of vehicles in operation and the incidence of serious accidents, as well as a consistent link between road length and accident occurrences [2].

The study conducted in Sri Lanka from 1997 to 2017 investigated the enduring factors that contribute to grievous road traffic accidents. These findings underscore the critical necessity for implementing robust measures to enhance road safety and mitigate the devastating impacts of traffic accidents. The ongoing rise in road traffic incidents calls for immediate action to establish a comprehensive framework for vehicle inspections and road safety management, ensuring that all vehicles on the road meet safety standards and contribute to a safer transportation environment for all users[3].

The study aims to address this challenge by developing a data-driven Warrant of Fitness (WOF) system with machine learning integration to enhance vehicle inspection decisions. The system will leverage historical vehicle inspection data to make accurate, data-driven decisions about a vehicle's roadworthiness, ensuring that only roadworthy vehicles are allowed on the roads. The proposed solution builds upon the existing research on roadworthy certification systems, which have been successfully implemented in various countries to enhance road safety and reduce accidents. The system will integrate advanced technologies like computerized testing and diagnostics to provide a comprehensive evaluation of a vehicle's roadworthiness [4].

The proposed system's implementation presents various advantages, particularly in enhancing road safety by ensuring that only vehicles deemed roadworthy are allowed on the roads, thereby minimizing accidents linked to mechanical failures. Successful execution of this system necessitates collaboration among pertinent government bodies, transportation authorities, technology suppliers, and stakeholders from the automotive industry. Additionally, it is vital to undertake comprehensive training and capacity-building initiatives to equip inspectors and technicians with the essential skills required for effective inspections.

1.2 Research Objectives & Deliverables

The objectives of this research study are to develop and integrate a machine learning model that leverages NZTA WOF vehicle inspection parameters and develop synthetic data to make accurate, automated decisions about vehicle fitness and roadworthiness, by reducing the need for human interactions. The model will be evaluated for its accuracy and reliability by quantifying its performance metrics, such as precision, recall, and overall prediction accuracy, using historical and synthetic vehicle inspection datasets.

The deliverable of this study includes a fully developed Minimum viable product (MVP) that fulfills the essential requirements with a trained machine learning model that can predict vehicle roadworthiness based on synthetic vehicle inspection data. Also, the scholarly paper will present the research approach and methodology, DSRM approach, findings, and implementation of the study, and working prototype of the automated WOF system demonstrating the integration of the machine learning model and showcasing human-less decision-making capabilities

1.3 Problem Statement

The absence of a thorough vehicle fitness inspection system in Sri Lanka has led to numerous critical issues, exacerbating the already high incidence of road accidents attributed to vehicles that do not comply with essential safety regulations [5]. Without a structured certification process, vehicle owners may overlook vital maintenance, resulting in prevalent problems such as defective brakes, malfunctioning lights, and other safety hazards. This situation has rendered the roads increasingly perilous, elevating risks for both drivers and pedestrians.

A recent article from July 2023 in The Federal underscores the gravity of the road safety crisis in Sri Lanka, reporting that approximately 12,000 individuals die annually in fatal road accidents, which translates to about two fatalities every 90 minutes [6]. These alarming figures highlight the pressing need for initiatives aimed at enhancing road safety and vehicle standards. The lack of a robust system, as outlined in this problem statement, is a significant factor contributing to the persistently elevated rates of accidents.

2. Literature Review

Road safety is a pressing concern in Sri Lanka, with the country grappling with a high incidence of road accidents and fatalities. The absence of an unbiased procedure to inspect vehicles has contributed to this issue [7], as poorly maintained and unsuitable vehicles continue to operate on the public roads [4]. In this literature review, we examine the existing research and best practices related to the warrant of fitness systems, their impact on road safety, and their successful implementation in other countries.

Existing research highlights the importance of warrant of fitness like decision support system can enhance road safety, with countries like New Zealand [8] [9], Australia [10], Spain [10] demonstrating significantly lower road accident-related death rates compared to Sri Lanka [11].

The experiences of developing nations provide valuable insights into best practices and lessons learned, emphasizing the critical importance of regular vehicle inspections and the associations between driver, vehicle, and environmental factors with roadworthiness violations. The adoption of a decision support system, such as a warrant of fitness, could effectively address challenges related to estimating the causal role of vehicle defects in road crashes by standardizing inspection procedures, minimizing human subjectivity, and generating precise, time-stamped records detailing vehicle conditions. However, the implementation of such a decision support system faces several challenges, including resistance to change [12], cultural barriers, lack of coordination and collaboration among stakeholders [13] [14], legal and regulatory challenges [15], and limited resources and funding [16]. To overcome these

hurdles, it is crucial to establish collaboration among relevant stakeholders, undertake adequate training and capacity-building initiatives, and conduct public awareness campaigns to promote the benefits of this kind of system [17]. By examining the experiences of other countries and addressing the unique challenges faced by Sri Lanka, the implementation of a data-driven warrant of fitness system has the potential to significantly enhance road safety and contribute to environmental sustainability. Overall, the literature review highlights the urgent need for comprehensive road safety measures in Sri Lanka and explains the potential benefits of implementing a decision support system to address the country's persistent road safety challenges.

3. Research Design

3.1 Design Science Research Methodology

This research adheres to the six phases of the Design Science Research Methodology (DSRM)-problem identification, objective definition, design and development, demonstration, evaluation, and communication. The study begins by recognizing the pressing problem of road safety in Sri Lanka, which stems from the absence of a standardized vehicle inspection system. The primary aim is to create a machine learning-integrated Warrant of Fitness (WOF) system that capitalizes on historical vehicle inspection data to make precise and impartial determinations regarding vehicle roadworthiness.

To achieve this objective, the research utilizes a quantitative method used to the collection and analysis of vehicle fitness parameters and outcomes (Pass or Fail) related to meeting safety standards. Due to the lack of a publicly available dataset, the research constructs a quality synthetic dataset derived from real-world NZTA criteria.

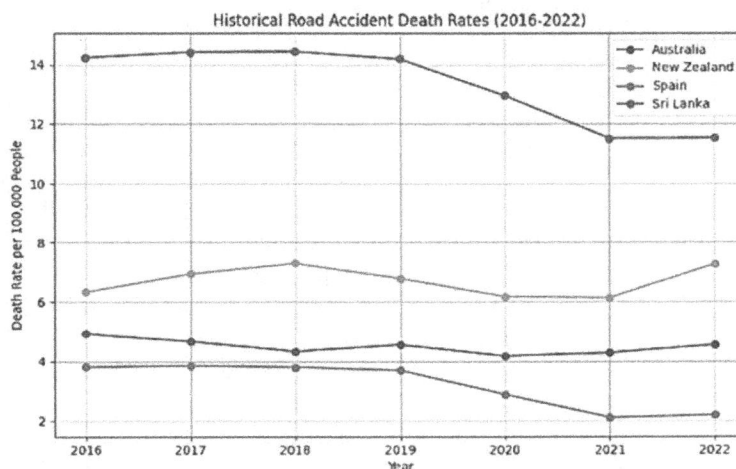

Fig. 7.1 Death rate comparison 2016-2022 [8], [9], [10], [11], [12]

Evaluation involves assessing the model's performance through metrics such as accuracy, precision, recall, and F1, with several machine learning models to get superior results. Finally, the research findings and the developed system are communicated to relevant stakeholders, emphasizing the potential benefits of improved road safety and reduced accidents in Sri Lanka through the implementation of this data-driven WOF system.

3.2 Data Collection

The data collection approach for this study utilizes quantitative methods to gather information on the number of vehicles that do not comply with critical safety standards. The data collection entirely depends on the New Zealand Transport Agency (NZTA) Warrant of Fitness (WOF) vehicle inspection criteria, which will be employed to generate a synthetic dataset. This synthetic dataset will be used for training and evaluating the machine-learning model.

The decision to use and rely on NZTA WOF parameters is justified due to the alignment of motor vehicle availability and regulations between Sri Lanka and New Zealand. Both countries have left-hand driving systems, and most vehicles in Sri Lanka are sourced from Japan, Korea, and the UK, which have similar left-hand driving orientations [18]. The synthetic data generation justification mainly lacks publicly available, verified datasets related to vehicle roadworthiness and WOF inspections in Sri Lanka, so that requires the use of a synthetic dataset. By leveraging NZTA WOF parameters.

The synthetic dataset will be developed using the following parameters:

Table 7.1 Vehicle inspection parameters and weight assignments [21]

Parameter	Weight
Tires	High
Brakes	High
Suspension	Medium
Body And Chassis	Medium
Lights	Medium
Glazing	Medium
Wipers	Low
Doors	Low
Seat Belts	Medium
Airbags	High
Speedometer	Low
Exhaust System	Medium
Fuel System	High

Each parameter has its critical level and to add weight to its critical level we have assigned it as High, Medium, and Low. These levels have predefined scores as follows.

Table 7.2 Weight table

Weight Level	Score
High	10
Medium	6
Low	4

3.3 Formula for Final Score Calculation

Weighted Score Calculation

- For each parameter, multiply the score by its weight.

$$\text{Weighted Score} = \text{Parameter Score} \times \text{Weight} \quad (1)$$

Total Weighted Score

- Sum up the weighted scores of all parameters.

$$\text{Total Weighted Score} = \Sigma(\text{Parameter Score} \times \text{Weight}) \quad (2)$$

Maximum Possible Weighted Score

- Calculate the maximum possible weighted score based on the weights of all parameters. Assuming each parameter score can be a maximum of 10:

$$\text{Maximum Possible Weighted Score} = \Sigma(10 \times \text{weight}) \quad (3)$$

Final Percentage Score

- Calculate the final percentage score

$$\text{Final Precentage Score} = \left(\frac{\text{Total Weighted Score}}{\text{Maximum Possible Weighted Score}}\right) \times 100 \quad (4)$$

3.4 Scoring System for Parameters

The scoring system for each vehicle inspection parameter is designed to reflect its contribution to overall vehicle safety. Each parameter is inspected manually with the aid of mechanical tools, depending on the specific requirement. For example, the Tire score is determined based on factors such as tread depth, tread wear indicators, visual inspection, and tire age. These factors help assess the overall condition of the tires.

It is important to note that the inspection process itself is conducted by domain experts in this phase, such as trained mechanics, who assess each parameter and assign a score ranging from 1 to 10. This manual or mechanical inspection is not a part of the machine learning-based WOF result assessment program. The program was only responsible for evaluating the inspected results, which are inputted as scores.

Each of the 12 parameters (e.g. Tires, breaks, suspension) has a weight (e.g. Tires - High) that reflects its criticality in ensuring vehicle safety.

These weights are applied when calculating the Final Score. The formula for the final evaluation is based on the weighted sum of all parameters, as outlined in the formula declaration area. The maximum possible score for each parameter is 10, and the Maximum Possible Weighted Score is calculated as:

"Maximum Possible Weighted Score = $\Sigma(10 \times weight)$" (5)

This weighted approach ensures that the model accurately reflects the importance of critical components, such as breaks and suspension when determining the vehicle's overall roadworthiness.

3.5 Outcome Determination

The outcome determination process will involve evaluating the final score against two criteria. First, if the final percentage score is greater than or equal to 70%, the vehicle is marked as passed the WOF inspection.

Secondly, if the final percentage score is less than 70% or if there are more than 2 high critical level parameters scored below 4 in that specific vehicle, the vehicle fails to meet WOF standards even final score is more than 70%. This outcome determination will ensure that the final score accurately reflects the overall conditions of the vehicle based on the critical importance of each parameter, providing a reliable and consistent assessment of the vehicle's safety and roadworthiness.

Table 7.3 Sample vehicle inspection parameters and outcomes

Parameters	Sample 1	Sample 2
Tyres	8	4
Brakes	7	8
Suspension	6	2
Body and Chassis	9	3
Lights	8	3
Glazing	6	6
Wipers	7	7
Doors	8	6
Seat Belts	7	3
Airbags	6	2
Speedometer	8	10
Exhaust System	9	10
Fuel System	7	5
Final Score	74.34	49.57
Outcome	Pass	Failed
TIres	8	4

The data collection process will involve the generation of a synthetic dataset using the New Zealand transport agency NZTA WOF vehicle inspection parameters, and as next step follow by the data preprocessing to ensure consistency and quality. After that, the preprocessed data will then be used to train the machine learning model.

3.6 Justification for 70% Threshold

The selection of a 70% threshold for vehicle inspection in this study is substantiated by empirical testing and alignment with industry standards. A systematic evaluation of various thresholds (60%, 65%, 70%, 75%, and 80%) revealed that a 70% threshold effectively balances safety and practicality, as vehicles scoring below this level were significantly more likely to exhibit critical safety issues.

This threshold aligns with real-world performance metrics, where well-maintained vehicles typically score between 7-9 out of 10, indicating that a score of 70% accurately reflects a vehicle's roadworthiness. Additionally, similar thresholds are utilized in established vehicle inspection systems globally, such as New Zealand's Warrant of Fitness (WOF), which emphasizes the importance of regular inspections in enhancing road safety.

To further substantiate this justification, future data analysis should include an examination of vehicle breakdown conditions and accident rates following the implementation of the 70% threshold. Such evidence-based evaluations can provide solid data demonstrating the effectiveness of this threshold in real-world scenarios. Unfortunately, due to time constraints, practical testing of this nature was not feasible within the current study's timeline.

3.7 Model Performance Comparison

Table 7.4 Compares the performance of the models across various metrics

Model	Accuracy	Precision	Recall
Logistic Regression	0.98	1.0	0.95
Random Forest	0.99	0.99	1.0
Model	Accuracy	Precision	Recall

3.8 Sample Dataset

In this study, a total of 968 records were utilized in the analysis. The dataset was derived from historical Warrant of Fitness data provided by the NZTA and supplemented with synthetic datasets created based on these parameters. The dataset was split into training and testing sets, with 80% of the data (576 records) used for training the model and 20% (394 records) reserved for testing. The Final Score feature represents a weighted (Table 7.1) sum of various inspection parameters. Each of these parameters is assigned a specific weight to emphasize the importance of relevant vehicle components. Critical parameters such as Tires and Brakes are given higher weights to reflect their greater influence on overall vehicle safety.

Table 7.5 Sample vehicle inspection data with its outcome

Parameters	Sample 1	Sample 2
Tyres	8	2
Brakes	7	3
Suspension	9	9
Body And Chassis	8	8
Lights	7	2
Glazing	8	8
Wipers	7	7
Doors	8	8
Seat Belts	9	9
Airbags	8	8
Speedometer	7	7
Exhaust System	8	8
Fuel System	7	7
Final Score	77.17	60.86
Outcome	Pass	Failed
Parameters	Sample 1	Sample 2

3.9 Model Prediction Results

Table 7.6 Model performance comparison with sample datasets

Sample ID	Model	Actual Outcome	Predicted Outcome	Confidence
1	Logistic Regression	Pass	Pass	0.99
2	Logistic Regression	Fail	Fail	1.0
1	Random Forest	Pass	Pass	0.96

3.10 Model Selection and Analysis

The Random Forest model outperformed the Logistic Regression model in terms of accuracy, precision, recall, and F1. The Random Forest model achieved an accuracy of 0.99, and a precision of 0.99. recall of 1.0 and F1 0.99 in contract the Logistic Regression model achieved an accuracy of 0.98, precision of 1.0 recall of 0.95, and F1 0.97.

The Random Forest model's superior performance and be attributed to its ability to handle complex interactions between and its robustness to overfitting. The model's high accuracy and precision indicate that it is effective in identifying roadworthy vehicles, while its high recall and F1 score suggest that it can detect a high proportion of failed vehicles.

4. Proposed Solution

4.1 Functional & Non-functional Requirements

The functional requirements include a complete inspection of critical vehicle components, including tires, brakes, suspension, lights, glazing, wipers, doors, seat belts, airbags, speedometer, exhaust system, and fuel system. The system will also integrate machine learning techniques to evaluate and generate decisions with input data. The non-functional requirements include accuracy, reliability, efficiency, scalability, user-friendliness, data security, and interoperability.

4.2 Implementation

Failed Sample Instance

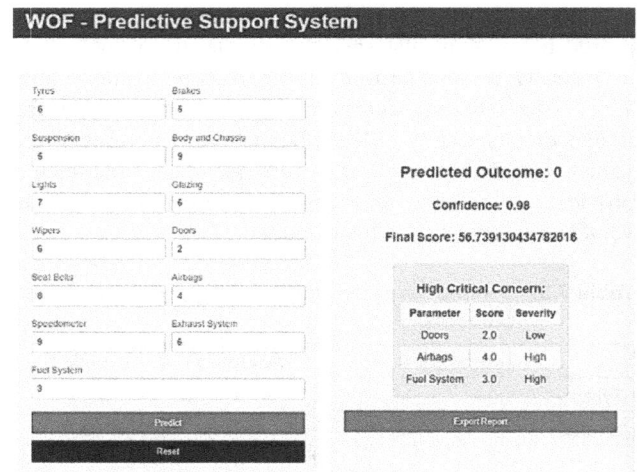

Fig. 7.2 Failed sample instances

Pass Sample Instance

These interfaces showcase the predictive interface that displays the outcomes of the vehicle fitness system. The "Pass" interface shows when a vehicle meets the safety standards, while the "Failed" interface indicates areas needing improvement. Some "Pass" vehicles also may receive a warning for parameters requiring immediate attention. This interface provides a clear demonstration of the system's predictions, allowing users to quickly identify vehicle roadworthiness issues that need to be addressed via generative detailed WOF report.

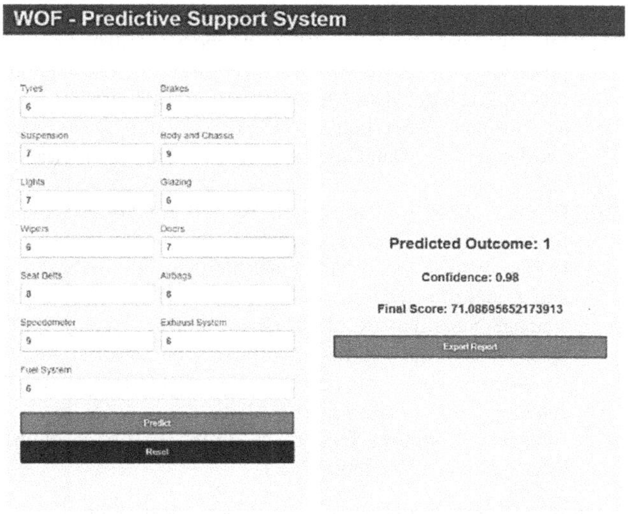

Fig. 7.3 Pass sample instance

5. Discussion

The proposed concept of the WOF system will improve road safety in Sri Lanka by making sure that only roadworthy and fitness cars are allowed only for public roads. The research showcases random forest as an effective algorithm to classify whether a vehicle is a "Pass" or "Fail" using high precision which is above 95%. This model's superior performance can be attributed to its ability to handle complex interactions between variables and its robustness to overfitting.

Due to the unavailability of relevant vehicle inspection data in Sri Lanka, this study utilizes historical Warrant of Fitness (WOF) parameters from New Zealand. This choice not only facilitates a strong analysis but also underscores that should comparable data become accessible in Sri Lanka, similar machine learning-based solutions could be effectively implemented. The integration of machine learning algorithms with the WOF system can improve the accuracy and reliability of vehicle inspection decisions, reducing the risk of biased outcomes and enhancing the overall safety of the transportation network.

The findings of the study emphasize the significance of collaboration among stakeholders, enough learning opportunities, and promoting the advantages of the system to the public through information campaigns. Future studies should focus on extending the current study to explore the application of machine learning models in vehicle inspection decision support processes and adapting the module to incorporate real-time data and make the decision support system fully automated by reducing human interactions. The implementation of this support

system has the potential to contribute to enhancing safer roads and a more efficient transportation network in Sri Lanka.

6. Conclusion

This research study aims to enhance road safety in Sri Lanka by deploying a data-driven vehicle inspection system with a predictive support system using ML. It will address the lack of vehicle inspection and maintenance practices in the country.

The research has employed a DSRM research method and quantitative approach, getting the original vehicle inspection parameters from the New Zealand Transportation Agency to construct a realistic synthetic dataset. This dataset was used to train and evaluate the machine learning model of Random Forest to predict vehicle roadworthiness.

The findings of the study demonstrate the performance of the Random Forest model, which achieved an accuracy of 0.99, precision of 0.99, recall of 1.0, and F1 score is 0.99 in identifying "Pass" and "Faile" vehicles. While the study presents a predictive support solution, its acknowledgment certain limitations, such as the reliance on a systematic dataset due to the lack of a publicly available dataset specific to vehicle inspections in Sri Lanka or worldwide. Future research should explore the application of transfer learning and domain adaptation techniques to improve the module's performance on diverse datasets, as well as the integration of real-time data to enable fully automated decision-support and making.

REFERENCES

1. Nirojan Donald Sinclair, "Three Ways to Improve Road Safety in Sri Lanka | Asian Development Blog," *Adb.org*. Adb.org, 2024.
2. C. T. Danthanarayana and S. N. Mallikahewa, "An Analysis of the Enduring Factors of Road Traffic Accidents in Sri Lanka," *Sri Lanka J. Econ. Res.*, vol. 8, no. 2, pp. 39–50, 2021, doi: 10.4038/sljer.v8i2.136.
3. C. T. Danthanarayana and S. N. Mallikahewa, "An Analysis of the Enduring Factors of Road Traffic Accidents in Sri Lanka," *Sri Lanka J. Econ. Res.*, vol. 8, no. 2, p. 39, 2021, doi: 10.4038/sljer.v8i2.136.
4. K. Weerasekera, "Towards Better Roads," UNSW, 2024.
5. EconomyNext, "One dies every 3 hour in Sri Lanka's road accidents – data," *EconomyNext*. EconomyNext, 2023.
6. T. Federal, "Sri Lanka : Road accidents the largest killers , says Health Ministry," 2023.
7. I. Ranasinghe, "Motor vehicle industry: Roadworthiness and suitability," *Latest in the News Sphere | The Morning*, 2024.
8. OECD, "New-Zealand-Road-Safety," *J. Penelit. Pendidik. Guru Sekol. Dasar*, vol. 6, no. August, p. 128, 2019.

9. W. Jones, "Road Crashes in New Zealand," *IATSS Res.*, vol. 30, no. 1, pp. 112–114, 2006, doi: 10.1016/s0386-1112(14)60161-8.

10. F. M. . Hassouna and I. Pringle, "Analysis and Prediction of Crash Fatalities in Australia," *Open Transp. J.*, vol. 13, no. 1, pp. 134–140, 2019, doi: 10.2174/1874447801913010134.

11. A. K. Somasundaraswaran, "Accident Statistics in Sri Lanka," *IATSS Res.*, vol. 30, no. 1, pp. 115–117, 2006, doi: 10.1016/s0386-1112(14)60162-x.

12. L. Olmstread, "Resistance to Change: 5 Causes & Best Practices," *Whatfix.* 2022.

13. R. Jayasekara, C. Siriwardana, D. Amaratunga, and R. Haigh, "Evaluating the network of stakeholders in Multi-Hazard Early Warning Systems for multiple hazards amidst biological outbreaks: Sri Lanka as a case in point," *Prog. Disaster Sci.*, vol. 14, no. April, p. 100228, 2022, doi: 10.1016/j.pdisas.2022.100228.

14. F. Ali and H. Haapasalo, "Development levels of stakeholder relationships in collaborative projects: challenges and preconditions," *Int. J. Manag. Proj. Bus.*, vol. 16, no. 8, pp. 58–76, 2023, doi: 10.1108/IJMPB-03-2022-0066.

15. M. Sirimane, "Sri Lanka - Data Protection Overview | Guidance Note | DataGuidance," *One Trust Data Guidance.* 2021.

16. R. Staff, "IMF says looking at options for Sri Lanka, no formal request," *Reuters*, 2015.

17. P. Plap, W. Tk, and N. Su, "Potential Drivers , Limitations, and Benefits in Implementing ISO 14001 Environmental ManagemenHillary, R. (2004). Environmental management systems and the smaller enterprise. Journal of Cleaner Production, 12, 561–569. doi.org/10.1016/j.jclepro.," *Environ. Sci. An Indian J.*, vol. 13, no. 2, pp. 1–15, 2017.

18. Aceable, "Countries That Drive on the Left Side of the Road - Aceable," Aceable, 2023.

Note: All the figures and tables (except Fig. 7.1 and Table 7.1) in this chapter were made by the authors.

Transformative Applied Research in Computing, Engineering, Science and Technology – Dr. Damayanthi Dahanayake et al. (eds)
© 2024 Taylor & Francis Group, London, ISBN 978-1-041-01782-0

8

Computational Discovery of *Glycyrrhiza Glabra*-based Anti-Androgen Drugs for the Management of Polycystic Ovarian Syndrome Hyperandrogenism— Molecular Docking Study

K.G.J. Shashimini*

Faculty of Humanities and Sciences,
Sri Lanka Institute of Information Technology,
Sri Lanka

M.A.S.H. Mirihana

Faculty of Humanities and Sciences,
Sri Lanka Institute of Information Technology,
Sri Lanka

C.R. Wijesinghe

School of Computing, University of Colombo,
Sri Lanka

Abstract

Polycystic Ovarian Syndrome is a complex, gynecological disorder. Being multifactorial, the most common risk associated with it is infertility. Hyperandrogenism is the major hallmark feature in distinguishing PCOS. CYP17, an enzyme essential for the androgen synthesis, when overexpressed, leads to hyperandrogenism. Inhibiting this overexpression would indeed prevent the increased production of androgens. Plant-based remedies have been emphasized as an emerging trend, in creating therapeutics with lesser side effects. In this study, the phytochemicals of *Glycyrrhiza glabra* were docked and visualized to identify potential inhibitors of target, CYP17 enzyme. Molecular docking was performed using PyRx, Auto Dock Vina Wizard. The visualization of the interactions was performed using the PyMol software. Metformin, Spironolactone, Clomiphene, Flutamide, and Ketoconazole were used as the control drugs. ADMET properties, drug-likeness, and bioavailability of the phytochemicals were analyzed using SWISS ADME and pKCSM servers. Twelve ligands out of the selected ligands showed good docking scores ranging from -4.2 kcal/mol to -10.1 kcal/mol. In comparison, the control drugs too ranged good docking scores from -4.7 kcal/mol to -10.1 kcal/mol. Furthermore, all the twelve ligands formed polar, hydrogen bond interactions, at a distance less than 3.0Å. The selected ligands exhibited varied physicochemical, drug-likeness, pharmacokinetic, and toxicokinetic properties, depicting their absorption, metabolism, bioavailability, and toxicity. The results of the present study reveal

---

*Corresponding author: janeeshashashimini@gmail.com

DOI: 10.1201/9781003616368-8

that twelve compounds from *Glycyrrhiza glabra* could be used as potential and promising drug candidates, for the treatment of PCOS hyperandrogenism via inhibition, which could create a significant medicinal impact in designing and synthesizing more potent drugs.

Keywords

CYP17, Glycyrrhiza glabra, Hyperandrogenism, Molecular docking, PCOS

1. Introduction

Polycystic ovarian syndrome (PCOS), being the most common, heterogeneous, gynaecological endocrine disorder, affects up to 10-15% of females of reproductive age, worldwide [1]. Being chronic and multifactorial, hyperandrogenism, polycystic structures of ovaries; on either one or both ovaries, chronic anovulation, and insulin resistance are considered to be the hallmark features that contribute to distinguishing PCOS [2]. PCOS is further characterized by; hormonal imbalances in Luteinizing hormone (LH) and Follicle stimulating hormone (FSH), disturbed menstrual cycle, and obesity. Most of the PCOS cases, narrate the symptom of increased level of androgens, referred to as hyperandrogenism. Clinically, hyperandrogenism in women will lead to hirsutism, androgenic alopecia, acne and anovulation [3].

Cytochrome P450 17-hydroxylase/17, 20-lyase (CYP17), a monoxygenase and a microsomal enzyme, encoded by the CYP17A1 gene, functions both as a hydroxylase and a lyase, while being essential for adrenal and gonadal steroid synthesis. Due to the overexpression of the CYP17A1 gene, androgen biosynthesis will be promoted more efficiently, and hence play a major role in hyperandrogenism. Currently, hormone therapy and anti-androgen drugs like Spironolactone, Metformin, and Flutamide are being used as prescriptive medicine for PCOS women. However, such therapeutics have shown unsatisfactory side effects in curing the syndrome; swelling of breasts, congenital heart diseases, nipple discharge, headache, and mental confusion. Hence traditional plant-based remedies have emerged as the driving trend, with safety, and fewer side effects among the community [4].

Glycyrrhiza glabra (Licorice), the oldest and most widely known medicinal herb, in the history of Ayurveda, is considered a therapeutic remedy for hyperandrogenism and PCOS [5]. *G. glabra*, belonging to the family Fabaceae, is a herbaceous perennial plant, cultivated in temperate and tropical regions, native to central and southwestern Asia, and also to the Mediterranean. The plant grows up to 1m in height, with pinnate leaves and flowers, having fruits of 2-3cm in length with several seeds. Constituents of *G. glabra* include simple sugars, polysaccharides, amino acids, proteins, starches, sterols, gums, pectin, and resins [6]. *G.glabra*, possesses varied pharmacological actions; antibacterial, antiviral, anti-fungal, anti-diabetic, anti-ulcer, anticancer, anti-malarial, anti-thrombotic, and anti-allergenic potentials. *G.glabra* also shows other remedial functions against depression, sore throat, coughs, asthma, hiccups, liver diseases, gastrointestinal disorders, oral and skin diseases, acidity, and jaundice [7].

Hasan et al. have reported that *G.glabra* can block the synthesis of androgen and estrogen by blocking 17,20-lyase enzymatic activity [8]. Also, Yang et al. have studied the effect of licorice intake on letrozol-enhanced rodents, while concluding that the extracts of licorice inhibit the symptoms of PCOS by regulating the disturbed hormone levels and irregular ovarian follicles, hence hyperandrogenism [9]. Further, Armanini et al., 2004 have concluded, that licorice could block 17-hydroxysteroid dehydrogenase and 17,20-lyase and could reduce serum testosterone, hence could be considered as an adjuvant therapy for hyperandrogenism [10].

Computer-aided drug design (CADD) provides tools and techniques to reduce the cost of research, biological testing efforts, and development time of the drug. Molecular docking is a computational technique, used to predict the binding affinities of ligands to their target proteins, hence finding the lead candidates and their chemical interactions, to predict the potential ligands that could act as drugs for that specific target receptor protein [11].

2. Methodology

2.1 Protein Preparation

The raw crystal structure of CYP17 protein (PDB ID: 3RUK) was retrieved from the Research Collaboratory for Structural Bioinformatics Protein Data Bank (RCSB PDB) (https://www.rcsb.org). Existing ligands and the water molecules were removed from the protein via the PDB Fixer. The final prepared protein was energy minimized via the SWISS PDB viewer and was used for further analysis.

2.2 Identification of Active Sites

The active site locations and the amino acids interacting with the active sites, of the target protein, CYP17 (3RUK) were determined via the CASTp Server 3.0. Thirteen (13) pockets were selected for the present study; based on surface area > 150.00Å^2.

2.3 Ligand Preparation

The ligands were selected, from Dr. Duke's Phytochemical and Ethnabotanical Database (https://phytochem. nal.usda.gov) and IMPPAT: Indian Medicinal Plants, Phytochemistry And Therapeutics (https://cb.imsc.res.in/imppat/home), and from published literature, based on their anti-androgenic activity, and CYP17 inhibition. The 3D structures of the fifteen (15) ligands were retrieved from the PubChem (https://pubchem.ncbi.nlm.nih.gov) database. Further, 3D structures of FDA-approved drugs (anti-androgenic) namely, Clomiphene, Flutamide, Ketoconazole, Metformin, and Spironolactone were retrieved from the PubChem database and were used in the molecular docking studies, as the control trial set. All the structures were converted from SDF to pdbqt format using Open Babel Wizard of PyRx.

2.4 Drug Likeness/ADMET Prediction

Drug likeness, physicochemical properties, pharmacokinetic properties, toxicity analysis of the ligands, and also the bioavailability radar analysis, BOILED-Egg analysis of the ligands were analyzed, using freely available online web servers; SWISS ADME (www.swissadme.ch) and pKCSMserver(https://biosig.lab.uq.edu.au/pkcsm/prediction).

2.5 Molecular Docking

Molecular docking was performed using the AutoDock Vina wizard of PyRx software. Docking was performed for all the selected active sites of CYP17, placing the grid box at the correct coordinates of the target protein.

2.6 Visualization of the Protein-Ligand Interaction

The visualization of the interaction between the ligand and the target protein was performed by using PyMol (version 2.5.5) visualization software.

3. Results and Discussion

The current study investigated the phytochemicals of *G.glabra*, to discover potential drug candidates against the target enzyme CYP17, causing hyperandrogenism of PCOS. Table 8.1 shows the selected fifteen phytochemicals.

3.1 Drug Likeness/ADMET Prediction

It is evident that computational approaches have enabled, the rapid selection of new drugs, by analyzing their drug-related properties. Despite the selection of the potential drug candidate or the inhibitors, the suitability of the inhibitors cannot be ensured, when in contact with biological systems. Hence, ADMET (Absorption, Distribution, Metabolism, Excretion, and Toxicity) including drug likeness should be inferred to make a rational decision on the selection of the potential outcomes. Table 8.1 shows the drug-likeness/ADMET results of the current study.

To investigate the drug-likeness of molecules, a rule of five, defined as, Lipinski's rule of five, has been widely accepted among drug discovery studies. Accordingly, if a molecule with a molecular weight <500, octanol/water Log P <5, number of hydrogen bond acceptors < 10, number of hydrogen bond donors < 5, and Topological polar surface area < 40 Å^2 is considered, such molecule obeys the Lipinski's rule of five, and hence possess the drug-likeness properties. If two or more rules are violated, the molecules will not be satisfied under Lipinski's rule of five [12]. According to the results shown in Table 8.1, all the compounds inferred with zero violations except, Beta Sitosterol, Glycyrrhetic acid and Isoliquiritin, violating only one rule.

The pharmacokinetic properties of the compounds are shown in Table 8.2. Accordingly, compounds with varied levels of gastrointestinal absorption, blood-brain barrier (BBB) permeant, and P-glycoprotein (P-gp) inhibitors could be inferred. Under the toxicity analysis, AMES toxicity, hERG inhibition, and hepatotoxicity were investigated and the results are shown in Table 8.2.

All compounds (except Eugenol and Liquiritin) showed no response in terms of AMES toxicity, depicting no carcinogenic effect. No compounds showed hERG I toxicity, whereas only Beta Sitosterol, Dehydroepiandrosterone, Glabrene, and Glabridin showed hERG II toxicity. No compounds were recorded with hepatotoxic effects.

The Brain Or IntestinaL EstimateD permeation predictive model (BOILED Egg) (Fig. 8.1) of all the compounds was graphically generated from the SWISS ADME server.

The graphical representation includes two major areas; the yellow region (yolk area) and the white region, depicting the BBB absorption and Human Intestinal Absorption (HIA) respectively [13]. BOILED – Egg also considers whether the ligands are P-gp substrates (PGP+) or inhibitors (PGP-).

Accordingly, Palmitic acid, Dehydroepiandrosterone, Anethole, Eugenol, Glabrene, Glabridin, Liquiritigenin,

Table 8.1 Drug likeness of the phytochemicals

Ligand	Molecular weight	LogP	Rotatable bonds	Acceptors	Donors	Surface Area	Lipinski Violations	Drug Likeness
Anethole	148.205	2.7283	2	1	0	67.315	0	Yes
Apigenin	270.24	2.5768	1	5	3	112.519	0	Yes
Beta Sitosterol	414.718	8.0248	6	1	1	187.039	1	Yes
Dehydroepiandrosterone	288.431	3.8792	0	2	1	127.551	0	Yes
Eugenol	164.204	2.1293	3	2	1	72.109	0	Yes
Glabrene	322.36	4.215	1	4	2	139.833	0	Yes
Glabridin	324.376	4.0007	1	4	2	140.522	0	Yes
Glycyrrhetic acid	470.694	6.4126	1	3	2	205.515	1	Yes
Isoliquiritigenin	256.257	2.6995	3	4	3	109.438	0	Yes
Isoliquiritin	418.398	0.1726	6	9	6	171.232	1	Yes
Liquiritigenin	256.257	2.8043	1	4	2	109.441	0	Yes
Liquiritin	418.398	0.2774	4	9	5	171.235	0	Yes
Naringenin	272.256	2.5099	1	5	3	114.235	0	Yes
Palmitic acid	256.43	5.5523	14	1	1	113.169	1	Yes
Quercetin	302.238	1.988	1	7	5	122.108	0	Yes

Table 8.2 Pharmacokinetic and toxicty analysis of the phytochemicals

Ligand	GI Absorption	BBB permeant	P-gp I inhibitor	P-gp II inhibitor	AMES toxicity	hERG I inhibitor	hERG II inhibitor	Hepatotoxicity
Anethole	High	Yes	No	No	No	No	No	No
Apigenin	High	No	No	No	No	No	No	No
Beta Sitosterol	Low	No	Yes	Yes	No	No	Yes	No
Dehydroepiandrosterone	High	Yes	Yes	No	No	No	Yes	No
Eugenol	High	Yes	No	No	Yes	No	No	No
Glabrene	High	Yes	Yes	No	No	No	Yes	No
Glabridin	High	Yes	Yes	No	No	No	Yes	No
Glycyrrhetic acid	High	No	No	Yes	No	No	No	No
Isoliquiritigenin	High	Yes	No	No	No	No	No	No
Isoliquiritin	Low	No	Yes	No	No	No	No	No
Liquiritigenin	High	Yes	No	No	No	No	No	No
Liquiritin	Low	No	No	No	Yes	No	No	No
Naringenin	High	No	No	No	No	No	No	No
Palmitic acid	High	Yes	No	No	No	No	No	No
Quercetin	High	No	No	No	No	No	No	No

and Isoliquiritigenin are predicted to permeate BBB, while Glycyrrhetic acid, Apigenin, Naringenin, Quercetin are predicted to be highly absorbed in the intestinal tract.

Bioavailability Radar was analyzed, to investigate six parameters; saturation (INSATU), lipophilicity (LIPO), polarity (POLAR), size (SIZE), solubility (INSOLU), and flexibility (FLEX). The radar analysis of the ligands is shown in Fig. 8.2 (on page 68), where the pink area represents the optimal range for each parameter and hence Dehyrdoepianderostone and Glabridin are predicted to have optimal characteristics.

3.2 Molecular Docking

Molecular docking being a computational approach, is used to model and predict the interactions between the

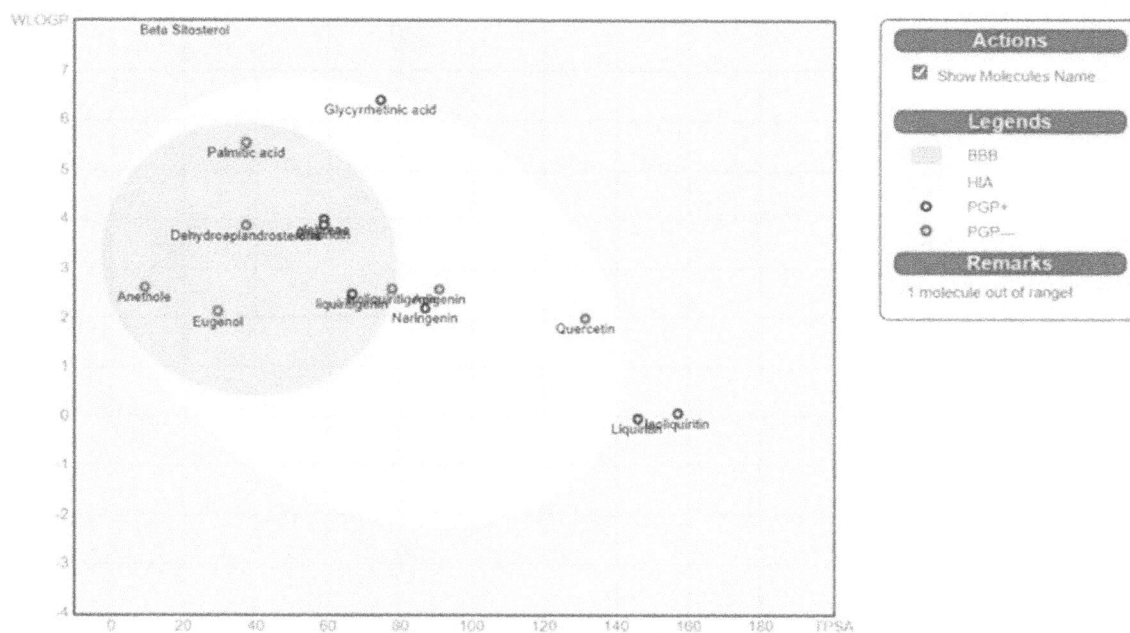

Fig. 8.1 Boiled – Egg analysis of the selected phytochemicals

ligand and the protein hence enabling to finding of better drug candidates. Greater negative docking scores indicate, more favorable and stronger binding confirmations (higher binding affinities) between the protein and the drug candidate. The control drugs have been used to validate the accuracy in comparing the docking scores of the ligands. All the docking energies were filtered, by considering a root mean square deviation (RMSD) value of 0.5 Å – 2.0 Å.

The binding energies of CYP17 with the ligands of *G.glabra*, at each active site, are shown in Table 8.3. Accordingly, many stable binding affinities show more negative scores, which also shows that several ligands can bind to several active sites. Such could be due to the shared chemistry between the active sites allowing the same ligand to bind with a greater affinity or possibly could be due to the ligand flexibility that allows the same ligand to adjust and reform when binding to another active site.

3.3 Visualization of the Protein-Ligand Interactions

The docked molecules were further studied for their interactions with the protein, by visualizing the hydrogen bond formation (polar bonds), using PyMol software. Hydrogen (H) -bonds, are indeed the most frequent interaction type in protein-ligand complexes, influencing the protein stability, and hence visualization of such interactions has always been a practice, in drug discovery research [14].

In the present study, H- bonds, interacting amino acid residues (under 5 Å distance), and the bond lengths have been analyzed and are shown in Table 8.4.

The ligands which showed H-bond formations are shown in Fig. 8.3 – Fig. 8.9.

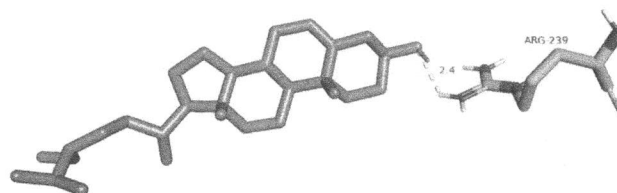

Fig. 8.3 Beta Sitosterol (2nd active site)

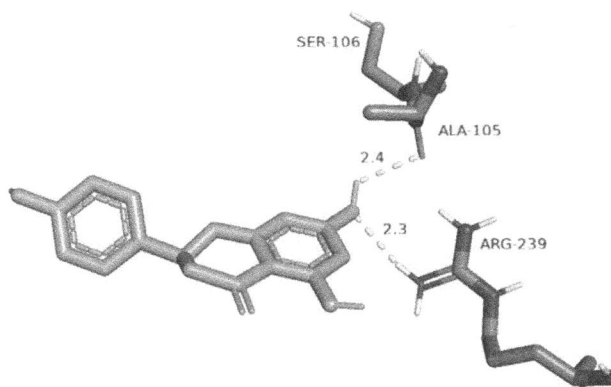

Fig. 8.4 Naringenin (3rd active site)

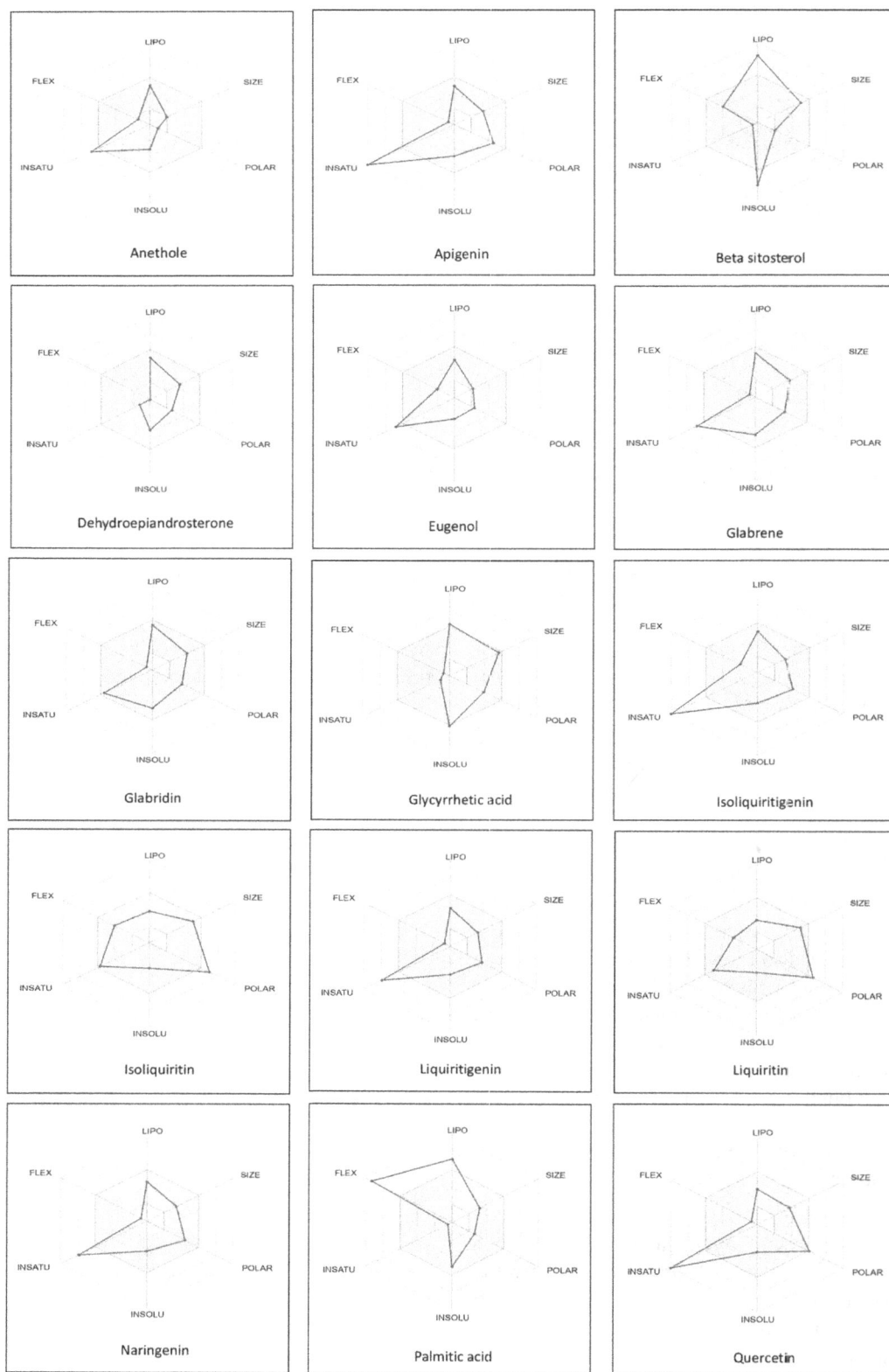

Fig. 8.2 Radar analysis of the selected phytochemicals

Table 8.3 Binding energies with the cyp17 at each active site

Active site	Ligand	Binding energy (kcal/mol)
1st	Clomiphene	-8.2
2nd	Beta-Sitosterol	-10
	Isoliquiritin	-8.6
	Ketoconazole	-10.1
3rd	Eugenol	-5.6
	Naringenin	-7.5
	Dehydroepiandrosterone	-8.7
	Liquiritigenin	-7.5
	Isoliquiritin	-8.8
	Flutamide	-7.3
4th	Naringenin	-7.5
	Liquiritin	-9.1
	Clomiphene	-6.6
5th	Apigenin	-7.4
	Naringenin	-7.4
	Palmitic Acid	-5.7
	Flutamide	-7.1
6th	Dehydroepiandrosterone	-6.9
	Clomiphene	-6.1
7th	Palmitic Acid	-4.2
	Liquiritigenin	-7.3
	Clomiphene	-7
	Ketoconazole	-6.3
8th	Naringenin	-6.3
	Liquiritigenin	-6.4
	Glycyrrhetic acid	-6.6
9th	Naringenin	-6.5
	Glabrene	-8.6
	Clomiphene	-5.5
10th	Beta-Sitosterol	-7.2
	Liquiritin	-7
	Ketoconazole	-7.7
11th	Apigenin	-6.8
	Beta-Sitosterol	-7.3
	Naringenin	-6.6
	Quercetin	-6.7
	Liquiritigenin	-6.6
	Liquiritin	-8.7
	Clomiphene	-6.6
	Flutamide	-5.9
	Ketoconazole	-7.8
12th	Isoliquiritigenin	-5.6
	Isoliquiritin	-7.1
	Metformin	-4.7
13th	Ketoconazole	-6.0

Table 8.4 Interactions between ligands and the cyp17

Active site	Ligand	Amino acids residues involved in the H-bond interaction
1st	Clomiphene	No H bond
2nd	Beta Sitosterol	Arg-239 (2.4 Å)
	Isoliquiritin	Ile-371 (2.5Å), Arg-239 (2.7Å)
	Ketoconazole	No H bond
3rd	Eugenol	Arg-239 (2.6Å and 2.4Å)
	Naringenin	Ala-105(2.4Å), Arg-239 (2.3Å)
	Dehydroepi-androsterone	No H bond
	Liquiritigenin	Ala-105(2.4Å),Arg-239(2.6Åand2.6Å)
	Isoliquiritin	Ala-302 (2.7 Å), Arg-440 (2.5 Å), Cys-442 (2.8 Å), Phe-435(2.4 Å), Pro-434(2.1 Å), Ala-367(2.5 Å)
	Flutamide	Arg -239 (2.5Å)
4th	Naringenin	Arg-239(2.3 Å)
	Liquiritin	Ala-105(2.6 Å)
	Clomiphene	No H bond
5th	Apigenin	Arg-239(2.3 Å)
	Naringenin	Arg-239(2.2 Å)
	Palmitic acid	Arg-239 (2.7 Å, 2.6 Å and 2.0 Å)
	Flutamide	No H bond
6th	Dehydroepi-androsterone	No H bond
	Clomiphene	No H bond
7th	Palmitic acid	Lys-71(2.1 Å), Thr-72 (2.2 Å)
	Liquiritigenin	No H bond
	Clomiphene	No H bond
	Ketoconazole	Asn-108 (2.5 Å)
8th	Naringenin	Asn-161(2.3 Å and 2.0 Å)
	Liquiritigenin	Asn-161(2.5Å) and Arg-500(2.6 Å)
	Glycyrrhetic acid	No H bond
9th	Naringenin	Lys-71(2.4 Å) and Glu-391 (2.4 Å)
	Glabrene	Leu-43(2.5 Å) and Glu-391(2.3 Å)
	Clomiphene	No H bond
10th	Beta Sitosterol	Asp-241(2.3 Å)
	Liquiritin	Glu-415(2.9Å), Lys-327(2.6A), Gln-334 (2.6 Å and 2.3 Å), Asn-335 (2.1 Å and 2.5 Å)
	Ketoconazole	No H bond
11th	Apigenin	No H bond
	Beta Sitosterol	No H bond
	Naringenin	Asn-402(2.2Å)
	Quercetin	Gly-77(1.9 Å)
	Liquiritigenin	His-78 (3.3A) and Asn-402(2.2A)
	Liquiritin	Gly-77(2.4A), Trp-397(2.6A), Asn-51(2.1A, 2.6A and 2.1A)
	Clomiphene	No H bond
	Flutamide	No H bonds
	Ketoconazole	Gly-77(2.0A)
12th	Isoliquiritigenin	Arg -67(2.2A), Lys-55 (1.9A), Lys-58 (2.5A)
	Isoliquiritin	Phe-224 (2.1A), Lys-71(2.7A)
	Metformin	Asp-216(2.3A), Thr-73(2.3A), Glu-391(2.7A and 2.3A)
13th	Ketoconazole	Gln-408(2.1A)

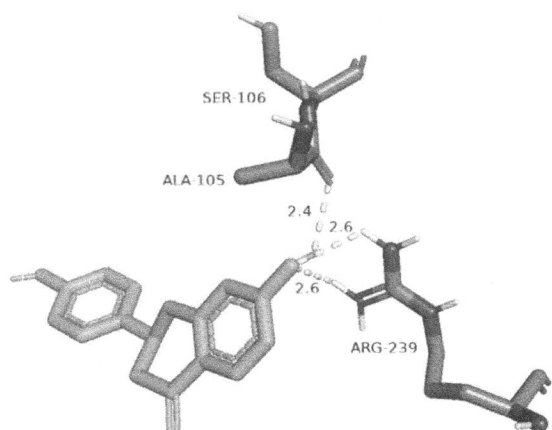

Fig. 8.5 Liquiritigenin (3rd active site)

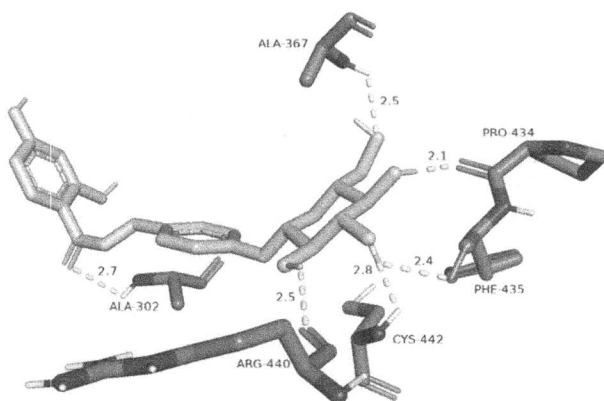

Fig. 8.6 Isoliquiritin (3rd active site)

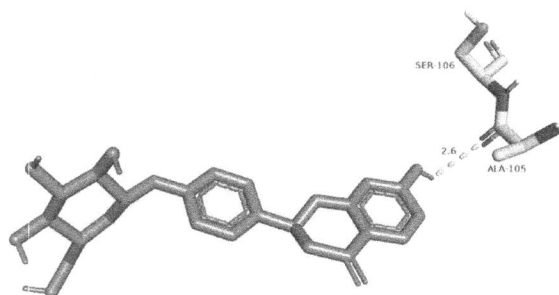

Fig. 8.7 Liquiritin (4th active site)

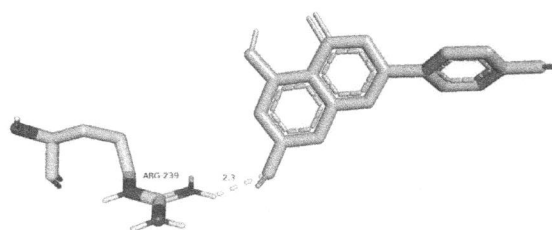

Fig. 8.8 Apigenin (5th active site)

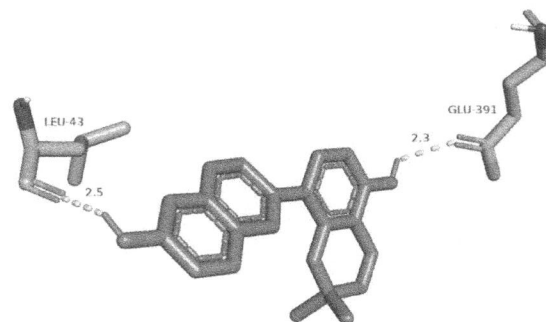

Fig. 8.9 Glabrene (9th active site)

4. Conclusion

In the present study, fifteen (15) phytochemicals of *G.glabra* were docked with the target protein, CYP17, to investigate their binding affinities (kcal/mol) and interactions, to identify possible potential drug candidates, against PCOS hyperandrogenism.

Out of the total fifteen (15), twelve (12) compounds; Beta Sitosterol, Isoliquiritin, Eugenol, Naringenin, Dehydroepiandrosterone, Liquiritigenin, Liquiritin, Apigenin, Palmitic acid, Glycyrrhetic acid, Glabrene and Quercetin, showed good docking scores ranged from -4.2 kcal/mol to -10kcal/mol. In contrast, Beta Sitosterol, Isoliquiritin, Naringenin, Dehydroepiandrosterone, Liquiritigenin, Liquiritin, Apigenin, and Glabrene depicted strong binding affinities ($\leq$7.0 kcal/mol), with CYP17. Clomiphene, Ketoconazole, Flutamide, and Metformin being the control drugs (Spironolactone showed no binding affinity with CYP17) too showed, good docking scores ranging from -4.7 kcal/mol to - 10.1 kcal/mol. These scores indeed emphasize that the ligands can bind more tightly with the protein, irrespective of the active site location. Furthermore, all the twelve (12) ligands (with good docking scores), formed H-bond interactions ranged from one (1) H - bond to six (6) H-bonds, at a distance less than 3.0 Å, depicting the structural stability of the protein-ligand complex. Also, all fifteen (15) compounds portrayed varied physicochemical, pharmacokinetic, and toxicokinetic properties, while depicting their absorption, metabolism, and toxicity.

The results of the present study showed that the selected compounds could be used as promising drug candidates, for the treatment of PCOS hyperandrogenism via inhibition, which could create a significant medicinal impact in designing and synthesizing more potent drugs. Although network pharmacology-related studies for PCOS were present, molecular docking studies for hyperandrogenism targeting CYP17 were lacking, where the present study could be an exception.

However, further research is encouraged, on structural modifications of the ligands with docking scores ≤ -6 kcal/mol. Other computational drug-based analyses such as Molecular dynamics simulations, and free energy perturbation (EFP) calculations, could also be performed, to understand better stability and flexibility in protein-ligand binding. Moreover, the present study also encourages in conducting in vivo and in vitro evaluations, to validate the computational findings, for the proposed compounds.

Acknowledgment

The authors acknowledge the Sri Lanka Institute of Information Technology for its relevant help regarding the software.

REFERENCES

1. Mansour, A., Mirahmad, M., Mohajeri-Tehrani, M. R., Jamalizadeh, M., Hosseinimousa, S., Rashidi, F., . . . Sajjadi-Jazi, S. M. (2023). Risk factors for insulin resistance related to polycystic ovarian syndrome in Iranian population. Scientific Reports, 13(1), 10269. doi:10.1038/s41598-023-37513-2

2. Teede, H., Deeks, A., & Moran, L. (2010). Polycystic ovary syndrome: a complex condition with psychological, reproductive and metabolic manifestations that impacts on health across the lifespan. BMC Medicine, 8(1), 41. doi:10.1186/1741-7015-8-41

3. Azziz, R., Sanchez, L. A., Knochenhauer, E. S., Moran, C., Lazenby, J., Stephens, K. C., . . . Boots, L. R. (2004). Androgen Excess in Women: Experience with Over 1000 Consecutive Patients. The Journal of Clinical Endocrinology & Metabolism, 89(2), 453–462. doi:10.1210/jc.2003-031122

4. Ashma, T., & Rani, D. V. E. (2022). Effect of Clitoria ternatea on PCOS - Molecular Docking Study.pdf. Int J Food Nutr Sci, 11(5), 49–53. doi:10.4103/ijfans_138–22

5. Khanage, S. G., Subhash, T. Y., & Bhaiyyasaheb, I. R. (2019). HERBAL DRUGS FOR THE TREATMENT OF POLYCYSTIC OVARY SYNDROME (PCOS) AND ITS COMPLICATIONS.pdf. Pharmaceutical Resonance, 2(1).

6. Pastorino, G., Cornara, L., Soares, S., Rodrigues, F., & Oliveira, M. (2018). Liquorice (Glycyrrhiza glabra): A phytochemical and pharmacological review. Phytother Res, 32(12), 2323–2339. doi:10.1002/ptr.6178

7. Kwon, Y.-J., Son, D.-H., Chung, T.-H., & Lee, Y.-J. (2020). A Review of the Pharmacological Efficacy and Safety of Licorice Root from Corroborative Clinical Trial Findings. Journal of Medicinal Food, 23(1), 12–20. doi:10.1089/jmf.2019.4459

8. Hasan, Md. K., Ara, I., Mondal, M. S. A., & Kabir, Y. (2021). Phytochemistry, pharmacological activity, and potential health benefits of Glycyrrhiza glabra. *Heliyon, 7*(6), e07240. https://doi.org/10.1016/j.heliyon.2021.e07240

9. Yang, H., Kim, H. J., Pyun, B. J., & Lee, H. W. (2018). Licorice ethanol extract improves symptoms of polycytic ovary syndrome in Letrozole-induced female rats. Integr Med Res, 7(3), 264–270. doi:10.1016/j.imr.2018.05.003

10. Armanini, D., Castello, R., Scaroni, C., Bonanni, G., Faccini, G., Pellati, D., . . . Moghetti, P. (2007). Treatment of polycystic ovary syndrome with spironolactone plus licorice. European Journal of Obstetrics and Gynecology and Reproductive Biology, 131(1), 61–67. doi:10.1016/j.ejogrb.2006.10.013

11. Ou-Yang, S. S., Lu, J. Y., Kong, X. Q., Liang, Z. J., Luo, C., & Jiang, H. (2012). Computational drug discovery. Acta Pharmacol Sin, 33(9), 1131–1140. doi:10.1038/aps.2012.109

12. Abdullahi, M., & Adeniji, S. E. (2020). In-silico Molecular Docking and ADME/Pharmacokinetic Prediction Studies of Some Novel Carboxamide Derivatives as Anti-tubercular Agents. Chemistry Africa, 3(4), 989–1000. doi:10.1007/s42250-020-00162-3

13. Abdullahi, S. H., Uzairu, A., Shallangwa, G. A., Uba, S., & Umar, A. B. (2022). Molecular Docking , ADMET and Pharmacokinetic properties predictions of some di-aryl Pyridinamine derivatives as Estrogen Receptor (Er+) Kinase Inhibitors. Egyptian Journal of Basic and Applied Sciences, 9(1), 180–204. doi:10.1080/2314808X.2022.2050115

14. Chen, D., Oezguen, N., Urvil, P., Ferguson, C., Dann, S. M., & Savidge, T. C. (2016). Regulation of protein-ligand binding affinity by hydrogen bond pairing. Science Advances, 2(3). https://doi.org/10.1126/sciadv.1501240

Note: All the figures and tables in this chapter were made by the authors.

Transformative Applied Research in Computing, Engineering, Science and Technology – Dr. Damayanthi Dahanayake et al. (eds)
© 2024 Taylor & Francis Group, London, ISBN 978-1-041-01782-0

9

Identifying the Potential Effect of *Citrus Reticulata* on Anxiety Based on Network Pharmacology and Molecular Docking

H. M. S. A. K. Herath*, M. A. S. H. Mirihana
Department of Humanities and Science,
Sri Lanka Institute of Information Technology,
Sri Lanka

C. R. Wijesinghe
School of Computing, University of Colombo,
Sri Lanka

Abstract

This study focuses on the medicinal properties of *C.reticulata*, a plant used to reduce anxiety in Sri Lankan Ayurveda medicine. The main objectives are to identify the active ingredients, describe the mechanism of action using network pharmacology and molecular docking, and to provide key objectives associated with *C.reticulata* in treating anxiety. The components of *C.reticulata* and anxiety-related genes were obtained from databases. Genes that overlapped with both the disease and its components were subjected to data analysis. Cytoscape 3.8.0 was used for analyzing the pharmaceutical components-targets-disease network. To determine a potential pathway of *C.reticulata* use in anxiety, several methods were used: protein-protein interactions (PPI) using the STRING platform, gene ontology (GO) and pathway enrichment (KEGG) using the DAVID and SR plot database, and molecular docking using the Autodock. Five bioactive components derived from *C.reticulata* and 34 overlapped genes between the active components of *C.reticulata* and anxiety. PPI analysis shows that key genes as BCL2, ESR1, PPARG, PTGS2, and MAOA. KEGG enrichment analysis showed genes linked to the endocrine resistance pathway, serotonergic synapse pathway, and alcoholism pathway. At −9.5 kcal/mol, 5, 7-dihydroxy-2-(3-hydroxy-4-methoxyphenyl) chroman-4-one has the lowest binding energy to PTGS2. Comparing the main components of *C.reticulata* to the binding energies of positive drugs, the results showed that the main component of *C.reticulata* bound into the key target proteins firmly. Many components, multiple targets, and multiple pathways are all involved in the processed *C. reticulata's* mechanism of action in the treatment of anxiety disorders.

Keywords

Anxiety, C.reticulata, Molecular docking, Network pharmacology, Signaling pathway

---
*Corresponding author: sanjalikaherath98@gmail.com

DOI: 10.1201/9781003616368-9

1. Introduction

Anxiety is a normal emotional experience that arises from anticipating possible dangers. However, anxiety can develop into anxiety disorder when it gets severe enough to interfere with behavior or cause suffering [1].

The first theory for anxiety disorder and the foundation of the majority of modern anti-anxiety treatments was the monoamine neurotransmitter hypothesis. It reveals that a decrease in several monoamine neurotransmitters, like 5-hydroxytryptamine (5-HT), Dopamine (DA), and Noradrenaline (NA), essentially causes anxiety.

Benzodiazepines and selective serotonin reptake inhibitors (SSRI) are the most widely used drugs for anxiety in Western medicine. It prevents the presynaptic membrane from reabsorbing 5-HT, raises neurotransmitter levels in the synaptic cleft, enhances 5-HT neuron transmission, and produces anxiolytic effects. Benzodiazepines exhibit central inhibitory effects, hyperpolarize nerve cells, enhance GABA activity, broadly open chloride ion channels, release large amounts of chloride ions into cells, and alleviate anxiety [2]. Nonetheless, continued use of these medications raises the possibility of brain damage, develops drug dependence, and impairs memory and cognitive function [3]. For this reason, researchers are looking into using traditional medicine to treat anxiety to reduce the negative reactions and side effects associated with Western medicine [4].

In Sri Lanka, mental disorders can be effectively addressed through Ayurveda approaches. Ayurveda therapies promote harmony, reduce stress, and restore the mental equilibrium.

The mandarin fruit commonly referred to by the name *Citrus reticulata*, has been recognized as a Traditional Chinese Medicine (TCM) and Ayurveda medicine to treat asthma, anxiety, depression, and headaches [5]. "Saththawadi Oil" and "Pas- pangiri oil" are some Ayurveda products made out of using *C. reticulata* plant and some other *Rutaceae* species, which are used to decrease insomnia, dementia, anxiety, and depression. Also, Traditional Chinese herbal medicine made using the *C. reticulata* plant called "Liu Yu Tang" and "Chaihu Shugan San" has been shown in Chinese clinical practice to be highly efficient in having antidepressant effects in the chronic restraint stress-induced depression mice models [6]. The main chemical in *C. reticulata* essential oils, limonene, has been shown in prior studies to be able to alleviate depressive symptoms in mice induced by chronic unpredictable mild stress (CUMS), possibly by re-establishing hippocampal Brain-Derived Neurotrophic Factor (BDNF) expression [4].

Even though, bbenzodiazepines and SSRIs may provide more potent, quicker relief, but they are not as good for long-term management due to their serious side effects. But long-term use of *C. reticulata* shows fewer risks and does not cause dependency, cognitive decline, or withdrawal symptoms. Additionally, its calming effects are less likely to sedate or dull emotions.

However, the components of Ayurveda and TCM are diverse and complex, and the medicine's mechanism is even more complicated. Therefore, there is a need to develop new techniques and analytical methods that can capture important features of them. For that, network pharmacology has been widely used to elucidate disease-drug relationships and to predict aspects of the medicine and therapeutic approaches. Molecular docking can predict drug binding, and provide free energy, protein surfaces, and information about their mechanism and function [7].

In the study, the key compounds of *C.reticulata* and potential targets for the treatment of anxiety were predicted using network pharmacology techniques. The active components of *C.reticulata* were identified and potential target molecules and signaling pathways were predicted using molecular docking and molecular dynamics. Visualization and analysis are then used to confirm actual ligand-protein interactions

2. Methodology

2.1 Identification of Active Components of C. Reticulata

C. reticulata's active ingredients' Simplified Molecular Input Line Entry System (SMILES) sequences were identified through Traditional Chinese Medicine Systems Pharmacology Database (http://lsp.nwu.edu.cn/tcmsp.php) [8] and Swiss target prediction (http://swisstargetprediction.ch/), and their 2D structures and ID numbers were obtained from PubChem (https://pubchem.ncbi.nlm.nih.gov/) [9]. Following their collection, the targets of these active components have been converted into gene symbols. A network containing medicine and components was built with Cytoscape 3.8.0 software. Active ingredients' chemical structures from TCMSP were redrafted using ChemBioDraw Ultra for clarity.

2.2 Screening of Targets Related to Anxiety

Target screening for anxiety began with exploring the National Center for Biotechnology Information (NCBI) Gene Database (https://www.ncbi.nlm.nih.gov/), using search terms "anxiety" and "anxiety-related diseases." Further expansion of the search led to disease databases, including GeneCards (https://www.genecards.org), Drugbank (https://go.drugbank.com), and Therapeutic Targets Database (TTD) (http://db.idrblab.net/ttd).

2.3 Identification of Genes that Overlap between Disease and Bioactive Components

The Venny software (https://bioinfogp.cnb.csic.es/tools/venny/index.html) [9] played a pivotal role in processing this intersection and presenting it as a Venn diagram, allowing for the automatic count of overlapping genes.

2.4 The Network of Medicine Components-Targets-Disease Construction

The intersection between *C.reticulata* and Anxiety was identified to create a network diagram using Cytoscape 3.8.0. (https://cytoscape.org/) [9]. The topological features of this network were studied using the Network Analyzer tool in the Cytoscape plugin.

2.5 Analysis of the Protein-Protein Interaction (PPI) Network

The core target proteins were selected based on topological analysis of the previous network and then input into the STRING database (https://string-db.org/). The chosen species for this analysis was "Homo sapiens," and a score cutoff of less than 0.4 was set as the correlation degree.

Subsequently, Cytoscape 3.8.0. (https://cytoscape.org/), a network visualization software was employed for further analysis. To generate a new PPI network for further study, only target nodes that had all six parameters above the relevant PPI network median values were chosen.

2.6 Gene Ontology and Kyoto Encyclopedia of Genes and Genome Pathway Enrichment Analysis

By utilizing the David database (https://david.ncifcrf.gov/), *C. reticulata's* targets for anxiety treatment were gathered and analyzed using GO functional annotation and KEGG pathway enrichment analysis. KEGG analysis was employed to map target genes onto pathways related to anxiety.

The SRplot (https://www.bioinformatics.com.cn/en) tool was used to perform KEGG analysis and utilized to further explanations of the action target of the chemical composition by conducting biological processes, molecular function, and cell components.

A significance threshold of $p < 0.05$ was set to obtain a dot plot for GO and KEGG analyses, revealing the principal functional enrichments and action pathways of *C.reticulata* in treating anxiety. Cytoscape3.8.0. (https://cytoscape.org/) software was utilized to construct networks for analyses.

2.7 Molecular Docking
Protein, Ligand, and Grid Box Preparation

Using Autodock tools 1.5.6, the target proteins' 3D structures were modified to eliminate ions, co-crystallized ligands, and water molecules. Using the RCSB protein Data Bank (https://www.rcsb.org/), the target proteins were obtained. By combining hydrogen atoms and Kollman partial charges, non-polar hydrogens were combined with matching carbons. These modified protein structures were stored in PDBQT format.

The 2D structures of active substances were retrieved from databases like PubChem (https://pub chem.ncbi.nlm.nih.gov/) and TCMSP (https://tcmspw.com/). These 2D structures were converted into 3D structures using ChemBio Draw 3D and Chem 3D software (https://www.chemdraw.com.cn/ChemBio3D.html) Hydrogens were added, protonation was performed, and non-polar hydrogens were merged. The resulting ligand structures were saved in PDBQT format.

Grid boxes determined the area in which docking would occur. The purpose is to make sure the center of the grid box is positioned correctly to cover the binding site and the entire protein.

Molecular Docking

The ligand and receptor structures, along with the grid box parameters, were inputted into the Autodock Vina software. The software calculated the binding affinity, and multiple docking runs were performed to obtain the lowest binding energy conformation. PyMol (https://pymol.org/2/) was used for 3D display and analysis of the molecular docking results.

3. Results and Discussion

2.1 Potential Targets of Citrus Reticulata and Anxiety

The 5 most suitable active components (Table 9.1) with 144 target genes were selected for Chemical absorption, distribution, metabolism, excretion, and toxicity (ADMET) screening criteria. A total of 840 target genes have been identified as particular human-related anxiety targets from the NCBI Gene Database.

2.2 The Intersection of Potential Targets

A total of 34 overlapping genes were calculated using the Venn diagram, as shown in Fig. 9.1. The fact that 3.6% of the total genes were overlapping suggests that overlapping genes may play a role in *C. reticulata's* anxiety-inducing effects.

2.3 Network Construction of Medicine-Components-Targets-Disease Construction

The creation of the medicine-components-targets disease network is shown in Fig. 9.2. There were 41 nodes, 115 edges, 34 genes that overlapped, and 5 bioactive components in the network. The Cytoscape 3.8.0 program was used to analyze additional parameters.

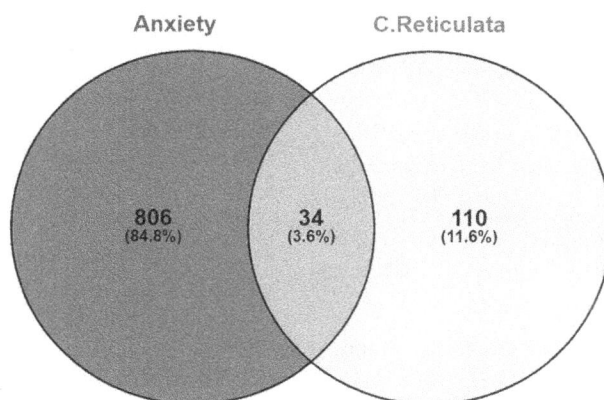

Fig. 9.1 The Venn diagram shows the genetic intersection between components derived from C.reticulata and anxiety. Human anxiety-related genes were shown as purple circle. C.reticulata bioactive component's target genes were represented as a yellow circle

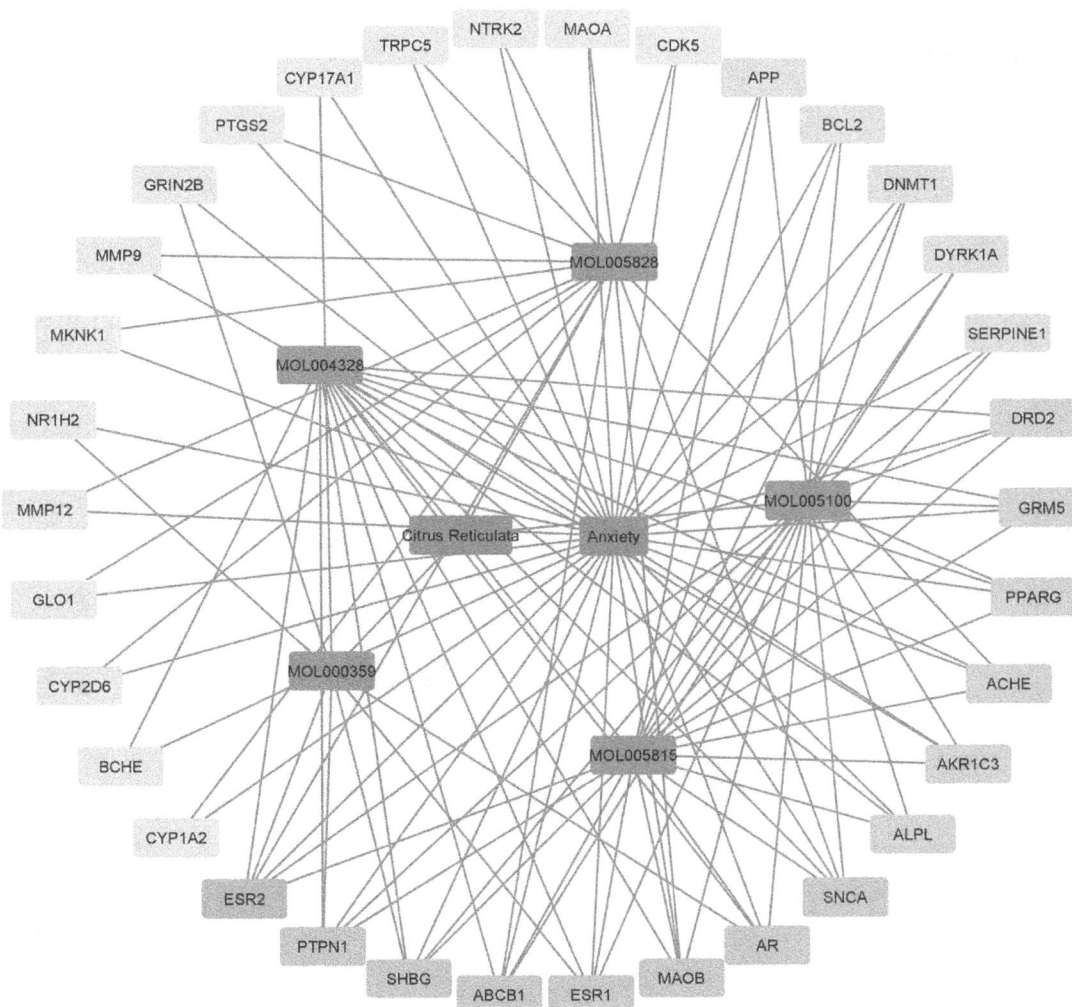

Fig. 9.2 This network of overlapping genes between *C.reticulata* bioactive component's target genes and human anxiety-related genes. Green shaded rectangles represented overlapping targets. Pink rectangles represented bioactive components, blue rectangles represented C.reticulata and anxiety disorders

2.4 Network of PPI

As shown in Fig. 9.3, all 34 overlapping genes were used to conduct the PPI network, by the STRING database. Additionally, each node's degree was examined and ESR1, BCL2, MAOA, PPARG, and PTGS2 were the five proteins selected for further investigations.

The estrogen receptor (ESR1) regulates the levels of oxytocin, serotonin, and the hypothalamic-pituitary-adrenal axis (HPA), all of which have anti-anxiety effects [10].

The limbic system, which is linked to emotions, mood, and behavior, contains estrogen receptors (ESRs). After menopause, decreased estradiol causes anxiety, indicating a connection between anxiety and ESR1 [4].

The effects of estrogen on cells are controlled by two estrogen receptors, ERα and ERβ. ERα has a major impact on mood, and estrogen receptor mutations can alter estrogen signaling and increase sensitivity to anxiety and depression in women.

Moreover, the development of anxiety and other psychiatric disorders is significantly influenced by monoamine oxidase A (MAOA). Numerous monoaminergic neurotransmitters, including dopamine, norepinephrine, and serotonin, are affected by MAOA [11].

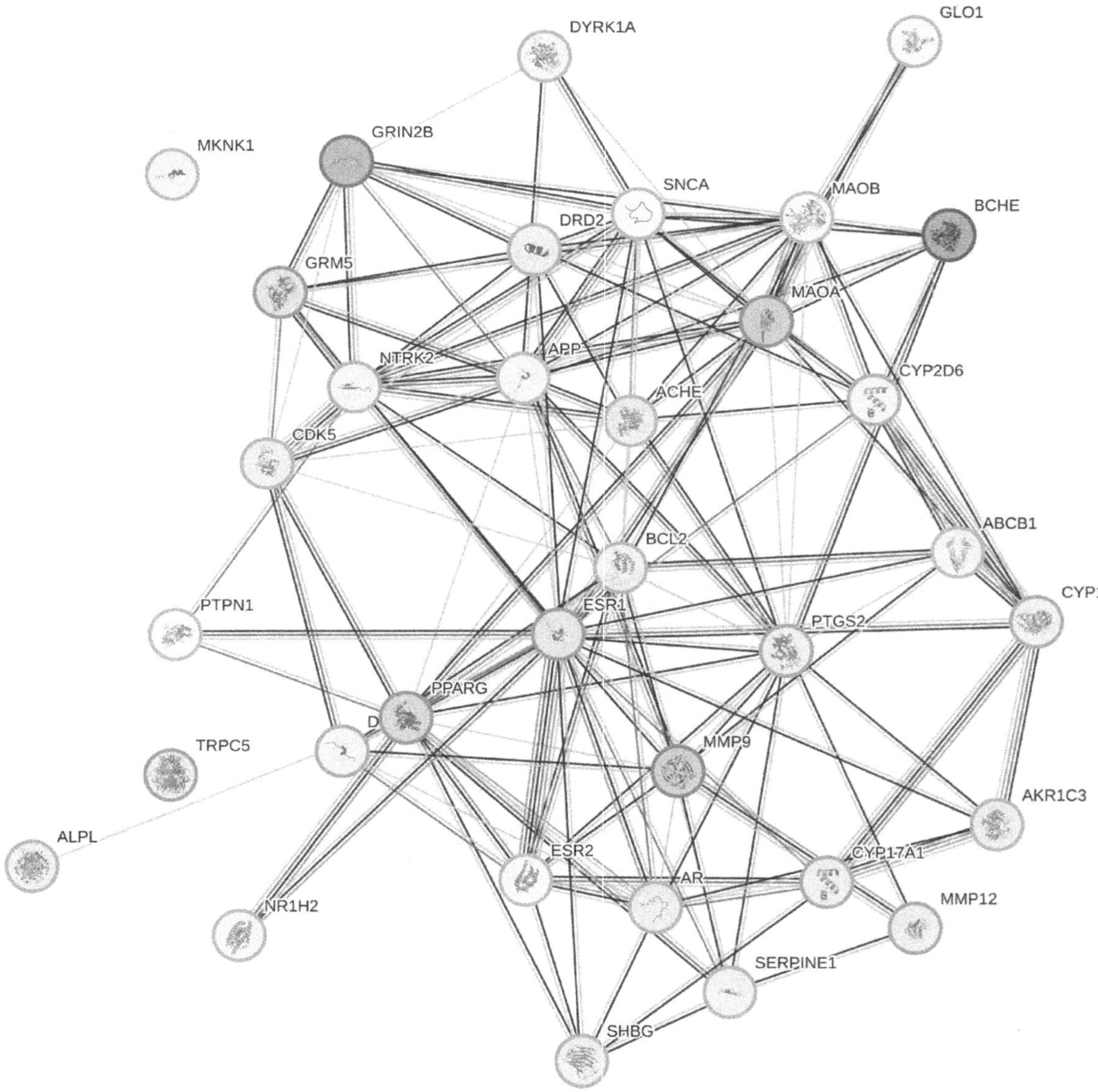

Fig. 9.3 Network of PPI analysis. PPI network analysis included the interaction of 34 overlapping proteins

Table 9.1   Details of five selected bioactive components of *C.reticulata*

Mol ID	Molecule Name	MW ≤500	OB (%) >30	BBB >(-0.3)	DL >0.2
MOL000359	Sitosterol	414.79	36.91	0.87	0.75
MOL004328	Naringenin	272.27	59.29	-0.3	0.21
MOL005100	Hesperetin	302.3	47.74	-0.3	0.27
MOL005815	Citromitin	404.45	86.9	0.16	0.51
MOL005828	Nobiletin	402.43	61.67	-0.08	0.52

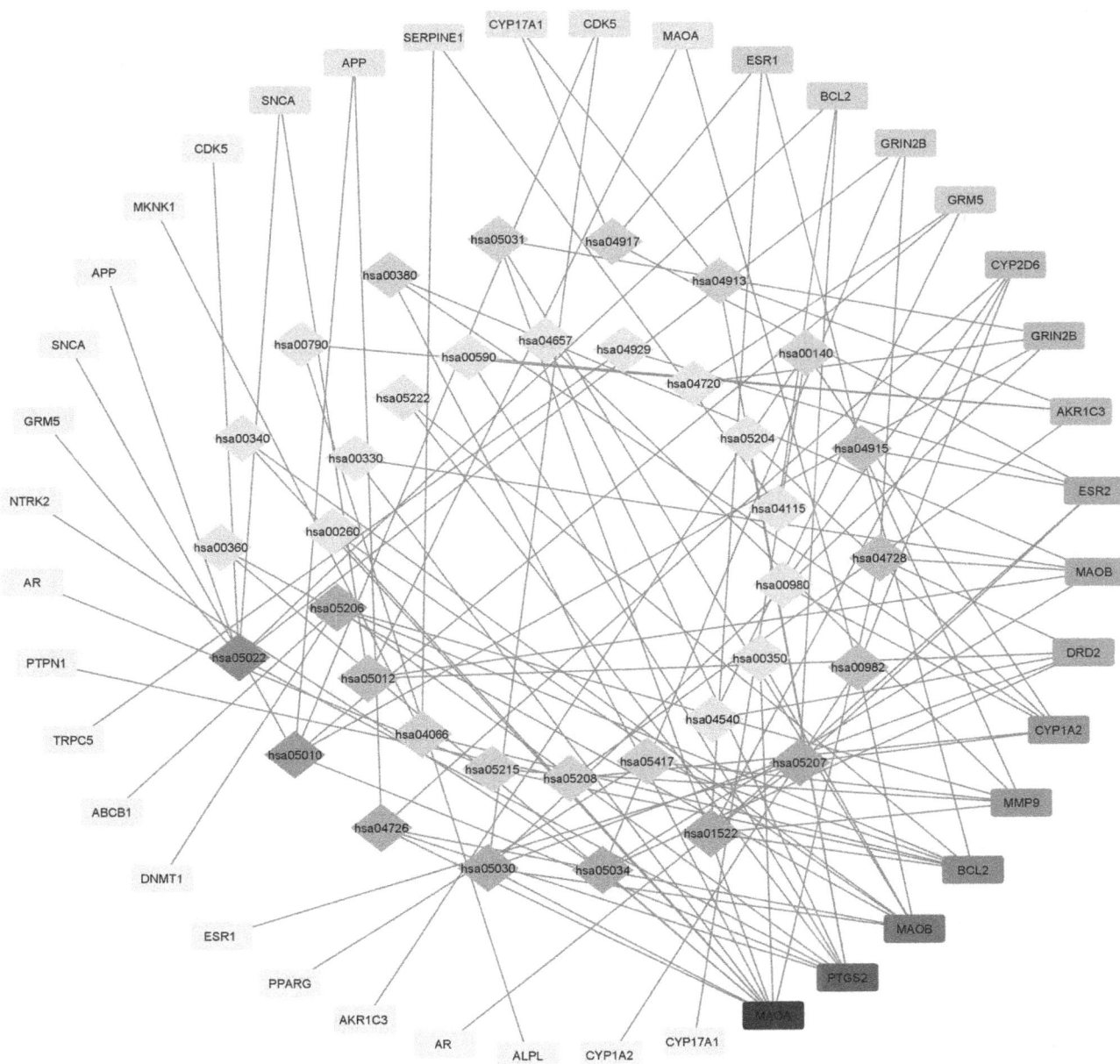

Fig. 9.4   The network shows the top 20 terms of KEGG pathway analysis, with 36 signaling pathways. The color range represents the lowest to highest node based on node degree

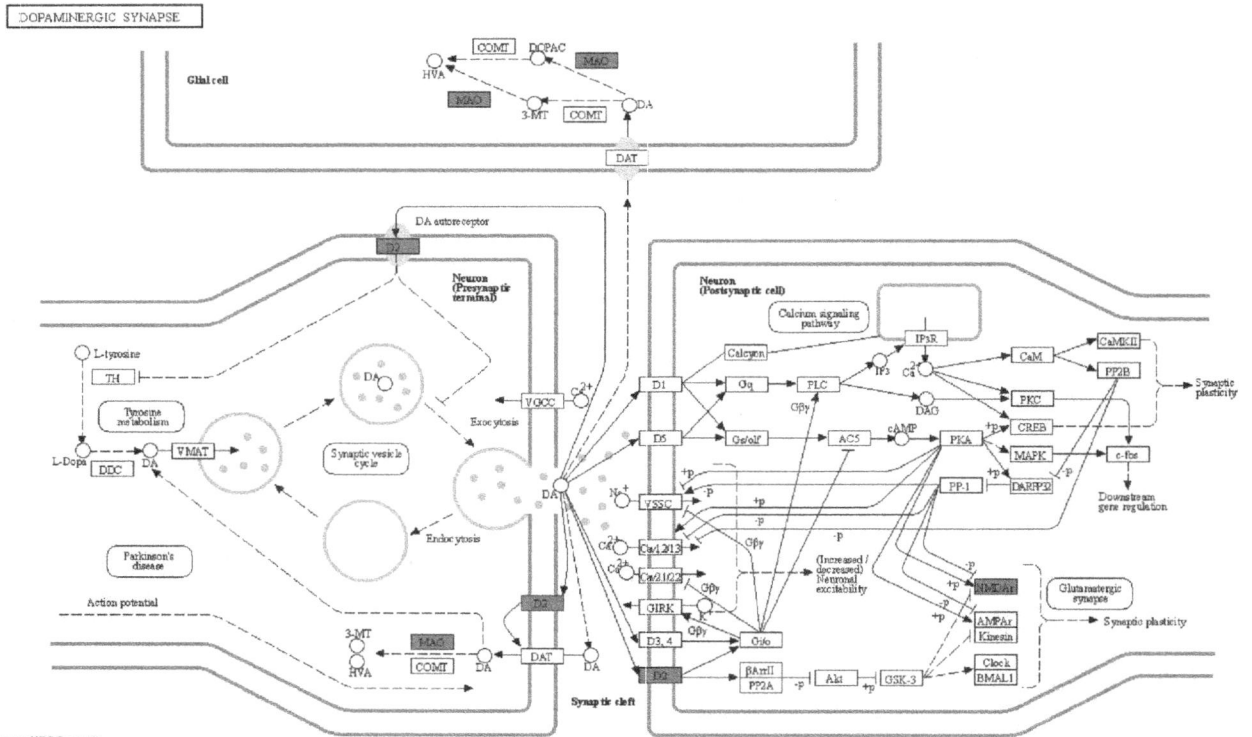

Fig. 9.5 Serotonergic pathway; Red color indicate the genes which are effect by *C. reticulata* medicine for anxiety

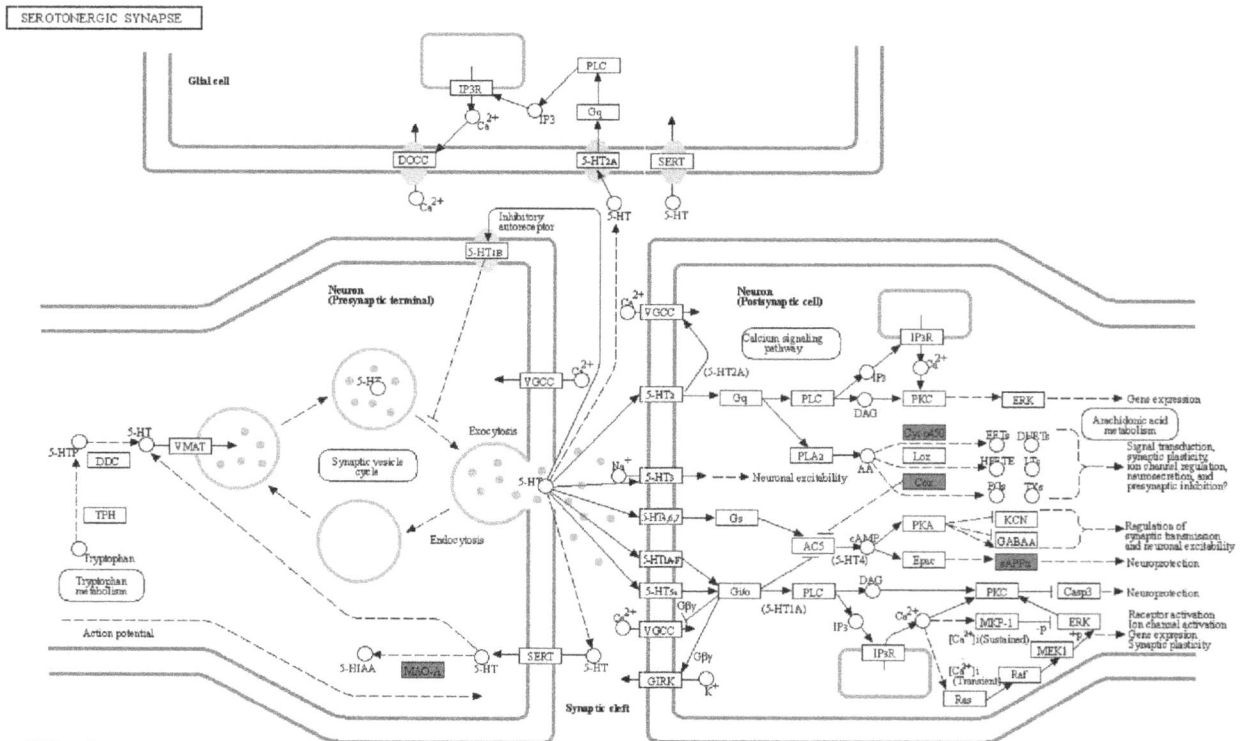

Fig. 9.6 Dopaminergic pathway; Red color indicate the genes which are effect by *C. reticulata* medicine for anxiety

The catecholamine depletion concept of anxiety and the mechanisms of MAOA inhibitors are both supported by the connection between anxiety and MAOA methylation. Also, patients with schizophrenia may exhibit severe anxiety-like symptoms when they have the T-allele of rs6323 in MAOA [12].

Prostaglandin-endoperoxide synthase 2 (PTGS2) gene, is a key enzyme that is implicated in mental diseases like stress disorder. It performs this by activating on downstream pathways such as PI3-K/AKT and PKA/CREB [11].

Furthermore, COX-2 is inhibited by PTGS2, and COX-2 expression is significantly upregulated; this elevation of the gene increases the oxidative stress response. The hippocampus and amygdala of people with anxiety disorders have been found to have a higher concentration of peroxisome proliferator-activated receptors (PPAR) [12].

2.5 GO Enrichment and KEGG Pathway Analysis of Target Genes

GO enrichment analysis is used to evaluate the function of overlapping genes from molecular function (MF), cellular components (CC), and biological processes (BP).Based on the threshold value of p < 0.05, the top three terms in the molecular function analysis were nuclear receptor activity, ligand-activated transcription factor activity, and steroid binding.

The top three terms of biological processes analysis were regulation of transporter activity, regulation of transmembrane transporter activity, and modulation of chemical synaptic transmission, based on the threshold value of p < 0.05.

The top three terms of cellular components analysis were distal axon, nuclear envelope lumen, and postsynaptic density, based on the threshold value of p < 0.05. 34 overlapping genes were significantly enriched in 36 signaling pathways (threshold value; p<0.05), according to KEGG enrichment analysis (Fig. 9.4). The top 3 signaling pathways of KEGG enrichment were Endocrine resistance (Fig. 9.5). and serotonergic synapse (Fig. 9.6).

The release and transmission of neurotransmitters including 5-HT, DA, and NA are closely linked with serotonergic and dopaminergic synapses.

Multiple neurotransmitter pathways can be broadly divided into two groups: (1) those linked to neurotransmitter synthesis, secretion, and recycling, such as the pathways involved in amphetamine addiction, tryptophan metabolism, dopaminergic synapse, serotonergic synapse, and phenylalanine metabolism; and (2) those linked to sedative or hypnotic effects, such as cocaine and morphine addiction [13].

5-HT has a significant impact on learning and memory, endocrine secretion, mood, sleep, pain, and motor function. Psychological and mental activity will function less effectively if there is a comparatively or completely insufficient amount of 5-HT in the synaptic cleft [13]. When 5-HT receptors are stimulated or inhibited, they can have antidepressant and anxiolytic effects.

Dopaminergic synapses regulate the reward system, which in turn controls mood. The primary neurotransmitter in the reward system, dopamine (DA), controls synaptic plasticity as well as neuronal activity [14].

2.6 Molecular Docking

Molecular docking is an effective technique for confirming how ligands and proteins interact. the top five core targets and the top three active compounds were chosen for molecular docking analysis based on PPI analysis results.

A lower binding energy corresponds to a higher affinity for binding. For successful docking, −5.0 kcal/mol is the available screening criterion [15]. Throughout the experiment, sertraline hydrochloride (FDA-approved) was used as the control drug. Autodock and PyMol 2.7 were used to conduct molecular docking modeling. The 3D structures of five core proteins were obtained from RCSB Protein Data Bank.

The data analysis shown in Table 9.2 reveals that the overall binding energies are less than −5 kcal/mol and the average binding energy is −7.5666 kcal/mol. This indicates that three separate active compounds can attach to five different core targets. The lowest binding energy of 5- 7-dihydroxy-2-(3-hydroxy-4-methoxyphenyl) chroman-4-one to PTGS2 is found at −9.5 kcal/mol, while nobiletin and Citromitin bind to PTGS2 with low strengths.

5,7-dihydroxy-2-(3-hydroxy-4-methoxyphenyl) chroman-4-one had lower binding energy than the positive control medication, indicating that it may be an important medication for the treatment of anxiety. Furthermore, ,7-dihydroxy-2-(3-hydroxy-4-methoxyphenyl)chroman-4-one, were ranked higher not only for their binding energy but also for the way they interacted with important ESR1 residues. This suggests that their potential efficacy may have been increased. These compounds were prioritized based on their known pharmacological properties, interaction stability, and binding affinity, which provides a more nuanced understanding of their potential therapeutic roles.

The primary targets of *C. reticulata*'s pharmacological effects on anxiety may be the major target proteins (PTGS2, MAOA, and ESR1). 5, 7-dihydroxy-2-(3-hydroxy-4-methoxyphenyl) chroman-4-one has anti-inflammatory

Table 9.2 Docking results of the main active compounds with the core target protein molecules

Active compound	Target Protein	PDB ID	Binding Energy (kcal/mol)
Citromitin	ESR1	7ujo	-7
	PTGS2	5f19	-8.4
	BCL2	6o0k	-6.3
	MAOA	2z5x	-7.3
	PPARG	8b8w	-7.2
5,7-dihydroxy-2-(3-hydroxy-4-ethoxyphenyl) chroman-4-one	ESR1	7ujo	-7.4
	PTGS2	5f19	-9.5
	BCL2	6o0k	-7
	MAOA	2z5x	-9.3
	PPARG	8b8w	-7.5
Nobiletin	ESR1	7ujo	-6.7
	PTGS2	5f19	-8.6
	BCL2	6o0k	-6.5
	MAOA	2z5x	-7.4
	PPARG	8b8w	-7.4
Sertraline hydrochloride	ESR1	7ujo	-8.3

and blood lipid-lowering properties in addition to being able to scavenge oxygen-free radicals.

Moreover, PTGS2 had a higher docking score than the positive control. Each target protein's average binding energy was displayed as follows: nobiletin (−7.32 kcal/mol), citromitin (−7.24 kcal/mol), 5,7-dihydroxy-2-(3-hydroxy-4 methoxyphenyl)chroman-4-one (−8.14 kcal/mol), and sertraline hydrochloride (−7.52 kcal/mol). Figure 9.7 shows the visualization of combined figures of the 3D molecular models.

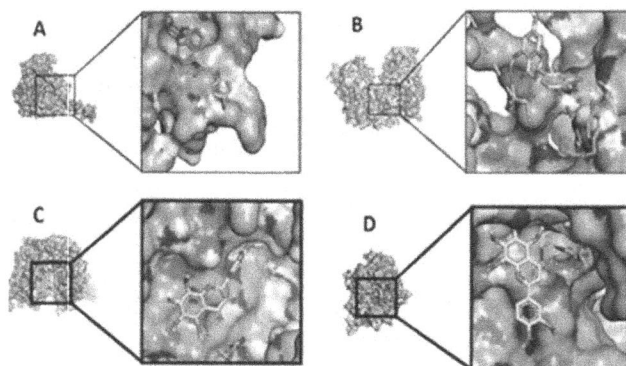

Fig. 9.7 The combined figures of the 3D molecular models are as follows: (A) Positive drug- ESR1, (B) ESR1- 5, 7-dihydroxy-2-(3-hydroxy-4-methoxyphenyl) chroman-4-one, (C) ESR1 - Citromitin, (D) ESR1- nobiletin

The identified overlapping genes demonstrate significant involvement in the anxiolytic pathway. However, the analysis of KEGG pathways reveals that these bioactive components target genes, found in *C. reticulata*, which may have broader implications.

Exploring these genes in the context of other disease pathways suggests that the core bioactive components of *C. reticulata* could potentially be utilized for the treatment of additional conditions such as the disease of anatomical entity, Disease of mental health, Central nervous system disease, Cognitive disorder, Disease metabolism, Neurodegenerative disease, Mood disorder, Major depressive disorder, Dementia, Gonadal disease, Vascular dementia and such.

This work has certain limitations because network pharmacology relies on pre-existing databases and known interactions, which could result to the exclusion of new, undiscovered, or improperly described bioactive compounds. Additionally, molecular docking also challenged by potential inaccuracies in binding affinities, protein conformational flexibility, and incomplete representation of environmental factors in the in silico environment.

5. Conclusion

Through molecular docking and network pharmacology, this study explored the mechanism of action of *C. reticulata* in treating anxiety disorder. Based on the results, the primary active ingredients in *C. reticulata*, the important targets, and numerous receptors and signaling pathways were found, and that explained how the herb exerts its anxiolytic effect. These results indicate the multicomponent, multitarget, and multi-pathway properties of *C. reticulata* in the treatment of anxiety.

In vitro and in vivo studies should be the main focus of future research in order to further validate these findings through experimental validation. Also, studying other less well-known signaling pathways, like neuroinflammatory or neuroendocrine pathways, could add new dimensions to the research, and provide a theoretical foundation for the clinical use of *C. reticulata* and indicate future research directions for the creation of anti-anxiety medications.

Acknowledgment

The authors acknowledge the Sri Lanka Institute of Information and Technology for providing the computational facilities.

REFERENCES

1. A. Kandola, D. Vancampfort, M. Herring, A. Rebar, M. Hallgren, J. Firth, et al., "Moving to beat anxiety:

Epidemiology and therapeutic issues with physical activity for anxiety," Curr. Psychiatry Rep., vol. 20, no. 8, p. 63, 2018, doi: 10.1007/s11920-018-0923-x.

2. E. M. Cornett, M. B. Novitch, A. J. Brunk, K. S. Davidson, B. L. Menard, R. D. Urman, et al., "New benzodiazepines for sedation," Best Pract. Res. Clin. Anaesthesiol., vol. 32, no. 2, pp. 149–164, 2018, doi: 10.1016/j.bpa.2018.06.007.

3. X. Geng, H. Wu, Z. Li, C. Li, D. Chen, J. Zong, et al., "Jie-Yu-He-Huan capsule ameliorates anxiety-like behaviours in rats exposed to chronic restraint stress via the cAMP/PKA/CREB/BDNF signalling pathway," Oxid. Med. Cell. Longev., vol. 2021, p. 1703981, 2021, doi: 10.1155/2021/1703981.

4. Y. Liu, D. Hu, Q. Fan, X. Zhang, Y. Zhu, M. Ni, and L. Sheng, "Mechanism of Chaihu shugan powder (柴胡疏肝散) for treating depression based on network pharmacology," Chin. J. Integr. Med., vol. 26, no. 12, pp. 921–928, 2019, doi: 10.1007/s11655-019-3172-x.

5. J. E. Yabesh, S. Prabhu, and S. Vijayakumar, "An ethnobotanical study of medicinal plants used by traditional healers in silent valley of Kerala, India," J. Ethnopharmacol., vol. 154, pp. 774–789, 2014.

6. Y. Jia, J. Zou, Y. Wang, X. Zhang, Y. Shi, Y. Liang, D. Guo, and M. Yang, "Action mechanism of Roman chamomile in the treatment of anxiety disorder based on network pharmacology," J. Food Biochem., vol. 45, no. 1, p. e13547, 2021.

7. J. Ru, P. Li, J. Wang, W. Zhou, B. Li, C. Huang, et al., "TCMSP: A database of systems pharmacology for drug discovery from herbal medicines," J. Cheminf., vol. 6, 2014.

8. Z. Liu, F. Guo, Y. Wang, C. Li, X. Zhang, H. Li, L. Diao, J. Gu, W. Wang, D. Li, and F. He, "BATMAN-TCM: A bioinformatics analysis tool for molecular mechanism of traditional Chinese medicine," Sci. Rep., vol. 6, p. 21146, 2016.

9. C. von Mering, M. Huynen, D. Jaeggi, S. Schmidt, P. Bork, and B. Snel, "STRING: A database of predicted functional associations between proteins," Nucleic Acids Res., vol. 31, no. 1, pp. 258–261, 2003.

10. H. B. Wu, Y. G. Xiao, J. S. Chen, and Z. K. Qiu, "The potential mechanism of Bupleurum against anxiety was predicted by network pharmacology study and molecular docking," Metab. Brain Dis., vol. 37, no. 5, pp. 1609–1639, 2022, doi: 10.1007/s11011-022-00970-1.

11. Y. Shi, M. Chen, Z. Zhao, J. Pan, and S. Huang, "Network pharmacology and molecular docking analyses of mechanisms underlying effects of the Cyperi rhizoma-Chuanxiong rhizoma herb pair on depression," Evid. Based Complement. Altern. Med., vol. 2021, p. 5704578, 2021, doi: 10.1155/2021/5704578.

12. M. Marin, J. G. Mejía, A. Flores, A. K. Cuchilla, and M. Moreno, "Integrating In Vivo model, molecular docking and network pharmacology to determine the mechanism of Theobroma cacao seed in treatment of diarrheal," J. Dis. Med. Plants, 2023, doi: 10.11648/j.jdmp.20230901.12.

13. M. Li, M. Jin, R. Hu, S. Tang, K. Li, X. Gong, et al., "Exploring the mechanism of active components from ginseng to manage diabetes mellitus based on network pharmacology and molecular docking," Sci. Rep., vol. 13, no. 1, 2023, doi: 10.1038/s41598-023-27540-4.

14. L. A. Hou, J. Yang, Y. Li, J. Kang, Z. Ma, X. Luo, et al., "Exploring the mechanism of action of Lobetyolin in the treatment of allergic rhinitis based on network pharmacology and molecular docking," Res. Square, 2023, doi: 10.21203/rs.3.rs-2477487/v1.

15. P. L. Liu, A. R. Song, C. D. Dong, Q. Chu, B. L. Xu, J. M. Liu, et al., "Network pharmacology study on the mechanism of the herb pair of prepared Rehmannia root-Chinese arborvitae kernel for anxiety disorders," Ann. Palliat. Med., vol. 10, no. 3, pp. 3313–3327, 2021, doi: 10.21037/apm-21-531.

Note: All the figures and tables in this chapter were made by the authors.

Transformative Applied Research in Computing, Engineering, Science and Technology – Dr. Damayanthi Dahanayake et al. (eds)
© 2024 Taylor & Francis Group, London, ISBN 978-1-041-01782-0

10

Unleashing the Antioxidant Property of β-Cryptoxanthin: A Potential Antioxidant in Mitigating Oxidative Stress

V. D. Hary,
D. R. Karunaratne, N. P. Katuwavila*
Department of Life Sciences,
Faculty of Science, NSBM Green University,
Sri Lanka

Abstract

Oxidative stress is caused by an imbalance between the body's antioxidant defenses and reactive oxygen species (ROS), which leads to serious health hazards. Aging and several age-related illnesses, including cancer, respiratory disorders, and cardiovascular diseases, are linked to oxidative stress. It causes harm to macromolecular structures like lipids, proteins, and nucleic acids, compromising cellular integrity and impairing cell function. β-cryptoxanthin is a carotenoid mostly present in citrus fruits, such as oranges. It has anti-inflammatory, antioxidative, and anticancer qualities. β-cryptoxanthin efficiently controls and reduces oxidative stress due to its strong antioxidant qualities. Using many processes such as quenching singlet oxygen, scavenging free radicals, inhibiting lipid peroxidation, and modifying signaling pathways linked to oxidative stress, β-cryptoxanthin fights oxidative stress. This review discusses the effect of oxidative stress on cellular components and how oxidative stress originates. It also provides a clear concise vision on the mechanisms of β-Cryptoxanthin as a potential antioxidant in mitigating oxidative stress and how this antioxidant ability helps in controlling a wide variety of diseases linked to oxidative stress.

Keywords

β-Cryptoxanthin, Oxidative stress, ROS, Antioxidant, Free radical scavenging

1. Introduction

The imbalance between the generation of reactive oxygen species (ROS) and the cell's capacity to counteract or repair the harm these molecules cause is known as cellular oxidative stress [1]. Mitochondrial activity, enzyme activity, and inflammation are internal contributions to the accumulation of ROS, as do external factors such as tobacco smoke, industrial smoke, and heavy metals[1, 2]. Higher levels of ROS promote oxidative stress which disrupts normal cell structure and function by affecting the structural integrity of nucleic acids, proteins, and lipids. Oxidative stress is linked to aging and multiple diseases like cancer and respiratory diseases that worsen with age [1–3].

---

*Corresponding author: nuwanthi.k@nsbm.ac.lk

DOI: 10.1201/9781003616368-10

Antioxidant enzymes (such as catalase and superoxide dismutase), non-enzymatic antioxidants, repair mechanisms, redox control, mitochondrial defense, and stress response proteins are some endogenous components and processes how cells reduce oxidative damage [4, 5]. Apart from the endogenous components, exogenous antioxidants such as Carotenoids, polyphenols, vitamin C and E are also crucial for oxidative stress defense[4–6].

β-Cryptoxanthin is a vital carotenoid with an oxygenated β-ring and multiple conjugated bonds. β-Cryptoxanthin is present in its pure form in human blood and tissue. β-Cryptoxanthin is also present in plant sources like citrus fruits like oranges, tangerines, squash and cruciferous vegetables. β-Cryptoxanthin is metabolized and converted to retinol with the aid of cleaving facilitated by β-Carotene oxygenases 1 and 2 (BCO1 and BCO2) enzymes. β-Cryptoxanthin poses numerous benefits by serving as an anti-inflammatory, antioxidant, and anticancer source[7, 8]. β-Cryptoxanthin's antioxidant properties enable it to efficiently reduce oxidative stress.

β-Cryptoxanthin has a multifaceted approach against oxidative stress due to the molecular structure and ability to regulate enzymes and pathways involved in lowering oxidative stress [7, 9, 10]. Because of the structural benefit of its conjugated bonds, β-cryptoxanthin participates in singlet oxygen quenching and free radical scavenging. Due to these processes the toxicity of ROS is reduced. Apart from the structural advantage, antioxidant enzymes like as superoxide dismutase are upregulated by β-cryptoxanthin to lower oxidative stress, the Nuclear Factor Kappa B (NF-κB) pathway is modulated to minimize inflammation, and AMP-activated protein kinase (AMPK) is activated to maintain energy balance and metabolic health.

With these multifaceted mechanisms against oxidative stress β-Cryptoxanthin serves as an effective therapeutic source against oxidative stress linked diseases like cancer. This review provides a clear vision on the antioxidative capability of β-cryptoxanthin in mitigating oxidative stress and the possible underlying mechanisms associated with lowering oxidative stress and targeting oxidative stress linked diseases.

2. Oxidative Stress, ROS and Involved Mechanisms

2.1 Oxidative Stress: Definition and Causes

Higher ROS in the body than antioxidant defense mechanisms result in cellular and tissue damage. This is referred to as oxidative stress. ROS are oxygen containing high reactive species with unpaired electrons [1]. Oxygen superoxide, hydroxyl groups, hydrogen peroxide and chlorine and nitrogen derivates like chloramines and nitric acid are examples of ROS [2, 11]. The cause of oxidative stress is multifactorial. Mitochondrial activity to produce (adenosine triphosphate) ATP, enzymatic pathways involving nicotinamide adenine dinucleotide phosphate (NADPH) oxidase, Myeloperoxidase and radical enzymes like cyclooxygenases result in ROS production and leads to oxidative stress. Neutrophils, eosinophils and macrophages during inflammatory conditions and exposure to environmental ROS sources like radiation that can ionize cellular molecules, heavy metals, pesticides, industrial smoke and tobacco abuse leads to excess ROS concentrations[1, 2, 11]. Deficiency of enzymes such as superoxide dismutase, catalase, glutathione peroxidase nutritional deficiencies due to low intake of vital vitamins like vitamin C and E minerals like zinc are some primary causes of oxidative stress [4, 12, 13].

2.2 Detrimental Effects of ROS on Cellular Components

At higher concentrations ROS becomes toxic to the cell as it affects the macromolecular structures of cell resulting to impaired cell function and altered structures [3, 14].

Proteins: Undergo ROS induced oxidation, fragmentation and aggregation which leads to the loss. Sulfur containing amino acids like cysteine, and methionine are prone to oxidative damage and after oxidation carbonyl products are formed. After oxidation the susceptibility to denature is high. Modification of proteins can occur via direct influence of ROS or by metal catalyzed oxidation and protein lipid adducts [1, 14].

Lipids: Lipid peroxidation which primarily occurs by OH- is an important hallmark of oxidative stress. Lipid peroxidation leads to formation of lipid hydroperoxides like polyunsaturated fatty acid hydroperoxide (PUFA-OOH) and lipid hyper peroxides degrade to form malonaldehyde and 4-hydroxynonenal (4-HNE). Lipid peroxidation leads to cell lysis due to loss of membrane integrity and increase membrane permeability due to alterations in membrane fluidity of functional 3D structure [1,8,15,16].

DNA and nucleic acid: ROS results in multiple DNA damages like DNA base modifications, strand breaks, DNA cross linkage. Hydroxyl group is a main ROS which results in DNA damage. 8-hydroxydeoxyguanosine (8-OHdG) and 5-(hydroxymethyl) uracil are key base modifications and prolonged DNA damage leads to fastened aging, carcinogenic and mutagenic modifications [1, 14, 17].

Oxidative stress is linked to the process of biological aging and age-related health risks like cardiovascular diseases (CVDs), cancer, diabetes, inflammatory and respiratory illnesses and male infertility [3, 18–22]. Below Fig. 10.1

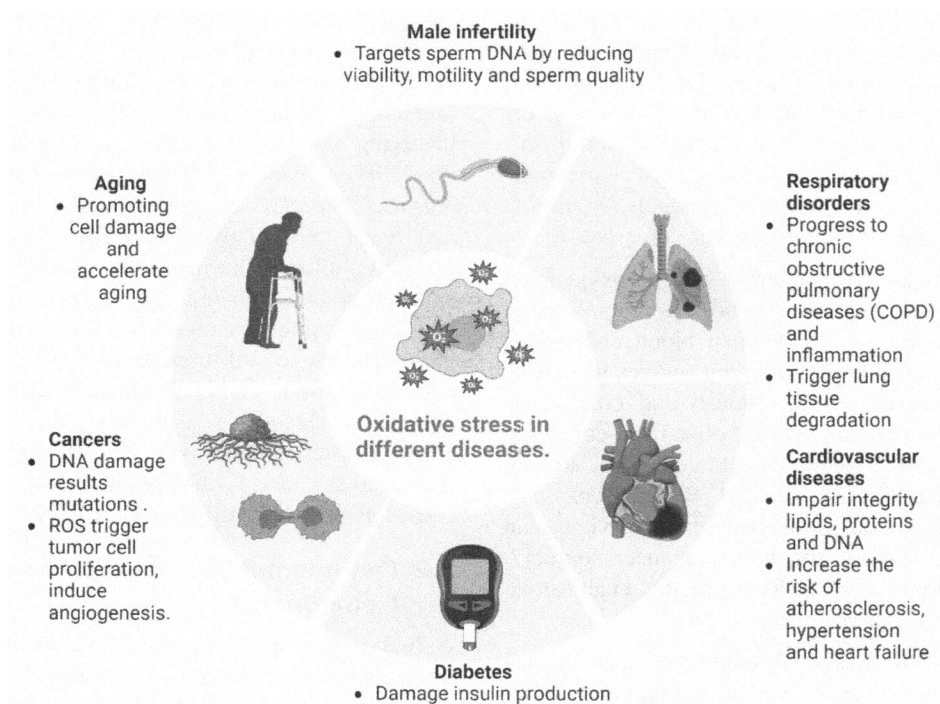

Fig. 10.1 The role of oxidative stress in different diseases namely diabetes, cancers, lung and cardiovascular diseases, male infertility and aging (Created with BioRender.com)

Source: Authors

provides an outline of the role of oxidative stress in different diseases.

3. Outline on β-Cryptoxanthin

3.1 Structure and Chemical Properties of β-Cryptoxanthin

β-Cryptoxanthin ($C_{40}H_{56}O$) is an oxygenated carotenoid due to the presence of a hydroxyl group at the third carbon of one of the β-rings. β-Cryptoxanthin possesses11 conjugated bonds including 2 located in the β-rings, which render the light adsorption, photoprotection and color properties[7,10]. The pure form of β-Cryptoxanthin is less stable and highly subjective to decomposition and isomerization resulting from UV light, pH alterations and oxygen thus the esterified form is more stable than the free form. Both unsaturated and saturated fatty acids are involved in esterification. Additionally, esterification increases thermal stability despite its unchanged light absorptive nature [4, 13].

3.2 Dietary Sources and Bioavailability of β-Cryptoxanthin

β-Cryptoxanthin is present freely in human blood and tissue and the ingested esterified forms are also transformed to free form. β-Cryptoxanthin is generally present in plant based dietary sources which are yellow orange in color. For example, fruits like oranges, tangerines, papaya, mango and cruciferous vegetables and leafy greens are rich sources of β-Cryptoxanthin. [7,10]. Including β-Cryptoxanthin rich food to feed livestock increases β-Cryptoxanthin levels in animal sources like butter and egg yolk [24].

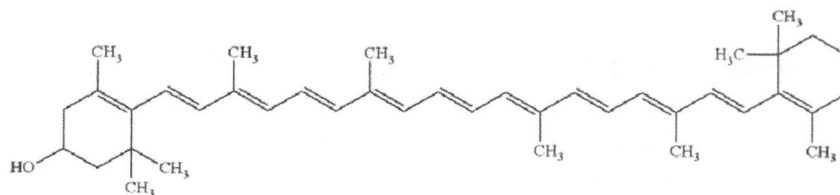

Fig. 10.2 Chemical structure of β-Cryptoxanthin [23]

Bioavailability of β-Cryptoxanthin is comparatively higher in fruits than in vegetables and the bioavailability is relatively higher than other carotenoids and Incorporation of oils and fats increases the bio accessibility and β-Cryptoxanthin is 725% more bioavailable than other provitamin A carotenoids. Bioaccessibility of both esterified and free form of β-Cryptoxanthin is identical. According to studies β-Cryptoxanthin is more bioavailable than β-Carotene, α-Carotene and lycopene and the absorption of β-Cryptoxanthin is more effectively absorbed and bioavailability is less altered even in fat malabsorption [7,9]

3.3 Metabolism and Absorption of β-Cryptoxanthin in the Human Body

β-Cryptoxanthin is released from food matrix and emulsified into oil droplets prior to absorption. Absorption occurs predominantly via facilitative transport by the involvement of protein transporters mainly the scavenger receptor class B type 1. β-Cryptoxanthin is converted to retinol within enterocytes and packed into chylomicrons. The transportation occurs via the lymphatic system and at fasting states β-Cryptoxanthin is distributed between lipoproteins. Liver serves as the primary site of storage whereas other storage sites are blood and adipose tissue. Excretion mainly occurs through feces. β-Cryptoxanthin is converted to retinol by BCO1 and BCO2 enzymes which cleaves β-Cryptoxanthin [9, 10].

3.4 β-Cryptoxanthin as a Potential Antioxidant in Mitigating Oxidative Stress the Possible Mechanisms Involved

Oxidative stress resulted by accumulation of ROS, results in impaired cell function and structural denaturation which leads onto chronic disease development. β-Cryptoxanthin possesses several antioxidant mechanisms such as free radical scavenging, restore DNA damage and inhibition of lipid peroxidation to restore oxidative stress. Additionally, β-cryptoxanthin modulates signaling pathways and incorporates with other antioxidants to harness maximum antioxidant potential in β-Cryptoxanthin.

3.5 Mechanisms Involved in Free Radical Scavenging by β-Cryptoxanthin

β-Cryptoxanthin possesses conjugate bonds which can donate electrons to neutralize free radicals and prohibit their involvement in oxidative reactions. Therefore β-Cryptoxanthin gains a structural advantage for effective free radical scavenging [10, 25–27] β-Cryptoxanthin also possess a unique singlet oxygen quenching ability, where unstable singlet oxygen is transformed to a stable form. Singlet oxygen quenching ability is because of conjugative double bonds that β-Cryptoxanthin possesses. The double bonds are involved in effective removal of excess energy without higher variation to the carotenoids molecular structure [27,28]

3.6 Inhibition of Lipid Peroxidation and Prevention of DNA Damage

Lipid peroxidation is the process in which ROS targets lipids, especially PUFA, in the membranes resulting in loss of membrane integrity and increasing membrane permeability. ROS scavenging mechanisms reduce ROS levels. This promotes inhibition of lipid peroxidation and aids in maintaining the structural integrity of plasma membranes. Antioxidant ability of β-Cryptoxanthin mitigates oxidative stress thereby showing inverse effects on lipid peroxidation [27, 29, 30].

Oxidative stress on DNA, which can break DNA strands, denaturize glycosidic linkages, and modify bases, especially damaging purines like guanine. As a result, 8-oxoguanine is created, which can attach to the DNA backbone and cause changes. Unrepaired DNA damage results in mutations producing permanent changes in DNA structure and functioning. This can also lead to tumor conditions . Due to the antioxidative mechanisms β-Cryptoxanthin protects human cells like HeLa cells from oxidative stress[1, 2, 31]. β-Cryptoxanthin improves repair processes by increasing base excision repair (BER) effectiveness. It improves DNA repair processes overall by increasing the activity of important BER enzymes, which make it easier to remove and replace damaged DNA bases. Due to this ability to protect DNA β-Cryptoxanthin is an effective anticancer source. β-Cryptoxanthin's potential to lessen smoke-induced oxidative stress is further supported by evidence found in lung tissue DNA damage indicators [9, 10, 32].

3.7 Other Mechanisms with β-Cryptoxanthin Involvement to Manage Oxidative Stress

β-Cryptoxanthin can reduce oxidative stress by regulating the activity of antioxidant enzymes and modulating signaling. The below table (Table 10.2) provides a clear outline of how β-cryptoxanthin is involved endogenously in antioxidative process.

4. Case Studies Proving the Antioxidant Potential of β-Cryptoxanthin in Disease Prevention

Rise in concentrations of ROS in the body leads to oxidative stress which is linked with aging, aging related diseases and wide array of diseases like CVDs, cancer. β- Cryptoxanthin possesses antioxidant mechanisms like

Table 10.1 Involvement of β-Cryptoxanthin in other endogenous antioxidant mechanisms

Mechanism/ process	Involvement of β-Cryptoxanthin
Regulating antioxidant enzymes and synergistic effect with them	β-Cryptoxanthin interacts with Superoxide Dismutase (SOD) and facilitates lowering oxidative stress. This was proved during an *in vitro* maturation of oocytes, where both SOD and β-Cryptoxanthin lowered oxidative stress. SOD is involved in conversion of more toxic superoxide to less toxic hydrogen peroxides [30,33,34] Based on several studies conducted β-Cryptoxanthin showed ability to enhance glutathione peroxidase activity promoting retinal and lung health. Glutathione peroxidase is involved in reduction of lipid hydroperoxides [30,35,36]
Modulation of signaling pathways and other molecular factors	
nuclear factor erythroid 2-related factor 2 (NRF2)	NRF2 is an important transcription factor regulating expression of antioxidant proteins and aid maintaining mitochondrial function. On an *in-vitro* study conducted on human renal tubular epithelial cells β-Cryptoxanthin was able to promote the NRF2 nuclear translocation and promoting NRF2 translocation was important for lowering damage to mitochondria [37]
NF-κB Pathway	NF-κB Pathway produce proinflammatory cytokines which cause inflammation and oxidative stress. Rats were treated with β-Cryptoxanthin supplementation, and the treatment resulted lowering of expression of NF-κB Pathway which reduced oxidative stress, inflammation and reduce myocardial ischemic damage to heart[38,39]
AMP-activated protein kinase (AMPK)	A study investigating β-Cryptoxanthin's effect on fatty liver in mice provided results suggesting activation of AMPK by β-Cryptoxanthin. AMPK is important in maintaining energy balance and activation of AMPK can activate Sirtuin 1 (SIRT1) action by controlling the $NAD^+/NADH$ ratio. This action can mitigate oxidative stress and lower inflammation levels [40]

Source: Authors

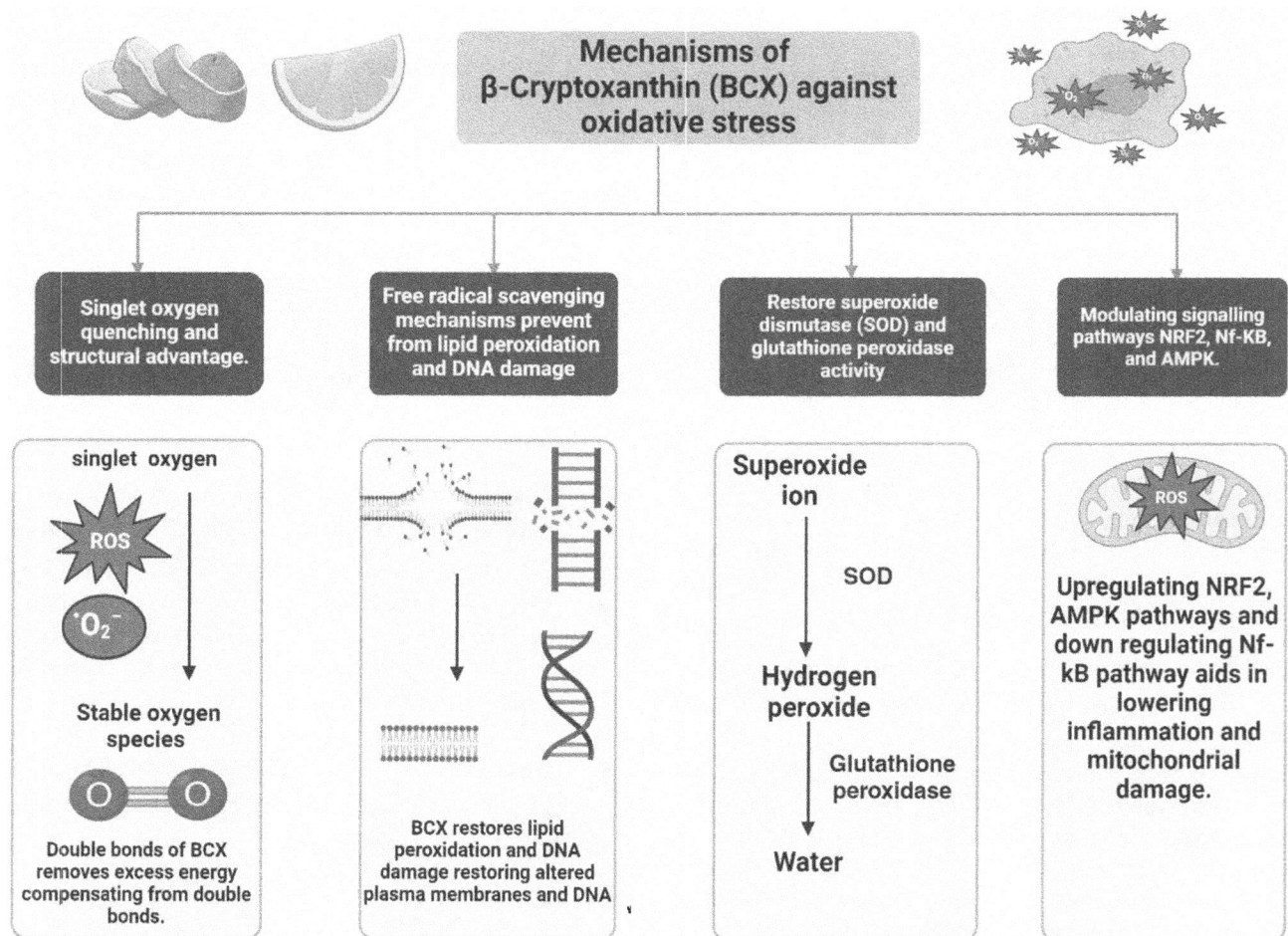

Fig. 10.3 Summary of different mechanisms how β-Cryptoxanthin lowers oxidative stress (created with BioRender.com)

Source: Authors

Table 10.2   Effect of B-cryptoxanthin against oxidative stress of multiple diseases

Study	Effect on oxidative stress	Disease prevention
A study on the effect of β-Cryptoxanthin against lung cancer developed in mice due to tobacco exposure. The study uses *Caenorhabditis elegans* (*C. elegans*) model to investigate the ability of β-cryptoxanthin to protect against oxidative stress and aid in fat reduction.	As a result of oxidative stress, the α7-nAChR pathway was lowered thus restoring this pathway lowered the inflammation and NADPH oxidase levels. β-Cryptoxanthin was able to lower oxidative stress in the model and prevented from oxidative damage	Multiplicity and motility of lung cancer cells were reduced in mice by upregulating α7-nAChR signaling. This action lowered the possibility of metastasis [41,42]. Antioxidant ability of β-Cryptoxanthin was beneficial to metabolic syndrome by controlling lipid metabolism and aging [43]
A study on carotenoid supplementation including β-cryptoxanthin for lowering the symptoms of Alzheimer's disease. An investigation on effect of β-Cryptoxanthin on cardioprotective effects on cardiac ischemia-reperfusion injury in mice. An investigation of the effect of β-Cryptoxanthin against the reproductive toxicity of chlorpyrifos in male rabbits.	β-cryptoxanthin was highly effective as an antioxidant due to the conjugate bonds and free radical scavenging ability. β-Cryptoxanthin can lower oxidative stress by increasing the antioxidant gene expression of enzymes like SOD and catalase. β-Cryptoxanthin was much effective than the antioxidant effect of vitamin E and astaxanthin. Chlorpyrifos is an organophosphorus insecticide which leads to oxidative stress by the free radicals. β-Cryptoxanthin was able to neutralize the free radicals and lower oxidative stress and restore the reproductive health.	β-cryptoxanthin was able to control lipid peroxidation a key factor in Alzheimer's disease and it was effective regardless of the carotenoid cleavage [44] By increasing antioxidant gene expression and minimizing mitochondrial dysfunction as a result reducing the infract, β-Cryptoxanthin function as an effective cardioprotective agent [45] As a result of the insecticide the testicle weight of the rabbits were reduced but β-Cryptoxanthin action lower the toxicity and oxidative stress and enhanced sperm production and quality [46]
Investigation on studying effects of β-cryptoxanthin on non-alcoholic fatty liver disease (NAFLD)	β-Cryptoxanthin neutralizes free radicals by preventing cell damage and thus lowering oxidative stress also lowers inflammation.	β-Cryptoxanthin increased insulin sensitivity, reduced elevated macrophage counts and regulated lipid metabolism by peroxisome proliferator-activated receptors (PPARs). Showed therapeutic effect against NAFLD and diabetes [8].

Source: Authors

free radical scavenging and singlet oxygen quenching which makes it a potential therapeutic source against oxidative stress related to different diseases. Below Table 10.2 depicts how β-Cryptoxanthin renders its antioxidant capability in mitigating oxidative stress of several illnesses.

The above table provides an insight on how the antioxidant capability of β-Cryptoxanthin can mitigate oxidative stress linked to various diseases. Apart from these studies and clinical investigations, there are higher number of studies which focuses on cumulative effect of carotenoids in lowering oxidative stress but there are less studies specifically targeting on the antioxidant capacity of β-Cryptoxanthin to safeguard and prevent worsening of diseases. Therefore, there is a necessity to focus on the specific effects of β-Cryptoxanthin against oxidative damage.

5. Why β-Cryptoxanthin is More Effective than Other Carotenoids

In general, astaxanthin is the most effective antioxidant due to its higher conjugation bonds and high free radical scavenging capacity but β-Cryptoxanthin is more effective than astaxanthin in mitigating oxidative stress linked to cardiac ischemia-reperfusion injury. Astaxanthin targets

plasma TBARS (Thiobarbituric Acid Reactive Substances) and cardiac TBARS the markers of lipid peroxidation but β-Cryptoxanthin is capable of directly targeting the genes related to antioxidative enzymes like SOD and catalase [45] Astaxanthin is highly present in algae and in seafood like Atlantic salmon, but β-Cryptoxanthin is readily available in citrus fruits and cruciferous vegetables[9, 10, 47, 48].

When compared to lycopene and β-carotene, β-Cryptoxanthin is more potent due to the structural advantage of having conjugated bonds and polar groups and β-Cryptoxanthin has higher bioavailability which is lacking in β-carotene and lycopene [7,9,10,47,48].

Lutein and zeaxanthin are 2 potent antioxidants in broccoli, kale, spinach. These antioxidants show strong action for oxidative stress in eye and has limited scope towards other regions, but β-Cryptoxanthin has a broad range of action as antioxidant by targeting lungs, bones, cardiovascular system and nervous system including eyes [10,41,49]

6. Conclusion

This review emphasizes the antioxidant potential of β-Cryptoxanthin that can counteract oxidative stress and avert further oxidative damage. Its antioxidant defense mechanisms, which include quenching singlet oxygen, scavenging free radicals, and inhibiting lipid peroxidation, are essential for preserving structural integrity and safeguarding cellular processes that are jeopardized by oxidative stress. β-Cryptoxanthin effectively limits oxidative damage and improves antioxidant protein performance by directly targeting ROS and influencing important antioxidant enzymes like SOD and glutathione peroxidase, as well as signaling pathways including AMPK, NRF2, and NF-κB. Numerous illnesses, such as cancer, cardiovascular diseases, and respiratory disorders are linked to oxidative stress. This article provides a concise summary of the ways in which the antioxidant characteristics of β-Cryptoxanthin might alleviate oxidative stress and even function as a therapeutic agent to lessen the susceptibility of disease. β-Cryptoxanthin has a noticeable significance over other carotenoids like astaxanthin, β-carotene, lycopene, Lutein and zeaxanthin under criteria such as bioavailability, border range of action as antioxidant, structural advantage of conjugated bonds and polar groups. Apart from these significant findings which emphasis potent antioxidant capability of β-Cryptoxanthin, there are limitations such as lack of clinical trials, standard dosage, unknown molecular mechanisms and bioavailability alterations in sources. Therefore, future research and investigations focusing on extensive clinical trials under controlled standard environments to find a standard dose and incorporating organoids and organ on chip models to analyze drug efficacy β-Cryptoxanthin, formulations to improve bioavailability and stability, standardized extraction procedures to produce nutraceuticals, incorporation of genomics technology to study molecular level effects and enhanced delivery systems utilizing nanoliposomes is necessary to unmask the full potential of β-Cryptoxanthin as an antioxidant.

REFERENCES

1. Sies H, Berndt C, Jones DP. Oxidative Stress. 2024;40:49.
2. Puppel K, Kapusta A, Kuczyńska B. The etiology of oxidative stress in the various species of animals, a review. J Sci Food Agric. John Wiley and Sons Ltd; 2015. p. 2179–2184.
3. Liguori I, Russo G, Curcio F, et al. Oxidative stress, aging, and diseases. Clin Interv Aging. Dove Medical Press Ltd.; 2018. p. 757–772.
4. Elsayed Azab A, A Adwas Almokhtar, Ibrahim Elsayed AS, et al. Oxidative stress and antioxidant mechanisms in human body. Journal of Applied Biotechnology & Bioengineering. 2019;6(1):43–47.
5. Srivastava S. Antioxidants and its functions in human body-A Review [Internet]. 2016. Available from: https://www.researchgate.net/publication/311674771.
6. Bjørklund G, Chirumbolo S. Role of oxidative stress and antioxidants in daily nutrition and human health. Nutrition. Elsevier Inc.; 2017. p. 311–321.
7. Burri BJ. Beta-cryptoxanthin as a source of vitamin A. J Sci Food Agric. John Wiley and Sons Ltd; 2015. p. 1786–1794.
8. Nishino A, Maoka T, Yasui H. Preventive effects of β-cryptoxanthin, a potent antioxidant and provitamin a carotenoid, on lifestyle-related diseases—a central focus on its effects on non-alcoholic fatty liver disease (Nafld). Antioxidants. MDPI; 2022.
9. Burri BJ, La Frano MR, Zhu C. Absorption, metabolism, and functions of β-cryptoxanthin. Nutr Rev. 2016;74(2): 69–82.
10. Jiao Y, Reuss L, Wang Y. β-Cryptoxanthin: Chemistry, Occurrence, and Potential Health Benefits. Curr Pharmacol Rep. Springer International Publishing; 2019. p. 20–34.
11. Li YR, Trush M. Defining ROS in Biology and Medicine. Reactive Oxygen Species. 2016;1(1).
12. Ahmed Amar SA, Eryilmaz R, Demir H, et al. Determination of oxidative stress levels and some antioxidant enzyme activities in prostate cancer. Aging Male. 2019;22(3):198–206.
13. Liu Z, Ren Z, Zhang J, et al. Role of ROS and nutritional antioxidants in human diseases. Front Physiol. Frontiers Media S.A.; 2018.
14. Caliri AW, Tommasi S, Besaratinia A. Relationships among smoking, oxidative stress, inflammation, macromolecular damage, and cancer. Mutat Res Rev Mutat Res. Elsevier B.V.; 2021.
15. Hernández JA, López-Sánchez RC, Rendón-Ramírez A. Lipids and Oxidative Stress Associated with Ethanol-Induced Neurological Damage. Oxid Med Cell Longev. Hindawi Publishing Corporation; 2016.
16. Ito F, Sono Y, Ito T. Measurement and clinical significance of lipid peroxidation as a biomarker of oxidative stress: Oxidative stress in diabetes, atherosclerosis, and chronic inflammation. Antioxidants. 2019;8(3).
17. Mikhed Y, Daiber A, Steven S. Mitochondrial oxidative stress, mitochondrial DNA damage and their role in age-related vascular dysfunction. Int J Mol Sci. MDPI AG; 2015. p. 15918–15953.
18. Gracia KC, Llanas-Cornejo D, Husi H. CVD and oxidative stress. J Clin Med. MDPI; 2017.
19. Hayes JD, Dinkova-Kostova AT, Tew KD. Oxidative Stress in Cancer. Cancer Cell. Cell Press; 2020. p. 167–197.
20. Maiese K. New insights for oxidative stress and diabetes mellitus. Oxid Med Cell Longev. Hindawi Limited; 2015.
21. Chatterjee S, Chakraborty K, Dalui S, et al. Oxidative Stress and Immune Regulation During Chronic Respiratory Diseases. Oxidative Stress in Lung Diseases: Volume 1. Springer Singapore; 2019. p. 187–194.
22. Takeshima T, Usui K, Mori K, et al. Oxidative stress and male infertility. Reprod Med Biol. John Wiley and Sons Ltd; 2021. p. 41–52.
23. Gammone MA, Riccioni G, D'Orazio N. Marine carotenoids against oxidative stress: Effects on human health. Mar Drugs. MDPI AG; 2015. p. 6226–6246.
24. Heying EK, Tanumihardjo JP, Vasic V, et al. Biofortified orange maize enhances β-Cryptoxanthin concentrations in egg yolks of laying hens better than tangerine peel fortificant. J Agric Food Chem. 2014;62(49):11892–11900.

25. Rodriguez-Amaya DB. Carotenes and xanthophylls as antioxidants. Handbook of Antioxidants for Food Preservation. Elsevier Inc.; 2015. p. 17–50.

26. Ribeiro D, Freitas M, Silva AMS, et al. Antioxidant and pro-oxidant activities of carotenoids and their oxidation products. Food and Chemical Toxicology. Elsevier Ltd; 2018. p. 681–699.

27. Mordi RC, Ademosun OT, Ajanaku CO, et al. Free radical mediated oxidative degradation of carotenes and xanthophylls. Molecules. MDPI AG; 2020.

28. Maoka T. Carotenoids as natural functional pigments. J Nat Med. Springer; 2020.

29. Zhang Y, Mao H, Li Y, et al. β-Cryptoxanthin Maintains Mitochondrial Function by Promoting NRF2 Nuclear Translocation to Inhibit Oxidative Stress-Induced Senescence in HK-2 Cells. 2023; doi: 10.3390/ijms.

30. Orhan C, Tuzcu M, Gencoglu H, et al. Different Doses of β-Cryptoxanthin May Secure the Retina from Photooxidative Injury Resulted from Common LED Sources. Oxid Med Cell Longev. 2021;2021.

31. Shin J, Song MH, Oh JW, et al. Pro-oxidant actions of carotenoids in triggering apoptosis of cancer cells: A review of emerging evidence. Antioxidants. MDPI; 2020. p. 1–17.

32. Slyskova J, Lorenzo Y, Karlsen A, et al. Both genetic and dietary factors underlie individual differences in DNA damage levels and DNA repair capacity. DNA Repair (Amst). 2014;16(1):66–73.

33. Badawi MS. The protective effect of β-cryptoxanthin against cyclophosphamide-induced lung injury in adult male albino rats. Bull Natl Res Cent. 2022;46(1).

34. Park YG, Lee SE, Son YJ, et al. Antioxidant β-cryptoxanthin enhances porcine oocyte maturation and subsequent embryo development in vitro. Reprod Fertil Dev. 2018;30(9): 1204–1213.

35. Gao YY, Xie QM, Ma JY, et al. Supplementation of xanthophylls increased antioxidant capacity and decreased lipid peroxidation in hens and chicks. British Journal of Nutrition. 2013;109(6):977–983.

36. Rai D, Sahin K, Sahin E, et al. Funding Sources: OmniActive Health Technologies [Internet]. Available from: https://academic.oup.com/cdn/article-abstract/4/ Supplement_2/126/5845343.

37. Zhang Y, Mao H, Li Y, et al. β-Cryptoxanthin Maintains Mitochondrial Function by Promoting NRF2 Nuclear Translocation to Inhibit Oxidative Stress-Induced Senescence in HK-2 Cells. 2023; doi: 10.3390/ijms.

38. Sahin K, Orhan C, Akdemir F, et al. β-Cryptoxanthin ameliorates metabolic risk factors by regulating NF-κB and Nrf2 pathways in insulin resistance induced by high-fat diet in rodents. Food and Chemical Toxicology. 2017;107: 270–279.

39. Zhang F, Shi D, Wang X, et al. β-cryptoxanthin alleviates myocardial ischaemia/reperfusion injury by inhibiting NF-κB-mediated inflammatory signalling in rats. Arch Physiol Biochem. 2022;128(4):1128–1135.

40. Lim JY, Liu C, Hu KQ, et al. Dietary β-Cryptoxanthin Inhibits High-Refined Carbohydrate Diet-Induced Fatty Liver via Differential Protective Mechanisms Depending on Carotenoid Cleavage Enzymes in Male Mice. Journal of Nutrition. 2019;149(9):1553–1564.

41. Lim JY, Wang XD. Mechanistic understanding of β-cryptoxanthin and lycopene in cancer prevention in animal models. Biochim Biophys Acta Mol Cell Biol Lipids. Elsevier B.V.; 2020.

42. Iskandar AR, Miao B, Li X, et al. β-cryptoxanthin reduced lung tumor multiplicity and inhibited lung cancer cell motility by downregulating nicotinic acetylcholine receptor α7 signaling. Cancer Prevention Research. 2016;9(11): 875–886.

43. Llopis S, Rodrigo MJ, González N, et al. β-Cryptoxanthin Reduces Body Fat and Increases Oxidative Stress Response in Caenorhabditis elegans Model. Nutrients. 2019;11(2).

44. Flieger J, Forma A, Flieger W, et al. Carotenoid Supplementation for Alleviating the Symptoms of Alzheimer's Disease. Int J Mol Sci. Multidisciplinary Digital Publishing Institute (MDPI); 2024.

45. Pongkan W, Takatori O, Ni Y, et al. β-Cryptoxanthin exerts greater cardioprotective effects on cardiac ischemia-reperfusion injury than astaxanthin by attenuating mitochondrial dysfunction in mice. Mol Nutr Food Res. 2017;61(10).

46. Mavedati O, Bandariyan E, Aminashayeri S, et al. β-Cryptoxanthin ameliorates the reproductive toxicity of chlorpyrifos in male rabbit. Comp Clin Path. 2015;24(2):409–415.

47. Caseiro M, Ascenso A, Costa A, et al. Lycopene in human health. LWT. Academic Press; 2020.

48. Olmedilla-Alonso B, Rodríguez-Rodríguez E, Beltrán-De-miguel B, et al. Dietary β-cryptoxanthin and α-carotene have greater apparent bioavailability than β-carotene in subjects from countries with different dietary patterns. Nutrients. 2020;12(9):1–21.

49. Mrowicka M, Mrowicki J, Kucharska E, et al. Lutein and Zeaxanthin and Their Roles in Age-Related Macular Degeneration—Neurodegenerative Disease. Nutrients. MDPI; 2022.

Transformative Applied Research in Computing, Engineering, Science and Technology – Dr. Damayanthi Dahanayake et al. (eds)
© 2024 Taylor & Francis Group, London, ISBN 978-1-041-01782-0

11

Evaluation of Naphthalene and Phenanthrene Degrdading Potential in Soil Bacteria from Automobile Repair Centres— An Innovative Bioremediation Approach

R Chandrasekaran,
RBN Dharmasiri*, HOTO Perera and AMVSS Polgolla
Department of Biomedical Science, BMS Campus,
Sri Lanka

Abstract

Polycyclic Aromatic Hydrocarbons (PAH) are organic chemical compounds with fused benzene rings that comprise carbon and hydrogen molecules. The incomplete combustion of carbonaceous compounds including petroleum products and wildfire frequently produces PAHs. They can be easily passed on to the plant due to their high accumulation tendency in the environment. They easily invade human systems via dietary sources and pose a high risk to human health since they are highly carcinogenic and genotoxic. This study focuses on PAHs; Naphthalene and Phenanthrene. The current study aims to isolate, identify, and evaluate the degradation percentages of such PAH-degrading soil bacteria. The soil samples were initially collected from automobile repair centres, which were polluted with PAHs. The environmental PAH analysis was done using High-Performance Liquid Chromatography (HPLC) to evaluate the PAH-pollution levels and morphologically different bacterial strains were isolated. The primary screening (plate assay) and a confirmatory tests (spectrophotometric analysis with methylene blue) were used to identify the PAH degraders and evaluate their degradation percentages respectively. Bacterial strains were cultured for seven days in Naphthalene and Phenanthrene-supplemented Bacto Bushnell Haas (BBH) broth following the starvation period to evaluate the degradation percentages. The molecular identification of bacteria was done using DNA extraction, PCR, and Sanger sequencing. This study identified new bacterial strains belonging to the genus *Bacillus* spp. and obtained NCBI Accession numbers as *Bacillus cereus* strain RCB-1210 and *Bacillus velezensis* strain RIA629. The population density of *B. cereus* and *B. velezensis* strains are calculated as 1×10^6 and 2×10^6 CFU/mL respectively. These bacteria exhibited more than 85% growth in the plate assay. The *B. cereus* strain RCB-1210 is the effective phenanthrene degrader with 79.47% and *B. velezensis* poses 52.87% of naphthalene degradation. Moreover, the statistical data confirms the dependency of PAH-degradation percentages on the supplements since the p-value > 0.05. These identified *Bacillus* spp. strains are potential biological agents that can mitigate PAHs from contaminated environments. Moreover, this PAH-degrading bacteria can improve soil quality by degrading the harmful pollutants from contaminated soil and can prevent the unnecessary passage of PAHs toward humans.

Keywords

Naphthalene, Phenanthrene, Bacillus cereus, Bacillus velezensis, Bioremediation, Degradation

*Corresponding author: nadeema.d@bms.ac.lk

DOI: 10.1201/9781003616368-11

1. Introduction

In 2021, the United Nations Environment Programme confronted the Triple Planetary Crisis: Climate, nature, and pollution. Anthropogenic activities are the major cause of environmental pollution. Soil pollution is one of the major convictions with an anomalous concentration of toxic compounds and pollutants in the soil resulting in high risk to human health and the ecosystem. The ability of future generations to satisfy their basic needs could be jeopardized by the current rate of soil pollution [20]. PAHs are the primary soil contaminant and the overall PAH contamination in soil generated by petroleum sources was given a high ecological risk [34]. Due to their high hydrophobicity and lipophilicity PAHs can easily accumulate in soil. It has been proven that PAHs are very harmful and toxic due to their immunotoxicity, genotoxicity, carcinogenicity, and teratogenicity [6] and are classified as Persistent Organic Pollutants (POPs) [10]. The incomplete combustion of carbonaceous compounds at high temperatures produces these PAHs. Agricultural, domestic, industrial, and mobile emissions are the main four categories of anthropogenic activities which release PAHs into the environment and can be controlled by proper management [23].

PAHs are classified according to the number of aromatic rings, chemical structure, and the origin of generation. Biogenic, petrogenic, and pyrogenic are other PAH categorizations based on their root of synthesis (living organisms, petroleum sources/ their by-products, and unintentional/ intentional incomplete combustion of organic compounds with low oxygen or high temperature respectively). In 2014, 16 PAHs were classified as priority pollutants including naphthalene and phenanthrene by the United States Environmental Protection Agency (US EPA). Naphthalene and Phenanthrene are petrogenic low molecular weight (LMW) PAHs which are often found to be pollutants.

Naphthalene ($C_{10}H_8$) is a two-fused aromatic ring as shown in Fig. 11.1 which is widely used in the industrial production of pest repellents however this in any form, can cause adverse effects including anaemia and cancer and its toxicity primarily affects the circulatory, respiratory, digestive, and ophthalmic systems. Previous studies state that naphthalene is very cancerous in both humans (especially in the larynx and intestine) and animals (especially in the nasal and lungs) [1]. Therefore, the US EPA classified naphthalene as a probable human carcinogen. Phenanthrene ($C_{14}H_{10}$) comprises three benzene rings which have "bay region" and "kay region" which are the ideal substrate region for metabolic studies. Phenanthrene toxicity can lead to respiratory irritation, skin allergies, and could pose carcinogenic risks to humans [12].

The atmospheric PAHs eventually deposit in the soil via dry and wet depositions, leading to further contamination in groundwater and plants [31]. Samarajeewa [27] has discussed the impact of PAH contamination on food safety and mentioned the regulations imposed in Sri Lanka to control excessive intake. In Sri Lanka, there are several studies have been taking place regarding PAH contamination in the environment such as aquatic, and phyllosphere in the past few years. Nevertheless, soil contamination considered studies are relatively low.

Some bacterial species that are identified to degrade naphthalene (e.g., *Acidovorax*, *Arthrobacter*, *Brevibacterium*) and phenanthrene (e.g., *Mycobacterium*, *Polaromonas*, *Pseudomonas*) use the PAHs as substrate in their metabolic pathway to obtain energy for their survival [29]. Microbial bioremediation techniques have drawn attention due to the drawbacks in chemical and physical processes such as incomplete degradation, expense complexity in implementation, regulatory burdens, and intervention of climate and seasons [18].

The primary goal of this study is to isolate, identify, and evaluate the PAH-degradation percentages of PAH-degrading soil bacteria. These identified bacterial strains can be used in microbial bioremediation, which is the most promising technology and the most eco-friendly way of removing pollutants from the soil as it produces relatively harmless molecules as byproducts (e.g., pyruvate and Krebs cycle intermediates), gases (e.g., CO_2), and water for their essential metabolic purposes such as nutrition and survival [16]. The simplest examples of the bioremediation process are composting and bioaugmentation [4]. Bacterial bioremediation is the most preferred technique due to its easy access to isolation, identification, growth rate, and non-complicated conditions.

2. Material and Methodology

2.1 Sample Collection and Environmental PAH Analysis

Soil samples (50 g) were collected from automobile repair centers in Peradeniya, Kandy (7°15'29" N, 80°35'26"

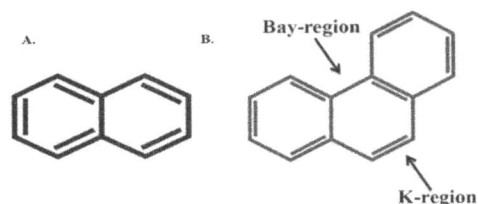

Fig. 11.1 Chemical structures of A) Naphthalene and B) Phenanthrene [12]

E) and Colombo (6°58'33" N, 79°52'33" E). PAH contamination levels in collected samples were evaluated using High-Performance Liquid Chromatography (HPLC) by obtaining chromatograms of standard naphthalene and phenanthrene solution and soil samples using 254 nm wavelength [26].

2.2 Bacterial Isoalation

Collected samples were separately dissolved in saline water and serially diluted up to 10^{-10}. Then 100 µL diluted samples with 10^{-5} and 10^{-10} were used to culture soil bacteria using the spread plate technique in nutrient agar (HiMedia, India). After 24 hours of incubation at 37°C, 12 morphologically different bacterial strains grown in the Petri dishes were selected and (1) was used to calculate the population density. The selected bacterial strains were cultured separately using the streak plate technique to obtain isolated pure cultures of each strain.

$$PD = IC / [DS \times DF] \qquad (1)$$

PD - Population Density (CFU/mL)
IC - No. of Isolated colonies
DS - Amount of the diluted sample used in spread plate
DF - Dilution factor

2.3 Plate Assay (Primary Screening)

After 48 hours of incubation at 37°C, pure cultures were cultured on Bacto Bushnell Haas (BBH) agar (MgSO$_4$ -0.200 g L^{-1}, CaCl$_2$ -0.020 g L^{-1}, KH$_2$PO$_4$-1.000 g L^{-1}, K$_2$HPO$_4$-1.000 g L^{-1} NH$_3$NO$_3$ - 1.000 g L^{-1}, FeCl$_3$-0.050 gL^{-1}, Final pH at 25 °C) [8]. After the starvation period of 3 days, the bacterial strains were transferred onto 100 ppm of naphthalene and phenanthrene (separately) spiked BBH agar plates which were divided into 25 squares. To achieve this process, a single starved colony was transferred onto each square. Finally, the grown colonies out of 25 squares were counted in each plate after 7 days of incubation at 30°C [8].

2.4 Spectrophotometric Analysis (Confirmatory Test)

Secondary screening was done using spectrophotometry analysis with methylene blue (MB) to evaluate the PAH degradation percentage of bacterial strains. Ten millilitres of naphthalene and phenanthrene (100 ppm) separately supplemented BBH broth was transferred into each tube. Three drops of methylene blue were added to each tube. Then 2 loops full of bacteria were taken from the initial streak plate culture and suspended in each tube where one was supplemented with naphthalene and the other one with phenanthrene. Negative control was maintained along with

the test. After 7 days of incubation at 30°C, the absorbance of each culture at 609 nm was obtained using a UV/Vis spectrophotometer with methylene blue. Then the PAH degradation percentages were calculated using (2) which was mentioned in previous studies [14, 37].

PAH-Degradation

$$\text{Percentage} = [(Mn\text{-}Ms) / Mn] \times 100 \quad (2)$$

Mn - Absorbance of Negative control

Ms - Absorbance of sample

2.5 Molecular Identification of PAH-Degrading Soil Bacteria

The DNA extraction from selected strains was done using the QIAGEN DNA Extraction Kit. The PCR was performed with 25 µL of the total sample including 2 µL of extracted DNA. Forward (27 F, AGAGTTTGATC MTGGCTCAG) and Reverse (1492 R, TACGGYTACCTTGTTACGACTT) primers [7] were used and the PCR conditions given in Table 11.1 were followed with 40 repeated cycles (denaturation to extension).

Table 11.1 PCR conditions

Step	Temperature	Time
Initial Denaturation	94°C	3 Minutes
Denaturation	94°C	30 Seconds
Primer Annealing	59°C	1 Minutes
Extension	72°C	1 Minutes
Final Extension	72°C	10 Minutes

The PCR products were visualized using Agarose Gel Electrophoresis (AGE) using 1% agarose gel. A 1 kb DNA ladder was used to determine the size of the DNA. Then the AGE was conducted under 55V for 75 minutes. The PCR products were visualized using a gel imager (Life Technologies, Israel). Finally, the PCR products were sent for sequencing to GENELABS, Sri Lanka. The 16s ribosomal RNA sequences were obtained using Sanger sequencing and bacteria were identified up to the species level using the nucleotide BLAST tool. Finally, the NCBI Accession numbers were obtained by submitting the sequences to NCBI GenBank.

2.6 Statistical Analysis

IBM Statistical Product and Service Solutions (SPSS) software version 16.0.1.0 was used to analyze statistical information. One-way ANOVA tests were conducted to analyze the confirmatory screening tests.

3. Results and Discussion

According to the Soil Quality Guidelines, PAHs are the primary soil contaminant and 95% of them are generated from petroleum sources [34]. Therefore, automobile repair centres were chosen as sample collection sites. There is a higher chance of isolating PAH-degrading bacteria from soil samples collected from these sites where the environment is very familiar with handling and releasing petrogenic PAHs to the environment. Environmental PAH levels of soil samples are given in Table 11.2.

Table 11.2 PAH levels in soil samples

CONCENTRATION (Ppm)		
Chemical	Ro2 (Kandy)	Ro3 (Colombo)
Naphthalene	4.2091	8.7338
Phenanthrene	35.6576	35.8259

According to the HPLC analysis, naphthalene contamination seemed to be much lower than phenanthrene contamination in Peradeniya and Colombo. During this environmental PAH analysis, the concentrations were found to be lower than expected. This could be due to the presence of such PAH-degrading soil bacteria in samples. However, proper measures should be taken to avoid any fluctuations to be caused in the near future.

Morphologically different bacterial strains were isolated using isolation techniques. Then further steps were followed to identify the PAH degraders among them. Molecular identification revealed that two *Bacillus* species can degrade naphthalene and phenanthrene with the ability to degrade at least one of the mentioned PAHs for higher than 50%. The population densities of these two bacteria were calculated as 2×10^6. CFU/mL. Table 11.3 contains the PAHs degrading *Bacillus* spp. and their NCBI Accession numbers.

Table 11.3 Bacterial strains and NCBI accession numbers

Strain Code	Identified Bacterial Strain	NCBI Accession Number
SRO3- R2 II	*Bacillus cereus strain* RCB-1210	PP518035
SRO2-R10	*Bacillus velezensis* strains RIA629	PP515578

Primary screening depended on the growth of bacterial strains under naphthalene and phenanthrene supplementation after the starvation period. The bacterial strains were starved in BBH agar, a recommended selective culture media for microbiological deterioration of fuels by microbes [15]. This contains all the essential nutrients and minerals except the carbon source which is necessary for bacterial growth. Therefore, only the bacteria that can utilize supplemented compounds can survive. The starvation period is the necessary process to identify the bacterial strains that use the supplemented PAHs as their sole carbon source in their metabolic activity to obtain energy for their survival [8].

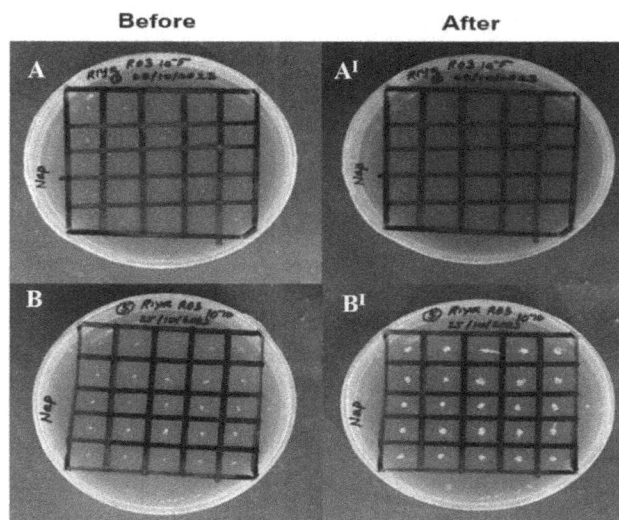

Fig. 11.2 Growth of bacterial strains in primary screening: A) Growth of a non-PAH degrader before the incubation. A^I) Growth of non-PAH degrader bacteria after incubation. B) Growth of a PAH degrader before the incubation. B^I) Growth of PAH degrader bacteria after incubation

Figure 11.2 shows the growth of non-PAH degrader (Top) and PAH degrader (bottom) in primary screening. According to the primary screening, approximately 30% of bacterial strains were able to grow in all 25 squares in both supplements and 58 % of isolated strains were able to grow in all 25 squares in at least one supplementation. *B. cereus* strain RCB-1210 exhibited growth in 25 squares in both supplements while *B. velezensis* strain RIA629 were grown in all 25 squares under phenanthrene supplement only.

In the spectrophotometric analysis, the calculation uses the absorbance of the samples at 609 nm [14]. The wavelength 609nm is the ideal wavelength to measure the absorbance of the methylene blue which acts as a bacterial PAH degradation indicator in the culture. The absorbance readings less than the negative control absorbance indicated the capability of the bacteria to degrade PAH. The ability of the strains to produce a colour change (less intense blue) in the cultures as in Fig. 11.3 presumably indicates the reduction of indicator in the culture by the oxidized byproducts of PAHs [7, 11]. This provides credence to the hypothesis that the isolates can degrade Naphthalene and Phenanthrene.

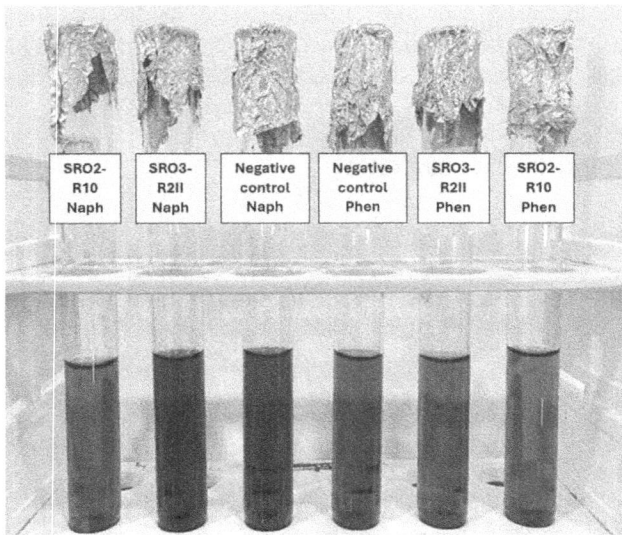

Fig. 11.3 Bacterial cultures after the incubation period along with the negative controls

Figure 11.4 contains the PAH-degradation percentages of respective strains where the Y-axis and X-axis indicate the PAH-degradation percentage and the identified new *Bacillus* spp. respectively. The *B. cereus* strain RCB-1210 is the effective phenanthrene degrader as it poses 79.47% of phenanthrene degradation. This strain exhibited a higher phenanthrene degradation percentage than all the other bacterial species experimented in this study. Its naphthalene degradation percentage is evaluated as 24.80%. The *B. velezensis* strain RIA629 exhibited naphthalene and phenanthrene degradation percentages up to 52.87% and 33.07% respectively. Moreover, the statistical data

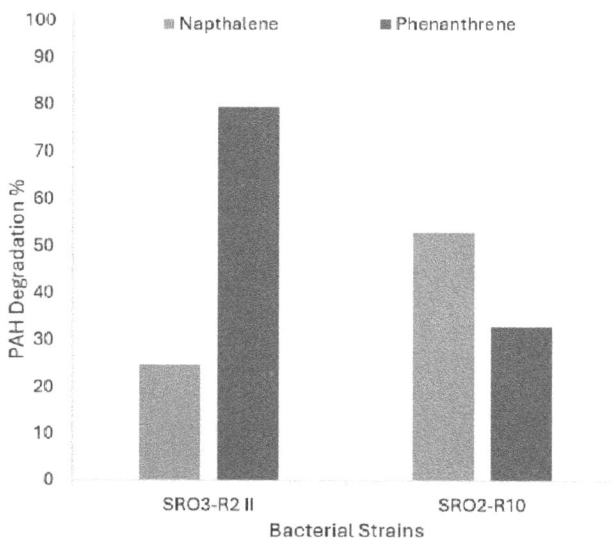

Fig. 11.4 PAH-degradation percentages of bacterial strains

confirms the dependency of PAH degradation percentages of the identified strains on the different PAH supplements since significant differences were identified (p-value> 0.05, statistically significant). These degradation percentages can be increased by implying several studied strategies. The addition of carbon source, nutrients and surfactants addition (improves the PAHs solubility) proved to be enhance the bioremediation of PAHs [38]. PAH-degrading bacterial consortium immobilized compost has proven to increase naphthalene and phenanthrene degradation [28].

PAH-degrading *Bacillus* spp. were abundantly identified in both inland and foreign countries. Sultana et al. studied the ability of *Bacillus velezensis* which was isolated from fermented foods (e.g., kimchi) to degrade PAHs and mentioned that as a probiotic from fermented foods, they have been identified to detoxify PAHs in humans [30]. Moreover, it was found to promote plant growth in sustainable agriculture [24, 39]. However, the special characteristics and importance especially in the environment as a biofertilizer of this bacterial species were studied by Alenezi et al. [3]. Dharmasiri et al. mentioned that a phyllosphere *B. velezensis* strain can completely degrade phenanthrene into CO_2 and water up to 94.79% within a week. In this study, *B. velezensis* strain RIA629 which was isolated from oil-contaminated soil samples was identified to degrade naphthalene and phenanthrene in moderate levels [8].

As mentioned, the PAH degradation ability of *Bacillus* spp. in oil-polluted areas was frequently studied [2, 16,19]. Tuhuloula et al. emphasized the bioremediation of petroleum-contaminated soil by a bacterial consortium which includes *B. cereus* [32]. Previous studies identified that some of the *B. cereus* strains can successfully degrade naphthalene [25,33] and phenanthrene [35]. [13] Hoang et al. studied about rhizo- degradation method of phenanthrene by *B. cereus* [13]. Moreover, it was found to degrade many other PAHs (e.g., anthracene) [21,22].

4. Conclusion

In this study, bacterial strains that can degrade PAHs were identified and their degradation percentages were evaluated. Two bacterial strains that belong to *Bacillus* spp. were identified and their NCBI accession numbers were obtained as *B.* cereus strain RCB-1210 and *B. velezensis* strain RIA629. The strain RCB-1210 is the most efficient phenanthrene degrader identified in this study as its degradation percentage was evaluated as the highest among the other strains, exhibiting 79.47% of degradation. *B. velezensis* strain RIA629 is the efficient naphthalene degrader among the identified *Bacillus* spp. as it can degrade up to 52.87% of naphthalene. These findings support that bacterial bioremediation of PAHs such as naphthalene and phenanthrene could be effective. Therefore, these identified strains can be used as potential biological agents to mitigate PAH pollution from contaminated soil and improve soil quality to promote plant growth and avoid unnecessary passage of PAHs toward humans.

Acknowledgement

The authors would like to acknowledge the Department of Biomedical Science, BMS Campus, Sri Lanka for their assistance in carrying out this research.

REFERENCES

1. Abdel-Shafy, Hussein I., and Mona SM Mansour. "A review on polycyclic aromatic hydrocarbons: source, environmental impact, effect on human health and remediation." *Egyptian journal of petroleum* 25, no. 1 (2016): 107–123.

2. Al-Dhabaan, Fahad A. "Morphological, biochemical and molecular identification of petroleum hydrocarbons biodegradation bacteria isolated from oil polluted soil in Dhahran, Saud Arabia." *Saudi Journal of Biological Sciences* 26, no. 6 (2019): 1247–1252.

3. Alenezi, Faizah N., Houda Ben Slama, Ali Chenari Bouket, Hafsa Cherif-Silini, Allaoua Silini, Lenka Luptakova, Justyna Anna Nowakowska, Tomasz Oszako, and Lassaad Belbahri. "Bacillus velezensis: A treasure house of bioactive compounds of medicinal, biocontrol and environmental importance." *Forests* 12, no. 12 (2021): 1714.

4. Alori, Elizabeth Temitope, Alhasan Idris Gabasawa, Chinyere Edna Elenwo, and Oluwadolapo Ololade Agbeyegbe. "Bioremediation techniques as affected by limiting factors in soil environment." *Frontiers in Soil Science* 2 (2022): 937186.

5. Aryal, M., 2024. Rhizomicrobiome dynamics: A promising path towards environmental contaminant mitigation through bioremediation. *Journal of Environmental Chemical Engineering*, p.112221.

6. Balint, Alexandru. "Physical, chemical and toxicological properties of polycyclic aromatic hydrocarbons (PAHs) in human exposure assessments to contaminated soil and groundwater." In *MATEC Web of Conferences*, vol. 342, p. 03016. EDP Sciences, 2021.

7. Benedek, T., I. Máthé, A. Táncsics, S. Lányi, and K. Márialigeti. "Investigation of hydrocarbon-degrading microbial communities of petroleum hydrocarbon contaminated soils in Harghita county, Romania." *Scientific bulletin series D: mining, mineral processing, non-ferrous metallurgy, geology and environmental engineering* 24, no. 2 (2010): 15.

8. Dharmasiri, R. B. N., L. J. S. Undugoda, A. H. L. Nilmini, N. N. R. N. Nugara, P. M. Manage, and D. Udayanga. "Phylloremediation approach to green air: phenanthrene degrading potential of Bacillus spp. inhabit the phyllosphere of ornamental plants in urban polluted areas." *International Journal of Environmental Science and Technology* 20, no. 12 (2023): 13359–13372.

9. Dharmasiri, R. B. N., A. H. L. Nilmini, L. J. S. Undugoda, N. N. R. N. Nugara, D. Udayanga, and M. M. Pathmalal. "Polyaromatic hydrocarbons (PAHs) degradation ability of Pseudomonas stutzeri isolated from phyllosphere of urbanareas in Sri Lanka." (2021).

10. Ejiako, Ejike Joel, Okechukwu Uzoma Iheme, and Camillus Uchenna Okonkwo. "Persistent organic pollutant: a review on the distribution of polycyclic aromatic hydrocarbons (PAHs) in aquatic ecosystem." *Int J Environ Sci Natl Resour* (2022).

11. George-Okafor, Uzoamaka, Floretta Tasie, and Florence Muotoe-Okafor. "Hydrocarbon degradation potentials of indigenous fungal isolates from petroleum contaminated soils." *Journal of Physical and natural sciences* 3, no. 1 (2009): 1–6.

12. Ghosal, Debajyoti, Shreya Ghosh, Tapan K. Dutta, and Youngho Ahn. "Current state of knowledge in microbial degradation of polycyclic aromatic hydrocarbons (PAHs): a review." *Frontiers in microbiology* 7 (2016): 1369.

13. Hoang, Son A., Dane Lamb, Balaji Seshadri, Binoy Sarkar, Girish Choppala, M. B. Kirkham, and Nanthi S. Bolan. "Rhizoremediation as a green technology for the remediation of petroleum hydrocarbon-contaminated soils." *Journal of Hazardous Materials* 401 (2021): 123282.

14. Kannangara, S., and L. Undugoda. "Naphthalene and phenanthrene degradation by phyllosphere bacteria from the ornamental plants in urbanized and polluted areas of Sri Lanka." *IJAER* 5 (2016): 1404–1419.

15. Kolsal, Fulya, Zeynep Akbal, Fakhra Liaqat, Oğuzhan Gök, Delia Teresa Sponza, and Rengin Eltem. "Hydrocarbon degradation abilities of psychrotolerant Bacillus strains." *AIMS microbiology* 3, no. 3 (2017): 467.

16. Kong, Fan-xin, Guang-dong Sun, and Zhi-pei Liu. "Degradation of polycyclic aromatic hydrocarbons in soil mesocosms by microbial/plant bioaugmentation: performance and mechanism." *Chemosphere* 198 (2018): 83–91.

17. Kong, Xianghui, Ranran Dong, Thomas King, Feifei Chen, and Haoshuai Li. "Biodegradation potential of Bacillus sp. PAH-2 on PAHs for oil-contaminated seawater." *Molecules* 27, no. 3 (2022): 687.

18. Kuppusamy, Saranya, Palanisami Thavamani, Kadiyala Venkateswarlu, Yong Bok Lee, Ravi Naidu, and Mallavarapu Megharaj. "Remediation approaches for polycyclic aromatic hydrocarbons (PAHs) contaminated soils: Technological constraints, emerging trends and future directions." *Chemosphere* 168 (2017): 944–968.

19. Mandree, Prisha, Wendy Masika, Justin Naicker, Ghaneshree Moonsamy, Santosh Ramchuran, and Rajesh Lalloo. "Bioremediation of polycyclic aromatic hydrocarbons from industry contaminated soil using indigenous bacillus spp." *Processes* 9, no. 9 (2021): 1606.

20. Münzel, Thomas, Omar Hahad, Andreas Daiber, and Philip J. Landrigan. "Soil and water pollution and human health: what should cardiologists worry about?." *Cardiovascular research* 119, no. 2 (2023): 440–449.

21. Bibi, Nadia, Muhammad Hamayun, Sumera Afzal Khan, Amjad Iqbal, Badshah Islam, Farooq Shah, Muhammad Aaqil Khan, and In-Jung Lee. "Anthracene biodegradation capacity of newly isolated rhizospheric bacteria Bacillus cereus S13." *PLoS One* 13, no. 8 (2018): e0201620.

22. Olowomofe, Temitayo O., J. O. Oluyege, B. I. Aderiye, and O. A. Oluwole. "Degradation of poly aromatic fractions of crude oil and detection of catabolic genes in hydrocarbon-degrading bacteria isolated from Agbabu bitumen sediments in Ondo State." *AIMS microbiology* 5, no. 4 (2019): 308.

23. Patel, Avani Bharatkumar, Shabnam Shaikh, Kunal R. Jain, Chirayu Desai, and Datta Madamwar. "Polycyclic aromatic hydrocarbons: sources, toxicity, and remediation approaches." *Frontiers in Microbiology* 11 (2020): 562813.

24. Rabbee, Muhammad Fazle, Buyng-Su Hwang, and Kwang-Hyun Baek. "Bacillus velezensis: a beneficial biocontrol agent or facultative phytopathogen for sustainable agriculture." *Agronomy* 13, no. 3 (2023): 840.

25. Rejiniemon, T. S., R. Lekshmi, Hissah Abdulrahman Alodaini, Ashraf Atef Hatamleh, Rengasamy Sathya, Palaniselvam Kuppusamy, Munirah Abdullah Al- Dosary, and M. Kalaiyarasi. "Biodegradation of naphthalene by biocatalysts isolated from the contaminated environment under optimal conditions." *Chemosphere* 305 (2022): 135274.

26. Rima, Jamil. "HPLC and spectrofluorimetric determination of pyrene in the Lebanese coast." *Journal of Black Sea/Mediterranean Environment* 19, no. 1 (2013): 58–69.

27. Samarajeewa, U. "Polycyclic aromatic hydrocarbons and food safety: A review." (2023).

28. Shahindha, F., J. M. U. D. Jayasundara, J. V. Arulnesan, R. Chandrasekaran, S. F. Sabra, P. Mayooran, R. Fernando, H. O. T. O. Perera, and R. B. N. Dharmasiri. "Microbiological Analysis of Phenanthrene and Naphthalene Degrading Soil Bacteria Isolated from Landfills and Filling Stations: Bioremediation Approach for a Green Environment." (2024).

29. Srivastava, Shaili, and Madan Kumar. "Biodegradation of polycyclic aromatic hydrocarbons (PAHs): a sustainable approach." *Sustainable green technologies for environmental management* (2019): 111–139.

30. Sultana, Omme Fatema, Saebim Lee, Hoonhee Seo, Hafij Al Mahmud, Sukyung Kim, Ahyoung Seo, Mijung Kim, and Ho-Yeon Song. "Biodegradation and removal of PAHs by Bacillus velezensis isolated from fermented food." *Journal of Microbiology and Biotechnology* 31, no. 7 (2021): 999.

31. Syed, Jabir Hussain, Mehreen Iqbal, Guangcai Zhong, Athanasios Katsoyiannis, Ishwar Chandra Yadav, Jun Li, and Gan Zhang. "Polycyclic aromatic hydrocarbons (PAHs) in Chinese forest soils: profile composition, spatial variations and source apportionment." *Scientific Reports* 7, no. 1 (2017): 2692.

32. Tuhuloula, Abubakar. "Biodegradation of Extractable Petroleum Hydrocarbons by Consortia Bacillus cereus and Pseudomonas putida in Petroleum Contaminated- Soil_Turnitin." (2019).

33. Tuleva, Borjana, Nelly Christova, Bojidar Jordanov, Boryana Nikolova-Damyanova, and Petar Petrov. "Naphthalene degradation and biosurfactant activity by Bacillus cereus 28BN." *Zeitschrift für Naturforschung C* 60, no. 7-8 (2005): 577–582.

34. Wang, Di, Jing Ma, Hao Li, and Xingchang Zhang. "Concentration and potential ecological risk of PAHs in different layers of soil in the petroleum-contaminated areas of the Loess Plateau, China." *International journal of environmental research and public health* 15, no. 8 (2018): 1785.

35. Yang, Zhilin, Bo Li, Shizong Wang, Qi Yang, and Yeyao Wang. "Investigation of degradation of phenanthrene by Bacillus cereus isolated from activated sludge and competitive inhibition kinetics." *Environmental Bulletin* 25 (2016): 5786–5794.

36. Yu-bin, Tang, Yang Xu, Chen Fang-yan, Jiang Rui-ling, and Wang Xin-gang. "Screening, identification and degrading gene assignment of a chrysene-degrading strain." *African Journal of Biotechnology* 10, no. 34 (2011): 6549–6557.

37. Yu-bin, Tang, Yang Xu, Chen Fang-yan, Jiang Rui-ling, and Wang Xin-gang. "Screening, identification and degrading gene assignment of a chrysene-degrading strain." *African Journal of Biotechnology* 10, no. 34 (2011): 6549–6557.

38. Zhou, Haixuan, Xiurong Gao, Suhang Wang, Youchi Zhang, Frederic Coulon, and Chao Cai. "Enhanced bioremediation of aged polycyclic aromatic hydrocarbons in soil using immobilized microbial consortia combined with strengthening remediation strategies." *International Journal of Environmental Research and Public Health* 20, no. 3 (2023): 1766.

39. Zhou, Jianping, Yunqiao Xie, Yuhong Liao, Xinyang Li, Yiming Li, Shuping Li, Xiuguo Ma et al. "Characterization of a Bacillus velezensis strain isolated from Bolbostemmatis Rhizoma displaying strong antagonistic activities against a variety of rice pathogens." *Frontiers in microbiology* 13 (2022): 983781.

Note: All the figures (except Fig. 11.1) and tables in this chapter were made by the authors.

Transformative Applied Research in Computing, Engineering, Science and Technology – Dr. Damayanthi Dahanayake et al. (eds)
© 2024 Taylor & Francis Group, London, ISBN 978-1-041-01782-0

12

Nano Formulations for Iron Deficiency Anemia

Y.G.C.D. Pitawala,
Nuwanthi P. Katuwavila*
Department of Life Sciences,
Faculty of Science, NSBM Green University,
Sri Lanka

Abstract

Iron deficiency was identified as the main cause of anemia, a most prevalent, and life-threatening illness across various age groups. The primary reasons for iron deficiency are the loss of iron or inadequate iron absorption, which damages cell growth, and the synthesis of oxygen-transporting proteins and DNA. There are conventional methods such as iron supplementation and food iron fortification to deal with the expanding disease. The most common method of administration is through oral iron supplements since it is more affordable, secure, and efficient than food iron fortification. This review summarizes conventional and novel nanotechnology applications for treating iron deficiency anemia (IDA), by outlining different types of nanoparticles, including polysaccharide, lipid, and metallic. This paper suggests that $FeSO_4$-loaded mucoadhesive microspheres may be useful as an efficient anemia treatment substitute. They may improve iron absorption, according to their strong mucoadhesive qualities, large swelling capacity, and effective encapsulation.

Keywords

Iron deficiency anemia, Nanotechnology, Nanoparticles, Nanoencapsulation

1. Introduction

Anemia is one of the most challenging deficiency conditions which is common worldwide and affects an estimated two billion individuals, primarily in South Asia, Central and West Africa [1-3]. This prevalence is common among infants, children, adolescents, pregnant and reproductive-age women [4]. World Health Organization shows that 40% of children between the ages of 0.5-5 years and 37% of expecting mothers are anemic worldwide in 2023.

Iron is a plentiful element on earth that is necessary for all life forms and can be converted into vital compounds that are necessary for every physiological function in blood and body organs, including aerobic metabolism, oxygen transport, energy metabolism, DNA synthesis, and electron

*Corresponding author: nuwanthi.k@nsbm.ac.lk

DOI: 10.1201/9781003616368-12

transport [5, 6]. Iron deficiency is the main cause of anemia and the most frequent type of anemia because it prevents the body from producing enough hemoglobin (Hb), typically caused by a diet that is low in iron. Low Hb levels can lead to fatigue, cognitive decline, and poor productivity, as well as increased maternal as well as neonatal mortality [4]. 70% of the body's total iron is bound to Hb as its primary component. Most of the iron is absorbed by enterocytes in the duodenum and proximal jejunum [5,7].

Currently, intravenous iron infusion, supplementation from the diet, or fortified products are utilized to raise the body's iron levels. Supplemental iron exists as either ferrous (Fe^{2+}) or ferric (Fe^{3+}). Salts of ferrous, like ferrous fumarate ($C_4H_2FeO_4$), ferrous sulfate ($FeSO_4$), or ferrous gluconate ($C_{12}H_{24}FeO_{14}$), are the types of iron supplements that are most quickly absorbed, with $FeSO_4$ being the first line of therapy for IDA because of its low-cost [1,4]. The bio-availability of different iron dosage forms varies notably because iron has a constrained absorption window [7]. To increase oral bio-availability, there has been an uptick in the development of drug-delivery systems based on nanotechnology [1,8]. It has been claimed that novel drug delivery strategies, such as polymeric iron nanoparticles (NPs) synthesized from magnetite, folic acid as well as other NPs can cure IDA [8,9].

Because of a number of benefits over conventional delivery methods for treating a wide range of illnesses, utilization of NPs for administration of drugs has become a viable option. Oral drug administration or inhalation is achievable for both hydrophilic and hydrophobic compounds to be included in NPs used as drug carriers without compromising stability. NPs are distinct because of their minor size, that set them apart from the substance's bulk counterpart. Their biological, chemical, mechanical, magnetic, electrical, and structural characteristics are all distinct, and able to move freely within the human body than larger materials [1,10]. This review gives an outline of established methods for IDA and describes therapeutic approaches that can be used to treat IDA with nanotechnology by reviewing current developments in iron supplementation by nanoparticle-based delivery systems critically. This study focuses on how these systems may be used to treat IDA. It will evaluate various forms of nanoparticles that have been investigated for iron delivery, such as metallic, lipid, and polysaccharide nanoparticles. In contrast to the majority of published research, which addresses a broad spectrum of nanoformulations, this study will only focus on nanoparticle-based strategies to determine the best option for increasing iron bioavailability and therapeutic efficacy. The review aims to present a thorough understanding of the mechanisms, benefits, and therapeutic prospects of nanoparticle-mediated systems by combining current research findings. "This will provide insight into which nanoparticle formulation holds the most promise."

2. Iron Deficiency Anemia

Deficiency of iron is the most prevalent type of anemia [11]. It comes from the blood's low iron content. Functional and absolute iron deficiency are the two basic forms. The supply of iron to the bone marrow is inadequate, despite overall iron levels being normal or even increased within the body, functional iron insufficiency develops [12]. Low or depleted total body iron reserves result in absolute iron insufficiency [13]. Absolute and functional deficiencies are not mutually exclusive. Numerous acute and chronic inflammatory conditions can exhibit functional iron deficiency, and hepcidin, the primary regulator of iron homeostasis [14] plays a crucial role in pathogenesis. Patients with IDA might appear with symptoms common to all anemias, yet they occasionally also have specific indicators related to iron deficiency. It is typical to have pallor in the nail beds, conjunctivae, and skin. When doctors can determine if the patient's existence of these symptoms represents a deviation from normal, the diagnostic value of these symptoms is increased. Fatigue, exertional dyspnea vertigo, deliquium, rapid heart rate, and a murmur in heart systolic flow are further symptoms and indicators for hypoxic functioning [15].

3. Conventional Therapies for Iron Deficiency Anemia

3.1 Iron Supplementation

Typically, iron supplements come in tablets, syrup, or powders that contain Fe^{2+} and Fe^{3+} salts such as $FeSO_4$, $C_{12}H_{24}FeO_{14}$, ferric citrate ($C_6H_5FeO_7$), and ferric sulfate (Fe_2SO_3) [1]. Fe^{2+} is more bioavailable than Fe^{3+} [16] because of their increased solubility. However, doses are elevated to improve bio-availability to make up for this low concentration, which brings us to the major disadvantage of this method. Constipation, nausea are among the long-term gastrointestinal adverse effects that could arise from taking supplemental iron at a dose of 45 mg or more per day [17].

3.2 Iron Infusion

Intravenous iron is advised for people who cannot tolerate oral iron, those with functional iron deficiency, and those who have had surgical operations since the IDA was diagnosed [18]. Additionally, there are times when the blood's iron levels are dangerously low, necessitating an emergency boost, which can be accomplished with an iron infusion [19]. Disadvantages include shock, anaphylaxis [18], and low blood pressure. In certain instances, the skin at the site of the injection has developed permanent scars [1].

3.3 Iron Fortification

Fortifying food with iron has been a widely used method that address the population's iron shortage. The most widely consumed basic foods (salt, flour, rice, and milk products) may use as carriers for adding iron [20]. Corn flour, rice, and milk products are currently being fortified [21]. Since young children do not consume these fortified food ingredients in substantial quantities, this strategy is nearly completely worthless for curing their anemia. The use of fortified foods is still up for controversy in several nations due to legal difficulties [1].

4. Nanotechnology in Iron Deficiency Anemia

Nanotechnology is being considered as a potential solution to reduce negative effects and enhance iron bioavailability in the blood [22]. One potential use of nanotechnology is to enhance nutrient bio-availability. minerals, drugs, and other molecules by reducing their size to the nanoscale. Researchers have found that this technique can significantly increase the efficiency of certain compounds [20]. Additionally, the NPs can be synthesized to satisfy specific needs, have improved stability, with a longer lifespan [19]. Moreover, the drug is released more effectively, resulting in a lower dosage and fewer adverse effects.

4.1 Nano-Encapsulation

Iron encapsulation in a nanostructure exhibits promising drug delivery outcomes. Drug stability and controlled release are ensured through nano-encapsulation [23]. Drugs are typically encapsulated in NPs to provide improved solubility rates, which increases the bioavailability of iron in the blood and increases absorption [19].Encapsulation tends to lessen the negative impact on the gastrointestinal tract while simultaneously increasing bioavailability [1, 25].

4.2 Amyloid Fibril Systems

Protein aggregations called amyloid fibrils are seen in biological systems. Development of amyloid fibril structures as fundamental components of biomaterials has been verified [1, 8, 26, 27, 28]. The study of Shen et al. presents a novel use for β-lactoglobulin and its biodegradable amyloid fibrils as effective iron fortification carriers. This mixture forms a stable protein-iron colloidal dispersion, releasing iron ions quickly and exhibiting reduced organoleptic alterations in food [28].

As a result, it is affordable and promising to use iron-amyloid fibrils to boost the body's iron availability. Further research has shown that iron-amyloid fibrils are useful as both liquids and powders, indicating a significant improvement atop the traditional modes of iron fortification because the conventional methods create potent colloidal aggregation when added to aqueous drinks. Consequently, there is currently a greater usage of iron-amyloid fibrils in liquid and solid foods, releasing iron during food breakdown [1].

5. Nanoparticles-Based Drug Delivery for Iron Deficiency Anemia

NPs are particles with nano dimensions ranging from a few nanometers to <100 nm in the pharmaceutical sciences [23]. Therapeutic substances can be distributed by NPs to desired region with required concentrations, possibly response to molecule's signals or environmental inducement [29]. As a theranostic nanomedicine, NPs have the potential to be utilized to track drug distribution, drug release, and drug efficacy [29]. They shield the load from early biochemical or chemical degradation [19]. Thus, delivery techniques employing nanoparticulates have demonstrated path aspired to get drug-like properties by modifying molecule's biopharmaceutical properties [30].

Researchers have studied various types of NPs for the treatment of IDA. These include polysaccharides, lipids, metallic, and others.

5.1 Polysaccharide Nanoparticles

Polysaccharides are monosaccharides with long straight or branched chains joined by glycoside bonds [30] and contain several theranostic benefits. Their reactive groups can be used to functionalize NPs, therapies and/or diagnostic agents. Polysaccharides are varied in size and charge, accessible, have low toxicity, *in vivo* [29]. Theranostic NPs based on polysaccharides are becoming prominent, since they are being exploited as platforms for imaging and medication delivery concurrently, making them good candidates to enhance iron delivery.

Alginate Nanoparticles

A naturally arising anionic polymer [31] has been extensively explored and exploited for numerous biomedical science and engineering applications. Alginate has fascinating biopharmaceutical features such as bio-resorbablity, perishability, pH sensitivity, mucoadhesiveness, low toxicity, and non-immunogenicity and physiochemical properties such as viscosity, thermostability, and the sol-gel transition making it appealing for drug modification [30].

Aynie's [32] research shows alginate nanoparticles efficiently transport oligonucleotides to the liver, spleen, and lungs, suggesting potential for iron delivery in the ferrous state. Encapsulation shields Fe^{2+} from other components and avoids direct contact with the gastrointestinal lumen, potentially lessening any negative consequences [33,34]. The most thoroughly studied mucoadhesive biomaterials with good cytocompatibility and biocompatibility are sodium alginate and alginic acid [34]. Utilizing alginate in oral delivery formulations has several benefits, one of which is its ability to maintain a solid-like structure under stomach circumstances as a result of the production of acid "alginic". Therefore, it protects the encapsulant inside its core. Additionally, Alginate beads disintegrate at basic and neutral pH values, that makes iron distribution efficient as the duodenum's pH ranges from 7.0 to 8.5 [34, 35, 36].

Chitosan Nanoparticles

A cationic linear polymer composed of -(14)-2-amino-D-glucose and -(14)-2-acetamido-D glucose units. [29]. A deacetylated derivative of chitin can be seen in fungal wall cells and crustacean exoskeletons [37]. Chitosan is soluble in acidic environments because of protonated amino groups and the cationic polyelectrolyte (transformed polysaccharide) [38]. To produce mucoadhesive polymer-coated microspheres with a good yield and great encapsulation efficacy, $FeSO_4$ has been coated with highly mucoadhesive polymers like hydroxypropylmethyl cellulose, chitosan, and carbopol [39].

It was previously explored how different polymers have been coated with $FeSO_4$ by using spray-drying [39,40]. Here polymers were used to coat $FeSO_4$ to supplement iron orally, changing drug-to-polymer ratios for improved efficiency and drug release.

It has concluded that mucoadhesive microspheres of $FeSO_4$ Possess good encapsulation efficiency, yield, swelling capacity, mucoadhesion capacity, increased cell uptake in Caco 2 cell lines, and efficacy comparable to $FeSO_4$ making them viable options for the treatment of anemia [39].

Pectin Nanoparticles

Pectin, a high-molecular-weight plant cell wall polysaccharide [41], is extracted from apples and citrus fruits [42], made up of galacturonic acid remnants with neutral sugars [43]. Its diverse functional groups stimulate various functionalities, making it safe, non-toxic, cost-effective, and widely available, making it a popular and versatile product [44].

Salima T. Minzanova [45] studied pectin polysaccharides as a potential organic matrix for proper metabolism. Rats were used in animal tests for new water-soluble pectin complexes containing various elements. The complexes improved health and avoided erythropoiesis problems in white rats with hemorrhagic anemia. Their anti-anemic activity was recommended for IDA treatment [45, 46].

5.2 Lipid Nanoparticles

Lipids' physicochemical features, like bio-resorbable, poor susceptibility to erosion events and a slower absorption of water, make them a suitable nanocarrier system for improving active pharmaceutical ingredients' Water solubility, bio-availability, and treatment effectiveness [47]. These NPs can overcome the drawbacks of polymeric NPs, such as cytotoxicity and a lack of adequate technologies for large-scale synthesis [48]. Solid lipid nanoparticles (SLNs), niosomes, liposomes, and nanostructured lipid carriers (NLCs) are examples of lipid nanocarriers.

Liposomes

Liposomes are sphere-like, colloid structures that form in solution when amphiphilic lipid molecules, like phospholipids, self-assemble [49].

Previous studies conclude that, microencapsulated $FeSO_4$ with lecithin [50, 51, 52] offers similar bio-availability as $FeSO_4$, however, it has the advantage of having a phospholipid membrane coating it, which keeps the iron away from other food ingredients and avoids unwanted interactions that can happen when using ordinary $FeSO_4$ [33].

In addition, liposomal $FeSO_4$ was introduced to fluid milk to assess the potential for application. They have claimed that the electrostatic with steric integrity of empty liposomes may generally be increased by adding particular cholesterol as well as Tween 80 concentrations. Additionally, microencapsulating $FeSO_4$ using the reverse phase evaporation approach yields $FeSO_4$ Liposomes having a high rate of encapsulation of 67% [33]. According to their preliminary findings, $FeSO_4$ liposomes may act as a potent iron fortifier and can enhance Fe^{2+} stability in foodborne conveyance.

Solid Lipid Nanoparticles

SLNs have multiple advantages, including the ability to produce huge quantities and improve medication absorption [11]. SLNs overcome liposome stability problems while retaining the benefits of classic liposome-based compositions like their biocompatibility and high absorption [53,54]. Utilization of SLNs for oral drug delivery indicates that they have high systemic bio-availability and favorable release characteristics of the encapsulated medications [54]. *In vivo* and *in vitro* characterization of SLN tolerance and toxicity was conducted [54-56].

Zariwala [54], investigated the likelihood of SLNs for administering iron orally. Research objective was to create $FeSO_4$-loaded SLNs and assess This used the well-researched human intestinal cell line Caco-2 for *in vitro* iron absorption. The measurement of iron absorption was assessed using formation of ferritin intracellularly [54,57]. They were able to investigate the impact of the mucoadhesive polysaccharide chitosan (Chi) incorporation on the particle's physiochemical and iron absorption capabilities via producing chitosan-coated solid-liquid nanoparticles (SLNs), *in vivo* study conducted by Hosny [11], using albino male rabbits to investigate the utilization of nanotechnology to formulate $FeSO_4$ into SLNs as a solution to the major problems associated with as a remedy for the main issues raised by the sold iron supplement pills. The results show that using iron in solid lipid nanoparticles (Fe-SLNs) enhances its penetration and absorption through the gastrointestinal tract membrane. Furthermore, compared to the oral tablet formulation that is currently on the market, the data show that Fe-SLNs can drastically change the drug's pharmacokinetic profile and enhance its bio-availability by over fourfold [11].

L. Hatefi and N. Farhadian [9], demonstrated that encapsulating FeSO4 in SLN via a secure and effective technique to protect $FeSO_4$ opposing to oxidation indicating that biodegradable iron-loaded SLNs may be a suitable delivery mechanism for conventional oral iron therapy [9].

5.3 Metallic Nanoparticles

Metal oxides derived from early transition metals have showed wave density charging behavior, electro-optic, dielectric, electromechanical, and catalytic charging behavior [58]. These characteristics enable their application in numerous processes such as photocatalysis, electrocatalysis, selective oxidation, and dehydration. For metal oxides to be used safely and effectively in biological applications, toxicity is an important factor to take into account [59].

Iron Oxide Nanoparticles

IONPs are at an advanced stage in nanomedicine and are currently being marketed for the treatment of IDA [60].

Some characteristics of IONPs include surface-to-volume ratio, enhanced surface area, super paramagnetism, straightforward separation technique, bio-resorbable, and bio-availability [20].

Using IONPs as a source of oral iron led to 1.35 times greater increases in iron absorption as opposed to $FeSO_4$

[61,62]. Therefore, it is anticipated that utilizing IONP will boost the drug's bioavailability, resulting in lower dosages being required and a reduction in the drug's gastric adverse effects, permitting the patient to keep taking the medication. With that finding, Gao have studied the potential effects of IONP supplementation over $FeSO_4$ therapy for treating *in vivo* IDA in rats. In that experiment, they found that when treating IDA, IONPs are more effective anti-inflammatory agents than $FeSO_4$ [62].

An appropriate coating must be employed in order to allow IONPs to travel across the stomach and enter the intestine. [63, 64, 65]. Garces [66] reported that beneficial bacteria Bifidobacteria breve and like Lactobacillus fermentum are utilized to tightly arrange microscopic IONPs on their external surfaces [66-69]. They have discovered that the bacteria remain alive after being grafted with NPs. The combined analysis of the findings reveals *L. fermentum* functions well as an agent to move maghemite NPs from the stomach environment into the intestine.

6. Conclusion

Application of nanotechnology in IDA can be used to improve outcomes in addition to overcoming the drawbacks of current treatments. Iron is delivered safely, steadily, and with almost no adverse effects when they are encapsulated. Further, research studies have shown that the drug in nanoform is much more readily absorbed than the drug in conventional form. Several types of NPs have been investigated by researchers for their potential in delivering iron and treating IDA. Studies on anemia could be separated into two categories according to the iron state Fe^{2+} and Fe^{3+} supplementation. In some investigations, iron insufficiency with Fe^{3+} supplementation is treated by IONPs. NPs made of polymers and lipids are frequently used for this. The gastrointestinal mucosa is shielded from oxidation and destruction by the inclusion of $FeSO_4$ inside the lipid shell, which restricts the contact of Fe^{2+} with the tissue. Mucoadhesive microspheres of $FeSO_4$ can be promising alternatives for the management of anemia because they have high yield, mucoadhesion capability, swelling ability, and encapsulation efficiency may increase the amount of iron absorption. It is important to do further studies, including preclinical and clinical trials to evaluate these NP's efficacy, safety, and practical applicability as a treatment option for IDA. Introducing laboratory-scale putting nanotechnology-based medications through clinical studies, producing them on a massive scale, and getting approval from drug regulators. permission are other important components to take into account to make them accessible to individuals in need.

REFERENCES

1. S. Iyer and Di. Chand, "Nanotechnology in Iron Deficiency Anemia: A review," ICRITO 2020 - IEEE 8th Int. Conf. Reliab. Infocom Technol. Optim. (Trends Futur. Dir., pp. 569–572, 2020, doi: 10.1109/ICRITO48877.2020.9197850.

2. WHO, "Anaemia Policy Brief," no. 6, pp. 1–7, 2012, [Online]. Available: http://www.who.int//iris/bitstream/10665/148556/1/WHO_NMH_NHD_14.4_eng.pdf

3. Mantadakis E, Chatzimichael E, and Zikidou P, "Iron Deficiency Anemia in Children Residing in High and Low-Income Countries: Risk Factors, Prevention, Diagnosis and Therapy. Mediterr J Hematol Infect Dis [revista en Internet] 2020 [acceso 23 de noviembre de 2022]; 12(1): 201–205.," Mediterr. J. Hematol. Infect. Dis., vol. 12, no. 1, p. e2020041, 2020, [Online]. Available: https://pubmed.ncbi.nlm.nih.gov/32670519/

4. M. M. Fathy, H. M. Fahmy, A. M. M. Balah, F. F. Mohamed, and W. M. Elshemey, "Magnetic nanoparticles-loaded liposomes as a novel treatment agent for iron deficiency anemia: In vivo study," Life Sci., vol. 234, no. June, p. 116787, 2019, doi: 10.1016/j.lfs.2019.116787.

5. F. Oliveira, S. Rocha, and R. Fernandes, "Iron metabolism: From health to disease," J. Clin. Lab. Anal., vol. 28, no. 3, pp. 210–218, 2014, doi: 10.1002/jcla.21668.

6. T. Maier, A. Kerbs, L. Fruk, and N. K. H. Slater, "Iron delivery from liquid-core hydrogels within a therapeutic nipple shield," Eur. J. Pharm. Sci., vol. 131, no. January, pp. 119–126, 2019, doi: 10.1016/j.ejps.2019.01.032.

7. B. K. Fuqua, C. D. Vulpe, and G. J. Anderson, "Intestinal iron absorption," J. Trace Elem. Med. Biol., vol. 26, no. 2–3, pp. 115–119, 2012, doi: 10.1016/j.jtemb.2012.03.015.

8. K. Span, "A novel oral iron-complex formulation: Encapsulation of hemin in polymeric micelles and its in vitro absorption," Eur. J. Pharm. Biopharm., vol. 108, pp. 226–234, 2016, doi: 10.1016/j.ejpb.2016.09.002.

9. L. Hatefi and N. Farhadian, "A safe and efficient method for encapsulation of ferrous sulfate in solid lipid nanoparticle for non-oxidation and sustained iron delivery," Colloids Interface Sci. Commun., vol. 34, no. July 2019, p. 100227, 2020, doi: 10.1016/j.colcom.2019.100227.

10. F. de Galiza Barbosa, "Genitourinary imaging," Clinical PET/MRI. pp. 289–312, 2022. doi: 10.1016/B978-0-323-88537-9.00012-X.

11. K. M. Hosny, Z. M. Banjar, A. H. Hariri, and A. H. Hassan, "Solid lipid nanoparticles loaded with iron to overcome barriers for treatment of iron deficiency anemia," Drug Des. Devel. Ther., vol. 9, pp. 313–320, 2015, doi: 10.2147/DDDT.S77702.

12. S. R. Pasricha, J. Tye-Din, M. U. Muckenthaler, and D. W. Swinkels, "Iron deficiency," Lancet, vol. 397, no. 10270, pp. 233–248, 2021, doi: 10.1016/S0140-6736(20)32594-0.

13. M. D. Cappellini, K. M. Musallam, and A. T. Taher, "Iron deficiency anaemia revisited," J. Intern. Med., vol. 287, no. 2, pp. 153–170, 2020, doi: 10.1111/joim.13004.

14. C. Camaschella and P. Strati, "Recent advances in iron metabolism and related disorders," Intern. Emerg. Med., vol. 5, no. 5, pp. 393–400, 2010, doi: 10.1007/s11739-010-0387-4.

15. A. Lopez, P. Cacoub, I. C. Macdougall, and L. Peyrin-Biroulet, "Iron deficiency anaemia," Lancet, vol. 387, no. 10021, pp. 907–916, 2016, doi: 10.1016/S0140-6736(15)60865-0.

16. R. Blanco-Rojo and M. P. Vaquero, "Iron bioavailability from food fortification to precision nutrition. A review," Innov. Food Sci. Emerg. Technol., vol. 51, no. April 2018, pp. 126–138, 2019, doi: 10.1016/j.ifset.2018.04.015.

17. A. S. Manoguerra, "Iron ingestion: An evidence-based consensus guideline for out-of-hospital management," Clin. Toxicol., vol. 43, no. 6, pp. 553–570, 2005, doi: 10.1081/CLT-200068842.

18. A. Kumar, E. Sharma, A. Marley, M. A. Samaan, and M. J. Brookes, "Iron deficiency anaemia: Pathophysiology, assessment, practical management," BMJ Open Gastroenterol., vol. 9, no. 1, 2022, doi: 10.1136/bmjgast-2021-000759.

19. K. Singh, D. Sethi Chopra, D. Singh, and N. Singh, "Nano-formulations in treatment of iron deficiency anaemia: An overview," Clin. Nutr. ESPEN, vol. 52, pp. 12–19, 2022, doi: 10.1016/j.clnesp.2022.08.032.

20. A. Kumari and A. K. Chauhan, "Iron nanoparticles as a promising compound for food fortification in iron deficiency anemia: a review," J. Food Sci. Technol., vol. 59, no. 9, pp. 3319–3335, 2022, doi: 10.1007/s13197-021-05184-4.

21. R. F. Hurrell, "The Potential of Iodine and Iron Double-Fortified Salt Compared with Iron-Fortified Staple Foods to Increase Population Iron Status," J. Nutr., vol. 151, no. 3, pp. 47S–63S, 2021, doi: 10.1093/jn/nxaa204.

22. R. Arshad, "Nanotechnology: A novel tool to enhance the bioavailability of micronutrients," Food Sci. Nutr., vol. 9, no. 6, pp. 3354–3361, 2021, doi: 10.1002/fsn3.2311.

23. S. M. Jafari, An overview of nanoencapsulation techniques and their classification. Elsevier Inc., 2017. doi: 10.1016/B978-0-12-809436-5.00001-X.

24. K. H. Min, "Hydrophobically modified glycol chitosan nanoparticles-encapsulated camptothecin enhance the drug stability and tumor targeting in cancer therapy," J. Control. Release, vol. 127, no. 3, pp. 208–218, 2008, doi: 10.1016/j.jconrel.2008.01.013.

25. C. Li, J. Adamcik, and R. Mezzenga, "Biodegradable nanocomposites of amyloid fibrils and graphene with shape-memory and enzyme-sensing properties," Nat. Nanotechnol., vol. 7, no. 7, pp. 421–427, 2012, doi: 10.1038/nnano.2012.62.

26. S. Bolisetty and R. Mezzenga, "Amyloid-carbon hybrid membranes for universal water purification," Nat. Nanotechnol., vol. 11, no. 4, pp. 365–371, 2016, doi: 10.1038/nnano.2015.310.

27. M. Kumar Teli, S. Mutalik, and G. K. Rajanikant, "Nanotechnology and Nanomedicine: Going Small Means Aiming Big," Curr. Pharm. Des., vol. 16, no. 16, pp. 1882–1892, 2010, doi: 10.2174/138161210791208992.

28. Y. Shen, "Amyloid fibril systems reduce, stabilize and deliver bioavailable nanosized iron," *Nat. Nanotechnol.*, vol. 12, no. 7, pp. 642–647, 2017, doi: 10.1038/nnano.2017.58.

29. M. Swierczewska, H. S. Han, K. Kim, J. H. Park, and S. Lee, "Polysaccharide-based nanoparticles for theranostic nanomedicine," *Adv. Drug Deliv. Rev.*, vol. 99, pp. 70–84, 2016, doi: 10.1016/j.addr.2015.11.015.

30. P. Severino, C. F. da Silva, L. N. Andrade, D. de Lima Oliveira, J. Campos, and E. B. Souto, "Alginate Nanoparticles for Drug Delivery and Targeting," *Curr. Pharm. Des.*, vol. 25, no. 11, pp. 1312–1334, 2019, doi: 10.2174/1381612825666190425163424.

31. K. Y. Lee and D. J. Mooney, "Alginate: Properties and biomedical applications," *Prog. Polym. Sci.*, vol. 37, no. 1, pp. 106–126, 2012, doi: 10.1016/j.progpolymsci.2011.06.003.

32. I. Aynié, C. Vauthier, H. Chacun, E. Fattal, and P. Couvreur, "Spongelike alginate nanoparticles as a new potential system for the delivery of antisense oligonucleotides," *Antisense Nucleic Acid Drug Dev.*, vol. 9, no. 3, pp. 301–312, 1999, doi: 10.1089/oli.1.1999.9.301.

33. S. Xia and S. Xu, "Ferrous sulfate liposomes: Preparation, stability and application in fluid milk," *Food Res. Int.*, vol. 38, no. 3, pp. 289–296, 2005, doi: 10.1016/j.foodres.2004.04.010.

34. N. P. Katuwavila, A. D. L. C. Perera, D. Dahanayake, V. Karunaratne, G. A. J. Amaratunga, and D. N. Karunaratne, "Alginate nanoparticles protect ferrous from oxidation: Potential iron delivery system," *Int. J. Pharm.*, vol. 513, no. 1–2, pp. 404–409, 2016, doi: 10.1016/j.ijpharm.2016.09.053.

35. K. I. Draget and C. Taylor, "Chemical, physical and biological properties of alginates and their biomedical implications," *Food Hydrocoll.*, vol. 25, no. 2, pp. 251–256, 2011, doi: 10.1016/j.foodhyd.2009.10.007.

36. S. R. Rout, "Recent advances in the formulation strategy to improve iron bioavailability: A review," *J. Drug Deliv. Sci. Technol.*, vol. 95, no. April, p. 105633, 2024, doi: 10.1016/j.jddst.2024.105633.

37. A. Acevedo-Fani, R. Soliva-Fortuny, and O. Martín-Belloso, "Photo-protection and controlled release of folic acid using edible alginate/chitosan nanolaminates," *J. Food Eng.*, vol. 229, no. c, pp. 72–82, 2018, doi: 10.1016/j.jfoodeng.2017.03.024.

38. Y. Luo and Q. Wang, "Recent development of chitosan-based polyelectrolyte complexes with natural polysaccharides for drug delivery," *Int. J. Biol. Macromol.*, vol. 64, pp. 353–367, 2014, doi: 10.1016/j.ijbiomac.2013.12.017.

39. R. B.S, L. S, S. L. S, S. M. M, and R. M J, "Mucoadhesive microspheres of ferrous sulphate – A novel approach for oral iron delivery in treating anemia," *Colloids Surfaces B Biointerfaces*, vol. 195, no. May, p. 111247, 2020, doi: 10.1016/j.colsurfb.2020.111247.

40. A. Sosnik and K. P. Seremeta, "Advantages and challenges of the spray-drying technology for the production of pure drug particles and drug-loaded polymeric carriers," *Adv. Colloid Interface Sci.*, vol. 223, pp. 40–54, 2015, doi: 10.1016/j.cis.2015.05.003.

41. A. Zdunek, P. M. Pieczywek, and J. Cybulska, "The primary, secondary, and structures of higher levels of pectin polysaccharides," *Compr. Rev. Food Sci. Food Saf.*, vol. 20, no. 1, pp. 1101–1117, 2021, doi: 10.1111/1541-4337.12689.

42. J. Cui, "Pectins from fruits: Relationships between extraction methods, structural characteristics, and functional properties," *Trends Food Sci. Technol.*, vol. 110, no. January, pp. 39–54, 2021, doi: 10.1016/j.tifs.2021.01.077.

43. D. qiang Li, "Pectin in biomedical and drug delivery applications: A review," *Int. J. Biol. Macromol.*, vol. 185, no. March, pp. 49–65, 2021, doi: 10.1016/j.ijbiomac.2021.06.088.

44. C. Maria, P. Freitas, S. Jane, V. Gomes, L. Souza, and C. Rita, "Maria, C., Freitas, P., Jane, S., Gomes, V., Souza, L., & Rita, C. (2021). and Pharmaceutical Industry : A Review. Coatings, 11(922), 1–22.," *Coatings*, vol. 11, no. 922, pp. 1–22, 2021.

45. S. T. Minzanova, "Complexation of pectin with macro- and microelements. Antianemic activity of Na, Fe and Na, Ca, Fe complexes," *Carbohydr. Polym.*, vol. 134, pp. 524–533, 2015, doi: 10.1016/j.carbpol.2015.07.034.

46. S. T. Minzanova, "Biological activity and pharmacological application of pectic polysaccharides: A review," *Polymers (Basel).*, vol. 10, no. 12, pp. 1–31, 2018, doi: 10.3390/polym10121407.

47. R. Kumar, *Lipid-Based Nanoparticles for Drug-Delivery Systems.* Elsevier Inc., 2018. doi: 10.1016/B978-0-12-814033-8.00008-4.

48. N. Dhiman, R. Awasthi, B. Sharma, H. Kharkwal, and G. T. Kulkarni, "Lipid Nanoparticles as Carriers for Bioactive Delivery," *Front. Chem.*, vol. 9, no. April, 2021, doi: 10.3389/fchem.2021.580118.

49. D. Guimarães, A. Cavaco-Paulo, and E. Nogueira, "Design of liposomes as drug delivery system for therapeutic applications," *Int. J. Pharm.*, vol. 601, no. February, 2021, doi: 10.1016/j.ijpharm.2021.120571.

50. A. E. Lysionek, "of Industrial Microencapsulated Method Ferrous to Determine Sulfate Its by Means Bioavailability of the Summary Radio-iron tests are frequently used to measure the bioavailability of different iron sources for food fortification . As the labeling procedur," pp. 125–129, 2000.

51. J. R. Boccio, M. B. Zubillaga, R. A. Caro, C. A. Gotelli, M. J. Gotelli, and R. Weill, "Bioavailability and stability of microencapsulated ferrous sulfate in fluid milk: Studies in mice," *J. Nutr. Sci. Vitaminol. (Tokyo).*, vol. 42, no. 3, pp. 233–239, 1996, doi: 10.3177/jnsv.42.233.

52. R. Uicich, "Bioavailability of microencapsulated ferrous sulfate in fluid cow's milk. Studies in human beings," *Nutr. Res.*, vol. 19, no. 6, pp. 893–897, 1999, doi: 10.1016/S0271-5317(99)00049-4.

53. F. Alexis, *Nanoparticle Technologies for Cancer Therapy Handbook of Experimental Pharmacology*, no. October. 2020.

54. M. G. Zariwala, "A novel approach to oral iron delivery using ferrous sulphate loaded solid lipid nanoparticles,"

Int. J. Pharm., vol. 456, no. 2, pp. 400–407, 2013, doi: 10.1016/j.ijpharm.2013.08.070.

55. V. Sanna, "Preparation and in vivo toxicity study of solid lipid microparticles as carrier for pulmonary administration," *AAPS PharmSciTech*, vol. 5, no. 2, pp. 1–7, 2004, doi: 10.1208/pt050227.

56. A. Fundarò, R. Cavalli, A. Bargoni, D. Vighetto, G. P. Zara, and M. R. Gasco, "Non-stealth and stealth solid lipid nanoparticles (SLN) carrying doxorubicin: Pharmacokinetics and tissue distribution after i.v. administration to rats," *Pharmacol. Res.*, vol. 42, no. 4, pp. 337–343, 2000, doi: 10.1006/phrs.2000.0695.

57. S. Fairweather-Tait, I. Phillips, G. Wortley, L. Harvey, and R. Glahn, "The use of solubility, dialyzability, and Caco-2 cell methods to predict iron bioavailability," *Int. J. Vitam. Nutr. Res.*, vol. 77, no. 3, pp. 158–165, 2007, doi: 10.1024/0300-9831.77.3.158.

58. S. Murthy, P. Effiong, and C. C. Fei, *Metal oxide nanoparticles in biomedical applications*. INC, 2020. doi: 10.1016/B978-0-12-817505-7.00011-7.

59. M. G. M. Schneider, "Biomedical Applications of Iron Oxide Nanoparticles: Current Insights Progress and Perspectives," *Pharmaceutics*, vol. 14, no. 1, 2022, doi: 10.3390/pharmaceutics14010204.

60. M. Sharon, "Nanoparticles for Therapeutic Applications," *Nanoparticles Ther. Appl.*, pp. 1–566, 2021, doi: 10.1002/9781119764205.

61. H. Gao, "Effect of nanometer pearl powder on calcium absorption and utilization in rats," *Food Chem.*, vol. 109, no. 3, pp. 493–498, 2008, doi: 10.1016/j.foodchem.2007.12.052.

62. M. Elshemy, "Iron Oxide Nanoparticles Versus Ferrous Sulfate In Treatment of Iron Deficiency Anemia In Rats,"

Egypt. J. Vet. Sci., vol. 49, no. 2, pp. 103–109, 2018, doi: 10.21608/ejvs.2018.3855.1039.

63. R. J. S. M. L. Dreyfuss, *Guidelines for the use of iron supplements to prevent and treat iron deficiency anemia prepared by Dr. Rebecca Stoltzfus and Ms.*, vol. 34, no. 23. 1998. [Online]. Available: http://www.univ-lille1.fr/pfeda/Ngonut/1998/9808e.html

64. É. C. M. Mimura, J. W. Breganó, J. B. Dichi, E. P. Gregório, and I. Dichi, "Comparison of ferrous sulfate and ferrous glycinate chelate for the treatment of iron deficiency anemia in gastrectomized patients," *Nutrition*, vol. 24, no. 7–8, pp. 663–668, 2008, doi: 10.1016/j.nut.2008.03.017.

65. M. E. Conrad and J. N. Umbreit, "Pathways of iron absorption," *Blood Cells. Mol. Dis.*, vol. 29, no. 3, pp. 336–355, 2002, doi: 10.1006/bcmd.2002.0564.

66. V. Garcés, "Bacteria-Carried Iron Oxide Nanoparticles for Treatment of Anemia," *Bioconjug. Chem.*, vol. 29, no. 5, pp. 1785–1791, 2018, doi: 10.1021/acs.bioconjchem.8b00245.

67. M. Martín, F. Carmona, R. Cuesta, D. Rondón, N. Gálvez, and J. M. Domínguez-Vera, "Artificial magnetic bacteria: Living magnets at room temperature," *Adv. Funct. Mater.*, vol. 24, no. 23, pp. 3489–3493, 2014, doi: 10.1002/adfm.201303754.

68. M. Martín, V. Garcés, J. M. Domínguez-Vera, and N. Gálvez, "Magnetism in living magnetically-induced bacteria," *RSC Adv.*, vol. 6, no. 97, pp. 95220–95226, 2016, doi: 10.1039/c6ra20295k.

69. M. Martín, "Magnetic study on biodistribution and biodegradation of oral magnetic nanostructures in the rat gastrointestinal tract," *Nanoscale*, vol. 8, no. 32, pp. 15041–15047, 2016, doi: 10.1039/c6nr04678a.

Transformative Applied Research in Computing, Engineering, Science and Technology – Dr. Damayanthi Dahanayake et al. (eds)
© 2024 Taylor & Francis Group, London, ISBN 978-1-041-01782-0

13

A Review of Psychological and Pharmacological Therapies for Anxiety Disorders

K.P. Ahangamage
Department of Life Sciences, NSBM Green University,
Sri Lanka

L. Jayasinha*
Department of Health Sciences, NSBM Green University,
Sri Lanka

Abstract

Anxiety disorders are the most prevalent subgroup of mental disorders. They can be classified into generalized anxiety disorder, social anxiety disorder, specific phobia, separation anxiety disorder, panic disorder, and agoraphobia. Anxiety disorders are less apparent than other psychiatric problems, hence they are frequently misdiagnosed and undertreated. Both psychological therapies and pharmacological therapies or a combination of both therapies are used in treating anxiety disorders. Cognitive Behavioral Therapy (CBT) and Virtual Reality Exposure Therapy (VRET) are the commonly used psychological therapies for anxiety. Psychological therapies can be done as individual therapy or group therapy. CBT is widely regarded as the gold standard in psychological therapy for anxiety disorders. VRET is a modified type of behavioral therapy that may be an alternative to traditional in vivo exposure. First-line pharmacological treatments for anxiety disorders include selective serotonin reuptake inhibitors (SSRIs) and serotonin-norepinephrine reuptake inhibitors (SNRIs). This review aims to evaluate the current psychological and pharmacological approaches to anxiety treatment.

Keywords

Anxiety disorders, Cognitive behavioral therapy, Pharmacological therapy, Psychological therapy, Virtual reality exposure therapy

1. Introduction

Anxiety disorders have features of excessive worry and arising avoidance, which is usually in response to a particular circumstance or an object in the absence of an actual threat [1]. The symptoms of an anxiety disorder must be prolonged (for example: Generalized Anxiety Disorder/GAD shows symptoms for at least six months),

*Corresponding author: lakshani.j@nsbm.ac.lk

DOI: 10.1201/9781003616368-13

cause severe distress, and interfere with regular or social functioning to be diagnosed [2]. Anxiety disorders are one of the most prevalent disorders among psychiatric disorders [3]. Women are diagnosed with anxiety disorders 1.5-2.0 times more than men [4].

Anxiety disorders are categorized into several types. They are separation anxiety disorder (Excessive fear or anxiety about being separated from attachment figures), specific phobia (Intense fear of a specific object or situation that poses little or no actual danger), social anxiety disorder (Fear of social situations or performance situations where the individual may be scrutinized by others), panic disorder (Recurrent, unexpected panic attacks accompanied by intense physical symptoms), selective mutism (Consistent failure to speak in specific social situations despite speaking in other situations), agoraphobia (Fear of being in situations where escape may be difficult or embarrassing in the event of a panic attack), GAD (Excessive worry and anxiety about a variety of events or activities), substance/medication-induced anxiety disorder (Anxiety symptoms caused by the use of a substance or withdrawal from a substance), and anxiety disorder due to other medical conditions (Anxiety symptoms directly caused by an underlying medical condition) [5].

Patients can be treated with psychological therapies, pharmacological therapies, or a combination of both therapies for anxiety disorders [6]. The settling between pharmacological therapy and psychological therapy is individualized and based on the patient's preference, past responses to treatments, and regional availability [2]. Although cognitive behavioral therapy (CBT) is the psychotherapy that has been studied the most, other psychotherapies such as virtual reality exposure therapy (VRET), eye movement desensitization reprocessing (EMDR), mindfulness meditation, psychodynamic psychotherapy (PDTh), interpersonal psychotherapy (IPT), and relaxation have also been the subject of studies [7].

Selective serotonin reuptake inhibitors (SSRIs), serotonin-noradrenaline reuptake inhibitors (SNRIs), tricyclic antidepressants (TCAs), antiepileptics, benzodiazepines, anxiolytics, and monoamine oxidase inhibitors (MAOIs) are some of the drug therapies used to treat anxiety disorders that are approved by U.S. Food and Drug Administration (FDA) [7, 8]. SSRIs and SNRIs are first-line treatments for social anxiety disorder, GAD, and panic disorder. MAOIs, benzodiazepines, and TCAs are second-line treatments due to considerations of tolerance and safety [8].

2. Methodology

Peer-reviewed research articles related to psychological and pharmacological therapies for anxiety disorders were gathered and analyzed as the first part of the methodology for this review. Keywords including "anxiety disorders", "CBT", "VRET", "SSRI", and "SNRI" were searched in databases such as "Google Scholar", "PubMed", and "APA PsychNet". Studies included in this review were taken into consideration according to the relevance, strength of evidence, and recency. The inclusion criteria for anxiety disorders were considered as GAD, panic disorder, social anxiety disorder, specific phobia, and separation anxiety disorder. As for therapy interventions, both group and individual therapy approaches, as well as pharmacological therapies were considered.

3. Results and Discussion: Psychological Therapy

Anyone struggling with anxiety disorders needs to have encouraging conversations and attention given to the emotional issues related to their condition [4]. The method of psychological therapy and the mode of delivery depends on the type and severity of the anxiety disorder. The mode of delivery can differ from individual to group psychological therapy due to economic advantage and the availability of treatment options in areas with limited development [3].

CBT and VRET are the main psychological therapies discussed in this review. One of the major privileges of CBT is the adaptability of the therapy to various arrangements such as individual, group, or online therapy [3]. VRET is unique compared to other psychological therapies as it can be customized according to the situation of each individual [9].

3.1 Cognitive Behavioral Therapy (CBT)

CBT is defined as "An amalgam of behavioral and cognitive interventions guided by principles of applied science" [1]. CBT is known as the golden standard of evidence-based therapy in psychological therapy for anxiety disorders [10]. The main features of CBT are problem-focused intervention techniques that are based on the fundamentals of both cognitive theory and learning theory. These methods of CBT are given a range of emphasis during therapy, depending on the anxiety issue [1]. Some patients do not respond to treatment, even though traditional CBT is very effective in treating the majority of anxiety disorders [10]. CBT is successful in the treatment of anxiety disorders in both randomized controlled studies and in realistic environments [11, 12]. However, the extent of the effect is still impossible to measure due to methodological problems [1]. The results of a meta-analysis indicate that despite small effect sizes and frequently insufficient or clinically irrelevant levels of accuracy, CBT—the most well-researched of the psychiatric therapies included—was frequently superior to other treatments [13].

People with GAD experience subjective frustration brought on by ongoing anxiety and struggle to manage it, which negatively affects their ability to function in social situations and their quality of life. CBT is now advised by clinical standards as the first line of treatment for GAD [14]. A study showed that social anxiety disorder responds well to therapy, even if many people continue to struggle with some symptoms long after the acute phase of treatment is through [15].

3.2 Individual vs Group CBT

There are some aspects of the group therapy technique that are different from individual therapy. Since numerous patients are treated at the same time, less therapist time is required for each patient when psychotherapy is provided in a group setting [17]. Treatment elements that have been suggested as being exclusive to groups include interpersonal and vicarious learning, feeling universal, altruism, and a sense of belonging and relatedness [16]. When individuals with anxiety disorders are treated in groups, there are additional drawbacks. The group may be a barrier to receiving therapy since those who struggle with anxiety disorders may find the environment stressful and consequently try to avoid it. Group psychotherapists advise pre-sessions when concerns and motivating difficulties are discussed to address this disadvantage. Less possibility to address unique issues and create unique etiological models is another drawback [3].

3.3 Virtual Reality Based Therapy

The primary development in the field of VR-based therapy is VRET [10]. Standard in vivo exposure may be replaced with VRET, a modified form of behavioral therapy. There has been research on the usefulness of VRET for phobias for enclosed spaces, flying, driving, heights, public speaking, spiders, and panic disorder with agoraphobia. Researchers have shown that exposure, particularly in the treatment of certain phobias, is quite beneficial, with experience being preferable to imaginal exposure. To fully engage patients in a digitally created virtual environment, virtual reality brings together real-time computer graphics, body tracking technology, visual displays, and other sensory input devices [18].

VRET is carried out in the same way as other types of graduated exposure therapy. Patients are exposed to fear-inducing stimuli. Patients must rate their anxiety frequently during the exposure session using subjective units of discomfort (SUDs) to provide them with a gradual and effective exposure treatment [18]. The phenomenon of presence and immersion experienced by the user, which means that the world is seen as being real and non-

mediated even when the user is aware that is computer-generated, is a key feature that sets VR apart from previous methods of human-computer interaction [10]. Patients are recommended to be exposed to the equal worlds in VRET and exposure in vivo for the same amount of time in order to compare the impact of the two [18]. Researchers have also started to treat adolescents with anxiety disorders with VR-based therapies [10]. In one study [19] VRET was able to greatly decrease the severity of school-related worries, but it had no discernible effect on general fears.

VRET has several advantages over exposure in vivo, including cost-effectiveness, the ability to produce subtler assignments (treatment order and intensity), the ability to create individual exposure, and the abundance of opportunities to repeat exposure assignments [20]. The disadvantage of VERT is known as the stimulation sickness with symptoms such as nausea, headaches, dizziness, warmth in the body, drowsiness, and stomach awareness [18].

CBT for anxiety disorders has many past literatures that support the efficacy of having long-term benefits [21]. CBT usually involves face-to-face interactions with the therapist while using VRET creates computer generated simulation or virtual environment that specify for patient's phobias [21, 22].

4. Results and Discussion: Pharmacological Therapy

Pharmacological therapy for anxiety disorders is often recommended for individuals based on the severity of the symptoms, and previous responses to other psychological therapy [2]. Finding the molecular and neurocircuit changes that cause anxiety has helped significantly in the field of neurobiology. According to the U.S. Food and Drug Administration treatment of anxiety disorders, the effectiveness of SSRIs and SNRIs as first-line therapies for GAD, social anxiety disorder, and panic disorder is supported by numerous randomized controlled trials [8].

Due to toxicity and tolerability concerns, TCAs, MAOIs, and benzodiazepines are typically used as second-line treatments for anxiety disorders despite having adequate efficacy data [8]. Different neurotransmitter systems, primarily gamma aminobutyric acid (GABA) and glutamate, have an impact on neuronal circuits. Serotonin, dopamine, and norepinephrine, the three main neurotransmitter systems, have been thoroughly investigated in both physiological and pathological anxiety states. Serotonin (5-hydroxytryptamine) is a neurotransmitter which is present in the central nervous system of vertebrates and invertebrates. Serotonin involved in mood regulation, managing impulses, and motor functions on presynaptic and postsynaptic receptors by regulating neuronal activities and influencing the release of other neurotransmitters such as dopamine, acetylcholine, GABA, and glutamate [23].

One or more of these systems are frequently the focus of efficient treatments for anxiety. However, a lack of any one neurotransmitter does not result in anxiety disorders. The diverse receptor architectures, numerous feedback mechanisms, and vast interrelationships in the networks controlled by these transmitters lead to unpredictable and occasionally counterintuitive drug reactions [6].

4.1 Selective Serotonin Reuptake Inhibitors (SSRIs)

The most prevalent pharmacological choices for all anxiety disorders are SSRIs because of their broad anxiolytic impact [2]. The recommended course of treatment may last three to six months, up to one to two years, or even longer [24]. Inhibiting the serotonin transporter and appearing to neutralize postsynaptic serotonin receptors, which restores normal serotonergic pathway activity, are the key properties of the treatments in this class [6]. These drugs are also typically well tolerated, with side effects such as nausea, headaches, dry mouth, diarrhea, or constipation that are normally tolerable or transient [25]. Sexual dysfunction is typically a more severe and bothersome side effect of SSRIs, but it is treatable with adjuvant therapies. SSRIs include fluoxetine, sertraline, escitalopram, citalopram, fluvoxamine, paroxetine, and paroxetine ER [24].

4.2 Serotonin- Norepinephrine Reuptake Inhibitors (SNRIs)

Typically, SNRIs are taken when an SSRI has failed or responded insufficiently. Due to the possibility of serotonin syndrome when these two medication groups are combined, they are used instead of SSRIs as augmentation. As a result of the improved norepinephrine-mediated signaling brought on by the blockage of the norepinephrine transporter, some patients may experience a worsening of the physiological symptoms of anxiety in response to SNRIs [6].

The elevated noradrenergic tonus may support these treatments' anxiolytic efficacy in those who do not suffer from this side effect [6]. Although some research favors the use of SNRI venlafaxine in the majority of anxiety disorders, it is only approved for use in GAD and social anxiety disorders. After venlafaxine withdrawal, withdrawal symptoms are frequent and can even occur from missing just one dosage [2]. Venlafaxine is contraindicated in people who are at high risk for cardiac arrhythmias or uncontrolled hypertension because it can raise blood pressure at larger doses [26]. Another SNRI with a GAD license, duloxetine, can likewise raise blood pressure. In a multiple-treatment meta-analysis, duloxetine was ranked first for the response but fourth for remission among the approved therapies for GAD [2]. Desvenlafaxine is used as a treatment for other than venlafaxine and duloxetine [24].

4.3 Tricyclic Antidepressants (TCAs)

Every TCA works as a norepinephrine reuptake inhibitor, and a few also inhibit serotonin reuptake. Although a lot of the drugs in this category are just as effective at treating anxiety disorders as SSRIs or SNRIs, TCAs have more side effects (Increased body weight, anesthesia, low blood pressure, and anticholinergic effects) and can be fatal if used in excess. TCAs should also be avoided or only used in very tiny doses for any patient who shows suicide risk. TCAs are therefore hardly utilized in the management of anxiety disorders [2].

4.4 Monoamine-Oxidase Inhibitors (MAOIs)

Due to their potentially fatal interactions with other serotonergic medications and dietary tyramine, MAOIs are rarely utilized in clinical settings. Tyramine, which is included in aged or cured meats, yeast extracts, dairy products, and other foods, as well as over-the-counter drugs containing ephedrine, must be strictly avoided when an MAOI is prescribed due to the possibility of a severe case of hypertension [2].

4.5 Benzodiazepines

Benzodiazepines have been prescribed to treat anxiety for many years and can quickly reduce the symptoms of acute anxiety disorders [2]. Benzodiazepines were previously often used to treat anxiety disorders, but due to the dangers involved with long-term usage, they are no longer regarded as first-line treatments [6]. Strong evidence supports the acute treatment of GAD, social anxiety disorder, and panic disorder with certain benzodiazepines. For the treatment of severe or fatal anxiety that is causing the patient unbearable distress, benzodiazepines should only be prescribed for two to four weeks. Benzodiazepines are not advised for people with panic disorder, according to NICE guidelines, as the long-term results are substandard. For instance, some patients said that stopping the benzodiazepines caused their panic attacks to worsen [2].

5. Conclusion

According to the analysis, CBT is considered as the most effective psychological therapy for anxiety disorders due to its adaptability. CBT can be used in various settings including group or individual therapy. Research also demonstrated the effectiveness of VRET in managing panic disorders and specific phobias. The first line pharmacological therapies for anxiety disorders include SSRIs and SNRIs while TCAs and MAOIs were found to be effective, but the usage is limited due to concern with side effects and patient risks.

The prevalence of anxiety disorders is high, and they are linked to considerable levels of personal distress, functional impairment, and unsatisfactory treatment outcomes. CBT and exposure therapy are the main psychological therapies that are used for anxiety disorders. CBT is preferably as efficient as medication. This strategy, in which therapy approaches are directly contrasted with one another, has the benefit that methodological variables are controlled for, and no further assumptions are required. CBT can be treated as individual therapy or group therapy depending on the patient's economic state and access to psychological therapy. CBT appears to be useful and effective in the treatment of anxiety disorders, although additional research of sufficient quality is needed to determine the extent of the benefits. Additionally, research studies in which VRET is evaluated as a stand-alone treatment, rather than as an aspect of a treatment package, are required.

SSRI and SNRI medications are presently the first-line therapies for anxiety disorders; benzodiazepines are best used as supplementary and short-term anxiolytics. Although TCAs and MAOIs are useful, their use has been restricted by tolerability concerns.

It is simpler to recognize the interest in creating new methods that would enable better distribution, as well as accessibility, efficacy/effectiveness, and lower costs of mental health services given the high prevalence of these disorders and the inaccessibility and/or unwillingness to access these treatments as discussed above.

REFERENCES

1. C. Otte, "Cognitive behavioral therapy in anxiety disorders: Current state of the evidence," *Dialogues in Clinical Neuroscience*, vol. 13, no. 4, pp. 413–421, Dec. 2022.

2. S. Bleakley and S. J. Davies, "The pharmacological management of anxiety disorders," *Progress in Neurology and Psychiatry*, vol. 18, no. 6, pp. 27–32, Nov. 2014.

3. S. Barkowski, D. Schwartze, B. Strauss, G. M. Burlingame, and J. Rosendahl, "Efficacy of group psychotherapy for anxiety disorders: A systematic review and meta-analysis," *Psychotherapy Research*, vol. 30, no. 8, pp. 1–18, Feb. 2020.

4. B. Bandelow, S. Michaelis, and D. Wedekind, "Treatment of Anxiety Disorders," *Generalized Anxiety Disorders*, vol. 19, no. 2, pp. 93–107, Jun. 2017.

5. American Psychiatric Association, *Diagnostic and statistical manual of mental disorders : DSM-5-TR*, 5th ed. Washington, DC: American Psychiatric Association Publishing, 2022.

6. A. Bystritsky, S. S. Khalsa, M. E. Cameron, and J. Schiffman, "Current diagnosis and treatment of anxiety disorders," *P & T : a peer-reviewed journal for formulary management*, vol. 38, no. 1, pp. 30–57, 2013.

7. B. Bandelow, M. Reitt, C. Röver, S. Michaelis, Y. Görlich, and D. Wedekind, "Efficacy of Treatments for Anxiety Disorders," *International Clinical Psychopharmacology*, vol. 30, no. 4, pp. 183–192, Jul. 2015.

8. J. W. Murrough, S. Yaqubi, S. Sayed, and D. S. Charney, "Emerging drugs for the treatment of anxiety," *Expert Opinion on Emerging Drugs*, vol. 20, no. 3, pp. 393–406, May 2015.

9. E. Carl *et al.*, "Virtual reality exposure therapy for anxiety and related disorders: A meta-analysis of randomized controlled trials," *Journal of Anxiety Disorders*, vol. 61, no. 61, pp. 27–36, Jan. 2019.

10. D. David, S.-A. Matu, and O. A. David, "New Directions in Virtual Reality-Based Therapy for Anxiety Disorders," *International Journal of Cognitive Therapy*, vol. 6, no. 2, pp. 114–137, Jun. 2013.

11. S. G. Hofmann, A. Asnaani, I. J. J. Vonk, A. T. Sawyer, and A. Fang, "The Efficacy of Cognitive Behavioral Therapy: a Review of Meta-Analyses," *Cognitive Therapy and Research*, vol. 36, no. 5, pp. 427–440, Jul. 2012.

12. R. E. Stewart and D. L. Chambless, "Cognitive–behavioral therapy for adult anxiety disorders in clinical practice: A meta-analysis of effectiveness studies.," *Journal of Consulting and Clinical Psychology*, vol. 77, no. 4, pp. 595–606, 2009.

13. A. Pompoli, T. A. Furukawa, H. Imai, A. Tajika, O. Efthimiou, and G. Salanti, "Psychological therapies for panic disorder with or without agoraphobia in adults: a network meta-analysis," *BJPsych Advances*, vol. 24, no. 1, pp. 2–2, Jan. 2018.

14. V. Hunot, R. Churchill, M. Silva de Lima, and V. Teixeira, "Psychological therapies for generalised anxiety disorder," *Cochrane Database of Systematic Reviews*, Oct. 2006.

15. E. Mayo-Wilson *et al.*, "Psychological and pharmacological interventions for social anxiety disorder in adults: a systematic review and network meta-analysis," *The Lancet Psychiatry*, vol. 1, no. 5, pp. 368–376, Oct. 2014.

16. P. J. Bieling, R. E. Mccabe, and M. M. Antony, *Cognitive-behavioral therapy in groups*. New York: Guilford Press, 2006.

17. L. Wolgensinger, "Cognitive behavioral group therapy for anxiety: recent developments," *Dialogues in Clinical Neuroscience*, vol. 17, no. 3, pp. 347–351, Sep. 2015.

18. M. Krijn, P. M. G. Emmelkamp, R. P. Olafsson, and R. Biemond, "Virtual reality exposure therapy of anxiety disorders: A review," *Clinical Psychology Review*, vol. 24, no. 3, pp. 259–281, Jul. 2004.

19. José Gutiérrez Maldonado, E. Magallón-Neri, Mar Rus-Calafell, and C. Peñaloza-Salazar, "Virtual reality exposure therapy for school phobia," vol. 40, no. 2, pp. 223–236, Dec. 2009.

20. M. B. Powers and P. M. G. Emmelkamp, "Virtual reality exposure therapy for anxiety disorders: A meta-analysis," *Journal of Anxiety Disorders*, vol. 22, no. 3, pp. 561–569, Apr. 2008.

21. A. C. Butler, J. E. Chapman, E. M. Forman, and A. T. Beck, "The Empirical Status of cognitive-behavioral therapy: a Review of meta-analyses," *Clinical Psychology Review*, vol. 26, no. 1, pp. 17–31, Jan. 2006.

22. T. D. Parsons and A. A. Rizzo, "Affective outcomes of virtual reality exposure therapy for anxiety and specific phobias: A meta-analysis," *Journal of Behavior Therapy and Experimental Psychiatry*, vol. 39, no. 3, pp. 250–261, Sep. 2008.

23. P. Celada, M. V. Puig, and F. Artigas, "Serotonin modulation of cortical neurons and networks," *Frontiers in Integrative Neuroscience*, vol. 7, 2013.

24. A. Garakani *et al.*, "Pharmacotherapy of Anxiety Disorders: Current and Emerging Treatment Options," *Frontiers in Psychiatry*, vol. 11, no. 595584, 2020.

25. M. Fava, "Prospective studies of adverse events related to antidepressant discontinuation," *The Journal of Clinical Psychiatry*, vol. 67 Suppl 4, pp. 14–21, 2006, Accessed: Mar. 30, 2022.

26. E. J. Hoffman and S. J. Mathew, "Anxiety disorders: a comprehensive review of pharmacotherapies," *Mount Sinai Journal of Medicine: A Journal of Translational and Personalized Medicine*, vol. 75, no. 3, pp. 248–262, Jun. 2008.

Transformative Applied Research in Computing, Engineering, Science and Technology – Dr. Damayanthi Dahanayake et al. (eds)
© 2024 Taylor & Francis Group, London, ISBN 978-1-041-01782-0

14

Decoction, Boiling and Solvent Extraction Methods in Extraction of Anticancer Compounds from Natural Plants

M.V.L. Charuka and U. Y. Bandara*

Department of Life Sciences, NSBM Green University,
Sri Lanka

Abstract

Cancer is the second leading cause of mortality worldwide, responsible for over 9 million deaths annually. The growing interest in natural compounds, particularly from plants, has led to the exploration of their anticancer properties due to fewer side effects compared to synthetic drugs. Various extraction methods, from traditional to modern, are used to extract these compounds. This review outlines the identification of compounds from plant materials to treat cancer using different extraction methodologies, focusing on boiling, decoction, and solvent extraction methods in the world as well as in Sri Lanka. Boiling and decoction are used in traditional practices due to its simplicity and eco-friendliness. Solvent extraction is a versatile and widely used method to extract a broad range of compounds using different solvents. This review focuses on some studies that highlight the effectiveness of using each of the two extraction methods to extract bioactive compounds with anticancer potential. The findings of these studies show the importance of selecting appropriate extraction methods to maximize the bioavailability of anticancer compounds. Understanding about this bioavailability helps in the development of effective cancer treatments. Collaborations between scientists, pharmacologists, and traditional medicinal practitioners can facilitate the formation of clinically useful medicines or drugs from these plant-derived compounds.

Keywords

Natural compounds, Decoction, Boiling, Solvent extraction

1. Introduction

Cancer is a noncommunicable, life-threatening, but treatable disease caused by the uncontrollable growth and spread of cells within the body. It poses a significant global health challenge, being the second-leading cause of death [1].

The World Health Organization (WHO) has reported approximately 20 million new cancer cases and 9.7 million deaths worldwide in 2022. It is projected that there will be around 35 million additional cancer cases by the year 2050. This gradual increase can be attributed to factors such as a lack of physical exercise, tobacco use, alcohol consumption, air pollution, and a high body mass index.

*Corresponding author: udeshika.y@nsbm.ac.lk

DOI: 10.1201/9781003616368-14

The most frequently diagnosed cancers among men are lung, stomach, liver, prostate, and colorectal cancers, while breast, cervical, lung, thyroid, and colorectal cancers are predominant in women [2].

The impact of cancer is also notable in Sri Lanka. In 2018, there were 23,530 total cancer cases and 14,013 cancer deaths. Breast and oral cavity cancers exhibit the highest incidence rate, while lung and breast cancers have the highest mortality rates in Sri Lanka [3].

To prevent the proliferation and spread of cancerous cells within the body, anticancer compounds are used. These anticancer compounds are obtained from various sources, like plants, marine organisms, and microbes. Currently, more than 30 natural compounds are undergoing clinical studies for cancer treatments due to their ability to minimize side effects compared to synthetic drugs [1]. Their ability to influence various signalling pathways involved in cancer development explains why only 29 out of the 240 antitumor drugs approved over the past 40 years are purely synthetic [4]. Among them, plants play a major role as a source of natural anticancer compounds due to the presence of secondary metabolites that have anticancer properties. Some of the anticancer compounds available in plants that have been investigated for their anticancer properties include polyphenols, flavanols like kaempferol and quercetin, flavones like luteolin and apigenin, alkaloids, and terpenoids. Recent research on plant-based anti-cancer compounds has focused on their capacity to induce cell death and apoptosis in different cancer types [5, 6].

To extract anticancer compounds from natural plant sources, it is essential to select the proper plants, use suitable extraction methods, and apply effective screening techniques to identify bioactive compounds that have been extracted [7]. Different extraction methods are used due to the complex chemical composition of natural products and variations in bioavailability [8]. To maximize the bioavailability of anticancer compounds, it is essential to select the best extraction methods. Factors such as temperature, extraction efficiency, and solvent selection affect the concentration and availability of bioactive compounds [4].

Each extraction method that can be used to extract anticancer compounds has its own advantages. Modern techniques, including ultrasound-assisted extraction, microwave-assisted extraction, tissue-smashing extraction, and solvent extraction; conventional techniques like Soxhlet extraction and maceration; and traditional methods, such as boiling and decoction, are examples of different extraction methods [8, 9].

This review focuses primarily on the importance of boiling/decoction, and solvent extraction, evaluates the

efficiency of those methods, and helps in understanding the bioavailability of anticancer compounds. Boiling/decoction are traditional methods that are simple, accessible, and cost-effective, while solvent extraction is an efficient method that is widely used due to its versatility [9].

2. Literature Review

2.1 Decoction and Boiling

Decoction and boiling are traditional extraction methods that are mainly used in Ayurveda medicine to extract compounds from plant materials. These techniques are frequently used in Sri Lanka, which has used Ayurveda practices since earlier periods. Through these processes, compounds from various plants and parts of the plants can be extracted. These two methods are used mainly to extract water-stable and heat-stable compounds, as they involve boiling plant materials [10, 11].

Decoction involves boiling plant matter in a specified volume of water or a solvent. It is one of the most used techniques to extract anticancer compounds, including polyphenols, alkaloids, terpenoids, and flavonoids, from medicinal plants [11]. Decoction can be done by using a single plant material or a mixture of plant materials [12]. Normally, in decoction, dried herbal components that are broken into small pieces or powdered are boiled until the volume is reduced to $1/8^{th}$ of the initial volume. This reduction concentrates the extracts which then increase the concentration of extracted bioactive compounds. Apart from that, if the material is soft, volume is reduced to $1/4^{th}$, and if it is very hard, volume is reduced to $1/16^{th}$ of the initial volume, respectively. Sometimes, aqueous ethanol or glycerol can be used instead of water [11, 13, 14].

Research done on a mixture of plant materials for the decoction method in Sri Lanka is described, and there are two decoctions done here. The first decoction is made from *Terminalia chebula* (Aralu), *Terminalia bellirica* (Bulu), *Phyllanthus emblica* (Nelli), and detoxified *Commiphora mukul* (Guggul). The second decoction is made from *Terminalia chebula*, *Terminalia bellirica*, *Phyllanthus emblica*, detoxified *Commiphora mukul*, *Nigella sativa* (black cummin), and *Smilax china* root (China root). Here, equal amounts of dried compounds are mixed and boiled, so that the volume reduces to 1/8th of the original volume. The results indicate that the total phenolic content and extraction yield are high in these two decoctions leading to a significant, dose-dependent reduction in cancer cell viability. This indicates the effectiveness of decoction methods for extracting anticancer compounds [13].

A mixture of plant matter, including *Hemidesmus indicus* root (Iramusu), *Nigella sativa Linn* seeds, and *Smilax glabra* rhizome, was decocted. These plant parts were mixed and heated in 1600 ml of water, then reduced to 200 ml after 3 hours. Apart from that, individual plants were also extracted separately. The results indicate that, after performing cytotoxic assays, the decoction made from the mixture of plant parts showed powerful cytotoxic properties toward human liver cancer cells. Generally, decoctions made from mixtures of plants show better effects than those of individual plants [12].

Adenanthera pavonina (Madatiya) and the barks of *Thespesia populnea* (Gan Sooriya) have been extracted using the decoction method to check their anticancer activity. Through MTT assay, sulforhodamine B(SRB) assay and lactate dehydrogenase activity, it was found that the decoction could inhibit the proliferation of human epithelial cell tumours [15].

The decoction of *Tinospora cordifolia* (Rasakinda) is prepared by hot water extraction, which contains the highest amount of extractable matter compared to other methods. In this extraction, *T. cordifolia* stems showed the presence of tannins, phenols, steroids, alkaloids, flavonoids, saponins, and terpenoids, which can be used as anticancer compounds after doing a qualitative analysis [16].

Another study has been conducted on six Indian herbal plants, *Manilkara zapota* (Sapodilla), *Azadirachta indica* (Neem), *Tinospora cordifolia*, *Psoralea corylifolia*, *Hemidesmus indicus,* and *Rubia cordifolia*, using this decoction method individually for each plant. According to this research, the extraction yield of all six plants is high in the decoction method, and they can be ranked as *M. zapota* > *R. cordifolia* > *H. indicus* > *T. cordifolia* > *P. corylifolia* > *A. indica*. All the plants show a high amount of phenol content, except *A. indica* [17].

For an experiment including a single plant, that the use of solvents instead of water in the decoction method includes *Eugenia jambolana* (Black Plum). Dried seeds are used in the decoction to extract the active compounds of the plant with the solvents, acetone, methanol, and ethanol. It is mainly reported that methanol extracts have antiproliferative effects against human tumour cells and induce apoptosis in methanol extracts, indicating their anticancer activity [18].

The advantage of using a mixture of plants in decoction rather than individual plants is that it provides better therapeutic effects, mainly due to the enhanced bioavailability [12]. The simplicity, well-established nature, environmental friendliness, and cost-effectiveness of this method make it suitable for large-scale or industrial extraction processes [11, 14].

Boiling is another traditional method that involves heating plant matter to a specific temperature for a defined time period [11]. There, water is commonly used as the solvent. At room temperature, water is so polar that it is not effective to extract compounds. But when water is subjected to specific temperatures and pressures, its polarity decreases, allowing it to dissolve a broader range of substances. This is a cost-effective and easily accessible technique [19].

Some researchers have used boiling as an extraction method to extract anticancer compounds from plants. To extract compounds from *Uvaria chamae* (bush banana), the boiling method has been used in Nigeria. There, the ground roots, and bark of this plant have been heated to 100 °C for 15 minutes. This method successfully identified some secondary metabolites, such as uvaretin and isouvaretin, which exhibit cytotoxic effects on cancer cells [20].

Punica granatum, commonly known as pomegranate, is a plant that is rich in polyphenols, including flavonoids like anthocyanins and catechins. Research has indicated that pomegranate has the potential to inhibit the proliferation of cancer cells, including those from the prostate, cervix, breast, pancreas, lungs, colon, and liver, through different mechanisms [21]. In Sri Lanka, the boiling method has been used to extract compounds from pomegranate peel and pericarp by subjecting the fine powder of the fruit parts to boiling water for 45 minutes. This technique is effective for extracting heat-stable compounds and unbreakable plant materials from pomegranate [10].

The efficiency of this method varies depending on the plant species and plant parts used. Therefore, each plant type has different ranges of temperatures and extraction times for this method. The advantages of this method are similar to those of the decoction method, as they both involve heating plant materials [19].

2.2 Solvent Extraction

Solvent extraction is a versatile method that uses various types of solvents to selectively extract bioactive compounds from plants. The various solvents used in the experiments influence the yield and composition of the extracted molecules [22]. Normally, solvents for extracting compounds are selected according to the polarity of the compounds being targeted. Solvents having a similar polarity to the target compounds tend to extract them more efficiently. The polarity ranking of common solvents from least to most polar is hexane, chloroform, ethyl acetate, acetone, methanol, and water [22, 23].

When selecting a solvent for the experiments, some factors, such as high selectivity according to the plant material used, low boiling point to facilitate removal of the solvent from the plant, reactivity of the solvent with other materials, and low vapour pressure to avoid solvent loss by evaporation, should be considered [11]. Solvents used in extraction should be inert, nontoxic, and easily removable to reduce issues like toxic residues in the final products [22].

In some experiments, sequential solvent extraction is used. This aids in extracting compounds with varying polarities from plant materials [22]. The sequential use of different solvents helps minimize the abundance of similar compounds in the final extraction. [23]. The collected plant parts are dried, ground into small pieces, and then subjected to sequential extraction using various solvents. This method uses a series of solvents like hexane, chloroform, ethyl acetate, and methanol with increasing polarities in a stepwise manner to extract different compounds and secondary metabolites from plant matter. Here, strongly non-polar compounds will be extracted by hexane. Chloroform, ethyl acetate, and methanol will extract compounds with increasing polarity, respectively, whereas methanol extracts highly polar compounds [24].

Several researchers have conducted solvent extractions using various solvents in order to extract anticancer compounds from plant parts, which can be used in forming novel anticancer drugs [25]. For example, ethanolic extraction was done to extract carbon tetrachloride from the *Fagonia schweinfurthii* (Bush candle), *angelicin* from the roots and rhizome of *Angelica archangelica* (Wild celery), and polyphenolic compounds from the fruit pericarp of *Litchi chinensis* [26-28]. Methanol extraction was done to extract benzophenones from the fruits and leaves of *Garcinia preussii*, diterpenes from the aerial parts of Andrographis paniculate, isoegoma-ketone from the leaves of Perilla frutescens (Beafsteak plant), steroidal saponins from the rhizome of *Paris polyphylla,* and xanthone from *Garcinia oblongifolia* [29-33]. Using ethyl acetate and methanol solvents, B-sitosterol was extracted from the leaves of *Asclepia scurassavica* (tropical milkweed) [34]. By chloroform extract, palmitic acid and B-sitosterol were extracted from the leaves of *Nitraria retusa*, and *chrysin* was extracted from the rhizomes of *Alpinia galangal* (Greater galangal) by using ethyl acetate solvent [35, 36].

Mangifera zeylanica (mango), a native plant in Sri Lanka, is known to have compounds with anticancer properties. *M. zeylanica* bark has mangiferin that induces an apoptotic effect, possibly by caspase activation, and a new resorcinolic lipid isolated from this plant, is said to have cytotoxic effects in ovarian cancer cells and breast cancer cells [37,38]. To extract these compounds, mainly sequential solvent extraction method can be used. There, powdered dried bark of the plant undergoes sequential solvent extraction using hexane, chloroform, ethyl acetate, and methanol to check the availability of polyphenols, flavonoids, lipids, sterols, and saponins as well. After the extraction, four fractions, namely hexane, chloroform, ethyl acetate, and water-soluble fractions, were obtained. The study findings demonstrate that the hexane extract exhibits cytotoxicity towards cancer cells, indicating the existence of anticancer compounds such as flavonoids [5]. Furthermore, chloromangiferamide, quercetin, and catechin compounds can be extracted from the chloroform extract of bark, which can be used for breast and ovarian cancer cells [39].

Garcinia species are found to contain many phytochemicals that have anticancer effects, such as garcinol, camboginol, xanthochymol, and garsubellin [40]. In Sri Lanka, *Garcinia quaesita* (Rath Goraka) was investigated to evaluate the anticancer effects of breast cancer stem cells using sequential solvent extraction. Dried powdered fruit was sequentially extracted with hexane, chloroform, ethyl acetate, and methanol to obtain four extracts. From the four extracts, both hexane and chloroform extracts showed significant anticancer effects. Hexane extract showed apoptotic effects as well as radical scavenging ability [41]. Another type of Garcinia, namely *Garcinia morella*, showed anti-tumour effects in lymphoma cells when using its leaf, bark, and fruits for solvent extraction [42].

Compounds from *Tinospora cordifolia* (Rasakinda) are extracted using methanol extraction by using a powder sample of *T. cordifolia* stem, adding it to the methanol solvent, and refluxing for 4 hours. Here, both cold and hot methanol extractions were done, and hot methanol extracts of *T. cordifolia* stems exhibited the presence of terpenoids, tannins, phenols, alkaloids, cardiac glycosides, steroids, and saponins, which have anticancer properties [16].

Hibiscus cannabinus (kenaf) is a plant abundant in bioactive molecules. Hibiscus leaf and seed powder was extracted with n-hexane, ethyl acetate, ethanol, and water solvent. According to the results of the experiment, ethanol extract showed the highest potential and extraction yield for bioactive compounds. Apart from that, n-hexane and ethanol extracts demonstrated anti-lung cancer activities at the same concentrations, with higher cytotoxicity levels [43].

To obtain high yields with a low extraction time, different types of solvent extraction methods, like pressurized solvent extraction and accelerated solvent extraction, can be used. Both methods perform at high temperatures and pressures that aid in the rapid extraction of anticancer compounds from plant matter, with advantages with respect to the amount of solvent used, yields and extraction time [11, 44].

Solvent extraction is beneficial as it aids in extracting compounds even from delicate or fragile flowers without degrading sensitive plant materials [22]. The process of solvent extraction is simple, widely used, and economical. Due to the versatility of solvent extraction, it allows for the extraction of specific bioactive compounds by selecting appropriate solvents and extraction conditions. As a result, this method is used for large-scale extractions [11].

3. Conclusion

Cancer is one of the major crises causing health problems around the world. To treat cancer patients effectively, it is necessary to identify novel compounds with anticancer properties. Plants play a significant role in the identification of novel anticancer compounds because natural compounds are now recognized as more efficient than synthetic drugs with minimal adverse effects. To find the therapeutic effects of the compounds in plants, they have to be extracted, and further investigations should be done.

To extract these compounds, different extraction methods are used. When selecting a suitable extraction method, the bioavailability of compounds with different extraction methods should be considered. Among the different extraction methods, decoction/boiling and solvent extraction play a key role. Decoction/boiling are well-established, cost-effective, and simple traditional methods that are suitable for extracting water-stable and heat-stable compounds from plants. It is mainly used in Ayurvedic medicine. Solvent extraction is a versatile method that can extract bioactive compounds efficiently using various types of solvents based on the compound's polarity. Both methods are efficient, making them suitable for large-scale extraction.

Boiling/decoction and solvent extraction methods can be used with advanced technologies to increase yields while reducing extraction times. Optimizing these techniques is essential, as they help in extracting a wider range of compounds more efficiently in an eco-friendly manner, that can be used to treat cancer.

REFERENCES

1. E.-H. Liu, L.-W. Qi, Q. Wu, Y.-B. Peng, and P. Li, Anticancer Agents Derived from Natural Products, Reviews in Medicinal Chemistry, 2009.
2. World Health Organization: WHO, Global Cancer Burden Growing, Amidst Mounting Need for Services, Geneva: WHO, 2024.
3. "Cancer Sri Lanka 2020 Country Profile." 2020. World Health Organization. https://www.who.int/publications/m/item/cancer-lka-2020.
4. C. A. Dehelean, I. Marcovici, C. Soica, M. Mioc, S. Iurcic "Plant-Derived Anticancer Compounds as New Perspectives in Drug Discovery and Alternative Therapy," *Molecules*, vol. 26, no. 4, p. 1109, Feb. 2021.
5. M. K. Ediriweera, K. H. Tennekoon, S. R. Samarakoon, I. Thabrew, and E. Dilip De Silva, "A study of the potential anticancer activity of Mangifera zeylanica bark: Evaluation of cytotoxic and apoptotic effects of the hexane extract and bioassay-guided fractionation to identify phytochemical constituents," *Oncology Letters*, vol. 11, no. 2, pp. 1335–1344, Jan. 2016.
6. M. Yuan, G. Zhang, W. Bai, X. Han, C. Li, and S. Bian, "The Role of Bioactive Compounds in Natural Products Extracted from Plants in Cancer Treatment and Their Mechanisms Related to Anticancer Effects," *Oxidative Medicine and Cellular Longevity*, vol. 2022, pp. 1–19, Feb. 2022.
7. A. Jawad, R. V. Balayeshwanth, A. Rami, R. Waleed, S. Hatem, and W. L. Nathan, "The influence of extraction solvents on the anticancer activities of Palestinian medicinal plants," *Journal of Medicinal Plants Research*, vol. 8, no. 9, pp. 408–415, Mar. 2014.
8. K. Yan, X. Cheng, G. Bian, Y. Gao, and D. Li, "The Influence of Different Extraction Techniques on the Chemical Profile and Biological Properties of Oroxylum indicum: Multifunctional Aspects for Potential Pharmaceutical Applications," *Evidence-based Complementary and Alternative Medicine*, vol. 2022, pp. 1–17, Sep. 2022.
9. J. Dai and R. J. Mumper, "Plant Phenolics: Extraction, Analysis and Their Antioxidant and Anticancer Properties," *Molecules*, vol. 15, 2010.
10. U. Y. Bandara, C. Witharana, and P. Soysa, "Extraction, Total phenol Content, Flavonoid content, Free Radical Scavenging Capacity and phytochemical screening of the Parts of Sri Lankan Pomegranate (Punica granatum L.) Fruit," *Current Trends in Biotechnology and Pharmacy*, vol. 14, no. 1, pp. 70–80, Jan. 2020.
11. S. S. Handa, S. P. S. Khanuja, G. Longo, and D. D. Rakesh, Extraction Technologies for Medicinal and Aromatic Plants, 2008.
12. M. I. Thabrew, R. R. Mitry, M. A. Morsy, and R. D. Hughes, "Cytotoxic effects of a decoction of Nigella sativa, Hemidesmus indicus and Smilax glabra on human hepatoma HepG2 cells," *Life Sciences*, vol. 77, no. 12, pp. 1319–1330, Aug. 2005.
13. N. Perera, P. Soysa, and T. U. Abeytunga, "Antioxidant and Cytotoxic Properties of Three Traditional Decoctions Used for the Treatment of Cancer in Sri Lanka," 2008.
14. M. G. Rasul, "Conventional Extraction Methods Use in Medicinal Plants, Their Advantages and Disadvantages," *International Journal of Basic Sciences and Applied Computing*, 2018.
15. K. S. Lindamulage and P. Soysa, "Evaluation of anticancer properties of a decoction containing Adenanthera pavonina L. and Thespesia populnea L.," *BMC Complementary and Alternative Medicine*, vol. 16, no. 1, Feb. 2016, doi: https://doi.org/10.1186/s12906-016-1053-9.

16. J. M. Dahanayake, P. K. Perera, P. Galappatty, P. Fernando, and L. Arawwawala, "Tinospora Cordifolia (Wild) Hook.f. (Thomas) Grown in Sri Lanka: Pharmacognostical, Physico-Chemical and Phytochemical Analysis of the Stem," *Journal of Ayurvedic and Herbal Medicine*, vol. 6, pp. 217–221, 2020.

17. M. Kaneria, B. Kanani, and S. Chanda, "Assessment of effect of hydroalcoholic and decoction methods on extraction of antioxidants from selected Indian medicinal plants," Asian Pacific *Journal of Tropical Biomedicine*, vol. 2, no. 3, pp. 195–202, Mar. 2012.

18. D. Mabeya Ogato, E. Mbaka Mauti, G. Omare Mauti, B. Ambrose, and D. Keno Kowanga, "Anticancer Activity of Eugenia Jambolana Seeds Against Hep2 Cell Lines," *The Journal of Phytopharmacology*, 2015.

19. H. Alwi and K. H. K. Hamid, "Momordica Charantia Extraction by Using Pressurized Boiling System and Compounds Identification through Gas Chromatography Mass Spectrometry," *International Journal of Engineering and Technology*, vol. 11, 2011.

20. C. C. Ogueke, J. N. Ogbulie, and B. N. Anyanwu, "The Effects of Ethanolic and Boiling Water Extracts of Root Barks and Leaves of Uvaria Chamae on Some Hospital Isolates," *Journal of American Science*, 2007.

21. G. Benedetti, Federica Zabini, Luca Tagliavento, F. Meneguzzo, V. Calderone, and V. Calderone, "An Overview of the Health Benefits, Extraction Methods and Improving the Properties of Pomegranate," *Antioxidants*, vol. 12, no. 7, pp. 1351–1351, Jun. 2023.

22. P. Kapadia, A. S. Newell, J. Cunningham, M. R. Roberts, and J. G. Hardy, "Extraction of High-Value Chemicals from Plants for Technical and Medical Applications," *International Journal of Molecular Sciences*, vol. 23, no. 18, p. 10334, Sep. 2022.

23. A. Altemimi, N. Lakhssassi, A. Baharlouei, D. Watson, and D. Lightfoot, "Phytochemicals: Extraction, Isolation, and Identification of Bioactive Compounds from Plant Extracts," *Plants*, vol. 6, no. 4, p. 42, Sep. 2017.

24. P. Jayarathna, K. Tennekoon, S. Samarakoon, I. Thabrew, E. Karunanayake, E.M. Ediriweera, "Cytotoxic, Antioxidant and Apoptotic Effects of Twenty Sri Lankan Endemic Plants in Breast Cancer Cells," *European Journal of Medicinal Plants*, vol. 15, no. 1, pp. 1–15, Jan. 2016.

25. M. A. Imran and H. Shahid, "A Review—Anti-Cancer Compounds from Medicinal Plants: Isolation, Identification, and Characterization," 2020. Available: https://doi.org/10.12692/ijb/17.6.442-468.

26. C. R. Oliveira, D.M. Garcia, D.G. Spindola, A. Bechara, S.S. Smaili, "Medicinal properties of Angelica archangelica root extract: Cytotoxicity in breast cancer cells and its protective effects against in vivo tumor development," *Journal of Integrative Medicine*, vol. 17, no. 2, pp. 132–140, Mar. 2019.

27. A. Pareek, A. Godavarthi, R. Issarani, and B. P. Nagori, "Antioxidant and hepatoprotective activity of Fagonia schweinfurthii (Hadidi) Hadidi extract in carbon tetrachloride induced hepatotoxicity in HepG2 cell line and rats," *Journal of Ethnopharmacology*, vol. 150, no. 3, pp. 973–981, Dec. 2013.

28. X. Wang, S. Yuan, J. Wang, P. Lin, G. Liu, Y. Lu, J. Zhang, W. Wang, Y. Wei, "Anticancer activity of litchi fruit pericarp extract against human breast cancer in vitro and in vivo," *Toxicology and Applied Pharmacology*, vol. 215, no. 2, pp. 168–178, Sep. 2006.

29. R. Ajaya Kumar, K. Sridevi, N. Vijaya Kumar, S. Nanduri, and S. Rajagopal, "Anticancer and immunostimulatory compounds from Andrographis paniculata," *Journal of Ethnopharmacology*, vol. 92, no. 2–3, pp. 291–295, Jun. 2004.

30. B. Biloa Messi, R. Ho, A. Meli, D Cressend, "Isolation and biological activity of compounds from Garcinia preussii," *Pharmaceutical Biology*, vol. 52, no. 6, pp. 706–711, Feb. 2014.

31. P. Li, H. Anandhi Senthilkumar, S. Wu, J.E. Yong, "Comparative UPLC-QTOF-MS-based metabolomics and bioactivities analyses of Garcinia oblongifolia," *Journal of Chromatography B*, vol. 1011, pp. 179–195, Feb. 2016, doi: https://doi.org/10.1016/j.jchromb.2015.12.061.

32. Y. Li, X. Zou, M.H. Zhang, J. Jiang, J.Y. Zhou, "The Anti-Lung Cancer Activities of Steroidal Saponins of P. polyphylla Smith var. chinensis (Franch.) Hara through Enhanced Immunostimulation in Experimental Lewis Tumor-Bearing C57BL/6 Mice and Induction of Apoptosis in the A549 Cell Line," vol. 18, no. 10, pp. 12916–12936, Oct. 2013.

33. H. Yan, Kyung Hee Jung, J. Kim, Marufa Rumman, Myung Sook Oh, and S.-S. Hong, "Artemisia capillaris extract AC68 induces apoptosis of hepatocellular carcinoma by blocking the PI3K/AKT pathway," *Biomedicine & Pharmacotherapy*, vol. 98, pp. 134–141, Feb. 2018.

34. A. A. Baskar, S. Ignacimuthu, G. M. Paulraj, and K. S. Al Numair, "Chemo preventive Potential of β-Sitosterol in Experimental Colon Cancer Model-An In Vitro and In Vivo Study," *BMC Complementary and Alternative Medicine*, vol. 10, 2010.

35. J. Boubaker, I. Ben Toumia, A. Sassi, I. Bzouich-Mokded "Antitumoral Potency by Immunomodulation of Chloroform Extract from Leaves of Nitraria retusa, Tunisian Medicinal Plant, via its Major Compounds β-sitosterol and Palmitic Acid in BALB/c Mice Bearing Induced Tumor," *Nutrition and Cancer*, vol. 70, no. 4, pp. 650–662, Apr. 2018.

36. S. Lakshmi, S. Suresh, B.S. Rahul, R. Saikant, V.Maya, "In vitro and in vivo studies of 5,7-dihydroxy flavones isolated from Alpinia galanga (L.) against human lung cancer and ascetic lymphoma," *Medicinal Chemistry Research*, vol. 28, no. 1, pp. 39–51, Nov. 2018.

37. M. K. Ediriweera, K. H. Tennekoon, A. Adhikari, S. R. Samarakoon, I. Thabrew, and E. D. de Silva, "New halogenated constituents from Mangifera zeylanica Hook.f. and their potential anti-cancer effects in breast and ovarian cancer cells," *Journal of Ethnopharmacology*, vol. 189, pp. 165–174, Aug. 2016.

38. M. K. Ediriweera, K. H. Tennekoon, S. R. Samarakoon, A. Adhikari, I. Thabrew, and E. Dilip de Silva, "Isolation of

a new resorcinolic lipid from Mangifera zeylanica Hook.f. bark and its cytotoxic and apoptotic potential," *Biomedicine & Pharmacotherapy*, vol. 89, pp. 194–200, May 2017.

39. P. Paranagama and R. De Silva, "Anticancer Potential of Natural Products: A Review Focusing on Sri Lankan Plants," 2019.

40. P. Jagtap, K. Bhise, and V. Prakya, "A Phytopharmacological Review on Garcinia Indica," *International Journal of Herbal Medicine*, vol. 3, 2015.

41. V. Colamba Pathiranage, J.N. Lowe, U. Rajagopalan, M.K. Ediriweera, "Hexane Extract of Garcinia quaesita Fruits Induces Apoptosis in Breast Cancer Stem Cells Isolated from Triple Negative Breast Cancer Cell Line MDA-MB-231," *Nutrition and Cancer*, pp. 1–11, Jun. 2020.

42. B. Choudhury, R. Kandimalla, R. Bharali, J. Monisha, "Anticancer Activity of Garcinia morella on T-Cell Murine Lymphoma Via Apoptotic Induction," *Frontiers in Pharmacology*, vol. 7, Jan. 2016.

43. Md. Adnan, K. K. Oh, M. O. K. Azad, M. H. Shin, M.-H. Wang, and D. H. Cho, "Kenaf (Hibiscus cannabinus L.) Leaves and Seed as a Potential Source of the Bioactive Compounds: Effects of Various Extraction Solvents on Biological Properties," *Life*, vol. 10, no. 10, p. 223, Sep. 2020.

44. B. Kaufmann and P. Christen, "Recent extraction techniques for natural products: microwave-assisted extraction and pressurized solvent extraction," *Phytochemical Analysis*, vol. 13, no. 2, pp. 105–113, 2002.

Transformative Applied Research in Computing, Engineering, Science and Technology – Dr. Damayanthi Dahanayake et al. (eds)
© 2024 Taylor & Francis Group, London, ISBN 978-1-041-01782-0

15

Evaluation of Classification Algorithms for Effective Spam Email Detection using Spam Email Dataset

Kalyani Shivaji Ubale*
Computer Engineering Department,
K K Wagh Institute of Research and Technology, SPPU,
Pune, Nashik, India

Kamini Ashutosh Shirsath
Computer Engineering Department,
Sandip Institute of Engineering and Management, SPPU,
Pune, Nashik, India

Abstract

This Abstract- The rapidly evolving digital landscape has resulted in a surge of spam emails, posing significant cybersecurity threats through methods like social engineering, malware distribution, and phishing. Traditional spam filtering techniques have proven insufficient in addressing the complexity of modern spam tactics. This paper presents a detailed evaluation of various classification algorithms on publicly available spam email datasets. By analyzing these datasets, we offer insights into the most effective data mining approaches for spam identification and prevention. The study involves a comparative analysis of classifiers such as Naive Bayes, K-Nearest Neighbors (KNN), Support Vector Machine (SVM), Logistic Regression, Decision Tree, and Random Forest. Our work not only examines the classifiers' performance but also highlights the datasets' characteristics, exploring factors like spam email percentage, the number of occurrences, feature types, and data attributes. The novelty of this research lies in its comprehensive approach to understanding spam email patterns, its emphasis on the dynamic nature of spam, and its use of diverse datasets to validate the effectiveness of different machine learning algorithms.

Keywords

Spam, Spam filtering method, Naive bayes, K-Nearest neighbors, SVM, Logistic regression, Decision tree, Random forest

1. Introduction

In the current era of digitalization, where communication is primarily accomplished through electronic channels, uninvited and undesired emails—also referred to as spam—are a typical occurrence. Worldwide, spam emails flood inboxes with unsolicited content, frauds, and promotions, clogging up both personal and professional accounts. It is

*Corresponding author: kalyaniubale110@gmail.com

DOI: 10.1201/9781003616368-15*

important for organizations to protect their networks and reputation as well as for individuals to maintain effective communication channels to comprehend the effects of spam emails. Currently, almost 85% of emails and texts that users receive are spam. The total number of emails sent daily has increased annually, growing from 269 billion in 2017 to 333.2 billion in 2022. This represents an increase of over 64 billion emails sent daily over the past five years. According to surveys, email is the most common medium for receiving spam, with nearly half (49%) of respondents indicating they most frequently receive spam through email. [1].

The volume of data makes it impractical to manually analyze spam communications. Using machine learning techniques, the most accurate spam classification may be accomplished. Junk email, sometimes known as spam, is unsolicited communication delivered by spammers by email [2]. The following are the primary categories of unsolicited emails: advertisements; Nigerian spam, which is spam sent by con artists attempting to extract money from letter recipients; Phishing is the practice of building a fake website that looks like it belongs to a reputable company in an effort to electronically gain sensitive or private information from visitors (typically with the intention of stealing it) [3]. This message lacks a valid return address. The carbon footprint of one spam email is around 0.03g CO2e. Thus, the amount of spam emails sent in 2021 may have contributed to the release of 4.5 tons of CO2e. Different kinds of spam emails are sent. Marketing, advertising, sexual content, financial matters, scams, and fraud are among the most prevalent categories of spam. According to a poll conducted in October 2021, the top 10 nations that send the highest percentage of spam emails are the United States, China, Russia, Brazil, India, Germany, Czech Republic, Poland, Bulgaria, and the United Kingdom [2]. To gain a better understanding of the scope of the spam problem caused by AT&T and Lucent subdomains over a six-month period starting at the end of April 1997, a case study was conducted.

Due to spammers' evolving strategies, a preliminary review of data gathered at the end of six months revealed a decline in filter performance [3]. Additionally, it was noted that, in the past, spammers would typically include messages in the body of their emails; this practice was termed as "traditional spamming." However, throughout the past ten years, email services have faced a new challenge in the form of image spam, which has evolved into a sophisticated form of spam since it makes the message more engaging for the user and makes it difficult for filters to identify as spam. Image spam filters use various techniques on their filters to be more effective because image spam is rich

in information and contains a range of data. Thus, there is a growing demand for trustworthy anti-spam filters due to the volume of unsolicited bulk emails. Thus far, these kinds of filters have primarily relied on manually created keyword patterns that yield subpar results. Using the publicly accessible email corpus, a comprehensive analysis of the Naïve Bayesian filter's performance is conducted, helping to establish industry standards [4]. The Reuters corpus, which is a publicly accessible collection of human categorized documents, has been beneficial to the field of text categorization research (Lewis, 1992). The same have served as reference points. One of the issues with having a standard email corpus publicly accessible is that it is difficult to provide resources for anti-spam filtering similar to this since users' incoming emails cannot be made public without breaking

Combining spam messages with ones taken from public mailing list archives that are free of spam is one of the most popular approaches to solving this kind of issue. In that perspective, we test Sahami et al.'s methodology using a combination of spam and communications submitted through the moderated (i.e., spam-free) Linguist list, which discusses the field and science of linguistics. The final corpus, known as Ling-Spam, is released to the public so that it can be used as a benchmark by others [5,6]. Making spam messages public is not a problem because spam is essentially already public knowledge because it is sent out blindly to a huge number of recipients. However, it is generally more difficult to publish genuine messages online without invading the privacy of those who send and receive them. In an attempt to provide a comprehensive analysis, we attempt to suggest a few of the most well-known publicly accessible spam email corpora. In order to help academics working with the spam data use the various email spam datasets more effectively, we attempted to emphasize in this paper their fundamental characteristics along with their benefits and drawbacks. Additionally, we suggested other dataset qualities by taking into account the characteristics associated with spam emails.

Modified in MS Word 2007 and saved as a "Word 97-2003 Document" for the PC, provides authors with most of the formatting specifications needed for preparing electronic versions of their papers. All standard paper components have been specified for three reasons: (1) ease of use when formatting individual papers, (2) automatic compliance to electronic requirements that facilitate the concurrent or later production of electronic products, and (3) conformity of style throughout a conference proceedings. Margins, column widths, line spacing, and type styles are built-in; examples of the type styles are provided throughout this document and are identified in italic type, within parentheses, following the example. Some components, such as multi-leveled equations, graphics, and tables are not prescribed, although the various table text styles are provided. The formatter will need to create these components, incorporating the applicable criteria that follow.

2. Literature Survey

The attempts to enact laws prohibiting spam emails have not had much of an impact. Creating tools to assist recipients in recognizing or deleting spam mail automatically is a more efficient approach. These devices are known as anti-spam filters, and their features range from content-based filters to blacklists of known spammers. A fresh benchmark corpus was created, containing a combination of spam and communications from moderated (thus, spam-free) email lists. The corpus is released to the public so that other academics can use it as a standard. An extensive analysis of the Naive Bayesian technique, which was employed in (Sahami et al. 1998), was carried out using this corpus [4]. An extensive analysis on a publicly available corpus was carried out, which helped establish common standards.

A comprehensive analysis was carried out on a publicly available corpus, which helped establish common standards. Moreover, previously unexplored topics such as the impact of stop lists, lemmatization, training corpus size, and attribute set size on the filter's performance were examined. In order to make the Naive Bayesian anti-spam filter to be practical, more safety nets must be included, it was determined after implementing suitable cost-sensitive assessment measures [5]. In the context of anti-spam filtering, which is a cost-sensitive application of text categorization, a method called stacked generalization, or stacking, was evaluated. The study showed that stacking can enhance the effectiveness of automatically generated anti-spam filters. These filters can be applied in real-world scenarios using a publicly available dataset known as Lingspam [6].

An assessment of memory-based learning referring to anti-spam filtering is presented in this research. The paper also suggested a unique, cost-sensitive use of text categorization in an effort to recognize automatically the bulk of unwanted commercial emails that arrive in inboxes. Using a publicly available corpus, a comprehensive study of memory-based anti-spam filter effectiveness is conducted with an emphasis on anti-spam filtering for mailing lists. A variety of attribute and distance-weighting approaches are examined, together with studies on the impact of neighborhood, attribute set, and training corpus sizes [7]. An investigation was conducted on four learning algorithms—Naive Bayes, Flexible Bayes, LogitBoost,

and Support Vector Machines—using four datasets created from different users' mailboxes. The study discussed the worst-case computational complexity of these algorithms. It is carried out a study on the impact of employing attributes that reflect token sequences rather than individual tokens on classification accuracy. It was also investigated how the size of the training set and attribute affected things within a budget-conscious framework [8]. Five supervised learning techniques are evaluated and presented in relation to statistical spam filtering. Using cost-sensitive metrics, the impact of different feature selection techniques and feature set sizes on each learner's performance was analyzed. The study found that the importance of feature selection varies significantly between classifiers. In particular, support vector machines, AdaBoost, and maximum entropy models performed well in the evaluation. These models share similar characteristics: they are not sensitive to feature selection strategies, can be easily scaled to very high feature dimensions, and perform well across different datasets. The four spam corpora used for the evaluation were PU1, Ling, SA, and ZH1 [9]. A comparison of the SVM, NB, boosted trees, and stacking algorithms was conducted using the benchmark spam filtering corpora LingSpam and PU1. For conventional semi-supervised co-training, the datasets must have two disjoint natural feature sets. However, most datasets have only one set of features, which limits the applicability of co-training. It was observed that in cases of high data redundancy, such as in spam email filtering, co-training with a random feature split is as effective as co-training with a natural feature split. [10].

The study compared a linear Support Vector Machine (SVM) used to automatically filter spam emails with seven different versions of Naive Bayes classifiers. Empirical studies were conducted using six large, publicly available datasets known as the Enron corpus. The results indicated that Boolean Naive Bayes, Multinomial Naive Bayes, and linear SVM were the best options for automatically filtering spam, with SVM showing the highest average performance across all datasets, achieving an accuracy rate of over 90% in every corpus examined. The performance of the seven Naive Bayes spam filters was compared after dimensionality reduction, which was performed using eight well-known term-selection strategies with varying degrees of popularity. This comparison was applied to classify messages from the six real, public, and large email datasets. [11,12,18].

3. Analysis of Dataset

The different publicly available email spam corpuses are described in this section. The spam email databases provide a wide range of data, including picture, text, and phishing email data. Recently, a significant rise in spam emails pertaining to all of the previously listed categories of spam data has been noted.

The field of cybersecurity and spam detection has evolved tremendously as a result of the availability of publicly available spam emails for study. We have examined the many advantages and ramifications of using these corpora throughout this review paper, highlighting their critical influence in molding the creation of efficient spam filtering methods and deepening our comprehension of spamming behavior. The fact that publicly accessible spam email corpora encourage creativity and teamwork among researchers is one of their main benefits.

These corpora facilitate the systematic evaluation and comparison of spam detection algorithms, allowing academics to identify new approaches and best practices by giving them access to standardized datasets with ground truth labels. Furthermore, this corpora's open nature promotes repeatability and transparency. The Table 15.1

shows comparison of various spam email datasets and the commonly considered features for spam filtering.

Furthermore, publicly accessible spam email corpora are priceless tools for researching the constantly changing techniques and approaches used by spammers. Researchers can learn more about the underlying patterns and trends that motivate spamming activity by examining large-scale datasets from a variety of sources and historical periods. The Table 15.2 shows publicly available email spam corpus and their data characteristics and the analysis of the number features that are commonly considered for spam detection.

This knowledge can then be used to inform the creation of more reliable and adaptable spam detection systems. Moreover, the incorporation of metadata, such as email headers and sender information, allows scholars to explore the technological and social dimensions of spam activity, providing insights into the mechanisms and incentives underlying spam campaigns. Additionally, the accessibility

Table 15.1 Comparing various datasets with their features

Dataset	Source	Size	Label (Spam/Ham)	Features
Spam Archive	Research dataset	15.4 MB	Binary	Text content, sender, recipient, subject, date/time, attachments
Spam email	Research dataset	Varies	Binary	- Subject line - Body text - Sender email address - Recipient email address
Spam base	UCI machine learning repository	0.4 MB	Binary	- Word frequency features (e.g., 'make', 'money', 'free'), character frequency, special characters, capitalization
Spam assassin	Spam Assassin public corpus	3.3 GB	Binary	- Email text (both body and headers) - Metadata (e.g., date, sender, subject)
Ling spam	Lingspam dataset	20 MB	Binary	- Bag of words features - Metadata (e.g., subject line, sender, date)
PU corpus	Research dataset	0.4 GB	Binary	- Bag of words features - Metadata (e.g., subject line, sender, date)
Phishing corpus	Research dataset	Varies	Binary	- HTML content features - Metadata (e.g., URL, domain)
Zh1	Research dataset	Varies	Binary	- Bag of words features - Metadata (e.g., subject line, sender, date)
Gen spam	Research dataset	Varies	Spam	Text content, sender, recipient, subject, date/time, attachments
Princeton spam image	Princeton university	Varies	Spam	Image pixels, image metadata, sender, recipient, subject, date/time
Dredze image spam	Johns Hopkins university	Varies	Spam	Image pixels, image metadata, sender, recipient, subject, date/time
Hunter	Public sources	Varies	Spam	Text content, sender, recipient, subject, date/time, attachments
Enron spam	Enron Corporation	12.8 MB	Binary	- Email text (both body and headers) - Metadata (e.g., subject line, sender, date)
Trec	TREC public spam corpora	Varies	Binary	- Email text (both body and headers) - Metadata (e.g., date, sender, subject)

Table 15.2 Publicly available email spam corpus [15]

Dataset Name TABLE 16.3	Number of messages		Rate of spam	Year of creation	References	Dataset characteristic	Associated tasks	Feature type	Features
	Spam	Non-spam							
Spam archive	15090	0	100%	1998	Almeida and yamakami	Multivariate	Classification	Integer	Varies
Spambase	1813	2788	39%	1999	Sakkis et al	Multivariate	Classification	Integer, Real	57
Lingspam	481	2412	17%	2000	Sakkis et al	Multivariate	Classification	Char, Integer	50
PU1	481	618	44%	2000	Attar et al	Multivariate	Classification	Integer	Varies
Spamassassin	1897	4150	31%	2002	Apache spam-assassin	Multivariate	Classification	Integer	100
PU2	142	579	20%	2003	Zhang et al	Multivariate	Classification	Integer	Varies
PU3	1826	2313	44%	2003	Zhang et al	Multivariate	Classification	Integer	Varies
PUA	571	571	50%	2003	Zhang et al	Multivariate	Classification	Integer	Varies
Zh1	1205	428	74%	2004	Zhang et al	Multivariate	Classification	Integer, Char	3000
Trec 2005	52,790	39,399	57%	2005	Androutsopoulos et al	Multivariate	Prediction	Integer, Char, Real	Varies
Phishing corpus	415	0	100%	2005	Abu-nimeh et al	Multivariate	Classification	Integer, Real	43
Enron-spam	20170	16545	55%	2006	Koprinska et al	Multivariate	Classification	Integer, Real	375
Trec 2006	24,912	12910	66%	2006	Androutsopoulos et al	Multivariate	Prediction	Integer, Char, Real	Varies
Trec 2007	50,199	25,220	67%	2007	Debarr and Wechsler	Multivariate	Prediction	Integer, Char, Real	135
Princeton spam image Benchmark	1071	0	100%	2007	Wang et al	Multivariate	Classification	Integer, Char, Real	50
Dredze image spam Dataset	3297	2021	62%	2007	Dredze, gevaryahu and elias-bachrach	Multivariate	Classification	Integer, Char, Real	23
Hunter	928	810	53%	2008	Gao et al	Multivariate	Classification	Integer, Char, Real	24
Spam email	1378	2949	32%	2010	Csmining group	Multivariate	Classification	Integer, Real	64

of spam email corpora has promoted cross-disciplinary cooperation between academics in computer science, linguistics, psychology, and other disciplines.

4. Proposed System

These days, the most widely used spam filtering techniques are as follows;

1. Systems that require confirmation. In order to guarantee that the original message is sent, the sender is invited to take action; if not, the message is deemed undelivered.

2. Utilizing provisional mailing addresses. When there are a lot of arriving letters, the user updates the address.

3. A blacklist. When an incoming message is received, the spam filter checks if the sender's IP address or email address is on a blacklist. If it is, the message is classified as spam and discarded. [8].

4. Whitelist. This method operates similarly to the blacklist method, but it checks for the absence of the sending IP address on the mail server's blacklist.

5. Spam recognition based on signatures. A signature is a unique identifier or characteristic of an email message. For each new message, its signature is calculated and compared to a database containing signatures of messages previously identified as spam. If the message's signature matches one in the database, it is marked as spam.

6. Linguistic heuristics. This method searches the body of the message for specific keywords and phrases that indicate the message may be spam.

Machine learning is a branch of artificial intelligence that concentrates on creating algorithms capable of learning from data and making predictions. The following section will explore the most popular machine learning methods for classifying spam and the current strategies used for spam detection. We will start by outlining the key phases of the machine learning process. First, the analysis stage: in this phase, processed and analyzed data are used to identify patterns. Second, train stage: Using the collected data, machine learning models are applied. Choosing the right hyperparameters can improve the models' quality. Testing comes next: On unutilized data, machine learning models are tested. The model can be assessed with a variety of indicators. Application, or implementing the best model, is the final step.

The six commonly used classification algorithms in machine learning were selected: Logistic Regression, K-Nearest Neighbors, AdaBoost, Naive Bayes, Gradient Boosting, and Random Forest.

A probabilistic algorithm that is good at classifying spam is called Naïve Bayes. It reduces a multidimensional problem to a collection of univariate problems, ignoring potential relationships or connections among inputs, which is why it is referred to as "naive" [9]. The following are the drawbacks of using this algorithm to process spam emails: The quality of classification will suffer if a term in the letter appears that has never been in the training sample.

KNN is a classification method that calculates the distances between items, representing them as points in space. It then proceeds to a learning phase where training data points are assigned to the cluster with the nearest center. [10]. One can optimize the tuning of the algorithm's input parameter, k.

The selected k value affects the classification accuracy. The training sample includes the k nearest neighbors of each categorized object. An object belongs to the class that is most common among its k closest neighbors. The algorithm does not work well with a high number of features and is sensitive to outliers. An appropriate analytical technique for modeling the data and elucidating the correlation between the explanatory variables and the binary answer variable is logistic regression. The chance of allocating a value to a certain class is the outcome, and it can only take values between 0 and 1 [11].

A prediction method called Random Forest makes advantage of the tree-building concept. The combined effect of multiple trees, or a forest, improves each tree's

capacity for prediction independently. The programmer creates several decision trees during training. These trees are then used to predict classes by considering the votes from each tree. The class with the most votes is chosen as the final prediction. [3].

5. Experimentaion and Results

The main stages of creating a classifier are: 1) Data collection; 2) Pre-processing and text cleaning; 3) Learning and obtaining prediction results. The main task of the algorithm is to find patterns.

The Lingspam dataset was used to evaluate the performance of various classifiers, including Logistic Regression, Neighbors Classifier, AdaBoost Classifier, Naïve Bayes, Gradient Boosting Classifier, and Random Forest Classifier. The Lingspam corpus consists of a collection of spam messages and messages from the Linguist list, a moderated mailing list about linguistics. The dataset includes 10 directories and a total of 2,893 messages. Of these, 2,412 are Linguist messages, collected by randomly downloading digests from the list's archives, splitting them into individual messages, and removing any server-added text. The remaining 481 messages are spam, received by the first author. Attachments, HTML tags, and duplicate spam messages from the same day are not included. Spam messages make up 16.6% of the corpus. The Fig. 15.1 represents the process that is followed to implement the model.

5.1 Data Processing and Algorithm Creation Process

The first step in data processing and algorithm creation is to prepare the data. This involves cleaning the data by removing gaps, duplicates, and undefined values. Even if many models permit the inclusion of gaps in the sets and undefined data, it is preferable to erase them before executing simple changes in order to reduce the likelihood of errors and enhance the quality of the classification.

The Table 15.3 shows the composition of lingspam dataset.

Table 15.3 Lingspam dataset

Dataset	Spam	Non spam	Rate of spam	Size	Year of creation	Features
Ling spam	481	2412	16.6%	20 MB	2000	50

Table 15.4 shows the performance of each spam classifier algorithm on the Lingspam dataset. For this dataset, each classifier evaluated only 14 randomly selected features at a time to identify the best feature out of the 50 available.

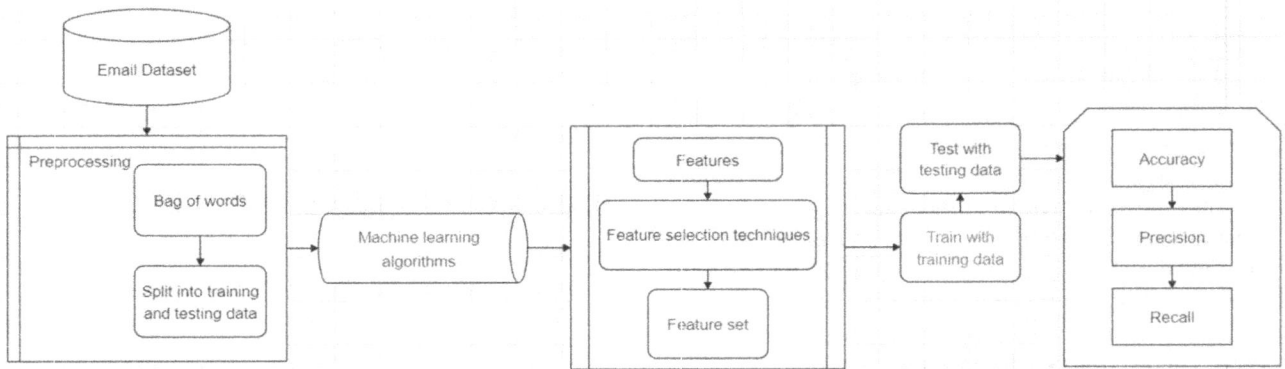

Fig. 15.1 Spam detection block diagram

Table 15.4 Performance comparison for the methods evaluated

Algorithm	Accuracy	Precision	Recall
Logistic Regression	0.972	0.977	0.972
K Neighbors	0.955	0.955	0.955
Ada Boost	0.986	0.986	0.986
Naïve Bayes	0.872	0.970	0.872
Gradient boosting	0.968	0.972	0.968
Random forest	0.982	0.984	0.982

5.2 Methodology

In this experiment, Kaggle platform was used for programming. The dataset was split into two sections: training data and testing data. The purpose of this process is to train a classifier using the training data from the Lingspam dataset and then test its ability to identify spam emails using the testing data. Experimental results show that the Adaboost and Random Forest methods greatly enhance the performance of the spam filter compared to other classifiers, such as logistic regression, nearest neighbors, Naïve Bayes, and gradient boosting algorithms. The Fig. 15.2 shows comparative analysis of the various spam classifier algorithms.

6. Conclusion

In conclusion, we can state that spam is an issue that bothers every user, which is why we have done study on the subject. To create spam protection, there are multiple approaches. Spam message classification is highly accurate thanks to machine learning algorithms. In this study, training was conducted using an available lingspam dataset. 481 spam mails and 2412 non-spam samples make up the data. These outcomes were attained using a variety of machine learning models, including Random Forest, Naive Bayes, K-Nearest

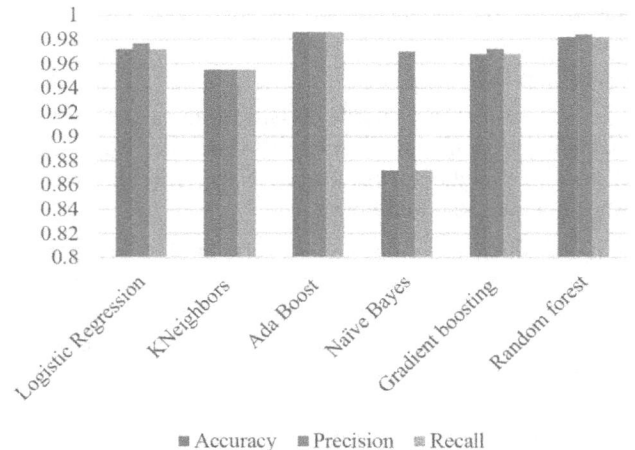

Fig. 15.2 Comparative analysis of the various spam classifier algorithms

Neighbors, Ada Boost, and Logistic Regression. In this work, we observe that, due to their highest accuracy, the most effective algorithms for spam filtering are Logistic Regression and Random Forest. It is now at 99%. It has reached 99%. The results can be used to develop a more effective spam detection classifier by combining different algorithms or filtering methods.

REFERENCES

1. Cai, Robert, "Spam statistics (2024): New data on junk email, AI scams and phishing", online blog, 19 Oct 2023.
2. Jyothiikaa Moorthy, "23 email spam statistics to know in 2024", online blog, 8 Aug 2023.
3. L. F. Cranor, B. A. Lamacchia, "Spam!", Communication of the ACM, vol. 41, issue 8, Aug 1998.
4. Androutsopoulos, J. Koutsias, K.V. Chandrinos, G. Paliouras, C.D. Spyropoulos, Learning to filter spam E-mail : a comparison of a naïve bayesian and a memory based approach, in: Proceedings of 4th European Conference

on Principles and Practice of Knowledge Discovery in Databases, Lyon, France, September 2000, 2000, pp. 1–12.

5. Androutsopoulos, J. Koutsias, K.V. Chandrinos, G. Paliouras, C.D. Spyropoulos, "An evaluation of naive bayesian anti-spam filtering", in: Proceedings of 11th European Conference on Machine Learning (ECML 2000), Barcelona, 2000, pp. 9–17.

6. G. Sakkis, I. Androutsopoulos, G. Paliouras, V. Karkaletsis, "A memory based approach to anti-spam filtering for mailing lists", in: Empirical Methods in Natural Language Processing, 2001, pp. 44–50.

7. G. Sakkis, I. Androutsopoulos, G. Paliouras, V. Karkaletsis, "Stacking classifiers for anti-spam filtering of E-mail", in: Kluwer academic publishers, 2003, pp. 49–73.

8. Androutsopoulos, G. Paliouras, E. Michelakis, "Learning to Filter Unsolicited Commercial E-Mail", National Centre for Scientific Research Demokritos, Athens, Greece, Oct 2006.

9. L. Zhang, J. Zhu, T. Yao, "An evaluation of statistical spam filtering techniques spam filtering as text categorization", ACM Trans. Asian Lang. Inf. Process 3 (4) (2004) 243–269.

10. Koprinska, J. Poon, J. Clark, J. Chan, "Learning to classify e-mail", Inf. Sci. 177 (10) (2007) 2167–2187.

11. G.V. Cormack, T.R. Lynam, "On-line supervised spam filter evaluation", ACM Trans. Inf. Syst. 25 (3) (2007).

12. T.A. Almeida, A. Yamakami, "Content-based spam filtering," in: The 2010 International Joint Conference on Neural Networks (IJCNN), Barcelona, 2010, pp. 1–7.

13. T.A. Almeida, A. Yamakami, "Spam filtering:how the dimensionality reduction affects the accuracy of Naïve Bayes classifiers," in: J Internet Serv Appl, 2011, pp. 183–200.

14. Attar, R.M. Rad, R.E. Atani, "A survey of image spamming and filtering techniques", Artif. Intell. Rev. 40 (1) (2011) 71–105.

15. D. DeBarr, H. Wechsler, "Spam detection using random forest", in: Pattern recognition letters, Elsevier, 2012, pp- 1237-1244.

16. B. Issac, "Spam detection approaches with case study implementation on spam corpora", in: Researchgate, 2010.

17. J.R. Mendez, F. Díaz, E.L. Iglesias, J.M. Corchado, "A comparative performance study of feature selection methods for the anti-spam filtering domain", in: Advances in Data Mining. Applications in Medicine, Web Mining, Marketing, Image and Signal Mining, Springer Berlin Heidelberg, 2006, pp. 106–120.

Note: All the figures and tables (except Table 15,2) in this chapter were made by the authors.

Transformative Applied Research in Computing, Engineering, Science and Technology – Dr. Damayanthi Dahanayake et al. (eds)
© 2024 Taylor & Francis Group, London, ISBN 978-1-041-01782-0

16

Nature's Defense—An Overview of Plant-Based Mosquito Repellents

A. J. Marinrojes and S. S. Uthumange*

Department of Life Sciences, NSBM Green University,
Sri Lanka

Abstract

As mosquito-borne diseases continue to present substantial global health challenges, the demand for effective repellents is crucial. Given the controversies surrounding the long-term safety and environmental impacts of existing synthetic repellents, exploring alternative options becomes increasingly advantageous. This review investigates the potential of natural mosquito repellents derived from plants present in Sri Lanka, focusing on their active ingredients, mechanisms of toxicity, safety concerns, and market viability. The findings exemplify the efficacy and potential of natural products as mosquito repellents. However, the comparative benefits of natural versus artificial repellents remain inadequately explored. Furthermore, significant emphasis must be placed on conducting rigorous safety testing of natural products to evaluate their viability as substitutes for synthetic repellents. Overall, the promising results observed with plant-derived repellents underscore their potential in the global market and warrant further exploration.

Keywords

Citronella, Mosquito-borne diseases, Natural repellents, Neem, Sri Lanka

1. Introduction

Mosquito-borne diseases pose a significant global public health threat. Each year, approximately 700 million people contract a mosquito-borne illness, resulting in over 725,000 deaths, according to the World Health Organization [1]. These diseases cause widespread infection and mortality, impacting millions of individuals worldwide and placing substantial burdens on public health systems. More than a dozen known mosquito-borne diseases vary in geographic distribution and health impact.

Increasing attention is being given to the role of mosquitoes in spreading several dangerous diseases, including malaria, filariasis, dengue, yellow fever, chikungunya, Zika virus, and West Nile virus, which threaten millions of humans and animals worldwide [2]. Despite significant scientific and medical advancements, these diseases continue to adversely affect human health, particularly in tropical and subtropical regions. Mosquito control measures are essential to reduce disease spread and alleviate the burden on healthcare systems in affected nations.

---
*Corresponding author: sahani.u@nsbm.ac.lk

DOI: 10.1201/9781003616368-16

The use of mosquito repellents minimizes human exposure to disease-carrying vectors, consequently lowering the incidence of mosquito-borne diseases. The effectiveness of mosquito repellents depends on proper usage, active ingredients and formulations, environmental conditions, and complementary measures. Synthetic repellents like N, N-diethyl-3-methylbenzamide (DEET), and picaridin have demonstrated significant effectiveness in repelling mosquitoes over decades [2]. However, concerns regarding their toxicity and environmental impact have sparked interest in safer and more environmentally friendly alternatives.

Nature offers an extensive arsenal of compounds with potential applications in various fields, including vector control against mosquito-borne diseases. Natural product chemistry presents several advantages over synthetic alternatives. Firstly, the diversity of naturally sourced bioactive compounds opens up many avenues for exploration. The molecular descriptors of natural products provide a foundation for further chemical optimization and diversification. These compounds often exhibit complex and novel structures, facilitating the discovery of lead candidates with strong therapeutic or preventive efficacy. Additionally, natural products typically produce fewer side effects than synthetic counterparts [3]. While synthetic approaches demand significant time, and resources, and generate substantial waste, natural products offer a cost-effective and accessible alternative, simplifying the isolation of bioactive molecules.

This review aims to investigate the utility and efficacy of natural mosquito repellents specifically focusing on plants present in Sri Lanka. A comprehensive analysis of historical usage, comparative efficacy, compound characterization, and mechanisms of toxicity provides essential knowledge for developing and optimizing natural mosquito repellents.

2. Literature Review

2.1 Historical use of Natural Mosquito Repellents

Historical evidence indicates that various insect-repellent methods were utilized by our ancestors. Records dating back to ancient Egypt report the use of essential oils and bed nets to deter insects. Additionally, large quantities of garlic found in their pyramids were likely employed for this purpose [2]. Over millennia, numerous civilizations have harnessed plants as insect repellents in diverse forms. These included hanging bruised plants in homes, burning leaves to create simple fumigants, and applying oil-based treatments to the body or garments [2]. Moreover, reports indicate that various primate species anoint their fur by rubbing it

with millipedes and plants such as *Piper marginatum*, and *Clematis dioica* [4]. Centuries later, studies revealed that millipedes contain benzoquinones, chemicals believed to deter biting insects, indicating that the anointing behavior was intended for insect repellency. Specifically, research has identified the effective compounds in millipedes as 2-methyl-1,4-benzoquinone and 2-methoxy-3-methyl-1,4-benzoquinone [4, 5]. Laboratory experiments have also demonstrated the repellent activity of benzoquinones against the *Aedes aegypti* and *Amblyomma americanum*, indicating that sources of natural insect deterrents extend beyond only plant-based products [4]. Ancestral usage of natural mosquito-repellent methods provides valuable insights into the historical context and efficacy of these practices.

2.2 Mosquito-Repellency: Synthetic vs Natural

While DEET and picaridin are recognized as the top synthetic repellents, other natural alternatives such as ethyl butylacetylaminopropionate (IR3535), pyrethrin and its derivatives, methyl jasmonate, methyl anthranilate, and para-methane-3,8- diol (PMD) also exhibit topical repellent activity akin to synthetic counterparts [6]. These compounds are derived from natural origins, although their carbon backbones may be artificially synthesized [6].

A survey-based study examining the public perception of mosquito repellents reported that 57% of respondents preferred mosquito repellents containing only natural ingredients. In comparison, 14% favored those with a combination of natural and artificial ingredients [7]. Although consumer opinion is heavily influenced by naturalness perceptions and chemophobia, concerns regarding the long-term use of synthetic repellents are not unjustified. Synthetic repellents have attracted considerable attention due to potential neurotoxic effects, especially with extensive use. DEET, a standard synthetic repellent, has been linked to nervous system disruption in mosquitoes by interfering with their neurotransmitter systems, which could translate into undesirable neurological effects in humans. Clinical studies report that DEET has been associated with numerous side effects, including dermatitis, allergies, cardiac problems, and encephalopathy in children [8]. Additionally, DEET interferes with sodium-potassium ion channels, which can lead to lip numbness [2]. Likewise, excessive use of synthetic pyrethroids can cause neurotoxic effects, fever, skin and eye irritation, reproductive problems, and changes in immune function [2]. Furthermore, it is estimated that the fine particulate matter emitted by a single synthetic mosquito coil is equivalent to over 137 cigarettes. Continuous use of similar products for 8-10 days could lead to respiratory disorders [9]. Synthetically formulated chemical repellents have disrupted ecosystems, fueled insecticide resistance, triggered a resurgence of mosquito populations, and produced harmful effects on non-target species [10].

It is worth noting that comparative repellency tests of DEET and natural essential oils showed that DEET consistently exhibited stronger repellent activity across all measured variables. This is likely due to the volatility of compounds within plant essential oils. Although alcohols, aldehydes, and terpenoids show repellent effects in the vapor phase, they generally provide a shorter protection time than synthetic alternatives. However, given the side effects and limitations of synthetic methods, exploring alternative approaches becomes advantageous.

2.3 Plant-Derived Mosquito Repellents and their Bioactive Compounds

Numerous plants have garnered interest as a source of natural chemicals, potentially offering viable alternatives to synthetic compounds for mosquito repellency. These medicinal plants possess diverse compound compositions, containing bioactive species of essential oils, terpenoids, and alkaloids. Recent experiments conducted in both laboratory and field settings have demonstrated their effectiveness as mosquito repellents [2,3,8]. An overview of natural products and their repellency spectrums can be found in Table 16.1.

Cymbopogon Nardus (Citronella)

Citronella oil, derived from various species of Cymbopogon grass, is recognized as a premier option among natural mosquito repellents. Isolated from the leaves and stems of citronella grass, this essential oil contains compounds like citronellal, eugenol, geraniol, and limonene, all known for their molecular-repellent properties in mosquitoes [11]. Citronella oil is widely recognized as an effective repellent, with potency comparable to DEET on a dose-for-dose basis. However, its efficacy diminishes rapidly as the oils evaporate, leaving the user exposed.

The essential oil of citronella is primarily produced from its leaves. A study reported that the younger leaves of *Cymbopogon nardus* contain higher levels of citronellal and citronellol, whereas the older leaves have a greater percentage of geraniol and citral [12]. Citral, which imparts an intense lemon odor, acts as an aroma compound [13]. Citronellal is a terpenoid compound that is derived from isoprene units. Citronella oil primarily comprises geraniol (35.7%), trans-citral (22.7%), cis-citral (14.2%), geranyl acetate (9.7%), citronellal (5.8%), and citronellol (4.6%) [14]. Variations in citronellal content have been observed among different citronella grass cultivars. For example, the oil extract from Maha Pengiri (Sri Lanka and Indonesia) has a citronellal concentration ranging from 40.5% to 60.7%. In contrast, the oil from *C. nardus var. confertiflorus* (India) contains significantly less, between 17.2-33.2% [14].

Citronellal, citronellol, geraniol, citral, and limonene have demonstrated repellent properties comparable to DEET [2]. Selecting citronella species with high concentrations of these compounds can enhance their effectiveness against mosquitoes. Iovinella et al., [15] reported that citronellal derivatives demonstrate high repellent efficacy against the mosquito vector species *Culex pipiens pallens* in both in-vitro and in-field tests. In a study by Hsu et al. [16], the effectiveness of *Cymbopogon* essential oils in repelling *Aedes aegypti* was evaluated using a Y-tube olfactometer. The results revealed that citronella grass, citral, and myrcene produced a low active response when administered at a concentration of 400 μL. Similarly, a 400 μL mixture of citral, myrcene, and citronellal oil in a 6:4:1 ratio significantly reduced host-seeking behavior, with a 42.5% active response and an 18% treatment response. When DEET was tested under the same conditions, the active response was 44%, and the treatment response was 22% at a 400 μL dose. These results indicate that citronella oil is a strong repellent against *A. aegypti*, producing results comparable to DEET [16, 17]. Citronellal derivatives optimized for reduced volatility and milder odor were found to provide longer protection than DEET at the same concentration against *Aedes albopictus* and *Anopheles gambiae* [15].

Azadirachta Indica (Neem)

Neem (*Azadirachta indica*), a member of the Meliaceae family, is recognized for its potent mosquito-repellent properties. Neem oil, derived from the seeds of neem plants, contains a limonid named azedarachin that exhibits repellent and incapacitating effects on insects. Azadirachtin has been effectively used to disrupt mosquito feeding behaviour and oviposition, thereby inhibiting the access of mosquitoes to human hosts [18].

In addition to neem seeds, neem leaves and bark exhibit mosquito-repellent properties. Aqueous crude extracts of neem leaves have demonstrated significant larvicidal activity against *Anopheles stephensi*. Additionally, a methanolic extract of neem seed kernels at a 0.02% concentration has been observed to decrease the hatching success of mosquito eggs and to impede larval development, population expansion, and adult emergence in *Culex pipiens* [19]. Azadirachtin lowers the levels of the insect hormone ecdysone, preventing immature larvae from developing into adults. It also disrupts the sexual communication of adult mosquitoes. Moreover, neem oil creates a layer on the insect's body that blocks the tracheal openings, leading to suffocation [19].

Studies have shown that neem oil can provide 100% protection for up to three hours and substantial protection for several additional hours [20]. Compared to synthetic repellents such as DEET, neem oil offers similarly effective protection against mosquitoes. As a result, neem oil is widely promoted as a natural alternative to DEET [2].

Eucalyptus Citriodora (Lemon Eucalyptus)

Lemon eucalyptus (*Eucalyptus citriodora*), a member of the Myrtaceae family, is well-regarded as an effective mosquito repellent. Originally native to Australia, it is now cultivated in tropical and subtropical regions of Asia. The leaves of this plant are commonly used to produce repellent oil. The primary constituents of eucalyptus oil include eucalyptol, limonene, terpinen-4-ol, citronellal, n-tetradecane, 2,2′-6,6′-tetramethylpiperidin-4-ol, and piperitone [21]. In Australia, PMD is classified as an extract derived from lemon eucalyptus, isolated via hydrodistillation. Experimental findings have indicated that a 30% PMD extract provides a comparable duration of protection against mosquito bites to that of low-dose (5-10%) DEET or picaridin-based repellents [22]. PMD's prolonged protection exceeds that of many other natural products because it is a monoterpene with lower volatility compared to most essential oil components, resulting in slower evaporation after application [2]. A mixture comprising 30% lemon eucalyptus oil was demonstrated to offer complete protection against *Anopheles darling*i for 4 hours in Bolivia, while a 50% extract was found to be fully effective for 6 hours against malaria vectors in Tanzania [23].

Curcuma Aromatica (Wild Turmeric)

Wild turmeric (*Curcuma aromatica*), belonging to the family Zingiberaceae, is commonly found in South Asian regions [24]. Eucalyptol (19.82%), curdione (15.31%), and 2-bornanone (12.25%) have been identified as the major phytochemical constituents in the essential oil of *C. aromatica* leaves [25]. Pitasawat et al. [26] showed that a 95% ethanol extract from this plant was highly effective in repelling *Aedes togoi* mosquitoes on human subjects, with ED_{50} and ED_{95} values of 0.061 and 1.55 mg/cm2, respectively. When applied topically at a concentration of 25% (w/w), the extract provided 3.5 hours of protection against mosquito bites. No dermal irritation or adverse effects were reported among the participants. Additionally, the ethanolic extract has shown protective efficacy against other mosquito species, including *A.s subalbatus*, *Cx. quinquefasciatus*, and *Cx. tritaeniorhynchus* under field conditions [24]. Choochote et al., [27] conducted a study on the antimosquito properties of hexane rhizome extracts and essential oil from *C. aromatica*, targeting *Aedes aegypti* mosquitoes. The results revealed that the oil exhibited notably greater larvicidal activity (LC_{50} of 36.30 ppm) against 4th instar larvae of *A. aegypti* compared to the hexane extracts (LC_{50} of 57.15 ppm). Conversely, the hexane extract demonstrated slightly stronger adulticidal activity (LC_{50} of 1.60 µg/mg) against female *A. aegypti* than the essential oil (LC_{50} of 2.86 µg/mg).

2.4 Mechanisms of Toxicity in Natural Repellents

Natural mosquito repellents employ various mechanisms to achieve their goal, targeting different aspects of mosquito behavior and physiology. These mechanisms include disrupting olfactory senses, creating antigenic aversions, and interfering with sensory receptors to deter mosquitoes from feeding on humans [28]. Olfactory disruption is the primary mechanism through which natural repellents function. This could lead to changes in insect behavior and migration, thereby reducing the risk of disease transmission. Most repellents disrupt the nasal receptors located on the antennae of mosquitoes, preventing them from detecting human odor and inhibiting their inclination to bite. These receptors play a crucial role in identifying chemical cues, including recognizing human odor. By blocking the normal chemoreception pathway, these repellents render mosquitoes unattracted to humans, as they no longer perceive the characteristic scent associated with human hosts [2].

Essential oils, derived from plant extracts, release volatile compounds that mask or interfere with scents emitted by other organisms, making it challenging for mosquitoes to pinpoint the source of the odor [29, 30]. Terpenoids such as limonene and citronellal, frequently found in essential oils, have been observed to disrupt olfactory receptors on mosquitoes' antennae [31]. This interference can impair the mosquito's ability to detect substances such as carbon dioxide and lactic acid, which are key indicators found in human breath [32].

Repellent plants can also exert physiological effects on mosquitoes by influencing nervous system activity, as well as development and reproduction cycles. Citronellal and eucalyptol, for instance, have been shown to interfere with the neural systems of mosquitoes, leading to behavioral abnormalities and a decrease in biting activity [32]. These chemicals disrupt the transmission of signals between nerve cells by targeting master pathways in mosquitoes, thereby preventing them from locating and feeding on hosts.

Table 16.1 Overview of primary active compounds and repellency spectrum of natural insect repellents

Insect repellent	Primary active compounds	Repellency spectrum	References
Citronella	Citronellal, Citronellol	*Cx .pipiens, A. aegypti, A. albopictus and A. gambiae*	[15], [16]
Neem	Azedarachtin	*A. stephensi, Cx. pipiens*	[19]
Lemon eucalyptus	PMD	*A. darlingi*	[8], [23]
Wild turmeric	Eucalyptol	*A.s subalbatus, Cx. quinquefasciatus, Cx. Tritaeniorhynchus, A. aegypti*	[24], [27]

Neem plants disrupt insect growth, act as antifeedants, and exhibit toxicity to insects primarily due to the presence of a complex tetranortriterpenoid limonoid [33]. Azadirachtin, a component of neem oil, interferes with mosquito development and reproduction by targeting their endocrine system, leading to developmental abnormalities [2]. Permethrin, extracted from the flowers of *Chrysanthemum cinerarifolium*, first stimulates the insect's nervous system by blocking sodium channels. This is followed by the inhibition of acetylcholinesterase, leading to lethal paralysis [33].

Citronella oil has been studied for its ability to act as a repellent by inhibiting acetylcholinesterase activity in mosquitoes [34]. Acetylcholinesterase is an enzyme crucial for neuromuscular transmission; inhibiting this enzyme can disrupt the normal nerve function in mosquitoes. As a result, mosquitoes may struggle to detect hosts and exhibit abnormal feeding behaviors. While it has been established that there are numerous ways in which natural repellents exert an effect on mosquitoes, a more detailed scientific investigation into the exact mechanisms of action would also be useful in maximizing their effectiveness and designing complementary mosquito control approaches.

2.5 Safety and Toxicity Concerns

Although plant-based repellents offer many benefits, thorough research into their safety and toxicity profiles is highly warranted. While the United States Food and Drug Administration states that synthetic repellents are safe for infants as young as two months, plant-derived lemon eucalyptus oil and its active ingredient PMD are not recommended for use in children under the age of 3 [35]. Furthermore, essential oil poisoning has been reported at low doses and both citronella and eucalyptus oil have been linked to human deaths [36, 37]. Several researchers have also identified the reproductive toxicity of natural insecticides on experimental animals [38]. As the "appeal to nature" fallacy drives consumers towards botanical products, appropriate safety testing is often neglected. However, it is essential to thoroughly investigate plants with potential repellent properties for any adverse effects before introducing them as alternative products. Furthermore, research has demonstrated that formulation plays a significant role in the longevity and safety of repellents [39]. Therefore, emphasis should also be placed on identifying the optimal choice of carriers, stability of active ingredients, effective concentrations, and cut-off levels to design effective formulations.

2.6 Market Potential of Natural Mosquito Repellents

Numerous natural mosquito repellents are available in the market. Most plant-derived repellent products provide less than 2 hours of complete repellent efficacy [40]. Over half of the topical mosquito repellents incorporate natural oils, either on their own or combined with synthetic ingredients [41]. Currently, citronella (5–10%) is among the most extensively used natural repellents; such concentrations are lower than those found in many other commercial repellents. Originally extracted for perfume production, citronella was first employed by the Indian Army to deter mosquitoes in the early 1900s. It was officially registered for commercial use in the USA in 1948 [2]. There are also various eucalyptus-based products available. Quwenling, an insect repellent sold in China, offers protection against *Anopheles* mosquitoes comparable to DEET and has supplanted the widely used synthetic repellent dimethyl phthalate. Quwenling contains a blend of PMD, citronellol, and isopulegone. Moreover, Mosiguard Natural, an internationally distributed repellent, contains 50% eucalyptus oil, while Buzz Away, a citronellal-based repellent, is marketed in China. These examples underscore the commercial viability of natural products in the repellent industry [2].

Consumer demand for sustainably sourced, plant-based products—particularly those using essential oils—has been steadily increasing [7]. However, a major obstacle to the widespread adoption of natural repellents is their limited duration of effectiveness, largely due to the high volatility of essential oil components. To address this, emphasis must be placed on developing physiologically acceptable vehicles/formulations that can extend the protective duration of these repellents and unlock their full market potential. For instance, a recent study by Hazarika et al. [42] has resulted in the creation of a mosquito-repellent cream formulated with essential oils from clove, citronella, and lemongrass. The efficacy of this innovative product was found to be comparable to a 12% N,N-diethyl benzamide commercial cream, providing a total protection time of 228 minutes [42]. These positive findings further reinforce the potential for natural repellents in the global market.

3. Conclusion

Natural mosquito repellents were found to possess significant activity and offer numerous benefits. Both synthetic and plant-based mosquito repellents provide various avenues for controlling mosquito-borne diseases. Although synthetic repellents have been associated with unwarranted toxicity and environmental harm, it remains unclear whether natural products can entirely circumvent these issues. Moreover, despite the potential of plant-based alternatives, the comparative benefits of natural versus artificial repellents remain inadequately explored. Extensive research is still needed to understand the precise mechanisms and potential adverse effects of both synthetic and natural repellent formulations on mosquitoes and other fauna in the environment. Careful evaluation of their toxicity and environmental impact is crucial to prevent misuse under the guise of improved mosquito control.

REFERENCES

1. A. Nandwana et al., "Evaluation of mosquito repellent activity of marigold petals extract," Naturalista Campano, vol. 28, no. 1, pp. 943–945, Feb. 2024.

2. H. F. Khater et al., "Commercial mosquito repellents and their safety concerns" in Malaria, F. H. Kasenga, Eds. IntechOpen, 2019. doi: https://doi.org/10.5772/intechopen.87436.

3. M. S. Butler, "The role of natural product chemistry in drug discovery," J. Nat. Prod., vol. 67, no. 12, pp. 2141–2153, Dec. 2004, doi: https://doi.org/10.1021/np040106y.

4. P. J. Weldon, J. R. Aldrich, J. A. Klun, J. E. Oliver, and M. Debboun, "Benzoquinones from millipedes deter mosquitoes and elicit self-anointing in capuchin monkeys (Cebus spp.)," Naturwissenschaften, vol. 90, no. 7, pp. 301–304, Jul. 2003, doi: https://doi.org/10.1007/s00114-003-0427-2.

5. A. B. Attygalle, S. C. Xu, J. Meinwald, and T. Eisner, "Defensive secretion of the millipede Floridobolus Penneri," J. Nat. Prod, vol. 56, no. 10, pp. 1700–1706, Oct. 1993, doi: https://doi.org/10.1021/np50100a007.

6. C. Grison, D. Carrasco, F. Pelissier, and A. Moderc, "Reflexion on bio-sourced mosquito repellents: nature, activity, and preparation," Front. Ecol. Evol., vol. 8, Feb. 2020, doi: https://doi.org/10.3389/fevo.2020.00008.

7. F. Eshun, J. Osei-Owusu, and W. K. Heve, "Public perception of the use of natural versus synthetic mosquito repellents in Ghana," J. Environ. and Sustain. Dev., vol. 3, no. 1, pp. 1–10, Aug. 2023.

8. M. F. Maia and S. J. Moore, "Plant-based insect repellents: a review of their efficacy, development and testing," Malar., vol. 10, no. S1, Mar. 2011, doi: https://doi.org/10.1186/1475-2875-10-s1-s11.

9. S. Gul, S. Ibrahim, N. Wasif, A. Zafari, A. Zafar, and R. Syed, "Mosquito repellents: Killing mosquitoes or yourselves," in Environ. Sci., Med., 2013.

10. J. Islam, K. Zaman, S. Duarah, P. S. Raju, and P. Chattopadhyay, "Mosquito repellents: An insight into the chronological perspectives and novel discoveries," Acta Trop., vol. 167, pp. 216–230, Mar. 2017, doi: https://doi.org/10.1016/j.actatropica.2016.12.031.

11. D. Shukla, S. Wijayapala, and P. Vankar, "Effective mosquito repellent from plant based formulation," Int. J. Mosq., vol. 5, no. 1, pp. 19–24, 2018,

12. H. P. Kusumaningrum, M. Zainuri, H. Endrawati, and E. D. Purbajanti, "Characterization of citronella grass essential oil of Cymbopogon winterianus from Batang region, Indonesia," J. Phys. Conf. Ser., vol. 1524, no. 1, p. 012057, Apr. 2020, doi: https://doi.org/10.1088/1742-6596/1524/1/012057.

13. S. N. H. M. Azmin, A. S. A. Halim, and M. S. M. Nor, "Physicochemical analysis of natural herbal medicated ointment enriched with Cymbopogon nardus and virgin coconut oil," IOP Conf. Ser.: Earth Environ. Sci., vol. 765, no. 1, p. 012040, May 2021, doi: https://doi.org/10.1088/1755-1315/765/1/012040.

14. K. Nakahara, N. S. Alzoreky, T. Yoshihashi, H. T. T. Nguyen, and G. Trakoontivakorn, "Chemical composition and antifungal activity of essential oil from Cymbopogon nardus (citronella grass)," JARQ, vol. 37, no. 4, pp. 249–252, 2013, doi: https://doi.org/10.6090/jarq.37.249.

15. I. Iovinella, B. Caputo, P. Cobre, M. Manica, A. Mandoli, and F. R. Dani, "Advances in mosquito repellents: Effectiveness of citronellal derivatives in laboratory and field trials," Pest Manag. Sci., vol. 78, no. 12, pp. 5106–5112, Sep. 2022, doi: https://doi.org/10.1002/ps.7127.

16. W. S. Hsu, J. H. Yen, and Y. S. Wang, "Formulas of components of citronella oil against mosquitoes (Aedes aegypti)," J. Environ. Sci. Health., Part B, vol. 48, no. 11, pp. 1014–1019, Nov. 2013, doi: https://doi.org/10.1080/03601234.2013.816613.

17. K. Harismah, D. Vitasari, M. Mirzaei, A. M. Fuadi, and Y. H. Aryanto, "Protection capacity of mosquito repellent ink from citronella (Cymbopogon nardus L.) and clove leaf oils (Syzygium aromaticum) againts Aedes aegypti," AIP Conf. Proc., vol. 1855, no. 1, 2017, doi: https://doi.org/10.1063/1.4985468.

18. B. Singh, P. R. Singh, and M. K. Mohanty, "Toxicity of a plant based mosquito repellent/killer," Interdiscip. Toxicol., vol. 5, no. 4, pp. 184–191, Dec. 2012, doi: https://doi.org/10.2478/v10102-012-0031-4.

19. G. Brahmachari, "Neem-An omnipotent plant: A retrospection," ChemBioChem, vol. 5, no. 4, pp. 408–421, Apr. 2004, doi: https://doi.org/10.1002/cbic.200300749.

20. E. Abiy, T. Gebre-Michael, M. Balkew, and G. Medhin, "Repellent efficacy of DEET, MyggA, neem (Azedirachta

indica) oil and chinaberry (Melia azedarach) oil against Anopheles arabiensis, the principal malaria vector in Ethiopia," Malar. J., vol. 14, no. 1, May 2015, doi: https://doi.org/10.1186/s12936-015-0705-4.

21. F. Manzoor, N. Naz, S. A. Malik, S. Arshad, and B. S. Siddiqui, "Chemical composition of essential oils derived from eucalyptus and lemongrass and their antitermitic activities angainst Microtermes mycophagus (Desneux).," Asian J. Chem., vol. 25, no. 5, pp. 2405–2408, Jan. 2013, doi: https://doi.org/10.14233/ajchem.2013.13335.

22. C. E. Webb and I. M. Hess, "A review of recommendations on the safe and effective use of topical mosquito repellents," PHRP, vol. 26, no. 5, Dec. 2016, doi: https://doi.org/10.17061/phrp2651657.

23. S. J. Moore, A. Lenglet, and N. Hill, "Field evaluation of three plant-based insect repellents against malaria vectors in Vaca Diez province, the Bolivian Amazon.," Malar J., vol. 18, no. 2, pp. 107–10, Jun. 2002.

24. A. Sikha, A. Harini, and L. Hegde Prakash, "Pharmacological activities of wild turmeric (Curcuma aromatica Salisb): A review Sikha A, Harini A, Hegde Prakash L," JPP, vol. 3, no. 5, pp. 1–4, 2015.

25. T. A. Aminu Sulhath, N. U. Visakh, Berin Pathrose, and Shiela Betsy George, "Investigating the insecticidal properties of essential oils extracted from wild turmeric (Curcuma aromatica salisb) leaves waste against three key stored product pests," Sustain. Chem. Pharm., vol. 38, pp. 101482–101482, Apr. 2024, doi: https://doi.org/10.1016/j.scp.2024.101482.

26. B. Pitasawat et al., "Repellency of aromatic turmeric Curcuma aromatica under laboratory and field conditions.," J Vector Ecol., vol. 28, no. 2, pp. 234–40, Dec. 2003.

27. W. Choochote et al., "Chemical composition and anti-mosquito potential of rhizome extract and volatile oil derived from Curcuma aromatica against Aedes aegypti (Diptera: Culicidae).," J Vector Ecol., vol. 30, no. 2, pp. 302–9, Dec. 2005.

28. F. Liu et al., "A dual-target molecular mechanism of pyrethrum repellency against mosquitoes," Nat. Commun., vol. 12, no. 1, p. 2553, May 2021, doi: https://doi.org/10.1038/s41467-021-22847-0.

29. G. Paluch, L. Bartholomay, and J. Coats, "Mosquito repellents: A review of chemical structure diversity and olfaction," Pest Manag. Sci., vol. 66, no. 9, pp. 925–935, Aug. 2010, doi: https://doi.org/10.1002/ps.1974.

30. S. A. Kreher, J. Y. Kwon, and J. R. Carlson, "The molecular basis of odor coding in the Drosophila larva," Neuron, vol. 46, no. 3, pp. 445–456, May 2005, doi: https://doi.org/10.1016/j.neuron.2005.04.007.

31. Z. Wang et al., "QSAR study of mosquito repellents from terpenoid with a six-member-ring," Bioorg. Med. Chem. Lett., vol. 18, no. 9, pp. 2854–2859, May 2008, doi: https://doi.org/10.1016/j.bmcl.2008.03.091.

32. E. Deletre, T. Martin, C. Duménil, and F. Chandre, "Insecticide resistance modifies mosquito response to DEET and natural repellents," Parasit. Vectors., vol. 12, no. 1, Mar. 2019, doi: https://doi.org/10.1186/s13071-019-3343-9.

33. J. H. Diaz, "Chemical and plant-based insect repellents: Efficacy, safety, and toxicity," Wilderness Environ Med, vol. 27, no. 1, pp. 153–163, Mar. 2016, doi: https://doi.org/10.1016/j.wem.2015.11.007.

34. S. Gade et al., "Acetylcholinesterase inhibitory activity of Stigmasterol & Hexacosanol is responsible for larvicidal and repellent properties of Chromolaena odorata," BBA, vol. 1861, no. 3, pp. 541–550, Mar. 2017, doi: https://doi.org/10.1016/j.bbagen.2016.11.044.

35. M. Shelomi, "Who's afraid of DEET? Fearmongering in papers on botanical repellents," Malar. J., vol. 19, no. 1, Apr. 2020, doi: https://doi.org/10.1186/s12936-020-03217-5.

36. A. Woolf, "Essential oil poisoning," J. Toxicol. Clin. Toxicol., vol. 37, no. 6, pp. 721–727, Jan. 1999, doi: https://doi.org/10.1081/clt-100102450.

37. L. Goodyer and R. H. Behrens, "Short report: The safety and toxicity of insect repellents.," Am J Trop Med Hyg., vol. 59, no. 2, pp. 323–324, Aug. 1998, doi: https://doi.org/10.4269/ajtmh.1998.59.323.

38. A. T. H. Mossa, S. M. M. Mohafrash, and N. Chandrasekaran, "Safety of natural insecticides: Toxic effects on experimental animals," Biomed Res. Int., vol. 2018, no. 4308054, pp. 1–17, Oct. 2018, doi: https://doi.org/10.1155/2018/4308054.

39. E. Lupi, C. Hatz, and P. Schlagenhauf, "The efficacy of repellents against Aedes, Anopheles, Culex and Ixodes spp. – A literature review," Travel Med. Infect. Dis., vol. 11, no. 6, pp. 374–411, Nov. 2013, doi: https://doi.org/10.1016/j.tmaid.2013.10.005.

40. N. Misni, Z. M. Nor, and R. Ahmad, "Repellent effect of microencapsulated essential oil in lotion formulation against mosquito bites," J. Vector Borne Dis., vol. 54, no. 1, pp. 44–53, Jan. 2017, doi: https://doi.org/10.4103/0972-9062.203183.

41. W. L. Lo, K. L. Mok, and S. D. Yu Pui Ming, "Which insect repellents should we choose? Implications from results of local market survey and review of current guidelines," Hong Kong J. Emerg. Med., vol. 25, no. 5, pp. 272–280, Apr. 2018, doi: https://doi.org/10.1177/1024907918773630.

42. H. Hazarika et al., "The fabrication and assessment of mosquito repellent cream for outdoor protection," Sci. Rep., vol. 12, no. 1, p. 2180, Feb. 2022, doi: https://doi.org/10.1038/

Transformative Applied Research in Computing, Engineering, Science and Technology – Dr. Damayanthi Dahanayake et al. (eds)
© 2024 Taylor & Francis Group, London, ISBN 978-1-041-01782-0

17

Analysing the S&P 500 Index in Relation to the Google Trends of Stock Market Related Words in the United States

T.A.H. Dilpriya*
Department of Computer and Data Science,
Faculty of Computing, NSBM Green University,
Sri Lanka

G.H.J. Lanel, M. T. M. Perera and B. V. N. C. Vidanage
Department of Mathematics,
Faculty of Applied Science, University of Sri Jayewardenepura,
Sri Lanka

Abstract

The Standard and Poor's five hundred (S&P 500) index, comprising five hundred leading companies, is a key benchmark for the New York stock market, reflecting the overall health of the New York Stock Exchange. It influences investor decisions, guides economic policies, and serves as a performance indicator for portfolios and mutual funds. This study explores the correlation between Google search term trends and the S&P 500 index over the past two decades and five years separately. Various keywords related to economic factors and global events were analysed in this paper. The data of Google trends were only related to the United States population. Also, Minitab and R- software used to the analysis under the methodology. The research offers valuable insights for investors, utilizing time series analysis and fitted line plots. The findings indicate a cubic relationship between most of these keywords and the index value. "Employment" shows the strongest correlation, suggesting it could be a reliable indicator of stock market movements. In contrast, "oil prices" displayed the highest relative error, indicating its limited predictability for stock market trends. Additionally, the study proposes adjusted fitted models with modified constant values to potentially improve accuracy and better capture the relationship between search term trends and the S&P 500 index.

Keywords

S&P 500 index, Stock market, Google trends words, Time series analysis, R programming

1. Introduction

The S&P 500 index, a key United States (US) stock market index, tracks five hundred major companies across diverse sectors, weighted by market capitalization. It serves as a benchmark for the US stock market's performance and holds global significance. Investors use it to gauge market health and guide investments. Numerous investment products, like

*Corresponding author: hirushi.d@nsbm.ac.lk

DOI: 10.1201/9781003616368-17

index funds and Exchange Traded Funds (ETFs), are based on the S&P 500's composition and performance. The S&P 500 index reflects the performance of 500 leading publicly traded companies in the US, serving as a key indicator of the nation's economic health. It offers investors a broad view of the equity market, guiding investment decisions. Early trend detection in the S&P 500 helps investors anticipate market directions, enabling informed decisions and the ability to capitalize on emerging opportunities. Early identification of S&P 500 index movements benefits investors in various ways. It allows predicting trends, making informed investment decisions, managing risks, and reducing losses. Capitalizing on emerging trends can lead to better returns, and the predictive advantage offers a competitive edge, potentially outperforming peers in the market.

2. Literature Review

The study of stock market prices and their determinants has long been a central focus in the field of finance. This literature review synthesizes findings from several key studies that explore various aspects of stock market dynamics, including the use of statistical models, the impact of index constituents, the role of taxation, and the effectiveness of monetary policy.

2.1 Stock Market Analysis Using Statistical Models

Alp, Ozbek, and Canbaloglu (2023) utilized the extended Kalman Filter to analyze stock market prices in the US and China [1]. Their study demonstrated the efficacy of this advanced filtering technique in predicting stock price movements, thereby providing a robust tool for investment analysis [2-5]. Similarly, Asem and Alam (2012) explored the role of S&P 500 index constituents in tracking the US equity market, emphasizing the significance of individual stock performance on the overall market index [6]. These research studies primarily focused on stock market prices and developed various tools to support analysis. However, they primarily explore established markets like the US and China, leaving other emerging or less developed markets underexplored, where different dynamics may influence stock behavior and the effectiveness of predictive models.

2.2 Index Replacements and Market Tracking

Beneish and Whaley (2002) examined the effects of S&P 500 index replacements on market dynamics [7]. They found that stock prices tend to exhibit significant movements upon inclusion or exclusion from the index, impacting investor behavior and market liquidity. Siegel and Schwartz (2006) provided a long-term perspective on

the returns of the original S&P 500 companies, highlighting the importance of historical performance in understanding current market trends [8]. While insightful, the literature does not delve into how other global indices or non-US markets react to index changes, nor does it explore how newer forms of indices (such as ESG or tech driven indices) might influence market behavior differently.

2.3 Taxation and Financial Markets

The influence of federal taxation on financial markets is another critical area of research [9-13]. Glick (2013) and Brave (2011) discussed the Federal Reserve's role and its interventions during financial crises, outlining how monetary policies affect market stability [14,15]. Burman, Gale, and Rohaly (2013) analyzed effective tax rates and their implications for tax reform, providing insights into how tax policies can influence investment decisions and economic behavior. Blanchard and Perotti (2002) and Lambert (2004) explored the complexities of federal income taxation, including its impact on individual and corporate behavior [16,17]. These studies underscore the interplay between taxation, economic incentives, and market outcomes.

2.4 Monetary Policy and Market Behavior

Campbell, Covitz, and Nelson (2011) evaluated the Term Asset-Backed Securities Loan Facility (TALF) and its effectiveness in stabilizing securitization markets during economic downturns [18]. Afonso and Armenter (2019) and Clark and McCracken (2001) investigated the evolution and forecasting of the federal funds rate, emphasizing the challenges and strategies in monetary policy implementation [19]. Arachchige et. al (2021) applied Artificial Neural Network on Federal Funds Rate [20]. Hamilton and Wu (2012) further examined alternative monetary policy tools in a zero lower bound environment, highlighting their potential to influence market behavior during periods of economic stress [21].

2.5 Effective Tax Rates and Policy Analysis

Wu and Zhu (2018) and Splinter (2019) provided comprehensive analyses of effective federal tax rates, offering valuable frameworks for policymakers and analysts to assess the impact of tax policies on different income groups and economic activities [22]. Atik and Austin (2017) extended this analysis by examining tax rates within the federal individual income tax system, highlighting disparities and suggesting avenues for reform [23,24]. Jayarathna and Lanel (2021) demonstrated the application of mathematical modeling in real-world scenarios [25], a concept further utilized by Dilpriya and

Lanel (2023) in their review of the efficacy of Federal Bank policies using time series analysis [26]. The literature primarily focuses on stock market analysis, emphasizing key areas such as statistical modeling, index dynamics, taxation, and monetary policy.

The integrated findings from these studies offer a holistic understanding of the factors influencing stock market behavior, providing valuable insights for investors, policymakers, and researchers in the field of finance. In summary, while the literature provides valuable insights into developed markets and established financial mechanisms, there is a lack of focus on emerging markets, newer indices, evolving tax policies, and unconventional monetary tools, all of which are becoming increasingly relevant in today's global financial landscape.

3. Methodology

3.1 The S&P 500 Index Calculation Procedure

The S&P 500 is a prominent index that tracks the performance of 500 major US stocks based on their market capitalization. To calculate the index, the market capitalization of each stock is determined by multiplying its current stock price by the total number of outstanding shares. The index divisor, a constant, is then computed to maintain index continuity despite changes in its components. The index value is derived by dividing the total market capitalization of the index by the index divisor, and adjustments are made for any changes in the index components, such as adding or removing stocks. Standard & Poor's, a subsidiary of S&P Global Inc., is responsible for computing the S&P 500 index. It is widely used as a benchmark to assess the performance of large-cap US stocks and to gauge the overall health of the US economy.

3.2 The Google Trend of the Word

Google Trends is a tool offered by Google that enables users to examine the popularity of specific search terms or topics within a specific period. It offers insights into the relative search interest for a particular keyword. It has changed over time. Additionally, Google Trends provides supplementary features like regional interest, related queries, and related topics to further explore the data. In summary, Google Trends is a valuable resource for understanding and analyzing trends in online search behavior by providing information on search volume and keyword popularity.

3.3 The Fitted Line Model

A fitted line plot, or regression line plot, visually represents the relationship between two variables by plotting data pairs on a scatter plot. It includes a regression line indicating the trend: upward for positive, downward for negative relationships. Created using statistical methods like linear regression, tools like Minitab and R-Software are commonly used.

3.4 Minitab and R - Software

Minitab is a user-friendly statistical software for data analysis, offering tools like hypothesis testing and regression analysis. In R, using ggplot2 and lubridate for time series plots involves loading libraries, importing data in POSIXct format, setting up a base plot with ggplot, specifying variables for axes, customizing aesthetics, adding geom_line for a line plot, and enhancing with additional layers like smoothing lines or confidence intervals. The S&P 500 index values from the past twenty years and Google trend data were obtained from Macro Trends historical data and Google. Inc respectively.

3.5 Error Determination and New Model Identification

Three relative errors were determined for each keyword, and the most optimal line plot was chosen based on the smallest error. The process involved analyzing data to find suitable line plots, generating new ones by modifying constants, and comparing their relative errors. The analysis focused on monthly data from the past two decades and weekly data from the past five years, calculating best-fitted line plots for each data set.

4. Research Design

Figure 17.1 Show indices research design for studying the S&P 500 index, divided into two parts. The first section uses Minitab software to create fitted line plots, evaluating linear, quadratic, and cubic models. Relative errors help identify the best model for each category in the last two decades and past five years. The second section analyzes Google trend word fluctuations using time series techniques, covering the past five years.

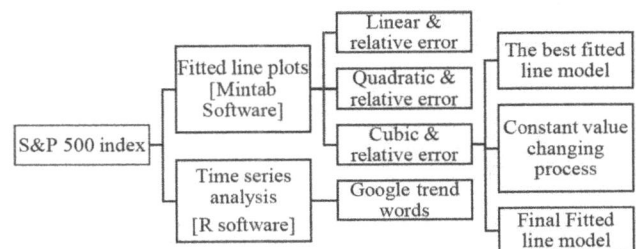

Fig. 17.1 The research design of the S&P 500 index analysis

5. Results

5.1 Asset

Assets like stocks provide economic benefits through trading on exchanges. Prices reflect financial performance, global trends, and market sentiment, impacting capital movement. Google trends in Fig. 17.2. show "assets" rising steadily over five years with annual fluctuations in the USA, peaking between 30 and 100.

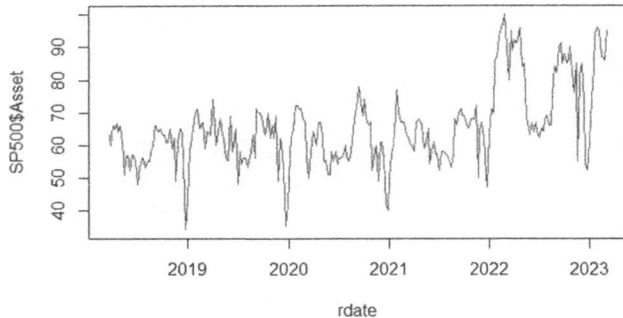

Fig. 17.2 The Google trends of the word "asset" over the last five years

5.2 Benefits

The stock market and benefits are closely linked, were financial performance impacts stock prices and portfolios. Positive results increase demand, while poor performance decreases it. External factors also influence stocks. Market performance affects company benefits: high prices support investment; low prices may reduce benefits. Investors should consider performance, benefits, and trends. Google Trends data in Fig. 17.3. for "benefits" from 2018 to 2023 shows a peak around mid-2020, with a gradual overall increase despite yearly fluctuations.

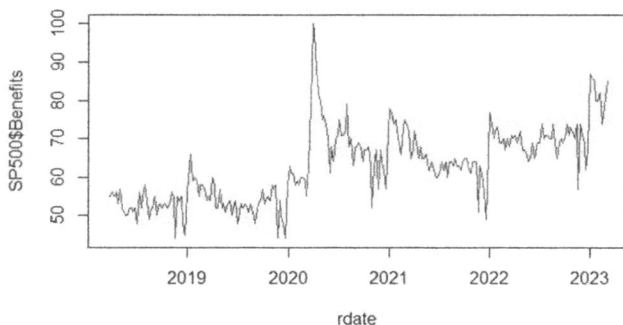

Fig. 17.3 The Google trends of the word "benefits" over the last five years

5.3 Budget

The relationship between a company's budget and the stock market is intricate, involving financial performance,

economic variables, and news events. Based on Fig. 17.4., the word "budget" has a zigzag pattern in Google searches. The data points typically range from 60 to 100, with the lowest value occurring at the end of 2021. Most of the values fall between 70 and 90. Additionally, there is a sharp increase in the Google trend for the word "budget" after 2022.

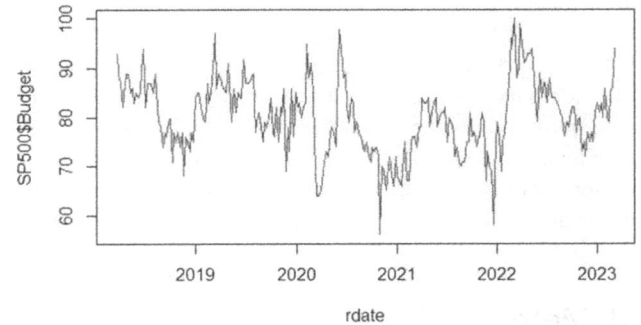

Fig. 17.4 The Google trends of the word "budget" over the last five years

5.4 Charity

Charity and the stock exchange have different goals but can connect through corporate social responsibility and philanthropy, benefiting society. Figure 17.5 shows a function that gradually declines from 2018 to 2020, but there is a sudden increase in the Google search trend for the word "charity" in the middle of 2020. The values then decrease until the middle of 2021, but they start to rise again after 2022. Most of the data falls between the ranges of 50 to 80.

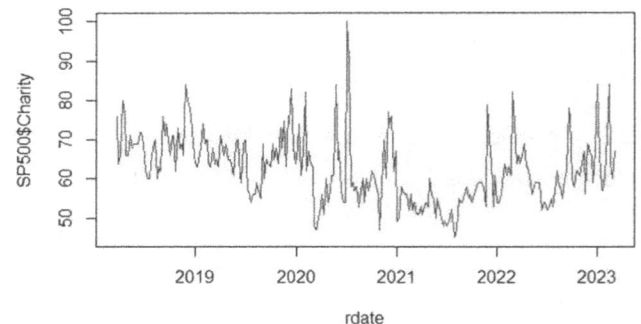

Fig. 17.5 The Google trends of the word "charity" over the last five years

5.5 Gross Domestic Product (GDP)

GDP fluctuations can notably affect the stock market due to their complex interdependence. Economic growth, investor sentiment, interest rates, and corporate earnings are crucial factors influencing this correlation. Figure 17.6 illustrates the Google search trend for the term "GDP" over the last five years.

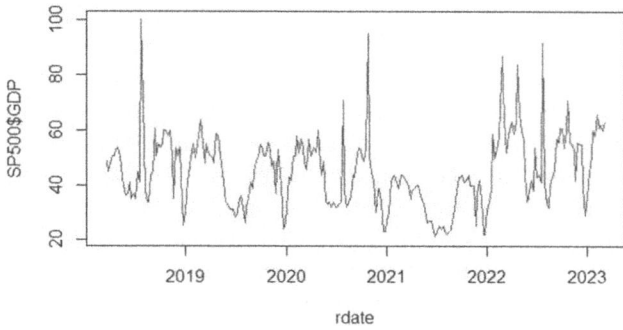

Fig. 17.6 The Google trends of the word "GDP" over the last five years

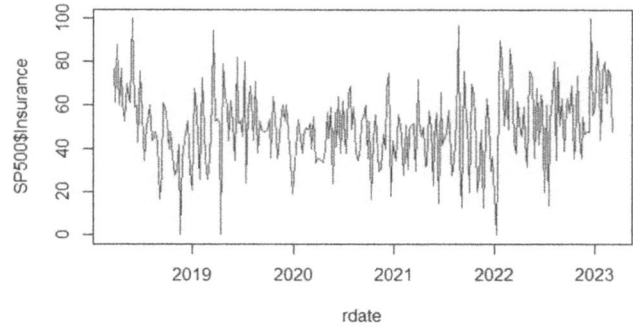

Fig. 17.8 The Google trends of the word "insurance" over the last five years

5.6 Inflation

Inflation's effect on the stock market is complex. Moderate inflation indicates growth and boosts stocks, but high inflation causes instability, concerns investors, and impacts interest rate-sensitive sectors. Currency erosion affects export-reliant firms. Figure 17.7 illustrates the Google search trend for the term "inflation" over the past five years. The data indicates a gradual increase in search interest until mid2022, followed by a decline toward the end of the year. The maximum value for this trend is 100.

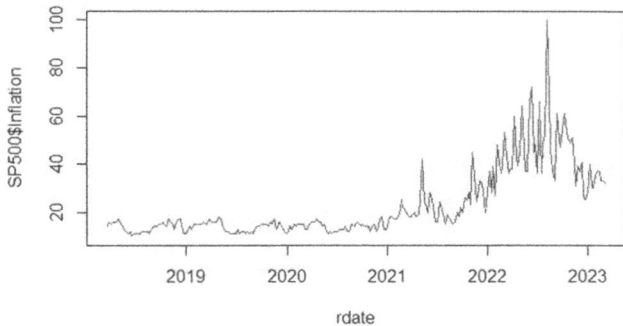

Fig. 17.7 The Google trends of the word "inflation" over the last five years

5.7 Insurance

Insurance firms invest premiums in the stock market for higher returns. Their performance affects the stock market; major company losses cause a decline, while profits lead to a rally. Both industries operate independently with unique features. Figure 17.8 depicting the Google search trend for the term "insurance" indicates that there has been no significant upward or downward trend over time. The data primarily falls within the range of 20 to 80. The years 2018, 2019, and 2022 had the lowest values recorded.

5.8 Monopoly

Monopolies wield significant market control, impacting prices and consumer options. Their stock market ties

fluctuate with regulatory shifts, tech advancements, and consumer trends, shaping stock values. Investors favor their stability and profits, yet antitrust laws promote market competition, potentially leading to breakup or asset sales. These concepts are distinct, each influenced by specific factors. Google search data in Fig. 17.9. shows declining annual interest in "monopoly," with peak values diminishing from 30 to 90, peaking notably in 2019.

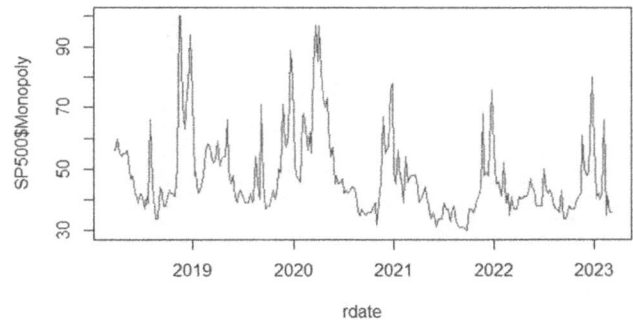

Fig. 17.9 The Google trends of the word "monopoly" over the last five years

5.9 Oil Price

Rising oil prices boost energy companies' stocks, while falling prices have the opposite effect. Additionally, oil price fluctuations indirectly influence interest rates, consumer spending, and market performance. In 2018, the Google search trend for "oil prices" remained almost unchanged, as shown in Fig. 17.10. However, there was a sudden spike in this trend in 2020, which quickly dropped off after a short period. The same pattern was observed again in 2022, but the spike was lower than the one observed in 2020.

Table 17.1 shows optimal models for the relationship between Google trend keywords and the S&P 500 index over twenty and five years. Most keywords have a cubic relationship, while "benefits," "budget," "GDP," "utility," and "capital" have quadratic relationships. "Oil prices" show a linear relationship. "Employment" has the lowest

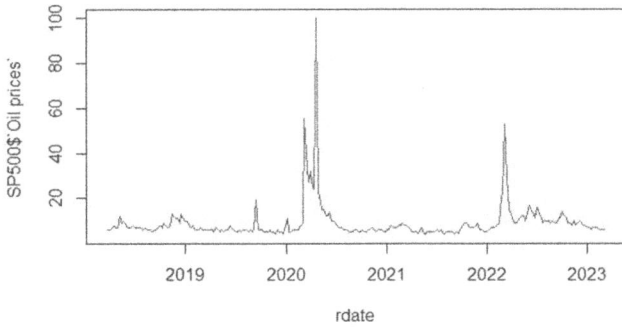

Fig. 17.10 The Google trends of the word "oil price" over the last five years

relative error, indicating a strong correlation, whereas "oil prices" have the highest relative error.

6. Discussion

Utilizing Google Trends, Minitab, and R, historical data from Macro Trends aids in visualizing and understanding economic concepts and stock performance. This analysis links economic factors like GDP, inflation, and oil prices with stock prices, highlighting the importance of a company's financial health. Visualizing these relationships underscores the need for cautious, data-driven investment decisions in volatile markets. The results emphasize the dynamic relationship between economic factors and the S&P 500 index, using Google Trends data. Rising search interest in assets like stocks highlights their role in market sentiment and capital movement. Terms such as "benefits" and "budget" fluctuate with global events and economic conditions, while "charity" spiked in mid-2020, likely due to increased corporate social responsibility during the COVID-19 pandemic. The correlation between GDP, inflation, and stock market performance is notable, with predictive models showing mostly cubic relationships between keywords and the S&P 500. "Oil prices," however, demonstrate a linear relationship. Although search trends for terms like "monopoly" and "insurance" were inconsistent, the analysis underscores the influence of economic factors

Table 17.1 The predicted models for S&P 500 index by considering the relative errors

Google Trend Words (x)	S&P 500 Index (y) [2000: 2023]	S&P 500 Index (y) [2018:2023]
Asset	$- 58922.42965 + 2588x - 35.98x^2 + 0.1640x^3$	$4512.01569 - 81.1x + 1.226x^2 - 0.00448x^3$
Benefits	$- 69.24118 + 76.39x - 0.5348x^2$	$408.2439 - 0.6x + 2.278x^2 - 0.02025x^3$
Budget	$6485.9614 - 114.2x + 0.6143x^2$	$44718.8443 + 1919x - 25.19x^2 + 0.1085x^3$
Charity	$19536.476 - 654.0x + 7.925x^2 - 0.03162x^3$	$8629.61456 - 142.1x + 0.8732x^2$
Employment	$10030.90388 - 313.7x + 3.90 X^2 - 0.01597x^3$	$4858.66614 + 513.8x - 9.489x^2 + 0.0514 X^3$
GDP	$3245.65743 - 63.02x + 0.7101x^2$	$7181.53884 - 220.9x + 3.730x^2 - 0.01928x^3$
Inflation	$2566.8648 - 63.14x + 2.738x^2 - 0.02055x^3$	$774.00547 + 217.7x - 4.273x^2 + 0.02452x^3$
Insurance	$71320.085 - 2849x + 38.07x^2 - 0.1654x^3$	$3537.78508 - 15.44 X + 0.1473x^2$
Monopoly	$4506.2746 - 171.4x + 3.157x^2 - 0.01818x^3$	$9545.9787 - 298.9x + 4.497x^2 - 0.02251x^3$
Oil Prices	$2070.2329 - 4.844x$	$3162.77975 - 13.29x + 0.0769x^2 - 0.000183x^3$
Phillps Curve	$1841.34658 + 60.61x - 1.887x^2 + 0.01264x^3$	$3170.29604 + 5.544x - 0.1329x^2$
Social Security	$696.5982 + 282.6x - 7.264x^2 + 0.04699x^3$	$5354.090176 - 186.6x + 3.841x^2 - 0.02137x^3$
Utility	$4300.88573 - 46.14x + 0.1544x^2$	$68148.2629 - 2608x + 34.10x^2 - 0.1452x^3$
Welfare	$22364.85 - 786.4x + 9.971x^2 - 0.04186x^3$	$5996.3142 + 571.1x - 10.14x^2 + 0.05423x^3$
Bankruptcy	$2937.00835 - 70.56x + 0.7538x^2 - 0.001466x^3$	$11721.37039 - 345.9x + 4.325x^2 - 0.01738x^3$
Business Cycle	$1816.36304 + 132.0x - 5.682x^2 + 0.04331x^3$	$3164.05644 - 5.027x + 0.1876x^2 - 0.001547x^3$
Capital	$16955.5589 - 373.4x + 2.308x^2$	$3305.29463 - 19.78x + 0.5660x^2 - 0.004170x^3$
Consumer Price Index	$8116.2249 - 313.4x + 4.852x^2 - 0.02338x^3$	$2280.54944 + 87.58x - 1.216x^2 + 0.004346x^3$
Exchange Rate	$9864.26828 - 313.7x + 3.982x^2 - 0.01656x^3$	$1585.40882 + 272.9x - 4.434x^2 + 0.02144x^3$
Interest Rate	$891.56344 + 3.7x + 1.022x^2 - 0.00785x^3$	$2072.18159 + 93.05x - 1.984x^2 + 0.01053x^3$
Liquidity	$7063.54811 - 305.6x + 5.581x^2 - 0.02963x^3$	$2810.72928 - 24.17x + 1.149x^2 - 0.008581x^3$
Market	$16896 - 875.3x + 15.85x^2 - 0.08521x^3$	$29549.1171 + 1484x - 21.40x^2 + 0.09765x^3$
Stock Market	$523.22464 + 352.4x - 8.706x^2 + 0.05526x^3$	$2208.55621 + 117.9x - 3.449x^2 + 0.02328x^3$

and public interest on market behavior. Among these, "employment" showed the strongest correlation with stock market movements.

Acknowledgement

The author thanks to the Department of Computer and Data Science at NSBM Green University for their support. Gratitude is also extended to family members, colleagues, and others for their encouragement and assistance. The project required significant work and dedication, which was made possible by the support of these individuals and organizations.

REFERENCES

1. O. S. Alp, L. Ozbek, and B. Canbaloglu, "An analysis of stock market prices by using extended Kalman filter: The US and China cases," *Investment Analysts Journal*, vol. 52, no. 1, pp. 67–82, Jan. 2023, doi: https://doi.org/10.1080/10 293523.2023.2179160.

2. K. Tang and W. Xiong, "Index Investment and the Financialization of Commodities," *Financial Analysts Journal*, vol. 68, no. 6, pp. 54–74, Nov. 2012, doi: https://doi.org/10.2469/faj.v68.n6.5.

3. J. A. Haslem, H. K. Baker, and D. M. Smith, "Identification and Performance of Equity Mutual Funds with High Management Fees and Expense Ratios," *The Journal of Investing*, vol. 16, no. 2, pp. 32–51, May 2007, doi: https://doi.org/10.3905/joi.2007.686410.

4. P. Nolan, "Effective Marginal Tax Rates: The New Zealand Case," *SSRN Electronic Journal*, 2018, doi: https://doi.org/10. 2139/ssrn.3172516.

5. K. Tang and W. Xiong, "Index Investment and the Financialization of Commodities," *Financial Analysts Journal*, vol. 68, no. 6, pp. 54–74, Nov. 2012, doi: https://doi.org/10.2469/faj.v68.n6.5.

6. E. Asem and S. Alam, "The Role of the S&P 500 Index Constituents in Tracking the U.S. Equity Market," *International Journal of Economics and Finance*, vol. 4, no. 12, Oct. 2012, doi: https://doi.org/10.5539/ijef.v4n12p15.

7. M. D. Beneish and R. E. Whaley, "S&P 500 Index Replacements," *The Journal of Portfolio Management*, vol. 29, no. 1, pp. 51–60, Oct. 2002, doi: https://doi.org/10.3905/jpm.2002.319863.

8. J. J. Siegel and J. D. Schwartz, "Long-Term Returns on the Original S&P 500 Companies," *CFA Digest*, vol. 36, no. 2, pp. 95–96, May 2006, doi: https://doi.org/10.2469/dig.v36.n2.4127.

9. L. M. Bartels, "Homer Gets a Tax Cut: Inequality and Public Policy in the American Mind," *Perspectives on Politics*, vol. 3, no. 1, pp. 15–31, Mar. 2005, doi: https://doi.org/10.1017/S1537592705050036.

10. J. A. Haslem, *Mutual funds: portfolio structures, analysis, management, and stewardship*. Hoboken, N.J.: Wiley, 2010.

11. C. L. Reynolds and S. M. Rohlin, "The effects of location-based tax policies on the distribution of household income: Evidence from the federal Empowerment Zone program," *Journal of Urban Economics*, vol. 88, pp. 1–15, Jul. 2015, doi: https://doi.org/10.1016/j.jue.2015.04.003.

12. N. N. Semenova, "Improvement of taxation of individuals' income in Russia in the context of formation of socially oriented tax policy," *Finance and Credit*, vol. 24, no. 1, pp. 129–142, Jan. 2018, doi: https://doi.org/10.24891/fc.24.1.129.

13. A. B. Atkinson, T. Piketty, and E. Saez, "Top Incomes in the Long Run of History," *Journal of Economic Literature*, vol. 49, no. 1, pp. 3–71, Mar. 2011, doi: https://doi.org/10.1257/jel.49.1.3.

14. R. Glick and M. Hutchinson, "China's Financial Linkages with Asia and the Global Financial Crisis," *Federal Reserve Bank of San Francisco, Working Paper Series*, May 2013, doi: https://doi.org/10.24148/wp2013-12.

15. S. A. Brave and Hesna Genay, *Federal Reserve Policies and Financial Market Conditions During the Crisis*. DIANE Publishing, 2011.

16. O. Blanchard and R. Perotti, "An Empirical Characterization of the Dynamic Effects of Changes in Government Spending and Taxes on Output," *The Quarterly Journal of Economics*, vol. 117, no. 4, pp. 1329–1368, Nov. 2002, doi: https://doi.org/10.1162/003355302320935043.

17. P. J. Lambert, "Income Taxation and Equity," *Baltic Journal of Economics*, vol. 4, no. 2, pp. 39–54, Mar. 2004, doi: https://doi.org/10.1080/1406099x.2004.10840410.

18. S. Campbell, D. Covitz, W. Nelson, and K. Pence, "Securitization markets and central banking: An evaluation of the term asset-backed securities loan facility," *Journal of Monetary Economics*, vol. 58, no. 5, pp. 518–531, Jul. 2011, doi: https://doi.org/10.1016/j.jmoneco.2011.05.003.

19. G. Afonso, R. Armenter, and B. Lester, "A model of the federal funds market: Yesterday, today, and tomorrow," *Review of Economic Dynamics*, vol. 33, pp. 177–204, Jul. 2019, doi: https://doi.org/10.1016/j.red.2019.04.004.

20. A. Arachchige, R. Sugathadasa, O. Herath, and A. Thibbotuwawa, "Artificial Neural Network Based Demand Forecasting Integrated with Federal Funds Rate," *Applied Computer Science*, vol. 17, no. 4, pp. 34–44, Dec. 2021, doi: https://doi.org/10.35784/acs-2021-27.

21. J. D. Hamilton and J. C. Wu, "The Effectiveness of Alternative Monetary Policy Tools in a Zero Lower Bound Environment," *Journal of Money, Credit and Banking*, vol. 44, no. s1, pp. 3–46, Feb. 2012, doi: https://doi.org/10.1111/j.1538-4616.2011.00477.x.

22. M. Wu and Z. Zhu, "The Impact of Restrictive Measures on the Price Discovery Function of Stock Index Futures – Evidence from CSI 500 Stock Index Futures," *International Journal of Financial Research*, vol. 9, no. 4, p. 117, Aug. 2018, doi: https://org/10.5430/ijfr.v9n4p117.

23. "Federal taxation in America: a short history," *Choice Reviews Online*, vol. 42, no. 04, pp. 42–231542–2315, Dec. 2004, doi: https://doi.org/10.5860/choice.42-2315.

24. A. B. Atkinson, T. Piketty, and E. Saez, "Top Incomes in the Long Run of History," *Journal of Economic Literature*, vol. 49, no. 1, pp. 3–71, Mar. 2011, doi: https://doi.org/10.1257/jel.49.1.3.

25. D. G. N. D. Jayarathna, G. H. J. Lanel, and Z. A. M. S. Juman, "Survey on Ten Years of Multi-Depot Vehicle Routing Problems: Mathematical Models, Solution Methods and Real-Life Applications," *Sustainable Development Research*, vol. 3, no. 1, p. p36, Feb. 2021, doi: https://doi.org/10.30560/sdr.v3n1p36.

26. T. A. H. Dilpriya, G. H. J. Lanel, and M. T. M. Perera, "Reviewing the Efficacy of Federal Reserve Bank Reserve Policies through a Time Series Analysis of the Effective Federal Funds Rate," *International journal of research and innovation in social science*, vol. VII, no. IV, pp. 869–880, Jan. 2023, doi: https://doi.org/10.47772/ijriss.2023.7472.

Note: All the figures and table in this chapter were made by the authors.

Transformative Applied Research in Computing, Engineering, Science and Technology – Dr. Damayanthi Dahanayake et al. (eds)
© *2024 Taylor & Francis Group, London, ISBN 978-1-041-01782-0*

18

Diversity and Ecological Significance of Vermicomposting Bacteria

H.N.S.D. Mediyawa and W. T. S. Munidasa*

Department of Life Sciences, NSBM Green University,
Sri Lanka

Abstract

Vermicomposting, a bioconversion process employing earthworms to decompose organic matter, has gained significant attention due to its eco-friendly waste management and soil-enriching properties. The microbial communities inhabiting the vermicompost matrices are central to the success of vermicomposting, which play pivotal roles in organic matter degradation, nutrient mineralization, and overall ecosystem functioning. A diligent investigation into various vermicompost samples has unveiled a diverse array of bacterial species such as Acidobacteria, Bacillus, Firmicutes, and Azotobacter presenting remarkable metabolic versatility and adaptive strategies to thrive in this specialized environment. Identification techniques scaling from traditional culture-based procedures to exceptional molecular approaches such as pyrosequencing have characterized these bacterial communities, revealing a wealth of previously unrecognized taxa and functional potentials. Moreover, copious literature has highlighted the ecological significance of vermicomposting bacteria in nutrient cycling, soil quality improvement, plant harvest promotion, and medicine. Furthermore, the practical implications of bacteria in vermicomposting in bioremediation, agricultural practices, and waste management underscore their immense potential in diverse applied domains. This review underscores the techniques for isolating and identifying different vermicomposting bacteria and the significance of understanding the composition and functions of vermicomposting bacteria for mobilizing their beneficial applications in agriculture and medicine.

Keywords

Bacteria, Earthworms, Vermicomposting, Organic waste

1. Introduction

Since the green revolution, chemical fertilizers (soluble acidic NPK fertilizers), insecticides, and herbicides have been used. Chemical fertilizers are often used to boost food yield in response to increased population and demand since they increase crop productivity by providing nutrients to plants, either directly or indirectly. Continuous use of chemical fertilizers leads to negative impacts on the agricultural ecosystem, including soil degradation, deterioration of crop genetics and microbiological diversity, groundwater contamination, and atmospheric pollution [1]. In recent

*Corresponding author: thushari.m@nsbm.ac.lk

DOI: 10.1201/9781003616368-18

decades, vermicompost has obtained increased attention due to its immense role in organic waste management and sustainable soil fertility management against chemical fertilizers. Vermicomposting is characterized as a process that can stabilize organic material in aerobic and mesophilic environments by the collaborative effort of both earthworms and microorganisms [2].

Vermicomposting is a non-thermophilic biodegradation where the organic matter gets transformed into humus-like material as a product of feeding earthworms [3]. Collateral to traditional composting, vermicomposting comprises bio-oxidative reactions and organic material stabilization. However, unlike traditional composting, vermicomposting also includes interactions between earthworms and microbes [2].

Vermicomposting involves two phases: an active stage throughout which earthworms and microbes undertake the substrate and a maturation phase where associated microbes act after the earthworms migrate to fresher layers of unprocessed waste or when the product is taken out from the vermireactor. Horticultural residues from processed potatoes, mushroom wastes, horse wastes, pig wastes, brewery wastes, sericulture wastes, municipal sewage sludge, agricultural residues, weeds, cattle dung, industrial unwanted substances such as paper wastes, sludge from paper mills and dairy plants, domestic kitchen scraps, urban residues, and animal wastes can be vermicompost [4]. Only a smaller number of more than 4000 species of earthworm that can be categorized into the three ecological groups of epigeic, anecic, and endogenic have been utilized for this process, For example, *Peronyx excavatus*, *Eudrilus eugeniae* (night crawler), and *Eisenia foetidia* (red earthworm). As red earthworms reproduce quickly and turn organic material into vermicompost within 45-50 days, they are the favorable option. Earthworms enhance soil quality by restoring porosity, structure, texture, drainage, water retention, and aeration. Moreover, they also reduce erosion and regulate the soil pH [5].

Although earthworms play a significant part in the vermicomposting operation, microorganisms carry through the actual biochemical decomposition of organic matter, whether those bacteria are from the soil or the earthworm's gut. The end product of vermicomposting provides various microbial communities, including phosphate solubilizers, nitrogen fixers, enzyme-producing bacteria, and bacteria that promote plant growth [2].

Vermicompost is recognized as a bioactive organic substance with various uses. It contains a variety of enzymes namely amylase, lipase, cellulase, and chitinase, which persist in decomposing organic matter in the soil even after being excreted [6]. This continuous breakdown contributes to soil fertility and health. Soil treated with vermicompost tends to have higher electrical conductivity (EC) and a near-neutral pH, both are favorable conditions for plant growth and microbial activity. Moreover, recent research on diverse vermicompost samples has identified a range of bacteria that possess the benefit of various biotechnological applications. This underscores the significance of vermicompost as a reservoir of valuable microorganisms [7].

Moreover, a few research have been pioneered to showcase the medicinal values of bacterial strains isolated from vermicompost. However, knowledge of bacterial communities in vermicompost of different substrates and their functional roles is yet to be discovered [2]. This review provides insight into the different approaches used for the isolation, identification, and characterization of vermicomposting bacteria and their potential applications in agriculture and medicine.

2. Literature Review

2.1 Microbial Diversity in Traditional Compost vs Vermicompost

Table 18.1 Comparison of traditional compost and vermicompost

Traditional compost	Vermicompost	References
B. Mesophilic, thermophilic, and maturation phase	C. Mesophilic and active and maturation phases	[8,9]
D. Microorganisms mainly bacteria, fungi, and actinomycetes drive the decomposition	E. Collaborative effort of both bacteria and earthworms drive the decomposition	[10]
F. 40 to 60 percent moisture content is needed	G. 70 to 90 percent moisture content is needed	[11]

Source: Authors

In conventional composting, thermophilic bacteria are the primary decomposers, and the process typically takes about 8 weeks to complete. However, an additional 4 weeks are often needed for curing, during which further aerobic decomposition occurs to break down remaining compounds, organic acids, and large particles. Compost must undergo proper curing because compost that has not been adequately cured may contain compounds that could potentially harm crops. In contrast, vermicomposting predominantly involves mesophilic bacteria and fungi, and this process typically takes about half the time of conventional composting. One of the key advantages of vermicompost is that it does not need curing; it can be used immediately after manufacture [10].

During the heating phase of traditional composting, there is a selective process where the material becomes invaded primarily by specially altered thermophilic bacteria, many of which have not been cultured yet. The microbial community in mature traditional compost mainly consists of facultative thermophiles, capable of surviving both high temperatures during composting and lower mesophilic temperatures. They either form spores or recolonize in the course of the mesophilic curing stage to endure the elevated temperatures. In contrast, vermicompost maintains a vivid array of organisms throughout the whole composting process, including saprophytic bacteria and fungi, as well as nematodes, protozoa, and microarthropods [12].

A study of the bacterial diversity in finished traditional compost and vermicompost showcases the compost material exhibited a prevalence of Firmicutes and Actinobacteria, known for containing spore-forming bacteria [13]. This characteristic enables them to thrive in the initial substrate and withstand the high temperatures during composting, ensuring their activity or survival. Meanwhile, the dominant bacteria found in vermicompost belong to the Phyla Chloroflexi, Bacteroidetes, and Gemmatimonadetes. Additionally, bacteria from the subclass Alphaproteobacteria and the phylum Acidobacteria were uniquely identified in vermicompost samples. Moreover, the notable contrast between traditional compost and vermicompost was evident in the composition of their 16S rRNA sequences.

It is mentioned that vermicomposting depicted significantly higher bacterial diversity compared to aerobic composting. Chao1 estimators and Shannon indices disclosed that the bacterial population in vermicomposting exhibited greater diversity and richness compared to that in composting. This increased microbial diversity may be credited to the mesophilic conditions, or the beneficial effects given by earthworm activity during vermicomposting, which create favorable conditions for distinct types of bacteria. Additionally, the lavish bacterial community present in earthworm guts and casts may also lead to the higher bacterial diversity observed during vermicomposting [8].

Different research has proposed varying factors that can affect bacterial diversity in vermicompost. The variances in microbial activity may arise from differences in the time duration of composting and the quality and complexity of the food sources consumed [14]. Furthermore, variations in microbial activity could be associated with varied species of earthworms, influenced by their morphological and physiological characteristics, including gut transit time and enzymatic profiles. It has been reported that earthworm activity significantly decreased the populations of bacteria within one month of vermicomposting [15].

Results obtained from the use of similar earthworm species (*Eisenia fetida*) across studies imply that distinct bacterial communities may develop in vermicompost derived from different waste materials [7]. However, this assumption may not be accurate because these studies employed methods that are not directly comparable when examining bacterial communities in specific vermicompost. Furthermore, discrepancies in vermicomposting procedures, such as differences in processing systems and durations, could result in variations among bacterial communities in vermicompost, even if they originate from similar waste sources.

During vermicomposting, Actinobacteria, represented by genera such as *Demequina, Arthrobacter Microbacterium, Nocardioides, Mycobacterium, and Streptomyces*, became the abundant Phylum, indicating significant alterations in bacterial communities within vermibeds due to the disintegration and stabilization of organic material [8].

While Bacilli were detected during vermicomposting, they were found in much lower numbers compared to traditional composting. This suggests that the microbial makeup during vermicomposting is influenced by both earthworm activity and the consistency or variability of the substrate, unlike composting. Additionally, the distinct physical and chemical properties of substrates resulting from composting and vermicomposting treatments play a significant role in determining the constitution of the bacterial community [8].

2.2 Isolation and Identification Techniques of Bacteria In Vermicompost

In the exploration of bacterial species residing in vermicompost, both culture-dependent and culture-independent methods have been used There are specificities between these two methods [16]. Characteristics such as colony appearance, staining properties like the Gram stain, biochemical reactions such as coagulase test, motility assessments, antibiotic resistance patterns, and other traits are traditionally used to identify and classify bacteria under culture-dependent methods. With the advancements in sequencing technologies, along with the progress in bioinformatics tools and the establishment of reference databases, researchers now have enhanced capabilities to apprehend microbial diversity without the partiality linked with culture-based methods. Culture-independent procedures for microorganisms' identification utilize a targeted amplicon approach, which employs highly conserved molecular markers distinct to microbes and does not depend on cultivating isolates in pure culture. The 16S ribosomal RNA gene for bacterial identification, and PCR amplification techniques such as quantitative

PCR, and reverse transcriptase PCR to identify and measure organisms, genes, or expression levels within the microbiome sample are a few examples of this method.

A study by Yasir et al. examined how earthworms impact the suppression of pathogenic fungi of plants in vermicompost by analyzing the bacterial communities and the diversity of chitinase genes [17]. Here, both culture-dependent (serial dilution, streaking) and culture-independent techniques (PCR techniques) have been used. Vivas et al. have done a study to explore how composting and vermicomposting influence the quantity and composition of bacterial populations in olive-mill residues, as well as the activity of primary enzymes engaged in decomposing organic material [18]. For this, culture-independent methods such as real-time PCR assays aimed at disclosing 16S rRNA genes, accompanied by denaturing gradient gel electrophoresis profiling coupled with sequence analysis of PCR-amplified 16S rRNA fragments (PCR–DGGE) have been used. A study by Gómez-Brandón et al. explored how the presence of *Eisenia fetida* an epigeic earthworm species affects both the structure and function of microbial communities in the course of the vermicomposting process of pig slurry with culture-independent methods [14]. (Phospholipid fatty acid (PLFA) analysis was utilized to assess the structure of the microbial community). Fernández-Gómez et al. used culture independent procedures [7]. (Denaturing Gradient Gel Electrophoresis (DGGE) and COMPOCHIP) for a deeper insight into the bacterial communities residing in vermicompost created from various wastes treated by *E. fetida* under dissimilar vermicomposting conditions.

Furthermore, both culture-dependent methods (isolation, identification, and biochemical tests, for example, production of catalase, urease, etc.) and culture-independent methods (16S rRNA sequence homology and molecular phylogeny analysis) have been used by a study for comprehensive insights and enhancements in understanding the divergent and functional capabilities of bacteria reside in vermicompost [19]. Chitrapriya et al. have assessed the quantity of phosphate solubilizing bacteria and *Azotobacter* in vermicompost processed by *Eudrilus eugeniae* and *Perionyx excavatus* using different mixtures of cow dung and sawdust using culture-dependent methods (Eg: Determining phosphate-solubilizing bacteria levels via Pikovskaya's medium and isolating *Azotobacter* in vermicompost using Jensen's medium) [20]. To explore the bacterial makeup and arrangement throughout the composting and vermicomposting processes of sewage sludge and cattle dung, Lv et al. have implemented culture-independent methods such as pyrosequencing [8]. In addition, the article states that pyrosequencing effectively unveiled a greater bacterial community diversity during composting and vermicomposting compared to traditional molecular biological approaches such as DGGE and clone library analysis. Another research has used culture-dependent methods (morphological, microscopic, and biochemical studies) to recognize the bacterial species participating in the vermicomposting of organic and agricultural wastes, including cow dung, neem leaves, straw, and vegetable scraps [21].

2.3 Common Bacterial Species Isolated from Vermicompost

Through the different isolation techniques discussed previously, a wide range of bacterial species have been identified. Vivas et al. [18], showed that the bacteria belonging to Betaproteobacteria, Gammaproteobacteria, Alphaproteobacteria, Actinobacteria, Firmicutes, and Acidobacteria are in the vermicompost. The bacterial species identified by the study [19], include *Bacillus* (57%), *Pseudomonas* (15%), *Microbacterium* (12%), *Acinetobacter*, *Chryseobacterium*, *Arthrobacter*, *Pseudoxanthomonas*, *Stenotrophomonas*, *Paenibacillus*, *Rhodococcus*, *Enterobacter*, *Rheinheimera* and *Cellulomonas*. Chitrapriya et al. have extracted Phosphate-solubilizing bacteria such as *Bacillus*, *Streptomyces*, and *Pseudomonas* sp. and nitrogen-fixing bacteria including *Azotobacter* colonies from both vermicompost and traditional compost samples [20]. During the processes of traditional composting and vermicomposting of sewage sludge and cattle dung, a total of 33 phyla were discovered with Proteobacteria, Bacteroidetes, Actinobacteria, Planctomycetes, and Firmicutes being the predominant ones. Notably, the dominant genus in vermicomposting varied from that in traditional composting. In vermicomposting, prevalent populations included *Rhodanobacter*, *Altererythrobacter*, *Lysobacter*, *Paenibacillus*, *Rhizomicrobium*, and *Luteimonas*. A significant distinction spotted during vermicomposting was the presence and notable increase of Acidobacteria, distinguishing it from traditional composting [8]. Eight species of bacteria were predominantly recognized, namely *Actinomyces israelli*, *Azotobacter*, *M. luteus*, *B. cereus*, *B. subtillis*, *P. aeruginosa*, and *Enterobacter* by Satpathy et al. during their studies.

2.4 Vermicomposting Bacteria: Enhancing Soil and Human Health

Agricultural Applications

The utilization of vermicomposting bacteria in agriculture has garnered considerable interest owing to their capacity to augment both soil fertility and plant growth. Numerous investigations have highlighted the positive impacts of vermicompost and its accompanying microbial populations on soil quality and agricultural output. The application of vermicompost has proven effective in ameliorating soil structure, enhancing water retention capabilities, and augmenting nutrient availability, consequently leading to improved crop yield and quality [22].

Azotobacter, a bacterium found in vermicompost, has garnered significant interest owing to its capability to fix nitrogen potentially enriching soil nitrogen levels. Furthermore, phosphate-solubilizing bacteria within vermicompost are vital in enhancing phosphorus accessibility to plants, leading to improved phosphorus absorption and crop output [20].

In addition, vermicomposting bacteria can produce extracellular enzymes that can degrade fungal cell walls and hydrolytic enzymes with valuable commercial applications such as protease, cellulase, xylanase, amylase, and DNase. Moreover, these bacteria are involved in the synthesis of enzymes and hormones that promote plant growth. They also produce siderophores, and hydrogen cyanide (HCN), and facilitate phosphate solubilization, enhancing nutrient availability for plants [19].

Actinomycetes present in herbal vermicompost exhibit antagonistic potential against Fusarium wilt, a common disease affecting various crops. Their ability to produce bioactive compounds, including antibiotics and enzymes, helps suppress the growth of *Fusarium* pathogens, thereby enhancing plant health and resilience [23]. In brief, employing vermicomposting bacteria in agriculture demonstrates considerable promise for sustainably maintaining soil fertility and boosting crop productivity.

Medicinal Applications

The medicinal application of vermicomposting bacteria has gained attention in the present years due to their potential therapeutic features and beneficial effects on human health. Atiyeh et al. have studied the act of earthworms in enhancing microbial populations through their digestive tract, leading to the proliferation of beneficial bacteria with potential pharmaceutical applications [22]. The work of Ganguly et al. has also depicted the antioxidant and anticancer properties of novel strains of *Bacillus anthracis* isolated from vermicompost [24].

Moreover, vermicomposting has been shown to increase the bioavailability of nutrients and bioactive compounds in organic waste [15] which could contribute to the production of bioactive metabolites with therapeutic properties. Furthermore, Arslan et al. have investigated the production of iron oxide nanoparticles using vermicomposting leachate and examined their potential uses [25]. It delves into their antimicrobial and antioxidant properties, along with their ability to inhibit biofilm formation and cleave DNA. The study emphasizes the nanoparticles' efficacy against diverse microorganisms and their potential applications in the biomedical field. Overall vermicomposting shows significant potential for finding and utilizing bacteria with pharmaceutical benefits, providing a sustainable and environmentally friendly method for tapping into the medicinal properties of microbial communities found in organic waste.

3. Conclusion

In conclusion, the literature review underscores the profound significance of isolating and identifying bacteria within vermicompost, shedding light on their multifaceted roles and potential applications. Through careful examination, scientists have revealed a wide range of microbial communities thriving within the organic materials of vermicompost. These bacteria showcase impressive metabolic abilities and adaptive tactics. They showcase a vital role in breaking down waste and cycling nutrients, and they also show great potential in practical applications.

The findings underscore the importance of vermicomposting as a sustainable and eco-friendly method for harnessing microbial biodiversity. By unraveling the microbial intricacies of vermicompost, potential applications across diverse fields, ranging from agriculture and environmental remediation to biotechnology and pharmaceuticals can be observed. However, while significant strides have been made, challenges persist, including refining isolation techniques, elucidating microbial interactions, and optimizing downstream processes for biotechnological applications.

Looking ahead, concerted efforts are warranted to bridge these knowledge gaps and unlock the full potential of vermicompost bacteria. Interdisciplinary collaborations and advanced technologies offer pathways to harness the transformative power of these microbial communities. This enriches our understanding of microbial ecology and holds promise for addressing pressing societal and environmental challenges through sustainable practices and innovation.

In essence, the segregation and recognition of bacteria in vermicompost not only deepens our knowledge of microbial ecosystems but also paves the way for innovative solutions that promote sustainable development and environmental stewardship.

REFERENCES

1. D. Maji, P. Misra, S. Singh, and A. Kalra, "Humic acid rich vermicompost promotes plant growth by improving microbial community structure of soil as well as root nodulation and mycorrhizal colonization in the roots of *Pisum sativum*," *Applied Soil Ecology*, vol. 110, pp. 97–108, Feb. 2017, doi: 10.1016/J.APSOIL.2016.10.008.

2. A. Vuković, M. Velki, S. Ečimović, R. Vuković, I. Štolfa Čamagajevac, and Z. Lončarić, "Vermicomposting—Facts, Benefits and Knowledge Gaps," *Agronomy*, MDPI, vol. 11, no. 10, p. 192, 2021. [Online]. Available: https://doi.org/10.3390/agronomy1110192

3. K. M. C. Fernando and K. K. I. U. Arunakumara, "Sustainable Organic Waste Management and Nutrients Replenishment in the Soil by Vermicompost: A Review," *AGRIEAST: Journal of Agricultural Sciences*, vol. 15, no. 2, p. 32, 2021. [Online]. Available: https://doi.org/10.4038/agriest.v15i2.105

4. J. Pathma and N. Sakthivel, "Microbial diversity of vermicompost bacteria that exhibit useful agricultural traits and waste management potential," *SpringerPlus*, vol. 1, no. 1, p. 26, Oct. 2012, doi: 10.1186/2193-1801-1-26.

5. T. Tiwari, C. S. Azad, T. Mishra, and D. Kumar, "Vermicomposting: How Earthworms Make Soil," *New Era Agriculture Magazine*. [Online]. Available: https://www.researchgate.net/publication/376184813

6. S. C. Tiwari, B. K. Tiwari, and R. R. Mishra, "Microbial populations, enzyme activities and nitrogen-phosphorus-potassium enrichment in earthworm casts and in the surrounding soil of a pineapple plantation," *Biol. Fertil. Soils*, vol. 8, no. 2, 1989

7. M. J. Fernández-Gómez, R. Nogales, H. Insam, E. Romero, and M. Goberna, "Use of DGGE and COMPOCHIP for investigating bacterial communities of various vermicomposts produced from different wastes under dissimilar conditions," *Science of The Total Environment*, vol. 414, pp. 664–671, Jan. 2012, doi: 10.1016/J.SCITOTENV.2011.11.045.

8. B. Lv, B. Lv, M. Xing, J. Yang, and L. Zhang, "Pyrosequencing reveals bacterial community differences in composting and vermicomposting on the stabilization of mixed sewage sludge and cattle dung," *Applied Microbiology and Biotechnology*, vol. 99, no. 24, pp. 10703–10712, Aug. 2015, doi: 10.1007/S00253-015-6884-7

9. J. Domínguez, M. Aira, A. R. Kolbe, M. Gómez-Brandón, M. Pérez-Losada, and M. Pérez-Losada, "Changes in the composition and function of bacterial communities during vermicomposting may explain beneficial properties of vermicompost.," *Scientific Reports*, vol. 9, no. 1, p. 9657, Jul. 2019, doi: 10.1038/S41598-019-46018-W

10. J. Dominguez, C. A. Edwards, and S. Subler, "A comparison of vermicomposting and composting," *Biocycle*, vol. 38, pp. 57–59, 1997.

11. C. Tognetti, F. Laos, M. J. Mazzarino, and M. T. Hernández, "Composting vs. Vermicomposting: A comparison of end product quality," *Compost Science & Utilization*, vol. 13, no. 1, pp. 6–13, Jan. 2005, doi: 10.1080/1065657X.2005.10702212.

12. N. Uphoff, A. S. Ball, E. Fernandes, H. Herren, O. Husson, M. Laing, and C. Palm, *Biological Approaches to Sustainable Soil Systems*, 1st ed. Boca Raton, FL: CRC Press, 2006.

13. L. Fracchia, A. B. Dohrmann, M. G. Martinotti, and C. C. Tebbe, "Bacterial diversity in a finished compost and vermicompost: differences revealed by cultivation-independent analyses of PCR-amplified 16S rRNA genes.," *Applied Microbiology and Biotechnology*, vol. 71, no. 6, pp. 942–952, Jan. 2006, doi: 10.1007/S00253-005-0228-Y.

14. M. Gómez-Brandón, M. Aira, M. Lores, and J. Domínguez, "Changes in microbial community structure and function during vermicomposting of pig slurry," *Bioresour. Technol.*, vol. 102, no. 5, pp. 4171–4178, May 2011. [Online]. Available: https://doi.org/10.1016/j.biortech.2010.12.057

15. J. Domínguez, M. Aira, and M. Gómez-Brandón, "Vermicomposting: Earthworms enhance the work of microbes," in *Microbes at Work: From Wastes to Resources*, Springer-Verlag, Berlin Heidelberg, pp. 93–114, 2010. [Online].

16. K. Findley and E. A. Grice, "The Skin Microbiome: A Focus on Pathogens and Their Association with Skin Disease," *PLOS Pathogens*, vol. 10, no. 11, Nov. 2014, doi: 10.1371/JOURNAL.PPAT.1004436.

17. M. Yasir, Z. Aslam, S. W. Kim, S.-W. Lee, C. O. Jeon, and Y. R. Chung, "Bacterial community composition and chitinase gene diversity of vermicompost with antifungal activity.," *Bioresource Technology*, vol. 100, no. 19, pp. 4396–4403, Oct. 2009, doi: 10.1016/J.BIORTECH.2009.04.015.

18. A. Vivas, B. Moreno, S. García-Rodríguez, and E. Benitez, "Assessing the impact of composting and vermicomposting on bacterial community size and structure, and microbial functional diversity of an olive-mill waste," *Bioresource Technology*, vol. 100, no. 3, pp. 1319–1326, Feb. 2009, doi: 10.1016/J.BIORTECH.2008.08.014.

19. P. Jayakumar and S. Natarajan, "Molecular and functional characterization of bacteria isolated from straw and goat manure based vermicompost," *Appl. Soil Ecol.*, vol. 70, pp. 33–47, Aug. 2013. [Online]. Available: https://doi.org/10.1016/j.apsoil.2013.03.011

20. K. Chitrapriya and R. Asokan, "Estimating the Level of Phosphate Solubilising Bacteria and Azotobacter in the Vermicompost of Eudrilus Eugeniae and Perionyx Excavatus with Various Combinations of Cow-Dung and Saw-Dust," *International Journal of Scientific and Research Publications*, vol. 3, no. 10, 2013.

21. J. Satpathy, M. H. Saha, A. S. Mishra, and S. K. Mishra, "Characterization of bacterial isolates in vermicompost produced from a mixture of cow dung, straw, neem leaf and vegetable wastes," *bioRxiv*, 2020.

22. R. M. Atiyeh, C. A. Edwards, S. Subler, and J. D. Metzger, "Earthworm-processed organic wastes as components of horticultural potting media for growing marigold and vegetable seedlings," *Compost Sci. Util.*, vol. 8, no. 3, pp. 215–223, 2000

23. S. Gopalakrishnan *et al.*, "Evaluation of actinomycete isolates obtained from herbal vermicompost for the biological control of Fusarium wilt of chickpea," *Crop Prot.*, vol. 30, no. 8, pp. 1070–1078, 2011

24. R. K. Ganguly, S. Midya, and S. K. Chakraborty, "Antioxidant and anticancer roles of a novel strain of *Bacillus anthracis* isolated from vermicompost prepared from Paper Mill sludge," *Biomed Res. Int.*, vol. 2018, pp. 1–7, 2018.

25. H. Arslan, S. Gonca, Z. Isik, S. Özdemir, M. Yalvac, N. Dizge, B. Deepanraj, and G. A. Ashraf, "Iron oxide nanoparticles synthesis from vermicomposting leachate and its antioxidant activities," *Front. Mater.*, vol. 9, Jun. 2022. [Online]. Available: https://doi.org/10.3389/fmats.2022.912066

Transformative Applied Research in Computing, Engineering, Science and Technology – Dr. Damayanthi Dahanayake et al. (eds)
© 2024 Taylor & Francis Group, London, ISBN 978-1-041-01782-0

19

Blue Chassis—Advances in Biochemical Synthesis in Engineered Marine Bacteria

Duleepa Pathiraja*

Department of Chemistry,
Faculty of Science, University of Colombo, Colombo 03,
Sri Lanka

Abstract

Marine ecosystems play a critical role in global ecological balance, carbon sequestration and nutrient cycling. It is a habitat for diverse marine bacterial communities with potential applications in biotechnology. Marine bacteria are emerging as promising hosts for the biosynthesis of various biochemicals and are referred to as "blue chassis". These organisms have highlighted their potential due to unique growth characteristics such as rapid growth, metabolic diversity, tolerance to extreme culture conditions, and ability to utilize marine biomass. Although most marine bacteria are resistant to genetic manipulation, recent advances in synthetic biology have paved the way to engineer a handful of marine microorganisms as potent microbial chassis. Heterologous expression of biosynthetic pathways in these microbial chassis has demonstrated the bioconversion of sustainable biomass, such as algal polysaccharides, into value-added biochemicals. Despite the rapid development, these chassis platforms still face challenges in characterization, genetic stability, downstream processing, and scale-up for industrial applications. This review summarizes the potential of marine bacteria as metabolic chassis, biochemical synthesis in marine bacteria, and recent advances in synthetic biology that enable genetic manipulation of marine bacteria as chassis platforms.

Keywords

Algal biomass, Synthetic biology, Biochemicals, Biorefinery, Microbial chassis

1. Introduction

Microbial chassis are fundamental tools in biotechnology, serving as engineered platforms for producing a wide range of value-added biochemicals, including pharmaceuticals, biofuels, and industrial chemicals [1]. These chassis are typically well-characterized microorganisms whose genetic and metabolic pathways can be modified and optimized for specific applications. Ideal microbial chassis are genetically tractable and can be easily manipulated with established genetic toolkits. These chassis exhibit high metabolic versatility with the ability to utilize different substrates and produce diverse metabolites. Microbial chassis exhibit rapid growth rates and high yields of

*Corresponding author: pmduleepa@chem.cmb.ac.lk

DOI: 10.1201/9781003616368-19

desired products. These microorganisms must exhibit high resistance to physiochemical stresses and tolerance to extreme conditions such as high heat, pH changes, and high salt concentrations. However, only a few naturally occurring microorganisms possess all these characteristics [1, 2]. Commonly used traditional microbial chassis such as *Escherichia coli* [3], *Saccharomyces cerevisiae* [4], *Bacillus subtilis* [5] and *Pseudomonas putida* [6] lack these characteristics.

Microbial diversity offers a vast source of solutions for addressing practical challenges in metabolic engineering and utilizing natural biological solutions for bioproduction and biorefinery. Current challenges include limiting growth rates and product yields in engineered bacteria, reducing production costs, and simplifying downstream processing. Promising bacterial chassis with attractive properties for bioproduction include *Vibrio natriegens* [7], *Shewanella* [8], *Geobacter sp.* [9], *Klebsiella sp.* [10], and *Deinococcus* [11]. Marine bacteria, often referred to as "blue chassis," are emerging as promising candidates for biotechnological applications due to their unique metabolic capabilities and adaptability to marine environments [12]. These microorganisms offer a wealth of advantages over traditional microbial chassis, particularly in the context of sustainable bioprocessing and biorefinery applications.

2. Marine Bacteria as Metabolic Chassis

Marine bacteria can naturally degrade complex marine polysaccharides, such as agar, alginate, and carrageenan, which are abundant in seaweeds [13]. Seaweed is considered a third-generation biomass that is receiving increasing attention as a sustainable feedstock for biorefineries. It is a sustainable alternative to first- and second-generation biomass and is readily available through harvesting from the natural environment and commercial seaweed farming [14]. These polysaccharides are chemically distinct from the terrestrial plant cell wall polysaccharides such as cellulose and hemicellulose. However, common metabolic chassis such as *E. coli*, *S. cerevisiae* or *B. subtilis* cannot metabolize complex algal polysaccharides. Marine microorganisms living in marine ecosystems are naturally capable of degrading and metabolizing algal polysaccharides [15]. Over the past decade, the metabolism of algal polysaccharides has been studied in marine bacteria. These microorganisms encode carbohydrate active enzymes (CAZymes) in specialized genomic regions called polysaccharide utilization loci (PULs) [16, 17]. CAZymes can depolymerize complex algal polysaccharides and convert them to simple monosaccharides which are then directed to the glycolytic pathway [16, 17]. This ability

allows the marine bacterial metabolic chassis to directly convert marine biomass into valuable chemicals without the need for extensive pretreatment [12].

Marine bacteria are adapted to thrive in saline environments, making them ideal for processes that use seawater as a culture medium. This reduces the need for fresh water, in line with sustainable industrial practices. Resistance to high concentrations of NaCl and high pH allows the selective growth of certain microorganisms, as conventional microorganisms cannot survive in these conditions. Therefore, culture conditions with high NaCl concentrations, high pH and minimal medium that favor the growth of marine bacteria can be used without sterilizing the culture medium [18].

3. Production of Value-Added Chemicals in Marine Bacteria

The metabolic versatility of marine bacteria enables them to produce a wide range of secondary metabolites, enzymes, and bioactive compounds. Their unique metabolic pathways can be exploited for the biosynthesis of novel chemicals and pharmaceuticals. *Vibrio natriegens,* which belongs to the class Gammaproteobacteria, is known for its widespread popularity as the fastest-growing bacterium used in molecular biology [7]. In addition, *V. natriegens* shows high protein expression ability and easy genetic manipulation, but it does not metabolize algal polysaccharides [19]. *V. natriegens* has been engineered to produce 3,4-dihydroxyphenylalanine (L-DOPA) from catechol, pyruvate, and acetate as substrates [20]. In addition, the conversion of glycerol to propane-1,3-diol [21] and glucose to succinate under anaerobic conditions are also reported [22]. In addition, the production of complex bioactive molecules, such as β-carotene and violacein, has also been reported using a range of substrates [23]. *Halomonas bluephagenesis* is a halophilic bacterium belonging to the class gammaproteobacteria, isolated from a salt lake in China [18]. *H. bluephagenes* prefers high salt concentrations and can be grown in non-sterile cultures with glucose as the sole carbon source [18]. It is one of the most successful chassis for the biosynthesis of polyhydroxyalkanoate (PHA) and polyhydroxybutyrate (PHB) [18]. Apart from these, *H. bluephagenes* has demonstrated the biosynthesis of 3-hydroxybutyrate-3-hydroxyvalerate from glucose and propionate [24], 3-hydroxybutyrate and 4-hydroxybutyrate copolymer from glucose and γ-butyrolactone [25], 3-hydroxypropionate from propane-1,3-diol [26]. The biosynthesis of the complex copolymer 3-hydroxybutyrate-4-hydroxybutyrate-5-hydroxyvalerate from glucose and appropriate precursor diols has also been demonstrated [27].

Recent attempts to utilize the algal polysaccharide degraders as non-model chassis organisms have successfully demonstrated the biosynthesis of valuable chemicals from algal biomass. *Vibrio* sp. dhg can degrade alginate in brown algae, and this strain was engineered to synthesize ethanol, butane-2,3-diol, and lycopene using dried brown algae [28]. *Vibrio* sp. SP1 is also a potent brown algal degrader that has been engineered to produce carotenoids directly from brown algae [29]. *Pseudoalteromonas atlantica* T6c is a potent red algal degrader that can metabolize agar and carrageenan. *P. atlantica* T6c was genetically engineered for red algal biorefinery and successfully demonstrated the bioconversion of dried red algal powder into value-added bioactive compounds β-carotene, violacein and prodeoxyviolacein. More interestingly this engineered *P. atlantica* T6c was used to up-cycle agaropectin, which is the waste product of commercial agarose production, into the same value-added bioactive compounds [30].

4. Marine Bacterial Genome Engineering

Synthetic biology has revolutionized the design and optimization of microbial chassis. By designing and constructing synthetic gene circuits, microorganisms can be programmed to perform complex tasks, such as dynamic control of metabolic pathways, biosensing, and biocomputing. Genome editing, metabolic engineering, and directed evolution are key to creating and refining microbial chassis with enhanced functionalities. *V. natriegens* is one of the most important marine bacterial chassis that has been extensively studied and modified with synthetic biology approaches. The development of genetic parts, genetic toolkits, DNA transformation and conjugation methods has established the framework for adapting *V. natriegens* as a potent microbial chassis. The repertoire of genetic parts developed for *V. natriegens* includes natural promoters, ribosomal binding sites, regulatory elements, synthetic promoters and synthetic 5'-UTR regions [31, 32]. The Marburg Collection is a Golden Gate Cloning toolbox consisting of 191 genetic parts to assemble genetic circuits for *V. natriegens* [33]. The natural competency of *V. natriegens* was successfully employed to develop a multiplex genome editing platform, known as Multiplex Genome Editing by Natural Transformation (MuGENT) [34], for *V. natriegens* and it was further improved for highly efficient mutant selection with CRISPR-Cas-based counterselection approach (NT-CRISPR) [35]. The wild-type strain of halophilic bacterium *H. bluephagenesis* is resistant to DNA transfer by electroporation and chemical transformation. However, partial suppression of the native restriction/methylation system show low efficient uptake of plasmids through conjugation and maintained stably [36].

Heterologous protein expression in *H. bluephagenesis* was demonstrated by chromosomal integration of the gene of interest downstream to the highly expressed porin gene forming an artificial operon. This was further improved by the integration of the *lac* repressor gene into the host chromosome and integration of the *lac* operator into the porin promoter. Core promoter region of the porin promoter was engineered to obtain a library of constitutive and inducible promoters along with the integrated *lac* operator [37]. In addition, genome mining has revealed several T7-like inducible expression systems, which were successfully implemented for tunable gene expression in *H. bluephagenesis* [38]. Furthermore, CRISPR-Cas9 and CRISPR-Cas12a have been used for genome editing in *H. bluephagenesis* with high efficiency [39, 40].

A library of genetic parts including a series of promoters, replication origins, and synthetic 5'-UTR regions was developed for the alginate metabolizing bacterium *Vibrio* sp. SP1 [29]. The expression of the biosynthetic gene cluster cloned into an extrachromosomal element was optimized using the genetic part library. Similarly, genome engineering of *Vibrio* sp. dhg has been achieved by developing a genetic toolbox containing a library of common promoters, synthetic promoters, and synthetic 5'-UTR regions [28]. Development of genetic parts and toolbox for both *Vibrio* sp. SP1 and *Vibrio* sp. dhg has improved the yield of produced biomaterials and the stability of the expression device in the host chassis [28, 29]. A different approach was used for the red algal polysaccharide degrading bacterium *P. atlantica* T6c, where a native promoter library, selected based on transcriptomics data, has been used for heterologous protein expression [30]. The engineering of these marine bacterial chassis for biorefinery has demonstrated the potential of synthetic biology to develop non-model organisms as metabolic chassis.

5. Challenges and Future Directions

Despite the rapid success of marine bacteria as efficient metabolic chassis, several challenges remain to be addressed. Marine bacteria often have complex genomes with many unique genes and regulatory elements whose function needs to be understood [12]. Understanding the metabolic pathways of complex algal polysaccharides encoded in marine bacterial genomes is also a critical component in the development of marine bacteria as metabolic chassis. Isolation of potent algal biomass degraders and high-throughput sequencing are continuously exploring undiscovered marine resources [13]. Unlike model organisms, many marine bacteria still lack well-developed genetic manipulation tools. This limits the ability to precisely engineer these organisms for desired metabolic pathways. With advances in synthetic biology, the number of engineered marine chassis is increasing over time. The integration of novel biosynthetic pathways into marine bacterial chassis may disrupt existing metabolic and regulatory pathways. Therefore, extensive studies on metabolic flux control, product toxicity, and feedback inhibition need to be conducted before being used as industrial chassis [12]. Marine bacteria are highly susceptible to horizontal gene transfer, which can complicate genetic stability and control in engineered strains.

Marine bacteria are adapted to specific growth conditions such as temperature, pH, and salinity and are highly sensitive to variations in these factors. Replicating optimal conditions in a large-scale bioreactor under industrial conditions can be energy intensive and costly. This can affect their growth and productivity when cultured outside their natural habitat. In addition, maintaining the specific conditions in bioreactors during scale-up and final bioprocessing can be labor-intensive and costly. All marine bacterial chassis developed have been tested and validated under laboratory conditions. However, many have not been extensively studied in large-scale fermentation processes. In addition, downstream processing can be more complicated because marine bacteria can contain unique metabolites and can quickly form biofilms under certain growth conditions.

Despite the challenges, marine bacteria hold great promise as metabolic chassis for biotechnology applications due to their unique metabolic capabilities and adaptability. Blue biotechnology is poised to become an essential field in the coming years, with increasing research into novel biotechnological applications for marine bacterial chassis. Advances are expected in technologies that enable the use of algal polysaccharides as sustainable feedstocks for bioproduction and synthetic biology approaches for efficient genome engineering. Overcoming these hurdles will require continued advances in synthetic biology, genetic engineering, and bioprocessing technologies. Collaboration between researchers, industry, and regulatory authorities will be essential to develop sustainable and efficient strategies for harnessing the potential of marine bacteria in various industrial applications.

REFERENCES

1. P. Calero and P. I. Nikel, "Chasing bacterial chassis for metabolic engineering: a perspective review from classical to non-traditional microorganisms," *Microb Biotechnol*, vol. 12, no. 1, pp. 98–124, 2019.
2. T. Beites and M. V Mendes, "Chassis optimization as a cornerstone for the application of synthetic biology based strategies in microbial secondary metabolism," *Front Microbiol*, vol. 6, p. 906, 2015.
3. S. Pontrelli, T.-Y. Chiu, E. I. Lan, F. Y.-H. Chen, P. Chang, and J. C. Liao, "Escherichia coli as a host for metabolic engineering," *Metab Eng*, vol. 50, pp. 16–46, 2018.
4. P. Jouhten, T. Boruta, S. Andrejev, F. Pereira, I. Rocha, and K. R. Patil, "Yeast metabolic chassis designs for diverse biotechnological products," *Sci Rep*, vol. 6, no. 1, p. 29694, 2016.
5. Y. Gu et al., "Advances and prospects of Bacillus subtilis cellular factories: from rational design to industrial applications," *Metab Eng*, vol. 50, pp. 109–121, 2018.
6. P. I. Nikel and V. de Lorenzo, "Pseudomonas putida as a functional chassis for industrial biocatalysis: from native biochemistry to trans-metabolism," *Metab Eng*, vol. 50, pp. 142–155, 2018.
7. J. Hoff, B. Daniel, D. Stukenberg, B. W. Thuronyi, T. Waldminghaus, and G. Fritz, "Vibrio natriegens: an ultrafast-growing marine bacterium as emerging synthetic biology chassis," *Environ Microbiol*, vol. 22, no. 10, pp. 4394–4408, 2020.
8. J. K. Fredrickson et al., "Towards environmental systems biology of Shewanella," *Nat Rev Microbiol*, vol. 6, no. 8, pp. 592–603, 2008.
9. J. M. Dantas et al., "Rational engineering of Geobacter sulfurreducens electron transfer components: a foundation for building improved Geobacter-based bioelectrochemical technologies," *Front Microbiol*, vol. 6, p. 752, 2015.
10. V. Kumar and S. Park, "Potential and limitations of Klebsiella pneumoniae as a microbial cell factory utilizing glycerol as the carbon source," *Biotechnol Adv*, vol. 36, no. 1, pp. 150–167, 2018.
11. E. Gerber et al., "Deinococcus as new chassis for industrial biotechnology: biology, physiology and tools," *J Appl Microbiol*, vol. 119, no. 1, pp. 1–10, 2015.
12. L. Schada von Borzyskowski, "Taking synthetic biology to the seas: from blue chassis organisms to marine aquaforming," *ChemBioChem*, vol. 24, no. 13, p. e202200786, 2023.
13. M. Martin, D. Portetelle, G. Michel, and M. Vandenbol, "Microorganisms living on macroalgae: diversity, interactions, and biotechnological applications," *Appl Microbiol Biotechnol*, vol. 98, no. 7, pp. 2917–2935, 2014.
14. R. Sachin Powar et al., "Algae: A potential feedstock for third generation biofuel," *Mater Today Proc*, vol. 63, pp. A27–A33, 2022, doi: 10.1016/j.matpr.2022.07.161.
15. J.-H. Hehemann, A. B. Boraston, and M. Czjzek, "A sweet new wave: structures and mechanisms of enzymes that digest polysaccharides from marine algae," *Curr Opin Struct Biol*, vol. 28, pp. 77–86, 2014.
16. L. Christiansen et al., "A multifunctional polysaccharide utilization gene cluster in Colwellia echini encodes enzymes for the complete degradation of κ-carrageenan, ι-carrageenan, and hybrid β/κ-carrageenan," *mSphere*, vol. 5, no. 1, pp. 10–1128, 2020.
17. E. Ficko-Blean et al., "Carrageenan catabolism is encoded by a complex regulon in marine heterotrophic bacteria," *Nat Commun*, vol. 8, no. 1, p. 1685, 2017.

18. D. Tan, Y.-S. Xue, G. Aibaidula, and G.-Q. Chen, "Unsterile and continuous production of polyhydroxybutyrate by Halomonas TD01," *Bioresour Technol*, vol. 102, no. 17, pp. 8130–8136, 2011.

19. J. Xu, S. Yang, and L. Yang, "Vibrio natriegens as a host for rapid biotechnology," *Trends Biotechnol*, vol. 40, no. 4, pp. 381–384, 2022.

20. X. Liu *et al.*, "Rapid production of l-DOPA by Vibrio natriegens, an emerging next-generation whole-cell catalysis chassis," *Microb Biotechnol*, vol. 15, no. 5, pp. 1610–1621, 2022.

21. Y. Zhang, Z. Li, Y. Liu, X. Cen, D. Liu, and Z. Chen, "Systems metabolic engineering of Vibrio natriegens for the production of 1, 3-propanediol," *Metab Eng*, vol. 65, pp. 52–65, 2021.

22. F. Thoma *et al.*, "Metabolic engineering of Vibrio natriegens for anaerobic succinate production," *Microb Biotechnol*, vol. 15, no. 6, pp. 1671–1684, 2022.

23. G. A. Ellis, T. Tschirhart, J. Spangler, S. A. Walper, I. L. Medintz, and G. J. Vora, "Exploiting the feedstock flexibility of the emergent synthetic biology chassis Vibrio natriegens for engineered natural product production," *Mar Drugs*, vol. 17, no. 12, p. 679, 2019.

24. X.-Z. Fu, D. Tan, G. Aibaidula, Q. Wu, J.-C. Chen, and G.-Q. Chen, "Development of Halomonas TD01 as a host for open production of chemicals," *Metab Eng*, vol. 23, pp. 78–91, 2014.

25. X. Chen *et al.*, "Engineering Halomonas bluephagenesis TD01 for non-sterile production of poly (3-hydroxybutyrate-co-4-hydroxybutyrate)," *Bioresour Technol*, vol. 244, pp. 534–541, 2017.

26. X.-R. Jiang, X. Yan, L.-P. Yu, X.-Y. Liu, and G.-Q. Chen, "Hyperproduction of 3-hydroxypropionate by Halomonas bluephagenesis," *Nat Commun*, vol. 12, no. 1, p. 1513, 2021.

27. X. Yan, X. Liu, L.-P. Yu, F. Wu, X.-R. Jiang, and G.-Q. Chen, "Biosynthesis of diverse α, ω-diol-derived polyhydroxyalkanoates by engineered Halomonas bluephagenesis," *Metab Eng*, vol. 72, pp. 275–288, 2022.

28. H. G. Lim *et al.*, "Vibrio sp. dhg as a platform for the biorefinery of brown macroalgae," *Nat Commun*, vol. 10, no. 1, pp. 1–9, 2019.

29. S. Park *et al.*, "Engineering Vibrio sp. SP1 for the production of carotenoids directly from brown macroalgae," *Comput Struct Biotechnol J*, vol. 19, pp. 1531–1540, 2021.

30. D. Pathiraja, B. Park, B. Kim, P. Stougaard, and I.-G. Choi, "Constructing Marine Bacterial Metabolic Chassis for Potential Biorefinery of Red Algal Biomass and Agaropectin Wastes," *ACS Synth Biol*, vol. 12, no. 6, pp. 1782–1793, 2023.

31. F. Wu *et al.*, "Design and reconstruction of regulatory parts for fast-growing Vibrio natriegens synthetic biology," *ACS Synth Biol*, vol. 9, no. 9, pp. 2399–2409, 2020.

32. L. Tietze, A. Mangold, M. W. Hoff, and R. Lale, "Identification and cross-characterisation of artificial promoters and 5′ untranslated regions in Vibrio natriegens," *Front Bioeng Biotechnol*, vol. 10, p. 826142, 2022.

33. D. Stukenberg *et al.*, "The Marburg Collection: A Golden Gate DNA assembly framework for synthetic biology applications in Vibrio natriegens," *ACS Synth Biol*, vol. 10, no. 8, pp. 1904–1919, 2021.

34. T. N. Dalia, C. A. Hayes, S. Stolyar, C. J. Marx, J. B. McKinlay, and A. B. Dalia, "Multiplex genome editing by natural transformation (MuGENT) for synthetic biology in Vibrio natriegens," *ACS Synth Biol*, vol. 6, no. 9, pp. 1650–1655, 2017.

35. D. Stukenberg, J. Hoff, A. Faber, and A. Becker, "NT-CRISPR, combining natural transformation and CRISPR-Cas9 counterselection for markerless and scarless genome editing in Vibrio natriegens," *Commun Biol*, vol. 5, no. 1, p. 265, 2022.

36. D. Tan, Q. Wu, J.-C. Chen, and G.-Q. Chen, "Engineering Halomonas TD01 for the low-cost production of polyhydroxyalkanoates," *Metab Eng*, vol. 26, pp. 34–47, 2014.

37. T. Li *et al.*, "Engineering of core promoter regions enables the construction of constitutive and inducible promoters in Halomonas sp.," *Biotechnol J*, vol. 11, no. 2, pp. 219–227, 2016.

38. H. Zhao *et al.*, "Novel T7-like expression systems used for Halomonas," *Metab Eng*, vol. 39, pp. 128–140, 2017.

39. X. Ao *et al.*, "A multiplex genome editing method for Escherichia coli based on CRISPR-Cas12a," *Front Microbiol*, vol. 9, p. 2307, 2018.

40. Q. Qin *et al.*, "CRISPR/Cas9 editing genome of extremophile Halomonas spp.," *Metab Eng*, vol. 47, pp. 219–229, 2018.

Transformative Applied Research in Computing, Engineering, Science and Technology – Dr. Damayanthi Dahanayake et al. (eds)
© 2024 Taylor & Francis Group, London, ISBN 978-1-041-01782-0

20

Role of Vitreous Humor Electrolyte Concentration in Postmortem Interval Estimation—A Mini Review

Y. B. Mulleriyawa and
M. S. K. Rabindrakumar*
Department of Life Sciences,
Faculty of Science, NSBM Green University,
Sri Lanka

Abstract

Determining the post-mortem interval (PMI) is a critical aspect of forensic medicine that plays a significant role in solving criminal and civil cases. Numerous methods have been developed to determine the PMI, with biochemical methods being particularly noteworthy. These biochemical methods include analysis of the concentration of various ions and compounds, including electrolytes, carbohydrates, proteins, and small molecules. In line with that, the emerging practices in PMI estimation are focusing on the analysis of vitreous humor electrolytes such as potassium, sodium, and chloride. Vitreous humor is the most reliable body fluid when determining the PMI, compared to other body fluids such as cerebrospinal fluid, serum, and blood due to its avascular nature and compartmentalization which can protect from putrefaction and decomposition. Studies have observed associations between vitreous humor electrolytes such as potassium, sodium, and chloride concentrations and PMI. Furthermore, studies indicate that electrolyte concentrations may be influenced by several internal and external factors including eye orientation (left/ right), sex, age, cause of death, and temperature. With the growing importance of forensic medicine, understanding the role of vitreous humor electrolyte concertation in PMI determination would be ideal for implementing these methods. Hence, this review summarizes the role of vitreous humor electrolyte concentrations in estimating PMI and the effect of different influencing factors.

Keywords

Electrolytes, Forensic medicine, Post-mortem interval, Vitreous humor

1. Introduction

Post-mortem interval (PMI) is the time between death and the time of post-mortem examination [1]. Determination of the PMI is important in many fields, particularly in the field of forensic medicine where they apply medical knowledge to legal investigations of crimes and civil circumstances [2]. Various methods are used in the estimation of PMI by using post-mortem changes. These methods can be broadly classified into physical methods, physiochemical methods,

*Corresponding author: miruna.r@nsbm.ac.lk

DOI: 10.1201/9781003616368-20

bacterial processes, autolysis, and biochemical methods [3].

Among these, biochemical methods, particularly the analysis of body fluids such as vitreous humor, blood, and cerebrospinal fluid, have gained increasing attention in forensic studies. Vitreous humor and cerebrospinal fluids are in a closed compartment which is well protected and less prone to contamination [4,5]. Vitreous humor, in particular, has become a focus of forensic research due to its relatively stable composition and slower autolytic degradation compared to cerebrospinal fluid [5]. Studies of vitreous humor are still possible even after a major head injury as it is anatomically protected by both its structure and the skull bones [5]. As a result, the assessment of electrolyte concentrations in vitreous humor has emerged as a significant method for PMI estimation. Many studies observed the associations between potassium, sodium, chloride, magnesium, calcium, and ammonium concentrations in the vitreous humor and PMI [6-9]. Certain studies have demonstrated that various internal and external factors can affect the concentrations of electrolytes in vitreous humor. Ambient temperature, cause of death, age, sex, physiological, and pathological state are some of them [3,10]. However, the effects of some of these factors are still under discussion. For example, while some studies suggest that temperature and pathological conditions can significantly alter electrolyte concentrations, others show minimal impact, leading to disagreement. Additionally, individual variability makes it difficult to create a universally applicable model for PMI estimation. Hence, the review focused on summarizing the current knowledge on using vitreous humor electrolytes concentration in estimating PMI.

2. Methods Used in Estimating PMI

2.1 Physical Methods

Post-mortem livor mortis and body cooling or algor mortis are examples of physical methods. Lividity and hypostasis are alternative terms for livor mortis [10, 11]. Lividity occurs as a result of the cessation of circulation. In the absence of circulatory pressure, blood passively accumulates in the lower regions, causing a red or dark purple discoloration of the skin. Postmortem lividity can be observed within 20 to 30 minutes after death as pink patches, with increasing PMI the color changes to red or dark purple. This can be observed within 2 hours of death [12]. This method is useful in determining the location, position, and any postmortem movement of the body. However, it is not a very useful method in determining the PMI as it is only useful for PMI estimation within the initial 12-hour window, beyond which it offers limited forensic value [3, 12, 13].

Thermoregulation of the body stops following the death. This results in the body losing temperature, and eventually equilibrate to the surrounding temperature. The temperature decrease inside the body is named 'algor mortis' also known as body cooling [12]. Surface area, clothing, humidity, temperature, wind, rain, the weight of the body, and surface area ratio has an impact on this strategy. This technique is less precise and less accurate for determining of PMI as body temperature depends on numerous factors. In a postmortem examination, temperature of different sites such as surface skin, liver, brain, and rectum can be measured. However, the body temperature is essentially only measured at the central cores (brain, rectum) for practical purposes [3, 12, 13].

2.2 Physiochemical Methods

Rigor mortis is a physiochemical method and refers to the stiffness of the muscles [11]. After death, muscles undergo two main phases: primary relaxation and secondary relaxation or rigor mortis. Immediately after death muscles loosen up and this is known as the primary relaxation. Then the rigor mortis occurs. Following death, the adenosine triphosphate (ATP) level decreases and causes calcium ions to enter the muscle fibers, resulting contractions in the muscles. The lack of ATP stops calcium ions from pumping out and muscles become rigid. Rigor mortis starts from the heart and then spreads from proximal to distal parts [3,12]. Within the first 3 – 4 hours, rigor mortis develops in the hands, legs, and face. After 12 hours the whole body completely stiffened and remains so for the next 12 hours. Subsequently following another 12 hours it becomes completely flaccid if not refrigerated [12,13]. Hence, the physiochemical methods are more suitable to determine the PMI within 24 hours of death.

2.3 Bacterial Process

Putrefaction is an example of bacterial process. The decomposition of the body due to microbial action is known as putrefaction. After death, natural flora of the digestive system enters the blood and is dispersed throughout the body. The respiratory system, alimentary canal, and open wounds are additional entry points for external bacteria that can further contribute to decomposition of the body. Putrefaction begins within the first few hours. Then the body starts to change color and eventually the bacterial activity increases. These changes last for days however it is influenced by temperature, underlying diseases, and body size [3,12]. Therefore, putrefaction is not an accurate method of estimating PMI as it gives a wide time range.

2.4 Autolysis

Autolysis is the self-destruction of the body [3,12]. Diffusion and loss of selective membrane permeability are examples of autolysis [3]. After death, cells break down and release enzymes that cause tissue destruction. Various hydrolytic enzymes in the liver, stomach, and pancreas start to degrade cells and tissues. Many changes are not observable except for the macroscopic changes (whitish appearance in the cornea). Since many aspects related to putrefaction and autolysis occur at the same time, it might be difficult to distinguish these two processes and this method is also not very useful in estimating PMI as they both give wide range of time as PMI [12,13].

2.5 Biochemical Methods

Biochemical methods in PMI estimation primarily involve the analysis of postmortem changes in various body fluids, with a focus on tracking the concentrations of key electrolytes and metabolites [3]. After death, cellular breakdown leads to measurable alterations in compounds such as potassium, sodium, chloride, magnesium, and calcium, as well as nitrogen-based metabolites like urea and ammonia. These biochemical markers follow predictable postmortem patterns, providing a useful framework for PMI estimation [9, 14, 15]. Given the rapid degradation of blood due to autolysis and bacterial activity, alternative body fluids such as cerebrospinal fluid, synovial fluid, pericardial fluid and vitreous humor have been explored. These fluids are more stable postmortem due to their containment in enclosed spaces, which shields them from early contamination and autolysis [16]. Compared to cerebrospinal fluid autolysis processes are much slower in vitreous humor. Consequently, research on PMI is primarily focused on vitreous humor studies [3,17,18].

3. Vitreous Humor

The vitreous humor, also known as the vitreous body as shown in Fig. 20.1, is located in the posterior cavity of the eye in vertebrates. It is a clear, viscoelastic, transparent, hydrophilic gel like mass that lies between the lens and the retina. About 4 to 5 ml volume of vitreous humor is contain in the eyeball [19]. It contains loose network of different types of collagen fibrils such as type II, IV, V, VI. Among these type II collagen is the most abundant [19]. Along with collagen fibrils vitreous humor contains 99% water and the balanced one percent consists of other components such as, sugar, amino acid, urea, creatine, electrolytes, hypoxanthine, and hyaluronic acid, and organic compounds such as carbohydrates and proteins [18, 19]. Presence of hyaluronic acid in the vitreous humor

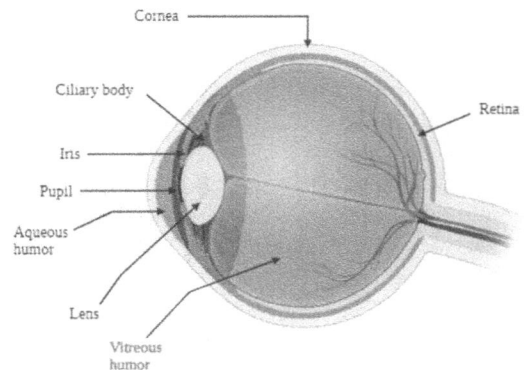

Fig. 20.1 Anatomy of the eye

Source: Authors (Biorender)

makes it more viscous than water. In addition to hyaluronic acid, the vitreous humor contains proteins such as albumin, globulin, and low-molecular-weight proteins, as well as lipids, carbohydrates, and electrolytes. These electrolytes include potassium, sodium, chloride, magnesium, calcium, ammonium, and nitrogen products like hypoxanthine, creatinine, and urea [19-21]. In the eye, the vitreous fluid has several functions. Its mechanical role is to maintain the eye's shape and positioning the retina. It also acts as a barrier to biomolecules, diffuses metabolic solutes that nourish the eye, stores and transports substances involved in the metabolic process of the surrounding ocular tissues, supports the growth and maintenance of the volume, elasticity, and resilience of the eye, protects against mechanical trauma, and permits light to reach the retina [19,21 22].

The location of vitreous humor is very useful in postmortem analysis, as it is anatomically isolated, sterile, stable for a longer period compared to other body fluids, and less influenced by microorganisms [18]. Studies have indicated that the electrolytes concentration in the vitreous humor can be used to determine the PMI over a long period.

3.1 Potassium (K+)

One of the main electrolytes identified in the vitreous humor is potassium which is abundantly found inside cells. Numerous studies using post-mortem vitreous humor are based on potassium-stimulated PMI [23,24,25]. The potassium concentration is slightly higher in vitreous humor (4.4 - 7.8 mmol/L) than in blood plasma (3.4 - 4.5 mmol/L) [19]. The ciliary body and the anterior capsule of the lens actively transport potassium into the posterior chamber of the eye, while the posterior capsule of the lens passively transports it into the vitreous humor. Potassium ions gradually flow out of the cells when the processes of selective membrane permeability and active membrane transport cease to function after death. The slow release of potassium ions from choroidal and retinal cells after death leads to an increase in potassium concentration in the extracellular fluid and the vitreous humor [18,19].

In 1959 Naumann establish a correlation between vitreous potassium concentration and the PMI. Later in 1964, Sturner suggested a linear correlation between the two variables [19]. Rathinam et al. confirmed a linear relationship between the rise in potassium concentration in both eyes and increasing PMI [24]. Similarly, Murthy et al. also observed that potassium concentration in the vitreous humor continue to increase with PMI, even under cold chamber condition [26]. Paul et al. found a consistent, fairly linear increase in potassium concentration with PMI throughout their study [26]. The same results were obtained by Akhtar et al [27]. Numerous studies have found that as vitreous potassium concentration and PMI have a strong positive linear correlation, vitreous potassium is the best electrolyte to determine PMI [4,16,28].

3.2 Sodium (Na⁺)

The most abundant cation in the extracellular fluid is sodium. It is one of the main cations found in the vitreous humor with 145.4 - 148.0 mmol/L of normal range [19]. It is an essential electrolyte that plays a vital role in maintaining normal cellular homeostasis and fluid and electrolyte regulation [18,19]. The studies showed that sodium concentration decreases with increasing PMI. Some studies observed a significant correlation between sodium and PMI [16,26] while some are not [7,28]. A weak correlation was observed between decreasing sodium concentration in the vitreous humor and postmortem cell death. This caused by loss of selective membrane permeability, which allows sodium to be absorbed into the retinal and choroidal cells after death. Zilg et al. discovered that every day after death, the sodium concentration in the vitreous reduces by roughly 2.2 mmol/L. According to Zilg research, vitreous sodium may regularly useful in identifying the cause of death. They have found that in cases of freshwater drowning, vitreous sodium concentrations were significantly lower compared to both non-drowning and brackish water drowning cases. Interestingly, brackish water drowning and non-water drowning cases exhibited similar sodium concentrations [29].

3.3 Chloride (Cl⁻)

Chloride is a significant anion in the vitreous humor, with a normal range of 120.6-122.7 mmol/L [19]. Also It regulates the fluid balance between the cells and maintains the pH in the cell [19]. Studies have shown that the vitreous chloride concentration decreases with the PMI [7, 29]. After death, the diffusion of chloride ions into the surrounding retinal and choroid cells due to a loss of function in selective

membrane permeability is most likely the cause of the decrease in vitreous chloride concentration [19]. Some studies showed that even though vitreous chloride ion concentration decreases with increasing PMI, it does not reach statistical significance [6,7,28] while some studies showed significant difference [26].

3.4 Magnesium (Mg²⁺)

Magnesium is another essential cation found in the vitreous humor. Magnesium ion plays a vital role in regulating various intracellular functions by acting as a cofactor for enzymatic reactions that regulate channels, cell cycle, energy metabolism and signaling pathways. The lack of oxygen supply to cells results in cellular hypoxia, which causes an elevation in the permeability of the cell membrane. As a consequence, magnesium ions diffuse through the membrane from inside the cell to the outside. Although a slow rise in the magnesium concentration in vitreous humor after death has been reported, the association was weaker than the association obtained between potassium and PMI. Hence, the studies claimed that magnesium cannot be utilized to estimate PMI [9,30,31]. However, limited studies are available on PMI and magnesium in vitreous humor and the use of magnesium in PMI estimation is still under debate [18].

3.5 Calcium (Ca²⁺)

One of the most prevalent cations in extracellular fluid is calcium. It is essential for several biological processes, including nerve impulse transmission, intracellular and extracellular communication, and muscle contraction. The serum calcium concentration is higher than the calcium ion concentration in the vitreous humor. Only a few studies are available on vitreous calcium concentration and the PMI estimation [6, 15, 30]. While Yang et al. and Siddamsetty et al. demonstrated a decline in vitreous calcium concentration with increasing PMI [6,30], Mihailovic et al claim that calcium ion concentration displays a significant rise with increasing PMI [15]. However, they did not obtain a strong regression coefficient or variation and suggested that vitreous calcium is not a precise indicator of PMI.

4. Factors Influencing Vitreous Humor Electrolyte Concentrations

Several factors have been reported to influence the vitreous humor electrolyte concentrations in deceased. These factors can be categorized as external and internal factors. External factors include the effect of different type of analytical instruments used for analysis, the sampling techniques employed, and the ambient temperature. For instance, the choice of analytical instruments, such as ion-selective electrodes or flame photometry, can introduce variability in the measured electrolyte concentration. Similarly, differences in sampling techniques, such as the site and method of vitreous humor collection, can impact the accuracy and precision of electrolyte measurements. Studies conducted by Rognum et al. and Zilg et al. found there is a positive correlation between the temperature and the postmortem vitreous potassium concentration [32, 33]. Their studies show that in higher ambient temperatures the rise of potassium concentration increases. Murthy et al. state that the potassium concentration gives a positive correlation with PMI in a cold chamber but sodium and chloride concentrations didn't show a negative correlation with PMI in a cold chamber. Their study showed that the temperature of a cold chamber has a significant effect on the rate of vitreous potassium change [26]. Ave et al. demonstrated that while ambient temperature and light can influence vitreous potassium concentration, freezing had no impact on the electrolyte concentration. They suggested that temperature changes may influence potassium concentration by causing membrane rupture or modifying potassium's binding to proteins in the vitreous humor [4]. However, Rathinam, et al. findings showed that there is no effect of temperature on vitreous electrolyte concentration [24].

Internal factors, on the other hand, refer to characteristics or conditions specific to the individual whose vitreous humor is being analyzed. These factors include sex, age, and body weight. The cause of death could be an external or internal factor [3]. Studies have measured the electrolyte concentrations separately in each eye and found no significant association between the eye orientation and the electrolyte concentration in the vitreous humor [8,24,34,35]. Further, recent studies have found that there is no significant effect of sex on the vitreous electrolyte concentrations [6,7,25].

Several studies reported that there is no significant difference between the age and the vitreous electrolytes concentrations [5-7,25]. However, Zilg et al. discovered that the vitreous potassium concentration increases exponentially with age, especially the younger the age, the faster the increase in vitreous potassium concentration [32].

When considering the cause of the death, a study conducted on saltwater drowning deaths observed a higher concentration of magnesium, sodium and chloride in saltwater drowning deaths than the non-saltwater drowning deaths. The study suggested that this may be due to the passive diffusion of salt water through eye covering during immersion [36]. A recent study showed that hanging, metabolic acidosis, and diabetic coma affect the vitreous potassium ion concentration. Hanging causes tightness around the neck and increases the venous pressure which leads to blood contamination with the vitreous humor. This influences the potassium ion concentration in the vitreous humor. Metabolic acidosis leads to hyperkalemia which changes the vitreous potassium concentration [37].

Limited studies have been conducted on body weight and vitreous humor electrolyte concentration. Zilg et al. study observed there is no effect of body weigh on vitreous electrolyte concentration [32]. However, Cordeiro et al. found that there is a relationship between body weight and PMI [5].

5. Conclusion

The current review highlights the significant role of vitreous humor potassium concentration in estimating the PMI, showing it to be a more accurate method compared to conventional techniques. Sodium and chloride estimations are not recommended to determine the PMI, however, it recommended for determining the cause of death. Research into magnesium and calcium concentrations remains limited and warrants further investigation. Although several factors have been identified, ambient temperature, cause of death and age are significant factors affecting potassium concentration and, consequently, PMI estimation. Despite these insights, the variability in findings across studies and the limitations in existing research highlight the need for more robust and consistent data. Developing and standardizing measurement protocols for potassium and other electrolytes is crucial to reduce variability and improve overall precision. It is also important to conduct further research on how environmental factors such as ambient temperature, cause of death, and age impact electrolyte concentrations and PMI, as this will refine existing models and contribute to more accurate estimations. Further, exploring additional variables, including postmortem eye orientation and sex, should be pursued despite current findings suggesting no significant effects. Addressing these research needs will contribute to more reliable and effective forensic practices, particularly in developing countries where enhanced accuracy in PMI estimation can significantly aid in solving criminal cases and advancing forensic capabilities.

REFERENCES

1. Gurpreet Singh, DK Sharma, Deepali Pathak, and Sumanta Dutta, "Comparative Study on Post Mortem Analysis of Sodium and Potassium Levels of Vitreous Humour and Synovial Fluid in Determining Time Since Death," *Indian J. Forensic Med. Toxicol.*, vol. 16, no. 3, pp. 393–398, 2022, doi: 10.37506/ijfmt.v16i3.18329.

2. P. D. I. Meilia, M. D. Freeman, Herkutanto, and M. P. Zeegers, "A review of causal inference in forensic medicine," *Forensic Sci. Med. Pathol.*, vol. 16, no. 2, pp. 313–320, 2020, doi: 10.1007/s12024-020-00220-9.

3. B. Madea, "Methods for determining time of death," *Forensic Sci. Med. Pathol.*, vol. 12, no. 4, pp. 451–485, 2016, doi: 10.1007/s12024-016-9776-y.

4. M. T. Ave, L. Ordóñez-Mayán, M. Camiña, M. Febrero-Bande, and J. I. Muñoz-Barús, "Estimation of the post-mortem interval: Effect of storage conditions on the determination of vitreous humour [K+]," *Sci. Justice*, vol. 61, no. 5, pp. 597–602, 2021, doi: 10.1016/j.scijus.2021.07.005.

5. C. Cordeiro, L. Ordóñez-Mayán, E. Lendoiro, M. Febrero-Bande, D. N. Vieira, and J. I. Muñoz-Barús, "A reliable method for estimating the postmortem interval from the biochemistry of the vitreous humor, temperature and body weight," *Forensic Sci. Int.*, vol. 295, pp. 157–168, 2019, doi: 10.1016/j.forsciint.2018.12.007.

6. A. K. Siddamsetty, S. K. Verma, A. Kohli, D. Puri, and A. Singh, "Estimation of time since death from electrolyte, glucose and calcium analysis of postmortem vitreous humour in semi-arid climate," *Med. Sci. Law*, vol. 54, no. 3, pp. 158–166, 2014, doi: 10.1177/0025802413506424.

7. H. V. Chandrakanth, T. Kanchan, B. M. Balaraj, H. S. Virupaksha, and T. N. Chandrashekar, "Postmortem vitreous chemistry-An evaluation of sodium, potassium and chloride levels in estimation of time since death (during the first 36 h after death)," *J. Forensic Leg. Med.*, vol. 20, no. 4, pp. 211–216, 2013, doi: 10.1016/j.jflm.2012.09.001.

8. Srettabunjong, S. Thongphap, W. Chittamma, and Anchalee, "Comparative and Correlation Studies of Biochemical Substances in Vitreous Humor and Synovial Fluid," *J. Forensic Sci.*, vol. 64, no. 3, pp. 778–785, 2019, doi: 10.1111/1556-4029.13966.

9. Z. Mihailovic, T. Atanasijevic, V. Popovic, and M. B. Milosevic, "The role of vitreous magnesium quantification in estimating the postmortem interval," *J. Forensic Sci.*, vol. 59, no. 3, pp. 775–778, 2014, doi: 10.1111/1556-4029.12286.

10. Z. Mihailovic, T. Atanasijevic, V. Popovic, M. B. Milosevic, and J. P. Sperhake, "Estimation of the postmortem interval by analyzing potassium in the vitreous humor: Could repetitive sampling enhance accuracy?," *Am. J. Forensic Med. Pathol.*, vol. 33, no. 4, pp. 400–403, 2012, doi: 10.1097/PAF.0b013e31826627d0.

11. G. D. Niturkar and S. G. Saraf, "Post Mortem analysis of electrolytes in vitreous humour to determine time since death," vol. 23, no. 4, 2023.

12. R. Shedge, K. Krishan, V. Warrier, and T. Kanchan, "Postmortem Changes," *StatPearls*, Jul. 2023, Accessed: May 26, 2024. [Online]. Available: https://www.ncbi.nlm.nih.gov/books/NBK539741/

13. A. E. Rattenbury, *Forensic taphonomy*. Elsevier Inc., 2018. doi: 10.1016/B978-0-12-809360-3.00002-3.

14. C. Pérez-Martínez, G. Prieto Bonete, M. D. Pérez-Cárceles, and A. Luna, "Influence of the nature of death in biochemical analysis of the vitreous humour for the estimation of post-mortem interval," *Aust. J. Forensic Sci.*, vol. 52, no. 5, pp. 508–517, 2020, doi: 10.1080/00450618.2019.1593503.

15. Z. Mihailović *et al.*, "The significance of post-mortem vitreous calcium concentration in forensic practice," *Leg. Med.*, vol. 47, no. August, p. 101779, 2020, doi: 10.1016/j.legalmed.2020.101779.

16. R. Swain *et al.*, "Estimation of post-mortem interval: A comparison between cerebrospinal fluid and vitreous humour chemistry," *J. Forensic Leg. Med.*, vol. 36, pp. 144–148, 2015, doi: 10.1016/j.jflm.2015.09.017.

17. P. M. Paul, S. Sneha, P. Pradhan, and P. S. Kumar, "Estimation of post-mortem interval from vitreous potassium : An autopsy based study," vol. 43, no. 4, pp. 370–373, 2021, doi: 10.5958/0974-0848.2021.00094.4.

18. W. Li *et al.*, "Vitreous humor: A review of biochemical constituents in postmortem interval estimation," *J. Forensic Sci. Med.*, vol. 4, no. 2, pp. 85–90, 2018, doi: 10.4103/jfsm.jfsm_13_18.

19. N. Pigaiani, A. Bertaso, E. F. De Palo, F. Bortolotti, and F. Tagliaro, "Vitreous humor endogenous compounds analysis for post-mortem forensic investigation," *Forensic Sci. Int.*, vol. 310, p. 110235, 2020, doi: 10.1016/j.forsciint.2020.110235.

20. K. R. Murthy *et al.*, "Proteomic analysis of human vitreous humor," *Clin. Proteomics*, vol. 11, no. 1, pp. 1–11, 2014, doi: 10.1186/1559-0275-11-29.

21. W. Murphy, J. Black, and G. Hastings, "Handbook of biomaterial properties, second edition," *Handb. Biomater. Prop. Second Ed.*, pp. 1–676, 2016, doi: 10.1007/978-1-4939-3305-1.

22. T. V. C. and Y. Hong, "The Vitreous Humor," *Handb. Biomater. Prop. Second Ed.*, pp. 1–676, 2016, doi: 10.1007/978-1-4939-3305-1.

23. R. Rathinam *et al.*, "Vitreous potassium concentration as a predictor of postmortem interval: A cross-sectional study among poisoning and burns cases at a tertiary care center in rural Haryana," *J. Dr. NTR Univ. Heal. Sci.*, vol. 4, no. 4, p. 214, 2015, doi: 10.4103/2277-8632.171701.

24. Rathinam *et al.*, "Vitreous potassium concentration as a predictor of postmortem interval: A cross-sectional study among natural death cases at a tertiary care center in rural Haryana," no. August, 2019.

25. A.-M. Bassam, H. Nofal, and M. Alhalabi, "Correlation between Vitreous Humor Potassium Levels and the Time of bleeding-caused Death and the Factors Affecting it," *Int. J. Pharm. Sci. Rev. Res.*, vol. 60, no. 1, pp. 1–5, 2020.

26. A. S. Murthy, S. Das, H. K. Thazhath, V. A. Chaudhari, and P. S. Adole, "The effect of cold chamber temperature on the cadaver's electrolyte changes in vitreous humor and plasma," *J. Forensic Leg. Med.*, vol. 62, no. September 2018, pp. 87–91, 2019, doi: 10.1016/j.jflm.2019.01.012.

27. N. Akhtar, R. Ali, A. R. Malik, A. Asghar, and K. Aziz, "Role of vitreous potassium level in postmortem interval estimation," *Pakistan J. Med. Heal. Sci.*, vol. 9, no. 1, pp. 88–92, 2015.

28. J. Garland *et al.*, "Using vitreous humour and cerebrospinal fluid electrolytes in estimating post-mortem interval - an exploratory study," *Aust. J. Forensic Sci.*, vol. 52, no. 6, pp. 626–633, 2020, doi: 10.1080/00450618.2019.1642956.

29. B. Zilg, K. Alkass, S. Berg, and H. Druid, "Interpretation of postmortem vitreous concentrations of sodium and chloride," *Forensic Sci. Int.*, vol. 263, pp. 107–113, 2016, doi: 10.1016/j.forsciint.2016.04.006.

30. M. Yang *et al.*, "A Study on the Estimation of Postmortem Interval Based on Environmental Temperature and Concentrations of Substance in Vitreous Humor," *J. Forensic Sci.*, vol. 63, no. 3, pp. 745–751, 2018, doi: 10.1111/1556-4029.13615.

31. R. Tse *et al.*, "Post mortem vitreous magnesium in adult population," *Forensic Sci. Int.*, vol. 284, pp. 46–52, 2018, doi: 10.1016/j.forsciint.2017.12.038.

32. B. Zilg, S. Bernard, K. Alkass, S. Berg, and H. Druid, "A new model for the estimation of time of death from vitreous potassium levels corrected for age and temperature," *Forensic Sci. Int.*, vol. 254, pp. 158–166, 2015, doi: 10.1016/j.forsciint.2015.07.020.

33. T. O. Rognum *et al.*, "Estimation of time since death by vitreous humor hypoxanthine, potassium, and ambient temperature," *Forensic Sci. Int.*, vol. 262, pp. 160–165, 2016, doi: 10.1016/j.forsciint.2016.03.001.

34. B. Zilg, K. Alkass, R. Kronstrand, S. Berg, and H. Druid, "A rapid method for postmortem vitreous chemistry—deadside analysis," *Biomolecules*, vol. 12, no. 1, pp. 1–12, 2022, doi: 10.3390/biom12010032.

35. H. S. Tatiya, A. A. Taware, V. T. Jadhav, and S. B. Punpale, "Between eye difference in vitreous electrolytes after death; for identical postmortme intervals," *Indian J. Forensic Med. Toxicol.*, vol. 11, no. 2, pp. 152–156, 2017, doi: 10.5958/0973-9130.2017.00086.X.

36. R. Tse *et al.*, "Postmortem Vitreous Humor Magnesium Does Not Elevate in Salt Water Drowning When the Immersion Time Is Less Than an Hour," *Am. J. Forensic Med. Pathol.*, vol. 38, no. 4, pp. 298–303, 2017, doi: 10.1097/PAF.0000000000000351.

37. S. Zięba, M. Wiergowski, B. M. Cieślik, J. S. Anand, and M. Krzyżanowska, "Uncertainty of Postmortem Time Estimation Based on Potassium Ion Determination in Vitreous Humor Using Potentiometric Ion-Selective Electrode and Microwave-Induced Plasma with Optical Emission Spectrometry Methods," *Separations*, vol. 10, no. 3, 2023, doi: 10.3390/separations10030201.

Transformative Applied Research in Computing, Engineering, Science and Technology – Dr. Damayanthi Dahanayake et al. (eds)
© *2024 Taylor & Francis Group, London, ISBN 978-1-041-01782-0*

21

Production of Biodiesel via Heterogeneous Catalytic Pathway

K.S.M.De Silva
Postgraduate Institute of Science,
University of Peradeniya,
Sri Lanka

T.M.M. Marso*
Postgraduate Institute of Science,
University of Peradeniya,
Sri Lanka
Department of Chemical Sciences,
South Eastern University of
Sri Lanka

Abstract

The quest for sustainable energy sources has led to intensified research into biodiesel production, with heterogeneous catalytic pathways emerging as promising alternatives. This review provides an extensive overview of recent advancements in biodiesel synthesis via heterogeneous catalysis. The review explores the principles and mechanisms underlying heterogeneous catalysis, beginning with an introduction to the significance of biodiesel as a renewable energy source and the drawbacks of traditional homogeneous catalytic methods. Various types of heterogeneous catalysts employed in biodiesel production, including solid acids, bases, and metallic catalysts, are discussed in detail, along with their advantages and limitations. Furthermore, recent developments in catalyst design and synthesis techniques are elucidated, highlighting strategies to enhance catalytic activity, selectivity, and stability. The review also delves into optimizing reaction parameters such as temperature, pressure, and catalyst loading to maximize biodiesel yield and quality. Additionally, the integration of heterogeneous catalytic processes with innovative technologies such as ultrasound and microwave irradiation are examined, showcasing their potential to enhance reaction kinetics and reduce energy consumption. Furthermore, the challenges associated with catalyst deactivation, regeneration, and waste management are addressed, along with strategies to mitigate these issues. Finally, the review concludes with insights into future research directions and the potential of heterogeneous catalytic pathways to play a pivotal role in the sustainable production of biodiesel.

Keywords

Biodiesel, Heterogeneous catalysis, Catalyst design, Reaction optimization, Sustainable energy

*Corresponding author: marso@seu.ac.lk

DOI: 10.1201/9781003616368-21

1. Introduction

Biodiesel is a renewable fuel derived from biological sources, typically vegetable oils, animal fats, or recycled cooking oils. It is produced through a process called trans-esterification, where triglycerides (found in oils and fats) react with an alcohol (usually methanol or ethanol) in the presence of a catalyst, such as sodium hydroxide or potassium hydroxide, to form fatty acid methyl esters (FAMEs) or fatty acid ethyl esters (FAEEs) - the main components of biodiesel - along with glycerol as a by-product [1]. Biodiesel can be used as a direct substitute for or blended with petroleum diesel in diesel engines, providing an alternative, renewable, and cleaner-burning fuel option [2, 3]. It is biodegradable, non-toxic, and emits lower levels of pollutants such as Sulfur oxides, particulate matter, and carbon monoxide compared to conventional diesel fuel, making it environmentally friendly and conducive to reducing greenhouse gas emissions and air pollution. Biodiesel production contributes to energy security, rural development, and promoting sustainable agriculture by utilizing domestically produced feedstocks and reducing dependence on fossil fuels [4].

The importance of biodiesel as a renewable energy source stems from its potential to address several critical environmental, economic, and social challenges.

1.1 Reduction of Greenhouse Gas Emissions

Biodiesel is derived from renewable feedstocks such as vegetable oils, animal fats, and used cooking oil. When burned, biodiesel releases carbon dioxide (CO_2), but the plants used to produce biodiesel absorb an equivalent amount of CO_2 during photosynthesis. This closed carbon cycle remarkably reduces net CO_2 emissions compared to fossil fuels, contributing to mitigation efforts against climate change.

1.2 Decreased Dependency on Fossil Fuels

Biodiesel provides an alternative to petroleum-based diesel fuel, helping to diversify energy sources and reduce reliance on finite fossil fuel reserves. This reduces the vulnerability of economies to fluctuations in global oil prices and geopolitical tensions associated with oil-producing regions.

1.3 Promotion of Rural Development and Agricultural Sustainability

Biodiesel production often utilizes crops, forestry residues, and waste materials as feedstocks. This creates opportunities for farmers, foresters, and rural communities to generate income from renewable resources, fostering economic development and job creation in rural areas. Additionally, sustainable cultivation practices can enhance soil fertility, biodiversity, and ecosystem health.

1.4 Energy Security

By producing biodiesel domestically, countries can enhance their energy security by reducing dependence on imported oil. This strengthens national resilience to supply disruptions and price volatility in the global oil market, thereby enhancing energy independence and sovereignty.

1.5 Improved Air Quality

Biodiesel combustion produces lower levels of particulate matter, sulfur oxides (SO_x), and other harmful pollutants compared to conventional diesel fuel. Consequently, the widespread use of biodiesel in transportation and stationary applications can help mitigate air pollution, protect public health, and alleviate respiratory illnesses in urban areas.

1.6 Support for Sustainable Development Goals (SDGs)

Biodiesel aligns with several Sustainable Development Goals outlined by the United Nations, including those related to climate action, affordable and clean energy, sustainable cities and communities, responsible consumption and production, and partnerships for the goals. By advancing these objectives, biodiesel contributes to a more sustainable and equitable global society.

Overall, the importance of biodiesel as a renewable energy source lies in its capacity to offer a cleaner, greener, and more sustainable alternative to conventional diesel fuel, thereby fostering environmental protection, economic development, and energy resilience on a global scale [4].

2. Limitations of Traditional Biodiesel Production Methods

Traditional biodiesel production methods face several challenges and limitations, which can hinder their widespread adoption and sustainability.

Many traditional biodiesel production methods rely on edible vegetable oils, such as soybean oil, palm oil, and rapeseed oil, as feedstocks. However, the cultivation of these crops for biodiesel can compete with food production, leading to concerns about food security, land use change, deforestation, and biodiversity loss [4].

The expansion of agricultural land for biodiesel feedstock cultivation can contribute to deforestation, habitat destruction, soil degradation, and water pollution. Land use change may also result in the displacement of Indigenous communities, loss of biodiversity, and disruption of ecosystems, exacerbating environmental degradation and climate change [5].

Traditional biodiesel production methods often require significant inputs of energy, water, fertilizers, and pesticides, leading to high resource consumption and environmental impacts. The energy balance of biodiesel production, particularly for feedstocks with low oil yields or grown under intensive agricultural practices, may be unfavorable, limiting its overall sustainability and energy efficiency.

While biodiesel offers potential reductions in net greenhouse gas emissions compared to fossil fuels, the carbon footprint of biodiesel production can vary remarkably depending on feedstock selection, cultivation practices, processing techniques, and transportation logistics. Certain feedstocks, such as palm oil, may have higher carbon intensity due to deforestation, land conversion, and peat land drainage associated with their production [2].

Traditional biodiesel production methods, such as trans-esterification, may involve complex chemical processes, catalysts, and equipment, leading to high capital and operating costs. Additionally, feedstock variability, impurities, and contaminants can pose technical challenges in biodiesel production, affecting yield, quality, and stability, and necessitating additional purification steps and process optimization.

The price and availability of biodiesel feedstocks, such as vegetable oils, animal fats, and used cooking oil, can be subject to market fluctuations, supply chain disruptions, weather events, and geopolitical factors [3]. Price volatility and market uncertainty may impact the profitability, competitiveness, and viability of biodiesel production, affecting investment decisions and industry growth.

Biodiesel production is subject to various regulations, policies, and sustainability standards aimed at ensuring environmental, social, and economic sustainability. Compliance with regulatory requirements, certification schemes, and sustainability criteria may entail additional costs, administrative burdens, and market access barriers for biodiesel producers, particularly small-scale and emerging enterprises [4].

3. Catalysts In Biodiesel Production

Catalysts play a crucial role in facilitating biodiesel synthesis by accelerating the conversion of triglycerides from renewable feedstocks such as vegetable oils, animal fats, and used cooking oil into fatty acid methyl esters (FAMEs), which constitute biodiesel [6, 7]. The primary role of catalysts is to facilitate the trans-esterification reaction, where triglycerides react with alcohol (usually methanol or ethanol) in the presence of a catalyst to yield FAMEs and glycerol. Catalysts enable this reaction by reducing the activation energy required for bond cleavage and formation, thus increasing the reaction rate, and promoting product formation. Additionally, catalysts can influence reaction selectivity, favoring the desired products while minimizing the formation of undesirable by-products. Common catalysts used in biodiesel synthesis include homogeneous catalysts such as alkaline and acidic catalysts (e.g., sodium hydroxide, potassium hydroxide, sulfuric acid) and heterogeneous catalysts such as solid acids, solid bases, and metal oxides (e.g., calcium oxide, magnesium oxide, zinc oxide). These catalysts exhibit varying catalytic activity, selectivity, stability, and ease of separation, depending on the specific reaction conditions and feedstock properties. Catalyst selection and optimization are crucial for maximizing biodiesel yield, quality, and process efficiency while minimizing costs and environmental impact.

Overall, catalysts play a pivotal role in facilitating biodiesel synthesis by enabling efficient and selective conversion of triglycerides into biodiesel, thus contributing to the advancement of sustainable and renewable energy technologies [8].

4. Principles and Mechanisms of Heterogeneous Catalysts

Heterogeneous catalysis, pivotal in various industrial processes including biodiesel production and petrochemical refining, operates at the interface between the catalyst surface and reactant molecules.

Here, reactants adsorb onto the catalyst surface, facilitated by physical or chemical interactions, leading to the activation of chemical bonds and the formation of reactive intermediates. Reaction pathways, influenced by catalyst properties and reaction conditions, involve adsorption-desorption cycles, surface diffusion, and surface-mediated redox processes. Active sites on the catalyst surface dictate catalytic activity and selectivity, influenced by factors such as type, size, and accessibility. Catalysis mechanisms encompass acid-base, metal, and bi-functional catalysis, facilitating diverse reactions [4, 8]. Catalyst deactivation may occur due to surface poisoning, necessitating regeneration techniques. Understanding these principles enables the development of innovative catalyst materials and optimized processes for sustainable and efficient catalysis across various applications, offering remarkable societal and economic benefits [7].

5. Advantages Over Homogeneous Catalysis in Biodiesel Production

Heterogeneous catalysis holds several advantages over homogeneous catalysis in biodiesel production, making it a preferred choice for industrial applications. Unlike homogeneous catalysts, heterogeneous catalysts are in a solid phase, enabling easier separation and recovery from the reaction mixture, thus allowing for catalyst reuse and minimizing waste generation [9]. Additionally, heterogeneous catalysis reduces undesirable interactions between reactants and catalysts, leading to improved catalytic activity, selectivity, and stability. Its flexibility in reaction conditions facilitates process optimization and scale-up, while compatibility with high-throughput screening techniques accelerates catalyst development and innovation. Moreover, heterogeneous catalysis minimizes environmental impact by utilizing solid catalysts and reducing the use of hazardous solvents, contributing to the sustainability of biodiesel production processes. With broad substrate compatibility, heterogeneous catalysis promotes resource utilization and feedstock flexibility, further enhancing its appeal for sustainable biofuel production. These advantages underscore the pivotal role of heterogeneous catalytic pathways in advancing efficient, environmentally friendly, and economically viable biodiesel production technologies to meet global energy needs [8].

6. Types of Heterogeneous Catalysts

Heterogeneous catalysts utilized in biodiesel production encompass various types, each with distinct properties and applications [10]. Common types of heterogeneous catalysts include:

6.1 Solid Acid Catalysts

Solid acid catalysts facilitate biodiesel production by promoting esterification and trans-esterification reactions. These catalysts typically consist of acidic functional groups supported on solid materials such as zeolites, sulfated metal oxides (e.g., sulfated zirconia), ion-exchange resins, or acidic clays [10]. Solid acid catalysts offer advantages such as high activity, stability, and ease of separation, making them suitable for biodiesel synthesis from low-quality feedstocks or in the presence of free fatty acids.

6.2 Solid Base Catalysts

Solid base catalysts are employed in biodiesel production to catalyze trans-esterification reactions, particularly in the presence of acidic feedstocks or high free fatty acid content. These catalysts comprise basic functional groups supported on solid materials, including alkali metal hydroxides (e.g., sodium hydroxide, potassium hydroxide) supported on alumina or silica, alkali metal carbonates, and hydrotalcite-like compounds [10]. Solid base catalysts offer rapid reaction kinetics, high selectivity, and ease of catalyst recovery, making them suitable for large-scale biodiesel production.

6.3 Metal Oxide Catalysts

Metal oxide catalysts are widely used in biodiesel synthesis to catalyze trans-esterification reactions through acid-base bi-functional mechanisms. These catalysts consist of metal oxide nanoparticles or supported metal oxides (e.g., magnesium oxide, calcium oxide, zinc oxide) with both acidic and basic sites on their surfaces [10, 11]. Metal oxide catalysts exhibit high catalytic activity, thermal stability, and resistance to catalyst poisoning, enabling efficient biodiesel production from a wide range of feed stocks under mild reaction conditions.

6.4 Enzymatic Catalysts

Enzymatic catalysts, including lipases and esterases, are utilized in biodiesel production to catalyze trans-esterification reactions under mild reaction conditions. These biocatalysts offer high catalytic efficiency, specificity, and environmental compatibility, enabling biodiesel synthesis from a variety of feedstocks, including waste oils and non-edible oils. Enzymatic catalysts exhibit biodegradability, recyclability, and compatibility with organic solvents, making them suitable for green and sustainable biodiesel production processes [10, 11].

Each type of heterogeneous catalyst offers unique advantages and limitations, depending on the specific reaction requirements, feedstock properties, process conditions, and desired product characteristics [12]. Selection of the appropriate catalyst type is critical for optimizing biodiesel yield, quality, and process efficiency while minimizing costs and environmental impact [9].

7. Effect of Temperature, Pressure, and Reaction Time on Biodiesel Yield

The yield of biodiesel in trans-esterification reactions is remarkably influenced by reaction temperature, pressure, and reaction time. Elevated temperatures generally accelerate the reaction kinetics by increasing the collision frequency and energy of reactant molecules, promoting the formation of biodiesel and glycerol. However, excessively high temperatures can lead to side reactions, catalyst deactivation, and thermal degradation of biodiesel, reducing overall yield and product quality [13]. Similarly, reaction pressure affects biodiesel yield by altering the equilibrium position of the reaction, with higher pressures favoring the formation of biodiesel. However, the effect of pressure is often less pronounced compared to temperature, and excessive pressure may lead to increased energy consumption and equipment costs without remarkable improvements in yield [9]. Reaction time also plays a crucial role, as longer reaction times allow for more extensive conversion of triglycerides into biodiesel and glycerol. However, prolonged reaction times may lead to diminishing returns and increased energy consumption, necessitating optimization to achieve maximum yield and efficiency. Therefore, careful control of temperature, pressure, and reaction time is essential for optimizing biodiesel yield while maintaining process efficiency, product quality, and economic viability [14], [15].

8. Optimization Strategies for Maximizing Biodiesel Production Efficiency

Optimizing biodiesel production efficiency involves various strategies aimed at maximizing yield, quality, and process sustainability while minimizing costs and environmental impact. These strategies include the selection of suitable feedstocks with high oil content and low free fatty acid levels, which can enhance biodiesel yield and reduce the need for additional pre-treatment steps [16]. Process optimization involves fine-tuning reaction parameters such as temperature, pressure, catalyst loading, and molar ratio of alcohol to oil to maximize conversion efficiency and minimize reaction time [13, 17]. Integration of innovative technologies such as ultrasound-assisted and microwave-assisted reactions can enhance mass transfer, reaction kinetics, and energy efficiency, leading to higher yields and reduced energy consumption. Additionally, catalyst selection, design, and regeneration techniques play a crucial role in improving catalytic activity, selectivity, and stability, thereby enhancing overall process efficiency [15, 18]. Furthermore, by-product utilization, waste minimization, and process integration strategies can improve resource efficiency and reduce environmental footprint, contributing to the sustainability of biodiesel production processes. Overall, a comprehensive approach combining feedstock selection, process optimization, technology innovation, and sustainability measures is essential for maximizing biodiesel production efficiency in a cost-effective and environmentally friendly manner.

9. Integration of Innovative Technologies

The integration of innovative technologies in biodiesel production holds important promise for enhancing process efficiency, productivity, and sustainability. One such technology is ultrasound-assisted trans-esterification, which utilizes high-frequency sound waves to improve mixing and mass transfer rates, thereby accelerating reaction kinetics and reducing reaction times [5]. Ultrasound can disrupt the boundary layer around catalyst particles and reactants, enhancing contact between reactants and catalyst surfaces and promoting biodiesel formation. Similarly, microwave-assisted trans-esterification employs electromagnetic radiation to heat reaction mixtures rapidly and uniformly, leading to higher reaction rates and reduced energy consumption compared to conventional heating methods. Microwave irradiation can enhance heat and mass transfer within the reaction medium, facilitating biodiesel production from various feedstocks with shorter reaction times and lower catalyst loading [1]. Additionally, the use of enzymatic catalysts in biodiesel synthesis offers advantages such as high catalytic activity, selectivity, and environmental compatibility. Enzymatic processes operate under mild reaction conditions, minimizing energy consumption, waste generation, and environmental impact while enabling biodiesel production from diverse feedstocks. Furthermore, the integration of continuous-flow reactors, membrane technologies, and process intensification techniques can enhance process control, scalability, and productivity, enabling cost-effective and sustainable biodiesel production on a commercial scale [4]. Overall, the integration of innovative technologies in biodiesel production holds tremendous potential for improving process efficiency, reducing costs, and mitigating environmental impact, thereby advancing the transition towards more sustainable and renewable energy in the future.

10. Challenges and Solutions in Biodiesel Production

Biodiesel production faces several challenges that must be addressed to ensure its viability as a sustainable alternative fuel source. One major challenge is the competition for feedstock resources with food production, which can lead to issues such as deforestation, land-use change, and food price volatility. To mitigate this, research focuses on developing biodiesel feedstocks that do not compete with food crops, such as algae, waste oils, and non-food crops like Jatropha and Camelina [13]. Another challenge is the variability of feedstock quality, which can affect biodiesel yield and quality. To address this, improved feedstock characterization methods and process optimization techniques are being developed to accommodate different feedstock compositions and properties [3].

Catalyst deactivation and efficiency are also remarkable challenges in biodiesel production. Catalyst poisoning, leaching, and deactivation over time can reduce process efficiency and increase costs. Solutions include the development of more stable and recyclable catalysts, as well as catalyst regeneration techniques to extend catalyst lifespan and reduce waste generation. Additionally, the energy-intensive nature of biodiesel production processes, particularly transesterification, presents a challenge in terms of environmental sustainability and cost-effectiveness [15]. Innovative technologies such as microwave and ultrasound-assisted reactions, enzymatic catalysis, and process intensification methods offer potential solutions by reducing energy consumption, reaction times, and waste generation.

The glycerol by-product generated during biodiesel production poses challenges in terms of disposal and utilization. Large-scale production of biodiesel results in a remarkable surplus of glycerol, which requires appropriate disposal or valorization to avoid environmental pollution and waste [12]. Solutions include the development of value-added products from glycerol, such as chemicals, pharmaceuticals, and bioplastics, as well as bio-refinery concepts that integrate biodiesel production with glycerol utilization to maximize resource efficiency.

Regulatory and policy challenges also affect biodiesel production, including fluctuating government incentives, tax credits, and sustainability certification requirements. Streamlining regulations, providing stable policy support, and incentivizing sustainable biodiesel production practices can help create a more favorable business environment for biodiesel producers and investors. Overall, addressing these challenges requires a multifaceted approach involving technological innovation, policy support, and stakeholder collaboration to ensure the continued growth and sustainability of the biodiesel industry [3].

11. Future Perspectives of Biodiesel Production

The future of biodiesel production holds promising developments driven by technological advancements, sustainability goals, and evolving market dynamics. One key trend is the increasing emphasis on feedstock diversification and utilization of non-food resources to mitigate competition with food production and address land-use concerns [7]. This includes the exploration of advanced feedstocks such as algae, microbial oils, waste oils, and lingo-cellulosic biomass, which offer higher yields, lower environmental impact, and reduced reliance on arable land.

The integration of bio-refinery concepts and advanced processing technologies enables the co-production of

biodiesel alongside value-added products, such as bio-based chemicals, biofuels, and biopolymers, enhancing overall process efficiency and economic viability [11]. Biorefineries leverage the utilization of all biomass components, including lipids, proteins, carbohydrates, and lignin, to maximize resource efficiency and minimize waste generation, contributing to a more circular and sustainable bio-economy [3].

Innovations in catalysis, including the development of novel catalyst materials, immobilization techniques, and process intensification methods, continue to drive improvements in biodiesel production efficiency, selectivity, and sustainability. Catalysts tailored for specific feedstocks, reaction conditions, and process requirements offer opportunities for optimizing reaction kinetics, minimizing energy consumption, and reducing environmental impact, thus enhancing the competitiveness of biodiesel as a renewable fuel source.

Additionally, the growing emphasis on environmental sustainability, carbon neutrality, and de-carbonization efforts worldwide is expected to drive increased demand for renewable fuels, including biodiesel. Policy support, regulatory incentives, and carbon pricing mechanisms aimed at reducing greenhouse gas emissions and promoting renewable energy adoption further bolster the growth prospects of the biodiesel industry [12].

Moreover, advancements in biotechnology, synthetic biology, and genetic engineering hold the potential to enhance feedstock productivity, lipid content, and oil quality in biodiesel feedstocks, contributing to higher yields, lower production costs, and improved resource efficiency [3]. Biotechnological approaches enable the development of tailored microorganisms and crops optimized for biodiesel production, as well as the production of designer oils with desired fatty acid compositions and properties.

Overall, the future of biodiesel production is characterized by innovation, sustainability, and diversification, with continued advancements in feedstock utilization, process optimization, and technology integration driving the transition towards a more sustainable, low-carbon, and resilient energy future.

12. Conclusion

In conclusion, biodiesel production stands at the threshold of remarkable advancements driven by technological innovation, sustainability imperatives, and evolving market dynamics. The future trajectory of biodiesel hinges on several key factors: feedstock diversification, bio-refinery integration, catalytic innovation, and policy support. By expanding the feedstock base to include non-food resources like algae and waste oils, biodiesel production can mitigate concerns regarding competition with food crops and land-use change, thus promoting environmental sustainability and resource efficiency. The integration of bio-refinery concepts, advanced processing technologies, and value-added product co-production offers opportunities to enhance process efficiency, reduce waste generation, and improve economic viability. Catalytic innovations, especially in heterogeneous catalysis, hold promise for optimizing reaction kinetics, minimizing energy consumption, and improving product quality. Additionally, policy incentives and regulatory frameworks aimed at promoting renewable energy adoption and carbon neutrality provide a conducive environment for the growth of the biodiesel industry. As we navigate towards a more sustainable energy future, biodiesel remains a key player in the transition to cleaner, greener fuels, offering a renewable alternative to conventional fossil fuels and contributing to the global efforts to combat climate change and achieve energy security.

REFERENCES

1. A. Abbaszaadeh, B. Ghobadian, M. R. Omidkhah, and G. Najafi, "Current biodiesel production technologies: A comparative review," *Energy Convers. Manag.*, vol. 63, pp. 138–148, 2012, doi: https://doi.org/10.1016/j.enconman.2012.02.027.

2. P. M. Felizardo, M. J. N. Correia, I. Raposo, J. F. Mendes, R. Berkemeier, and J. Bordado, "Production of biodiesel from waste frying oils.," *Waste Manag.*, vol. 26 5, pp. 487–494, 2006, [Online]. Available: https://api.semanticscholar.org/CorpusID:28567196

3. S. N. Gebremariam and J. M. Marchetti, "Economics of biodiesel production: Review," *Energy Convers. Manag.*, vol. 168, pp. 74–84, 2018, doi: https://doi.org/10.1016/j.enconman.2018.05.002.

4. F. Ma and M. A. Hanna, "Biodiesel production: a review1Journal Series #12109, Agricultural Research Division, Institute of Agriculture and Natural Resources, University of Nebraska–Lincoln.1," *Bioresour. Technol.*, vol. 70, no. 1, pp. 1–15, 1999, doi: https://doi.org/10.1016/S0960-8524(99)00025-5.

5. A. P. S. Chouhan and A. K. Sarma, "Modern heterogeneous catalysts for biodiesel production: A comprehensive review," *Renew. Sustain. Energy Rev.*, vol. 15, no. 9, pp. 4378–4399, 2011, doi: https://doi.org/10.1016/j.rser.2011.07.112.

6. J. M. Marchetti, V. U. Miguel, and A. F. Errazu, "Possible methods for biodiesel production," *Renew. Sustain. Energy Rev.*, vol. 11, no. 6, pp. 1300–1311, 2007, doi: https://doi.org/10.1016/j.rser.2005.08.006.

7. S. V. Ranganathan, S. L. Narasimhan, and K. Muthukumar, "An overview of enzymatic production of biodiesel.," *Bioresour. Technol.*, vol. 99, no. 10, pp. 3975–3981, Jul. 2008, doi: 10.1016/j.biortech.2007.04.060.

8. M. Hara, "Environmentally Benign Production of Biodiesel Using Heterogeneous Catalysts," *ChemSusChem*, vol. 2, no. 2, pp. 129–135, Feb. 2009, doi: https://doi.org/10.1002/cssc.200800222.

9. S. Sahani and Y. C. Sharma, "Economically viable production of biodiesel using a novel heterogeneous catalyst: Kinetic and thermodynamic investigations," *Energy Convers. Manag.*, vol. 171, pp. 969–983, 2018, doi: https://doi.org/10.1016/j.enconman.2018.06.059.

10. A. Ruhul, M. A. Kalam, H. H. Masjuki, I. M. R. Fattah, S. Shahed, and M. M. Rashed, "State of the art of biodiesel production process: A review on heterogeneous, homogeneous, biocatalytic and non-catalytic process.," *RSC Adv.*, vol. 5, Nov. 2015, doi: 10.1039/C5RA09862A.

11. X. Ma et al., "Current application of MOFs based heterogeneous catalysts in catalyzing transesterification/esterification for biodiesel production: A review," *Energy Convers. Manag.*, vol. 229, p. 113760, 2021, doi: https://doi.org/10.1016/j.enconman.2020.113760.

12. S. F. Basumatary et al., "Production of renewable biodiesel using metal organic frameworks based materials as efficient heterogeneous catalysts," *J. Clean. Prod.*, vol. 358, p. 131955, 2022, doi: https://doi.org/10.1016/j.jclepro.2022.131955.

13. J. V. L. Ruatpuia and S. L. Rokhum, "Biodiesel Production through Heterogeneous Catalysis Route: A Review," *Sci. Vis.*, vol. 22, Apr. 2022, doi: 10.33493/scivis.22.01.01.

14. P. T. Vasudevan and M. Briggs, "Biodiesel production—current state of the art and challenges," *J. Ind. Microbiol. Biotechnol.*, vol. 35, no. 5, p. 421, May 2008, doi: 10.1007/s10295-008-0312-2.

15. A. Mukhtar et al., "Current status and challenges in the heterogeneous catalysis for biodiesel production," *Renew. Sustain. Energy Rev.*, vol. 157, p. 112012, 2022, doi: https://doi.org/10.1016/j.rser.2021.112012.

16. M. Cozier, "Business highlights: Collaboration: Bigger and beta," *Biofuels, Bioprod. Biorefining*, vol. 8, no. 6, p. 743, 2014, doi: 10.1002/BBB.

17. Y. Zhang, L. Duan, and H. Esmaeili, "A review on biodiesel production using various heterogeneous nanocatalysts: Operation mechanisms and performances," *Biomass and Bioenergy*, vol. 158, p. 106356, 2022, doi: https://doi.org/10.1016/j.biombioe.2022.106356.

18. B. Wang, B. Wang, S. K. Shukla, and R. Wang, "Enabling Catalysts for Biodiesel Production via Transesterification," *Catalysts*, vol. 13, no. 4, 2023, doi: 10.3390/catal13040740.

19. M. Mathiyazhagan, and, A Ganapathi., 2011. Factors affecting biodiesel production. Research in plant Biology, 1(2).

20. R. Romero, S.L. Martínez, and, R. Natividad, 2011. Biodiesel production by using heterogeneous catalysts. Alternative fuel, pp.3–20.

Transformative Applied Research in Computing, Engineering, Science and Technology – Dr. Damayanthi Dahanayake et al. (eds)
© 2024 Taylor & Francis Group, London, ISBN 978-1-041-01782-0

22

In Silico Design and Computational Validation of a Novel Synthetic Genetic Logic Gate Circuit for the Detection and Degradation of Benzene, Toluene, Ethylbenzene, and Xylene in Petroleum

S. Sooriyapperuma,
M.A. Shahan, D. Abeysekara, L. Wedamulla
Department of Biotechnology,
Faculty of Agriculture and Plantation Management,
Wayamba University of Sri Lanka, Makandura,
Gonawila (NWP), 60170, Sri Lanka

A. Gamage
International Institute of Health Sciences, No 704
Negombo Rd, Welisara, Sri Lanka

D. Rajapaksha, S. Amath,
Department of Biotechnology,
Faculty of Agriculture and Plantation Management,
Wayamba University of Sri Lanka, Makandura,
Gonawila (NWP), 60170, Sri Lanka

R. P. Jayasingha
Centre for Advanced Materials and Devices (CAMD),
Department of Chemistry, Faculty of Science,
University of Colombo, Sri Lanka

G. Dikkumburage
Department of Biotechnology,
Faculty of Agriculture and Plantation Management,
Wayamba University of Sri Lanka, Makandura,
Gonawila (NWP), 60170, Sri Lanka

H.M.L.P.B. Herath*
Centre for Advanced Materials and Devices (CAMD),
Department of Chemistry, Faculty of Science,
University of Colombo, Sri Lanka
Department of Biomedical Science, Faculty of Science,
NSBM Green University, Sri Lanka

---

*Corresponding author: lalinka.h@nsbm.ac.lk

DOI: 10.1201/9781003616368-22

Abstract

Petroleum pollution, particularly from Benzene, Toluene, Ethylbenzene, and Xylene (BTEX) compounds, poses significant environmental and health risks. Bioremediation, using microorganisms to degrade pollutants, offers a promising solution. This study designed a dual-purpose synthetic genetic logic gate circuit for the detection and degradation of BTEX compounds in petroleum pollution. The novel gene circuit integrated genetic elements will trigger enzyme production and included a biomonitoring component for real-time assessment. Key genes for BTEX degradation and biomonitoring were identified, and a logical framework was developed to activate these genes in response to BTEX detection. The genetic construct comprised three promoters which are genetic "on-switches" that control when specific genes are activated (Pu, BFP, and Blind), BTEX signalling genes (*TodS, TodT, and El222*), degrading genes for benzene, xylene, and ethylbenzene (*Ben, Xyl, and EdoA2*), terminators for enzyme production genes, and a Blue Fluorescent Protein (BFP) reporter gene for biomonitoring. Time-course simulation results indicated efficient activation and degradation processes, with pollutant breakdown occurring within 70 seconds. Enzyme activation was observed at 0.8 seconds, and BFP production began within 0.5 seconds. COPASI simulations confirmed the robustness of the biomodel under various conditions. In conclusion, this study demonstrated the efficient activity of the newly designed biocircuit, with an 80% confidence level determined bioinformatically for the detection and degradation of BTEX compounds in petroleum. However, further *in vitro* and *in vivo* validation tests are necessary to confirm the feasibility and potential of this approach for environmental remediation and biosensing applications. Future work could explore using prokaryotes, particularly those incapables of naturally degrading BTEX, as hosts for genetic circuits, leveraging their genetic engineering potential.

Keywords

Biomonitoring, Bioremediation, BTEX compounds, Genetic logic gate, Synthetic biology

1. Introduction

The annual release of petroleum hydrocarbons into the marine environment is estimated to be between 1.5 and 10 million tons, significantly altering the physical and chemical properties of seawater and increasing its viscosity [1, 2, 3]. The aromatics in petroleum include monocyclic aromatic hydrocarbons (MAHs) like BTEX (benzene, toluene, ethylbenzene, and xylene) and polycyclic aromatic hydrocarbons (PAHs) [4]. BTEX compounds, prioritized by the U.S. EPA, pose significant health and ecological risks [5].

To address this, bioremediation emerges as a cost-effective and sustainable method. Advances in genetic engineering and synthetic biology offer promising methods for addressing petroleum pollution. These disciplines enable the creation of custom gene circuits for environmental solutions, allowing precise assembly of gene cassettes using computational tools [6]. Notably, there is a lack of research that incorporates genetic logic circuit construction with the use of blue fluorescence for real-time assessment of BTEX. In petroleum pollution management, gene circuits can be designed to detect and degrade BTEX compounds, integrating biosensing for real-time monitoring and interventions. Thus, the present study aimed to design a genetic circuit for detecting and degrading BTEX compounds in petroleum providing a comprehensive approach to address a significant research gap while offering a potential effective solution to BTEX in petroleum.

2. Literature Review

2.1 Petroleum Pollution

Petroleum, commonly known as crude oil, is a naturally occurring fossil fuel formed from the remains of ancient marine organisms. These organisms were buried under layers of sediment and rock, subjected to intense heat and pressure over millions of years, resulting in the formation of hydrocarbons, which are the primary components of petroleum [7]. Petroleum pollution can occur during various stages of petroleum production, including exploration, extraction, transportation, refining, and storage. Accidental spills, leaks, and operational discharges are common sources of petroleum pollution [8].

2.2 BTEX Bioremediation by Microorganisms

Some microorganisms can degrade BTEX compounds aerobically. Key microorganisms include *Acidocella*, *Pseudomonas*, *Burkholderia*, *Cupriavidus*,

Streptomyces, Acinetobacter, Bacillus, Microbacterium, Paraburkholderia, Variovorax, Pseudoxanthomonas spadix BD-a59, and *Rhodococcus* [9, 10, 11, 12, 13]. Additionally, consortia such as *Pseudomonas, Mesorhizobium, Achromobacter, Stenotrophomonas,* and *Halomonas* have significant BTEX degradation capabilities [14].

2.3 Synthetic Biology and Genetic Logic Gate Circuits

Synthetic biology is an interdisciplinary field that combines principles from biology, engineering, and computer science to design and construct new biological parts, devices, and systems, or to redesign existing biological systems for useful purposes [15]. Genetic circuits are analogous to electronic circuits, however they use biological molecules such as DNA, RNA, proteins, to perform logical operations and control cellular processes [16]. These circuits are designed to sense environmental signals, process information, and produce specific outputs, such as the expression of a particular gene or the production of a metabolite. Genetic circuits offer a promising solution for bioremediation of BTEX contamination. These circuits can detect the presence of BTEX compounds using biosensors, trigger appropriate degradation pathways, and adapt to changing environmental conditions. By optimizing for efficiency and specificity, genetic circuits can effectively degrade BTEX compounds while minimizing damage to non-target organisms. This approach provides a cost-effective alternative to traditional methods, for addressing environmental pollution [14, 15, 16].

3. Methodology

3.1 Identification of Potential Genes

This study used in silico design and analysis for the development of genetic design incorporating logic gates. The genes in respect to detection and remediation of BTEX were derived from literatures [17, 18]. These potential genes associated with the degradation of BTEX were verified using Ugene and Uniprot by reverse BLAST.

3.2 Preparation of the Logical Framework and Biomodel

The logic gate framework was designed using the draw.io tool (https://app.diagrams.net/). An "OR gate" was used for biomonitoring, and an "AND gate" was used for bioremediation. The biomodel, which explains the entire metabolic pathway for the genetic system along with logic gates, was designed using Tinker Cell software [19]. *Pseudomonas putida* DOT-T1E was chosen as the basis for this biomodel [17].

3.3 BTEX – Receptor Docking and Statistical Analysis

The TodS receptor, composed with domains PAS-1, HK-1, REC, PAS-2, and HK-2. It uses PAS-1 as the binding site for BTEX compounds. TodS receptor's PAS-1 domain, 1jx, 5gta, AF-O87939-F, AF-Q8KIY1-F1, and TlpQ chemoreceptor was used to identify the most suitable receptor for BTEX sensing in the genetic circuit. These receptor structures were prepared using BIOVIA Discovery Studio. PyRx software with AutoDock Vina [20], was used for receptor-ligand docking analysis of the BTEX compounds with those receptors.

To confirm the most suitable receptor for the ligands, the affinity values were statistically analyzed with a "Two-Way ANOVA," and the mean separation test was conducted using the "TukeyHSD" test in R-Statistical Software.

3.4 Preparation of Genetic Construct

The genetic construct was designed by adding all the identified genes using SBOL Designer [21]. First, all the validated genes were added one by one to the proper parts of the construct, and the design was downloaded as GenBank (".gb") format. Then the exported genetic construct was finalized using the Genes smart tool of the Genscript. TinkerCell was used to visually represent the genetic circuit according to the logical framework and gene selection [19].

3.5 Test Simulation of the Synthesized Genetic Logic Circuit

The time-course simulation was conducted using Cell Designer. The behaviour of the signalling pathway in response to the presence of BTEX degradation compounds was observed. Additionally, the genetic construct and biomodel were imported to COPASI. Steady-state, Lyapunov exponent analysis and sensitivity analysis (including metabolic control) were conducted using COPASI [22].

4. Results and Discussion

4.1 Preparation of the Logical Framework

The genetic circuit, as shown in Fig. 22.1, responds to BTEX compounds, which include benzene, toluene, ethylbenzene, and the three xylene isomers. When the TodS receptor detects any of these compounds, it generates a signal. Subsequently, downstream genes encoding enzymes like xylene/toluene monooxygenase, benzene dioxygenase, and ethylbezene dioxygenase are activated. These enzymes play a crucial role in the detection of BTEX compounds.

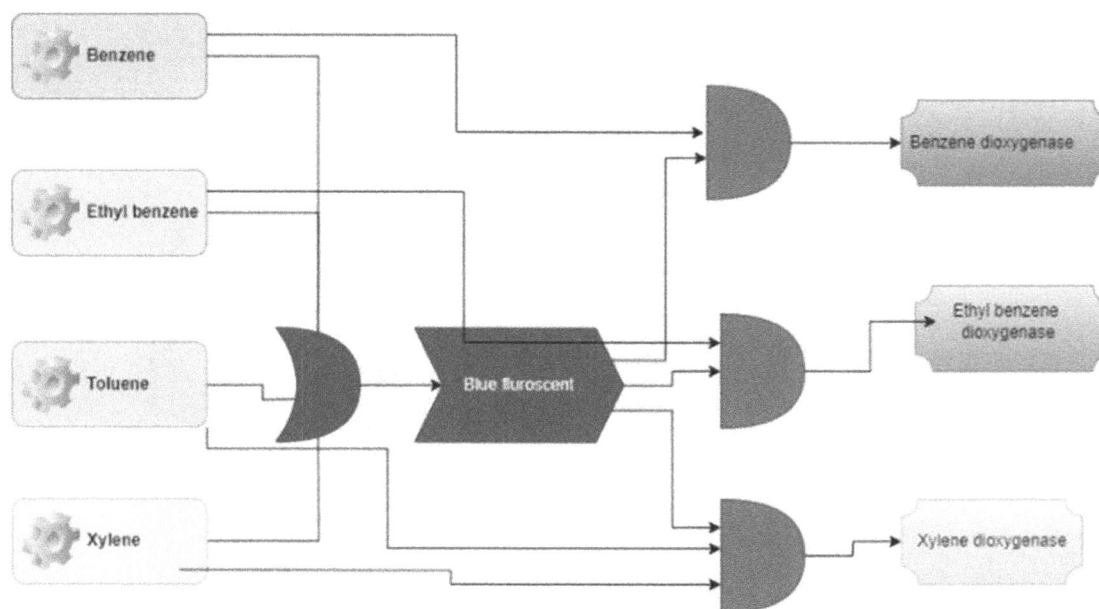

Fig. 22.1 Genetic circuit based on AND and OR gate logic, featuring four inputs for detecting and degrading BTEX compounds in petroleum pollution. *The circuit senses BTEX pollutants, triggers degrading enzymes, and uses the BFP reporter gene for biomonitoring*

4.2 Designing the Biomodel

The engineered pathway in *Pseudomonas putida* DOT-T1E detects BTEX pollutants using the TodS receptor. In the presence of BTEX pollutants in the environment, TodS forms a ligand-receptor complex, activating the signalling pathway. The signal then proceeds to TodT. *TodT* activates the *BFP* promoter, leading to the production of BFP. Concurrently, in the presence of the transcription factor and the signal from the blue fluorescence, El222 protein is activated. EL222 binds to the *Blind* promoter region, thereby activating genes encoding degrading enzymes, as depicted in Fig. 22.2.

4.3 Binding Affinity of Receptors to BTEX Compounds

The docking simulations predicted binding affinities between BTEX compounds and receptors. Statistical analysis revealed that PAS-1 exhibited the highest affinity for all six ligands, with statistical significance at the 95% confidence level. Consequently, PAS-1 was identified as the most suitable receptor for the study (Table 22.1). Specifically, among the BTEX compounds, toluene demonstrated the highest affinity for the TodS receptor, followed by benzene, p-xylene, m-xylene, and ethylbenzene (Table 22.1). O-xylene acted as an antagonist among the three xylene derivatives [23].

Table 22.1 Binding affinity values of BTEX compounds with receptors

Receptor	T	B	p-X	m-X	EB
PAS-1	6.5[a]	5.7[c]	5.4[d]	5.4[d]	5.1[g]
1jx	4.6[j]	3.9[o]	5.1[g]	5.2[f]	5.1[g]
5gta	6[b]	5.3[e]	4.2[n]	4.2[n]	3.9[o]
AF-O87939-F	4.3[m]	5.1[g]	4.5[k]	4.5[k]	4.8[h]
AF-Q8KIY1-F1	4.8[h]	5.7[c]	5.2[f]	5.2[f]	5.3[e]
TlpQ	3.7[p]	4.4[l]	4.2[n]	4.7[i]	4.5[k]

Source: Author's compilation

Note: T-Toluene, B-Benzene, p-X-p-Xylene, m-X-m-Xylene, EB-Ethylbenzene. All values are in -kcal/mol. Values denoted by the same superscript letter are not significantly different ($p < 0.05$).

4.4 Preparation of Genetic Construct

The genetic construct incorporates selected genes and their sequences to efficiently detect and degrade BTEX pollutants. Key components include the Pu promoter from *Pseudomonas putida*, which activates BTEX signalling genes (*TodS, TodT*, and *El222*). The *BFP* promoter was used to activate genes for producing BFP, serving as a visual indicator of promoter activity. Additionally, the circuit included a *Blind* promoter, sensitive to blue light, to activate BTEX-degrading enzymes such as *ben*, *xyl*, and *edoA2* genes. This promoter ensured enzyme expression

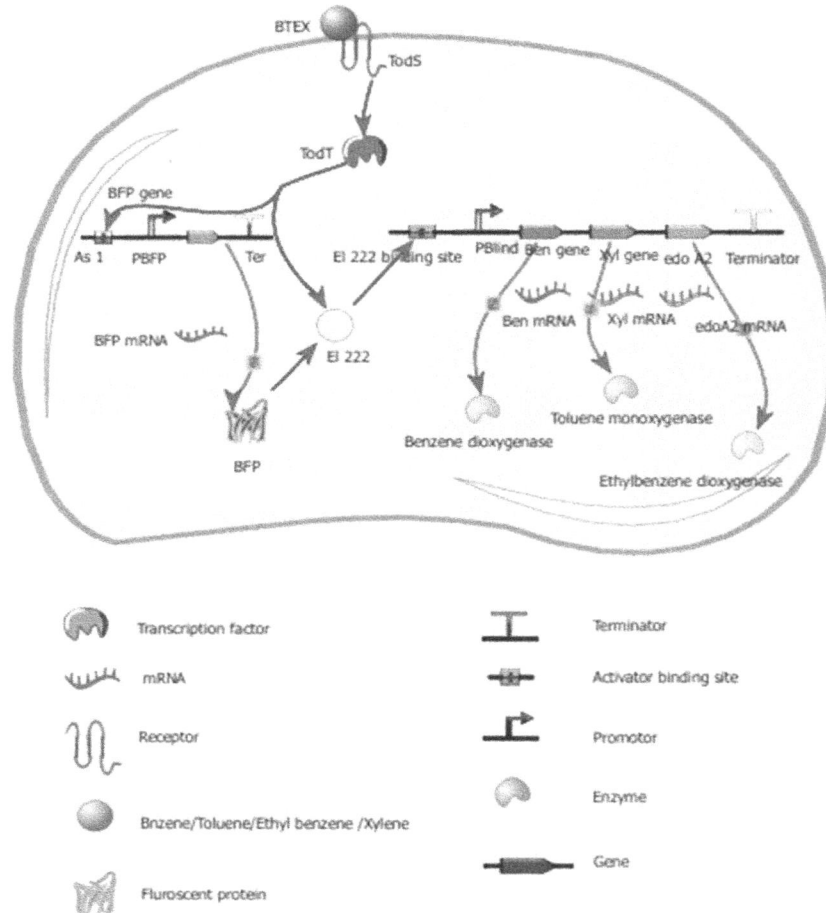

Fig. 22.2 Proposed signalling pathway for the genetic logic gate circuit designed to detect and degrade BTEX compounds in petroleum pollution. *The pathway shows sequential activation of genes for enzyme production in response to BTEX pollutants, with biomonitoring*

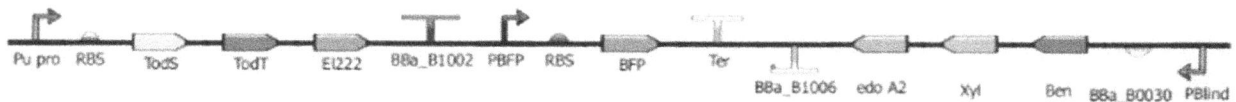

Fig. 22.3 Genetic Circuit for BTEX detection and degradation. *The figure depicts the genetic circuit designed for the detection and degradation of BTEX compounds. The circuit includes the Pu promoter, RBS, TodS gene, TodT gene, EL222 gene, and terminator sequence (BBa_B1002). Following this sequence, the circuit includes a BFP promoter, RBS, gene, and terminator. Finally, the circuit includes a Blind promoter, RBS (BBa_B0030), ben gene, xyl gene, edoa2 gene, and terminator sequence (BBa_B1006)*

was triggered specifically by the blue light signal from BFP (Fig. 22.3).

4.5 Simulation of the Biomodel

Upon ligand binding to TodS, the concentration of the ligand-receptor complex rapidly increases, reaching its peak within 0.6 seconds. This elevated state is sustained between 0.6 and 0.8 seconds. As the ligand undergoes degradation, the complex concentration gradually decreases, ultimately reaching zero by 62 seconds (Fig. 22.4).

At 0.1 seconds, TodT, a transcription factor, becomes active upon ligand binding to TodS. The binding of the ligand to TodS activates TodT, leading to the expression of the *BFP* gene. The promoter activity and *TodT* return to baseline levels by 62 seconds. BFP production begins at 0.5 seconds and increases rapidly, ending within 66 seconds (Fig. 22.5).

Ligand-Receptor complex formation with time

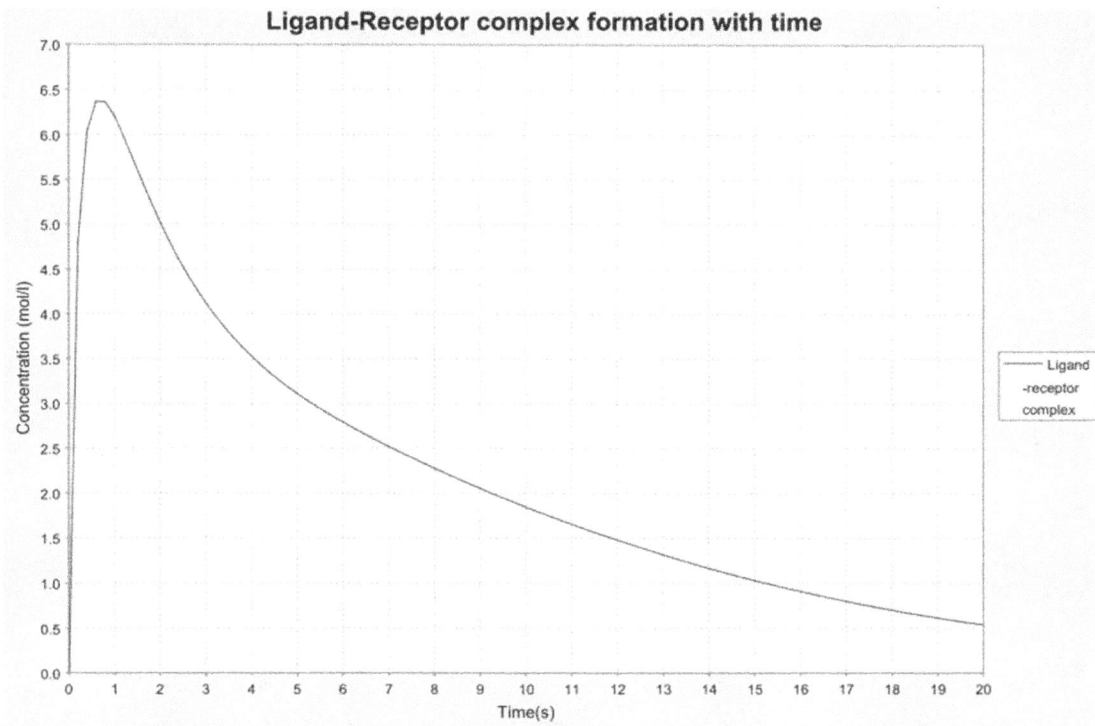

Fig. 22.4 Time-course analysis showing the concentration of the TodS-ligand receptor complex. *The graph illustrates how the concentration of the complex changes over a specified period, indicating the dynamics of ligand binding and receptor interaction*

Blue flurescence protien promoter with blue fluroscence protien production

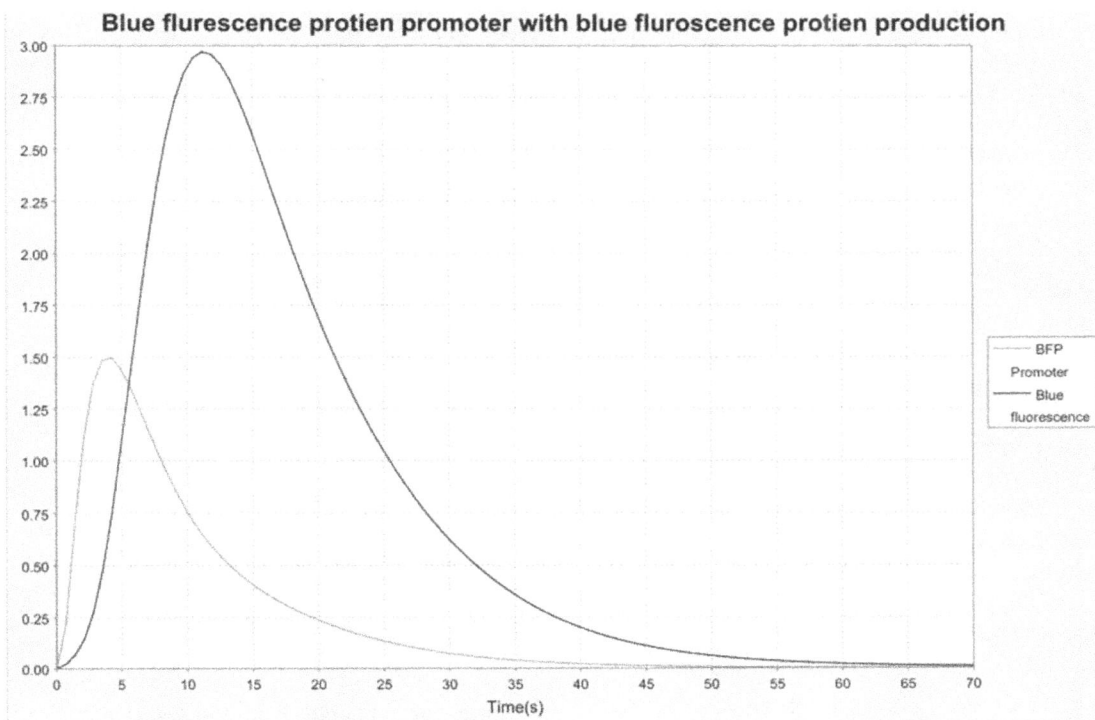

Fig. 22.5 Time-course analysis of BFP production. *The graph illustrates the changes in BFP levels over a specified period, highlighting the kinetics of BFP expression in response to the activation of the genetic circuit*

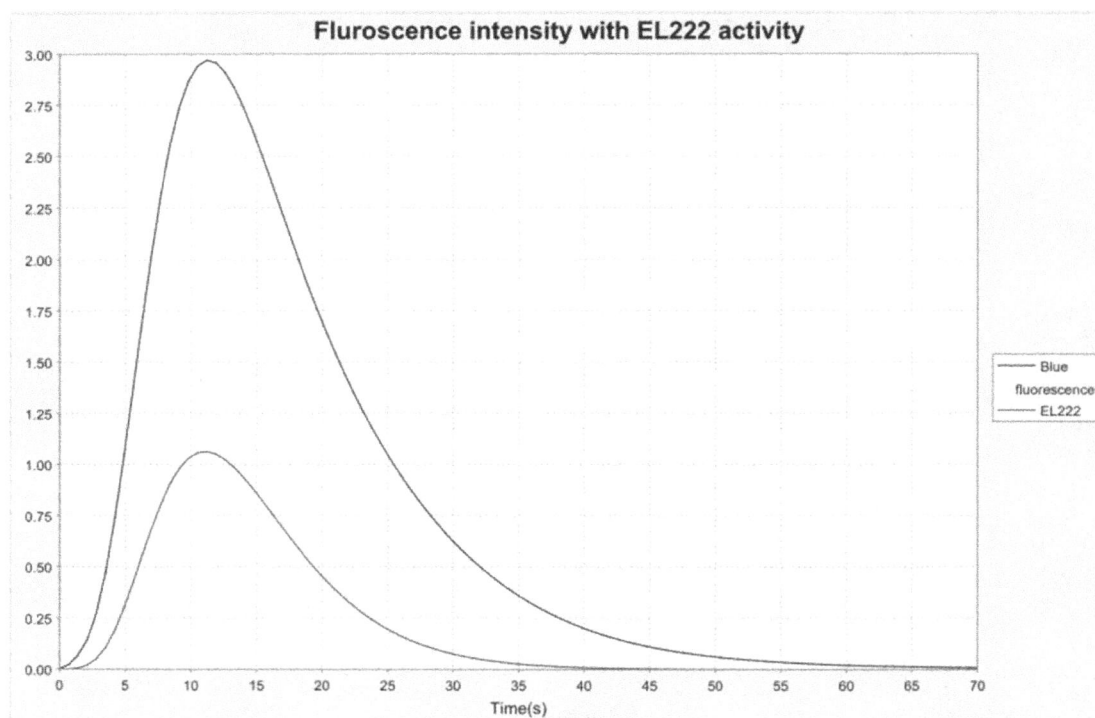

Fig. 22.6 Time-course analysis of EL222 activation in response to BFP production. *The graph demonstrates the temporal relationship between the activation of EL222 and the expression of BFP, indicating the regulatory role of EL222 in the genetic circuit*

EL222, a blue light-dependent protein, becomes active upon exposure to blue fluorescence emitted by BFP. Once activated, EL222 binds to a specific promoter region, known as the *Blind* promoter. This binding event triggers the expression of genes encoding enzymes such as benzene dioxygenase, ethylbenzene dioxygenase and xylene/toluene monooxygenase. EL222 activation occurs 0.1 seconds after BFP production (Fig. 22.6).

As the cascade activates the expression of genes encoding enzymes such as benzene dioxygenase, ethylbenzene dioxygenase and xylene/toluene monoxygenase, these enzymes begin to be produced at 0.8 s. These enzymes are responsible for the degradation of the pollutants, leading to a decrease in pollutant concentration over time. The enzyme-mediated degradation process is crucial for effectively bioremediating environments contaminated with BTEX compounds. This degradation process continued for 70 seconds, ensuring the effective remediation of the contaminated environment, marked by reducing the pollutant concentration from 5 mol/L to 0 mol/L (Fig. 22.7).

According to the COPASI results, in the simulated system, a stable steady state is achieved, characterized by no net molecular flow through reactions. This stability is confirmed by zero fluxes and the absence of oscillations. Metabolic Control Analysis (MCA) reveals low sensitivity to metabolites, as indicated by close to zero elasticity values. Additionally, Lyapunov exponent analysis demonstrates system stability, with all negative exponents and an average divergence of -16.1798.

5. Conclusion

This study demonstrated the potential of a novel genetic logic gate circuit for the detection and degradation of BTEX compounds in petroleum pollution. The genetic construct was validated bioinformatically with an 80% confidence level to detect BTEX by producing fluorescence and can be remediated them within a few minutes. However, further *in vitro* and *in vivo* validation tests are warranted to confirm the feasibility and potential of this approach for environmental remediation and biosensing applications. Future work could explore the use of prokaryotes, particularly those incapables of naturally degrading BTEX, as hosts for the genetic circuit, leveraging their genetic engineering potential. Additionally, potential applications include integration with the Internet of Things for real-

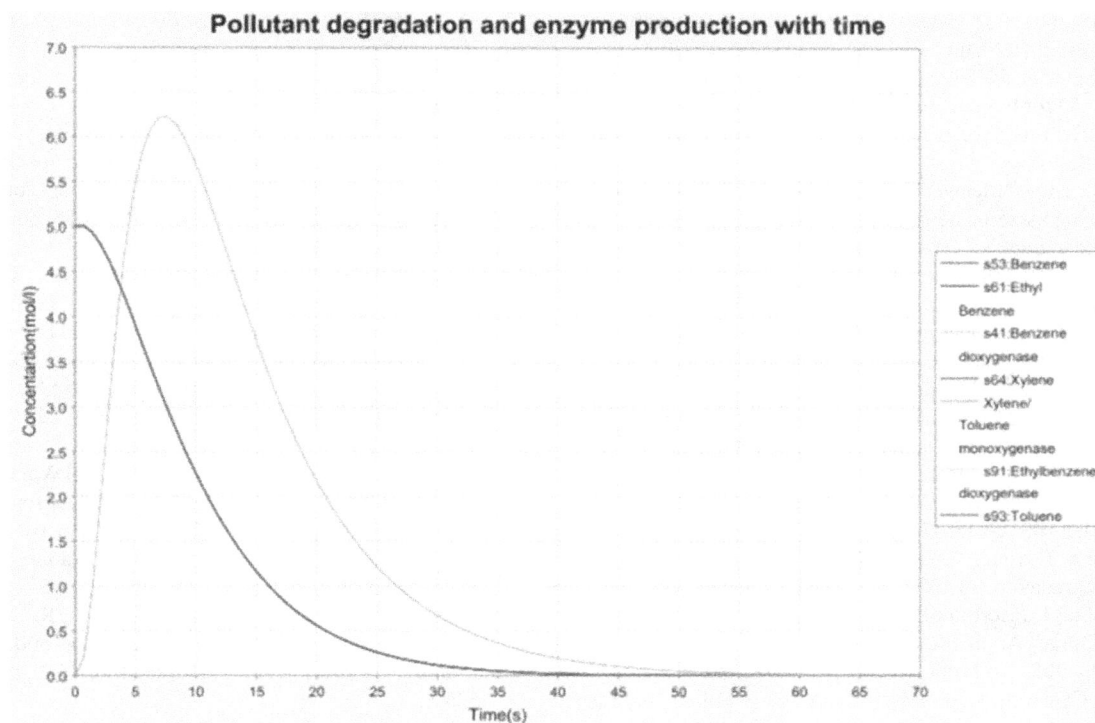

Fig. 22.7 Enzymatic degradation of BTEX compounds. *Toluene degradation by Xylene/Toluene monooxygenase, xylene degradation by Xylene/Toluene monooxygenase, benzene degradation by Benzene dioxygenase, and ethylbenzene degradation by Ethylbenzene dioxygenase. These enzymes catalyze the conversion of the respective BTEX compounds into less harmful substances, facilitating bioremediation processes*

time monitoring, hybrid bioremediation strategies, and large-scale industrial deployment to manage and mitigate pollution more effectively.

Acknowledgment

The authors express gratitude to the staff of the Department of Biotechnology at Wayamba University and the Centre for Advanced Materials and Devices at the University of Colombo for their assistance in completing the research project successfully.

REFERENCES

1. B. Lukić, A. Panico, D. Huguenot, M. Fabbricino, E. D. van Hullebusch, and G. Esposito, "A review on the efficiency of landfarming integrated with composting as a soil remediation treatment," Environ. Technol. Rev., vol. 6, no. 1, pp. 94–116, 2017, doi: 10.1080/21622515.2017.1310310.

2. Z. Wang, Y. Xu, J. Zhao, F. Li, D. Gao, and B. Xing, "Remediation of petroleum contaminated soils through composting and rhizosphere degradation," J. Hazard. Mater., vol. 190, no. 1–3, pp. 677–685, 2011, doi: 10.1016/j. jhazmat.2011.03.103.

3. E. Bani-Hani, M. Tawalbeh, A. Al-Othman, and M. El Haj Assad, "Rheological study on seawater contaminated with oil components," Polish J. Environ. Stud., vol. 28, no. 4, pp. 2585–2591, 2019, doi: 10.15244/pjoes/92121.

4. M. Farhadian, C. Vachelard, D. Duchez, and C. Larroche, "In situ bioremediation of monoaromatic pollutants in groundwater: A review," Bioresour. Technol., vol. 99, no. 13, pp. 5296–5308, 2008, doi: 10.1016/j.biortech.2007.10.025.

5. H. Services, "Toxicological Profile for Total Petroleum Hydrocarbons (TPH)," ATSDR's Toxicol. Profiles, no. September 2002, doi: 10.1201/9781420061888_ch155.

6. Y. Xiang, N. Dalchau, and B. Wang, "Scaling up genetic circuit design for cellular computing: advances and prospects," Nat. Comput., vol. 17, no. 4, pp. 833–853, 2018, doi: 10.1007/s11047-018-9715-9.

7. B. P. Tissot and D. H. Welte, Sedimentary Processes and the Accumulation of Organic Matter. doi: 10.1007/978-3-642-96446-6_5.

8. K. A. Kvenvolden and C. K. Cooper, "Natural seepage of crude oil into the marine environment," Geo-Marine Lett., vol. 23, no. 3–4, pp. 140–146, 2003, doi: 10.1007/s00367-003-0135-0.

9. A. Hocinat, A. Boudemagh, H. Ali-Khodja, and M. Medjemadj, "Aerobic degradation of BTEX compounds by Streptomyces species isolated from activated sludge and

agricultural soils," Arch. Microbiol., vol. 202, no. 9, pp. 2481–2492, 2020, doi: 10.1007/s00203-020-01970-4.

10. T. Benedek et al., "Potential of Variovorax paradoxus isolate BFB1_13 for bioremediation of BTEX contaminated sites," AMB Express, vol. 11, no. 1, 2021, doi: 10.1186/s13568-021-01289-3.

11. M. O. Eze, "Metagenome analysis of a hydrocarbon-degrading bacterial consortium reveals the specific roles of btex biodegraders," Genes (Basel)., vol. 12, no. 1, pp. 1–14, 2021, doi: 10.3390/genes12010098.

12. J. Son, H. Lee, M. Kim, D. U. Kim, and J. O. Ka, "Massilia aromaticivorans sp. nov., a BTEX Degrading Bacterium Isolated from Arctic Soil," Curr. Microbiol., vol. 78, no. 5, pp. 2143–2150, 2021, doi: 10.1007/s00284-021-02379-y.

13. Y. Y. Zhou, H. Huang, and D. Shen, "Multi-substrate biodegradation interaction of 1, 4-dioxane and BTEX mixtures by Acinetobacter baumannii DD1," Biodegradation, vol. 27, no. 1, pp. 37–46, 2016, doi: 10.1007/s10532-015-9753-2.

14. Y. Deng, F. Yang, C. Deng, J. Yang, J. Jia, and H. Yuan, "Biodegradation of BTEX Aromatics by a Haloduric Microbial Consortium Enriched from a Sediment of Bohai Sea, China," Appl. Biochem. Biotechnol., vol. 183, no. 3, pp. 893–905, 2017, doi: 10.1007/s12010-017-2471-y.

15. D. E. Cameron, C. J. Bashor, and J. J. Collins, "A brief history of synthetic biology," Nat. Rev. Microbiol., vol. 12, no. 5, pp. 381–390, 2014, doi: 10.1038/nrmicro3239.

16. P. E. M. Purnick and R. Weiss, "The second wave of synthetic biology: From modules to systems," Nat. Rev. Mol. Cell Biol., vol. 10, no. 6, pp. 410–422, 2009, doi: 10.1038/nrm2698.

17. M. A. Matilla et al., "Cellular Ecophysiology of Microbe: Hydrocarbon and Lipid Interactions," Cell. Ecophysiol. Microbe Hydrocarb. Lipid Interact., no. January 2018, doi: 10.1007/978-3-319-50542-8.

18. H. jun Wu, X. yuan Du, W. jing Wu, J. Zheng, J. yu Song, and J. cai Xie, "Metagenomic analysis reveals specific BTEX degrading microorganisms of a bacterial consortium," AMB Express, vol. 13, no. 1, pp. 0–11, 2023, doi: 10.1186/s13568-023-01541-y.

19. D. Chandran, F. T. Bergmann, and H. M. Sauro, "TinkerCell: Modular CAD tool for synthetic biology," J. Biol. Eng., vol. 3, no. October 2009, doi: 10.1186/1754-1611-3-19.

20. S. Dallakyan and A. J. Olson, "Small-molecule library screening by docking with PyRx," Methods Mol. Biol., vol. 1263, no. January, pp. 243–250, 2015, doi: 10.1007/978-1-4939-2269-7_19.

21. M. Zhang, James Alastair McLaughlin, Anil Wipat, and C. J. Myers, "SBOLDesigner 2: An Intuitive Tool for Structural Genetic Design," ACS Synthetic Biology, vol. 6, no. 7, pp. 1150–1160, May 2017, doi: https://doi.org/10.1021/acssynbio.6b00275.

22. A. Navid, C. Ghim, A. T. Fenley, S. Yoon, S. Lee, and E. Almaas, Methods in Molecular Biology 500: Systems Biology, vol. 500, no. 1. 2009. doi: 10.1007/978-1-59745-525-1.

23. J. Lacal, A. Busch, M. E. Guazzaroni, T. Krell, and J. L. Ramos, "The TodS-TodT two-component regulatory system recognizes a wide range of effectors and works with DNA-bending proteins," Proc. Natl. Acad. Sci. U. S. A., vol. 103, no. 21, pp. 8191–8196, 2006, doi: 10.1073/pnas.0602902103.

Note: All the figures and table in this chapter were made by the authors.

Transformative Applied Research in Computing, Engineering, Science and Technology – Dr. Damayanthi Dahanayake et al. (eds)
© 2024 Taylor & Francis Group, London, ISBN 978-1-041-01782-0

23

The Therapeutic Potential of *Osbeckia Octandra*—A Comprehensive Review of its Antidiabetic and Other Pharmacological Properties

D.N. Chathurangi and S. L. Lavan Kumar

Department of Life Sciences, NSBM Green University,
Sri Lanka

Abstract

Type 2 diabetes mellitus is a global concern affecting approximately more than 95% of the people with diabetes. Numerous studies have been conducted so far to find a cure for Type 2 diabetes mellitus. As the use of many clinically approved antidiabetic drugs such as thiazolidinediones (TZDs) causes adverse side effects, the development of antidiabetic drugs using natural plants is one of the major objectives of current drug-based research. Many studies summarizing promising medicinal plants and their active compounds and their function in glucose homeostasis have been done so far to provide hope for the future development of drugs to treat diabetes. Among them is an indigenous plant of Sri Lanka, *Osbeckia octandra*, also commonly known as "Heen bovitiya" in Sinhala. It is a herbal plant that has been utilized for thousands of years by Ayurvedic practitioners in Sri Lanka in traditional medicine to treat diabetes mellitus, hepatitis, and hemorrhoids. This literature review discusses the existing evidence on *Osbeckia octandra's* hypoglycemic, immunomodulatory, antioxidative, anticancerous, hepatoprotective, antimicrobial, cholinesterase and protease inhibitory properties through numerous in vitro and in vivo research.

Keywords

Antidiabetic drugs, Glucose homeostasis, Herbal medicine, Type 2 diabetes mellitus

1. Introduction

Diabetes is a disease that is quite common in both developed and developing nations. This long-term condition is marked by hyperglycemia and glycosuria [1], resulting from β – cell failure and insulin resistance [2]. Based on the data obtained from the International Diabetes Federation (IDF), a count of 463 million individuals aged between 20 to 79 had diabetes in 2019, and by 2045, it is expected that to be increased up to 700 million. According to statistics from 2019, there are 87.9 million people with Diabetes mellitus in the Southeast Asia Region, which is the epicenter of the disease while Sri Lanka has a prevalence of 8.7% in the adult population (20–79 years old) [3]. The common risk factors for the development of diabetes-related problems are mostly oxidative stress, inflammation,

*Corresponding author: lavan.k@nsbm.ac.lk

DOI: 10.1201/9781003616368-23

and dyslipidemia. Patients with diabetes mellitus who experience uncontrolled hyperglycemia may experience increased lipid peroxidation, glucose oxidation, and nonenzymatic protein glycation. Thus, the development of antidiabetic medicines that specifically target diabetes and its related problems was found to be crucial. [3].

However, for a very long time before modern western medicine was developed, medicinal flora has been used to treat a variety of illnesses, including diabetes mellitus [3]. One significant turning point in the history of antidiabetic pharmacology was the discovery of Galegine and similar compounds in the first half of the 1900s, which came from the plant *Galega officinalis*. This work led to the discovery of metformin, which is now used as the first line of treatment for type 2 diabetes [3]. In-depth research on the pathophysiology of diabetes mellitus has led to the development of drugs from several medicinal plants with potent antioxidant, antihyperlipidemic, antihyperglycemic, hepatoprotective, anti-inflammatory and anticancer properties. The pharmacological use of medicinal plants for the treatment of diabetes has resurged due to their low side effects, cost-effectiveness and high availability. Some of these plants which were used as oral hypoglycemic medications contained well-known groups of biguanides, sulfonylureas, meglitinides, thiazolidinediones, α-glucosidase inhibitors, and dipeptidyl peptidase-IV inhibitors [3].

In Sri Lanka, the very rich and diverse flora has helped the native population acquire an extensive legacy of traditional medicine for a wide range of illnesses including diabetes mellitus. The book "Arka Prakasha," penned by the prehistoric King Ravana, is a treatise on herbal medicine that demonstrates a very high level of in-depth knowledge and comprehension of herbal and natural substances and their effects [1]. Since ancient times, Sri Lanka has embraced four systems of traditional medicine: Ayurveda, Siddha, Unani, and Deshiya Chikitsa while Ayurveda and Deshiya Chikitsa commonly utilized herbal remedies and, whereas mineral remedies were used in Siddha [3]. Nowadays, ayurvedic treatment is the most widely used traditional medical system in the country and this system makes use of around two thousand therapeutic herbs.

One such therapeutic herb is 'Heen bovitiya' (*Osbeckia octandra*), one of the endemic plants to Sri Lanka, found in the dry, moist and intermediate zones [4]. It is a small, finely textured shrub [4], grown as an aesthetically pleasing herb because of its large beautiful violet blossoms [5] that blooms thrice a year [4]. Figure 23.1 and 23.2 shows the *Osbeckia octandra* flower and leaves respectively. It is considered as a medicinal plant with hepatoprotective qualities that is used by ayurvedic and other traditional medical

practitioners to treat hepatitis, diabetes, and hemorrhoids [6]. To this day, majority of people in rural Sri Lankan districts use fresh salad made from *Osbeckia octandra* leaves in their meals to regulate their blood sugar levels. In Sri Lankan traditional medicine, 'kolakenda' (herbal porridge) composed of *Osbeckia octandra* is advised for patients with hepatitis and diabetes [6]. Nevertheless, the use of 'kolakenda' from *Osbeckia octandra* is becoming rare due to its availability and hardships in its medicinal preparation. A study was done by Gunathilake and Gamlath to create an instant herbal porridge mixture using *Osbeckia octandra* leaves [7] thereby, providing a far more convenient way for people to incorporate the medicinally rich herb into their diet. However, there has been limited research work conducted on the medical effects of the plant so far [5]. This review outlines the scientific validity and the potential antidiabetic and other protective effects of *Osbeckia octandra*.

2. Methodology

ScienceDirect, PubMed and Google Scholar search engines were employed to identify the related published studies of the hypoglycemic, immunomodulatory, antioxidative,

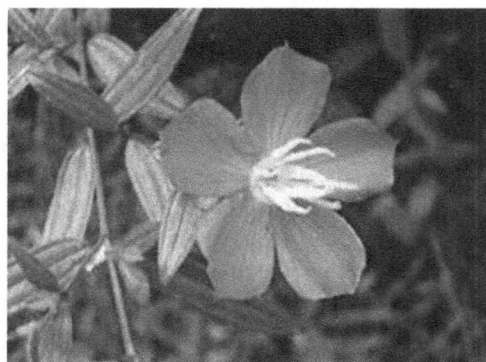

Fig. 23.1 Flower of *Osbeckia octandra* [5].

Fig. 23.2 Leaves of *Osbeckia octandra* [5].

anticancerous, hepatoprotective, antimicrobial, cholinesterase and protease inhibitory properties of *O. octandra* from 1950 to 2023. "*O. octandra*", "diabetes" "antidiabetic" "hypoglycemic", "hepatoprotective", "antiglycation", "antioxidative", "antimicrobial", "anticancerous", "immunomodulator", "anti-fibrotic", "cholinesterase", antidyslipidemic and "protease inhibitor" were the main search terms used to carry out the literature search.

3. Experimental Evidence on Hypoglycaemic Effects

In a study by Wasana et al., the administration of two spoonsful of powdered *O. octandra* leaves dissolved in 30 ml of warm water, taken twice daily for 30 days, was shown to decrease the level of fasting blood glucose [3].

Furthermore, in a review done on herbs that are being used in the treatment of diabetes, Ediriweera and Ratnasooriya obtained information from traditional and ayurvedic physicians whose experience showed that in addition to its leaves, *Osbeckia octandra*'s chyme also had anti-diabetic properties. The blood glucose level had been noted to decrease with a decoction that was made with 120 g of fresh *O. octandra* leaves and 120 ml of water when administered twice a day to diabetic patients [1].

In another study, patients aged between 30 and 65 who had fasting blood sugar levels between 115 and 200 mg/dL were administered two spoonfuls of *Osbeckia octandra* leaf powder in 30 ml of warm water for 15 minutes, twice a day, for one month. This lowered the mean value of their fasting blood sugar levels with a p-value of 0.01, which was less than the significant level of 0.05 [5]. Table 23.1 below shows the results of the T-test done for the fasting blood glucose levels and Fig. 23.3 below shows the graph indicating the hypoglycemic effect after treatment with *O. octandra*. Moreover, a liver function test was carried out to determine the presence of adverse effects of the plant leaves and, all the results were within the normal range, indicating that the powder consumption had no negative health effects [5].

Jayaweera reported that diabetes could also be alleviated when the mature leaves of this plant are put into a salad and

Table 23.1 Results of the t-test for the fasting blood sugar levels

	No	Mean	St. Dev	Se Mean
AFTER	30	142.033	24.462	4.466
BEFORE	30	155.300	20.115	3.673
DIFFERENCE	30	-13.2667	29.414	5.370

Source: Aurhors

Fig. 23.3 Hypoglycemic effect after treatment with *O. octandra*. [5]

the tender leaves are cooked into a curry and consumed in large quantities with both meals for 5-7 days [6]. All these studies suggested the promising antidiabetic properties of *O. octandra*. However, no clinical trials have been done to prove these effects although it is widely used in the ayurvedic treatment of diabetes mellitus.

4. Extended Pharmacological Benefits

Many studies have been done to examine the antimicrobial, hepatoprotective, immunomodulatory, hypoglycemic, antioxidant, and anti-cancerous effects of *Osbeckia octandra* species [8].

4.1 Hepatoprotective Effects

Jayaweera had reported that the *Osbeckia octandra* and roots are used as a drink to cure hepatitis [6].

An in-vivo investigation was carried out by Thabrew and Jayatilaka to compare the preventive effects of aqueous leaf extracts of Osbeckia aspera and Osbeckia octandra against liver damage caused by carbon tetrachloride (CCl4) in Sprague Dawley rats. Administration of O. octandra or O.aspera extract 24 hours after CCl4 exposure indicated a quicker recovery of the liver function as shown by serum enzyme activities, compared to animals that were treated with the toxin and allowed to recover on their own for four days without the plant extracts. The toxin-mediated alterations were significantly less pronounced in rat livers pre- or post-treated with *O. octandra* or *O. aspera* than the changes that were found in the livers of CCl_4 controls which were not treated with the plant extracts [9].

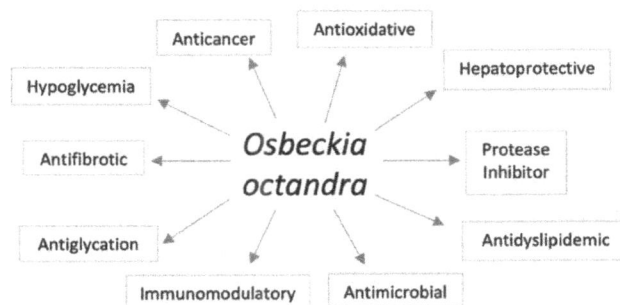

Fig. 23.4 Scientifically proven protective effects of *Osbeckia octandra*

Source: Aurhors

Aqueous extracts of the aerial parts of *Melothria maderasptana* and the leaves of *Osbeckia octandra* have been compared with (+)-3-cyanidanol, a flavonoid that has been frequently used as a therapeutic and protective agent in several types of liver diseases to assess how well these drugs protect the liver against CCl_4 mediated changes. The studies indicated that *Osbeckia octandra* was found to be just as effective as (+)-3-cyanidanol in preventing CCl_4 mediated alterations in serum enzyme levels and preserving the normal architecture of liver cells. The plant was noticeably more effective when rats who were pre-treated with *Osbeckia octandra* for seven days before CCl_4 administration showed fewer necrotic alterations in their livers compared to the rats that received only CCl_4 [10].

When given together with paracetamol, the plant extract was able to considerably prevent liver damage caused by the drug. Fewer zones of severe necrosis and reduced eosinophilia were evident as the paracetamol-induced hepatic lesions were significantly reduced after the treatment with the plant extract. The plant extract was able to provide significant protection against toxin-mediated damage by providing protection against lipid peroxidation [11].

In another study, an aqueous extract of *Osbeckia octandra* were used to examine the harm caused by D-galactosamine and tert-butyl hydroperoxide (TBH) against newly obtained rat hepatocytes. The plant extract provided dose-dependent protection at 500 pg/ml to hepatocytes damaged by galactosamine or TBH with the highest protection against both toxins. Although the plant extract which had a concentration of 500 pg/ml provided nearly total protection, the degree of protection declined as the duration of hepatocyte exposure to the toxin before treatment increased [12].

A study has been conducted to determine if the leaf extracts of *Osbeckia octandra* or 'Pavetta' may protect against liver injury caused by the well-known hepatotoxin CCl_4 and whether *Osbeckia octandra* is a superior hepatotonic than 'Pavetta'. It only took three days of pre-treatment to produce a noticeable resistance to CCl_4's effects and the liver recovered more quickly when the plant extract was administered 24 hours after the exposure to CCl_4, compared to 'Pavetta'. No apparent differences were observed between liver slices from pre-treated rats for seven days and then treated with CCl_4 compared to the liver slices obtained from untreated rats [13].

4.2 Antiglycation Effects

The primary source of spontaneous protein damage is non-enzymatic glycation, which results in oxidative stress and the production of non-reversible Advanced Glycation End Products (AGEs), which can cause several issues including chronic diabetes mellitus complications [14]. Numerous studies have demonstrated the link between diabetes mellitus and an increase in free radical generation that results in oxidative stress. Advanced Glycation End Products are formed mostly by the persistent increased blood glucose levels in diabetes and oxidation. Hence, plant-derived medications with anti-glycation and antioxidant properties were crucial in averting problems associated with diabetes. In an investigation, water extracts of dried and milled powdered *Osbeckia octandra* leaves were prepared according to the traditional "Kwatha" preparation method. These leaf decoctions of *Osbeckia octandra* showed the highest level of antiglycation activity of 23.0 ± 1.2 µg/ml followed by 25.2 ± 2.2 µg/ml and 28.5 ± 1.3 µg/ml, from southern, western and uva provinces respectively [14]. In another study, the antiglycation capability of decoctions made from *Osbeckia octandra* leaves taken from various locations was seen to be much higher than that of the positive control, arbutin (65.0 pg/ml), which corresponded to the highest anti-glycation activity [15].

4.3 Antioxidant Effects

All living things naturally produce free radicals as a normal cellular function of their physiological processes. However, excessive levels of free radicals may lead to oxidative stress and can also cause chronic illnesses including diabetes mellitus [15]. These harmful effects of free radicals can be counteracted by antioxidants [16]. When present in lower concentrations than the substrates, antioxidants can either delay or prevent the oxidation of oxidizable substrates, thereby protecting cells from oxidative damage produced by reactive oxygen and nitrogen species.

One primary molecular cause of the macro and microvascular problems linked to persistent diabetes is oxidative stress. In a certain study, 2,2-diphenyl-1-picrylhydrazyl (DPPH) radical scavenging activity of five anti-diabetic herbs was examined. Among the decoctions, fresh and dry *O. octandra* samples exhibited strong DPPH radical scavenging potentials (55.7-98.4 pg/ml). These findings demonstrated that *Osbeckia octandra* 's antidiabetic properties stem from its ability to block protein glycation and delay the onset of oxidative stress [15].

An in-vitro study done to investigate the radical scavenging and antioxidant properties of the aqueous extract of *Osbeckia octandra* leaf revealed, it to have the best radical scavenging activity as well as the greatest levels of total phenolic and flavonoid content among the twelve therapeutic herbs tested [17]. These researchers conducted another study to create herbal tea bags with *Osbeckia octandra* leaves as the main component and assessing how infusion conditions affected the in-vitro antioxidant power of the biologically active chemicals derived from the herbal tea bags. When compared to tea samples made without the inclusion of *O. octandra*, tea bags containing the leaves of the plant had higher total phenol and total flavonoid concentrations. At both infusion conditions, the tea bags with *O. octandra* leaves as the primary constituent (87%) demonstrated noticeably high values of antioxidant activity [18].

4.4 Anticancer Effects

Recent research on oral squamous cell carcinoma (OSCC) has demonstrated that *Osbeckia octandra* extracts exhibit anti-cancer effects, reducing OSCC cell migration and increasing DNA fragmentation. The cytotoxic effect of the extract on OSCC cells were assessed by treating with an extract of *O. octandra* of concentrations ranging from 50–300 µg/ml for 72 hours using the MTT assay. The results exhibited a significant decrease in the viability of different OSCC cell lines as compared to the control, Dimethylsulfoxide (DMSO) [19]. Through cell cycle arrest in the G1 phase and disruption of DNA replication, the *O. octandra* leaf extract was reported to decrease the development of OSCC cells in vitro to initiate the apoptotic response [20]. The leaf extracts from *O. octandra* have been found to have a strong in vitro anti-cancer potential, mainly through the inhibition of cell migration and the induction of cellular DNA damage, as opposed to direct cytotoxicity induced by current drugs used in chemotherapy. An in-vitro investigation carried out using the oral cancer cell line YD-38 showed a significant reduction ($p < 0.05$) in cell viability, with all the doses of leaf extract starting at 24 hours exposure time compared to the non-treated control. The highest concentration (30 µg/ml) of *O. octandra* showed the most significant ($p < 0.05$) reduction of cell viability compared to both the non-treated control and the positive control, Doxorubicin, a widely used chemotherapeutic agent [20]. A qualitative phytochemical analysis also revealed the presence of Terpenoids which have been identified as a promising anti-cancer agent in the boiled leaf extract of *O. octandra* [8].

4.5 Antidyslipidemic Effects

The presence of Diabetes disrupts the lipid metabolism which in turn increases the risk of cardiovascular diseases [21]. However, in a study aimed to determine the antioxidant capacity of 12 medicinal plants in Sri Lanka, *Osbeckia octandra* showed the highest flavonoid concentration (111.49 mg Rutin Equivalent/ g dry weight of leaves). Flavonoids are a major family of phenolic chemicals that have a direct role in preventing atherosclerosis. It has been demonstrated to lower blood levels of total cholesterol, which lowers the risk of cardiovascular disease, teratogenicity, and arthritis[22]. However, sufficient studies have not been carried out so far to examine the antidyslipidemic effect of *O. octandra* and hence more scientific validation is required for the exact confirmation of its effect.

4.6 Antimicrobial Effects

Osbeckia octandra is believed to show antimicrobial activities where traditional Sri Lankan ayurvedic practitioners have used aqueous preparations of the plant for the treatment of viral hepatitis [23]. However, promising scientific evidence regarding the antimicrobial aspect of *O. octandra* is lacking.

4.7 Anti-fibrotic Effects

A study by Bogahawaththa et al. indicated that a crude leaf suspension, boiled leaf extract and sonicated leaf extract from *O. octandra* exhibited promising hepatic anti-fibrotic effects in thioacetamide-induced liver cirrhosis in male Wistar rats. By preventing angiogenesis and the release of pro-inflammatory and pro-fibrotic cytokines, these extracts improved liver fibrosis in cirrhotic rats [24].

4.8 Cholinesterase Inhibitory Effects

A study was carried out by Samaradivakara et al to examine the cholinesterase inhibitory activity of ethanolic extracts of 17 different medicinal plants. The whole plant extract of *O. octandra* showed cholinesterase inhibitory action at a concentration of 71.72 ± 6.00 µg/ml (IC50) in the acetylcholinesterase inhibition test [16].

4.9 Protease Inhibitory Effects

Protease overexpression has been linked to several illnesses, including Alzheimer's disease, respiratory, cardiovascular, and inflammatory conditions and malignancy [16]. A study showed that the ethanol extract of the whole *O. octandra* plant had protease inhibitory activity at 15.88 µg/ml in the elastase inhibition assay [16].

4.10 Immunomodulatory Effects

In a study by [25] the immunomodulatory properties of *Phyllanthus debelis*, *Melothria maderaspatana*, and *Osbeckia octandra* were demonstrated. Among them, *Osbeckia octandra* had the highest inhibitory action on luminol-induced chemiluminescence of human polymorphonuclear leucocytes (PMNs) in both the classical pathway (17.5 µg/ml) and the alternative pathway (850.0 µg/ml) of the human complement (C) system [25].

Furthermore, being a close relative of *Osbeckia octandra*, *Osbeckia aspera* leaf extract has also shown an inhibitory effect on the lymphocyte proliferation stimulated by antigens and mitogens in a study by [26]. In this study, *Osbeckia* extract concentrations of 300 g/ml and 1 mg/ml significantly decreased the proliferation of peripheral blood mononuclear cells stimulated by phytohaemagglutinin.

5. Conclusion

Osbeckia octandra, also known as 'Heen bovitiya' in Sinhala has been used for hundreds of years in Sri Lankan Ayurvedic medicine to cure diabetes mellitus and hepatitis. The main focus of this review is to demonstrate the available scientific data on *O. octandra*'s antidiabetic properties. The available data supports the use of *O. octandra* in the treatment of diabetes mellitus and demonstrates the plant's hypoglycemic, antidyslipidemic, antioxidative, anticancer, antihepatotoxic, anti-inflammatory, immunomodulatory, and cholinesterase and protease inhibitory properties. Even though *O. octandra* extract is commonly used in the treatment of diabetes in Sri Lankan traditional medicine, there is no scientific data to show its mechanism of action in diabetic control. Therefore, it is crucial to conduct a scientific validation of the effectiveness of *O. octandra* and to find its mechanism of action in diabetes management.

6. Future Perspectives

To date, the studies evaluating the antidiabetic potential of *Osbeckia octandra* have been focused mainly on in-vitro and in-vivo studies, and no in-silico studies have been conducted so far to explore this aspect. Hence this highlights an area for future research. Although *O. octandra* is widely used in Ayurvedic medicine for the treatment of diabetes, no clinical trials have been conducted so far. Moreover, the mechanism/s by which *O. octandra* controls diabetes mellitus and lowers the blood glucose level is also yet to be investigated. Furthermore, the chemical components of *O. octandra* responsible for the hypoglycemic and other pharmacological effects have not yet been discovered and hence this can be researched on, and this will allow the specific chemical components to be used in the development of anti-diabetic drugs and in the drug development for various other conditions.

REFERENCES

1. E.R.H.S.S Ediriweera, and W.D. Ratnasooriya, "A review on herbs used in treatment of diabetes mellitus by Sri Lankan ayurvedic and traditional physicians," AYU. Vol. 30. 2009.
2. F. Picard, and J. Auwerx, "PPARγ and glucose homeostasis," Annu Rev Nutr, pp. 167–97, 2002.
3. K.G.P. Wasana, A.P. Attanayake, K.A.P.W. Jayatilaka, and T.P. Weerarathna, "Antidiabetic activity of widely used medicinal plants in the Sri Lankan traditional healthcare system: New insight to medicinal flora in Sri Lanka," Evid Based Complement and Alternat Med 2021.
4. K. Yakandawala, M. D. C. P. Weerasinghe, and S. A. E. C. Wijesinghe, "*Osbeckia octandra*: A potential shrub for urban environment," Acta Horticulturae, no. 999, pp. 301–305, Jun. 2013.
5. M.G. Balasooriya, W.D. Karunarathna, and W.J. Wickramarachchi, "Evaluation of the clinical efficacy of heen bowitiya leaves (*Osbeckia octandra*) power in the management of diabetes mellitus," World Journal of Pharmaceutical Research, pp. 2541–7, 2020.
6. D.M.A. Jayaweera, "Medicinal plants (indigenous and exotic) used in Ceylon," The National Science Council of Sri Lanka, part IV, pp. 280-281, 1982.
7. K.D.P.P. Gunathilake, and G.G.S. Gamlath, "Development of instant herbal porridge mixtures from heenbowitiya (*Osbeckia octandra* L.) Leaves," Tropical Agricultural Research Vol. 14. 2002.
8. S. Vivekanandarajah, V. Shanmugalingam, and P. Rajamanoharan, "Bioactivities of *Osbeckia octandra* DC. Extracts," Matrix Science Pharma, vol. 8, no. 1, pp. 7–9, Jan. 2024.
9. M.I. Thabrew, and K.A.P.W. Jayatilaka, "A comparative study of the beneficial effects of *Osbeckia octandra* and *Osbeckia aspera* in liver dysfunction in rats," Ceylon Journal of Medical Science. vol. 42, no. 1, p. 1, Jun. 1999.
10. K. Jayathilaka, M. Thabrew, C. Pathirana, D. de Silva, and D. Perera, "An evaluation of the potency of *Osbeckia octandra* and *Melothria maderaspantana* as antihepatotoxic agents," Planta Medica. vol. 55, no. 02, pp. 137–139, Apr. 1989.
11. M.I. Thabrew, R.D. Hughes, C.D. Gove, B. Portmann, R. Williams, and I.G. Mcfarlane, "Protective effects of *Osbeckia octandra* against paracetamol-induced liver injury," Xenobiotica, vol. 25, no. 9, pp. 1009–1017, Jan. 1995.
12. M.I.Thabrew, C.D. Gove, R.D. Hughes, I.G. Mcfarlane, and R. Williams, "Protective effects of *Osbeckia octandra* against galactosamine and tert-butyl hydroperoxide induced hepatocyte damage," Journal of Ethnopharmacology. vol. 49, no. 2, pp. 69–76, Dec. 1995.
13. M.I. Thabrew, P.D.T.M. Joice, and W. Rajatissa, "A comparative study of the efficacy of *Pavetta indica* and *Osbeckia octandra* in the treatment of liver dysfunction," Planta Medica, vol. 53, no. 03, pp. 239–241, Jun. 1986.
14. P.R.D. Perera, S. Ekanayake, and K.K.D.S. Ranaweera, "In vitro study on antiglycation activity, antioxidant activity and phenolic content of *Osbeckia octandra* L. leaf decoction," Journal of Pharmacognosy and Phytochemistry, pp. 198–201, 2013.
15. P.R.D. Perera, S. Ekanayake, and K.K.D.S. Ranaweera, "Comparison of antiglycation and antioxidant potentials and total phenolic contents of decoctions from antidiabetic plants," Procedia Chemistry, vol. 16, pp. 519–524, 2015.
16. S.P. Samaradivakara, R. Samarasekera, S.M. Handunnetti, and O.V.D.S.J. Weerasena, "Cholinesterase, protease

inhibitory and antioxidant capacities of Sri Lankan medicinal plants," Industrial Crops and Products, vol. 83, pp. 227–234, May 2016.

17. S.K. Hettihewa, and P.D.S.A Silva, "Phytochemical evaluation, in-vitro radical scavenging and antioxidant activities of aqueous leaf extract of heen bovitiya (*Osbeckia octandra* L. (DC.) grown in Sri Lanka," Asian Journal of Pharmacognosy. Vol. 5. 2021.

18. S.K. Hettihewa, and P.D.S.A Silva, "Effects of infusion conditions on in vitro antioxidant power of extracts obtained from nutraceutical tea products developed with *Osbeckia octandra* and black tea leaves," Asian Journal Of Pharmacognosy. Vol. 5. 2021.

19. J.Y. Kim, J. Kim, B.M.R. Bandara, W.M.Tilakaratne, and D. Kim, "Leaf extract of *Osbeckia octandra* induces apoptosis in oral squamous cell carcinoma cells," BMC Complementary Medicine and Therapies, vol. 22, p. 20, Jan. 2022.

20. M. Prasadani, S. Bogahawaththa, R.P. Illeperuma, and S.P. Kodithuwakku, "Leaf extract of *Osbeckia octandra* L. (heen bovitiya) suppresses human oral squamous cell carcinoma cells migration and induces cellular DNA damage," Journal of Oral and Maxillofacial Surgery, Medicine, and Pathology, vol. 33, no. 2, pp. 215–220, Mar. 2021.

21. H. Perera, "Antidiabetic effects of *Pterocarpus marsupium* (Gammalu)," European Journal of Medicinal Plants, vol. 13, no. 4, pp. 1–14, Jan. 2016.

22. M.I.S. Safeena, J.S.M. Nethmi, and N. Samarakoon, "Antioxidant potential of 12 medicinal plants of Sri Lanka." Journal of Medicinal Plants Studies 2020.

23. S. Das, and A. Coku, "Antimicrobial and antioxidant activities of *Osbeckia stellata* buch.-ham. ex d. don (melastomataceae) prevalent of darjeeling hills," International Journal of Pharmacy and Pharmaceurtical Sciences, vol.5, 2013.

24. S. Bogahawaththa *et al.*, "Anti-fibrotic and anti-angiogenic activities of *Osbeckia octandra* leaf extracts in thioacetamide-induced experimental liver cirrhosis," Molecules, vol. 26, no. 16, p. 4836, Jan. 2021.

25. M.I. Thabrewa, K.T.D. De Silva, R.P. Labadie, P.A.F. De Bie, and B. Van Der Bergc, "Immunomodulatory activity of three Sri-Lankan medicinal plants used in hepatic disorders," Journal of Ethnopharmacology, vol. 33, no. 1–2, pp. 63–66, May 1991.

26. D.S. Nicholl, H.M. Daniels, M.I. Thabrew, R.J. Grayer, M.S.J Simmonds, and R.D.Hughes, "In-vitro studies on the immunomodulatory effects of extracts of *Osbeckia aspera*," Journal of Ethnopharmacology, vol. 78. 2001.

Transformative Applied Research in Computing, Engineering, Science and Technology – Dr. Damayanthi Dahanayake et al. (eds)
© 2024 Taylor & Francis Group, London, ISBN 978-1-041-01782-0

24

Unlocking Machine Learning Potential— Simplified Automated Model Development

D.T. Wijesinghe*

Department of Software Engineering and Information Systems,
Faculty of Computing, NSBM Green University,
Sri Lanka

G. Perera

Department of Computer and Data Science,
Faculty of Computing, NSBM Green University,
Sri Lanka

Abstract

Model ML is an innovative platform designed to democratize machine learning (ML) by simplifying model development for users with limited expertise. By integrating advanced algorithms with a highly intuitive interface, Model ML addresses key barriers such as high computing costs, complex model selection, and the need for specialized knowledge in areas like feature selection and hyperparameter optimization. Unlike traditional AutoML tools, the platform offers a seamless experience through its web and mobile applications, featuring automated dataset encoding, dynamic data visualization, instant model testing, and transparent workflows. Validated through a user study with undergraduate students, Model ML demonstrated an 85% success rate in enabling model development without prior ML experience, underscoring its accessibility and efficiency. User feedback highlighted its intuitive design and ease of use, while the platform's scalability ensures it can accommodate both small and large organizations. By lowering the entry barriers to ML, Model ML fosters broader adoption and innovation across various sectors, positioning it as a versatile tool for advancing machine learning accessibility.

Keywords

Automated machine learning (AutoML), User-friendly interface, Model training, Data visualization, Machine learning accessibility

1. Introduction

Recent years have witnessed profound advancements in machine learning (ML), leading to its widespread adoption across various industries and daily life. The versatility and robustness of ML techniques have significantly enhanced profitability and market value. However, widespread integration of ML among small and medium-sized enterpris-

*Corresponding author: diluka.w@nsbm.ac.lk

DOI: 10.1201/9781003616368-24

es (SMEs), novices, students, graduates, and non-experts remains challenging. Factors such as high computing costs, inadequate knowledge of ML technologies, and lengthy development cycles [1] hinder broader adoption.

To address these barriers, the "Model ML" project introduces a novel approach to democratize ML model development. This platform aims to empower users with minimal coding experience to create efficient ML models efficiently and intuitively. Even seasoned ML practitioners encounter complexities in model development, underscoring the significant learning curve for newcomers [2]. Existing ML development tools are often complex and lack user-friendly interfaces, further complicating adoption for beginners and small organizations.

1.1 Problem Statement

Machine learning has revolutionized data processing and analysis, supported by frameworks like Scikit-Learn, TensorFlow, and CNTK, which have simplified access to ML capabilities. Despite these advancements, gaps persist in making ML accessible to non-experts due to the technical intricacies involved. Automated ML (AutoML) platforms have emerged to streamline model development, yet they require substantial theoretical knowledge and coding skills to operate effectively. This complexity poses a barrier to entry for many potential users, limiting the democratization of ML across industries.

Current ML development platforms often lack transparency in algorithm selection, hyperparameter tuning, and model evaluation, hindering users' ability to understand and trust their outcomes. Moreover, the absence of user-friendly interfaces and limited mobile functionality restricts accessibility for beginners and SMEs [3]. These challenges underscore the need for a more intuitive, accessible, and transparent solution to democratize ML model development.

1.2 Contribution

The "Model ML" platform addresses these challenges by providing a user-centric, no-code environment accessible via web and mobile applications. Key features include dataset encoding, customized model training, statistical analysis, and intuitive data visualization tools. The platform's interface facilitates seamless workflow management and instant model testing, promoting transparency through detailed algorithm evaluations and export capabilities in various formats. By focusing on usability and accessibility, "Model ML" aims to empower SMEs, students, and novices to harness ML's potential without extensive technical expertise.

This approach not only fills existing gaps in current ML platforms but also enhances the democratization of ML technologies across diverse sectors. The platform's integration of automated tools and user-friendly design sets a new standard for accessibility and transparency in ML model development, paving the way for broader adoption and innovation in the field.

2. Literature Review

2.1 Automated Machine Learning (AutoML)

Automated Machine Learning (AutoML) aims to automate complex tasks traditionally performed by experts during the development of machine learning models. These tasks include data preprocessing, feature engineering, algorithm selection, and hyperparameter tuning, which are critical for achieving accurate models but often require significant expertise and time [4]. AutoML can be categorized into several levels, such as identifying target data, preparing data, engineering features, selecting algorithms, and tuning hyperparameters, each aiming to democratize machine learning by making it accessible to a broader audience [5].

Several AutoML platforms have emerged to streamline the model development process. [6] introduced AUTO-SKLEARN, which utilizes Bayesian optimization with meta-learning to automate model development. Despite its effectiveness in optimizing model parameters, AUTO-SKLEARN lacks a user-friendly interface, requiring manual coding by users [7] proposed TPOT, employing genetic programming for pipeline identification, yet it too lacks an intuitive interface.

To address these limitations, [8] introduced Azure Machine Learning, leveraging advanced AI techniques to solve both supervised and unsupervised learning problems without expert intervention. Despite its capabilities, Azure Machine Learning is a paid platform, limiting accessibility for non-experts and small organizations. Another prominent platform, H2O, as discussed by [9], utilizes fast random search and stacked ensembles for model training but may be daunting for non-experts.

H2O.ai remains a widely adopted open-source AutoML platform offering a user-friendly interface for data preparation, model training, and deployment. However, [10] identified limitations in handling unstructured data and large datasets. In contrast, DataRobot provides a commercial platform with a drag-and-drop interface for model building and deployment, yet its cost may pose a barrier to smaller enterprises and lack full control over the ML pipeline [11]. Google Cloud AutoML addresses cloud-based AutoML, supporting both structured and unstructured data, but its expense may deter users requiring extensive pipeline control [12].

2.2 Identified Gaps

Despite the proliferation of AutoML platforms, transparency and robust model performance evaluation remain critical challenges [3]. Users express concerns about model interpretability and the effectiveness of data visualization features within these platforms. Simple and intuitive user interfaces are essential for maximizing the utility of AutoML tools across diverse user demographics.

2.3 Development Technologies

[13] advocates for Python and Flask technologies in implementing AutoML platforms, citing advantages such as flexibility, compatibility with modern technologies, customization capabilities, security features, and reduced development time. These technologies are crucial for ensuring that AutoML platforms remain adaptable to evolving user needs and technological advancements[14].

3. Methodology and Model Specifications

3.1 Platform Design and Architecture

The "Model ML" platform is designed to democratize machine learning model development, focusing on accessibility and usability for users with varying levels of expertise in machine learning and artificial intelligence (AI).

 1) Frontend Development: Developed using HTML5, CSS3, and JavaScript frameworks with responsive design principles to ensure optimal user experience across web and mobile platforms.

 2) Backend Infrastructure: The backend is implemented using Python and Flask, which facilitate seamless communication between the frontend interface and backend services. This architecture is designed for scalability, leveraging Flask's lightweight structure and modular capabilities to accommodate increasing user demand and data processing needs. The platform utilizes RESTful APIs to ensure efficient data exchange, enabling horizontal scaling as user activity grows.

 3) Framework Reliance: The backend architecture incorporates existing frameworks like SQLAlchemy for ORM (Object-Relational Mapping) and Flask-RESTful for building APIs, allowing for rapid development and maintainability. These frameworks support scalable data processing and storage while ensuring a robust foundation for future enhancements.

 4) Database Management: Utilizes Firebase Realtime Database for efficient storage and synchronization of user data, datasets, trained models, and metadata [15]. Real-time capabilities enable collaborative model development and deployment.

3.2 Identify the Headings

"Model ML" integrates Auto-Sklearn, an advanced automated machine learning (AutoML) tool, to streamline the model development process.

Data Preprocessing

 (a) **Dataset Encoding:** Categorical variables are encoded using techniques like one-hot encoding or ordinal encoding to transform them into numerical formats suitable for machine learning algorithms.

 (b) **Data Cleaning:** Implements robust techniques such as mean imputation and outlier detection to handle missing data and ensure dataset integrity.

 (c) **Feature Scaling:** Applies normalization techniques (e.g., Min-Max scaling, Standardization) to standardize numerical features, preventing bias during model training.

Model Selection and Hyperparameter Optimization

 (a) **Algorithm Selection:** Auto-Sklearn evaluates a variety of supervised learning algorithms (e.g., Random Forests, Gradient Boosting) based on dataset characteristics and performance metrics.

 (b) **Hyperparameter Tuning:** Utilizes Bayesian optimization to optimize model hyperparameters (e.g., learning rate, regularization strength) iteratively. Bayesian optimization employs a probabilistic surrogate model, such as Gaussian Processes, to maximize objective functions like accuracy or AUC.

$$\theta_{t+1} = ar\, gmax_\theta\, \alpha(\theta) \qquad (1)$$

Where,

θ_{t+1} Represents the updated hyperparameters at iteration t+1

Indicates that we are finding the value θ that maximizes the function $\alpha(\theta)$

Model Training and Evaluation

 (a) **Cross-validation:** Implements kk-fold cross-validation to assess model generalization performance, partitioning the dataset into kk subsets for training and validation.

 (b) **Performance Metrics:** Evaluates models using standard metrics (e.g., accuracy, precision, recall, F1-score) to quantify prediction performance and validate model efficacy.

Integration and Deployment

 (a) **Model Export:** Serializes trained models into formats (e.g., pickle, joblib) compatible with deployment environments, enabling seamless integration into production systems for real-time predictions.

4. Evaluation and Results

4.1 Experimental Design

The evaluation of the "Model ML" platform focused on assessing its user-friendliness and effectiveness compared to existing AutoML solutions. A controlled study involving 50 undergraduate students with limited machine learning experience was conducted. The study emphasized multiple usability metrics, task completion times, model performance, and user satisfaction.

(a) **Participants:** 50 undergraduate students, with varying levels of familiarity with machine learning, participated in the study.

(b) **Assessment of Familiarity:** Participants' familiarity with machine learning was assessed using a pre-study survey comprising:

- **Multiple Choice Questions:** Questions on fundamental machine learning concepts (e.g., supervised vs. unsupervised learning, common algorithms, etc.).

- **Self-Assessment Scale:** A scale of 1 to 10 (1 = no experience, 10 = expert level) for participants to rate their confidence in machine learning.

(c) **Classification of Skill Levels:** Based on survey responses, participants were categorized into three skill levels:

- Beginner: Score of 1-3
- Intermediate: Score of 4-7
- Advanced: Score of 8-10

(d) **Tasks:** Participants were required to develop machine learning models using both "Model ML" and an existing AutoML platform (e.g., Auto-Sklearn).

(e) **Metrics:** Data was collected on usability (using the System Usability Scale), task completion times, model accuracy, and user satisfaction ratings.

4.2 User Study Results

Usability and User Experience

Participants rated the usability of "Model ML" significantly higher than existing AutoML platforms, as shown in Fig. 24.1. Usability was measured using the System Usability Scale (SUS), which ranges from 0 to 100.

(a) **Mean SUS Scores:**

- "Model ML": 85 ± 5
- Existing Platforms: 68 ± 7

(b) **Statistical Significance:** A paired t-test revealed a significant difference in SUS scores between "Model ML" and existing platforms ($t(49) = 8.25$, $p < 0.001$).

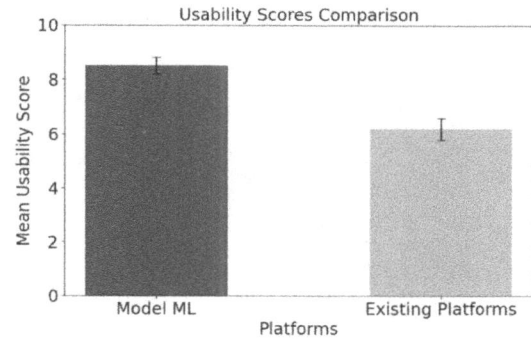

Fig. 24.1 Usability scores comparison

Task Completion Times

Participants completed tasks significantly faster using "Model ML" compared to existing platforms, as illustrated in Fig. 24.2.

(a) **Average Task Completion Time:**

- "Model ML": 20 ± 4 minutes
- Existing Platforms: 35 ± 6 minutes

(b) **Statistical Significance:** A Wilcoxon signed-rank test confirmed a significant reduction in task completion time with "Model ML" ($W = 1235$, $p < 0.001$).

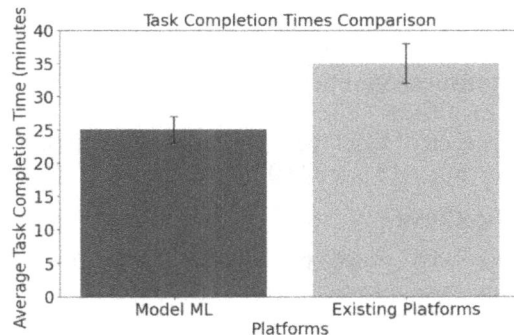

Fig. 24.2 Task completion times comparison

Model Performance

The accuracy of the models developed using both platforms was evaluated on a standardized dataset as depicted in Fig. 24.3.

(a) **Average Model Accuracy:**

- "Model ML": $92\% \pm 3\%$
- Existing Platforms: $88\% \pm 4\%$

(b) **Statistical Significance:** A paired t-test indicated a significant difference in model accuracy between "Model ML" and existing platforms ($t(49) = 4.12$, $p < 0.001$).

User Satisfaction

Participants expressed higher satisfaction levels with "Model ML" compared to existing platforms, as shown in Fig. 24.4.

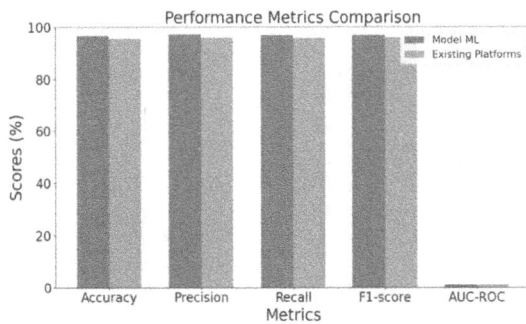

Fig. 24.3 Performace metrics comparison

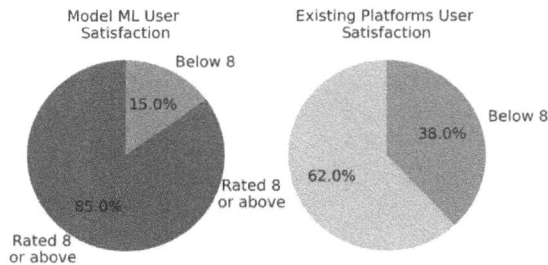

Fig. 24.4 User satisfaction comparison

(a) **User Satisfaction Ratings (scale of 1 to 10):**
- "Model ML": 8.5 ± 1.2
- Existing Platforms: 6.2 ± 1.4

(b) **Statistical Significance:** A Chi-square test indicated a significant difference in user satisfaction ratings between "Model ML" and existing platforms ($\chi^2(1,$ N = 50) = 15.6, p < 0.001).

Learning Curve

The ease with which participants learned to use the platforms was assessed through a pre-and post-study survey, as illustrated in Fig. 24.5.

(a) **Pre-study Survey (Baseline Knowledge):**
- Average Score: 3.1 ± 1.0 (out of 10)

(b) **Post-study Survey (Knowledge Gain):**
- "Model ML": 7.8 ± 1.5
- Existing Platforms: 5.5 ± 1.8

(c) **Statistical Significance:** An ANOVA test showed a significant difference in knowledge gain between "Model ML" and existing platforms (F(1, 98) = 21.45, p < 0.001).

4.3 Comparative Analysis

The study's results clearly indicate that "Model ML" offers a more user-friendly and effective experience compared to existing AutoML platforms. Key findings include:

1. **Ease of Use:** "Model ML" scored significantly higher in usability, demonstrating its effectiveness

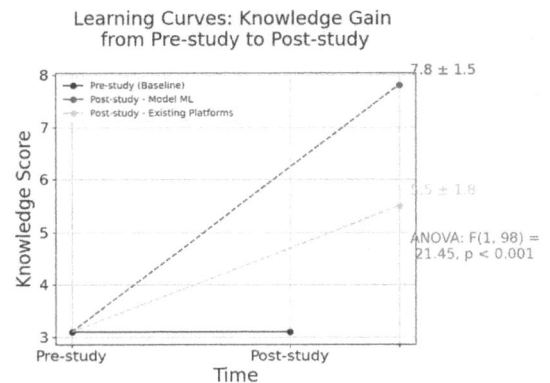

Fig. 24.5 Learning curves

in lowering the entry barrier for users with limited machine learning expertise.

2. **Efficiency:** Participants completed tasks faster using "Model ML", highlighting the platform's streamlined workflow and intuitive design.

3. **Model Performance:** Models developed with "Model ML" had higher accuracy, showcasing the platform's ability to produce reliable results.

4. **User Satisfaction:** Higher satisfaction ratings for "Model ML" suggest that users find it more enjoyable and less frustrating to use.

5. **Learning Curve:** Participants showed a greater increase in their understanding of machine learning concepts after using "Model ML".

5. Discussion

The evaluation of "Model ML" compared to existing AutoML platforms reveals several noteworthy findings. Firstly, the ease of use of "Model ML" is significantly higher, as evidenced by higher user satisfaction scores. Participants found the platform more intuitive and less cumbersome, which can be attributed to its user-centric design and accessible interface. This aligns with our aim to lower the entry barrier for users with limited machine learning expertise.

Secondly, the efficiency in completing tasks was superior on "Model ML." Participants could develop models faster, which is crucial for both novice users and seasoned practitioners seeking rapid prototyping. This efficiency is due to the streamlined workflow and integrated automated features, such as dataset encoding and model training, which reduce the time and effort required to build and test models.

Moreover, the performance of the models generated using "Model ML" was higher in accuracy compared to those created on existing platforms. This performance boost can be attributed to the platform's robust algorithm selection and hyperparameter optimization processes, facilitated by Auto-Sklearn. The platform's ability to consistently produce reliable results demonstrates its potential as a valuable tool for various ML tasks.

User satisfaction ratings further emphasize the platform's effectiveness. Participants rated "Model ML" significantly higher in terms of overall satisfaction, reflecting its usability and the positive user experience. This satisfaction is critical for broader adoption, as it indicates that users are more likely to continue using the platform and recommend it to others.

However, the study also highlights areas for improvement. While "Model ML" performed well with structured data, future enhancements should focus on better handling of unstructured data and expanding the platform's capabilities to accommodate a wider variety of datasets. Additionally, integrating more advanced visualization tools could further enhance user understanding and trust in the model development process.

6. Conclusion

"Model ML" successfully addresses several barriers to the widespread adoption of machine learning by providing an intuitive, efficient, and powerful AutoML platform. By focusing on user experience and accessibility, it empowers individuals with minimal coding experience to create sophisticated machine-learning models. The platform's superior performance in model accuracy, user satisfaction, and efficiency demonstrates its potential to democratize ML technology across various sectors.

The study validates "Model ML" as a valuable tool for SMEs, students, and novice users, enabling them to harness the power of machine learning without extensive technical expertise. Its user-centric design and comprehensive feature set position it as a leading solution in the AutoML landscape, facilitating broader adoption and fostering innovation in the field.

7. Future Work

Future work will focus on several key areas to enhance the capabilities of "Model ML." Firstly, improving the platform's handling of unstructured data will be a priority, allowing users to work with a broader range of datasets. This will involve integrating advanced data preprocessing techniques and expanding support for diverse data formats.

Secondly, enhancing the data visualization tools within "Model ML" will be crucial. Providing more interactive and detailed visualizations will help users better understand their data and the results of their models, fostering greater transparency and trust in the platform. Additionally, extending the platform's scalability and performance to support larger datasets and more complex models will be important. This will involve optimizing the backend infrastructure and exploring the integration of more powerful machine learning algorithms.

Finally, ongoing user feedback will be essential in guiding future developments. Regular updates based on user suggestions and emerging trends in machine learning will ensure that "Model ML" remains a cutting-edge tool that meets the evolving needs of its users.

REFERENCES

1. V. A. Chastikova and S. A. Zherlitsyn, "Developing the platform model for problem-solving of automated machine learning," *Journal of Physics: Conference Series*, vol. 2094, no. 3, p. 032049, 2021. [Online].
2. J. Han, K. S. Park, and K. M. Lee, "An automated machine learning platform for non-experts," in *Proc. Int. Conf. Res. Adaptive Convergent Syst.*, 2020, pp. 84–86.
3. J. Drozdal *et al.*, "Trust in AutoML," in *Proc. 25th Int. Conf. Intell. User Interfaces*, 2020. [Online].
4. K. M. Lee *et al.*, "Autonomic machine learning platform," *Int. J. Inf. Manag.*, vol. 49, pp. 491–501, 2019. [Online].
5. K. Chauhan, S. Jani, D. Thakkar, R. Dave, J. Bhatia, S. Tanwar, and M. S. Obaidat, "Automated machine learning: The new wave of machine learning," in *2020 2nd Int. Conf. Innovative Mechanisms Industry Appl. (ICIMIA)*, 2020, pp. 205–212. IEEE.
6. M. Feurer, A. Klein, K. Eggensperger, J. Springenberg, M. Blum, and F. Hutter, "Efficient and robust automated machine learning," in *Advances in Neural Information Processing Systems*, vol. 28, 2015.
7. R. S. Olson and J. H. Moore, "TPOT: A tree-based pipeline optimization tool for automating machine learning," in *Workshop on Automatic Machine Learning*, PMLR, Dec. 2016, pp. 66–74.
8. J. Barnes, *Microsoft Azure Essentials: Azure Machine Learning*. Redmond, WA: Microsoft Press, 2015.
9. E. LeDell and S. Poirier, "H2O AutoML: Scalable automatic machine learning," in *Proc. AutoML Workshop at ICML*, vol. 2020, 2020.
10. D. Zhang, C. Yin, J. Zeng, X. Yuan, and P. Zhang, "Combining structured and unstructured data for predictive models: a deep learning approach," *BMC Med. Inform. Decis. Mak.*, vol. 20, pp. 1–11, 2020.
11. M. A. Kaliszewski, D. A. D. Gonçalves, and H. S. Santos, "A comparison of three AutoML tools: H2O, TPOT, and Auto-Sklearn," *arXiv preprint arXiv:2104.07734*, 2021.
12. M. Budiman, K. Huang, L. Weng, Z. Li, and S. Zhang, "AutoML tools review: H2O.ai, TPOT, and Auto-Sklearn," *arXiv preprint arXiv:2104.14389*, 2021.
13. F. Malik, "Flask — Host your Python machine learning model on web," *FinTechExplained*, 2019. [Online]..
14. Y. Mao, Y. Chen, X. Zhang, S. Zhang, and Y. Zhu, "A survey of automated machine learning," *IEEE Trans. Neural Netw. Learn. Syst.*, vol. 32, no. 5, pp. 1955–1982, 2021.
15. E. LeDell and S. Poirier, "H2O AutoML: Scalable automatic machine learning," in *Proc. AutoML Workshop at ICML*, vol. 2020, 2020.

Note: All the figures in this chapter were made by the authors.

Transformative Applied Research in Computing, Engineering, Science and Technology – Dr. Damayanthi Dahanayake et al. (eds)
© 2024 Taylor & Francis Group, London, ISBN 978-1-041-01782-0

25

Treatment Services, Stigma and Mental Health Problems—Impact of Stigmatizing Attitudes of Medical Professionals on Help-Seeking Behavior in Colombo District

K. A. Epasinghe*
Department of Sociology, University of Colombo,
Sri Lanka

M.D.D. Manathunga
Department of Health Science,
Faculty of Science, NSBM Green University,
Sri Lanka

Abstract

Stigma, rooted in misconceptions and biases, profoundly impacts individuals experiencing mental illnesses. Importantly, the negative beliefs and attitudes held by mental health professionals perpetuate stigma, influencing how individuals access services and seek help. This study aims to explore how stigma from mental health professionals discourages psychiatric patients from seeking necessary treatment. This mixed-method research study was conducted in Colombo District, Western Province, Sri Lanka covering four main hospitals with psychiatric units. Four psychiatrists were selected through judgmental sampling, while 100 caretakers were chosen via convenience sampling. Consequently, 104 individuals were included in the sample. Qualitative data was gathered through in-depth interviews with the 4 psychiatrists, while the quantitative data was collected by incorporating the questionnaires filled out by the 100 caretakers. Thematic analysis was conducted to analyze qualitative data while bar graphs and pie charts generated by Microsoft Excel were employed for quantitative data analysis The study found no solid evidence of overt discriminatory treatment by healthcare professionals in the Colombo district, Sri Lanka, towards individuals with mental illnesses. However, underlying stigmatizing attitudes and beliefs among healthcare providers were uncovered in the subtle form of labelling. The study findings highlight the importance of addressing covert forms of stigma which significantly impact patient care and help-seeking behaviors. These attitudes can be mitigated by implementing training programs, awareness campaigns, enforcing strict diagnostic guidelines as well as encouraging open dialogue and patient feedback.

Keywords

Mental illness, Medical professionals, Stigma, Treatment services

*Corresponding author: amanda.e@nsbm.ac.lk

DOI: 10.1201/9781003616368-25

1. Introduction

The prevalence of mental illness and other mental health issues is staggeringly widespread. According to reports by WHO, in 2019, pre-pandemic, 970 million people worldwide were living with a mental disorder, with depression and anxiety being the most common [1]. The presence of mental illness profoundly impacts a person's life [2]. For instance, distress from symptoms can be debilitating. It disrupts everyday life and interferes with one's ability to make plans, leaving individuals in a state of coping. Moreover, severe mental illnesses lead to low self-esteem and feelings of hopelessness which can both be a cause and a consequence of the condition [2].

Goffman et al. have defined stigma as an attribute that is "deeply discrediting", reducing a person's value [3]. Stigma is said to arise from a discrepancy between one's "virtual social identity" (the identity assigned by society based on stereotypes, assumptions and generalizations dictating how an individual should behave) and "actual social identity" (the actual attributes and characteristics of the individual). It can impact the well-being of individuals with mental health conditions, acting as a barrier to treatment [4]. Brewis and Wutich et al. have highlighted how stigmatization can prevent people with severe symptoms from getting care in high-income countries such as the United States. Even when therapy is sought, patients often receive insufficient or harsh care. For example, research shows that patients with schizophrenia are often mistreated compared to those seeking treatment for diabetes, leading to frequent dropouts from therapeutic appointments [5].

A review of the literature finds several recurrent themes about the stigma attached to mental health issues. Initially, stigma associated with being classified as having a mental illness makes people reluctant to seek help, worsened by unfavorable care from medical personnel. Knaak, Mantler, and Szeto et al. found that people with mental illnesses frequently feel mistreated and undervalued by medical personnel. Labelling someone who has depression as a "depressive patient" or someone who has schizophrenia as a "schizophrenic patient" furthers this stigma[6]. This perception of mentally ill individuals as less capable, hazardous, and unpredictable has a substantial influence on their desire to seek treatment [6]. Clement et al. note a research gap since the extent to which help-seeking delay takes place within Sri Lanka is still not established. This discrepancy between the patients' actual conditions and the medical professionals' perceptions can lead to inadequate treatment, impairing their quality of life and fulfilment of needs, and even misdiagnosis [7].

While previous research has shown common stigma-related patterns in treatment-seeking, the present investigation was unable to locate any evidence in favor of these themes in Sri Lanka [7, 8]. Rather, a distinct topic emerged from the research, which was the 'prevalence of stigmatizing attitudes and beliefs among medical professionals toward people with mental disorders', which may discourage patients from seeking treatment. Despite the lack of overt discriminatory treatment by medical professionals, the research indicates a tendency to overlook the unique abilities of individuals with mental illness, thus further perpetuating stigma which will consequently hinder effective treatment. Therefore, the primary aim of this study is to examine the effects of medical professionals' stigmatizing ideas and the trend towards devaluing the uniqueness of persons with mental illness. Additionally, this study seeks to understand why poor treatment by healthcare workers and medical personnel has been identified as a major issue in Sri Lanka.

2. Literature Review

Despite the prevalence of mental health conditions in the modern day, there remains a substantial gap between those needing and receiving help, largely due to stigma. Stigma expressed as cues, stereotypes, prejudice, and discrimination, often discourage individuals from seeking treatment [9, 10]. Factors influencing help-seeking behavior include the preference to handle problems alone, low perceived need, low mental health literacy, and financial limitations [11]. Additionally, self-stigmatization and anticipated discrimination are major reasons patients avoid professional help [12]. Patients might anticipate discrimination and may avoid healthcare environments due to unwelcoming care takers, reinforcing any negative self-perceptions the patients might have. This is particularly concerning given the high prevalence of mental disorders and the low treatment rates worldwide. Evidence suggests that 30% of the global population acquires some form of psychological disorder with only one-third receiving treatment while others remain untreated [8]. In the USA, 31% of the population acquires mental disorders annually, however, 67% remain untreated. In Europe, 27% of the population is diagnosed with some form of mental illness while 74% remain untreated [8]. Despite the prevalence of untreated mental illness, stigma from mental health professionals such as downplaying the severity of mental health conditions or prioritizing physical symptoms invalidates patients' experiences and worsens the issue. While various factors contribute to low treatment rates, the role healthcare professionals play which inadvertently contributes to this stigma is critical yet overlooked. Their perpetuation of stigma can be a significant barrier to treatment. If a patient who finally seeks treatment encounters judgmental or dismissive attitudes, it could reinforce negative self-perceptions associated with mental illnesses. This can discourage future appointments or seeking help elsewhere, validating patient's fears and prejudices causing them to avoid treatment at all [10].

Therefore, the stigma perpetuated by some healthcare professionals creates a negative and unwelcoming environment for people with mental illnesses, discouraging them from seeking help due to the fear of judgment, lack of support, and concerns about receiving suboptimal care [13] . In reference to the Sri Lankan context, mental health care service is not considered a priority compared to other health services. Specifically, Sri Lankans tend to seek help from traditional healers before considering "Western" medicine, eventually resulting in delays in accessing appropriate care [14]. A reason for this preference may be beliefs regarding the causes of mental illnesses. Many hold the belief that spirits, and "Gods and Devils" cause mental illnesses or factors related to academic stress like excessive studying, inability to pass exams or secure employment —can lead to a mental disorder or that it develops as atonement for one's past life [14]. This lack of understanding results in poor help-seeking behaviors. Individuals seek help from a long line of traditional spiritual healers before considering "Western" healing. This results in significant delays in receiving timely treatments, late diagnosis and reduced efficacy of allopathic medicine. This, in turn, further reinforces the belief that Western medicine is "ineffective" [14]. This cultural preference paired with the stigma present within the healthcare system itself, impedes timely and effective mental treatment in Sri Lanka.

Few studies have identified the stigmatizing attitudes held by medical professionals towards persons undergoing mental illnesses. Fernando et al. have found that medical students and doctors in Sri Lanka often harbor stigmatizing attitudes, believing patients are responsible for their condition, possess weak character, lack ability, pose a threat, and should not live near others. Similarly, Baminiwatta et al. have examined stigma among nurses in Sri Lanka revealing widespread negative attitudes towards patients with mental disorders [15,16]. Nurses with higher levels of mindfulness and compassion were more supportive while those that expressed low levels tended to avoid and discriminate against psychiatric patients.

Additionally, comparisons in attitudes towards mental illness among medical professionals in Sri Lanka [15], Pakistan [17] and the UK [18] present a complex view of stigma. Professionals in Sri Lanka and Pakistan displayed more stigmatizing attitudes, attributing blame for mental health conditions such as depression, schizophrenia, and substance use disorders than their counterparts in the UK. High perceptions of dangerousness were notable for substance use disorders in Sri Lanka and Pakistan. Conversely, health campaigns in the UK aimed at reducing mental health stigma may have contributed to more positive attitudes among British healthcare professionals. Thus, the pervasive stigma surrounding mental health, perpetuated by negative stereotypes and discriminatory attitudes among healthcare professionals, significantly patients' willingness to seek treatment. However, there is a critical research gap in understanding how individuals with mental illness may experience stigma from mental health professionals and how it impacts their help-seeking behavior. Therefore, the present study aims to address this gap potentially reducing treatment delays and improving treatment engagement by addressing and minimizing specific stigmatizing attitudes and behaviors.

3. Materials and Methods

The present study focuses on the Colombo District in the Western Province of Sri Lanka. The study selected Colombo District due to its accessibility and high level of urbanization that makes it an ideal location for studying daily living and work-related conditions. As a highly urbanized region, Colombo likely provided a larger and more diverse sample, including individuals from various occupations, living arrangements, and socioeconomic backgrounds. The urban environment also exposed participants to a greater number of environmental stressors, which are associated with elevated stress levels. These factors, in turn, have a significant impact on mental health, making Colombo a relevant choice for the research. The data was collected at four major hospitals in Colombo including National Hospital Colombo, Police Hospital Colombo, Colombo South Teaching Hospital, and Base Hospital Homagama. A sample of four psychiatrists, one from each of the selected hospitals, was incorporated using the judgmental sampling methods (also known as purposive sampling). This technique was used to guarantee that the selected psychiatrists could offer pertinent and essential information. This approach was selected to guarantee that medical specialists who could supply the required data for the research were included. Additionally, 100 informal caretakers (25 from each hospital) comprising family members and relatives of individuals undergoing treatment for mental illnesses were chosen by the convenience sampling method. Convenience sampling was selected since it was an effective method to identify people who were readily available and interested in offering pertinent information. Using a combination of survey and interview methods, the study uses a mixed-method research design to collect quantitative and qualitative data. The use of quantitative and qualitative methods improved the study's validity and reliability. Quantitative data provided measurable insights, while qualitative data added depth, making the findings more accurate and credible. In-depth interviews with the four psychiatrists yielded qualitative data. In contrast, formal questionnaires under the survey method were used to gather quantitative data from 100 caretakers. As a result, each psychiatrist gave information about five patients with mental health disorders, culminating in a dataset of 20 individuals. It is crucial to note that questioning people who are undergoing mental illness directly about their condition might be upsetting and detrimental to their mental well-being. Therefore, instead of gathering data directly from the patients, data were gathered from 100 caretakers and four psychiatrists to allay ethical concerns. To ensure participants' willingness to take part in the study, oral informed consent was obtained from each psychiatrist and care giver upon their agreement. To protect patient privacy, pseudonyms were employed instead of real names. Thematic analysis was utilized as an inductive strategy to analyze qualitative data. By coding the data based on recurrent and common patterns, relevant themes were identified. Furthermore, the efficacy of this approach in locating pertinent themes and codes within the qualitative information obtained from the four in-depth interviews with the psychiatrists led to its selection. Quantitative information was gathered from the 100 questionnaires that the sample of 100 caretakers filled out for numerical analysis based on the identified themes. This quantitative data was subsequently analyzed using graphical representations made with Microsoft Excel since data could be represented graphically through pie charts and bar charts.

4. Results and Discussion

Based upon his book Asylums in 1961, Goffman [19] argues that the motives within asylums were not to cure patients but rather to mold their attitudes and behavior in such a way that would make it easier for the caretakers to manage them. As Goffman argued, the labeling of someone as crazy is a product of consensus, and stigma is at the heart of this process [5]. The mental health professionals in Colombo, tended to view mentally ill individuals through a stigmatized lens. Reflecting Goffman's views on mental illness being a result of social consensus than objective diagnosis, data collected showcased medical professionals in the Colombo business district to exhibit patterns of labelling individuals as mentally ill irrespective of their actual competence to manage their lives.

The case of Chamath, a 27-year-old male who was diagnosed with depression, could be defined as an example.

The medical professional explained that: "Chamath did not have any sleep disturbances, he had no cognitive impairments, no recorded hallucinations or delusions, and he had not lost his appetite."

Importantly, lack of appetite and sleep disturbances are major indicators of depression, yet Chamath was reported to have no sleep disturbance or lack of appetite even if the medical professional had diagnosed him as suffering from moderate depression. In addition, according to Pellegrino et al. depression was regarded as a common feature within cognitive impairments, whereas in the case of Chamath, even though he was diagnosed with depression, the medical professional also reported him to have no cognitive impairments [20]. This argument sheds light on how, regardless of the true nature of the persons or their abilities and resilience, the medical professionals are strictly adhering to a stigmatized pattern of diagnosing persons with mental illness, which may motivate these professionals to label persons as mentally ill at the presence of the slightest trace of a symptom. Corrigan et al. supports this by highlighting how diagnostic labelling and classification can intensify the public's perception of people with mental illness as a distinct group, diminishing their individual identities as well as exacerbating the sense of "groupness" and "differentness" contributing to stigma [21].

Another case that illustrates the stigmatizing beliefs held by medical professionals is the case of Dinesh, a 32-year-old male who was diagnosed with conduct disorder and was admitted to the general hospital in Colombo due to his aggressive behavior. The medical professional explained that Dinesh was an individual who holds a degree in video editing and is involved in video editing as a self-employed. He was quite interesting to talk to as he talked about unique topics such as the astral body, timeline, and multiverse changes. He stated that he has done a great deal of reading regarding such topics since childhood. When talking to him, one can't feel that he has a mental disorder at all. He seems very presentable and knowledgeable.

Dinesh had complained that, because of having to be "stuck between walls" at the hospital, he could not get any new ideas to do any creative writings or any form of video editing as he did not have the equipment needed at the hospital. He was desperate to go home and "get on with his work."

Even though the medical professional himself was able to take note of Dinesh's uniqueness as an individual and stated that he "can't feel he has a mental disorder," still Dinesh was diagnosed and hospitalized restricting his needs and further development.

The above-mentioned cases highlight the importance of recognizing that diagnosing persons with specific mental illnesses may not always align with their own realities and uniqueness. This may lead to certain disparities in care outcomes for these patients and may make them question the usefulness of such treatment services where the medical professionals have failed to address their subjective ideologies. This may, in turn, motivate disruptions in the continuation of the treatment process

In conclusion, apart from the strict adherence to the biomedical model which disregards the actual realities of the individuals and causes the perpetuation of beliefs that promote stigma, there was no significant evidence of the 'discriminatory treatments directed by the doctors or other hospital staff towards the mentally ill patients' within the hospitals in Colombo district. Yet in contradiction, previous studies extracted from other countries have regarded the negative treatment offered by doctors and other healthcare staff to be quite prominent. A study by Lam et al. presented that primary care physicians held negative stereotypes of dangerousness and unpredictability towards psychiatric patients showcasing fewer negative attitudes towards patients with depression over those with schizophrenia [22]. Studies also suggest that stigma and distrust of psychiatric treatment are key factors delaying help-seeking. For example, African Americans in Chicago believe that spiritual mental health care provided by the church is more effective than treatment from the mental healthcare system, which contributes to their reluctance to address psychiatric symptoms with primary caretakers [10]. Tirintica et al. showcased how healthcare professionals perpetuate stigma by hesitating to recommend mental healthcare services, creating a negative and unwelcoming environment for those seeking treatment [23]. In addition, this argument in relation to the Colombo district could further be proved through the data gathered from the questionnaires under survey method. Survey data indicate that most healthcare professionals do not perceive themselves as engaging in discriminatory treatment with 72% disagreeing that doctors treat mentally ill patients negatively (Fig. 25.1). However, the qualitative cases, such as Chamath's misdiagnosis of depression despite lacking key symptoms reveal subtler forms of stigma. Similarly, Figure 25.3 (Being labelled as having a mental illness) highlights that 65% of respondents agreed that labelling patients with mental illness hinders treatment, as that of Dinesh's case who was unnecessarily labelled and hospitalized This demonstrates that although overt discrimination may be rare, subtle stigma through labelling still affects patient care.

In reference to Fig. 25.1 (Discriminatory treatment offered by doctors), it is clear it supports the stated argument

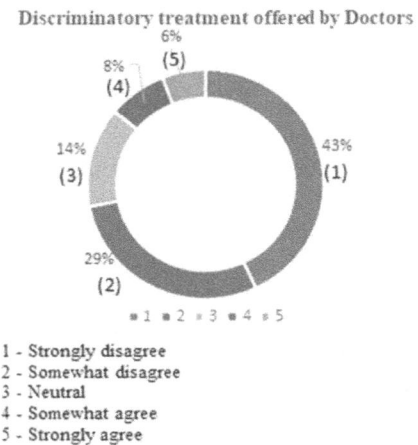

Fig. 25.1 Discriminatory treatment offered by doctors

that doctors have not offered any form of negative or discriminatory treatments towards the patients suffering from mental illnesses. Since almost 43% strongly disagree in saying that there was a prevalence of negative treatment practiced by doctors, 29% somewhat disagree. While a percentage of 14 remains neutral upon this statement, only a minority agrees that there had been some form of discriminatory treatment exercised by the doctors (Strongly agree – 6% & somewhat agree – 8%). Similarly, Figure 25.2 (Discriminatory treatment offered by the hospital staff) also indicates how there were no discriminatory treatments.

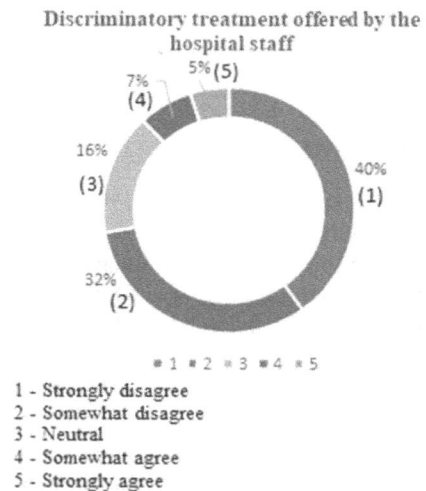

Fig. 25.2 Discriminatory treatment offered by the hospital

Demonstrated by the hospital staff either. For instance, the above chart illustrates most respondents having rated a higher percentage on 'disagreeing' (Strongly disagree – 40% & somewhat disagree – 32%) on the assumption that there could be negative treatment offered by the hospital staff towards the mentally ill persons. Moreover, only a quite small number of respondents agreed (Strongly agree – 5% & somewhat agree 7%) with discriminatory treatment practiced by hospital staff, whereas a percentage 16 remained neutral.

As shown in Fig. 25.3 (Being labelled as having a mental illness), was rated positively within the questionnaire. For instance, many participants have agreed upon the fact that patients are being labelled on their mental illness and that in turn, it may hinder their process of gaining treatment services. Additionally, 26% strongly agreed while 39% of the respondents agreed upon this statement. Consequently, while a percentage of 19 remained neutral, 16 disagreed on the occurrence of the labelling process (Strongly disagree – 9% & somewhat disagree 7%).

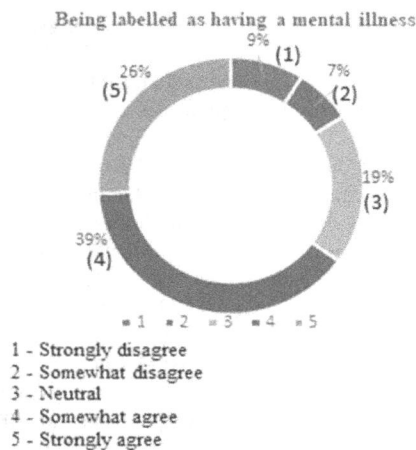

1 - Strongly disagree
2 - Somewhat disagree
3 - Neutral
4 - Somewhat agree
5 - Strongly agree

Fig. 25.3 Being labelled as having a mental illness

In reference to Fig. 25.4 (Feeling reluctant to obtain services due to stigma), this statement was once again supported by a majority, where 29% strongly agreed, and 25% somewhat agreed. Only 11% strongly disagreed, while 15% somewhat disagreed with the above statement and 19 respondents were neutral. Therefore, pertaining to the data from Fig. 25.4 (Feeling reluctant to obtain services due to stigma), it is understandable how, there is a positive inclination towards encountering barriers in obtaining treatment services, because of being labelled on one's mental illness and feeling reluctant to obtain treatment services due to stigma.

In conclusion, it is worth noting that, even though there was no significant discriminatory treatment offered by either doctors or hospital staff, the revealing of a prominent theme traces stigmatizing beliefs and attitudes practiced by medical professionals. Therefore, the study underscores important insights into how this very process of being

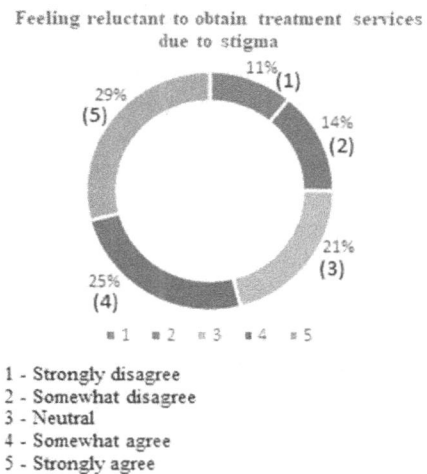

1 - Strongly disagree
2 - Somewhat disagree
3 - Neutral
4 - Somewhat agree
5 - Strongly agree

Fig. 25.4 Feeling reluctant to obtain services due to stigma

labelled with a mental illness, which eventually promotes stigma, could contribute to the reluctance of the patients to obtain treatment services.

5. Conclusion

This study explored the impact of stigma on individuals with mental health issues within the Colombo district, focusing on the influence of stigma from mental health professionals on help-seeking behavior. Contrary to expectations and previous research, the findings indicate no strong evidence of overt discriminatory treatment. Both interview and questionnaire responses consistently showed that healthcare professionals in Colombo do not engage in negative treatment based on mental health status. However, despite this positive finding, the research uncovered underlying stigmatizing views and beliefs. These subtle biases, despite not being overt discrimination, could still influence patient interactions and treatment experiences. This dichotomy highlights the complex nature of stigma in mental healthcare settings.

The study faced several limitations, including time-consuming interviews, difficulties in scheduling medical professionals, and the need for multiple visits to hospitals to reach the target of 20 patients. This increased both time and travel costs, while also making it difficult to identify individuals with mental disorders or their caretakers for the questionnaire.

Addressing these attitudes through targeted training programs and awareness campaigns are essential to eliminate stigma in healthcare. These initiatives help dispel misconceptions, challenge harmful stereotypes, and reduce unconscious bias, while humanizing mental illness in the process. Stricter diagnostic protocols can reduce diagnoses based on minimal symptoms and prevent unnecessary stigma. Encouraging open dialogue and patient feedback can foster discussions on mental health stigma, promoting empathy and corrective action. Additionally, encouraging professionals to adopt a more individualized approach, considering a patient's unique characteristics over isolated symptoms, promotes more accurate and compassionate care. Finally, regular evaluations of staff attitudes and performance related to mental health care can ensure continuous improvement and accountability in reducing stigma across all levels of care.

In conclusion, this research emphasizes a critical and hopeful discovery: the absence of discriminatory treatment by healthcare providers in Colombo towards individuals with mental health issues. It demonstrates the positive aspects of the healthcare system while also stressing the need to establish a truly stigma-free environment.

REFERENCES

1. M. Freeman, "The World Mental Health Report: transforming mental health for all," *World Psychiatry*, vol. 21, 2022, [Online]. Available: https://api.semanticscholar.org/CorpusID:252112340

2. J. Connell, J. Brazier, A. O'Cathain, M. Lloyd-Jones, and S. Paisley, "Quality of life of people with mental health problems: A synthesis of qualitative research," Nov. 22, 2012. doi: 10.1186/1477-7525-10-138.

3. E. Goffman, "Stigma; Notes On The Management Of Spoiled Identity," 1964. [Online]. Available: https://api.semanticscholar.org/CorpusID:143845069

4. A. Shrivastava, M. Gath, and Y. Bureau, "Stigma of Mental Illness-1: Clinical Reflections," *Mens Sana Monogr*, vol. 10, pp. 70–84, Mar. 2012, doi: 10.4103/0973-1229.90181.

5. A. A. Brewis and A. Wutich, "Lazy, Crazy, and Disgusting: Stigma and the Undoing of Global Health," 2019. [Online]. Available: https://api.semanticscholar.org/CorpusID:213414966

6. S. Knaak, E. Mantler, and A. Szeto, "Mental illness-related stigma in healthcare: Barriers to access and care and evidence-based solutions," Mar. 01, 2017, *SAGE Publications Inc.* doi: 10.1177/0840470416679413.

7. S. Clement *et al.*, "What is the impact on mental health-related stigma on help-seeking? A systematic review of quantitative and qualitative studies," Jan. 12, 2015, *Cambridge University Press.* doi: 10.1017/S0033291714000129.

8. G. Thornicroft, "Stigma and discrimination limit access to mental health care," 2008, *Il Pensiero Scientifico Editore s.r.l.* doi: 10.1017/S1121189X00002621.

9. P. W. Corrigan, B. G. Druss, and D. A. Perlick, "The Impact of Mental Illness Stigma on Seeking and Participating in Mental Health Care," *Psychological Science in the Public Interest*, vol. 15, no. 2, pp. 37–70, Sep. 2014, doi: 10.1177/1529100614531398.

10. P. Corrigan, "How Stigma Interferes With Mental Health Care," *Am Psychol*, vol. 59, pp. 614–625, Oct. 2004, doi: 10.1037/0003-066X.59.7.614.

11. N. Schnyder, R. Panczak, N. Groth, and F. Schultze-Lutter, "Association between mental health-related stigma and active help-seeking: Systematic review and meta-analysis," Apr. 01, 2017, *Royal College of Psychiatrists*. doi: 10.1192/bjp.bp.116.189464.

12. G. Schomerus and M. Angermeyer, "Stigma and its impact on help-seeking for mental disorders: What do we know?," *Epidemiol Psichiatr Soc*, vol. 17, pp. 31–37, Mar. 2008, doi: 10.1017/S1121189X00002669.

13. S. Gunasekaran, G. T. H. Tan, S. Shahwan, C. M. J. Goh, W. J. Ong, and M. Subramaniam, "The perspectives of healthcare professionals in mental health settings on stigma and recovery - A qualitative inquiry," *BMC Health Serv Res*, vol. 22, no. 1, Dec. 2022, doi: 10.1186/s12913-022-08248-z.

14. Samarasekare, M. Lloyd, M. Davies, and S. Siribaddana, "The Stigma of Mental Illness in Sri Lanka: The Perspectives of Community Mental Health Workers," *Stigma Res Action*, vol. 2, no. 2, pp. 93–99, 2012, doi: 10.5463/SRA.v1i1.13.

15. S. M. Fernando, F. P. Deane, and H. J. McLeod, "Sri Lankan doctors' and medical undergraduates' attitudes towards mental illness," *Soc Psychiatry Psychiatr Epidemiol*, vol. 45, no. 7, pp. 733–739, Jul. 2010, doi: 10.1007/s00127-009-0113-6.

16. A. Baminiwatta, H. Alahakoon, N. Herath, K. Kodithuwakku, and T. Nanayakkara, "Trait Mindfulness, Compassion, and Stigma Towards Patients with Mental Illness: A Study Among Nurses in Sri Lanka," *Mindfulness (N Y)*, vol. 14, pp. 1–13, Mar. 2023, doi: 10.1007/s12671-023-02108-5.

17. F. Naeem, A. Ayub, Z. Javed, M. Irfan, and F. Haral, "Stigma & psychiatric illness: A survey of attitude of medical students and doctors in Lahore, Pakistan," *J Ayub Med Coll Abbottabad*, vol. 18, pp. 46–49, Jul. 2006.

18. R. Mukherjee, A. Fialho, A. Wijetunge, K. Checinski, and T. Surgenor, "The stigmatisation of psychiatric illness: The attitudes of medical students and doctors in a London teaching hospital," *Psychiatric Bulletin*, vol. 26, no. 5, pp. 178–181, 2002, doi: 10.1192/pb.26.5.178.

19. E. Goffman, "Asylums: Essays on the Social Situation of Mental Patients and Other Inmates," 1961. [Online]. Available: https://api.semanticscholar.org/CorpusID:74288080

20. L. D. Pellegrino, M. E. Peters, C. G. Lyketsos, and C. M. Marano, "Depression in cognitive impairment," *Curr Psychiatry Rep*, vol. 15, no. 9, Sep. 2013, doi: 10.1007/s11920-013-0384-1.

21. P. Corrigan, "How Clinical Diagnosis Might Exacerbate the Stigma of Mental Illness," *Soc Work*, vol. 52, pp. 31–39, Feb. 2007, doi: 10.1093/sw/52.1.31.

22. T. P. Lam, K. F. Lam, E. W. W. Lam, and Y. S. Ku, "Attitudes of primary care physicians towards patients with mental illness in Hong Kong," *Asia-Pacific Psychiatry*, vol. 5, no. 1, Mar. 2013, doi: 10.1111/j.1758-5872.2012.00208.x

23. A. R. Tirintica *et al.*, "Factors that influence access to mental health services in South-Eastern Europe," *Int J Ment Health Syst*, vol. 12, no. 1, Dec. 2018, doi: 10.1186/s13033-018-0255-6.

Note: All the figures in this chapter were made by the authors.

Transformative Applied Research in Computing, Engineering, Science and Technology – Dr. Damayanthi Dahanayake et al. (eds)
© 2024 Taylor & Francis Group, London, ISBN 978-1-041-01782-0

26

BioCrypt—The DNA Cryptography Framework

Ravindu Wickramasinghe*
School of Engineering,
Computing and Mathematics, University of Plymouth,
United Kingdom

Chamara Disanayake, Chamindra Attanayake
Department of Computer Security and Network Systems,
NSBM Green University, Sri Lanka

BAS Dilhara
Macquarie University, Australia

Abstract

With the exponential growth in computer storage demands, driven by current human data requirements, accommodating these needs has become a critical concern. Traditional data storage methods face numerous problems, prompting researchers to explore alternative solutions. One promising development is DNA-based data storage systems, which offer significant advantages over conventional approaches. However, the gap between electronic and biological domains in real-world applications involving general users and genetic engineers can introduce security issues. The proposed framework addresses these challenges by integrating DNA computing and cryptography, promoting the adoption of synthetic DNA as a viable data storage medium. This research proposes a homomorphic encryption approach designed to enhance security in DNA data storage, specifically targeting the issues introduced by the inter-domain knowledge gap. The methodology includes developing algorithms that enable secure data encoding and retrieval while preserving data privacy. The system empowers researchers, businesses, and general users with a versatile toolkit with multiple cryptographic functionalities. Key deliverables include user authentication, file management, encryption, decryption, steganography, DNA sequence visualization, and more. Expected outcomes include improved data security, increased efficiency in data management, and adaptability to various applications in both research and commercial settings. This paper provides a comprehensive overview of the research objectives, methodologies, deliverables, and requirements, highlighting its potential to revolutionize data security and storage paradigms.

Keywords

DNA. Cryptography, Data security, DNA data storage

*Corresponding author: rviz@pm.me

DOI: 10.1201/9781003616368-26

1. Introduction

DNA computing and cryptography represent a cutting-edge intersection of biology and computer science, offering innovative solutions to complex computational challenges. DNA's unique characteristics make it particularly suitable for cryptography. Its molecular structure provides a high level of advantages for data storage and security. This surpasses several aspects of emerging security fields and cryptographic methods, including quantum cryptography. [3].

In DNA computing, researchers explore the potential of DNA strands as fundamental components for information storage and processing. Unlike conventional computers that rely on binary code, DNA computing uses the four nucleotide bases—adenine (A), thymine (T), cytosine (C), and guanine (G)—to encode data. This capability enhances the security of stored information.

Within this framework, DNA cryptography emerges as a specialized field focused on safeguarding information through molecular biology principles. The distinctive properties of DNA not only offer innovative data storage solutions but also enhance information security.

This document provides a comprehensive overview of the BioCrypt framework, outlining its objectives, methodologies, and anticipated outcomes. Subsequent chapters will cover the literature review, project requirements, design and implementation specifics, testing and validation methods, and a concise summary of key findings and future development prospects.

2. Problem Statement

The challenge of accommodating the exponential surge in computer storage needs to meet the current requirements of human data has become a critical concern. The data stored on these devices is anticipated to surpass the daily data consumption of our society, with projections estimating 5000 zettabytes by the year 2024 [2]. In the 21st century, the significance of certain digital information is widely acknowledged. Recognising the heightened value of data, especially sensitive and vital information, current storage methods, such as tape or solid-state storage, are deemed average. While tape technology, commonly used for long-term archiving, has witnessed significant density improvements, reaching 330 terabytes [1], these mediums may struggle to meet the future demand for data storage. The existing process for converting digital files to DNA lacks adequate security measures when considering practical applications from molecular and electronic, inter-domain perspectives. For instance, a user without expertise in molecular biology must directly share their digital file with an expert to facilitate the storage of digital files in DNA. The proposed framework systematically addresses this challenge.

DNA computing-based algorithms and various DNA cryptography algorithms have been proposed in recent years, yet not all of them prove as secure as initially perceived. For instance, the substitution cypher based on DNA cryptography developed by the University of India and the University of Mumbai, utilising the Bio Java framework, lacks proper security and can be easily decrypted if the substitution alphabet is known [3]. Symmetric cryptographic algorithms based on DNA cryptography involve key generation, encryption, and decryption processes. While these areas are still undergoing research and development, proposed systems often rely on One Time Pad (OTP) or substitution ciphers, with different key generation algorithms. Although some algorithms align with current encryption standards and DNA properties, especially in the case of Asymmetric algorithms, they tend to be computationally intensive. Thus, the substitution cyphers discussed earlier cannot be deemed secure. The evaluation of these algorithms is insufficient, lacking a common toolkit or framework for proper testing. A significant challenge in DNA cryptography lies in the gap between its two domains: the molecular domain and the electronic domain. This dual-domain nature introduces a potential proficiency gap, as experts in one domain may lack expertise in the other. Computation at the molecular level is a research area still under development, posing challenges in bridging the expertise divide.

One prevalent issue in DNA cryptography is the tendency to encrypt only highly sensitive files, neglecting medium to low-level sensitive files. This practice increases the risk of data leaks and subsequent chain attacks. Addressing this, there exists a research gap in the molecular domain, which, though problematic in the electronic domain, remains unaddressed. Despite the computational and financial limitations, there's a need for higher security for the most sensitive data. While some organizations currently employ advanced security measures, many are yet to do so. The evolution of computational power, evident from early computers to contemporary quantum computers, clearly indicates the need to secure large data sets against potential computational threats.

In response to emerging challenges, new cryptographic fields have surfaced in recent years, including quantum cryptography, elliptic cryptography, and DNA cryptography. However, quantum and elliptic cryptography have demonstrated vulnerabilities to Person in The Middle Attacks (PiTM) and Denial of Service Attacks

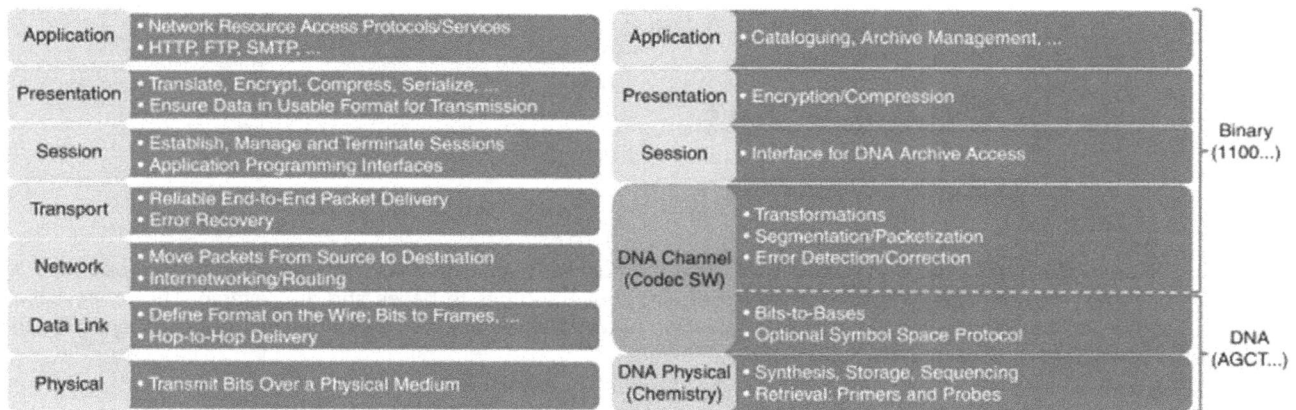

Fig. 26.1 The layers of the OSI model and the DNA data storage model. [6]

(DoS). [3]. Despite being a field under constant research and development, there is a lack of an organised toolkit or software application to operate within the electronic domain of DNA computing and cryptography. This deficiency, coupled with the shortage of research and development in DNA cryptography, underscores the necessity for collaboration among experts in computer science, molecular biology, and cryptography to address these challenges.

3. Project Objectives

The proposed system (hereafter referred to as BioCrypt) aims to address some common issues in DNA computing and Cryptography within the electronic domain by creating a framework (toolkit) that helps researchers and be used in the future by general users.

With the use of BioCrypt, the process of moving to the new data storage medium DNA would be more straightforward and secure for a general computer user. With the hyper-dense feature of synthetic DNA, it is possible to store up to 455 exabytes per gram (EB g−1) [5]. Another property is that the ultra-persistent feature of synthetic DNA can last about 10 times longer than the storage media used today. DNA synthetic fossils last 2000 to 2,000,000 years. Since DNA has no obsolescence, it won't change as a medium along with time like other storage mediums and computers. [4].

DNA cryptography is not something that should be considered as a field planned to be implemented in the future; it's already actively used by different kinds of organizations and big technical companies. For example: The military in Tel Aviv is using DNA cryptography for its computer storage. The US military also uses DNA cryptography for storing their very confidential files. [3].

But there's no common toolkit or framework designed or developed to work with DNA cryptography as a complete framework to work within the electronic domain. BioCrypt framework is the system proposed to solve many problems around this and to streamline the DNA cryptography process.

When it comes to securely storing digital data in DNA, the knowledge gap between users in between the domains will be addressed by the proposed BioCrypt framework. The user doesn't have to provide their raw data to the molecular domain for the DNA storage directly which can be insecure because the people who work in the molecular domain will have access to that user's data. Instead with the BioCrypt framework users can take a homomorphic encryption approach where they can encrypt the files first using a digital key and then provide the encrypted data for DNA computing and storage. This is one of the main objectives of BioCrypt. Another gap between the two domains is that electronic domain users can help the molecular domain users by providing a proper visualisation of the DNA sequences that they want to create, it would be helpful when it comes to creating the DNA sequences because there are specific proteins and chemical reactions that required to be done to create synthetic DNA sequences.

Another objective of BioCrypt is to provide an organised output file following a common standard DNA sequence file format like FASTA format along with visualisation of DNA sequences. The BioCrypt project aims to foster an open and collaborative environment for research in DNA-based cryptography. By encouraging interdisciplinary cooperation among molecular biologists, computer scientists, and cryptographers, the project seeks to advance the understanding and application of DNA as a secure storage medium. This collaborative approach is intended to enhance innovation and drive the field forward, addressing

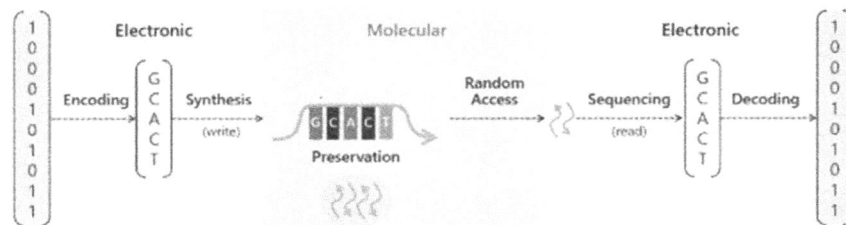

Fig. 26.2 Diagram illustrating the end-to-end DNA data storage process: The DNA data storage system operates by encoding and decoding information electronically, converting bits to bases and the reverse. The processes of synthesis and sequencing serve as the gateways between the electronic and molecular domains, enabling the creation and retrieval of DNA sequences

Source: Microsoft Research

the high costs associated with DNA storage and promoting greater inter-domain research.

4. Literature Review

4.1 DNA Encoding

In the work proposed by Raj, Bonny B; Sharmila, and others proposed using DNA encoding techniques. They advocated for a conventional yet versatile strategy, combining cryptography with DNA as an information carrier. The authors emphasised the potential of Deoxyribonucleic Acid (DNA) as a promising technique, showcasing its enhanced parallelism, unparalleled energy efficiency, and capabilities in storage and computation. [7]

4.2 DNA Data Storage System

In the paper published in July 2023, Landsman and Strauss present an insightful exploration of DNA data storage within the Open Systems Interconnect (OSI) model, aligning the synthetic DNA storage process with traditional storage technologies. The authors emphasise DNA's potential as an archival solution and discuss its hyper density, retention characteristics, sustainability, and cost advantages. Detailing the encoding-to-decoding process, they highlight the unique features of synthetic DNA, such as its on-the-fly manufacturing during write operations and distinctive error characteristics. Parallels between the DNA data storage and OSI models are drawn, focusing on layers from application to session. The DNA channel layer, related to traditional network channels, employs packetization, error correction, translation, and transformations, while the physical layer encompasses synthesis, sequencing, storage, and retrieval. The retrieval process, crucial for logical storage operations, is explained with methods like PCR and DNA pull-out. In this, the processes, especially processes within the electronic domain will be useful and additional cryptographic applications will be added in BioCrypt. [6]

4.3 DNA Cryptography

Md. Rafiul Biswas and other authors introduced a DNA cryptographic technique that employs dynamic DNA encoding and asymmetric cryptosystems to enhance data security performance. This approach involves employing a mathematical method to partition the plaintext into specific-sized chunks. The algorithm is applied to each chunk individually, and the resulting ciphertexts are merged using dynamic DNA encoding. The authors incorporated the concept of converting text into ASCII equivalent, subsequently dividing it into a finite sequence. For encryption, the equivalent binary representation is utilised for DNA bases. To complete the merging operation for each chunk, a set of random strings is generated to introduce diffusion and confusion, utilising the Fibonacci series for these random strings to increase the security levels. [8]

Marwan, Shawish, and Nagaty (2017) present a DNA-based steganography algorithm that enhances data storage and security. This method encodes diverse data types into DNA, encrypts it, and hides it within noncoding regions of a selected DNA sequence. The encryption and use of a key sequence matching the fake DNA length improve security. The algorithm doubles data storage capacity and prevents full data extraction by excluding the hidden key sequence from the transmitted fake DNA. Experimental studies validate its effectiveness as a secure alternative in DNA-based steganography. [9] Their approach uses a substitution cipher they point out the fact that this cracking probability can occur in case the attacker knows the ciphering technique. Security of this method depends on the substitution table which cannot be considered very secure with modern technology. [9]

5. Methodology, Model Specification and System Architecture

The underlying logic of BioCrypt is to use the general DNA mapping that maps the binary values of digital data to

Table 26.1 Binarybinary data to DNA mapping

Binary Data	DNA Sequence
00	A – Adenine
01	C – Cytosine
10	G – guanine
11	T - thymine

Source: Adapted from the Blog of Mitja Felicijan

nucleotides of DNA using a particular algorithm and create a DNA sequence as output BioCrypt framework is more than simply using DNA mapping and there are many more features, it provides the DNA cryptographic application of.

- Current algorithms
- Proposed algorithm
- Encodings
- Compression algorithms,
- Steganography techniques and algorithms,
- Standard key-generation processes,
- DNA-based key generation processes
- Standard processes to follow before writing Synthetic DNA
- Algorithms can be introduced since it's template/module-based architecture.

Those standard processes that must follow before the DNA writing process include processes like indexing and adding redundant data which can be used in the reading process to recover any data corruption or loss. [4] Processes like these would be added as features of the BioCrypt framework, and these processes can be automated. Insecure algorithms and some improved secure algorithms have been proposed for the last few years related to DNA cryptography and it also supports research and development there would be a separate section within the software to highlight and test these algorithms as well. However, within the tool, there are options to show the security level of the algorithm used clearly. The BioCrypt framework is composed of several components that can be used to address functionalities within the electronic domain.

In the framework, it would follow a template-based architecture to create and work with new algorithms or techniques. For example, if there's a new proposed algorithm the contributors can add them to the public repository as a new module or template and every other user can use it. If the user prefers to keep it private, a new template can be created and used only on the personal computer. There are features to visualise the DNA sequences of the final output. This can be helpful for researchers' people who work in the molecular domain and general users as well. Especially when it comes to DNA-based steganography

techniques this feature can be used to analyse the output with molecular-level visualisation.

The development of BioCrypt involves two distinct domains: the molecular and electronic realms. While the project's applications operate electronically, a crucial understanding of molecular biology, specifically DNA functionality and the intricacies of DNA storage processes, is essential. Even though creating a software design for the electronic domain is feasible, ensuring that the output aligns with the requirements of the molecular domain is particularly important. Simultaneously, studying and getting a comprehensive understanding of cryptographic algorithms, steganography algorithms, associated tools, and their security levels are mandatory. Therefore, one of the initial steps involves studying and comprehending the fundamentals of cryptography.

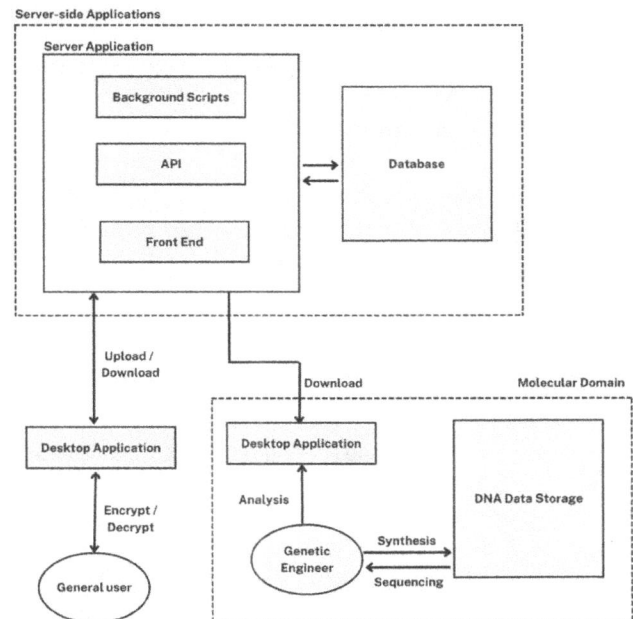

Fig. 26.3 High-level architecture diagram

Source: Author's compilation

BioCrypt Desktop Application's development is done using Python3 mainly using the Tkinter library and custom Tkinter libraries are used to create the user-friendly graphical user interface. The application's windows, user input fields, buttons and other key features were developed with the help of these custom Tkinter libraries while some extended windows were developed with Tkinter directly. The current development is going in a way to support both UNIX-based and Windows operating systems and based on the operating system type two different functionalities were added to support these two operating systems. Other than

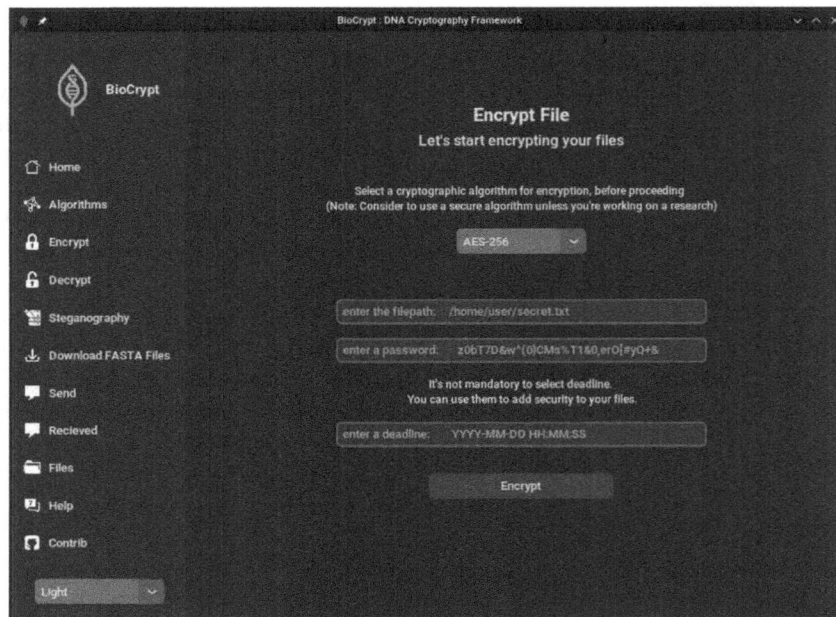

Fig. 26.4 Bio-crypt desktop application interface

Source: Author's compilation

that, multiple background scripts are developed to add the expected functionality and perform the main functionalities, for example, cryptographical functionalities, handling API calls, etc.

Development of the server-side applications was also done using Python FAST API framework, and the common web application development languages HTML, JavaScript and CSS were also used. The FAST API framework was used to host the setup files and to handle main functionality-based API calls. During the development, the security of the application was prioritized, and multiple background scripts were developed as well to handle the file storage and security. In the backend, a lightweight and fast SQLite database model was developed to provide optimal performance on data handling and CRUD operations.

Main components of the proposed system:

1. Web application Front-end
2. Desktop GUI application
3. API in the server application
4. Background scripts in the server application

The system architecture of BioCrypt is designed to facilitate secure interactions among users, the server, and Application Programming Interfaces (APIs). At its core, the architecture comprises a centralized server application that provides multiple endpoints to support the functionality of the desktop application and various server-side scripts. Users interact with the BioCrypt framework primarily through the desktop application, which utilizes the API to communicate securely with the server.

This API is designed for handling requests related to all the core functionalities including, encryption, decryption, secure messaging, and file management. The server application is responsible for maintaining user data, cryptographic keys, and configurations, leveraging a proper database to ensure data integrity and performance. Key features include encryption and decryption of files, management of cryptographic algorithms, secure messaging, file locking and unlocking, and there are server-side applications like the "DelDead" feature, which automatically purges outdated files for security and to optimize storage resources. This architecture ensures a user-friendly experience while upholding high-security standards.

To illustrate the interaction process, consider a user who wishes to encrypt a file. The process begins when the user logs into the BioCrypt desktop application using their credentials. Upon successful authentication, the application queries the server via the API to retrieve available cryptographic algorithms and user settings. The user then selects a file for encryption and chooses an appropriate algorithm. The application formulates a request, including the file data and algorithm, and sends it to the server. Upon receiving this request, the server verifies the user's permissions, retrieves the specified algorithm from the database, and processes the encryption. The resulting encrypted file is then securely stored in the database.

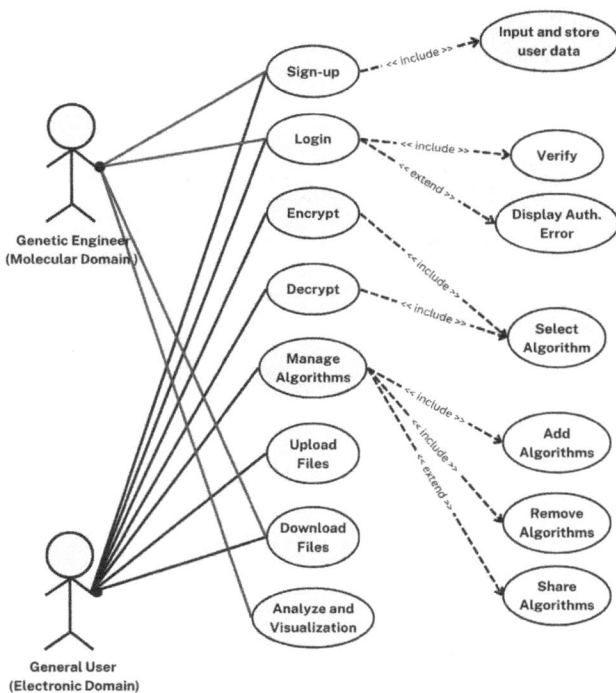

Fig. 26.5 Bio-Crypt desktop application use-case diagram

Source: Author's compilation

6. Conclusion

In conclusion, the BioCrypt DNA cryptography framework represents a significant advancement in information security, offering a pioneering solution for the secure storage and transmission of digital data using DNA molecules. Through a meticulous integration of molecular biology and computer science principles, BioCrypt empowers businesses, researchers, and individuals to harness the vast potential of DNA as a storage medium while fortifying data security with cryptographic techniques. By bridging the gap between the electronic and molecular domains, BioCrypt facilitates seamless collaboration and innovation, ushering in a new era of secure and efficient data management.

Moreover, the development and implementation of the BioCrypt framework have illuminated the challenges and opportunities inherent in DNA cryptography. Key challenges, such as the high cost of DNA storage and the current limitations of inter-domain research, have been identified as areas requiring further exploration. Our rigorous research, experimentation, and testing have paved the way for continued innovation and refinement in the field.

Looking ahead, there are several promising avenues for future research and implementation. These include investigating cost-reduction strategies for DNA synthesis and sequencing, exploring the integration of DNA storage solutions into existing digital infrastructures, and addressing the scalability of DNA-based cryptographic systems. By expanding on these areas, BioCrypt aims to catalyse advancements in DNA computing and cryptography, pushing the boundaries of what is possible in secure data storage and transmission.

REFERENCES

1. S. Furrer, M. A. Lantz, P. Reininger, A. Pantazi, H. E. Rothuizen, R. D. Cideciyan, G. Cherubini, W. Haeberle, E. Eleftheriou, J. Tachibana, N. Sekiguchi, and et al., "201 Gb/in² recording areal density on sputtered magnetic tape," IEEE Trans. Magn., vol. 54, no. 10, pp. 1–8, 2018, doi: 10.1109/TMAG.2017.2727822

2. D. Rydning, J. Reinsel, and J. Gantz, The Digitization of the World from Edge to Core, Framingham, MA: International Data Corporation, 2018. [Online]. Available: https://www.seagate.com/files/www-content/our-story/trends/files/idc-seagate-dataage-whitepaper.pdf

3. T. Sellschop, "Bio-Lock: The future and ethics around DNA cryptography," Besides Munich, 2023. [Online]. Available: https://www.youtube.com/watch?v=B-LOWAqrcuU.

4. K. Strauss and A. B. Nguyen, "Toward nanoscale DNA writers: Unlocking scalable DNA data writing technology," Microsoft Research AI4Science, Dec. 1, 2021. [Online]. Available: https://www.microsoft.com/en-us/research/blog/toward-nanoscale-dna-writers-unlocking-scalable-dna-data-writing-technology/.

5. R. R. Garafutdinov, D. A. Chemeris, A. R. Sakhabutdinova, O. Y. Kiryanova, C. I. Mikhaylenko, and A. V. Chemeris, "Encoding of non-biological information for its long-term storage in DNA," Biosystems, vol. 215–216, p. 104664, 2022. doi: 10.1016/j.biosystems.2022.104664.

6. D. Landsman and K. Strauss, "The DNA data storage model," Computer, vol. 56, no. 7, pp. 78–85, 2023. doi: 10.1109/MC.2023.3272188.

7. B. B. Raj and V. C. Sharmimila, "A survey on DNA-based cryptography," in Proc. IEEE Int. Conf. Emerging Trends and Innovations in Engineering and Technological Research (ICETIETR), Ernakulam, India, Jul. 11–13, 2018, doi: 10.1109/ICETIETR.2018.8529075.

8. M. R. Biswas, K. M. R. Alam, A. Akber, and Y. S. Morimoto, "A DNA cryptographic technique based on dynamic DNA encoding and asymmetric cryptosystem," in 2017 4th Int. Conf. Networking Systems and Security (NSysS), 2017, doi: 10.1109/NSYSS2.2017.8267782

9. S. Marwan, A. Shawish, and K. Nagaty, "Utilizing DNA strands for secured data-hiding with high capacity," Int. J. Interactive Mobile Technol. (iJIM), vol. 11, p. 88, 2017. doi: 10.3991/ijim.v11i2.6565.

10. E. Soni, "Innovative field of cryptography: DNA cryptography," Computer Science & Information Technology, vol. 2, pp. 161–179, 2012. [Online]. Available: http://dx.doi.org/10.5121/csit.2012.2115.

Transformative Applied Research in Computing, Engineering, Science and Technology – Dr. Damayanthi Dahanayake et al. (eds)
© 2024 Taylor & Francis Group, London, ISBN 978-1-041-01782-0

27

Thermostable Microbial Proteases: Advances, Applications, and Industrial Impact—A Review

D. K. H. Hettiarachchi and M. S. N. Samaranayake*

Department of Life Sciences NSBM Green University,
Sri Lanka

Abstract

Microbial proteases are ubiquitous and can be found in living organisms, involved in the breakdown of proteins. Thermostable microbial proteases are essential in various industrial applications due to their robustness under extreme conditions. This review explores the advancements and applications of thermostable microbial proteases, highlighting their discovery, molecular and genetic enhancements, and diverse industrial uses. The types of microbial proteases, their sources, and the mechanisms underlying their thermostability are discussed in detail. Additionally, the review addresses challenges in maintaining enzyme stability, cost-effective production, and genetic stability. Emerging trends in protein engineering, synthetic biology, and enzyme immobilization are also examined. The alignment of these enzymes with green chemistry principles underscores their role in promoting sustainable industrial practices. This review provides a comprehensive overview, emphasizing the potential of thermostable proteases in advancing industrial biotechnology and fostering eco-friendly processes.

Keywords

Microbial enzymes, Protein engineering, Sustainable biotechnology, Thermostable proteases

1. Introduction

Enzymes are crucial biological catalysts that facilitate various biochemical reactions [1, 2]. Among these, proteases, a diverse class involved in protein degradation (Fig. 27.1), stand out due to their significant industrial relevance [3].Classified under the Enzyme-Commission Classification as EC3.4.x.x, proteases vary based on substrate-active site specificity, active pH, temperature range, and stability profiles [1, 4]. Proteases are essential in industrial applications due to their stereo-specificity, biodegradability, and ability to produce natural products, addressing environmental concerns and promoting sustainable manufacturing processes [5]. However, their inherent fragility necessitates the search for robust enzymes capable of functioning in harsh industrial conditions [6]. Thermostable proteases, which maintain catalytic activity at elevated temperatures, are particularly valuable. This review provides an overview of advances in thermostable microbial proteases and their industrial applications.

---

*Corresponding author: sharini.s@nsbm.ac.lk

DOI: 10.1201/9781003616368-27

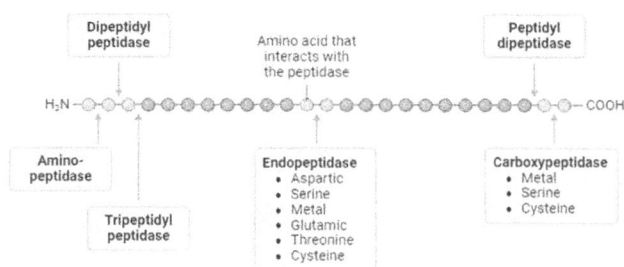

Fig. 27.1 Proteases and their action [4]

2. Microbial Proteases and Their Thermostability

2.1 Types of Microbial Proteases

Proteases are classified based on their active sites and modes of action [7]. Principal types include serine proteases (alkaline, EC 3.4.21-24, 99), aspartic proteases (acidic, EC 3.4.23), cysteine proteases (neutral, EC 3.4.22), and metalloproteases (EC 3.4.17, 24). Microorganisms, mainly bacteria and fungi, offer promising prospects for thermostable protease production due to their broad biochemical variety and easy genetic manipulation [4]. Bacterial proteases, which are generally alkaline, are significant in industrial sectors such as leather, food, textile, and detergent industries. Fungal species contribute significantly to the production of thermostable proteases due to characteristics such as substrate specificity, diversity, and high stability. Archaeal sources, particularly hyperthermophilic archaea, are gaining attention for their thermostable proteases. Although viral sources have been explored for protease production, they have yet to gain significant commercial importance [8].

2.2 Mechanisms of Thermostability

Thermostable proteases exhibit several structural features that enhance their stability. Increased proline content within the protease structure enhances protein rigidity, helping maintain structural integrity under thermal stress [9]. Hydrogen bonding and ionic interactions are pivotal in stabilizing these enzymes, forming a network that supports the enzyme's structural framework, making it less susceptible to thermal denaturation [10, 11]. Disulfide bridges provide substantial energy stabilization by reinforcing the protein fold, ensuring the protein maintains its structural conformation even at high temperatures [12, 13].

Heat shock proteins (HSPs) and molecular chaperones are crucial for maintaining protein stability and functionality under stress conditions. Heat shock proteins function as molecular chaperones, aiding the correct folding of new proteins, refolding misfolded proteins, and preventing protein aggregation [14]. Post-translational modifications, including glycosylation, phosphorylation, and ubiquitylation, enhance protein stability and help organisms adapt to harsh environments [15].

3. Advances in Thermostable Microbial Proteases

3.1 Discovery and Isolation

Thermostable proteases are isolated from extreme environments such as hot springs, hydrothermal vents, and compost piles. These environments provide the necessary conditions for microorganisms that produce thermostable enzymes. Enrichment cultures and selective media are designed to favor the growth of thermophiles by maintaining high temperatures that mimic their natural habitats [8, 16].

3.2 Screening Techniques

- **Thermal Shift Assays:** These assays, also known as differential scanning fluorimetry, assess the thermal stability of enzymes by measuring the change in their melting temperature (Tm). By monitoring the unfolding of the enzyme in response to increasing temperature, these assays help identify thermostable proteases and screen stabilizing agents or mutations [17, 18].
- **Enzyme Activity Assays:** These assays evaluate enzymes' catalytic activity by measuring the substrate conversion rate to the product. Factors such as temperature, pH, ionic strength, and concentration is meticulously controlled to ensure accurate and reproducible results. By determining the enzyme's velocity under various conditions, researchers can identify the optimal conditions for enzyme function and stability [17], [19].

3.3 Molecular and Genetic advances

Recent advances in genetic engineering have significantly enhanced the thermostability and activity of proteases. Techniques such as site-directed mutagenesis, gene shuffling, and CRISPR-Cas9 have been instrumental in these advancements [20-25]. The power of genetic manipulation has been shown by [26], using Site-directed mutagenesis, where they have changed more than 50% of the amino acids to enhance enzyme stability and catalytic activity. Gene shuffling accelerates the evolution and development of proteases by recombining DNA from similar genes to create new genes with improved characteristics [22]. CRISPR-Cas9 enables precise, quick, and cost-effective genome modifications, research done by [27] has introduced salt bridges to the enzyme subtilisin E using this CRISPR-Cas9 method, thereby enhancing its catalytic efficiency by 46.5%. Synthetic biology techniques integrate metabolic pathways and gene circuits to optimize enzyme production and stability in microbial hosts. These strategies enable precise control of enzyme expression and the refinement of metabolic networks, thereby enhancing both the yield and stability of the enzymes [28, 29]. For instance, studies have successfully enhanced the thermostability of subtilisin by introducing mutations that increase its structural rigidity [30]. Additionally, the catalytic efficiency of thermolysin has been improved by optimizing its active site architecture [31, 32]. It can be difficult to analyze a wide variety of enzymes for substrate specificity and ideal conditions using only laboratory work. However, the investigation of these factors using computational approaches is made more effective by synthetic biology technologies including molecular modeling, nanotechnology, molecular docking, *in silico* studies, and artificial intelligence (Fig. 27.2) [29, 33].

3.4 Structural and Functional Characterization

Structural analysis techniques: Advanced structural analysis techniques, such as X-ray crystallography, NMR spectroscopy, and cryo-electron microscopy, have provided valuable insights into the structural basis of protease thermostability. These techniques allow researchers to determine the three-dimensional structures of proteins at atomic resolution, providing a detailed understanding of the mechanisms that contribute to their stability [34-36].

Functional Characterization: Functional characterization involves evaluating the enzymatic activity and kinetics of thermostable proteases under various conditions. Enzyme kinetics studies determine parameters such as maximum velocity (Vmax) and substrate affinity (Km), which are critical for understanding the efficiency and specificity of the proteases. Thermal stability tests, including determining enzyme half-life and melting temperature, are essential for assessing the stability of these enzymes. Activity assays evaluate enzyme performance across different parameters, such as temperature, pH, and the presence of metal ions, to identify optimal operating conditions [8, 18, 43].

4. Industrial Applications of Thermostable Proteases

Thermostable proteases are integral to various industries due to their ability to maintain activity under extreme conditions. Below are key applications of these enzymes in different sectors.

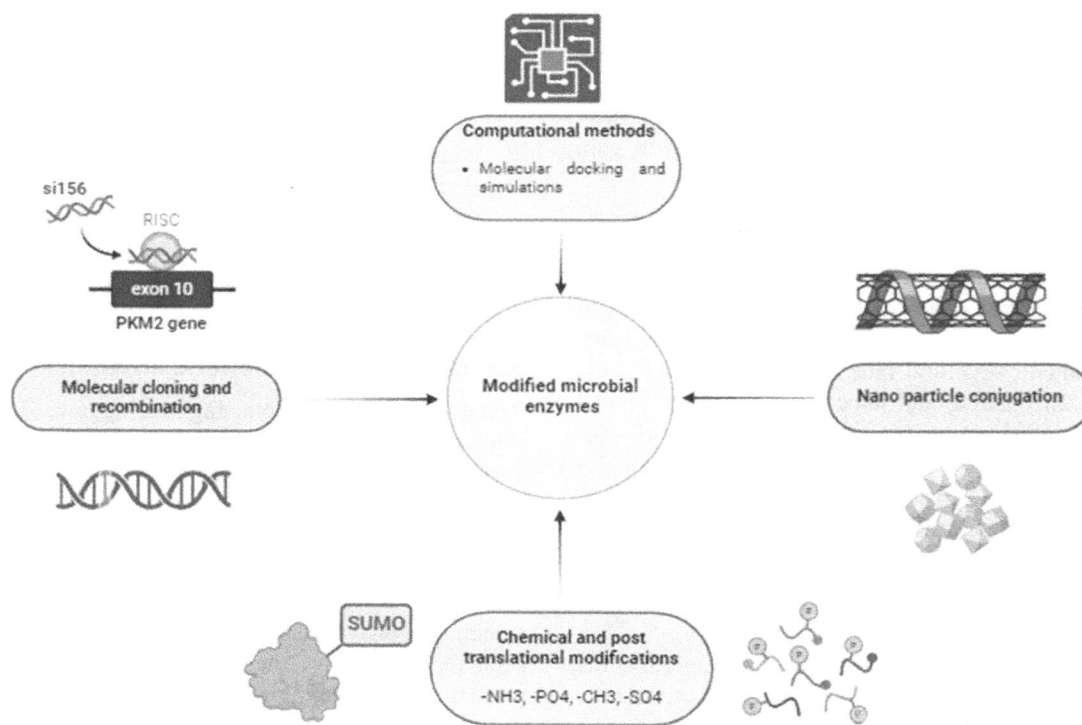

Fig. 27.2 Synthetic biology for modification of microbial enzymes [29], [33]

4.1 Detergent Industry

Thermostable proteases are essential in the detergent industry for removing protein-based stains. They remain active at high temperatures and alkaline pH, compatible with surfactants and bleaches. Proteases from *B. subtilis* and *A. niger* are commonly used in detergent formulations to enhance cleaning efficiency [1, 44]. In the United States, proteases are present in 25% of powdered detergents, 50% of liquid detergents, and nearly all powdered bleaches.

4.2 Eather and Textile Industry

In the leather industry, proteases are used for soaking, dehairing, and bating processes, effectively degrading non-collagenous components and removing non-fibrillary proteins. Microbial alkaline proteases from *Bacillus* species and *A. tamarii* are particularly effective [1, 4].

Table 27.1 Microbial sources of thermostable proteases

Source	Microorganism	References
Bacterial	*Bacillus subtilis, B. licheniformis* (subtilisin)	[19], [37]
	Geobacillus stearothermophilus	[38]
	B. megaterium, B. cereus strain S8, *B. megaterium*-TK1	[37], [39]
	B. infantis SKS1, *B. amyloliquefaciens, B. clausii*	[40]
	B. halodurans, B. lentus, B. pumilus, B. circulans	[4]
	B. safensis, Thermus thermophilus HB8	[1], [39]
Fungal	*Aspergillus niger, A. clavatus, A. flavus, A. oryzae*	[1], [4]
	A. fumigates, A. melleus, A. nidulans HA-10	[41]
	A. tamari URM4634, *A. sojae, A. terreus*	[4], [41]
	A. oryzae Y1, *Cephalosporium, Fusarium* species, *Rhizopus, Penicillium italicum*	[1], [7]
Archaeal	*Pyrococcus furiosus*	[42]
	Deinococcus geothermalis	[39]
Viral	Adenovirus, Hepatitis C Virus (cysteine and serine proteases)	[8]

Enzymes from *B. subtilis* IIQDB32 have been reported for effective dehairing of sheep's skin [45]. Additionally, enzymes from *B. amyloliquefaciens, B. cereus, and P. furiosus* are noted for their thermostability, making them suitable for leather and textile applications [42, 46].

4.3 Food Industry

Proteases play an essential role in the food industry, particularly in baking, cheese making, and meat tenderization. They improve dough elasticity, reduce viscosity, and enhance the solubility of soy and fish proteins. Enzymes from *B. subtilis* and *Mucor miehei* have replaced traditional calf enzymes in cheese manufacturing, hydrolyzing specific peptide bonds to produce casein and macro peptides [1, 12]. In the baking industry, proteases modify gluten in the dough, essential for producing baked goods like wafers, cookies, and biscuits. Thermostable proteases from *Thermoactinomyces vulgaris* and *B. licheniformis* help prolong the freshness of baked goods [47].

4.4 Waste Management

Microbial proteases are utilized in waste management to degrade complex organic compounds. Fungi like *A. niger* and bacteria like *B. subtilis* produce proteases that are used for applications such as cleaning clogged pipe and deproteinizing shrimp waste [48, 49]. Proteases from *Micromonospora chaiyaphumensis* S103 and *B. safensis* S406 have shown outstanding deproteinization of chitin in shrimp waste processing [49]. In waste-activated sludge management, microorganisms contribute to anaerobic fermentation processes aimed at producing short-chain fatty acids, which can be utilized in biogas production [50].

Microbial proteases enhance nutrient utilization and feed efficiency in the animal feed industry. Protease supplementation improves growth performance in livestock and aquaculture, with notable examples including *B. licheniformis* and keratinolytic proteases that transform poultry feathers into protein-rich feed [51, 52]. Protease mixtures, including cysteine and serine endopeptidases, improve productivity in dairy cattle, enhancing milk and meat production efficiency [53].

4.5 Silver Recovery

Thermostable proteases are used to recover silver from photographic and X-ray films by degrading the gelatinous coating, providing an eco-friendly alternative to chemical methods. Microorganisms such as *B. subtilis* and *A. versicolor* are commonly used in this application [2, 4]. Fungal sources like *A. versicolor* have shown promising results in silver recovery by rapidly degrading the gelatin layer under optimal conditions.

5. Challenges and Future Directions

5.1 Technical and Industrial Challenges

1. **Stability and Activity Under Diverse Conditions:** Maintaining the stability and activity of thermostable proteases in diverse industrial settings with extreme pH levels, high salt concentrations, and

various solvents remains challenging [18, 19]. The development of proteases that can withstand these conditions without losing activity is crucial for expanding their industrial applications.

2. **Scalability and Cost-Effectiveness:** For thermostable proteases to be viable for industrial applications, their large-scale production must be cost-effective. This includes optimizing fermentation processes, reducing production costs, and ensuring consistent enzyme quality [54]. Developing more efficient and economical purification methods is essential. The use of low-cost substrates and improving microbial strains can significantly reduce production costs [4, 55]. Efficient purification methods, such as affinity tags, simplify the process and reduce costs [56, 57].

3. **Genetic Stability and Expression in Host Organisms:** Ensuring genetic stability and high-level expression in host organisms like Escherichia coli or B. subtilis is crucial for reliable production. Techniques such as integrating genes into host chromosomes and using strong promoters can enhance stability and expression [58, 59]. Overcoming these challenges requires ongoing advancements in genetic engineering and fermentation technology.

6. Emerging Trends and Innovations

6.1 Advances in Protein Engineering

Advances in protein engineering, supported by AI and machine learning, are accelerating the development of thermostable proteases. These technologies enable the rapid identification and improvement of new proteases, enhancing their stability and catalytic activity. Techniques such as rational design, directed evolution, and de novo design have been employed to create enzymes with enhanced properties (Fig. 27.3) [60, 61]. Recent developments in protein engineering have led to the development of novel proteins with improved characteristics and cutting-edge uses. These include optimizing enzyme structures to improve stability and activity under industrial conditions.

Table 27.2 Industrial applications of thermostable microbial proteases

Industry	Applications	Microorganism	References
Detergent	Removal of protein-based stains	B. subtilis, A. niger	[1], [44]
Leather and Textile	Soaking, dehairing, and bating processes	Bacillus spp., A. tamarii	[1], [4]
Food	Baking, cheese making, meat tenderization	B. subtilis, Mucor miehei	[1], [12]
Waste Management	Degrading complex organic compounds	A. niger, B. subtilis	[48], [49]
Animal Feed	Enhancing nutrient utilization and feed efficiency	B. licheniformis,	[51], [52]
Silver Recovery	Recovering silver from photographic and X-ray films	B. subtilis, A. versicolor	[2], [4]

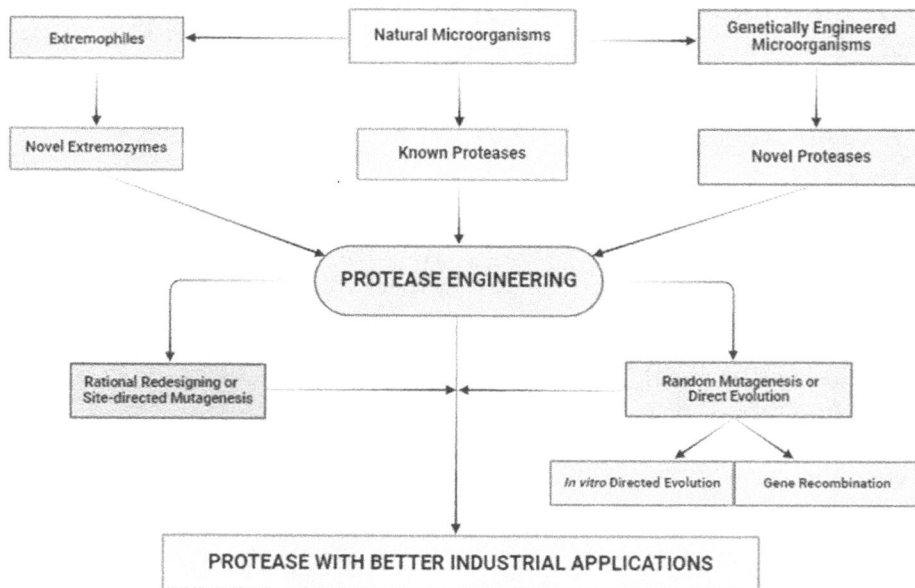

Fig. 27.3 Basic principles of protease engineering [60, 68]

6.2 Synthetic Biology

Synthetic biology integrates metabolic pathways and gene circuits to optimize enzyme production and stability in microbial hosts, enhancing biotechnological processes [28], [29]. This field is essential for the development of specialized microbial strains that exhibit elevated thermostable protease production. Techniques such as combining metabolic pathways artificial gene circuits, and synthetic biology enhance the stability and synthesis of enzymes, improving the efficiency and productivity of biotechnological processes.

6.3 Enzyme Immobilization Techniques

Enzyme immobilization on solid supports boosts their stability and reusability, enhancing their practicality for industrial use. Innovations in immobilization techniques, such as new materials and covalent binding methods, improve the performance and lifespan of thermostable proteases [62]. This approach also cuts costs by enhancing enzyme stability, increasing loading capacity, and simplifying recycling and downstream processing. Various interactions, including reversible adsorption, ionic linkages, and stable covalent bonds, are used to affix enzymes to supports, collectively improving enzyme efficiency in industrial applications.

6.4 Integration with Biotechnological Processes

Thermostable proteases are crucial in various biotechnological processes due to their stability and efficiency under extreme conditions. In biofuel production, these enzymes facilitate the pretreatment and hydrolysis of biomass, converting it into fermentable sugars more effectively. For instance, incorporating thermostable proteases into bioethanol production from lignocellulosic biomass significantly improves yield and efficiency, maintaining enzyme activity under harsh process conditions [63]. In bioremediation, thermostable proteases can degrade pollutants and contaminants in the environment, aiding in the cleanup of polluted sites [64]. These enzymes operate in extreme environments, such as high temperatures or pH levels, making them suitable for diverse bioremediation scenarios.

7. Sustainability and Environmental Impact

7.1 Green Chemistry and Environmental Impact

The use of thermostable proteases aligns with the principles of green chemistry, offering environmentally friendly alternatives to traditional chemical processes [65]. These enzymes reduce the need for harsh chemicals and high energy inputs, minimizing the environmental footprint of industrial operations. Traditional industrial processes often rely on strong acids, bases, or other toxic chemicals to achieve desired reactions. Thermostable proteases, being robust at high temperatures, can catalyze reactions efficiently without the need for such harsh chemicals. This shift not only makes processes safer for workers but also reduces the risk of environmental contamination [66].

Traditional leather processing techniques are carried out by utilizing large amounts of poisonous chemicals such as lime and sodium sulfide, which cause serious damage to the environment. However, the current trend towards using proteases has shown promising results in leather processing, thus replacing these toxic chemicals and minimizing environmental harm [2]. Furthermore, thermostable proteases enhance waste reduction and resource efficiency by enabling complete utilization of raw materials and reducing by-products. They facilitate the effective degradation of complex organic waste, converting it into valuable resources such as amino acids [67]. This application is particularly beneficial in industries like food processing, leather manufacturing, and waste treatment, where they also help reduce sludge volume, lowering disposal costs and environmental burden.

8. Conclusion

Thermostable microbial proteases have significant industrial applications due to their stability and catalytic activity under extreme conditions. Advances in protein engineering, synthetic biology, and enzyme immobilization have enhanced their properties and broadened their applications. However, challenges such as maintaining stability, cost-effective production, and genetic stability must be addressed. Emerging trends in AI, machine learning, and synthetic biology hold promise for future developments. Aligning these enzymes with green chemistry principles underscores their role in promoting sustainable industrial practices. Collaborative efforts are essential to fully realize their potential, driving greener, more efficient, and sustainable industrial processes.

REFERENCES

1. M. Naveed, F. Nadeem, T. Mehmood, M. Bilal, Z. Anwar, and F. Amjad, "Protease—A Versatile and Ecofriendly Biocatalyst with Multi-Industrial Applications: An Updated Review," *Catal Letters*, vol. 151, no. 2, pp. 307–323, Feb. 2021.
2. M. Sharma, Y. Gat, S. Arya, V. Kumar, A. Panghal, and A. Kumar, "A review on microbial alkaline protease: An essential tool for various industrial approaches," Apr. 01, 2019.

3. K. Rani, R. Rana, and S. Datt, "Review on latest overview of proteases," 2012.

4. A. Razzaq et al., "Microbial proteases applications," 2019.

5. R. Ahmad Bayoumi, "International Journal of Advanced Research in Biological Sciences Production, Purification and Applications of Thermostable Slaughterhouse (SH), Fish (FW) and Poultry (PW) Wastes Protease(s) Under Solid State Fermentation (SSF) Conditions," *Int. J. Adv. Res. Biol. Sci*, vol. 5, no. 2, pp. 108–132, 2018.

6. Z. Dadshahi, A. Homaei, F. Zeinali, R. H. Sajedi, and K. Khajeh, "Extraction and purification of a highly thermostable alkaline caseinolytic protease from wastes Litopenaeus vannamei suitable for food and detergent industries," *Food Chem*, vol. 202, pp. 110–115, Jul. 2016.

7. I. Ramadan Matter, "Industrial Applications of Microbial Protease: A Review," *Academic Science journal*, vol. 1, no. 3, pp. 141–160, Jul. 2023.

8. G. Z. L. Dalmaso, D. Ferreira, and A. B. Vermelho, "Marine extremophiles a source of hydrolases for biotechnological applications," Apr. 01, 2015.

9. Y. Li, P. J. Reilly, and C. Ford, "Effect of introducing proline residues on the stability of Aspergillus awamori.," *Protein Engineering, Design and Selection*, vol. 10, no. 10, pp. 1199–1204, Oct. 1997.

10. C. N. Pace et al., "Contribution of Hydrophobic Interactions to Protein Stability," *J Mol Biol*, vol. 408, no. 3, pp. 514–528, May 2011.

11. D. Sun, J. Zhang, C. Li, T. F. Wang, and H. M. Qin, "Biochemical and structural characterization of a novel thermophilic and acidophilic β-mannanase from Aspergillus calidoustus," *Enzyme Microb Technol*, vol. 150, Oct. 2021.

12. F. Rigoldi, S. Donini, A. Redaelli, E. Parisini, and A. Gautieri, "Review: Engineering of thermostable enzymes for industrial applications," Mar. 01, 2018.

13. A. Kruglikov, Y. Wei, and X. Xia, "Proteins from Thermophilic Thermus thermophilus Often Do Not Fold Correctly in a Mesophilic Expression System Such as Escherichia coli," *ACS Omega*, vol. 7, no. 42, pp. 37797–37806, Oct. 2022.

14. H. V. Edwards, R. T. Cameron, and G. S. Baillie, "The emerging role of HSP20 as a multifunctional protective agent," *Cell Signal*, vol. 23, no. 9, pp. 1447–1454, Sep. 2011.

15. J. A. Cain, N. Solis, and S. J. Cordwell, "Beyond gene expression: the impact of protein post-translational modifications in bacteria," *J Proteomics*, vol. 97, pp. 265–286, Jan. 2014.

16. N. Merino et al., "Living at the extremes: Extremophiles and the limits of life in a planetary context," *Front Microbiol*, vol. 10, no. MAR, p. 447668, Apr. 2019.

17. H. Bisswanger, "Enzyme assays," *Perspect Sci (Neth)*, vol. 1, no. 1–6, pp. 41–55, May 2014.

18. A. Karray, M. Alonazi, H. Horchani, and A. Ben Bacha, "A novel thermostable and alkaline protease produced from bacillus stearothermophilus isolated from olive oil mill sols suitable to industrial biotechnology," *Molecules*, vol. 26, no. 4, Feb. 2021.

19. F. Hailemichael, "Production and Industrial Application of Microbial Aspartic Protease: A Review," *International Journal of Food Engineering and Technology*, vol. 5, no. 2, p. 85, 2021.

20. C. L. Fisher and G. K. Pei, "Modification of a PCR-based site-directed mutagenesis method," *Biotechniques*, vol. 23, no. 4, pp. 570–574, 1997.

21. J. Bachman, "Site-Directed Mutagenesis," *Methods Enzymol*, vol. 529, pp. 241–248, Jan. 2013.

22. A. J. Meyer, J. W. Ellefson, and A. D. Ellington, "Library Generation by Gene Shuffling," *Current protocols in molecular biology / edited by Frederick M. Ausubel ... [et al.]*, vol. 105, no. SUPPL.105, p. Unit, 2013.

23. H. Zhao and F. H. Arnold, "Optimization of DNA shuffling for high fidelity recombination.," *Nucleic Acids Res*, vol. 25, no. 6, p. 1307, Mar. 1997.

24. M. Redman, A. King, C. Watson, and D. King, "What is CRISPR/Cas9?," *Arch Dis Child Educ Pract Ed*, vol. 101, no. 4, p. 213, Aug. 2016.

25. F. Jiang and J. A. Doudna, "CRISPR-Cas9 Structures and Mechanisms," *Annu Rev Biophys*, vol. 46, pp. 505–529, May 2017.

27. M. A. Price, R. Cruz, S. Baxter, F. Escalettes, and S. J. Rosser, "CRISPR-Cas9 In Situ engineering of subtilisin E in Bacillus subtilis," *PLoS One*, vol. 14, no. 1, Jan. 2019.

28. N. S. McCarty and R. Ledesma-Amaro, "Synthetic Biology Tools to Engineer Microbial Communities for Biotechnology," *Trends Biotechnol*, vol. 37, no. 2, pp. 181–197, Feb. 2019.

29. P. Shukla, "Synthetic Biology Perspectives of Microbial Enzymes and Their Innovative Applications," *Indian J Microbiol*, vol. 59, no. 4, p. 401, Dec. 2019.

30. K. H. Bae, J. S. Jang, K. S. Park, S. H. Lee, and S. M. Byun, "Improvement of Thermal Stability of Subtilisin J by Changing the Primary Autolysis Site," *Biochem Biophys Res Commun*, vol. 207, no. 1, pp. 20–24, Feb. 1995.

31. H. Takagi et al., "Enhancement of the thermostability of subtilisin E by introduction of a disulfide bond engineered on the basis of structural comparison with a thermophilic serine protease," *Journal of Biological Chemistry*, vol. 265, no. 12, pp. 6874–6878, 1990.

32. V. G. H. Eijsink et al., "Rational engineering of enzyme stability," *J Biotechnol*, vol. 113, no. 1–3, pp. 105–120, Sep. 2004.

33. P. Gainza-Cirauqui and B. E. Correia, "Computational protein design-the next generation tool to expand synthetic biology applications," *Curr Opin Biotechnol*, vol. 52, pp. 145–152, Aug. 2018.

34. B. Alberts, A. Johnson, J. Lewis, M. Raff, K. Roberts, and P. Walter, "Analyzing Protein Structure and Function," 2002, Accessed: Jun. 08, 2024.

35. N. R. Mohamad, N. H. C. Marzuki, N. A. Buang, F. Huyop, and R. A. Wahab, "An overview of technologies for immobilization of enzymes and surface analysis techniques for immobilized enzymes," 2015.

36. A. Bolje and S. Gobec, "Analytical Techniques for Structural Characterization of Proteins in Solid Pharmaceutical Forms: An Overview," *Pharmaceutics*, vol. 13, no. 4, Apr. 2021.

37. T. Manavalan, A. Manavalan, S. Ramachandran, and K. Heese, "Identification of a novel thermostable alkaline protease from Bacillus megaterium-TK1 for the detergent and leather industry," *Biology (Basel)*, vol. 9, no. 12, pp. 1–14, Dec. 2020.

38. I. Iqbal, M. N. Aftab, M. S. Afzal, A. Zafar, and A. Kaleem, "Characterization of geobacillus stearothermophilus

protease for detergent industry," *Revista Mexicana de Ingenieria Quimica*, vol. 19, pp. 267–279, 2020.

39. L. B.K.M, M. K. D, M. Sowjanya, Ch. Venkatrayulu, and H. K.P.J, "Industrial Applications of Alkaline Protease with Novel Properties from Bacillus Cereus Strain S8," *Journal of Advanced Zoology*, vol. 44, no. S-3, pp. 1314–1322, Nov. 2023.

40. S. K. Saggu and P. C. Mishra, "Characterization of thermostable alkaline proteases from Bacillus infantis SKS1 isolated from garden soil," *PLoS One*, vol. 12, no. 11, Nov. 2017.

41. O. Soares da Silva, R. Lira de Oliveira, J. de Carvalho Silva, A. Converti, and T. Souza Porto, "Thermodynamic investigation of an alkaline protease from Aspergillus tamarii URM4634: A comparative approach between crude extract and purified enzyme," *Int J Biol Macromol*, vol. 109, pp. 1039–1044, Apr. 2018.

42. J. Varghese, G. J. John, and J. J. Georrge, "Structural features and industrial uses of thermostable proteins," 2020.

43. Y. Xie *et al.*, "Enhanced enzyme kinetic stability by increasing rigidity within the active site," *Journal of Biological Chemistry*, vol. 289, no. 11, pp. 7994–8006, Mar. 2014.

44. M. Alias *et al.*, "Production and characterisation of thermostable alkaline protease from Bacillus subtilis isolated from LA hot spring, Terengganu," *Res J Biotechnol*, vol. 16, no. 7, pp. 84–91, Jun. 2021.

45. "Production, Purification and Applications of Therm_240224_222454," 2018.

46. N. Thakur, M. Goyal, S. Sharma, and D. Kumar, "Proteases: Industrial Applications and Approaches used in Strain Improvement," 2018.

47. P. Akbaş Ondokuz and M. Üniversitesi, "USES OF PROTEASES OBTAINED FROM MICROORGANISMS IN THE FOOD INDUSTRY," 2023.

48. K. S. Pawar, P. N. Singh, and S. K. Singh, "Fungal alkaline proteases and their potential applications in different industries," 2023.

49. S. Mhamdi, N. Ktari, S. Hajji, M. Nasri, and A. Sellami Kamoun, "Alkaline proteases from a newly isolated Micromonospora chaiyaphumensis S103: Characterization and application as a detergent additive and for chitin extraction from shrimp shell waste," *Int J Biol Macromol*, vol. 94, pp. 415–422, Jan. 2017.

50. H. Pang *et al.*, "Enhanced short-chain fatty acids production through a short-term anaerobic fermentation of waste activated sludge: Synergistic pretreatment of alkali and alkaline hydrolase blend," *J Clean Prod*, vol. 342, p. 130954, Mar. 2022.

51. S. Park *et al.*, "Dietary protease improves growth performance, nutrient digestibility, and intestinal morphology of weaned pigs," *J Anim Sci Technol*, vol. 62, no. 1, pp. 21–30, 2020.

52. Y. Wang, P. Zhao, Y. Zhou, X. Hu, and H. Xiong, "From bitter to delicious: properties and uses of microbial aminopeptidases," *World J Microbiol Biotechnol*, vol. 39, no. 3, pp. 1–12, Mar. 2023.

53. H. Yang *et al.*, "Characterization of an Intracellular Alkaline Serine Protease from Bacillus velezensis SW5 with Fibrinolytic Activity," *Curr Microbiol*, vol. 77, no. 8, pp. 1610–1621, Aug. 2020.

54. J. Neetu, N. Chaudhary, N. Jabalia, and P. C. Mishra, "Applications, Challenges and Future Prospects of Proteases: An Overview."

55. D. Sakhuja, H. Ghai, R. K. Rathour, P. Kumar, A. K. Bhatt, and R. K. Bhatia, "Cost-effective production of biocatalysts using inexpensive plant biomass: a review," *3 Biotech*, vol. 11, no. 6, p. 280, Jun. 2021.

56. J. A. Bornhorst and J. J. Falke, "[16] Purification of Proteins Using Polyhistidine Affinity Tags," *Methods Enzymol*, vol. 326, p. 245, 2000.

57. N. Kaur, P. Sharma, S. Jaimni, B. A. Kehinde, and S. Kaur, "Recent developments in purification techniques and industrial applications for whey valorization: A review," *Chem Eng Commun*, vol. 207, no. 1, pp. 123–138, Jan. 2020.

58. F. Baneyx, "Recombinant protein expression in Escherichia coli," *Curr Opin Biotechnol*, vol. 10, no. 5, pp. 411–421, Oct. 1999.

59. K. Terpe, "Overview of bacterial expression systems for heterologous protein production: From molecular and biochemical fundamentals to commercial systems," *Appl Microbiol Biotechnol*, vol. 72, no. 2, pp. 211–222, Sep. 2006.

60. M. Baweja, L. Nain, Y. Kawarabayasi, and P. Shukla, "Current technological improvements in enzymes toward their biotechnological applications," *Front Microbiol*, vol. 7, no. JUN, p. 206451, Jun. 2016.

61. D. Kumar and A. Kumar, "Production optimization and characterization of an alkaline thermostable protease and its application as laundry additive," 2016.

62. A. Liese and L. Hilterhaus, "Evaluation of immobilized enzymes for industrial applications," *Chem Soc Rev*, vol. 42, no. 15, pp. 6236–6249, Jul. 2013.

63. K. Vasić, Ž. Knez, and M. Leitgeb, "Bioethanol production by enzymatic hydrolysis from different lignocellulosic sources," Feb. 01, 2021.

64. R. Margesin and F. Schinner, "Biodegradation and bioremediation of hydrocarbons in extreme environments," *Appl Microbiol Biotechnol*, vol. 56, no. 5–6, pp. 650–663, 2001.

65. P. Kumar Assistant Professor, S. Sharma Associate Professor, P. Kumar, and S. Sharma, "Impact Factor: 5.2 IJAR," vol. 2, no. 6, pp. 337–341, 2016.

66. R. A. Sheldon and J. M. Woodley, "Role of Biocatalysis in Sustainable Chemistry," *Chem Rev*, vol. 118, no. 2, pp. 801–838, Jan. 2018.

67. R. Gupta, Q. Beg, and P. Lorenz, "Bacterial alkaline proteases: Molecular approaches and industrial applications," *Appl Microbiol Biotechnol*, vol. 59, no. 1, pp. 15–32, 2002.

68. M. Baweja, R. Tiwari, P. K. Singh, L. Nain, and P. Shukla, "An alkaline protease from Bacillus pumilus MP 27: Functional analysis of its binding model toward its applications as detergent additive," *Front Microbiol*, vol. 7, no. AUG, Aug. 2016.

Note: All the tables in this chapter were made by the authors.

Transformative Applied Research in Computing, Engineering, Science and Technology – Dr. Damayanthi Dahanayake et al. (eds)
© 2024 Taylor & Francis Group, London, ISBN 978-1-041-01782-0

28

Zero to Hero—Enhancing Zero-Shot Accuracy in Low Parameter LLMs Through Prompt Engineering and User Sentiment Integration

A. Jayakody*
Department of Data Science and Computer Science,
NSBM Green University,
Sri Lanka

T. Perera
University of Vocational Technology,
Kandawala, Rathmalana,
Sri Lanka

Abstract

Artificial Intelligence (AI) and Natural Language Processing (NLP) have revolutionized technology in recent years, with Large Language Models (LLMs) becoming a focal point of interest for researchers and enthusiasts alike. Despite their potential, the high computational demands and costs associated with LLMs often restrict their accessibility for individual developers. This study investigates how a prompt engineering pipeline can enhance the zero-shot accuracy of open-source, low-parameter LLMs. By customizing and automating prompts, the approach aims to optimize prompt-based learning for the model. Furthermore, the study explores the impact of integrating user sentiment into prompts. Through comprehensive analysis and experimentation, the findings reveal that strategic prompt engineering significantly improves the performance of lower-tier LLMs such as BLOOM-560M. Specifically, BLOOM-560M with prompt engineering achieved ROUGE-1 (F1) of 0.584, ROUGE-2 (F1) of 0.300, and ROUGE-L (F1) of 0.514, compared to the base model's scores of ROUGE-1 (F1) 0.462, ROUGE-2 (F1) 0.200, and ROUGE-L (F1) 0.453. These results offer new insights into enhancing the capabilities of low-parameter LLMs in NLP.

Keywords

Natural language processing, Large language models, Prompt engineering, Prompt optimization

1. Introduction

Artificial Intelligence (AI) has become a cornerstone of modern technology, driving innovations across various domains. One of the most transformative areas within AI is Natural Language Processing (NLP), which enables machines to understand, interpret, and generate human language. In recent years, Large Language Models (LLMs)

*Corresponding author: anton.j@nsbm.ac.lk

DOI: 10.1201/9781003616368-28

have emerged as powerful tools in NLP, demonstrating remarkable capabilities in tasks such as text generation, translation, summarization, and question-answering. These models, exemplified by GPT-3 and similar architectures, have set new benchmarks in performance, driving substantial interest and research in the field.

However, the immense computational resources and financial investment required to develop and deploy high-parameter LLMs pose significant barriers to their widespread use, particularly among individual developers and smaller organizations. This limitation has spurred interest in exploring ways to optimize and leverage smaller, more accessible models without compromising performance. In this context, prompt engineering has gained attention as a promising technique to enhance the functionality of low-parameter LLMs.

Prompt engineering involves designing and refining input prompts to guide the model's output more effectively. This study focuses on the potential of a prompt engineering pipeline to improve the zero-shot accuracy of an open-source low-parameter LLM, specifically the BLOOM-560M model. Zero-shot learning, where a model performs tasks, it has not been explicitly trained on, represents a significant challenge and a valuable capability for AI systems.

The research presented in this paper explores several key aspects: the customization and automation of prompts to facilitate better prompt-based learning, and the integration of user sentiment into the prompt to further refine the model's responses. By conducting a detailed analysis and a series of experimental evaluations, this study aims to demonstrate that even lower-tier LLMs can achieve substantial performance improvements through strategic prompt engineering.

The results of this study indicate a marked improvement in the performance metrics of the BLOOM-560M model when enhanced with prompt engineering techniques. Specifically, the model achieved higher ROUGE-1, ROUGE-2, and ROUGE-L scores, indicating better alignment with human-like text generation and comprehension.

In conclusion, this paper offers new perspectives on leveraging prompt engineering to enhance the capabilities of low-parameter LLMs, providing a pathway for more accessible and cost-effective applications in NLP. The findings underscore the importance of innovative approaches to model optimization, paving the way for broader adoption and utilization of AI technologies.

2. Literature Review

2.1 Zero-Shot Text Generation

Zero-shot text generation refers to the capability of language models to generate coherent and contextually appropriate text for tasks they have not been explicitly trained on. This capability relies heavily on the model's ability to generalize from the training data to unseen tasks. Recent advancements in large language models (LLMs) have significantly improved zero-shot learning capabilities.

GPT-3, a cutting-edge model that exhibited exceptional zero-shot performance on a diverse array of NLP tasks, was introduced by Brown *et al.* [1]. The model's ability to perform zero-shot text generation was largely attributed to its massive scale and extensive pre-training on diverse datasets. The authors highlighted that the model could generate text for tasks such as translation, question answering, and summarization without task-specific training data.

The capabilities of GPT-2 in zero-shot settings were the subject of discussion by Lin *et al.* [2]. They emphasized the importance of unsupervised learning from large corpora and demonstrated that with sufficiently large and diverse pre-training data, models could generalize well to new tasks. The zero-shot performance of GPT-2 on tasks like reading comprehension and language translation underscored the potential of pre-trained models in zero-shot scenarios

2.2 Sentiment Analysis through Texts

Sentiment analysis involves extracting and determining the emotional tone of text data, which is crucial for applications ranging from customer feedback analysis to social media monitoring. Traditional sentiment analysis relies on supervised learning methods with labeled datasets, but recent advancements have explored unsupervised and semi-supervised approaches.

Pre-trained language models, such as BERT, were employed to investigate sentiment analysis by Sanh *et al.* [3]. They showed that fine-tuning BERT on sentiment analysis tasks resulted in state-of-the-art performance, illustrating the effectiveness of transfer learning in this domain.

2.3 Prompt Engineering

Prompt engineering is the process of designing and optimizing input prompts to elicit desired responses from language models. This technique has become increasingly important with the rise of large pre-trained models, as it allows users to guide model outputs without extensive retraining.

The utilization of prompt-based learning for the comprehension and production of natural language was discussed by Kim *et al.* [4]. Their work demonstrated that carefully crafted prompts could significantly enhance the performance of models on diverse NLP tasks, including text classification and summarization.

A comprehensive overview of prompt engineering strategies and their influence on model performance is provided by Liu [5]. He discussed various techniques such as prompt templates, few-shot prompting, and instruction-based prompts, highlighting their effectiveness in improving task-specific outcomes.

3. Methodology

3.1 Data Collection

In this study, we utilized an extract from the DailyDialog dataset for evaluating our model's performance. DailyDialog, created by Yanran Li and colleagues, is a manually labeled, human-written dataset recognized for its high quality and relevance in assessing conversational models [6]. Li et al.'s dataset [6] comprises dialogues covering a wide range of topics and emotional expressions, including joy, sadness, anger, fear, surprise, disgust, and neutral tones, making it an ideal benchmark for evaluating language model outputs in conversational contexts, as shown by Butler et al. [7].

These emotional tones play a critical role in determining the quality of a model's responses, particularly when evaluating the coherence and sentiment appropriateness as in conversations, as mentioned Socher, *et al.* [8]. In our study, we specifically focused on how the model handled sentiment-aware response generation. By leveraging the dataset's emotional annotations, we ensured that the model's ability to produce responses aligned with the expected emotional tone of the dialogue was rigorously tested. This allowed us to assess the zero-shot capabilities of the BLOOM-560M model, particularly in generating contextually appropriate and sentiment-consistent responses across diverse conversational scenarios.

The dataset's structured format and comprehensive annotations provided a robust foundation for testing the model's conversational fluency and emotional accuracy, ensuring a thorough evaluation of its performance in realistic settings.

3.2 Model Description

The BLOOM-560M model, used in this study, is a transformer-based language model designed for efficiency in low-resource environments. It utilizes approximately 1.2GB of weights in half precision, allowing it to run smoothly on consumer GPUs with around 8GB of RAM. For CPU usage, the model requires about 2.4GB of RAM in full precision, making it suitable for systems with 8-16GB of RAM. Its architecture, incorporating multi-head attention and feed-forward networks, effectively captures linguistic patterns, making BLOOM-560M an excellent choice for zero-shot tasks in constrained computational settings.

3.3 Prompt Engineering Pipeline & Sentiment Integration

The prompt engineering pipeline as shown in "Fig. 28.1" begins with user input, processed through a series of steps to optimize the model's response. Initially, a NumPy zeros array is created and modified throughout the pipeline. The user input is checked for punctuation and special characters, as these can influence sentiment analysis [4, 7].

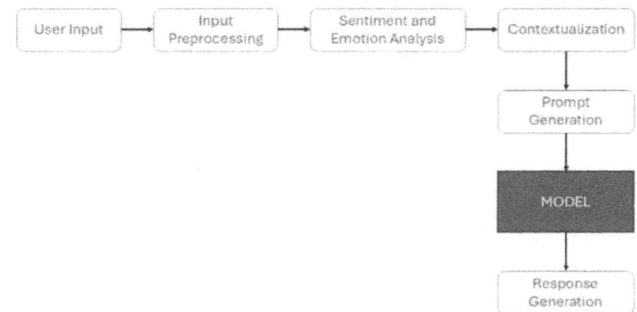

Fig. 28.1 Refined prompt engineering pipeline

Next, sentiment and emotion analysis are conducted using the distilbert-base-uncased-emotion and twitter-roberta-base-sentiment-latest models. These models were selected for their high accuracy in detecting user sentiment, providing context to the user's current state of mind [9].

Subsequently, previous user dialogues are appended to the model input using local storage. An optimum number of five dialogues are included, as fewer dialogues had little impact on context, while more exceeded the model's token length [10].

Finally, the processed input and contextual information are combined to generate the final prompt, which is then fed into the BLOOM-560M model for response generation. This structured approach ensures that the model's outputs are contextually relevant and sentiment aware.

4. Results and Analysis

4.1 Evaluation Methodology

We utilized an extract from the DailyDialog dataset, recognized for its quality and relevance in evaluating conversational models [6]. Our evaluation approach involved the following steps:

- Prompting and Response Generation: Using questions from the dataset to prompt our model and obtaining generated responses [11].

- Comparison with Reference Answers: Comparing generated responses to actual answers from the dataset.
- Evaluation Metric: Employing the ROUGE (Recall-Oriented Understudy for Gisting Evaluation) method to measure overlap with reference texts [12, 13, 14]. Specifically, we used:
  - ROUGE-1: Measures unigram (single word) overlap.
  - ROUGE-2: Measures bigram (two consecutive words) overlap.
  - ROUGE-L: Measures the longest common subsequence, which reflects structural coherence.

ROUGE-1 Evaluation

As shown in Table 28.1, the enhanced model achieved a ROUGE-1 F1 score of 0.584, which is significantly higher than the base model's score of 0.462. This indicates that the enhanced model was better at generating individual words that matched the reference answers, suggesting a substantial improvement in lexical accuracy.

ROUGE-2 Evaluation

The enhanced model's ROUGE-2 F1 score improved from 0.200 in the base model to 0.300. This shows that the enhanced model was more capable of generating correct pairs of consecutive words, demonstrating better short-range coherence and context understanding.

ROUGE-L Evaluation

The enhanced model outperformed the base model in ROUGE-L as well, with a score of 0.514 compared to 0.453. This improvement indicates that the enhanced model generated responses that more closely followed the structural pattern of the reference answers, reflecting better overall sentence-level coherence.

4.2 Analysis

The results in Table 28.1 demonstrate that the enhanced model showed consistent improvements across all three ROUGE metrics, validating the effectiveness of our prompt engineering strategy against the normal procedure shown in "Fig. 28.2".

Table 28.1 ROUGE scores for base and enhanced models

Metric	Base BLOOM-560M	Enhanced Model
ROUGE-1 F1	0.462	0.584
ROUGE-2 F1	0.200	0.300
ROUGE-L F1	0.453	0.514

Source: Author's compilation

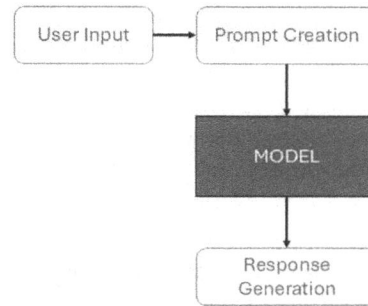

Fig. 28.2 Normal LLM pipeline

Improved Unigram and Bigram Overlap

The significant increase in ROUGE-1 (from 0.462 to 0.584) and ROUGE-2 (from 0.200 to 0.300) indicates that the enhanced model was able to generate responses with more relevant content. The higher unigram overlap suggests that it was better at identifying and using appropriate vocabulary, while the higher bigram score reflects an improvement in the model's ability to generate meaningful short phrases [15, 16].

Improved Structural Coherence

The increase in the ROUGE-L score (from 0.453 to 0.514) shows that the enhanced model maintained better structural coherence in its responses, resulting in answers that were not only accurate at the word level but also made more sense as complete sentences. This improvement is critical for conversational models, as it allows for more fluid and natural-sounding interactions.

5. Conclusion

This study has demonstrated the efficacy of prompt engineering in enhancing zero-shot text generation capabilities of low-parameter language models, exemplified by our use of the BLOOM-560M model. By systematically customizing prompts based on user input, sentiment analysis, and previous dialogues, we achieved significant improvements in model performance.

Our contributions to the field are twofold:

1. **Practical Framework for Prompt Customization and Automation:** We introduced a systematic framework that allows developers to optimize prompt structures tailored to user interactions. This framework not only enhances the performance of low-parameter models but also makes sophisticated NLP techniques more accessible to individual developers and smaller organizations.

2. **Integration of User Sentiment for Enhanced Coherence:** Incorporating sentiment analysis

into our prompt engineering pipeline enriched the contextual relevance and coherence of generated text. This integration ensures that the model's outputs align closely with the user's current state of mind and conversational context, improving overall user interaction quality.

Moving forward, the insights gained from this study underscore the potential of prompt engineering in advancing zero-shot text generation capabilities. Future research could explore further refinements in prompt strategies and their applications across different domains and languages, fostering broader adoption and innovation in natural language processing.

REFERENCES

1. B. Brown, et al., "Language Models are Few-Shot Learners," NeurIPS, 2020. [Online]. Available: https://neurips.cc/

2. Lin, et al., "Exploring Token Length Limits in Transformer Models," Journal of Computational Linguistics, 2020.

3. Sanh, et al., "DistilBERT, a distilled version of BERT: smaller, faster, cheaper and lighter," arXiv, 2019. [Online]. Available: https://arxiv.org/abs/1910.01108

4. Kim, et al., "Effect of Special Characters in Text Classification Tasks," Proceedings of the ACL, 2020.

5. Liu, et al., "Pre-train, Prompt, and Predict: A Systematic Survey of Prompting Methods in Natural Language Processing," arXiv, 2021. [Online]. Available: https://arxiv.org/abs/2107.13586

6. Li, Y., et al. 2017. "DailyDialog: A Manually Labelled Multi-turn Dialogue Dataset." Proceedings of the IJCNLP.

7. D. Butler, et al., "Punctuation Influence in Sentiment Analysis," Computational Linguistics Journal, 2006.

8. Socher, et al., "Recursive Deep Models for Semantic Compositionality Over a Sentiment Treebank," EMNLP, 2013.

9. Z. L. Jiang, et al., "Sentiment Analysis with distilBERT and RoBERTa: A Comparative Study," Proceedings of the ICML, 2020.

10. Lin, et al., "Optimization of Contextual Information in Dialogue Systems," Journal of Artificial Intelligence Research, 2020.

11. Y. Tay, et al., "Efficient Transformers: A Survey," arXiv, 2021. [Online]. Available: https://arxiv.org/abs/2009.06732

12. Liu, "Sentiment Analysis and Opinion Mining," Synthesis Lectures on Human Language Technologies, 2012.

13. Radford, et al., "Language Models are Unsupervised Multitask Learners," OpenAI, 2019. [Online]. Available: https://openai.com/research/language-models

14. Raffel, et al., "Exploring the Limits of Transfer Learning with a Unified Text-to-Text Transformer," JMLR, 2020. [Online]. Available: http://jmlr.org/

15. Reynolds and K. McDonell, "Prompt Programming for Large Language Models: Beyond the Few-Shot Paradigm," arXiv, 2021. [Online]. Available: https://arxiv.org/abs/2102.07350

16. Schick and H. Schütze, "Exploiting Cloze Questions for Few-Shot Text Classification and Natural Language Inference," EACL, 2021.

29

Multimodal Approaches in the Therapeutic Focus and Clinical Management of Gestational Diabetes Mellitus—A Narrative Review

S.M. Thennakoon*
Department of Life Sciences,
Faculty of Science, NSBM Green University,
Sri Lanka

N.D. Withanage
Department of Medical Laboratory Sciences,
Faculty of Allied Health Sciences, University of Sri Jayewardenepura,
Sri Lanka

K.L.M.D. Seneviwickrama
Department of Community Medicine,
Faculty of Medical Sciences, University of Sri Jayewardenepura,
Sri Lanka

M.A.M.M. Jayawardane
Department of Obstetrics and Gynecology,
Faculty of Medical Sciences, University of Sri Jayewardenepura,
Sri Lanka

L.V. Athiththan
Department of Biochemistry,
Faculty of Medical Sciences, University of Sri Jayewardenepura,
Sri Lanka

Abstract

Gestational diabetes mellitus (GDM) has a prevalence of 2-5% among all pregnant women and is one of the pregnancy-associated complications reported during the past ten years. The definition of GDM manifests the defects in the metabolism of carbohydrates that initially appear during pregnancy. Being a major public health problem, it causes notable clinical concomitants for expectant mothers and their children. This narrative review summarizes treatments and management of GDM considering recent research findings. Monitoring blood glucose levels, dietary therapy, and exercising exhibit well management of GDM while insulin is the gold standard therapeutic focus being safe and effective in comparison to other treatments. Systematic and narrative reviews and randomized and non-randomized studies published in the databases of Google Scholar, SCOPUS, Web of Science, MEDLINE, and PubMed were used

*Corresponding author: Sachini.t@nsbm.ac.lk

DOI: 10.1201/9781003616368-29

to conduct this review. Short-term impacts and long-term outcomes of both mothers and fetuses can be improved by diagnosing GDM at an early stage directing the patient to proper control over blood glucose levels. Lifestyle and pharmacological interventions will be the main focus of treatments that aid in effective management as well as prevention of GDM. Adequate treatment and management of GDM is of utmost importance with the advancing disease progression in the community. It symbolizes the need for the establishment of appropriate interventional strategies in the management of GDM in affected pregnant women.

Keywords

Clinical complications, Diagnosis, Gestational diabetes mellitus, Management, Treatment

1. Introduction

Gestational diabetes mellitus (GDM) is recognized as one of the most significant complications that arise during pregnancy leading to increased blood glucose levels [1]. Expectant mothers diagnosed with GDM present an increased risk of pregnancy-associated medical complications and complications at delivery namely infants of small-for-gestational-age (SGA), hyperglycaemia, and macrosomia, with caesarean delivery [2]. Furthermore, GDM mothers have a greater risk of developing type 2 diabetes mellitus (T2DM). Being hyperglycaemic during infancy, they become vulnerable to emerging glucose intolerance in the advancing years of their lives [1]. The initial diabetes classification during gestation introduced by Priscilla White has been subjected to several amendments until the publication of the latest classification in 1978 [3]. Moreover, the American College of Obstetricians and Gynecologists (ACOG) has challenged White's classification by focusing further on metabolic complications. However, the term "diabetes in pregnancy" includes all hyperglycaemic pregnancies such as GDM and pre-existing diabetes. The current defined category of GDM includes overt diabetes that is diagnosed at an early stage of pregnancy and actual GDM condition that will develop later [4]. GDM tends to recur in pregnancy later even though it generally resolves into a normal glucose tolerance (NGT) state following delivery. Different criteria used in the diagnosis of GDM, and the heterogeneity of the disease provide various rates of recurring GDM in varying populations [5].

Asian (5-10%), Arab, and Mexican American (5-7%) populations show high prevalence rates whereas Caucasians have reported comparatively lower prevalence (2-4%) [5]. The heterogeneity in the GDM prevalence among different ethnicities and regions is thought to underpin variations in body composition, insulin sensitivity, diet and lifestyle, genetic susceptibility, and socioeconomic factors [6].

It is evident that GDM shows progressive growth with the increased prevalence of type 2 diabetes and obesity. Meanwhile, pre-existing diabetes in pregnant females is misclassified as GDM [3].

Evidence reported by intervention studies focusing on treatments of GDM is found to be inconsistent and controversial. Conflicting results are considered due to different diagnostic criteria and interventions used, various populations studied, and varying time durations of conduction which directs the concern of the scientific community towards emerging research on the treatment and management modalities of GDM.

The objective of this narrative review is to evaluate and pinpoint the significance of diversified treatment strategies for GDM management to date. Hence, we discuss the possible treatment strategies to incorporate for GDM and the management of the disease by following up with affected populations of GDM mothers and their offspring which would aid in the clinical management of obstetric complications of GDM. Further, this review elaborates on the multi modes of treatment and management for GDM beyond insulin.

2. Methodology

A literature search was conducted with the purpose of obtaining evidence-based data from the narrative and systematic reviews, as well as randomized and non-randomized studies (from 2000 to 2024) published in English language using Google Scholar, SCOPUS, Web of Science, MEDLINE, and PubMed databases. The specific keywords that guided the search were "Gestational diabetes", "Gestational diabetes treatment methods", "GDM and dietary treatments", "Insulin, metformin, and sulfonylureas supplementation", "Myo-inositol", "Bariatric surgery and GDM" AND "Prevention of gestational diabetes". Studies were included based on which treatment modalities they have studied and the appropriateness of use for GDM management. Studies of non-human investigations, which focused on forms of diabetes other than pre-existing diabetes and GDM were excluded.

3. Treatments Focused on Gestational Diabetes Mellitus

Wellness in mothers and reducing perinatal morbidity elicits significant importance when implementing treatment for GDM. Despite that, GDM and its consequential effects on both the mother and offspring can be managed and thereby reduced with the treatments recommended, certain studies have reported that treatments did not provide proper therapeutic management over GDM. A meta-analysis carried out in the US indicated that the treatments are not capable of decreasing the rates of labor induction, neonatal hypoglycaemia, caesarean delivery, SGA, birth trauma, respiratory complications, hyperbilirubinemia, or admission to neonatal intensive care unit (NICU) [7,8] which was confirmed by another meta-analysis conducted recently in China [6]. Further, pregnancy-associated adverse outcomes showed an association with postprandial hyperglycaemia [9]. However, GDM mothers needed to be well enlightened that proper blood glucose management would reduce the above complications [3].

Treatment approaches require self-care of the affected subjects for clinical management with necessary information on GDM, self-tracking of blood glucose levels, and counseling on healthy diet and lifestyle measures that could be facilitated by an experienced educator [10].

3.1 Assessment of Blood Glucose Concentration

Regular blood glucose assessment will aid in confirming the state of glycaemic control in response to nutritional treatments [10]. The American Diabetes Association (ADA) states assessing glucose concentrations following fasting and after a meal. Besides, ACOG recommends tracking blood glucose levels in blood drawn following fasting and after 1-2 hours of each respective meal which illustrates measuring glucose four times in a single day. Glycaemic testing is further advised by the National Institute for Clinical Excellence (NICE) to be performed bedside in patients receiving insulin injection therapy daily. Additionally, one fasting glycaemic test and 2-3 postprandial glycaemic testing are recommended by the International Federation for Gynecology and Obstetrics (FIGO). Assessment of postprandial glucose levels could be done following 1-2 hours of meals. An increase in the fat mass of the neonate is predicted by the mean levels of fasting glucose. As per the evidence, postprandial glucose tracking presents an association with reduced macrosomia and pre-eclampsia alongside advancements in glycaemic control [9, 11,12].

As per the recommendations of ACOG, NICE, and ADA, target blood glucose at the pre-prandial state is < 95 mg/dL, and at the one-hour postprandial state < 140 mg/dL, and two-hours postprandial state < 120 mg/dL [9, 11,12]. Peak postprandial glucose levels in blood eventuate at 69 ± 24 minutes. Continual tracking of blood glucose levels is urged for mothers with GDM who receive insulin therapy. Frequent evaluation of glycaemic control is not required following stabilization of the glucose levels while weekly assessment will be needed in place until then [11]. Haemoglobin-A1c (HbA1c) analysis is a strong suggestion for the verification of reliable self-glucose monitoring [3]. Different glucose targets in achieving glycaemic control recommended by the established international guidelines are mentioned in Table 29.1.

3.2 Lifestyle Interventional Strategies

Modifications to the diet and advised physical activity will encourage suppressing the postprandial elevations of glucose. However, a minority of GDM mothers will require pharmacotherapy [13].

Dietary Treatment for Gestational Diabetes Mellitus

Fetal growth is mainly governed by glucose alongside the involvement of other nutrients. Elevated maternal hyperglycaemia exhibits direct associations with several complications and fetal overgrowth as stated by Pedersen's hypothesis. With regard to that, the management of maternal hyperglycaemic state in maternal blood stands as the key focus of remedial therapy for GDM [13]. Evidence from two studies demonstrated a reduction of fetal overgrowth and shoulder dystocia by lifestyle interventional strategies with advised supplementary insulin therapy by about 50% [14,15]. Medical attention and therapy with appropriate lifestyle modifications are regarded as the cornerstone of remedial treatment for GDM [16,17]. The recommended diet for a GDM mother shares similarities with that for a diabetic patient and needs to be composed of adequate micronutrients and macronutrients, restricting post-prandial glucose drive and thereby preventing gestational weight gain in mothers.

The diet would best comprise mainly carbohydrates of low-glycaemic index and three meals of apportions daily dietary caloric intake with 2-4 snacks. The daily carbohydrate inclusion of ≥175 g into the diet is recommended by the Institute of Medicine (IOM) for proper growth, development, and function of the fetus [18,19].

Table 29.1 Established plasma glucose targets by international guidelines

International Recommendation	ADIPS (mmol/L)	ADA (mmol/L)	CDA (mmol/L)
Fasting	5.5	5.8	5.3
One-hour postprandial	8.0	8.6	7.8
Two-hour postprandial	7.0	7.2	6.7

Source: Obstetricians and Gynecologists 2013 [20]

Abbreviations: ADIPS- Australasian Diabetes in Pregnancy Society, ADA- American Diabetes Association, CDA- Canadian Diabetes Association

Such conditions of ketonuria and/or ketonemia in pregnant women are known to pose an association with reduced motor function and mental health development in children. The established carbohydrate intake for GDM mothers by IOM ensures that the mother is safe from starvation and ketonemia. Randomized trials conducted provide sufficient proof that lower birth weight and frequent insulin therapy can be managed with a diet with a low glycaemic index. These trials advised that an average total daily calory intake of 1,600 kcal in expectant mothers alongside a caloric restriction of up to 30% in obese pregnant women [17, 18]. No such evidence is suggestive for non-obese pregnant women to date [13].

Treatment with Exercise and Physical Activity

Daily physical activity is appreciated and recommended for women with GDM [12]. As per the recorded data, the glycaemic control in about 70-85% of mothers with GDM can be presided over by diet and sufficient physical activity [12, 17]. This implication also would aid in reducing postnatal depression [14]. Moreover, interventional exercises were reported to affect weight retention during the postpartum period in mothers as given by a systematic review [13, 21]. Physical activity during pregnancy exhibited a link with the risk of GDM incidence in meta-analyses carried out by Tobias et al. and Mijatovic-Vukas et al. [22,23].

3.3 Pharmacological Interventional Strategies

Pharmacological interventions are advised in pregnant women with GDM when glycaemia cannot be controlled. In such circumstances, daily monitoring of glucose and the introduction of pharmacotherapy are required. Individual glycaemic control and its intensity are monitored bordering on fetal growth. A fetal abdominal circumference of <75th percentile proposes to postpone the commencement of pharmacological therapy. Contrariwise, an escalation of the focus of treatments for glycaemic control is highlighted by uncontrolled excess growth of the fetus [24].

3.4 Insulin Therapy

Insulin is commonly used and remains the mainstay of GDM therapy with its outstanding performance and its inability to cross the placenta. Ineffective implication and glycaemic control by lifestyle modifications within 1-2 weeks signals to initiate insulin therapy. Human insulin and certain analogs of insulin demonstrate safe use. Such analogs include insulin detemir, insulin lispro, and insulin aspart [12]. Despite that, insulin treatment is recognized as presenting certain stressed considerations for women involving hypoglycaemic risk, discomfort, costly treatments, and trypanophobia. GDM patients suffer from mild episodes of hypoglycaemia during insulin therapy whereas severe hypoglycaemic cases are less frequent and require further attention and treatments [13].

Insulin therapy focuses on controlling maternal weight gain while presenting control over glucose as per the goals of lifestyle interventional strategies. It is regarded as a basal-bolus routine which illustrates basal insulin to be an intermediate- or long-acting and injected once per day and the bolus insulin to be a rapid-acting form and given prior to each main meal. Effectiveness was elaborated with a mixture of both long-acting and rapid-acting insulin twice per day. The initial insulin dosage is established per Kg body weight and for a period of 24 hours, it is required to be 0.3 international units (IU) whereas the final dosage is suggestive to be closer to 1 IU per kg [25].

There are several categories of insulin therapies available as follows.

1. Rapid-acting insulin: Aspart (Novolog) and Lispro (Humalog)
2. Short-acting insulin: Regular insulin
3. Intermediate-acting insulin: Neutral Protamine Hagedorn (NPH)
4. Long-acting insulin: Glargine, Detemir
5. Ultra-long-acting insulin: Degludec
6. Premixed: NPH/ REGULAR 70/30

The convenience of using oral drugs makes them more attractive for managing hyperglycaemia in GDM [26]. A large, randomized control trial compared the effective application of regular short-acting insulin with aspart in 322 pregnant women who were diagnosed with type 1 diabetes. The authors reported similar neonatal outcomes in both groups revealing its safe use compared with regular insulin. The efficacy of rapid-acting analogs of insulin was investigated in comparison with regular insulin by certain small randomized controlled studies which also have demonstrated comparable results [10].

Furthermore, pregnant mothers with GDM have been studied for the effective application of well-established oral medications for glycaemia mainly including sulfonylurea glibenclamide and metformin. The use of oral drugs except for these two which lower glucose levels is not advised due to consequential unforeseen complications in the fetus with epigenetic and metabolic derangements and neonatal hypoglycaemia. Given that, due to time consumption and the requisition of training for insulin treatments for GDM mothers, metformin gains more attention. It shares similarities with insulin in treating hyperglycaemia as per certain randomized clinical trials but is associated with some benefits as well as drawbacks [13].

4. Metformin Therapy

The significance of metformin as a therapeutic drug includes its key role in treating pre-diabetes mellitus, gestational diabetes, and polycystic ovary syndrome (PCOS) with further elaborated implications in the treatment of preeclampsia as per recent randomized clinical trials [27].

It plays an appreciable role in being the primary therapy for glyceamia in non-pregnant, non-insulin-dependent diabetic individuals. It efficaciously reduces fasting blood glucose levels and HbA1c with suppression of the production of glucose in the liver [28]. Metformin poses certain drawbacks such as lowering vitamin B_{12} levels, resulting in gastrointestinal complications, and on rare occasions causing elevated risk of having lactic acidosis. Furthermore, metformin might affect the development of the fetus as it is capable of crossing the placenta. However, mothers at a high risk of GDM development would benefit from metformin treatment due to its ability to enhance insulin sensitivity [3]. Evidence from some randomized trials suggests the characteristics of metformin treatments correspond to that of insulin in controlling the glycaemic status resulting in expeditious outcomes in the neonate [29,30]. The majority of GDM mothers would respond to metformin therapy while approximately one-third of GDM mothers need to be treated additionally with insulin [26]. Metformin exhibits certain long-term impacts on offspring that are necessary to be focused on as it could transfer across the placenta [31]. Studies conducted by Battin et al. and Rowan et al. have elaborated that the offspring of two years of age of women with GDM presented subcutaneous fat to a greater extent in the forehand upon exposure to metformin treatments in utero[32,33]. Concerning these studies, the blood pressure and adiposity in these children were similar to that of insulin therapy.

Rowan et al. (2018) further provided evidence that children aged nine years who were born to mothers who presented GDM and undergone metformin therapy exhibited significant height compared to the children whose mothers had the insulin treatment [34]. Another similar study revealed that the one-year-old and 18-month-old offspring who were exposed in utero to metformin medication demonstrated increased weight and both increased weight and height respectively [35].

Additionally, recent studies indicated sufficient evidence for the safe therapeutic application of metformin minimizing obstetrical complications in comparison to the novel therapy of bariatric surgery (BS) in women with GDM [27, 36]. Therefore, metformin could be suggested as a first-line therapy for GDM in patients who undergo lifestyle modifications and experience inefficient glycaemic management [37].

5. Treatment with Sulfonylureas

Sulfonylureas are reported to decrease fasting blood sugar concentrations and glycated haemoglobin levels by a mechanism that augments insulin secretion and thereby reduces plasma glucose. Glyburide or glibenclamide was found an effective sulfonylurea medication for glycaemic therapy similar to insulin.

Comparable outcomes were evident in the neonates associated with GDM and the percentage of neonates born large for gestational age (LGA) in sulfonylureas and insulin [38]. Nevertheless, further studies present evidence that glibenclamide could cross the placenta exhibiting considerable consequences in the development of the fetus [39]. There is lacking evidence on complications that might be experienced and manifested by children who exposed to glibenclamide in utero [13].

Balsells et al. carried out a meta-analysis in the year 2015 and the study revealed that the development of hypoglycaemia in neonates (pooled risk ratio 2.04 (95% Confidence interval (CI) 1.30-3.20)), increased birth weight (pooled mean difference 109 g (95% CI: 35.9-181.0)), and elevated rates of fetal macrosomia (pooled risk ratio 2.62 (95% CI: 1.35-5.08)) have a significant association with glibenclamide than insulin. The study focused on the safe application and efficacy of metformin, insulin, and glibenclamide. As per the study, increased rates of macrosomia and increased birth weight showed associations with glibenclamide than metformin. Adhering to the given proof, metformin and/or insulin denote the more efficient glycaemic treatment for mothers with GDM in comparison to glibenclamide therapy [26].

Besides, Camelo et al. indicated that glibenclamide therapy would be associated with neonatal complications counting birth injuries, increased LGA percentage, hypoglycaemia, and neonatal emergency treatment care. However, glibenclamide has been an established medication for pregnant women diagnosed with GDM in the USA [40]. The findings of these studies would not suggest and therefore argue the implication of glibenclamide drug in first-line glycaemic pharmacotherapy in mothers present with GDM requiring further research in order to investigate complications associated with glibenclamide therapy for GDM.

Summarizing the treatment of GDM, insulin remains the centerpiece of GDM therapy whereas cost and the ease of use decide on choosing metformin or glibenclamide depending on the particular individual consideration [13].

6. Nutritional Supplementation

Nutritional supplementations are known to enhance insulin resistance in pregnancy which mainly includes inositol and probiotics. Therefore, an increasing trend can be observed in the scientific community for the focus on inositol and probiotics-based supplementation for the treatment and prevention of GDM. These novel insights suggest the role of nutritional intervention of inositol and probiotics in pregnancy while promoting fetal health. Evidence-based approaches reported by the studies propose their usage to manage adverse maternal and neonatal outcomes associated with GDM [41]. Pointedly, the efficacy of dietary supplementation with myo-inositol was proven to treat GDM while revealing its potency to prevent GDM during gestation [3].

Inositol regulates several human biological processes including the growth and survival of cells, osteogenesis, reproduction and endocrine function, development of the central nervous system, and lipid and glucose metabolism [42]. Myo-inositol is recognized as a member of structural isomers of the group inositol of which nine isomers are possible to be present. Myo-inositol plays a significant role in this regard which is found to be efficient and safe [3].

The GDM incidence is thought to have declined with the probiotics and myo-inositol in pregnant women. Glucose control could be achieved with myo-inositol in conditions of insulin resistance indicating the 3rd trimester of the gestation in which GDM was identified and PCOS. Evidence from two clinical trials revealed a decline in risk and the incidence of GDM with supplementation of myo-inositol [43,44]. Contrarily, Farren, et al. suggested with the evidence from their clinical trial that inositol supplementation in early pregnancy was not effective on women present with GDM whose family line discovered to have diabetes [45]. Being a new treatment strategy, its quality needs to be assessed with more established findings though the detailed metabolism is not well understood.

Probiotic supplementation prevents GDM based on the effects of benefit on the metabolism of glucose apart from pregnancy. A randomized controlled trial performed in Finland demonstrated positive evidence for this regard with the decline in prevalence of GDM from 35-13% [46]. It was achieved by preparation of probiotics with the inclusion of *Bifidobacterium animalis* subsp. *lactis* BB-12 and *Lactobacillus rhamnosus* GG. Literature does not support the implementation of probiotics to prevent GDM as the findings are inconclusive [47].

Concisely, the ADA, FIGO, the NICE, and the Endocrine Society are the foremost leading international guidelines that have established treatment recommendations for pregnant women diagnosed with GDM [13, 48]. As per their guidelines, lifestyle interventional strategies and insulin therapy stand as the centerpiece for GDM with the applied possibility of using metformin or glibenclamide during gestation. Individual circumstances would decide the glibenclamide or metformin to be chosen whereas insulin is recommended for pharmacotherapy [13].

6.1 Perspective of Surgical Intervention for Gestational Diabetes Mellitus

Bariatric surgery (BS) is a medical intervention for morbidity associated with obesity and other complications [49]. Evidence reveals an increasing trend of BS in obese women of childbearing age. Bariatric surgery aids in reducing the incidence of GDM in the next five years [50] and BS has been performed on a considerable number of women expecting motherhood [51]. The frequency of the occurrence of GDM and non-insulin-dependent diabetes mellitus (NIDDM) seems to have declined with BS [52, 53]. Any significant rise in perinatal mortality is not detailed except for certain adverse outcomes including preemies, SGA, and indication for admitting to NICU [52]. Subcategories of BS involve malabsorptive, restrictive, or combined [54]. It is appreciably beneficial to the majority as this surgical procedure improves glycaemic control and would even direct the discontinuation of diabetic therapy [55, 56]. Pregnancy following BS seems secure and safer in comparison to obese gestation [57, 58].

The probability of GDM would have a significant reduction and thereby reduce obesity-associated complications [51, 52, 56, 57, 59, 60]. BS is associated with a higher incidence of SGA neonates but a lower risk of fetal macrosomia and obstetrical hypertensive disorders during pregnancy [59, 61-63]. Aricha-Tamir et al. demonstrated an appreciable decrease in hypertensive disorders following BS with pregnancies before BS [58]. In accordance with that, Weintraub et al. demonstrated a significant decline in severe pre-eclampsia (95% CI: 0.1-0.7, $P=0.005$) and hypertension (95% CI: 0.3-0.6, $P<0.001$) in women who conceived post-BS [57]. Nevertheless, Sheiner et al. suggested the absence of an association between BS and adverse outcomes in neonates [64]. A persistently reduced rate of GDM risk in proceeding pregnancies was another notable consequence of BS. When a woman conceives post-BS and develops GDM, a significant risk elevation was not demonstrated in fetus and mother in comparison with the GDM mothers who have not undergone BS [65].

As per the established recommendations, the conception is advised to be avoided for 1-2 years following BS, with the expectation of avoiding variations in nutritional fluctuations during 6-18 months due to rapid weight reduction [66, 67].

7. Medical Management of Gestational Diabetes during Gestation, at Delivery, and Postpartum

Euglycaemia can be achieved in GDM patients by adequate control of diet or by medication. Surveillance of the fetus is recommended in mothers diagnosed with GDM. ACOG suggests monitoring the fetus from 32 weeks of pregnancy when other risk factors for the fetus are absent. The GDM mothers who undergo dietary therapy only and have good glycaemic control need to be managed for about 40 plus 6 to 7 weeks, which indicates until the delivery and postpartum. The delivery for mothers with well-controlled GDM by medication is recommended between 39-40 weeks whereas for women with poor glycaemic control, is suggested between 37-39 weeks of pregnancy. Obstetric complications in mother and fetus with uncontrolled glycaemia direct late preterm delivery between 34-36 weeks and need to be managed for glycaemia up until 6 weeks postpartum. As per NICE guidelines, the volume of amniotic fluid and fetal growth needs to be monitored during gestation at the 28th, 32nd, and 36th weeks to manage birth. Hourly capillary blood glucose measurements are recommended during labor in diabetic women, with insulin or dextrose administered to maintain blood glucose levels between 72 and 126 mg/dL [9].

Mothers with GDM are encouraged to discontinue glycaemic treatments following birth and to breastfeed for 4 months postpartum minimally. It declines the risk of the occurrence of neonatal hypoglycaemia, metabolic syndrome, and obesity in offspring. Even if the glucose intolerance status in GDM is reported to resolve following delivery, might proceed to undiagnosed T2DM. Given that, they are advised to undergo an OGTT of 75 g glucose to detect glycaemic management following childbirth. Moreover, as stated by the Canadian guidelines, OGTT needs to be repeated following 6 months postpartum. NICE prescribes performing fasting blood glucose tests 13 weeks postpartum. Mothers with GDM who received negative results for postnatal testing are required to undergo annual testing for HbA1c. Lifestyle interventions are strongly suggested by ADA in postpartum mothers with GDM due to the risk of pre-diabetes and 30-84% risk of recurring probability of GDM in the succeeding pregnancies [3].

8. Sri Lankan Guidelines for Treatment and Management of Gestational Diabetes

Concerning treatments and management of hyperglycaemia in pregnancy employed in Sri Lanka, self-monitoring of blood glucose (SMBG), non-pharmacological treatments and pharmacological treatments are being used upon the recommendation of physicians depending on the individual case [68]. Daily SMBG for fasting and 2 hours following a meal for at least 4 times per day is established effective. This will prevent adverse pregnancy outcomes and aid in achieving patients' glycaemic targets. Non-pharmacological therapy includes Medical Nutrition Therapy (MNT) and exercise/ physical activity. Over and above, the commencement of MNT is strictly recommended by a nutritionist soon following GDM diagnosis. It mainly comprises a diet-based approach which is required to be continued throughout the pregnancy. MNT alone is competent to manage GDM in about 80-90% of GDM mothers. An ideal diet should contain 45-55% carbohydrates, 20-30% fat including saturated fat <10%, and 15-20% protein which always should be in accordance with the nutritional status of the mother [68].

Obstetricians recommend a physical activity plan of 30 minutes per day after evaluating the patient's capacity including arm exercises and brisk walking. In an inability of non-pharmacological treatments to achieve glycaemic control within the expected days, the patient will be guided for pharmacological therapy. This should be followed by SMBG to proceed with pharmacological treatment. Insulin and metformin are the recommended pharmacological treatments with which metformin, an oral antidiabetic drug, is the 1st line of therapy [68]. Furthermore, it also can be continued on GDM mothers present with PCOS who were taking metformin medication before conception. Nevertheless, insulin will be required to be used in the ineffective management of plasma glucose levels with metformin alone. The 2nd line pharmacological therapy recommended is insulin including rapid-acting, intermediate-acting insulin, and ultra-short-acting analogs lispro and aspart for safe use. Detemir is a long-acting analog of insulin. Apart from the aforementioned pharmacological therapy, sulfonylureas are not recommended for safe use during pregnancy as per the guidelines, but glibenclamide is being used in such conditions where insulin and/or metformin use is considered not safe. Alongside GDM therapy, maternal blood glucose series assessment is conducted with the assessment of fetal growth [68].

As per the guidelines currently practiced in Sri Lanka, proper antenatal care from the first appointment which further continues with intrapartum, and postpartum management is of utmost importance to promote maternal and fetal care preventing adverse complications associated with GDM mainly including fetal loss [68].

However, the treatment strategy will be heavily reliant on the respective diagnostic criteria utilized by the country. In terms of diagnosis, Sri Lanka approaches specific national guidelines with certain variations to the World Health Organization (WHO) and International Association of Diabetes and Pregnancy Study Groups (IADPSG) based on the population-specific differences, ethnicity, prevalence of GDM and hyperglycemia in pregnancy, and availability of healthcare resources. It thereby aids in the appropriate diagnosis and implication of proper treatment for GDM while preventing misdiagnosis and/or overdiagnosis [68-70].

9. Concluding Remarks

The rising prevalence of GDM makes it a global health concern not only throughout pregnancy but also after birth with a significant elevation risk of morbidity and mortality in the fetus. GDM carries significant adverse health effects in both mother and neonate that might be either short-term or long-term. Further, offspring has a possibility of developing metabolic dysfunction and diabetes mellitus in their later life. Incorporation of adequate preventive measures is of utmost importance in the management of these complications. Preventive strategies focusing on lifestyle intervention including nutrition, diet, and physical activity play a major role. Among the pharmacological treatment strategies for mothers with GDM, insulin plays an invincible role. Metformin and glyburide are suggested to be reserved for GDM cases in which insulin therapy is reported unsafe. Treatment with myo-inositol was recently recognized as an effective non-pharmacological agent in preventing GDM. Proper obstetric and medical care are beneficial to minimize the potential hurdles of pregnancy. This review elaborates on the essential requirement of further research to be carried out for a better understanding of the appropriate clinical management of expectant mothers with GDM.

Disclosure

The author(s) declare the absence of conflicts of interest with regard to the authorship and publication of the article.

Acknowledgment

A special thanks to the University of Sri Jayewardenepura, Sri Lanka, and NSBM Green University, Sri Lanka for providing the necessary facilities, and to the academia for cultivating a supportive environment for research and development.

REFERENCES

1. G. López Stewart, "Diagnostic criteria and classification of hyperglycaemia first detected in pregnancy: A World Health Organization Guideline," *J Diabetes Res.* vol. 103, pp. 341–3633, 2014.
2. A. M. Dirar and J. Doupis, "Gestational diabetes from A to Z," *World J Diabetes,* vol. 8, pp. 489, 2017.
3. G. Zito, L. Della Corte, P. Giampaolino, M. Terzic, S. Terzic, F. Di Guardo, *et al.*, "Gestational diabetes mellitus: Prevention, diagnosis and treatment. A fresh look to a busy corner," *JNPM,* vol. 13, pp. 529–541, 2020.
4. J. Dahlgren, "Pregnancy and insulin resistance," *Metabolic Syndr Relat Disord,* vol. 4, pp. 149–152, 2006.
5. N. Shaat and L. Groop, "Genetics of gestational diabetes mellitus," *Curr Med Chem,* vol. 14, pp. 569–583, 2007.
6. W. Ye, C. Luo, J. Huang, C. Li, Z. Liu, and F. Liu, "Gestational diabetes mellitus and adverse pregnancy outcomes: systematic review and meta-analysis," *BMJ,* vol. 377, 2022.
7. D. A. Schoenaker, G. D. Mishra, L. K. Callaway, and S. S. Soedamah-Muthu, "The role of energy, nutrients, foods, and dietary patterns in the development of gestational diabetes mellitus: a systematic review of observational studies," *Diabetes Care,* vol. 39, pp. 16–23, 2016.
8. L. Hartling, D. M. Dryden, A. Guthrie, M. Muise, B. Vandermeer, and L. Donovan, "Benefits and harms of treating gestational diabetes mellitus: a systematic review and meta-analysis for the US Preventive Services Task Force and the National Institutes of Health Office of Medical Applications of Research," *Ann. Intern. Med,* vol. 159, pp. 123–129, 2013.
9. M. Hod, A. Kapur, D. A. Sacks, E. Hadar, M. Agarwal, G. C. Di Renzo, *et al.*, "The International Federation of Gynecology and Obstetrics (FIGO) Initiative on gestational diabetes mellitus: A pragmatic guide for diagnosis, management, and care," *IJGO,* vol. 131, pp. S173–S211, 2015.
10. N. W. Cheung, "The management of gestational diabetes," *Vasc Health Risk Manag,* pp. 153–164, 2009.
11. J. Walker, "NICE guidance on diabetes in pregnancy: management of diabetes and its complications from preconception to the postnatal period. NICE clinical guideline 63. London, March 2008," *Diabet Med,* vol. 25, pp. 1025–1027, 2008.
12. A. D. Association, "13. Management of diabetes in pregnancy: standards of medical care in diabetes—2018," *Diabetes Care,* vol. 41, pp. S137–S143, 2018.

13. H. D. McIntyre, P. Catalano, C. Zhang, G. Desoye, E. R. Mathiesen, and P. Damm, "Gestational diabetes mellitus," *Nat Rev Dis Primers*, vol. 5, p. 47, 2019.

14. C. A. Crowther, J. E. Hiller, J. R. Moss, A. J. McPhee, W. S. Jeffries, and J. S. Robinson, "Effect of treatment of gestational diabetes mellitus on pregnancy outcomes," *NEJM*, vol. 352, pp. 2477–2486, 2005.

15. M. B. Landon, C. Y. Spong, E. Thom, M. W. Carpenter, S. M. Ramin, B. Casey, *et al.*, "A multicenter, randomized trial of treatment for mild gestational diabetes," *NEJM*, vol. 361, pp. 1339–1348, 2009.

16. A. D. Association, "14. Management of diabetes in pregnancy: standards of medical care in diabetes—2019," *Diabetes Care*, vol. 42, pp. S165–S172, 2019.

17. E. P. Gunderson, "Gestational diabetes and nutritional recommendations," *Curr Diab Rep*, vol. 4, pp. 377–386, 2004.

18. L. V. Viana, J. L. Gross, and M. J. Azevedo, "Dietary intervention in patients with gestational diabetes mellitus: a systematic review and meta-analysis of randomized clinical trials on maternal and newborn outcomes," *Diabetes Care*, vol. 37, pp. 3345–3355, 2014.

19. K. M. Rasmussen, P. M. Catalano, and A. L. Yaktine, "New guidelines for weight gain during pregnancy: what obstetrician/gynecologists should know," *Curr Opin Obstet Gyn*, vol. 21, pp. 521–526, 2009.

20. A. C. O. Obstetricians and Gynecologists, "Gestational diabetes mellitus," *Practice Bulletin*, vol. 137, pp. 1–11, 2013.

21. S.-M. Ruchat, M. F. Mottola, R. J. Skow, T. S. Nagpal, V. L. Meah, V. James, *et al.*, "Effectiveness of exercise interventions in the prevention of excessive gestational weight gain and postpartum weight retention: a systematic review and meta-analysis," *BJSM*, vol. 52, pp. 1347–1356, 2018.

22. D. K. Tobias, C. Zhang, R. M. Van Dam, K. Bowers, and F. B. Hu, "Physical activity before and during pregnancy and risk of gestational diabetes mellitus: a meta-analysis," *Diabetes Care*, vol. 34, pp. 223–229, 2011.

23. J. Mijatovic-Vukas, L. Capling, S. Cheng, E. Stamatakis, J. Louie, N. W. Cheung, *et al.*, "Associations of diet and physical activity with risk for gestational diabetes mellitus: a systematic review and meta-analysis," *Nutrients*, vol. 10, p. 698, 2018.

24. S. L. Kjos and U. M. Schaefer-Graf, "Modified therapy for gestational diabetes using high-risk and low-risk fetal abdominal circumference growth to select strict versus relaxed maternal glycemic targets," *Diabetes Care*, vol. 30, 2007.

25. M. R. Mikkelsen, S. B. Nielsen, E. Stage, E. R. Mathiesen, and P. Damm, "High maternal HbA1c is associated with overweight in neonates," *Dan Med Bull*, vol. 58, p. A4309, 2011.

26. M. Balsells, A. García-Patterson, I. Solà, M. Roqué, I. Gich, and R. Corcoy, "Glibenclamide, metformin, and insulin for the treatment of gestational diabetes: a systematic review and meta-analysis," *BMJ*, vol. 350, 2015.

27. R. Romero, O. Erez, M. Hüttemann, E. Maymon, B. Panaitescu, A. Conde-Agudelo, *et al.*, "Metformin, the aspirin of the 21st century: its role in gestational diabetes mellitus, prevention of preeclampsia and cancer, and the promotion of longevity," *AJOG*, vol. 217, pp. 282–302, 2017.

28. Y. Jia, Y. Lao, H. Zhu, N. Li, and S. W. Leung, "Is metformin still the most efficacious first-line oral hypoglycaemic drug in treating type 2 diabetes? A network meta-analysis of randomized controlled trials," *Obes Rev*, vol. 20, pp. 1–12, 2019.

29. J. A. Rowan, W. M. Hague, W. Gao, M. R. Battin, and M. P. Moore, "Metformin versus insulin for the treatment of gestational diabetes," *NEJM*, vol. 358, pp. 2003–2015, 2008.

30. H. Ijäs, M. Vääräsmäki, L. Morin-Papunen, R. Keravuo, T. Ebeling, T. Saarela, *et al.*, "Metformin should be considered in the treatment of gestational diabetes: a prospective randomised study," *BJOG*, vol. 118, pp. 880–885, 2011.

31. L. A. Barbour and D. S. Feig, "Metformin for Gestational Diabetes Mellitus: Progeny, Perspective, and a Personalized Approach," *Diabetes Care*, vol. 42, pp. 396–399, 2019.

32. M. R. Battin, V. Obolonkin, E. Rush, W. Hague, S. Coat, and J. Rowan, "Blood pressure measurement at two years in offspring of women randomized to a trial of metformin for GDM: follow up data from the MiG trial," *BMC Pediatrics*, vol. 15, pp. 1–5, 2015.

33. J. A. Rowan, E. C. Rush, V. Obolonkin, M. Battin, T. Wouldes, and W. M. Hague, "Metformin in gestational diabetes: the offspring follow-up (MiG TOFU) body composition at 2 years of age," *Diabetes Care*, vol. 34, pp. 2279–2284, 2011.

34. J. A. Rowan, E. C. Rush, L. D. Plank, J. Lu, V. Obolonkin, S. Coat, *et al.*, "Metformin in gestational diabetes: the offspring follow-up (MiG TOFU): body composition and metabolic outcomes at 7–9 years of age," *BMJ Open Diabetes Research and Care*, vol. 6, p. e000456, 2018.

35. H. Ijäs, M. Vääräsmäki, T. Saarela, R. Keravuo, and T. Raudaskoski, "A follow-up of a randomised study of metformin and insulin in gestational diabetes mellitus: growth and development of the children at the age of 18 months," *BJOG*, vol. 122, pp. 994–1000, 2015.

36. M. J. Paglia and D. R. Coustan, "The use of oral antidiabetic medications in gestational diabetes mellitus," *Curr Diab Rep*, vol. 9, pp. 287–290, 2009.

37. J. Khan and A. Ali, "Metformin and Gestational Diabetes Mellitus: A Systematic Review," *The Stetho*, vol. 5, 2024.

38. O. Langer, D. L. Conway, M. D. Berkus, E. M.-J. Xenakis, and O. Gonzales, "A comparison of glyburide and insulin in women with gestational diabetes mellitus," *NEJM*, vol. 343, pp. 1134–1138, 2000.

39. R. A. Schwartz, B. Rosenn, K. Aleksa, and G. Koren, "Glyburide transport across the human placenta," *OBGYN*, vol. 125, pp. 583–588, 2015.

40. W. C. Castillo, K. Boggess, T. Stürmer, M. A. Brookhart, D. K. Benjamin, and M. J. Funk, "Association of adverse pregnancy outcomes with glyburide vs insulin in women with gestational diabetes," *JAMA Pediatrics*, vol. 169, pp. 452–458, 2015.

41. E. Vitacolonna, M. Masulli, L. Palmisano, L. Stuppia, and M. Franzago, "Inositols, Probiotics, and gestational Diabetes: clinical and epigenetic aspects," *Nutrients,* vol. 14, p. 1543, 2022.

42. F. A. Gulino, E. Leonardi, I. Marilli, G. Musmeci, S. G. Vitale, V. Leanza, *et al.*, "Effect of treatment with myo-inositol on semen parameters of patients undergoing an IVF cycle: in vivo study," *Gynecol Endocrinol,* vol. 32, pp. 65–68, 2016.

43. A. Santamaria, A. Di Benedetto, E. Petrella, B. Pintaudi, F. Corrado, R. D'Anna, *et al.*, "Myo-inositol may prevent gestational diabetes onset in overweight women: a randomized, controlled trial," *J Matern- Fetal Neonatal Med,* vol. 29, pp. 3234–3237, 2016.

44. C. Celentano, B. Matarrelli, P. A. Mattei, G. Pavone, E. Vitacolonna, and M. Liberati, "Myo-inositol supplementation to prevent gestational diabetes mellitus," *Curr Diab Rep,* vol. 16, pp. 1–7, 2016.

45. M. Farren, N. Daly, A. McKeating, B. Kinsley, M. J. Turner, and S. Daly, "The prevention of gestational diabetes mellitus with antenatal oral inositol supplementation: a randomized controlled trial," *Diabetes Care,* vol. 40, pp. 759–763, 2017.

46. R. Luoto, K. Laitinen, M. Nermes, and E. Isolauri, "Impact of maternal probiotic-supplemented dietary counselling on pregnancy outcome and prenatal and postnatal growth: a double-blind, placebo-controlled study," *Br J Nutr,* vol. 103, pp. 1792–1799, 2010.

47. S. J. Davidson, H. L. Barrett, S. A. Price, L. K. Callaway, and M. D. Nitert, "Probiotics for preventing gestational diabetes," *CDSR,* 2021.

48. J. Webber, M. Charlton, and N. Johns, "Diabetes in pregnancy: management of diabetes and its complications from preconception to the postnatal period (NG3)," *BJD,* vol. 15, pp. 107–111, 2015.

49. K. Willis, N. Lieberman, and E. Sheiner, "Pregnancy and neonatal outcome after bariatric surgery," *Best Pract Res Clin Obstet Gynaecol,* vol. 29, pp. 133–144, 2015.

50. S. Farahvar, A. Walfisch, and E. Sheiner, "Gestational diabetes risk factors and long-term consequences for both mother and offspring: a literature review," *Expert Review of Endocrinol & Metab,* vol. 14, pp. 63–74, 2019.

51. M. A. Maggard, I. Yermilov, Z. Li, M. Maglione, S. Newberry, M. Suttorp, *et al.*, "Pregnancy and fertility following bariatric surgery: a systematic review," *JAMA,* vol. 300, pp. 2286–2296, 2008.

52. K. Willis, C. Alexander, and E. Sheiner, "Bariatric surgery and the pregnancy complicated by gestational diabetes," *Curr Diab Rep,* vol. 16, pp. 1–11, 2016.

53. H. Buchwald, "The evolution of metabolic/bariatric surgery," *Obes Surg,* vol. 24, pp. 1126–1135, 2014.

54. E. Akkary, "Bariatric surgery evolution from the malabsorptive to the hormonal era," *Obes Surg,* vol. 22, pp. 827–831, 2012.

55. M. d. F. H. S. Diniz, M. T. C. Diniz, S. R. A. Sanches, P. P. C. de Almeida Salgado, M. M. A. Valadão, C. P. Freitas, *et al.*, "Glycemic control in diabetic patients after bariatric surgery," *Obes Surg,* vol. 14, pp. 1051–1055, 2004.

56. H. Buchwald, Y. Avidor, E. Braunwald, M. D. Jensen, W. Pories, K. Fahrbach, *et al.*, "Bariatric surgery: a systematic review and meta-analysis," *JAMA,* vol. 292, pp. 1724–1737, 2004.

57. A. Y. Weintraub, A. Levy, I. Levi, M. Mazor, A. Wiznitzer, and E. Sheiner, "Effect of bariatric surgery on pregnancy outcome," *IJGO,* vol. 103, pp. 246–251, 2008.

58. B. Aricha-Tamir, A. Y. Weintraub, I. Levi, and E. Sheiner, "Downsizing pregnancy complications: a study of paired pregnancy outcomes before and after bariatric surgery," *SOARD,* vol. 8, pp. 434–439, 2012.

59. E. Sheiner, T. S. Menes, D. Silverberg, J. S. Abramowicz, I. Levy, M. Katz, *et al.*, "Pregnancy outcome of patients with gestational diabetes mellitus following bariatric surgery," *AJOG,* vol. 194, pp. 431–435, 2006.

60. I. Guelinckx, R. Devlieger, P. Donceel, S. Bel, S. Pauwels, A. Bogaerts, *et al.*, "Lifestyle after bariatric surgery: a multicenter, prospective cohort study in pregnant women," *Obes Surg,* vol. 22, pp. 1456–1464, 2012.

61. E. Sheiner, K. Willis, and Y. Yogev, "Bariatric surgery: impact on pregnancy outcomes," *Curr Diab Rep,* vol. 13, pp. 19–26, 2013.

62. K. Willis and E. Sheiner, "Bariatric surgery and pregnancy: the magical solution?," *J Perinat Med,* vol. 41, pp. 133–140, 2013.

63. D. Shai, I. Shoham-Vardi, D. Amsalem, D. Silverberg, I. Levi, and E. Sheiner, "Pregnancy outcome of patients following bariatric surgery as compared with obese women: a population-based study," *J Matern- Fetal Neonatal Med,* vol. 27, pp. 275–278, 2014.

64. E. Sheiner, A. Levy, D. Silverberg, T. S. Menes, I. Levy, M. Katz, *et al.*, "Pregnancy after bariatric surgery is not associated with adverse perinatal outcome," *AJOG,* vol. 190, pp. 1335–1340, 2004.

65. D. Amsalem, B. Aricha-Tamir, I. Levi, D. Shai, and E. Sheiner, "Obstetric outcomes after restrictive bariatric surgery: what happens after 2 consecutive pregnancies?," *SOARD,* vol. 10, pp. 445–449, 2014.

66. J. R. Wax, M. G. Pinette, A. Cartin, and J. Blackstone, "Female reproductive issues following bariatric surgery," *OGS,* vol. 62, pp. 595–604, 2007.

67. A. Karmon and E. Sheiner, "Timing of gestation after bariatric surgery: should women delay pregnancy for at least 1 postoperative year?," *Am J Perinatol,* vol. 25, pp. 331–333, 2008.

68. M. M. M. Jayawardane, M. Rajakaruna, K. S. A. Perera, U. Chandradeva, H. L. T. C. Abeywickrama, and A. Fernando, "Is it HAPO/IADPSG and NICE/National Consensus Document criteria for diagnosis of GDM best suit for Sri Lanka; Outcomebased comparative study," *Sri Lanka J Obstet Gyn,* vol. 44, 2022.

69. T. Dias, S. H. M. Siraj, I. M. Aris, L.-J. Li, and K. H. Tan, "Comparing different diagnostic guidelines for gestational diabetes mellitus in relation to birthweight in Sri Lankan women," *Front Endocrinol,* vol. 9, p. 682, 2018.

70. A. Kumarage, A. Kaluarachchi, S. Wijeratne, and P. Udagama, "A Sri Lankan pilot case–control study on gestational diabetes mellitus: oxidative stress and a potential diagnostic marker panel," *Int J Diab Dev Ctries,* pp. 1–7, 2024.

Transformative Applied Research in Computing, Engineering, Science and Technology – Dr. Damayanthi Dahanayake et al. (eds)
© *2024 Taylor & Francis Group, London, ISBN 978-1-041-01782-0*

30

Trends in Forensic Microbiology and the Future Directions in Sri Lanka

A. I. Karunanayake
Department of Life Sciences,
Faculty of Science, NSBM Green University,
Sri Lanka

M. A. Thilakarathna
Department of Life Sciences,
Faculty of Science, NSBM Green University,
Sri Lanka
Department of Microbiology,
Faculty of Medicine, Wayamba University,
Sri Lanka

I. Khan, N. Ullah
Department of Biotechnology,
Faculty of Chemical and Life Sciences,
Abdul Wali Khan University,
Pakistan

B. Deepachandi*
Department of Life Sciences,
Faculty of Science, NSBM Green University,
Sri Lanka

Abstract

Forensic science is known to be a broad field in which scientific methods are used as solutions to resolve criminal cases and legal concerns. As for the subdivision of forensic science, forensic microbiology has been extensively utilized for the evaluation of the cause and manner of death, individual recognition, crime scene detection, and postmortem interval estimation. Globally, there is an emphasis on creating novel techniques for microbial identification to tackle challenging forensic problems. Therefore, current research is broadening the applications of forensic microbiology. Since the beginning of the pre-20th century, forensic microbiology has evolved from simple culture techniques to culture-independent techniques and ultimately to advanced methods such as machine learning algorithms and artificial intelligence (AI). These techniques can be used to find microbial evidence in different criminal investigations. However, in the Sri Lankan situation, the field of forensic microbiology is infrequently used and is in the primary stages of

*Corresponding author: bhagya.d@nsbm.ac.lk

DOI: 10.1201/9781003616368-30

usage in local investigations. The use of microorganisms in the field of forensics can be further strengthened through the development of deep learning techniques and AI. However, further actions should be taken to minimize their limitations, and more consideration should be given regarding the application of these current advanced techniques to be implemented in Sri Lanka.

Keywords

Forensic microbiology, Artificial intelligence, Forensic science, Sri Lanka

1. Introduction

Forensic science is known as the use of scientific methods and ideas to resolve legal issues and criminal cases. It involves acquiring, analyzing, and deciphering tangible evidence from crime scenes to ascertain the truth, pinpoint suspects, and support the administration of justice [1]. It is a broad field including the subdivisions of forensic toxicology, forensic anthropology, forensic odontology, forensic pathology, digital forensics, forensic microbiology, and other disciplines [2].

Within the specialized subject of forensic science, forensic microbiology uses microbiological concepts to resolve legal and criminal problems. It entails the examination of microorganisms, including bacteria, viruses, fungi, and other microscopic organisms to give evidence and insights for investigations [3]. During the pre-20th century, forensic microbiology began with simple culture techniques and evolved with the introduction of culture-independent techniques like DNA analysis, fingerprinting, and advanced PCR techniques. In the 21st century, DNA sequencing techniques like next generation sequencing (NGS) were introduced. Later in the 21st century, the development of metagenomics, microbial profiling, bioinformatics, artificial intelligence (AI), and machine learning algorithms were established [2]. The development of tools in the forensic microbiology field has strengthened their use in investigations including instances of finding geolocation, personal identification, tracing evidence of a crime scene, determining the manner and cause of death, involvement of sexual contact and, cases regarding drowning [4].

However, the Sri Lankan situation of forensic science is still evolving. Currently, the use of DNA analysis, fingerprint analysis, ballistics, toxicology, and digital forensics is present. Nevertheless, the use of forensic microbiology in Sri Lanka is very uncommon [5].

Therefore, understanding the field of forensic microbiology, the development of its tools and applications, and how classical techniques can be incorporated with the current development of AI and machine learning algorithms are important for the local forensic field to gain accurate and efficient results regarding legal issues and criminal cases.

2. History of Forensic Microbiology

Microbiology played a modest role in the field of forensic science for more than a decade. In the pre-20th century, forensic microbiology began with simple culture techniques where microbes were isolated and viewed under the microscope, which enabled the involvement of microbes in crime scenes [6]. In the late 1980s, the only methods for identifying and detecting microorganisms were phenotypic procedures linked to antigenic and/ or antimicrobial resistance profiles [2]. These methods depended on culture-dependent techniques and only allowed determination at the genus and/or species level [4].

Afterwards, the introduction of DNA analysis revolutionized the field of forensic microbiology [3]. DNA fingerprinting, applied for the identification of individual organisms, contributes to crime investigation by connecting the biological samples found at a crime scene [6]. The sensitivity of using microbes in an investigation increased with the development of advanced PCR technologies for efficient DNA analysis [8]. In the early 21st century, microbial DNA sequencing technologies were introduced [7]. NGS techniques allowed for high throughput sequencing, enabling the analysis of entire microbial genomes [8]. During the period 2000-2010, improvements in metagenomics occurred, involving the analysis of the collective genome of microbial communities [3]. This method is significantly useful for unique samples, such as those from soil or mixed body fluids. During the decomposition process, patterns of bacterial community activity were detected and identified using pyrosequencing at specific time intervals [9].

In 2010, the foundation of microbial profiling and forensic analysis was established, allowing for the observation of specific microbial communities associated with individuals or environments [6]. The employment of microbiomes in criminal investigations is extending beyond bio-crime, bioterrorism, and epidemiology [7]. They are utilized to determine the causes of death, including drownings, toxicology, hospital-acquired diseases, unanticipated child death, and shaken baby syndrome, and also aid in the identification of mortals via skin, hair, and body fluid microbiomes [7]. Furthermore, soil microbiomes aid with proper geolocation and posthumous age prediction using thanato-microbiome and epinecrotic microbial communities [10]. Bioinformatics contributes to microbial identification which links samples to unique sources, building associations between microbial profiles and crime scenes. In this method, microbiomes are used in localization, personal identity, trace evidence, determining the cause of death, and estimating the postmortem interval (PMI) [3].

From the year 2020's and beyond, emerging technologies such as nanopore sequencing and advanced bioinformatics algorithms are further improving the field of forensic microbiology [3]. Furthermore, the integration of AI and machine learning enables to comprehend the intricate microbial data sets [11]. Researchers have created and proven machine-learning algorithms for analyzing bacterial cultures, detecting microbes in images, and predicting antimicrobial susceptibility patterns due to the growing desire for faster turnaround times and better results [12].

3. Classical Forensic Microbiology Techniques

The techniques used in forensic microbiology can be categorized into two major groups, namely, culture-dependent and culture-independent methods. The culture-dependent methods allow for the separation of viable microorganisms from materials by growing certain kinds of bacteria in restricted microbiological media. This method offers a way to describe these microbes with a high level of precision and taxonomic resolution [2]. This technique has drawbacks because of the lengthy cultivation times needed by certain microbes, nonetheless, its capability to squarely recognize taxa makes it essential in forensic investigations. Furthermore, the identification of bacteria utilizing these methods can be difficult in forensic analysis since up to 80% of bacterial species found in the human body are deemed to be "unculturable", and roughly 99% of environmental bacteria cannot be effectively grown in laboratory conditions [2].

Culture-independent techniques are more comprehensive and sensitive compared to the culture-dependent techniques [13]. In 16s rRNA gene sequencing, a forensic scientist can recognize and describe the types of microbes found in samples taken from crime scenes. This technique helps to profile the microbial populations linked to a particular location or individual [4]. Although accurate, they take much longer to reach an end point, which is an undesirable feature in every criminal inquiry [14]. With metagenomic analysis, the complete microbial population found in forensic evidence can be identified. Researchers have detected marine bacteria in the blood and organs of drowning victims through high-throughput metagenomic analysis using 454-pyrosequencing. The current cost of 454-pyrosequencing may be too expensive for regular testing. However, this is anticipated to decrease gradually. Additional blood and organ samples from different victims, including those who did not drown, should be studied in upcoming studies [15]. High-throughput NGS can investigate microbial DNA samples efficiently in large volumes. These techniques allow detailed profiling of microbial populations present in forensic samples. Research shows that bacterial populations can be used as a "microbial clock" to estimate the PMI. However, high-throughput sequencing is too costly for everyday inspections, and various other forensic methods have required significant evaluation and improvement decades after they were first created [8].

Matrix-associated laser desorption/ionization time-of-flight mass spectroscopy (MALDI-TOF MS) is another powerful tool in forensic microbiology used for quick and suitable identification of microorganisms, including bacteria, viruses, and fungi based on their specific mass spectrum. MALDI-TOF mass spectrometry was investigated as an alternate approach for identifying organisms linked with the thanatomicrobiota and epinecrotic communities [16].

Microbial forensic markers can be genomic regions or genera that are exclusive to a particular strain of a microbe. A study depicts the potential use of mRNA, miRNA, DNA methylation, and microbiological indicators for tissue recognition in a forensic setting. However, the selection of an appropriate marker to infer a specific bodily fluid or tissue type may be difficult. [17]. A novel molecular technique for determining drowning as an explanation of death by real-time PCR with TaqMan probes detected eight bacterioplankton species simultaneously. PCR detection of bacterioplankton types offered valuable insights into the aspirated water type. As for its development, quick, simpler, and high-throughput PCR testing for determining water aspiration and type, along with traditional diatom analysis and/or several other techniques, could boost the likelihood that a drowning-related mortality judgment is correct [15].

The microbial forensic database includes microbial genome data that helps in the comparison of forensic samples with known microbial profiles. A study depicts forensic examination of skin and bodily fluids for the human microbiota across different geographical locations, focusing on the skin, saliva, vaginal fluid, and stool. It discovered variations in microbiome distribution based on body component and location, utilizing microbiome data from different parts of the human body across 35 different nations sourced from the Forensic Microbiome Database. The limitations of these comparative analyses impact worldwide comparisons, including those of human parts, bodily fluids, and geographic regions. More research is required to ascertain the strength and determination of microbial diversity and the availability of vigorous forensic biomarkers, considering geographic locations and lifestyle variables [18, 19, 20].

4. Microbial Evidence Role in Criminal Investigations

Humans have a rich microbial community that interacts with and influences their surroundings and analyzing these microbial profiles of humans and their surroundings can provide valuable insights for forensics [4]. Therefore, forensic microbiology finds application in various areas such as geolocation, personal identification, trace evidence analysis, determination of manner and cause of death, assessment of sexual contact, and investigation of drowning incidents, respectively.

By studying the distinctive microbiological content in various settings, forensic scientists can pinpoint the geographical origin of a sample, assist in the location of crime scenes, or identify the source of evidence [3]. One study showed that soil taken from the sole of a shoe decoded the resemblance of soil bacterial 16S rDNA profiles produced by the method for denaturing gradient gel electrophoresis [22]. Also, individualized microbial signatures provide an extra degree of identification, enhancing conventional techniques like DNA analysis and providing forensic investigators with more comprehensive tools for identifying individuals [3]. Researchers examined microbial profiles specific to several body sites and tried to correlate them with 25–105 microbiome profiles on the individual's initial and follow-up visits to the sampling site. According to the researchers, 30% of the individuals could still be individually identified many months after the initial sampling, demonstrating the value of these profiles in distinguishing individuals over time [22].

Microbes are also involved in the tracking of a material's origin. Microbe pattern analysis can be used to connect proof to certain places or people, which helps to clarify the events surrounding a case. One study conducted in a controlled environment, proved that distinct modes of death were linked with Lactobacillus, Rhizobiales, and Enterobacteriaceae, Sediminibacterium. These correlations may eventually serve as predictive markers that aid in identifying the cause of death through additional study [23]. Postmortem changes in microbial populations reveal information about the method and reason for death [3]. According to the studies, *Actinomyces* sp. proved to be more common in suicide instances, while *Xanthomonadaceae* was more common in cases involving hospital related fatalities [23]. Forensic microbiology can be employed to investigate sexual assaults. Comprehensive research revealed that the pubic microbiota remains stable for six months, even under varying storage conditions and temperatures. This stability appears to be influenced by gender differences, as men are more likely to have *Bacillales* or *Corynebacterium*, whilst women may have *Bifidobacteriales* and/or *Lactobacillales* [2].

When victims are rescued from wet surroundings, drowning is a common cause of death; pathology results are used whenever possible to rule out other potential causes. Diatoms, aquatic algae from the phytoplankton family, are examined to determine the type and quantity of water inhaled into the lungs prior to death, provided their density is sufficiently high. However, this method has limitations: it is less effective if diatoms are too large, if their concentration is too low to enter the bloodstream and organs, or if they are present in non-drowned bodies. Consequently, research increasingly investigates the role of small aquatic microorganisms such as bacteria, cyanobacteria, and bacterioplankton as potential indicators of drowning [2].

5. Deep Learning In Forensic Science and the Future Challenges

Traditional forensic analysis approaches have undergone an evolution in recent years, due to the tremendous breakthroughs produced by the merging of forensic science and deep learning [12]. Deep learning is a branch of machine learning that utilizes multi-layered artificial neural networks to discover intricate patterns and characteristics from unprocessed data. This technology enables forensic scientists to improve the automation, productivity, and precision of a variety of forensic activities [12]. The use of artificial intelligence combined with whole genome sequencing is expected to increase and become widespread in forensic microbiology [12].

Currently, forensic microbiology uses a variety of machine learning models such as random forest (RF), support vector machine (SVM), and AdaBoost, and they have emerged as viable approaches for several forensic incidents [12]. Identification of individual humans is among the main uses of forensic microbiology in situations where a microbiological method offers an overview of scenarios with the identification of the microbiota on skin, saliva, hair, or objects that are contaminated in the case of blood or tissue evidence [25]. Therefore, the Unique Fraction metric (UniFrac) and hierarchical clustering are employed for the identification of salivary microbiomes and microorganisms linked with the skin. The RF model is used for examining bacteria found in pubic hair [27].

Furthermore, there is proof that forensic microbiology, combined with machine learning, may determine geolocation to a considerable degree. A study showed that geolocation inference heavily relies on the human gut microbiota and is backed by correlations derived from conventional statistical techniques like Wilcoxon's rank-sum test and similarity analysis [1]. The Analysis of Similarities (ANOSIM) network, and UniFrac were utilized in 2014 to examine the human saliva microbiota [27].

Deep neural networks (DNNs) were also effectively utilized later in 2020 to detect human blood specimens that were significant to forensics [28]. According to recent research, Convolutional neural network (CNN) is capable of distinguishing between bacteria and algae from microbiome photos. The use of microbiological computer image analysis is mostly concerned with the division, aggregation, categorization, and count of microbes [1]. In 2019, witnessed the use and training of a CNN model with a validation rate based on the GoogLeNet Inception V3 architecture to detect diatoms, with 97.33% demonstrating the effectiveness and affordability of deep learning as an automatic diatom identification technique [1].

AI's new algorithms will help with micro-biotic analysis for forensic applications. The main tactic to help AI perform better is to concentrate on building a larger microbiota collection. The creation of a forensic microbial bank is critically required given the diversity of microbial populations needed [1]. Furthermore, there is still a need for more standardization of the processes for forensic microorganism sampling and analysis. Additionally, combining the microbiome data from animal experiments, rendering the intricate influences of sample types, locations, environmental factors, and postmortem alterations, is necessary. Further, consideration should be given to human samples as well as specific items found at the crime scene [1].

Therefore, it is possible to overcome these challenges and limitations by building extensive microbial genomic databases to help identify particular microbial strains discovered at crime scenes by creating techniques to describe distinct microbiological signatures connected to particular settings or people. It may help identify culprits and connect them to crime scenes, investigating the evolution and interactions of microbial communities in forensic environments like decomposition, soil, or water. It further shed light on the origin of a sample or its PMI [2].

6. Conclusion

Forensic microbiology is a gradually growing field that started with the birth of simple culture techniques. Afterwards, by passing the milestones of DNA fingerprinting, advanced PCR techniques, NGS, metagenomics, microbial profiling, and bioinformatics, the recent integration of deep learning techniques has been established. These advancements in the forensic microbiology field expand investigations' powers in ways that were never before possible. Using modern deep learning algorithms in conjunction with conventional techniques like DNA analysis and microbial culture, forensic specialists may analyze complicated biological evidence with greater capacity, accuracy, and rapidity.

Currently, in Sri Lanka, DNA analysis, fingerprint analysis, ballistics, toxicology, and digital forensics are mostly used. However, the use of forensic microbiology is very scarce in Sri Lanka [5]. The development of this field should evolve by integrating classical forensic microbiology techniques with deep learning trends, which have enormous potential to transform forensic microbiology and improve justice in contemporary times.

REFERENCES

1. Y. Huiya, et al. "Trends in Forensic Microbiology: From Classical Methods to Deep Learning." Front. Microbiol. 14 (March) 2023.
2. M.Oliveria and A. António. "Microbial Forensics: New Breakthroughs and Future Prospects." Appl. Microbiol. Biotechnol. 102 (24): 10377–91, 2018
3. J. Robinson, Z. Pasternak, C. Mason and E. Elhaik. "Forensic Applications of Microbiomics: A Review." Front. Microbiol. 11 (January), 2021.
4. S. Mateusz, A. Piecuch, J. Borzecka, M. Kadej and R.Ogórek. "Microbial Traces and Their Role in Forensic Science." J. Appl.Microbiol. 132 (4): 2547–57, 2022.
5. Gunathilake and I. Gooneratne. "Drowning Associated Diatoms in Sri Lanka." SLJFMSL 1 (2): 23, 2011.
6. A. Cláudia-Ferreira, et al. "The Future Is Now: Unraveling the Expanding Potential of Human (Necro)Microbiome in Forensic Investigations." Microorganisms 11 (10): 2509–9, 2023.
7. K. Palvi, P. Prakash, Yadav, Sand, V. Saran. "Microbiome Analysis: An Emerging Forensic Investigative Tool." Forensic Sci. Int. 340 (November): 111462, 2022.

8. G. Juanjuan, et al. "Potential Use of Bacterial Community Succession for Estimating Post-Mortem Interval as Revealed by High-Throughput Sequencing." Sci. Rep. 6 (1), 2016.

9. J. Pechal, et al. "The Potential Use of Bacterial Community Succession in Forensics as Described by High Throughput Metagenomic Sequencing." Int. J. Legal Med. 128 (1): 193–205,2013.

10. G, Javan, et al. "An Interdisciplinary Review of the Thanatomicrobiome in Human Decomposition." Forensic Science, Med and Pathol15 (1): 75–83,2018.

11. H. Johnson, et al. "A Machine Learning Approach for Using the Postmortem Skin Microbiome to Estimate the Postmortem Interval." Edited by Raymond Schuch. *PLOS ONE* 11 (12): e0167370,2016.

12. A.Mishra , S.Khan, A.Das and B.Das. "Evolution of Diagnostic and Forensic Microbiology in the Era of Artificial Intelligence." Cureus, September,2023.

13. "South Asian Journal of Research in Microbiology." n.d. Journalsajrm.com. Accessed June 29, 2024.

14. C. Ismail, G. Javan, A. Pozhitkov and P. Noble. "Distinctive Thanatomicrobiome Signatures Found in the Blood and Internal Organs of Humans." J. Microbiol. Methods 106 (November): 1–7,2014.

15. T. Uchiyama, et al "A New Molecular Approach to Help Conclude Drowning as a Cause of Death: Simultaneous Detection of Eight Bacterioplankton Species Using Real-Time PCR Assays with TaqMan Probes." Forensic Sci. Int. 222 (1-3): 11–26,2012.

16. F.Dell'Annunziata, et al. "Postmortem Interval Assessment by MALDI-TOF Mass Spectrometry Analysis in Murine Cadavers." J. Appl. Microbiol. 132 (1): 707–14, 2021.

17. Sijen. T. "Molecular Approaches for Forensic Cell Type Identification: On MRNA, MiRNA, DNA Methylation and Microbial Markers." Forensic Sci. Int. Genet 18 (September): 21–32, 2015.

18. Hye-Won.C, and E. Yong-Bin."Forensic Analysis of Human Microbiome in Skin and Body Fluids Based on Geographic Location." Front. Cell. Infect. Microbiol. 11 (August), 2021.

19. S.Tridico, D, Murray, J. Addison, K.Kirkbride and B.Michael ."Metagenomic Analyses of Bacteria on Human Hairs: A QualitativeAssessment for Applications in Forensic Science." Investig. Genet 5 (1),2014.

20. M.Upadhyay, P.Shrivastava, K.Verma,and B.Joshi. "Recent Advancements in Identification and Detection of Saliva as Forensic Evidence: A Review." Egypt. J. Forensic Sci. 13 (1),2023.

21. S.Anothai,S. Katekeaw and K.Lomthaisong . "Forensic Soil Investigation from the 16S RDNA Profiles of Soil Bacteria Obtained by Denaturing Gradient Gel Electrophoresis." Chiang Mai J. Sci. 43 (4): 748,2016.

22. E.Franzosa,et al. "Identifying Personal Microbiomes Using Metagenomic Codes." Proc. Natl. Acad. Sci. U.S.A. 112 (22): E2930–38,2010.

23. A.Advenier, N. Guillard,J Alvarez.,L.Martrille, and G.Grandmaison . "Undetermined Manner of Death: An Autopsy Series." J. Forensic Sci. 61 (August): S154–58,2015.

24. J. Li.et al. "Long-Term Effects of Xuezhikang on Blood Pressure in Hypertensive Patients with Previous Myocardial Infarction: Data from the Chinese Coronary Secondary Prevention Study (CCSPS)." Clin. exp. hypertens. (N.Y.N.Y., 1993, Online) 32 (8): 491–98,2010.

25. D.Butzbach. "The Influence of Putrefaction and Sample Storage on Post-Mortem Toxicology Results." Forensic Sci Med Pathol 6 (1): 35–45,2009.

26. N.Fierer,et al."Forensic Identification Using Skin Bacterial Communities." Proc. Natl. Acad. Sci. U.S.A. 107 (14): 6477–81,2010.

27. J.Escobar, B.Klotz, B.Valdes and G.Agudelo . "The Gut Mi7crobiota of Colombians Differs from that of Americans, Europeans and Asians." BMC Microbiol. 14 (1),2014.

28. E.Costello, "Bacterial Community Variation in Human Body Habitats across Space and Time." N. Y. sci. j. 326 (5960): 1694–97,2009.

Transformative Applied Research in Computing, Engineering, Science and Technology – Dr. Damayanthi Dahanayake et al. (eds)
© 2024 Taylor & Francis Group, London, ISBN 978-1-041-01782-0

31

Importance of Studying the Bioactive Compounds in *Vateria Copallifera* (Hal), an Endemic Plant in Sri Lanka— A Narrative Review

N.M. Hettiarachchi,
D. Dahanayake*, and M.S.K. Rabindrakumar

Faculty of Science,
NSBM Green University, Pitipana, Homagama,
Sri Lanka

Abstract

Vateria copallifera, Hal is a seasonal fruiting, Sri Lankan endemic plant that belongs to the Dipterocarpaceae family. It has been used in food preparations and traditional medicine to maintain the health of traditional Sri Lankan communities. Various bioactive properties of *V. copallifera* extracts or scrapes have been reported in many studies such as antioxidant, antibacterial, anti-inflammatory, anticancer, larvicidal activity, sedative activities, and other therapeutic practices. However, the isolation, identification, and characterization studies of *V. copallifera* bioactive compounds in those extracts or scrapes are limited. Hence, it is crucial to understand the importance of studying their bioactive compounds and properties to utilize in many applications including modern integrated food therapies as an endangered, endemic plant in Sri Lanka. This review paper describes the significant potential of *V. copallifera's* bioactive compounds while discussing their properties and their active chemical nature.

Keywords

Bioactive compounds, Bioactive properties, Integrated food therapy, Sri Lankan traditional medicine, Vateria copallifera (Hal)

1. Introduction

Hal (*Vateria copallifera*) is an endemic plant in Sri Lanka that belongs to the Dipterocarpaceae family and inherits a rich legacy as an indigenous food source. It has been used to make traditional foods like hal pittu, hal gutti, and hal helapa, which could be replaced by refined flour nowadays

[1]. In Sri Lankan traditional practices, the extracts, and scrapes of *V. copallifera* have been used to fulfill the people's medical requirements. Figure 31.1 shows the parts of *V. copallifera* that compose many traditional usages and treatments in ethnomedicine.

The extracts and scrapes of *V. copallifera* are comprised of many bioactive properties that have been shown in

*Corresponding author: damayanthi.d@nsbm.ac.lk

DOI: 10.1201/9781003616368-31

Fig. 31.1 The parts of *V. copallifera* plant that compose traditional uses and treatments in ethnomedicine

Source: dilmahconservation.org and wikipedia.org

and scrapes is the pioneer drive for the progress of natural bioactive-related studies during the recent decades. With the huge technological improvements that emerged recently, pharmaceuticals, nutraceuticals, medicine, food additives, and even natural pesticide sectors in agriculture have become interested in bioactive compounds from natural plant sources such as *V. copallifera*. However, the importance of revealing active chemical compounds discretely in *V. copallifera* has created a huge potential for scientific research by isolating, identifying, characterizing, and screening their bioactive properties. Thus, this review paper describes the importance of studying the bioactive compounds in *V. copallifera* and their utilization as medicaments in many applications including modern integrated food therapies. Further, it would provide indirect protection to *V. copallifera* as an endangered, endemic plant in Sri Lanka.

2. Ethnomedicinal Uses of *V. Copallifera*

The classical findings have shown that every part of Hal has been used in traditional medicine. Many reported classical studies have revealed that it has been used for diabetes mellitus for a long time [3]. Furthermore, the decoction of the stem bark of *V. copallifera* by boiling with water has been treated for ulcers, diarrhea, and rheumatic pain in Sri Lankan traditional medicine [4]. The curing of cognitive damage and mental disorders with ethnomedicine treatments using the herbal extract of Hal for steam bathing, oil treatments, and water-extracted decoctions has been popular in Sri Lankan village communities. Essential oils of the root and bark of *V. copallifera* have been used in Sri Lankan ethnomedicine as a wound-washing medicament based on their antibacterial properties, as well as for the treatments of hemorrhoids, bile-related disorders, diarrhea, rheumatic pains, and diabetes mellitus [5]. Many disorders such as nervous system diseases, vision problems, gastrointestinal tract infections, ear diseases, skin diseases, and cardiovascular diseases have been cured using the extracts of seeds and the flowers of *V. copallifera* [4]. The oils extracted from seeds have been used for curing medical conditions related to mucus, bile, and rheumatoid arthritis in traditional medicine [6]. The smoke from the *V. copallifera* resin has been used in the treatment of hemorrhoids, and internal bleeding. Furniture has also been made using the wood of *V. copallifera* to heal cognitive problems [5].

classical studies. Fig. 31.2 illustrates the schematic diagram for the properties of *V.copallifera* extracts/scrapes with their bioactive compounds. Accordingly, they have been reported as antimicrobial (antibacterial), anti-inflammatory, antioxidant, wound healing, anti-cancer, analgesic, larvicidal, sedative activities, and other therapeutic properties [2]. However, the studies of isolated bioactive compounds from Hal extracts and scrapes that comprised the unique properties have been done limitedly. Thus, those classical studies have demonstrated the properties as a synergistic effect of various bioactive compounds of extract and scrapes of *V.copallifera*.

The increased understanding of the active chemical nature of the diverse bioactive compounds of *V. copallifera* extracts

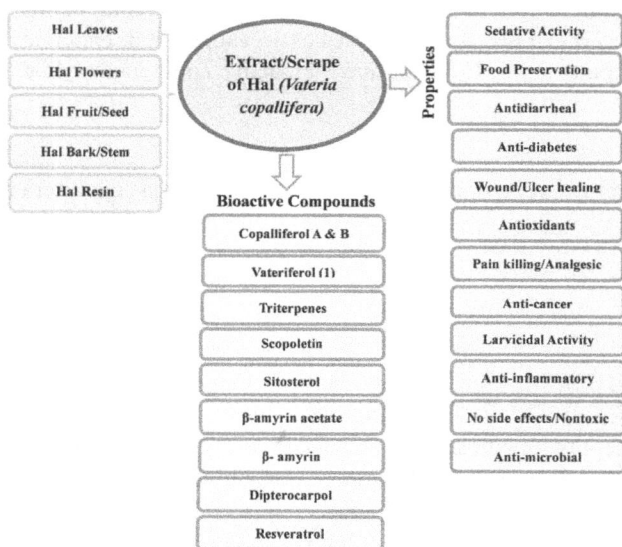

Fig. 31.2 The schematic diagram for the properties of *V. copallifera* plant extracts/scrapes with their bioactive compounds

Source: Author

3. Food-Related uses of *V. Copallifera*

Dried flour or wet scrapes of Hal seed, with a unique bitter taste, have been used in traditional healthy food preparations after debittering [7]. This debittering treatment developed by intuition among the Sri Lankan community over time highlights the connection between therapeutic and nutritional values. The resin and stem bark of *V. copallifera* have been used in coconut and kithul tapping as preservatives to prevent sap from yeast fermentation in sugary-related food preparations such as treacle, candies, and honey. Hal resin has been used as a food coating to prevent pests and post-harvest losses in fruits and vegetables.

4. Other Traditional uses of *V. Copallifera*

V. copallifera resin oil has been used for the protection of palm-leaf manuscripts by Sri Lankan ancestors since ancient times. It has been applied to keep away the bacteria, mold, and insects that deteriorate the palm leaf manuscripts [8]. Moreover, different combinations of extract/smoke/resin emulsions of *V. copallifera* have been used for pest control in traditional agriculture. The mixing of *V. copallifera* parts on the field has been done to get a natural fertilizing and pesticide effect when they decompose in the agricultural field. As they are organic and biodegradable, the negative impact on the environment is minimal. Furthermore, resin-coated ropes have been used to control pests by dragging them on the field with two farmers to stick eggs and larvae. The stem of *V. copallifera* has been used for packing wooden boxes in the tea industry due to its pest-controlling effect.

5. Bioactive Compounds of *V. Copallifera*

The secondary metabolites of *V. copallifera* plant play defensive functionalities and can influence biological systems, hence, they are identified as 'bioactive' compounds [9]. The oligostilbenoids are important polyphenols in the Dipterocarpaceae family that are rarely found in other plants [10]. The phenolic acids and stilbenes are present at higher levels in *V. copallifera*. Amongst, resveratrol plays a significant role [11]. The resveratrol trimers exist in Hal as an interesting bioactive candidate for many remedies exhibiting many active biological properties. Studying and isolation of these bioactive compounds in *V. copallifera* and distinguishing their potential properties are extremely vital.

A few reported bioactive compounds of *V. copallifera* were copalliferol A, copalliferol B, vateriferol (1), triterpenes, scopoletin, hexamethylcoruleoellagic acid, sitosterol, hexamethylcoruleoellagic acid, pentamethylflavellagic acid, tetramethylellagic acid, chrysophanol, resveratrol, β-amyrin acetate, β-amyrin, and dipterocarpol, etc.

6. Significance of Bioactive Compounds in *V. Copallifera*

The distinguished bioactive compounds have played a significant role. Sufficient studies are rare and limited. A few bioactive compounds have been reported by isolating, identifying, characterizing, and generating their chemical structures such as copalliferol A, copalliferol B, and vateriferol (1) which are given in Fig. 31.3. These are antibacterial, polyphenolic resveratrol trimers.

The copalliferol A and B are isomers that have revealed antibacterial properties of Hal bark extract [12]. They have been isolated and reported as two new resveratrol trimers from the cold acetone extraction of Hal bark [13, 14]. Uvais et al. have proposed the chemical structure of copalliferol A with a $C_{42}H_{32}O_9$ formula formed with the three units of the oligomer of resveratrol ($C_{14}H_{12}O_3$) by oxidative phenolic coupling [11]. The filter paper disc method with the Mueller Hinton Agar (MHA) medium was used to identify the antibacterial properties of copalliferol A and B. The study has been observed that copalliferol A and B inhibit the growth of *Oxford staphylococcus* and *Escherichia coli*. It has been proven that using bark and

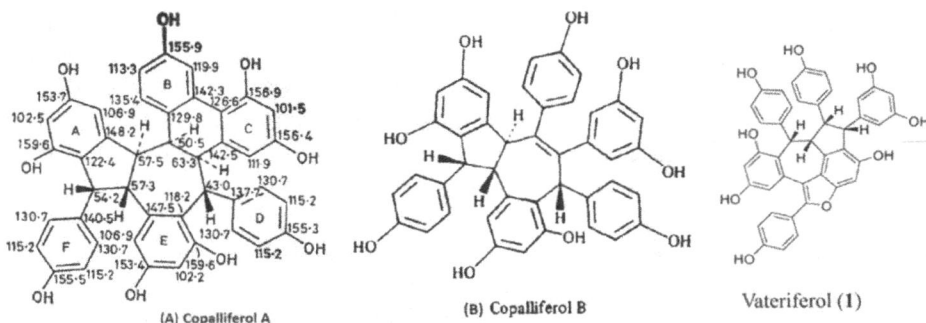

Fig. 31.3 The chemical structures of *V. copallifera* bioactive compounds (A) Copalliferol A[11], (B) Copalliferol B[14], and (C) Veteriferol (1)[15]

resin as food preservatives in Sri Lankan jaggery industry due to those bioactive compounds [11].

Additionally, copalliferol B has a powerful fluorescence under UV irradiation representing a stilbene system that controls the positions of double bonds. The role of stilbenoids has been identified for inhibiting fungal and bacterial attacks on Halwood [14]. Stemonoporol is isomeric with copalliferol A and an unstable polyphenol that can convert into copalliferol A when treated with formic acid or toluene-p-sulphonic acid [11].

Isolation, characterization, and revealing of the biological activity of vateriferol (1) from *V. copallifera* bark extract has been done by Samaradivakara et al. It has been proven for all-cis configurations using chromatography techniques [15]. A bioactivity assessment has been performed for its antioxidant, growth-inhibitory activities on cancer cell lines, enzyme inhibitory, neuroprotective, and anti-inflammatory activity. The extractions of ethanol, hexane, and ethyl acetate of *V.copallifera* bark have been used here [15]. Vateriferol (1) was found as a brown-amorphous solid with the $C_{42}H_{30}O_9$ formulation from NMR spectroscopic studies. Vateriferol (1) has revealed its weak ability on the 2,2-diphenyl-1-picrylhydrazyl (DPPH) free radical scavenging assay and the Oxygen Radical Absorbance Capacity (ORAC) activity compared to the positive standard Trolox. The neuroprotective activity has been investigated compared to enzymes, such as acetylcholine esterase (AChE), and butyrylcholinesterase (BChE). The inhibition of ChE enzymes of vateriferol (1) can be a potential treatment or potential healing candidate for the cognitive damages associated with Alzheimer's disease, senile dementia, myasthenia gravis, and Parkinson's disease [16]. The protease enzyme inhibitory activity of vateriferol (1) has been revealed with two enzymes called elastase, and serine proteases α-chymotrypsin. Vateriferol (1) has been shown 56% α-chymotrypsin inhibition [15]. The literature reports glutathione S-transferase (GST) inhibitors are important adjuvants in chemotherapy to enhance the efficacy of cancer chemotherapeutical drugs.

Vateriferol (1) has shown weak growth inhibition activity or weak cytotoxic potency of less than 50% against several cancer cell lines. It has been confirmed that various cancer cells (such as human breast, colon, and liver cancer cells) have weak growth inhibition activity by these resveratrol compounds [17].

7. Proven Properties of *V. Copelifera* Scrape/Extract by Classical Methods

Various properties of *V. copallifera* extract and scrape have been revealed in many studies. For instance, a stem bark aqueous extract of *V. copallifera* has been confirmed for its sedative activity using a rat hole-board model with Wistar male rats. The aqueous extract has exhibited its significant and dose-dependent sedative activity on male rats and revealed the effectiveness of rheumatic pain and ulcer treatments which were used in Sri Lankan traditional medicine [4].

Somarathna et al. have investigated the antidiarrheal potential of decoction of the *V. copallifera* stem bark using a rats-castor oil-induced diarrheal model. The rat feces improvement from a watery condition to a solid scientifically has justified the decoction of stem bark as an antidiarrheal remedy in Sri Lankan traditional medicine [18]. Samaradivakara et al. have revealed the volatile compounds of the n-hexane fraction of *V. copallifera* bark analysis with GC-MS and in-vitro bioactivities [19].

The integration of *V. copallifera* stem bark scrapes into foods has been practiced as a preservation technique based on controlling yeast fermentations in sugar solutions [3] and has been revealed in many ways [20]. Roshinie et al. have reported that cooling with dehumidifying of stem bark was the best drying method to use in foods due to its less bubble formation in the sugar solutions. The 60% sugar solution has been revealed as having the best antibacterial properties and the reducing-sugar content was decreased from 38.6 g/100 ml to 32.2 g/100 ml. The weight of the Hal bark scrapes/pieces to integrate with the sugar solution has been observed at a 1% (w/v%) concentration. The amount of water extraction of bark with 2% concentration (v/v%) can be used without varying the sensory properties [3].

Moreover, the resin of *V. copallifera* bark has been revealed as a food preservative [21], natural food coating, flavoring agents, and traditional recipes by classical methods. Methanol and acetone extracts of *V. copallifera* roots' essential oils have been reported to have higher antibacterial activity than the extract of essential oil of their seeds by Athukorala et al. It confirms the usage as a wound-washing medicament in Sri Lankan traditional Ayurveda [5].

The leaf, bark, pericarp, and seed extracts of *V. copallifera* with crude acetone have been stated for the mosquito larvicidal activity compared to *Culex quinquefasciatus* and *Aedes aegypti* (third-instar larvae) by Senadeera et al. The antibacterial activity of those extractions based on methicillin-resistant *Staphylococcus aureus* (MRSA) bacteria also has been revealed in that study [6].

Mihiranie et al. have reported macronutrients, functional, and textural properties of twenty-five Sri Lankan traditional sweetmeats prepared with standardized recipes using traditional food sources. Antioxidant potential (AP) has been analyzed with the methanol (80%, v/v%) extracts of those products by 2,2-Azino-bis (3-ethylbenzothiazoline-6-sulfonic acid) (ABTS) scavenging activity, ferric reducing antioxidant potential (FRAP), and DPPH free radical scavenging assays. The AP of Hal helapa made with rice flour, finger millet flour, and Hal seed scrape have been found pointedly ($p<0.05$) higher than the rest of the twenty-four Sri Lankan traditional sweetmeats. The AP was measured here as 222.44 ± 5.34 mM TEAC/g dry matter by DPPH assay and 240.28 ± 5.62 mM TEAC/g dry matter by ABTS assay for Hal helapa. Amongst the non-deep-fried sweetmeats, Hal helapa has been stated with the highest contents of total phenolic content (TPC), as 1.82 ± 0.06 GAE mg/g DM, and total flavonoid content (TFC), as 0.72 ± 0.07 QE mg/ g DM [2] .As the glycemic index (GI) of *V. copallifera* food sources has been recorded as the lowest in comparison to the other Sri Lankan underutilized flour sources and wheat flour, it has been proven its significance as an integrated solution in food therapies [7]. The TPC in raw flour of *V. copallifera* had been found as the highest phenolic content of 1162 ± 26 GAE mg/100g FW, as well as the highest antioxidant potential of 225 ± 7 μmol/g TEAC, reported by Senevirathna et al. [22].

8. Conclusion

This review expresses the importance of the stated bioactive properties of *V. copallifera* extracts, scrapes, and isolated bioactive compounds. Isolated, specific bioactive compounds from extracts/scrapes have been studied rarely. Amongst, copalliferol A and B have been reported frequently and found that they can be potential treatment or therapeutic candidates for medical conditions and other related integrated applications regarding antimicrobial properties. Different properties of them have not been scientifically reported in depth using isolated bioactive compounds. Vateriferol (1), as an all-cis configured resveratrol trimer has been shown to have high effectiveness as a potential therapeutic applicant for mental damages related to Parkinson's disease, Alzheimer's disease, etc. It is value mentioning that, there are limited or lacking findings about other bioactive compounds of Hal and in vivo and cell-based studies of isolated bioactive compounds.

9. Future Perspectives

In-depth scientific investigations from those identified gaps in the high-potential bioactive compounds of *V. copallifera* to reveal their bioactive properties are a must. However, there can be a valuable potency to the integration of these unique bioactive compounds of Hal as the applications in therapeutics and other fields. Aforementioned findings show the high potential of *V. copallifera* to integrate through

the food therapies as therapeutic candidates with the bioactive compounds' properties such as neuroprotective and other capacities. Studying the food-related properties of the isolated active compounds of *V. copallifera* may be advantageous as integrated food therapies for human well-being as a seasonal, endemic food source in Sri Lanka. Moreover, integrated pest management to gain sustainable environmental management is also an extra upcoming field that is indirectly related to these bioactive compounds of Hal and their novel products such as eco-friendly bio-fertilizers, pesticides, and fungicides. They can be economical, environmentally sound, and easy to practice by enhancing the cultivation of this endemic plant Hal within the country.

REFERENCES

1. Y. A. Geevananda, P. Gmawmmat, M. Uvais, S. ! Hjltanesawa'b, and S. Balasubramaniam$, "Distribution of some triterpenes and phenolic compounds in the extractives of endemic Dipterocarpaceae species of Sri Lanka," @ Pergamon Press Ltd. Printed in England, 1980.
2. M. K. S. Mihiranie, J. M. J. K. Jayasinghe, J. P. D. Wanasundara, and C. V. L. Jayasinghe, "Macronutrient Composition, Functional and Textural Properties of Selected Traditional Sweetmeats of Sri Lanka," *Journal of Agricultural Sciences - Sri Lanka*, vol. 18, no. 1, pp. 14–39, 2023, doi: 10.4038/jas.v18i1.10096.
3. Roshinie M.K.K., Navaratne S.B., and Jayamanne V.S., "Evaluation o f the Effect o f H al Bark (Vateria copallifera) on Controlling Yeast in Sugar Ferm entations," 2009.
4. W. D. Ratnasooriya, L. H. D. S. Lelwala, K. N. K. Kannangara, S. D. D. Sandanayaka, and E. R. H. S. S. Ediriweera, "Sedative activity of stem bark of the Sri Lankan endemic plant, Vateria copallifera," *Fitoterapia*, vol. 77, no. 4, pp. 331–332, Jun. 2006, doi: 10.1016/j.fitote.2006.03.012.
5. Athukorala D.A.D.O.D., Sivasinthujah S., Gnanakarunyan T. J., and Srikaran R., "Antibacterial activity of extracts of roots and seeds essential oil of Sri Lankan endemic plant, Vateria copallifera," 2022.
6. S. P. D. Senadeera, C. D. Wijayarathna, I. S. Weerasinghe, and K. A. K. C. Kulatunga, "Antibacterial and larvicidal activities of Sri Lankan endemic plant, Vateria copallifera," *Pharmacognosy Journal*, vol. 3, no. 19, pp. 75–81, 2011, doi: 10.5530/pj.2011.19.14.
7. Senavirathna R.M.I.S.K., Ekanayake S., and Jansz E.R., "Traditional and novel foods from indigenous flours: Nutritional quality, glycemic response, and potential use in food industry," *Starch/Staerke*, vol. 68, no. 9–10, pp. 999–1007, Sep. 2016, doi: 10.1002/star.201500175.
8. Udaya C. and Rathnabahu R.M.N., "Development of policies for access, management and preservation of the Palm-leaf manuscript collection of the University of Peradeniya library," *Sri Lankan Journal of Librarianship and Information Management*, vol. 1, no. 1, pp. 42–58, Mar. 2009, doi: 10.4038/sllim.v1i1.431.

9. Sytar O. and Iryna S., "Special Issue 'Bioactive Compounds from Natural Sources (2020, 2021),'" Mar. 01, 2022, *MDPI*. doi: 10.3390/molecules27061929.

10. Seo E.K. and Kinghorn A.D., "Bioactive constituents of the family Dipterocarpaceae," 2000.

11. Sotheeswaran S., Uvais M., Sultanbawa S., Surendrakumar S., and Bladon P., "Polyphenols from Dipterocarp Species. Copalliferol A and Stemonoporol," 1983.

12. Navaratne S.B., "Determination of the Effectiveness of Hal Bark (Vateria copallifera) as a Natural Preservative for Food Security of Confectionery Industry," 2015.

13. Geevananda Y A, Gunawardhana P, Uvais M, Sultanbawa S, and Balasubramaniam S, "Distribution of some triterpenes and phenolic compounds in the extractives of endemic Dipterocarpaceae species of Sri Lanka," @ Pergamon Press Ltd. Printed in England, 1980.

14. Geewananda Y.A. *et al.*, "Another antibacterial polyphenol, copalliferol B, from Vateria copallifera (dipterocarpaceae)," 1986.

15. Samaradivakara S.P. *et al.*, "A Bioactive Resveratrol Trimer from the Stem Bark of the Sri Lankan Endemic Plant Vateria copallifera," *J Nat Prod*, vol. 81, no. 8, pp. 1693–1700, Aug. 2018, doi: 10.1021/acs.jnatprod.7b00892.

16. Mukherjee P.K., Kumar V., Mal M., and Houghton P.J., "Acetylcholinesterase inhibitors from plants," *Phytomedicine*, vol. 14, no. 4, pp. 289–300, Apr. 2007, doi: 10.1016/j.phymed.2007.02.002.

17. Schroete A. and Marko D., "Resveratrol modulates the topoisomerase inhibitory potential of doxorubicin in human colon carcinoma cells," *Molecules*, vol. 19, no. 12, pp. 20054–20072, Dec. 2014, doi: 10.3390/molecules191220054.

18. Somarathna K.I.W.K., Rathnasooriya W.D., Jayakody J.R.A.C., and Ediriweera E.R.H.S.S., "Antidiarrhoeal activity of stembark of the Sri lankan endemic plant Vateria copallifera Retz," 2010. [Online]. Available: https://www.researchgate.net/publication/347936319

19. Samaradivakara S.P. *et al.*, "Bioactivities of n-hexane fraction of Vateria copallifera and GC–MS analysis of its phytoconstituents," *Ind Crops Prod*, vol. 97, pp. 87–92, Mar. 2017, doi: 10.1016/j.indcrop.2016.12.011.

20. H. P. D. T. Hewapathirana, H. T. R. Wijesekara, D. M. De Costa, U. M. A. Kumara, L. L. W. C. Yalegama, and T. M. S. G. Weerasinghe, "Evaluation of microbial quality of unfermented coconut sap with different collection methods," *Carpathian Journal of Food Science and Technology*, vol. 15, no. 4, pp. 91–98, 2023, doi: 10.34302/CRPJFST/2023.15.4.7.

21. Abeygunawardena S.I., "Studies on anti-fermentative activity of Vateria Copallifera Alston (Dipterocarpaceae)," 1981.

22. R. Mudiyanselage, I. Sanjeewa, and K. Senavirathna, "Study of the phenolics and the antioxidant capacities of some breakfast foods," 2013. [Online]. Available: https://www.researchgate.net/publication/267099046

Transformative Applied Research in Computing, Engineering, Science and Technology – Dr. Damayanthi Dahanayake et al. (eds)
© *2024 Taylor & Francis Group, London, ISBN 978-1-041-01782-0*

32

Cryptographic Technologies for Guaranteeing Compliance of Data Privacy to International Data Protection Laws— A Preliminary Study

Pawani Maheshika Bandara*,
Pabudi Abeyrathne
Department of Networking and Security,
NSBM Green University,
Sri Lanka

Manjula Sandirigama
Department of Computer Engineering,
Faculty of Engineering, University of Peradeniya,
Sri Lanka

Abstract

With the advent of interconnectivity in today's digital world, compliance with data protection laws has become a prime factor for protecting privacy. In turn, cryptographic technologies, like data encryption, authentication, and integrity, go a long way toward meeting compliance. Organizations seeking to ensure security in data privacy and security face numerous challenges in times of an ever-increasing data breach rate and the strict implementation of data protection laws like the California Consumer Privacy Act (CCPA) and the General Data Protection Regulation (GDPR). It presents connections between regulatory compliance and cryptographic technologies, hence showing how technical implementations interact with legal constraints. We put together broad regulatory compliance frameworks that would link international data protection legislation and cryptography solutions. This review conducts using case studies in establishing the importance of cryptographic techniques in maintaining data privacy standards prescribed by international regulations. Additionally, it provides clear guidance and best practices to organizations for delivering both robust confidentiality of information and compliance with the law. According to the findings from this review encryption and anonymization plays a crucial role in GDPR and CCPA compliance. Essential resources address encryption methods along with laws and cryptographic uses.

Keywords

Data privacy, Cryptographic technologies, Data protection laws, GDPR, CCPA, Data encryption

*Corresponding author: pawanimaheshika2003@gmail.com

DOI: 10.1201/9781003616368-32

1. Introduction

To ensure the data privacy regulatory frameworks organizations are face numerous cyber threats and stringent making compliance with international data protection laws. Cryptographic technology is a mechanism to ensure privacy and data security while making it essential for achieving compliance. This review article shows cryptographic methods and their alignment with global data protection regulations, highlighting their importance in modern data privacy. Stronger data protection rules, such as the CCPA and GDPR, have been introduced by regulatory agencies globally in response to the growing concerns over data privacy and the proliferation of data breaches. Strong data security measures are required by these standards, which frequently stipulate the use of cryptographic technology for data integrity, anonymisation, and encryption. However, organizations frequently struggle to balance compliance with these regulations while leveraging advanced cryptographic solutions. This discrepancy poses substantial challenges in achieving regulatory compliance and ensuring robust data security. This research focus on develops comprehensive regulatory compliance to framework which align with cryptographic technologies with international data protection laws, providing organizations with practical guidelines to navigate the complex landscape of data protection regulations.

The structure of this paper is as follows: Literature Review gives focus to such aspects as international legislation related to data protection, cryptographic technologies, and problems of business regulation. This paper will be succeeded by an Analysis of Cryptographic Solutions according to the Data Protection Laws section, examining the way cryptographic solutions address legal demands. Section Emerging Trends and Future Directions outlines new technologies relating to data privacy and security. The Compliance Challenges section elaborates on the problems organizations face in the quest to be compliant. Finally, the Conclusion and the Future Works sections reiterate the key insights drawn from the study and indicate the directions further research shall take in a bid to enhance data privacy and security using cryptography.

2. Methodology

This review utilises a qualitative methodology by examining detailed literature reviews and investigations. A wide range of resources, including theory-based articles and law documents, was examined for insight. These data sources reveal a detailed view of the cryptographic systems utilized for enforcing compliance with worldwide data protection laws, including GDPR and CCPA. The exploration compared relevant content and aimed to reveal patterns and weaknesses within existing implementations of cryptography in legal systems. This strategy allowed the retrieval of useful facts and laid the groundwork for the results and suggestions outlined in this review.

3. Literature Review

While sharing data, it is difficult to protect the data from being disclosed, and at the same time meet various countries' data protection regulations. This review gives information about the international legislations on data protection, the current state regarding cryptographic technologies and the compliance issues, which companies encounter and the way cryptographic solutions can match these criteria.

3.1 Data Protection Laws

CCPA in USA and GDPR in EU are two important data protection laws currently in force. These regulations have laid down several strict measures for accuracy of data, right to be forgotten, and data security. The GDPR instructs the organizations on the need to protect personal data by ensuring that they take reasonable measures such as encryption and anonymization of data. Information should also be safeguarded from changes by anyone who is not allowed to do so [1]. The CCPA mandates businesses to implement reasonable security measures and grants individuals three core rights: the right of control over their personal data, the right to deletion, and the right to object to the use of their data, especially the sale of the same [2].

3.2 Cryptography

Cryptography is the key to assuring the protection of data and particularly when in the process of being transmitted. These include encryption, decryption, hash functions, digital signatures, and security protocols.

Encryption is a fundamental security type because it converts plain text messages into cipher text so that only those who are authorized can understand them. The symmetric encryption routines are Data Encryption Standard (DES) and the Advanced Encryption Standard (AES), while the asymmetric encryption utilizes Rivest-Shamir-Adleman (RSA) [3,4]. For example, the type of public key cryptography called elliptic curve cryptography (ECC) is useful in a low-resource environment [5,6]. The practical applications of these technologies include cryptography for securing data communication over the internet, key management techniques for use in banking, and data archival for storage in clouds [4,7,8].

Hash functions have significance for ensuring data integrity since they generate fixed-size outputs from input data. For digital signatures and blockchain validation, secure hash algorithms (SHA) are necessary to confirm data integrity and authenticity [8,9,10]. To facilitate blockchain operations, ensure secure password storage, and check software integrity, hash functions are frequently utilized [4,8,11].

Further, data protection measures like Secure Multi-Party Computation (SMPC) and homomorphic encryption also adds to the privacy feature. It is possible to analyze and make calculations on the data without actually revealing the information [1, 2, 12, 13, 14]. Yao's SMPC protocols enable several parties to compute a function of their inputs without divulging individual inputs, and this is useful in privacy-preserving data mining and collaborative analysis in healthcare [15, 16].

Homomorphic Encryption facilitates mathematical actions and operations on data that are encrypted to be performed in a useful manner while ensuring security. These concepts were pioneered by Gentry on fully homomorphic encryption and allowed the encryption of data to enable secure data processing, especially in cases involving outsourcing and cloud computing [1,8]. Homomorphic encryption is applicable in secure voting systems, confidential data analysis, and private information retrieval as noted by [17,18].

3.3 Data Protection Laws and Cryptography

This part eliminates the division between technology and regulation by examining how cryptographic solutions comply with and fulfil the criteria of data protection regulations.

The GDPR has made encryption as one of the fundamental principles that aim at protecting the data by applying the principle of protection by design and by default. Kosta et al., [19] point out that encryption greatly assists in

contributing to the GDPR goals and precautions related to data protection during various periods of its life cycle. Writing for the Journal of Enterprise Information Management,[7] also back this up by establishing that strong measures of encryption are needed to safeguard individual data from unauthorized access and aggregation. Collectively, these insights show encryption as a vital concept for organizations to protect the privacy of personal data and to meet the GDPR regulation.

Similarly, the CCPA provides consumers with substantial privacy rights as those individuals have a right to data privacy and protection. To satisfy CCPA regulations, organizations propose processes like Information data deletion, Anonymization of data among other controls to protect personal information. Employing the concepts on this review paper, and reference [16] also affirm that anonymization techniques pose fundamental difficulties and challenges in our society due to risks of privacy violation; thus, the need for reliable cryptographic processes. Furthermore, "Evaluating the utility of anonymity" [15] and "Towards a global data privacy standard" [2] provide further insight about the importance of these protocols in ensuring privacy. compliance with the CCPA. Combined, these papers underscore the need to use highly robust cryptographic strategies in protecting data and meeting CCPA regulation.

3.4 Emerging Trends and Future Directions

This section discusses new and evolving technologies in data privacy and cryptography, considering how they may impact future data protection strategies and compliance efforts.

In the modern world driven by technological advancement, the issues concerning data privacy and security are increasingly complex. Advancements in new technologies such as blockchain, artificial intelligence, and cryptographic methods are revolutionizing the field of data protection and

Table 32.1 Illustrates how encryption and anonymization comply with GDPR and CCPA

Regulation	Emphasis	Key Measures	References	How it has been Used
GDPR	Data protection by design and by default	Encryption	[29]	Encryption techniques are applied to ensure compliance with GDPR's data protection requirements, particularly emphasizing data security by design and by default.
GDPR	Data protection by design and by default	Encryption	[12]	Used to establish privacy-preserving mechanisms and secure data processing in IT environments to comply with GDPR.
CCPA	Consumer privacy rights	Anonymization	[3]	Anonymization methods are employed to uphold consumer privacy rights as mandated by CCPA, particularly in the auditing architecture's data handling processes.
CCPA	Consumer privacy rights	Anonymization	[12]	Utilized to anonymize personal data and ensure compliance with CCPA's requirements for protecting consumer privacy.

data management. The role of cryptographic solutions in data accountability and future trends of data privacy is also discussed in this section.

Blockchain technology uses cryptographic methods to safeguard records' integrity, which is beneficial in uses like identity validation and supply chain management [17,20]. It makes data exchange clear and responsible and, at the same time, secure [21, 22].

This has, however, been fueled by the increased use and adoption of artificial intelligence in the modern world. Research on data protection relates to current solutions in the context of AI and the given works propose privacy-preserving technologies [17,23]. Some of the methods used to promote data privacy within artificial intelligence include Federated learning and Differential privacy [14,24,25].

In a recent review, "Data privacy and security in IT: a review of techniques and challenges" [22] identify principles, methods, and issues in data privacy and security in IT environments. On the same note, the review asserts that protocols such as zero-knowledge proofs and differential privacy should be applied to enhance data integrity and confidentiality [22]. As a result, it covers such topics as the incorporation of privacy-preserving machine learning models, the contribution of secure enclaves to the strengthening of data protection, and the incorporation of new cryptographic strategies to address newly arising privacy challenges [22].

Crypto technology is key in preserving core rights that include the right to privacy as well as freedom of speech. In "Cryptography as the Means to Protect Fundamental Human Rights." [26] argued that cryptographic technologies enable individuals to protect their privacy against intrusive technologies by ensuring that their rights to privacy are respected in the digital world [21]. By ensuring secure communication channels and protecting sensitive information, cryptographic methods support the broader human rights framework and promote trust in digital interactions.

3.5 Compliance Challenges

This section identifies the tough anti-compliance hurdles that an organization is likely to encounter socially, technologically, legally, and operationally. There are a number of issues that organizations encounter in their struggle to meet the requirements of data protection laws. Dependable encryption as well as anonymization technologies require significant investment in costly equipment, software, and qualified personnel and can be classified as technical constraints. The need to make these systems compatible with current structures complicates the factors and results in legal issues. While implementing data protection measures for cross-border organizations, it becomes challenging due to disparity in data protection regulations, which constitutes an operational hindrance. Compliance is a constant process that needs to be updated and audited from time to time, which consumes resources including time and may disrupt normal business. Awareness and training of staff are also important factors that will help avoid any breaching of compliance. Hence, compliance with data protection laws remains an endeavour that poses substantial technical, legal and operational challenges. These risks could be addressed through procuring high-grade cryptographic tools, ensuring compliance of data protection laws across geographic regions, and incorporating stringent check-and-balances and staff education.

3.6 Alignment of Cryptographic Solutions with Regulatory Requirements

Here we present how particular cryptographic methods satisfy legal requirements of data protection regulations to practitioners. Finding the match between cryptographic technologies and the regulation is owed to the fact that regulatory requirements need to be met by these technologies. For example, the GDPR and CCPA require organizations to have adequate safeguards for the encryption and anonymization of data. These requirements may be fulfilled by employing cryptographic algorithms such as AES or RSA as well as adopting more complex techniques like homomorphic encryption for the protection of the data when it is in transit and even when it is at rest. Further, the application of blockchain technology offers accuracy in data management through decentralization of the information, which cannot be tampered with, as required by the regulations of integrity and accountability. For additional support of the compliance, privacy-preserving protocols and cryptographic auditing tools allow to keep a record all processing operations, which can be necessary in cases of required accountability and transparency according to the regulations.

4. Conclusion

In this study, we have reviewed significant contributions to the field of data privacy and security. The critical contributions of significant studies are summarized in Table 32.2. These studies highlight the development and application of various cryptographic techniques and regulatory frameworks essential for ensuring data protection and privacy in an increasingly digital world.

In an increasingly interconnected world, cryptographic technologies are vital for organizations to meet international

Table 32.2 Key contribution of significant studies

References	Type of Study	Focus Area	Key Contribution
[1]	Policy Paper	Global Data Privacy Standards	Discussion on creating a global standard for data privacy
[2]	Legal Document	Data Protection Regulation	Establishes data protection and privacy regulations
[3]	Standard Document	Encryption	Specification of the AES encryption standard
[4]	Review Paper	Cloud Security	Survey of cryptographic algorithms for cloud data security
[5]	Theoretical Paper	Identity-Based Encryption	Proposal of an identity-based encryption scheme using Weil pairing
[6]	Theoretical Paper	Digital Signatures	Introduction of a fast digital signature scheme
[7]	Review Paper	Cloud Security	Analysis of security and privacy issues in cloud storage and computation
[8]	Theoretical Paper	Homomorphic Encryption	Proposal of a fully homomorphic encryption scheme without bootstrapping
[9]	Theoretical Paper	Secure Computation	Introduction of secure multi-party computation protocols
[10]	Review Paper	International Data Protection	Comparative analysis of privacy and data protection laws globally
[11]	Theoretical Paper	Blockchain Protocols	Analysis and applications of the Bitcoin Backbone protocol
[12]	Theoretical Paper	Homomorphic Encryption	The first practical construction of fully homomorphic encryption
[13]	Critical Comment	Privacy Regulation	Critique of the "privacy by design" approach in data protection law
[14]	Theoretical Paper	Public-Key Cryptography	Introduction of the RSA algorithm
[15]	Theoretical Paper	Data Anonymization	Evaluation of anonymization techniques
[16]	Theoretical Paper	Secure Computation	Development of secure multiparty computation protocols for data mining
[17]	Review Paper	AI and Data Privacy	Examination of data protection challenges and solutions in the AI era
[18]	Review Paper	Cloud Security	Discussion on security and privacy protection issues in cloud computing
[19]	Policy Paper	Privacy by Design	Discussion on implementing privacy by design principles
[20]	Theoretical Paper	Blockchain Protocols	Analysis and applications of the Bitcoin Backbone protocol
[21]	Policy Paper	Cryptography and Human Rights	Emphasizes the role of cryptographic technologies in safeguarding personal data and upholding human rights
[22]	Review Paper	Data Privacy and Security	Highlights key techniques and challenges in data privacy and security within IT environments
[23]	Review Paper	AI and Data Privacy	Examination of data protection challenges and solutions in the AI era
[24]	Theoretical Paper	Differential Privacy	Introduction of the concept of differential privacy
[25]	Theoretical Paper	Cryptographic Proofs	Introduction of the concept of knowledge complexity in interactive proof systems
[26]	Theoretical Paper	Blockchain and Privacy	Proposes a blockchain-based data usage auditing architecture for enhancing privacy and availability
[27]	Review Paper	Cloud Security	Examination of cryptographic mechanisms for data security and privacy in cloud storage environments
[28]	Review Paper	Cloud Security	Overview of security challenges in public cloud environments
[29]	Theoretical Paper	Public-Key Cryptography	Introduction of public-key cryptography
[30]	Legal Document	Consumer Privacy Rights	Establishes consumer privacy rights and regulations
[31]	Theoretical Paper	Cloud Security	Proposal of attribute-based encryption for secure sharing of personal health records in the cloud
[32]	Book	Privacy Law	Comprehensive analysis of privacy concepts and laws
[33]	Theoretical Paper	Secure Voting	Introduction of a receipt-free secret-ballot election protocol
[34]	Theoretical Paper	Identification and Signatures	Practical solutions for identification and signature problems
[35]	Theoretical Paper	Cryptographic Proofs	Analysis of the complexity of computationally sound proofs
[36]	Theoretical Paper	Cryptographic Proofs	Development of non-interactive zero-knowledge proofs of knowledge

data security requirements. Fundamental technologies such as encryption, homomorphic encryption, and privacy-preserving protocols like secure multi-party computation (SMPC) help fulfill data protection principles and regulatory requirements. Ongoing efforts and collaboration are necessary to address challenges posed by shifting legislation and emerging technologies. The final section elaborates on the relevance of cryptographic technologies in developing better data protection solutions and suggests potential areas for future research to address the dynamic nature of privacy threats.

5. Future Works

Future research in cryptographic technologies must address several critical areas to enhance data privacy and security. One key focus is the development of cryptography resistant to quantum computing. With the advent of quantum computing, existing cryptographic systems are vulnerable to quantum attacks, necessitating the standardization of post-quantum cryptography algorithms to ensure long-term security against these emerging threats [8,27].

Additionally, scalable privacy-preserving technologies are essential as data volumes continue to grow exponentially. Solutions that can manage large-scale data analysis while maintaining confidentiality are needed, and future research should explore differential privacy and secure multi-party computation to address scalability issues and improve user experience [15, 22, 24, 28].

User-centric privacy solutions are also crucial, as giving users more control over their information can significantly enhance data privacy. Future studies should focus on developing readily available privacy-preserving technologies that empower average users to protect their data effectively [2,17,23].

Moreover, designing continuous and dynamic regulatory compliance frameworks is imperative given the evolving landscape of data protection laws and privacy. Research should investigate how cryptographic technologies can aid in compliance across various jurisdictions and reconcile differing regulatory standards [10,13,19].

Finally, the implications for society and ethics must be considered in future research. Addressing data privacy within the broader context of ethical concerns is essential, focusing on issues such as algorithmic bias, discrimination, and equitable use and distribution of privacy-enhancing technologies. This approach ensures that cryptographic solutions serve the greater societal good and uphold ethical standards [14, 17].

REFERENCES

1. Cate, F. H., and R. Cullen. "Towards a global data privacy standard." International Data Privacy Law 9.3 (2019): 173–191.
2. European Union. "Regulation (EU) 2016/679 of the European Parliament and of the Council (GDPR)." Official Journal of the European Union 59 (2016): 1–88.
3. National Institute of Standards and Technology. "FIPS PUB 197: Advanced Encryption Standard (AES)." Proceedings of federal information processing standards publications, national institute of standards and technology 19 (2001): 22.
4. Xu, J., and H. Jin. "Outlines of data privacy preservation." Tsinghua Science and Technology 14.1 (2009): 1–9.
5. Miller, V. S. "Use of elliptic curves in cryptography." Proceedings of Advances in Cryptology (1985): 417–426.
6. Koblitz, N. "Elliptic curve cryptosystems." Mathematics of Computation 48.177 (1987): 203–209.
7. Wang, C., and K. Ren. "Security and privacy for storage and computation in cloud computing." Information Sciences 179.19 (2009): 2892–2901.
8. Chen, Y., and R. Sion. "To cloud or not to cloud?" Proceedings of the 11th ACM Workshop on Hot Topics in Operating Systems (2007): 13–18.
9. Yao, A. C. "Protocols for secure computations." Proceedings of the 23rd Annual Symposium on Foundations of Computer Science (1982): 160–164.
10. Solove, D. J. "Privacy and data protection in an international perspective." Washington University Law Review 87.4 (2010): 1027–1053.
11. Garay, J., A. Kiayias, and N. Leonardos. "The bitcoin backbone protocol: Analysis and applications." Annual International Conference on the Theory and Applications of Cryptographic Techniques (2014): 281–310.
12. Gentry, C. "Fully homomorphic encryption using ideal lattices." Proceedings of the 41st Annual ACM Symposium on Theory of Computing (2009): 169–178.
13. Kallinikos, J., A. Aaltonen, and A. Marton. "Privacy regulation cannot be hardcoded." Information Technology & People 23.3 (2010): 306–322.
14. Zyskind, G., O. Nathan, and A. Pentland. "Decentralizing privacy: Using blockchain to protect personal data." Proceedings of the 2015 IEEE Security and Privacy Workshops (2015): 180–184.
15. Sweeney, L., and A. Machanavajjhala. "Evaluating the utility of anonymity." Proceedings of the National Academy of Sciences 110.30 (2013): 12266–12271.
16. Shokri, R., G. Theodorakopoulos, and J. P. Hubaux. "Privacy games along location traces." Proceedings of the 2011 ACM Conference on Computer and Communications Security (2011): 417–428.
17. Katz, J., and Y. Lindell. "Introduction to modern cryptography." Proceedings of the 2014 ACM Conference on Computer and Communications Security (2014): 1565–1567.

18. Bent, R., and D. Dean. "Data security and privacy protection issues in cloud computing." International Journal of Computer Applications 60.19 (2012): 12–16.

19. Kosta, E., et al. "Privacy and data protection by design—from policy to engineering." Computer Law & Security Review 33.5 (2017): 677–688.

20. Narayanan, A., and J. Clark. "Bitcoin's academic pedigree." Communications of the ACM 60.12 (2017): 36–45.

21. Kaaniche, N., and M. Laurent-Maknavicius. "A blockchain-based data usage auditing architecture with enhanced privacy and availability." Proceedings of the 2024 IEEE International Symposium on Network Computing and Applications (2024): 1–8.

22. Farayola, O. A., O. L. Olorunfemi, and P. O. Shoetan. "Data privacy and security in IT: a review of techniques and challenges." Computer Science & IT Research Journal 5.3 (2024): 606–615.

23. Garfinkel, S. L. "Data protection in the era of artificial intelligence." Journal of Privacy and Confidentiality 8.1 (2018): 1–16.

24. Dingledine, R., N. Mathewson, and P. Syverson. "Tor: The second-generation onion router." Proceedings of the 13th USENIX Security Symposium (2004): 303–320.

25. Rivest, R. L., A. Shamir, and L. Adleman. "A method for obtaining digital signatures and public-key cryptosystems." Communications of the ACM 21.2 (1978): 120–126.

26. Limniotis, K. "Cryptography as the Means to Protect Fundamental Human Rights." Cryptography 3.1 (2024): 1–10.

27. Sarathy, R., and D. C. Robertson. "Data security and privacy preservation in cloud storage environments." Information Systems Research 25.4 (2014): 678–694.

28. Ren, K., and C. Wang. "Security challenges for the public cloud." IEEE Internet Computing 16.1 (2012): 69–73.

29. Diffie, W., and M. Hellman. "New directions in cryptography." IEEE Transactions on Information Theory 22.6 (1976): 644–654.

30. California Legislative Information. "Assembly Bill No. 375, Chapter 55 (CCPA)." California Civil Code Title 1.81.5 (2018): 1–24.

31. Li, M., S. Yu, Y. Zheng, K. Ren, and W. Lou. "Scalable and secure sharing of personal health records in cloud computing." IEEE Transactions on Parallel and Distributed Systems 24.1 (2013): 131–143.

32. Liu, X., Q. Wu, and Q. Wu. "A survey on privacy protection in cloud computing." Journal of Network and Computer Applications 52 (2015): 59–73.

33. Curtis, A., and B. Ledvina. "Privacy preservation for cloud computing." Proceedings of the 2018 IEEE International Conference on Big Data (2018): 2222–2227.

34. Bellare, M., and P. Rogaway. "Random oracles are practical: A paradigm for designing efficient protocols." Proceedings of the 1st ACM Conference on Computer and Communications Security (1993): 62–73.

35. Goldwasser, S., and S. Micali. "Probabilistic encryption." Journal of Computer and System Sciences 28.2 (1984): 270–299.

36. Menezes, A. J., and S. A. Vanstone. "Elliptic curve cryptosystems and their implementations." Journal of Cryptology 6.4 (1993): 209–224.

Note: All the tables in this chapter were made by the authors.

Transformative Applied Research in Computing, Engineering, Science and Technology – Dr. Damayanthi Dahanayake et al. (eds)
© 2024 Taylor & Francis Group, London, ISBN 978-1-041-01782-0

33

Invasive Alien Plant *Lantana Camara*— A Promising Antibacterial Agent for Combatting Multidrug Resistance

J. M. H. M. Jayasinghe and D. R. Karunaratne*
Department of Life Sciences,
Faculty of Science, NSBM Green University,
Sri Lanka

Abstract

Invasive alien plants pose a severe threat to native habitat by spreading rapidly causing the degradation and fragmentation of the ecosystem. These plants have been found to possess medicinal properties including antibacterial effects due to the presence of various phytochemicals. On the other hand, multidrug resistance is a critical aspect that affects global health. Multidrug resistant (MDR) bacterial strains are resistant to several antibiotics and are continuously increasing day by day. This is turning out to be a silent epidemic which can lead to a catastrophic health crisis. This situation has made researchers develop novel antibacterial agents using invasive alien plants and thereby developing a solution to meet two global threats efficiently. *Lantana camara* is an invasive plant with diverse bioactive compounds and has drawn attention for its potential antibacterial properties. This review investigates the antibacterial activity of *Lantana camara* against MDR bacterial strains. Research shows that *Lantana camara* has inhibitory effects on methicillin-resistant *Staphylococcus aureus* (MRSA) and multidrug resistant *Escherichia coli*, two clinically important multidrug resistant bacteria. Although these findings are promising, challenges such as standardization of extracts still exist. Further research is needed to identify specific bioactive components showing antibacterial properties and to study synergistic effects in combination with conventional antibiotics.

Keywords

Antibacterial activity, Invasive alien plants, Lantana camara, Multidrug resistance, Multidrug resistant bacteria

1. Overview of Invasive Alien Plants

1.1 Threats and Medicinal Value of Invasive Alien Plants

Invasive alien plants are non-native species that have proliferated and established populations in new environments, where they pose substantial risks to local ecosystems, economic stability, and public health [4]. These species can severely impact agriculture and fisheries, leading to economic losses. Moreover, they threaten indigenous flora through a range of mechanisms, both deliberate and inadvertent. Invasive alien species

*Corresponding author: devanji.k@nsbm.ac.lk

DOI: 10.1201/9781003616368-33

affect ecosystems by altering trophic structures, altering the availability of resources like nutrients and water, and altering disturbance regimes [2]. As a result, invasive alien plants pose a serious danger to global biodiversity and have a marked negative impact on both environmental integrity and the economic stability of affected nations [8].

Various parts of invasive plants are utilized in traditional folk medicine for treating a range of ailments. Notably, these invasive species have demonstrated significant antibacterial activity against a variety of pathogenic bacteria, including *Pseudomonas aeruginosa, Staphylococcus aureus, Escherichia coli*, and *Enterococcus* spp. The therapeutic potential of these plants is largely attributed to the diverse array of phytochemicals they contain, which contribute to their efficacy in combating bacterial infections [21].

1.2 Phytochemicals Present in Invasive Alien Plants

Phytochemicals are biologically active, natural chemical components which are found in plants. They protect plants from some plant diseases and damages due to environmental factors and contribute to the plants flavour, aroma and colour. They provide benefits for human health than those attributed to micronutrients and macronutrients [29].

The medicinal potential of invasive plants is attributed to their rich array of phytochemical compounds, including alkaloids, deoxymikanolides, tannins, flavonoids, xanthoxylenes, phenolic compounds, terpenoids, glycosides, saponins, anthocyanins, coumarins, anthraquinones, polyacetylenes, catechins, and hydroxyquinolines. These diverse phytochemicals support the pharmacological efficacy of these plants, mediating a range of physiological effects and offering therapeutic benefits against various diseases [1].

2. Overview on Multidrug Resistance

Multidrug resistance (MDR) represents the phenomenon whereby pathogenic microorganisms develop resistance to multiple therapeutic agents, even after initially demonstrating susceptibility to these drugs. This escalating resistance not only exacerbates the prevalence and severity of infectious diseases but also leads to heightened mortality rates. Consequently, there is an ongoing and urgent quest within the research community to discover and develop novel therapeutic agents to effectively combat these resistant infections [14]. The basis for treating bacterial infections is antibiotics [13]. Since the advent of antibiotics and their subsequent use as chemotherapeutic agents, there has been considerable optimism about their potential to eradicate infectious diseases. However, a significant factor driving the emergence and proliferation of MDR strains across various bacterial species is the excessive and often indiscriminate use of these antibiotics [3].

Approximately 2.8 million neonatal deaths globally are ascribed to bacterial infections, which remain a leading cause of mortality among children under five years of age. These infections encompass conditions such as meningitis, sepsis, pneumonia, and diarrhea. Particularly in developing nations, the incidence of lower respiratory illnesses is notably higher. While antibiotics play a crucial role in mitigating mortality and morbidity associated with bacterial diseases, their indiscriminate use fosters the emergence of resistant bacterial strains, complicating treatment and management efforts [25]. Additionally, bacterial species such as *Streptococcus pneumoniae* have progressively acquired resistance to a range of antibiotics, including erythromycin, penicillin, and levofloxacin. The emergence of methicillin-resistant *Staphylococcus aureus* (MRSA) was first documented in 1962, following the widespread use of penicillin. Similarly, a tetracycline-resistant strain of *Shigella* was identified after the introduction of tetracycline in 1959 [14]. Data from sources such as the Centers for Disease Control and Prevention (CDC) underscore the global impact of drug-resistant bacterial infections, which contribute to millions of cases and thousands of deaths each year due to these resistant strains [25]. Table 33.1 includes the current antibiotics that are ineffective against MDR bacteria.

Table 33.1 Some antibiotics that are ineffective against MDR bacteria

Multidrug resistant bacteria	Antibiotics that are ineffective	References
Methicillin-resistant *S. aureus*	Methicillin, oxacillin, cloxacillin, nafcillin, dicloxacillin, cephalosporins (such as cephalexin, cefazolin), carbapenems and monobactams	[12],[24]
Carbapenem-resistant *A. baumannii*	Imipenem, meropenem, doripenem, ertapenem, penicillins, cephalosporins and monobactams	[26], [30]
Carbapenem-resistant *P. aeruginosa*	Imipenem, meropenem, doripenem, ertapenem, penicillins, cephalosporins, monobactams, fluoroquinolones ad aminoglycosides	[12],[24]
Clarithromycin-resistant *H. pylori*	Amoxicillin, erythromycin, cefuroxime, ceftriaxone azithromycin, levofloxacin and clarithromycin	[22], [26]
Fluoroquinolone-resistant *Campylobacter* spp	Erythromycin, ciprofloxacin, levofloxacin, ofloxacin, moxifloxacin, gemifloxacin, tetracyclines and aminoglycosides	[26], [31]

Source: Author's compilation

It is now clear that invasiveness and MDR bacteria are two global threats that need to be addressed. The antibacterial qualities of invasive plants merit further research. In fact, invading terrestrial plant species typically exhibit greater sizes, higher rates of growth, and more shoot allocation than non-invasive species. Given their wide dispersion and ease of cultivation for potential large-scale exploitation, these traits may prove advantageous if the extracts from these plants turn out to be antibacterial. In addition, since MDR is another silent pandemic that keeps growing, a solution for two global threats will be addressed efficiently.

3. Invasive Alien Plant *Lantana Camara (L. Camara)*

Lantana camara, as seen in Fig. 33.1, belonging to the Verbenaceae family, is an evergreen shrub originating from South America [7]. Initially spread globally through human activity, animal dispersal, and natural means, it has become an invasive plant, posing significant challenges to agricultural and natural ecosystems worldwide. Despite its invasive nature, L. camara is valued by some animal species and is known as 'Gadhapana' in Sri Lanka, with various other names globally [10].

Fig. 33.1 Parts of *L. camara* plant: a. Leaves, b. Flowers, c. Fruits [9]

In addition to its significant ecological impact, *Lantana camara* boasts a distinguished history in traditional medicine, where it is acclaimed for its diverse therapeutic properties and efficacy in treating a range of ailments. Extensive scientific research has explored its chemical composition and pharmacological potential, highlighting its use in contemporary medicine and drug discovery efforts. Phytochemical investigations have revealed a diverse array of biologically active compounds in *Lantana camara*, such as alkaloids, phenolic compounds, tannins, flavonoids, steroids, terpenoids, saponins, and cardiac glycosides.

These constituents support its wide-ranging medicinal properties, which include antibacterial, antifungal, antiviral, anticarcinogenic, anti-inflammatory, antiallergic, nematocidal, insecticidal, and immunosuppressive activities [14,16,33]. While *Lantana camara* has been recognized for its medicinal properties, its specific efficacy against MDR bacteria requires further exploration. Therefore, *Lantana camara* stands out not only as an invasive plant but also as a potential source of novel antibacterial agents against MDR pathogens. Its rich chemical diversity and therapeutic potential make it a promising candidate for future pharmaceutical applications.

4. Key Findings of Antibacterial Properties of *Lantana Camara* Extracts

Table 33.2 provides an overview of each study's methodology, phytochemical analysis, antibacterial activity results, bacterial strains tested, and key findings regarding the potential antibacterial properties of extracts of *Lantana camara*.

5. Discussion of Key Findings of Antibacterial Activity of *Lantana Camara*

Lantana camara, notorious as an invasive alien plant, has garnered attention beyond its ecological impact due to its potential therapeutic properties, specifically its antibacterial activity against MDR pathogens. The studies reviewed here underscore its diverse bioactive compounds and their efficacy against a range of bacterial strains.

5.1 Phytochemical Diversity and Extraction Methods

Studies utilized various extraction methods including Soxhlet extraction, maceration, and cold extraction, employing solvents such as methanol, ethanol, and petroleum ether. These methods aimed to extract a spectrum of phytochemicals including alkaloids, flavonoids, tannins, and saponins, known for their antimicrobial potential. Each study highlighted the efficacy of different solvent extracts against specific bacterial strains, reflecting the complex interplay between extraction techniques and phytochemical profile.

5.2 Antibacterial Activity Against MDR Pathogens

The extracts from *Lantana camara exhibited* remarkable antibacterial efficacy against MDR bacteria, a growing global health concern. Methanol and dichloromethane

Table 33.2 Studies on antibacterial activity of extracts of *lantana camara*

Study Reference	Extraction Method	Solvents Used	Phytochemicals Identified	Antibacterial Activity	Bacterial Strains Tested	Results
[6]	Soxhlet extraction	Water, methanol, acetone, petroleum ether, dichloromethane, ethyl acetate, ethanol	Reducing sugars, alkaloids, saponins, flavonoids, steroids, glycosides, terpenoids,	Methanol and dichloromethane extracts showed the highest zones of inhibition against *P. mirabilis* (29 mm) and MRSA (29 mm). Methanol extract showed 29 mm against VRE.	Gram-positive (MRSA, *Streptococcus pyogenes,* VRE), Gram-negative (*Acinetobacter baumannii, Proteus mirabilis, Citrobacter freundii, Proteus vulgaris, Pseudomonas aeruginosa*)	Dichloromethane extracts and methanol displayed the most potent antibacterial efficacy against the strains tested.
[21]	Maceration	95% petroleum ether, 95% methanol, distilled water	Alkaloids, flavonoids, glycosides, phenolics, saponins, tannins	Methanol extract is most effective against MDR clinical isolates, particularly *S. aureus* 43300 (28 mm) and *S. typhi* B69.	*S. typhi* B69, *S. aureus* 43300, *S. aureus* 29213, *S. pneumonia, E. coli* 35218, *P. aeruginosa*	Methanol leaf extract displayed the highest antibacterial activity against tested clinical isolates. Water extract showed no efficacy.
[19]	Maceration	Hexane, ethyl acetate, ethanol	Alkaloids, flavonoids, tannins, phenols, steroids, cardiac glycosides	Ethanol extract exhibited the strongest antibacterial effect against *E. coli* (25.50 mm).	*Salmonella typhi, P. aeruginosa, E. coli, Proteus vulgaris, Klebsiella oxytoca, S. aureus*	Ethanol extract showed higher antibacterial activity compared to conventional antibiotics like ciprofloxacin and ofloxacin.
[27]	Maceration	Methanol, chloroform, water	Not specified	Methanolic extract showed activity against all tested strains of *M. tuberculosis*, with varying MIC values.	*Mycobacterium tuberculosis* strains (H37Rv, TMC-331, wild type)	Methanolic extract demonstrated antimycobacterial activity across all tested strains.
[17]	Maceration	Methanol, diethyl ether, ethyl acetate, n-butanol	Not specified	Methanol extract showed highest efficiency against Gram-negative bacteria.	*Escherichia coli, Klebsiella pneumoniae, Enterococcus faecalis, S. aureus, Pseudomonas aeruginosa*	Methanol extract demonstrated highest antibacterial activity among tested solvents.
[28]	Soxhlet extraction	99% methanol	Alkaloids, flavonoids, phenolic compounds, saponins, tannins, terpenoids	Methanolic extract had higher MIC values compared to conventional anti-TB drugs.	*Mycobacterium tuberculosis* strains (H37Rv, TMC-331, M. smegmatis)	Methanolic extract showed higher MIC values compared to standard anti-TB medications.
[23]	Cold extraction	Ethanol	Quinones, alkaloids, saponinssteroids, flavones, tannins, phlobaphenes, flavonols, flavonones, chalcones, pyrogallates, catechins, proanthocyanidins, triterpenoids	Leaf extract showed MICs of 256 µg/mL against *E. coli* and 512 µg/mL against *S. aureus*.	*Staphylococcus aureus, Escherichia coli*	Leaf extract displayed antibacterial activity against tested strains, with significant MIC reductions in combination with antibiotics.

Study Reference	Extraction Method	Solvents Used	Phytochemicals Identified	Antibacterial Activity	Bacterial Strains Tested	Results
[5]	Cold extraction	Ethanol	Not specified	Leaf extract showed MIC values of 512 µg/mL for *S. aureus* and 256 µg/mL for *E. coli*.	*Staphylococcus aureus, Escherichia coli*	Leaf extract demonstrated MIC values against tested strains.
[18]	Cold extraction	Acetone, water, benzene	Not specified	Acetone extract showed 12 mm zone of inhibition against *S. aureus*.	*Staphylococcus aureus, Escherichia coli*	Acetone extract demonstrated MICs of 0.53 mg/ml for S. aureus.
[6]	Soxhlet extraction	Water, methanol, acetone, petroleum ether, dichloromethane, ethyl acetate, ethanol	Reducing sugars, alkaloids, glycosides, terpenoids, saponins, flavonoids, steroids	Methanol and dichloromethane extracts showed the highest zones of inhibition against MRSA (29 mm) and *P. mirabilis* (29 mm). Methanol extract showed 29 mm against VRE.	Gram-positive (MRSA, *Streptococcus pyogenes*, VRE), Gram-negative (*Acinetobacter baumannii, Citrobacter freundii, Proteus mirabilis, Proteus vulgaris, Pseudomonas aeruginosa*)	Methanol and dichloromethane extracts displayed the highest antibacterial activity against tested strains.
[21]	Maceration	95% petroleum ether, 95% methanol, distilled water	Alkaloids, flavonoids, glycosides, phenolics, saponins, tannins	Methanol extract is most effective against MDR clinical isolates, particularly *S. aureus* 43300 (28 mm) and *S. typhi* B69.	*S. typhi* B69, *S. aureus* 43300, *S. aureus* 29213, *S. pneumonia, E. coli* 35218, *P. aeruginosa*	Methanol leaf extract displayed the highest antibacterial activity against tested clinical isolates. Water extract showed no efficacy.

Source: Author's compilation

extract consistently exhibited significant inhibitory effects, particularly against Gram-positive pathogens like Vancomycin resistant *Enterococci* (VRE), MRSA, and various clinical isolates of *Staphylococcus aureus*. These extracts often surpassed the efficacy of conventional antibiotics, suggesting their potential as alternative or adjunct therapies in combating antibiotic resistance.

5.3 Variability in Effectiveness Across Studies

Despite promising findings, variability in the efficacy of extracts was observed across studies. Factors such as extraction method, solvent choice, and bacterial strain variability likely contributed to these discrepancies. For instance, while methanol extracts showed strong activity in some studies, water extracts in others demonstrated minimal effectiveness, underscoring the importance of extraction parameters in utilizing the bioactive potential of *Lantana camara*.

6. Challenges and Future Directions

Challenges in utilizing *Lantana camara as* an effective antibacterial agent include the variability in extraction

methods and solvent choices, which influence the phytochemical composition and thus the efficacy of extracts. Standardization of extraction protocols is critical to ensure consistency and comparability across studies. Moreover, while the plant shows potent antibacterial activity against MDR pathogens in vitro, the mechanisms underlying these effects remain largely unexplored. Future research should study deeper about the mode of action of bioactive compounds in *Lantana camara* to elucidate their interactions with bacterial targets and potential synergies with existing antibiotics. In addition, the antibacterial activity of these invasive plant extracts can be studied in combination with antibiotics in order to get a synergistic antibacterial activity against multidrug resistant bacteria. Moreover, translating these promising in vitro findings into clinical applications necessitates comprehensive preclinical and clinical trials to rigorously evaluate safety, efficacy, and optimal dosage regimens. For the purpose of verifying therapeutic potential in humans, clinical studies are essential. To guarantee uniformity and dependability, standardized procedures for extract preparation and testing should be developed. Furthermore, investigating the mode of action of bioactive substances in *Lantana camara* is essential in understanding the antibacterial actions and planning further research. Addressing these challenges will not only validate the therapeutic potential of *Lantana camara* but also pave the way for its integration into mainstream antimicrobial strategies, addressing the pressing global challenge of antibiotic resistance effectively.

7. Conclusion

In conclusion, *Lantana camara* presents a promising reservoir of natural antibacterial agents, particularly against MDR bacteria. The synergy between its diverse phytochemical composition and extraction techniques offers a compelling opportunity for future drug discovery and development. However, careful consideration of extraction methods, phytochemical characterization, and clinical validation is crucial to utilizing its full therapeutic potential. Furthermore, investigating how *Lantana camara* extracts work in combination with conventional antibiotics may improve the effectiveness of treatment. By integrating all these approaches, researchers can improve the understanding of *Lantana camara and* develop potential interventions to combat multidrug resistance.

REFERENCES

1. A. C. Akinmoladun, E. O. Ibukun, and I. A. Dan-Ologe, "Phytochemical Constituents and Antioxidant Properties of Extracts from the Leaves of Chromolaena Odorata," Scientific Research and Essay, vol. 2, no. 6, pp. 191–194, 2007. [Online]. Available: http://www.academicjournals.org/SRE.

2. A. Alghamdi, "Phytoconstituents Screening and Antimicrobial Activity of the Invasive Species Nicotiana Glauca Collected from Al-Baha Region of Saudi Arabia," Saudi Journal of Biological Sciences, vol. 28, no. 3, pp. 1544–1547, 2021, doi: 10.1016/j.sjbs.2020.12.034.

3. M. Arip, M. Selvaraja, R. Mogana, et al., "Review on Plant-Based Management in Combating Antimicrobial Resistance - Mechanistic Perspective," Frontiers in Pharmacology, 2022, doi: 10.3389/fphar.2022.879495.

4. B. Baral and B. L. Maharjan, "Antagonistic Characteristics and Phytochemical Screening of Invasive Alien Species of Nepal Himalaya," International Journal of Pharmaceutical & Biological Archives, vol. 2, 2011. [Online]. Available: www.ijpba.info.

5. F. S. Barreto, E. O. Sousa, A. R. Campos, J. G. M. Costa, and F. F. G. Rodrigues, "Antibacterial Activity of Lantana camara Linn and Lantana montevidensis Brig Extracts from Cariri-Cear, Brazil," Journal of Young Pharmacists, vol. 2, no. 1, pp. 42–44, 2010, doi: 10.4103/0975-1483.62211.

6. D. Dubey and R. N. Padhy, "Antibacterial Activity of Lantana camara L. against Multidrug Resistant Pathogens from ICU Patients of a Teaching Hospital," Journal of Herbal Medicine, vol. 3, no. 2, pp. 65–75, 2013, doi: 10.1016/j.hermed.2012.12.002.

7. M. Falcone, M. Bassetti, G. Tiseo, et al., "Time to Appropriate Antibiotic Therapy Is a Predictor of Outcome in Patients with Bloodstream Infection Caused by KPC-Producing Klebsiella Pneumoniae," Critical Care, vol. 24, no. 1, 2020, doi: 10.1186/s13054-020-2742-9.

8. P. Fan and A. Marston, "How Can Phytochemists Benefit from Invasive Plants?" [Online]. Available: http://www.cps-skew.ch (accessed Mar. 10, 2024).

9. K. Girish, "Antimicrobial Activities of Lantana camara Linn," Asian Journal of Pharmaceutical and Clinical Research, 2017, doi: 10.22159/ajpcr.2017.v10i3.16378.

10. IUCN, "AsESG Report on Invasive Plant Species in EleHabitats_LE," 2012.

11. A. Kali, "Antibiotics and Bioactive Natural Products in Treatment of Methicillin Resistant Staphylococcus Aureus: A Brief Review," Pharmacognosy Reviews, 2015, doi: 10.4103/0973-7847.156329.

12. S. S. Kanj and Z. A. Kanafani, "Current Concepts in Antimicrobial Therapy against Resistant Gram-Negative Organisms: Extended-Spectrum β-Lactamase-Producing Enterobacteriaceae, Carbapenem-Resistant Enterobacteriaceae, and Multidrug Resistant Pseudomonas aeruginosa," Mayo Clinic Proceedings, vol. 86, pp. 250–259, 2011, doi: 10.4065/mcp.2010.0674.

13. B. J. Lourenço, C. F. O. Niconte, A. A. João, L. G. Cuinica, and P. A. Vintuar, "Identification Data of Secondary Metabolites and Antibacterial Action of Leaf Extract of Lantana camara L. on Multidrug Resistant Microorganisms," Data in Brief, Jun. 2024, doi: 10.1016/j.dib.2024.110338.

14. J. Mamangkey, L. W. Mendes, A. Z. Mustopa, and A. Hartanto, "Endophytic Aspergillii and Penicillii from Medicinal Plants: A Focus on Antimicrobial and Multidrug Resistant Pathogens Inhibitory Activity," BioTechnologia, vol. 105, no. 1, pp. 83–95, 2024, doi: 10.5114/bta.2024.135644.

15. H. J. Morrill, J. M. Pogue, K. S. Kaye, and K. L. LaPlante, "Treatment Options for Carbapenem-Resistant Enterobacteriaceae Infections," Open Forum Infectious Diseases, vol. 2, no. 2, 2015, doi: 10.1093/ofid/ofv050.

16. C. R. Nirmal, R. S. Ebenezer, P. Kannan, M. Balasubramanian, I. Thirunavukkarasu, R. Mondal, and A. Dusthackeer, "Anti-Tuberculosis Activity of Bio-Active Compounds from Lantana camara L., Euphorbia Hirta L., Mukia Maderaspatana (L.) M. Roem, and Abutilon Indicum (L.)," European Journal of Integrative Medicine, vol. 35, Apr. 2020, doi: 10.1016/j.eujim.2020.101105.

17. S. Noor, "Synergistic Effect of the Methanolic Extract of Lemongrass and Some Antibiotics to Treat Urinary Tract Bacteria," Journal of Biosciences and Medicines, vol. 4, no. 11, pp. 48–58, 2016, doi: 10.4236/jbm.2016.411006.

18. D. Ojha, C. Maity, P. D. Mohapatra, et al., "In Vitro Antimicrobial Potentialities Of Different Solvent Extracts Of Ethnomedicinal Plants Against Clinically Isolated Human Pathogens," Journal of Phytology, vol. 4, pp. 57–64, 2010. [Online]. Available: https://www.researchgate.net/publication/258886016.

19. S. O. Oladoye, "Lantana camara: Phyto-Constituents and Antimicrobial Activity Study," Pan African Journal of Life Sciences, vol. 5, no. 2, pp. 289–298, 2021, doi: 10.36108/pajols/1202.50.0270.

20. P. Pasrija, M. Girdhar, M. Kumar, S. Arora, and A. Katyal, "Endophytes: An Unexplored Treasure to Combat Multidrug Resistance," Phytomedicine Plus, 2022, doi: 10.1016/j.phyplu.2022.100249.

21. I. N. Ruburika, C. Izere, T. Habyarimana, and F. N. Niyonzima, "Antimicrobial Activity of Lantana camara Extracts against Selected Clinical Isolated Bacteria," International Journal of Health Sciences, pp. 10828–10837, Jun. 2022, doi: 10.53730/ijhs.v6ns3.8437.

22. M. Safavi, R. Sabourian, and A. Foroumadi, "Treatment of Helicobacter Pylori Infection: Current and Future Insights," 2016, doi: 10.12998/wjcc.v4.i1.

23. . O. Sousa, F. F. G. Rodrigues, A. R. Campos, and J. G. M. Costa, "Phytochemical Analysis and Modulation in Aminoglycosides Antibiotics Activity by Lantana camara L.," Acta Scientiarum - Biological Sciences, vol. 37, no. 2, pp. 213–218, 2015, doi: 10.4025/actascibiolsci.v37i2.22877.

24. S. L. Sukanya, J. Sudisha, P. Hariprasad, S. R. Niranjana, H. S. Prakash, and S. K. Fathima, "Antimicrobial Activity of Leaf Extracts of Indian Medicinal Plants against Clinical and Phytopathogenic Bacteria," African Journal of Biotechnology, vol. 8, no. 23, pp. 6677–6682, 2009. [Online]. Available: http://www.academicjournals.org/AJB.

25. W. Tafroji et al., "Antibacterial Activity of Medicinal Plants in Indonesia on Streptococcus Pneumoniae," PLoS ONE, vol. 17, no. 9, Sep. 2022. doi: 10.1371/journal.pone.0274174.

26. J. Tanwar, S. Das, Z. Fatima, and S. Hameed, "Multidrug Resistance: An Emerging Crisis," Interdisciplinary Perspectives on Infectious Diseases, 2014. doi: 10.1155/2014/541340.

27. N. Tuyiringire et al., "Three Promising Antimycobacterial Medicinal Plants Reviewed as Potential Sources of Drug Hit Candidates against Multidrug Resistant Tuberculosis," Tuberculosis, 2020. doi: 10.1016/j.tube.2020.101987.

28. N. Tuyiringire et al., "In Vitro Antimycobacterial Activity of Medicinal Plants Lantana camara, Cryptolepis Sanguinolenta, and Zanthoxylum Leprieurii," Journal of Clinical Tuberculosis and Other Mycobacterial Diseases, vol. 27, May 2022. doi: 10.1016/j.jctube.2022.100307.

29. S. Velavan, "Phytochemical Techniques – A Review," World Journal of Science and Research, vol. 1, 2015. [Online]. Available: http://www.harmanpublications.com.

30. J. A. Viehman, M. H. Nguyen, and Y. Doi, "Treatment Options for Carbapenem-Resistant and Extensively Drug-Resistant Acinetobacter Baumannii Infections," Drugs, 2014. doi: 10.1007/s40265-014-0267-8.

31. K. Wieczorek and J. Osek, "Antimicrobial Resistance Mechanisms among Campylobacter," BioMed Research International, 2013. doi: 10.1155/2013/340605.

32. W. Wijesundara and S. Wijesundara, "Invasive Alien Plants in Sri Lanka," Biodiversity Secretariat of the Ministry of Environment, 2010.

33. Z. Zare, "Investigating of Anti-Bacterial and Anti-Fungal Activities of Lantana camara L. Against Human Pathogens," International Journal of Basic Science in Medicine, vol. 6, no. 4, pp. 139–144, 2021. doi: 10.34172/ijbsm.2021.25.

Transformative Applied Research in Computing, Engineering, Science and Technology – Dr. Damayanthi Dahanayake et al. (eds)
© 2024 Taylor & Francis Group, London, ISBN 978-1-041-01782-0

34

A Review on the Food Allergies and Blood Groups in Sri Lanka

Y. Kavindi, N. Uthayarajan
Department of Life Sciences,
Faculty of Science, NSBM Green University,
Sri Lanka

T. Gunathilaka
Department of Basic Science and Social Science for Nursing,
Faculty of Nursing, University of Colombo,
Sri Lanka

B. Deepachandi*
Department of Life Sciences,
Faculty of Science, NSBM Green University,
Sri Lanka

Abstract

When it comes to the diseases that involve the immune system and certain reactions to antigens and antibodies, food allergy can be rightly ranked as one of the most widespread ones. Examining the possible connection between blood types and food allergies can improve overall health management reducing the symptoms of inflammatory and autoimmune diseases in worldwide. Exploring the connection between ABO blood groups and food allergies has the potential to enhance patient care and doctor consultations by identifying blood-type-specific patterns in food allergies which can inform personalized risk assessment and tailored management strategies. Although there have not been any in- depth studies on this subject in Sri Lanka, evidence from study points of other countries to a potential connection between blood type and food allergies. This literature review focuses on existing research, exploring the frequency, characteristics, and potential risk factors associated with food allergies, with a specific focus on examining the possibility of connection with ABO blood groups. To address existing knowledge gaps and pave the way for improved healthcare and well-being for individuals with food allergies in Sri Lanka, a multidisciplinary approach considering clinical, genetic, and environmental aspects is required.

Keywords

Allergy, Blood groups, Food allergy

---
*Corresponding author: bhagya.d@nsbm.ac.lk

DOI: 10.1201/9781003616368-34

1. Introduction

Food is one of the fundamental needs of life which produces energy for daily activities. However, food allergies are a vital problem among humans. Therefore, it is essential to study food allergies. Food allergies cannot be cured, despite getting medications and developing treatments [1]. Asia is a vast continent with many different ethnic groups, cultural and culinary traditions [2]. Due to their distinctive cuisine and the tendency for rare or varied food allergies, South Asians may exhibit different food allergy patterns than other ethnic groups. Traditionally Sri Lankans and most Indians are vegetarians and their staple diet comprises vegetables, lentils, and rice [3]. The South Asian cuisine also includes a range of many other spices, such as red pepper, cumin (*Cuminum cyminum*), coriander (*Coriandrum sativum*), mustard seed (*Brassica nigra*), fenugreek (*Trigonella foenum-graecum*), ginger, turmeric, and curry leaves. Some spices have been linked to spice allergies according to studies [4].

Notably, besides blood groups, genetic and environmental risk factors for the development of allergic diseases are multiple. This includes family history, which is among the major determinants [5]. In addition, asthma, atopic dermatitis, acute illness, drug or alcohol usage, strenuous exercise, or psychological distress, obesity, and vitamin D insufficiency, are some of the other risk factors that contribute to inducing allergic reactions in the body [6]. Also, blood types were identified as a biomarker for food allergies.

2. Food Allergy

Adverse food responses, as they are often called, can occur in people through various mechanisms. These reactions can be classified as toxic or non-toxic. When compared to immune-mediated reactions, non-immune-mediated reactions arise far more frequently. Some examples would be those in which sensitivity to particular substances such as lactose intolerance or inadequacy in enzymes such as those in vasoactive amines. Nonetheless, the food choices and social lives of most people are affected by immune-mediated responses, which are a leading cause of morbidity and healthcare expenses, and may even outcome in lethal reactions due to their severe life-threatening activity [7].

They are characterized as any adverse food-induced immune-mediated reactions involving both the adaptive and innate immune systems. Eosinophilic esophagitis, allergic proctocolitis, and dietary protein-induced enterocolitis are a few examples of both non-IgE-mediated and IgE-mediated illnesses.

Allergy can be divided into four primary types based on the pathogenic mechanisms, type I, II, III, and IV. The generation of IgE against food allergens is the most prevalent type of immune-mediated adverse food reaction (type I hypersensitivity). T cell-dependent type IV reactions are also implicated in diseases like celiac disease and food protein-induced enterocolitis. Certain food components also induce immunological reactivity driven by the innate immune system, which includes complement, Toll-like receptors, and innate immune cells [8]. In developed countries, 1–3% of adults and 3%–8% of children struggle with IgE-associated food allergies [9].

2.1 Commonly Reported Food Allergies

Food allergies linked to IgE are frequently triggered by fish, fruits, vegetables, milk, eggs, wheat, peanuts, almonds, and sesame [9]. Patients usually outgrow food allergies to milk, eggs, and wheat. Allergies to fish, tree nuts, and peanuts seem to persist throughout life [10] and, can appear at any age in childhood or later in adulthood. This includes allergies to eggs, milk, soy, and wheat, which develop mostly in infancy, before age two. In general, children are less likely to overcome allergies to fish, peanuts, tree nuts, or shellfish than they are to outgrow allergies to wheat, soy, milk, and eggs with aging [11].

Marker allergens have been identified within some of the most common sources of food allergens sources, such as apples, peanuts, milk, and wheat that can only be found in particular food sources and are useful for identifying food sources of sensitization. There are more allergens in various food sources [12]. Some patients, although sensitive to some food, will still develop symptoms even after consuming foods seemingly unrelated to the allergens [8].

Symptoms may manifest at the sites of allergen interaction (such as the mouth, oesophagus, and/or gut) or in other organs when food allergens enter the circulation through the gastrointestinal tract. Systemic responses result when allergens that can cross-link IgE bound to effector cells penetrate the mucosal barrier and enter the circulation. The cardiovascular and neurological systems may be impacted by allergen uptake. The type and degree of reactions depend on the amount of the consumed allergen, its resistance to digestion, and the epithelial barrier permeability. The development of food allergies and symptoms that go along with food allergies occurs before the development of respiratory system-related allergies. Later in life, there is a possibility in the opposite direction; food allergies are frequently outgrown, and respiratory allergies rise to the top [8, 13].

3. Blood Groups and Allergy Disease

The blood types are grouped based on the presence or absence of specific antigens that are carbohydrate or protein chains attached to either the lipid or the protein component of the membrane on the surface of the red blood cells. The two major grouping systems are ABO and Rhesus; the major antigens are A, B, and D [14]. The matching antibody against an ABO blood group antigen will naturally be present in a person's plasma if that antigen is lacking from their red blood cells. Four primary categories of blood types; A, B, AB, and O are distinguished, each group can be either RhD positive (agglutination with anti-d) or RhD negative, with varied prevalence in various populations [15]. The genomes of people dictate which variety of enzymes they will have to catalyze the transfer of sugar units to form antigens, and which variety of antigens end up on their red blood cell surfaces [16].

To avoid life-threatening transfusion reactions including agglutination, hemolysis, fever, and shock, it is essential to understand blood types and their characteristics. Further, some diseases and disorders, such as cancer and cardiovascular diseases, and infection by *Helicobacter pylori*, were connected with antigens of blood groups [17, 18].

It is, for example, known that individuals with blood group O have a reduced risk of pancreatic cancer, whereas blood group A, is more common in gastric cancer than other blood types. Also, compared to individuals with type O blood, individuals of non-O blood type are at higher risk of having cardiovascular diseases [19]. People with O blood type have lower levels of von Willebrand Factor, which is very important in blood clotting [20].

Functioning as receptors or surface markers, the majority of blood group antigens exhibit relevant in-cell/in-cell recognition and self-declaration processes [21]. These antigens could represent potential receptors for microorganisms or other substances, like toxins or allergens, and their interaction with antibodies that may predispose an individual's susceptibility to disease [17]. Certain blood types may be more prone to developing specific types of allergies according to existing studies [19].

Based on observational studies, it was proposed that ABO agglutinins, which are present in various grass, flower, and tree pollens could interact with respiratory epithelial cells that carry blood group antigens [22]. The ABO allele responsible for vulnerability to atopic disorders is the main source of variation between the studies. Atopic bronchial asthma, rhinitis, hay fever, and conjunctivitis were found to be linked with blood group A and/or B antigens in two studies, and the link was attributed to female patients with pollinosis. Most of the investigations revealed a link between the blood group O and atopic disorders including rhinitis, whereas resistance was linked to A phenotypes [22].

To explain more about this association of ABO phenotypes with allergic rhinitis in patients, the case-control study conducted in India included 100 cases of allergic rhinitis and 100 controls. According to this, Allergic rhinitis is associated with the phenotype of blood group O, and this is the most prevalent in the study population; on the other hand, blood group AB is the most protected in the population [23]. However, the exact way that blood type can influence how an allergic condition develops is still unknown. The association of ABO blood groups with susceptibility to allergic diseases, including asthma and food allergies, has been an area of investigation in only a very few studies [24] including rhinitis, and dermatitis.

The geographic data gap regarding the association between allergy illnesses and ABO blood groups has been observed in some studies. That means allergies can vary according to the geographical state of the population around the world [19]. Blood group O is the most frequent in the study population, at a very high risk of acquiring allergic rhinitis, and the most secure in this population is blood group B, based on a cohort study from Iraq [25].

The Biotype Diets approach is a diet plan developed after extensive research that showed a statistical correlation between blood types and the severity of food allergies. Due to their easy, quick, and affordable identification; their interaction with the immune system; and association with gastrointestinal and allergy disease, blood types were selected as biological markers for this investigation. The ABO markers are also expressed on many tissues of the human body that are sensitive to allergy [26].

One study suggested that the B-negative and AB-negative blood groups are more prone to sensitization to alpha-gal [27]. Another study suggested that Rh-negative blood types have higher allergic sensitization all types to meats, seafood, gluten grains, nightshades, and fruits, because they lack antigens [28]. But another study suggested that the frequencies of getting alpha-gal allergies in patients who have type B or AB were significantly lower [29]. However, those studies suggest various associations between specific blood groups and food allergies. There is also doubt whether food allergies have an association with blood groups or not. And another study suggested that there was no association between food allergies and the ABO or Rh blood groups [30].

4. Reported Food Allergies in Sri Lanka

However, certain allergies might be brought on by regional eating patterns. Compared to the Western developed world,

Asia has a different pattern of food allergies. Bird's nest soup was in first place as the most common cause of food allergy in China [31]. Nonetheless, the pattern of food allergy seen in this study differs substantially from that in other Asian countries, and those in Europe and the United States. South Asia has limited information on food allergies. The current study focuses on the assessment of native foods that cause immediate type I hypersensitivity in Sri Lanka and comparing them with Western-developed countries and Asia [2]. Foods that can cause food-induced anaphylaxis in Sri Lanka are cows' milk, pork, fish, mutton, gelatin, eggs, beef, shellfish, cuttlefish, wheat, sesame [32].

Sri Lanka has limited data. In a survey of 449 school children, from the Colombo District, 30% of the food allergies were claimed by the participants, with pineapple being the most often reported allergic food. Involved foods also included rambutan (*Nephelium lappaceum*), tomato, cuttlefish, breadfruit (*Artocarpus altilis*), prawns, tuna, and canned fish. However confirmatory tests were not conducted [33]. In a survey of 1255 patients from all over the nation who visited the allergy clinic, the most prevalent food allergy diagnosis made in childhood was cow's milk allergy [2]. The second most common allergy was red meat, but the study claimed it was due to a low consumption of red meat for cultural and religious reasons. Confirming these correlations and identifying the underlying mechanisms will require more investigation. In Sri Lanka, quite a higher percentage of patients than in other countries experienced anaphylaxis to red meat. There have been two cases of novel food allergies that resulted in anaphylaxis over the last 20 years [2]. The food-dependent exercise-induced anaphylaxis (FDEIA) triggered by food alone, occurs when the consumption of the suspected food is followed by exercise within 4 hours, either just before or just after [7]. In Sri Lanka, wheat is the main cause of FDEIA and red meat (mainly beef) was reported [32]. The allergy to red meat comes as a result of an IgE-mediated antibody response to one molecule found in a variety of mammals-Alpha gal. Although coconut (*Cocos nucifera*) is a common food material among Asians, allergies to it are not uncommon in Sri Lanka one of the studies discovered adverse reactions after consuming foods containing coconut (milk, cream, oil, and water) in some individuals in Sri Lanka [34].

4.1 Native Food Allergens and Categories

Studying the causes of food allergies is essential given that the prevalence of allergy-related disorders has been rising in Sri Lanka. It is challenging to provide suitable preventative and treatment measures, which can result in misdiagnosis and inadequate delayed treatment which puts the health and there is a potential threat to the lives of those who are suffering from food allergies in Sri Lanka. The lack of research into this topic places the safety and well-being of persons who have native food allergies at risk. In considering Sri Lanka's unique cuisine, it is necessary to close this knowledge gap to properly care for and safeguard these people.

Rare foods such as mustard, tangerine, *Moringa oleifera* (Moringa), Sarana, and cassava (*Manihot esculenta*) caused anaphylaxis [32]. To better understand and manage, foods are classified into 7 distinct categories; vegetables, fish and seafood, fruits, meat and eggs, milk, spices, and "other foods." Fruits were the food group that caused hypertension in most people who had been diagnosed with it. Fish and sea foods were the second most frequently problematic food category. It was discovered that certain percentages of the research group were hypersensitive to vegetables, the "other foods" category, meat and eggs, milk, and spices [33]. "Other foods" include jackfruit (*Artocarpus heterophyllus*), peanuts, walnuts, Sarana, soy, legumes, mushrooms, spinach, and [2].

5. Native Food Allergies and Blood Types

Research on the genetics of food allergies in different ethnic groups has also highlighted the need to take blood type into account when developing food allergies. Even though these results cannot be directly applied to the Sri Lankan situation, those studies do raise the possibility that there is a biological mechanism at play relating to blood type and native food allergies in Sri Lanka that deserves further investigation.

6. Conclusion

This literature review shows the possible relationship between blood types and native food allergies in Sri Lanka. Although previous research in other countries suggests possible correlations, limitations such as insufficient data and regional differences require additional Sri Lanka-specific studies to observe the potential association between blood types and native food allergies in Sri Lankan patients. Understanding the prevalence, characteristics, and risk factors of local food allergies, alongside delving into the biological mechanisms linking them to blood types, will be crucial. Overall, addressing these knowledge gaps can pave the way for the potential advantages of a deeper comprehension of this subject in improving personalized healthcare and well-being, ultimately enhancing the lives of individuals with food allergies in Sri Lanka.

REFERENCES

1. T. U. Food and D. Administration, "Food allergies: what you need to know what are the major food allergens?," pp. 2–4, 2021, [Online]. Available: https://www.accessdata.fda.gov/scripts/medwatch/index.cfm.

2. R. de Silva, C. Karunatilake, J. Iddagoda, and D. Dasanayake, "Food allergy in Sri Lanka – A comparative study," *World Allergy Organ. J.*, vol. 15, no. 12, p. 100723, 2022.

3. S. L. Prescott *et al.*, "A global survey of changing patterns of food allergy burden in children," *World Allergy Organ. J.*, vol. 6, no. 1, p. 21, 2013.

4. J. L. Chen and S. L. Bahna, "Spice allergy," *Ann. Allergy, Asthma Immunol.*, vol. 107, no. 3, pp. 191–199, 2011.

5. C. S. Rosario, C. a Cardozo, D. C. Chong e Silva, H. J. Chong Neto, C. a Riedi, and N. A. Rosario, "Epidemiology and risk factors of allergic diseases in adolescents," *J. Allergy Clin. Immunol.*, vol. 141, no. 2, p. AB223, 2018.

6. b. y. patel and g. w. volcheck, "food allergy: common causes, diagnosis, and treatment," *Mayo Clin. Proc.*, vol. 90, no. 10, pp. 1411–1419, 2015.

7. D. Atkins, "Food allergy: diagnosis and management," *Prim. Care - Clin. Off. Pract.*, vol. 35, no. 1, pp. 119–140, 2008.

8. R. Valenta, H. Hochwallner, B. Linhart, and S. Pahr, "Food allergies : the basics," *Gastroenterology*, vol. 148, no. 6, pp. 1120-1131.e4, 2015.

9. G. Longo, I. Berti, A. W. Burks, B. Krauss, and E. Barbi, "IgE-mediated food allergy in children," *Lancet*, vol. 382, no. 9905, pp. 1656–1664, 2013.

10. S. H. Sicherer and H. A. Sampson, "Food allergy: Epidemiology, pathogenesis, diagnosis, and treatment," *J. Allergy Clin. Immunol.*, vol. 133, no. 2, pp. 291-307.e5, 2014.

11. R. Ganesh and M. Sathiyasekeran, "Food allergy in children," *Indian J. Pract. Pediatr.*, vol. 15, no. 3, pp. 180–188, 2013.

12. M. Fernández-Rivas *et al.*, "Apple allergy across Europe: How allergen sensitization profiles determine the clinical expression of allergies to plant foods," *J. Allergy Clin. Immunol.*, vol. 118, no. 2, pp. 481–488, 2006.

13. M. Kulig, R. Bergmann, U. Klettke, and V. Wahn, "Food and drug reactions and anaphylaxis Natural course of sensitization to food and inhalant allergens during the first 6," pp. 1173–1179, 1999.

14. R. Mitra, N. Mishra, and G. P. Rath, "Blood groups systems," vol. 58, no. 5, pp. 524–529, 2014.

15. B. Roy, I. Banerjee, B. Sathian, M. Mondal, and S. Cg, "Blood group distribution and its relationship with bleeding time and clotting time : A medical school based observational study among Nepali , Indian and Sri Lankan students," vol. 1, no. 4, pp. 135–140, 2011.

16. L. Dean and B. MD, "Blood group antigens are surface markers on the red blood cell membrane," in *Blood Groups and Red Cell Antigens*, National Center for Biotechnology Information (US), 2005.

17. L. Cooling, "Blood groups in infection and host susceptibility," *Clin. Microbiol. Rev.*, vol. 28, no. 3, pp. 801–870, 2015.

18. G. M. Liumbruno and M. Franchini, "Beyond immunohaematology: The role of the ABO blood group in human diseases," *Blood Transfus.*, vol. 11, no. 4, pp. 491–499, 2013.

19. N. H. Dahalan, S. A. Tuan DIn, and S. M. B. Mohamad, "Association of ABO blood groups with allergic diseases: A scoping review," *BMJ Open*, vol. 10, no. 2, pp. 1–8, 2020.

20. J. C. Gill, "Diagnosis of von willebrand disease in people with type O Blood," *Clin. Adv. Hematol. Oncol.*, vol. 12, no. 2, pp. 119–121, 2014.

21. M. Chigira, "Origin of blood-group antigens: A self-declaration mechanism in somatic cell society," *Med. Hypotheses*, vol. 46, no. 3, pp. 290–294, 1996.

22. C. Carpeggiani, "Allergic rhinitis and association with the O blood group," *Rev. Bras. Hematol. Hemoter.*, vol. 33, no. 6, pp. 406–407, 2011.

23. N. Topno, V. P. Narvey, and A. K. Jain, "The correlation of allergic rhinitis with abo phenotype," *Indian J. Otolaryngol. Head Neck Surg.*, vol. 71, no. s3, pp. 1827–1831, 2019.

24. J. T. Schroeder *et al.*, "Red meat allergy in Sweden: Association with tick sensitization and B-negative blood groups," vol. 132, no. 6, 2013.

25. O. N. Hamad, "A relationship between allergic rhinitis and ABO blood group and related it with genetics in population based cohort study in Kut," vol. 2, no. 2, pp. 9–12, 2016.

26. U. Power, Laura W. Rockville, MD, "BIOTYPE DIETS SYSTEM: PREDICTING FOOD ALLERGES BY BLOOD TYPE," 2006.

27. K. S. Hofmeier, S. Link, and I. Heijnen, "Food allergy to the carbohydrate galactose-alpha-1,3-galactose (alpha-gal): four case reports and a review," 2007.

28. L. Power, "Biotype Diets System®: Blood types and food allergies," *J. Nutr. Environ. Med.*, vol. 16, no. 2, pp. 125–135, 2007.

29. Andreas J.Bircher, A. J., K. S. Hofmeier, S. Link, and I. Heijnen, "The B antigen protects against the development of red meat allergy," *HHS Public Access*, 2018.

30. I. C. R. Leite, J. C. dos Santos Júnior, C. C. S. de Sousa, A. V. Lima, and A. L. Miranda-Vilela, "Recognition of phenylthiocarbamide (PTC) in taste test is related to blood group B phenotype, females, and risk of developing food allergy: a cross-sectional Brazilian-based study," *Nutr. Res.*, vol. 52, no. 2018, pp. 22–38, 2018.

31. D. L. M. Goh, Y. N. Lau, F. T. Chew, L. P. C. Shek, and B. W. Lee, "Pattern of food-induced anaphylaxis in children of an Asian community," pp. 84–86, 1999.

32. N. R. De Silva, W. M. D. K. Dasanayake, C. Karunatilake, G. D. Wickramasingha, B. D. De Silva, and G. N. Malavige, "Aetiology of anaphylaxis in patients referred to an immunology clinic in Colombo , Sri Lanka," *Allergy, Asthma Clin. Immunol.*, pp. 1–9, 2018.

33. Y. S. G. Wimalasiri, R. M. U. Ratnayake, T. D. N. Karunaratne, and K. K. D. S. Ranaweera, "Food allergy and anaphylaxis - 2063. Identification of foods causing hypersensitivity/ allergy among school children in two sub-urban schools in Colombo District, Sri Lanka," *World Allergy Organ. J.*, vol. 6, no. Suppl 1, p. P146, 2013.

34. J. Iddagoda *et al.*, "Identification of allergens in coconut milk and oil with patients sensitized to coconut milk in Sri Lanka," *Clin. Mol. Allergy*, vol. 20, no. 1, pp. 1–11, 2022, doi: 10.1186/s12948-022-00181-0.

Transformative Applied Research in Computing, Engineering, Science and Technology – Dr. Damayanthi Dahanayake et al. (eds)
© 2024 Taylor & Francis Group, London, ISBN 978-1-041-01782-0

35

Sex Determination Using Cluster Analysis of Femur Fragments in a Sri Lankan Population

Madhavi M Gamage*
Department of Electrical,
Electronic and Systems Engineering, NSBM Green University,
Sri Lanka

Lakshika S Nawarathna
Department of Statistics and Computer Science,
University of Peradeniya,
Sri Lanka

Deepthi Nanayakkara[3]
Department of Basic Sciences, University of Peradeniya,
Sri Lanka

Abstract

Identifying the sex of unidentified human skeletons is crucial in bioarchaeology and forensic anthropology. This study develops a clustering-based approach using 22 measurements from proximal, distal ends, and shafts of both femur bones to determine sex in the current population of Sri Lanka. K-means with hierarchical clustering techniques were evaluated using elbow, silhouette, and gap statistics for K-means, while Ward's method for hierarchical clustering demonstrated higher accuracy in identifying sex. Specifically, Ward's hierarchical clustering method showed an accuracy of 90.6%. Both methods identified two clusters as optimal for sex classification, making them suitable for determining sex in unknown, mutilated, or dismembered skeletal remains.

Keywords

Femur bone, Hierarchical clustering, K-means clustering, Sex determination

1. Introduction

The femur constitutes the largest and most prominent bone in the human skeleton [1]. In forensic anthropology, a primary objective is identifying whether male or female, a critical aspect in identifying the remains of a skeleton, including those that are mutilated, decomposed, or reduced to cremains [2]. Figure 35.1 illustrates the structure and the

*Corresponding author: madhavi.m@nsbm.ac.lk

DOI: 10.1201/9781003616368-35

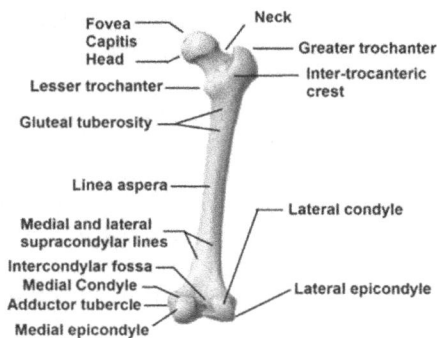

Fig. 35.1 The anatomy of the femur bone [3]

anatomy of the femur bone highlighting its importance in anthropological studies.

Sex identification of human bones or bone fragments plays a crucial role in estimating unknown human bodies [4]. Therefore, it has been extensively studied for sex identification and estimation using various statistical methods such as discrimination analysis, linear regression, t-test, F-test, correlation, and univariate analysis [5,6]. Typically, these analyses use a small set of variables, such as specific bone measurements, that are highly relevant to sex determination. This is done to simplify the models and focus on the most significant features for accurate results.

Identifying sex is one of the initial steps in constructing an individual's biological profile, which is essential for forensic and bioarcheological investigations [7]. However, this task becomes particularly challenging when skeletal remains are damaged or incomplete, especially in scenarios involving mass fatalities like aircraft accidents, earthquakes, floods, landslides, and tsunamis.

This study extends the scope by considering a comprehensive set of variables, specifically 22 measurements from not only the left side but also the right side of the femur bone. The primary objective can be to explore sex dimorphism in femur bone measurements and develop a robust classification method for identifying sex in the contemporary Sri Lankan population.

The reliable identification of males and females from the remains of human skeletons can be essential not only for personal identification in forensic contexts but also for studying ancient populations through archaeological cemetery data. DNA has increasingly been employed for this purpose in forensic investigations [8]. Researchers have developed innovative methods across various disciplines to address this need.

While various statistical methods, such as logistic regression [9], decision tree, and discriminant analysis [10], have traditionally been employed for sex determination in most

research, clustering methods may be more suitable due to the categorical nature of sex. Previous studies indicate that clustering methods have not been extensively utilized in bone research. Therefore, this study introduces clustering techniques to enhance the accuracy and reliability of sex determination using femur bone data. Additionally, comparisons between measurements from the left and right femur bones are conducted to explore potential asymmetry in sex dimorphism.

2. Literature Review

According to the literature, metric standards for sex determination using femur measurements have been extensively studied. Univariate and multivariate analyses have proven highly effective in assessing sexual dimorphism in femora, with significant utility in forensic studies [6]. Key parameters such as maximum length, head dimensions, midshaft circumference, and epicondylar diameters have demonstrated high accuracy rates, emphasizing their importance in sex identification, often achieving up to 90.2% accuracy [6].

Early studies by Steyn and İşcan et al. have established methodologies for sex classification from the femur and tibia among South African whites, underscoring the reliability of skeletal measurements in forensic investigations [2]. Similarly, research conducted in 2015 assessed the measurements of the femur in Austrians born from the 19th century to the mid-20th century, highlighting traditional statistical approaches in skeletal studies [4].

In specific studies focusing on isolated femur bones, researchers have found statistically significant differences in parameters such as the average width in the medial epicondyle between both sexes. These findings contribute significantly to forensic osteology and anthropometry, aiding in identifying skeletal remains [11].

Earlier research has predominantly employed discrimination analysis, linear regression, and other statistical methods using limited variables to estimate femur bone sex. These methods have laid the groundwork for current advancements in clustering algorithms and machine learning techniques, which promise further improvements in accuracy and reliability [12].

In a recent study, researchers found that bone stress injuries (BSIs) in sprinters are influenced by multiple factors and are not fully understood. Unsupervised machine learning techniques could identify runner subgroups with varying BSI risks. Martin and Heiderscheit utilized hierarchical clustering to categorize runners from different countries based on pelvis-proximal femur geometry derived from dual-energy X-ray absorptiometry scans. They identified seven clusters, primarily segmented by gender, revealing distinct geometric differences that corresponded with incidences of lower body BSIs. Lower pelvis shape factor values, indicative of specific geometric characteristics, were linked to higher BSI risks, particularly among males. This study highlights the importance of pelvis and proximal femur geometry in evaluating BSI risk and offers a methodological framework for developing predictive injury matrices [13].

Recent advancements have introduced machine learning and clustering algorithms as innovative tools for improving sex determination accuracy. Bischl et al. have explored machine learning applications in forensic research, highlighting the efficacy of clustering algorithms like K-means and hierarchical clustering in handling complex femur bone data [12]. These methods offer robust alternatives to traditional statistical approaches by identifying inherent patterns in multidimensional skeletal measurements.

3. Material and Methods

3.1 Methods

A total of 43 pairs of adult femora (30 male and 13 female) from a contemporary Sri Lankan population were obtained from the skeleton collection at the Division of Anatomy, Department of Basic Sciences, Faculty of Dental Sciences, University of Peradeniya, Sri Lanka. All individuals were born after 1924, and the study included femora from individuals aged between 26 and 62. Any femurs that were incomplete, had pathological lesions or showed signs of healed fractures were eliminated from the study. Before commencing the study, ethical approval (ERC/FDS/UOP/1/2017/04) was obtained from the institutional ethics committee.

Despite the limited sample size, we employed multiple approaches to enhance the accuracy of our dataset. These included assessing variable distributions using skewness and kurtosis tests, applying min-max normalization for classification purposes, and conducting comprehensive reliability analyses. These measures were pivotal in ensuring the robustness and validity of our research findings.

3.2 Measurement Protocol

Twenty-two measurements from both the right and left femora were utilized, including maximum length (FML), the vertical diameter of the neck (VND), transverse diameter of the neck (TND), vertical diameter of the head (VHD), transverse diameter of head (THD), subtrochanteric anteroposterior diameter (SAPD), subtrochanteric medial-lateral diameter (SMLD), mid-shaft anteroposterior diameter (MAPD), mid-shaft medial-

lateral diameter (MMLD), and epicondylar breadth (EpB). Detailed descriptions of these measurements are provided in Table 35.1. The maximum length was assessed using an osteometric board, while other dimensions were determined with digital calipers, and recorded to the nearest 0.01 mm. To ensure consistency, a single investigator performed all measurements, with each measurement repeated three times to obtain the mean value for subsequent analysis.

Table 35.1 Description of measurements of the femur bone [14,15]

Measurement	Description
Femur Maximum Length (FML)	The straight-line distance from the highest point on the femoral head to the lowest point on the condyles.
Epicondylar breadth (EpB)	The straight-line distance between the inner edge of the medial condyle and the outer edge of the lateral condyle.
Vertical Head Diameter (VHD)	The greatest vertical diameter of the head, measured from its highest to its lowest point.
Transverse Head Diameter (THD)	The greatest diameter of the head, measured from medial to lateral, is perpendicular to the VHD.
Vertical (superior-inferior) Neck Diameter (VND)	The smallest diameter of the femoral neck in the superior-inferior direction.
Transverse Neck Diameter (TND)	The smallest diameter of the femoral neck in the anteroposterior direction.
Length Neck Diameter (LND)	For neck lengthening, the acetabular version angle (AS) should be 0 degrees or less, and the dorsal acetabular rim angle should be within normal range.
Subtrochanteric medial-lateral (transverse) diameter (SMLD)	The distance between the medial and lateral surfaces at the proximal end of the diaphysis, measured at the point of its greatest lateral expansion just below the lesser trochanter
Subtrochanteric anteroposterior diameter (SAPD)	The distance between the anterior and posterior surfaces at the proximal end of the diaphysis was measured perpendicular to the SMLD, at the point of its greatest lateral expansion.
Midshaft anteroposterior diameter (MAPD)	The anteroposterior diameter was measured near the midpoint of the diaphysis, at the highest point of the linear aspera.
Midshaft medial-lateral (transverse) diameter (MMLD)	Measurement is taken perpendicular to the anteroposterior diameter of the shaft.

3.3 Statistical Analysis

Descriptive statistics were used to graphically represent the data. Clustering techniques, including hierarchical and K-means clustering, were applied to sex classification. Clustering methods are particularly suitable for sex identification from skeletal remains due to several advantages. Firstly, sex is a categorical variable, and clustering algorithms are adept at handling categorical data, effectively grouping similar data points based on bone measurements or sex dimorphism indicators. Secondly, these methods facilitate pattern recognition, enabling the detection of distinctive traits that differentiate between male and female skeletal structures. Thirdly, they offer flexibility in data handling, accommodating diverse data types and sizes commonly encountered in forensic and archaeological contexts. Moreover, clustering allows for exploratory analysis, unveiling hidden structures within datasets that traditional statistical methods may overlook. Additionally, their scalability makes them practical for analyzing large datasets prevalent in these fields. Overall, clustering methods complement traditional statistical approaches by enhancing accuracy and providing deeper insights into sex determination from skeletal remains.

All computations in this study were performed using statistical software packages R and SPSS [12].

3.4 Hierarchical Clustering

Hierarchical clustering builds a cluster tree (dendrogram) to represent data, merging clusters based on their similarity. This study employed agglomerative hierarchical clustering methods, including complete linkage, single linkage, average linkage, and Ward's method. Ward's method, known for its ability to minimize variance within clusters, was selected for its suitability in this context [16]. Dendrogram analysis was used to visualize clustering results. We chose the hierarchical clustering method for this study because it is especially effective when the number of clusters is unknown and when a thorough understanding of the data's hierarchical relationships is needed [17].

3.5 K-means Clustering

K-means clustering is an iterative, partition-based method where each cluster is defined by its mean value. It is preferred for its efficiency and simplicity, particularly with spherical cluster structures. Despite our smaller sample size, we validated our dataset and employed three methods to identify optimal clusters. Distance metrics such as Euclidean, Manhattan, and Minkowski distances were utilized to measure dissimilarities between objects. The optimal number of clusters was established using the Elbow method, Silhouette analysis, and Gap statistic techniques [18].

4. Results and Discussion

Based on skewness and kurtosis tests, all variables demonstrated a normal distribution. Min-max normalization

was applied for classification methods, and the study achieved a reliability of 0.952. These factors collectively underscore the accuracy and robustness of the dataset.

Figure 35.2 depicts the variation in measurements between the left and right femora using boxplots. The green color represents measurements from the right femur, while the red color represents measurements from the left femur. Epicondylar breadth (EpB) exhibits the greatest variability, whereas the transverse neck diameter (TND) of both the left and right femoral shows minor variability. All measured characteristics of the left and right femora exhibit similar variability. Normality was assessed using the statistical values and standard errors of skewness and kurtosis within a 5% confidence interval. Since all variables fell between -1.96 and 1.96, they followed a normal distribution. The average values, standard deviations, and p-values of the t-test for each variable categorized by male and female femur bone are given in Table 35.2. Significant differences (p-value < 0.05) were observed between male and female measurements, indicating measurable differences in these dimensions between genders. These differences may be attributed to biological factors such as skeletal structure, density, or overall size, which often vary between males and females. Our study found that males generally have larger femoral dimensions than females.

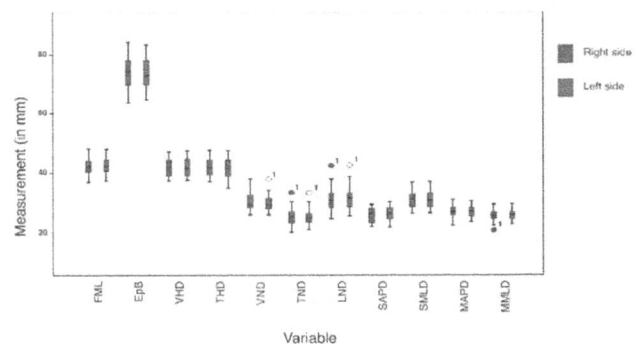

Fig. 35.2 The variation in measurements between left and right femur bone

4.1 K-means Clustering

For K-means clustering, all femoral measurements were normalized using min-max normalization. The optimal number of clusters was determined using the Elbow method, Silhouette analysis, and Gap statistic, all of which indicated a two-cluster solution. The Elbow method shows a sharp reduction in the within-cluster sum of squares at k=2, marking it as the "elbow" point. The Silhouette method yields the highest average silhouette score at k=2, indicating well-defined clusters. Similarly, the Gap Statistic peaks at k=2, confirming this as the point where the clustering structure is most distinct from random reference data. Cluster 1 predominantly consisted of male records (67% males, 33% females), while Cluster 2 predominantly consisted of female records (85% females, 15% males). This clustering pattern effectively separated males into one cluster and females into another, as depicted in Fig. 35.4.

Table 35.2 The average values, standard deviations, and p-values from the t-test for each variable, separated by male and female femur bones

Side	Variable	Female (n = 13)	Male (n = 30)	p-value
Left	FML	40.12 ± 1.51	43.10 ± 2.48	<0.001
	EpB	69.45 ± 3.82	75.72 ± 4.85	<0.001
	VHD	38.91 ± 1.72	42.89 ± 2.84	<0.001
	THD	38.78 ± 2.05	42.30 ± 2.93	<0.001
	VND	27.87 ± 1.89	30.37 ± 2.69	<0.001
	TND	23.03 ± 1.41	25.57 ± 2.68	<0.001
	LND	30.50 ± 2.02	31.31 ± 2.75	<0.001
	SAPD	24.86 ± 2.30	26.21 ± 21.40	<0.001
	SMLD	28.41 ± 1.92	31.41 ± 2.75	<0.001
	MAPD	25.09 ± 1.62	27.19 ± 1.83	<0.001
	MMLD	24.28 ± 1.37	25.99 ± 1.49	<0.001
Right	FML	39.93 ± 1.88	43.01 ± 2.52	<0.001
	EpB	69.57 ± 3.88	76.22 ± 4.85	<0.001
	VHD	38.89 ± 1.93	42.73 ± 2.56	<0.001
	THD	39.13 ± 2.08	42.48 ± 2.77	<0.001
	VND	27.72 ± 1.69	30.46 ± 2.81	<0.001
	TND	22.29 ± 2.19	25.68 ± 2.52	<0.001
	LND	28.97 ± 2.76	31.17 ± 4.10	<0.001
	SAPD	23.94 ± 2.25	26.04 ± 2.02	<0.001
	SMLD	28.62 ± 2.50	31.55 ± 2.74	<0.001
	MAPD	25.42 ± 1.47	27.01 ± 2.06	<0.001
	MMLD	24.22 ± 1.42	25.93 ± 1.50	<0.001

4.2 K-means Clustering

For K-means clustering, all femoral measurements were normalized using min-max normalization. The optimal number of clusters was determined using the Elbow method, Silhouette analysis, and Gap statistic, all of which indicated a two-cluster solution. The Elbow method shows a sharp reduction in the within-cluster sum of squares at k=2, marking it as the "elbow" point. The Silhouette method yields the highest average silhouette score at k=2, indicating well-defined clusters. Similarly, the Gap Statistic peaks at k=2, confirming this as the point where the clustering structure is most distinct from random reference data. Cluster 1 predominantly consisted of male records (67% males, 33% females), while Cluster 2 predominantly

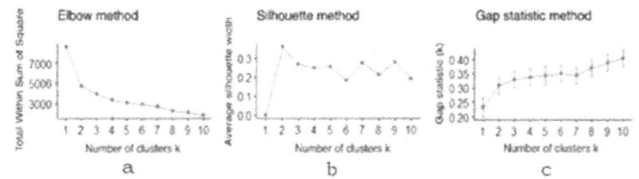

Fig. 35.3 The results of the methods of K-means clustering a) Elbow method, b) Silhouette method, and c) Gap statistic method

consisted of female records (85% females, 15% males). This clustering pattern effectively separated males into one cluster and females into another, as depicted in Fig. 35.4.

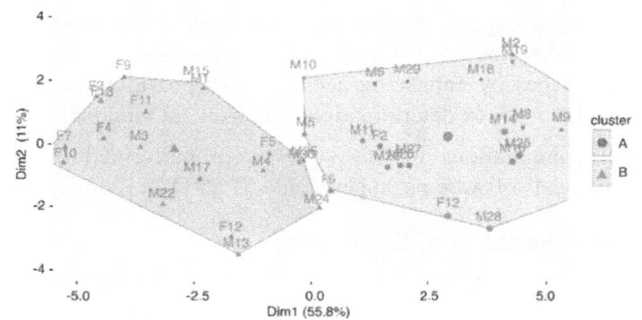

Fig. 35.4 Cluster plot for the optimal number of clusters

4.3 Hierarchical Clustering

Figure 35.5 displays dendrograms for four hierarchical clustering methods: Complete Linkage, Single Linkage, Average Linkage, and Ward's Method. Ward's Method showed the highest accuracy (0.906), effectively clustering females and males into two distinct groups (Clusters A and B).

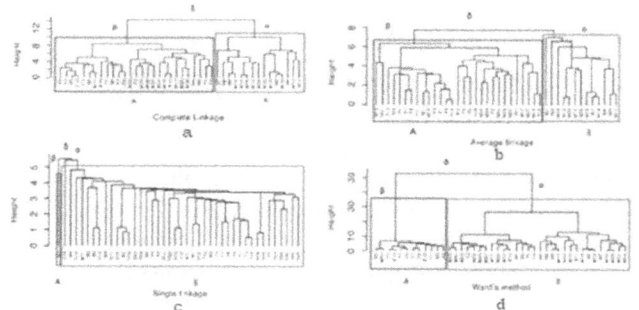

Fig. 35.5 Dendrograms of the hierarchical clustering using the four methods: a) complete linkage, b) Average linkage, c) Simple linkage, and d) Ward's method

Cluster A predominantly comprised females (100% females, 46% males), while Cluster B predominantly comprised males (0% females, 54% males). This method provided the most accurate classification of sex based on femoral measurements, as illustrated in the statistical values of Table 35.3 and Fig. 35.6.

Table 35.3 Summary of accuracies of agglomerative hierarchical algorithms used to classify the gender

Method	Accuracy
Complete Linkage	0.817
Single Linkage	0.546
Average Linkage	0.679
Ward's method	0.906

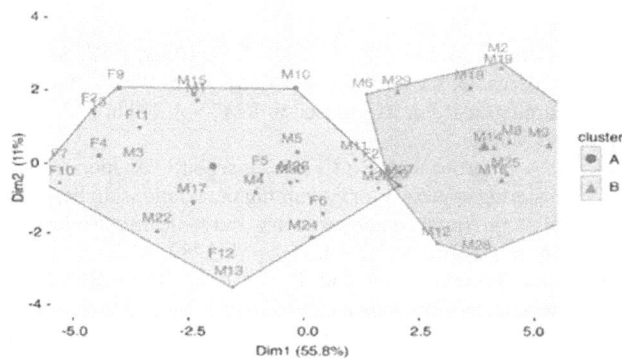

Fig. 35.6 Clusters of ward's method

a) Algorithm

```
#Non hirachichal method
#Kmeans Clustering
set.seed(247)
k2 <- kmeans(femur.data, centers = 4)
fviz_cluster(k2,data=femur.data,    xlim=    c(-5:5),
ylim=c(-4:4))
#plot the compare
k2 <- kmeans(femur.data, centers = 2)
k3 <- kmeans(femur.data, centers = 3)
k4 <- kmeans(femur.data, centers = 4)
k5 <- kmeans(femur.data, centers = 5)
p1 <- fviz_cluster(k2, geom = "point", data = femur.data)
+ ggtitle("k = 2")
p2 <- fviz_cluster(k3, geom = "point", data = femur.data)
+ ggtitle("k = 3")
p3 <- fviz_cluster(k4, geom = "point", data = femur.data)
+ ggtitle("k = 4")
p4 <- fviz_cluster(k5, geom = "point", data = femur.data)
+ ggtitle("k = 5")
library(gridExtra)
grid.arrange(p1, p2, p3, p4, nrow = 2)
```

```
#Determine the optimal Number of Clusters
set.seed(247)
# Elbow method
m1 <- fviz_nbclust(femur.data, kmeans, method = "wss")
+
 geom_vline(xintercept = 4, linetype = 2)+
 labs(title = "Elbow method")
# Silhouette method
m2 <- fviz_nbclust(femur.data, kmeans, method =
"silhouette")+
 labs(title = "Silhouette method")
# Gap statistic
# nboot = 50 to keep the function speedy.
# Use verbose = FALSE to hide computing progression.
m3 <- fviz_nbclust(femur.data, kmeans, nstart = 25,
method = "gap_stat", nboot = 50)+ labs(title = "Gap
statistic method")
library(gridExtra)
grid.arrange(m1, m2, m3,nrow=2, ncol=2)
#Determine the optimal Number of Clusters
set.seed(247)
# Elbow method
m1 <- fviz_nbclust(scaled.data, kmeans, method = "wss")
+
 geom_vline(xintercept = 4, linetype = 2)+
 labs(title = "Elbow method")
# Silhouette method
m2 <- fviz_nbclust(scaled.data, kmeans, method =
"silhouette")+
 labs(title = "Silhouette method")
# Gap statistic
# nboot = 50 to keep the function speedy.
# Use verbose = FALSE to hide computing progression.
m3 <- fviz_nbclust(scaled.data, kmeans, nstart = 25,
method = "gap_stat", nboot = 50)+ labs(title = "Gap
statistic method")
library(gridExtra)
grid.arrange(m1, m2, m3,nrow=2, ncol=2)
#According to the best suggested
k2 <- kmeans(femur.data, centers = 2)
fviz_cluster(k2, data = femur.data, xlim= c(-5:5), ylim= c(-
4:4)) + ggtitle("k = 2")
k2
```

5. Conclusion

The study successfully utilized clustering methods to classify sex based on femoral measurements from a contemporary Sri Lankan population. K-means clustering identified distinct clusters based on normalized measurements, while hierarchical clustering, especially Ward's Method, provided highly accurate clustering of male and female femora. In previous studies, researchers identified sex using univariate and multivariate analyses with an accuracy of 90% [6]. In our study, we achieved an accuracy of 91% using Ward's method. This demonstrates that clustering methods can accurately determine the sex of femur bones. These findings underscore the utility of clustering techniques in forensic and anthropological studies for sex estimation using skeletal remains.

The relatively small number of female femur bone measurements presents a significant limitation. Therefore, it is recommended that further research be conducted with a larger sample size to enhance the accuracy of the findings.

Acknowledgment

The authors are thankful to the Faculty of Dental Sciences, University of Peradeniya, for providing the data.

REFERENCES

1. Francis, A. Shrivastava, C. Masih, N. Dwivedi, P. Tiwari, R. Nareliya, and V. Kumar, "Biomechanical analysis of human femur: a review," J. Biomed. Bioeng., vol. 3, no. 1, 2012.
2. M. Steyn and M. Y. İşcan, "Sex determination from the femur and tibia in South African whites," Forensic Sci. Int., vol. 90, no. 1–2, pp. 111–119, 1997.
3. F. H. Netter, Netter's Atlas of Human Anatomy, 3rd ed. Philadelphia: Elsevier, 2003, "Osteology of the Femur."
4. F. Kanz, C. Fitzl, A. Vlcek, and F. Frommlet, "Sex estimation using the femur of Austrians born in the 19th to the middle of the 20th century," Anthropologischer Anzeiger, vol. 72, no. 1, 2015.
5. G. Soni, U. Dhall, and S. Chhabra, "Determination of sex from femur: discriminant analysis," J. Anat. Soc. India, vol. 59, no. 2, pp. 216–221, 2010.
6. U. Sembian, M. Muhil, T. Srimathi, T. Muthukumar, and S. D. Nalina Kumari, "A study of sexual dimorphism in femora of rural population of South Tamilnadu, India," J. Clin. Diagn. Res., vol. 6, no. 2, pp. 163–165, 2012.
7. T. D. White, M. T. Black, and P. A. Folkens, Human Osteology, 3rd ed. San Diego: Academic Press, 2011.
8. S. Mays and M. Cox, "Sex determination in skeletal remains," in Human Osteology in Archaeology and Forensic Science, 2000, pp. 117–130.
9. S. Aslan, Ş. D. Kekeç, E. G. Ateş, C. İncekaş, A. Kürkçüoğlu, and İ. C. Pelin, "Sex determination of proximal and distal end of femur on radiological images," Eurasian J. Anthropol., vol. 14, no. 1, pp. 15–33, 2024.
10. N. Madushani, V. Vadysinghe, and N. Nanayakkara, "Identification of gender using fragments of femur bone in Sri Lankan population," in Proc. Int. Conf. Math. Math. Educ., 2019, p. 36.
11. O. Gulhan, K. Harrison, and A. Kiris, "A new computer-tomography-based method of sex estimation: Development of Turkish population-specific standards," Forensic Sci. Int., vol. 255, pp. 2–8, 2015.
12. B. Bischl, M. Lang, L. Kotthoff, J. Schiffner, J. Richter, E. Studerus, G. Casalicchio, and Z. M. Jones, "mlr: Machine learning in R," J. Mach. Learn. Res., vol. 17, no. 170, pp. 1–5, 2016.
13. J. A. Martin and B. C. Heiderscheit, "A hierarchical clustering approach for examining the relationship between pelvis-proximal femur geometry and bone stress injury in runners," J. Biomech., vol. 160, p. 111782, 2023.
14. P. H. Moore-Jansen and R. L. Jantz, Data Collection Procedures for Forensic Skeletal Material. Forensic Anthropology Center, Dept. of Anthropology, Univ. of Tennessee, 1990.
15. J. E. Buikstra and D. H. Ubelaker, Standards for Data Collection from Human Skeletal Remains. Fayetteville: Arkansas Archaeological Survey, 1994.
16. F. Murtagh and P. Legendre, "Ward's hierarchical agglomerative clustering method: which algorithms implement Ward's criterion?," J. Classif., vol. 31, pp. 274–295, 2014.
17. A. Jatain, A. Nagpal, and D. Gaur, "Agglomerative hierarchical approach for clustering components of similar reusability," Int. J. Comput. Appl., vol. 68, no. 2, 2013.
18. J. Yadav and M. Sharma, "A review of K-mean algorithm," Int. J. Eng. Trends Technol., vol. 4, no. 7, pp. 2972–2976, 2013.

Note: All the figures and tables (except Fig. 35.1 and Table 35.1) in this chapter were made by the authors.

Transformative Applied Research in Computing, Engineering, Science and Technology – Dr. Damayanthi Dahanayake et al. (eds)
© 2024 Taylor & Francis Group, London, ISBN 978-1-041-01782-0

36

Evaluate The Learning Experience of Interior Design Students in Community Participatory Design

W.P.G.U. Pathirathna*
Department of Design Studies, NSBM Green University,
Sri Lanka

L.K.Y.S. Lihiniyakumara and R.M.S. Pramod
Department of Design Studies,
Faculty of Engineering, NSBM Green University,
Sri Lanka

Abstract

This research delves into the deep impact of involving interior design students in community participatory processes. Through a qualitative approach, the study seeks to assess the effectiveness of engaging students in real-world design projects within local communities. It investigates how participating in community-based interior design influences various learning parameters, including cognitive, affective, and contextual factors, as well as instructional and learning characteristics among students. The insights derived from this research will be helpful for educators and curriculum developers, highlighting the significance of integrating community participatory projects with a learn-by-doing approach in design education to foster a vibrant and applied learning environment.

Keywords

Interior design education, Community participatory design, Design process, Learning experiences, Learn-by-doing approach

1. Introduction

In the realm of interior design education, a notable evolution in learning methodologies, which have increasingly embraced community participatory design processes can be witnessed as a transformative educational approach. [1]. Traditionally, the focus was on studio-based practices that emphasized technical proficiency and theoretical knowledge. However, contemporary education now places greater emphasis on experiential learning and real-world engagement. One of the most prominent approaches in this evolution is community participatory design, which provides interior design students with unparalleled opportunities to directly collaborate with local communities. This goes beyond conventional classroom settings, allowing students to grapple with authentic design

*Corresponding author: wpgupathirathna@students.nsbm.ac.lk

DOI: 10.1201/9781003616368-36

challenges in real-world contexts. As a result, students not only enhance their practical skills in spatial planning and aesthetic considerations but also develop a deeper understanding of how to integrate social and cultural dynamics into their design solutions.

Students immersed in diverse community contexts have the unique opportunity to gain a deep understanding of the ethical, cultural, technical, and environmental implications of their design work. [1]. This experience equips them to navigate the complexities of professional practice in our rapidly globalizing world. The primary aim of this research is to thoroughly explore the impact of community participatory design on the learning experiences of interior design students. This study seeks to understand how these experiences shape students' cognitive development and emotional engagement, offering a nuanced understanding of the effects of community engagement. Using in-depth qualitative research methods, including detailed case studies, this investigation aims to provide comprehensive insights into the multifaceted benefits of community-engaged learning.

This research aims to assess interior design students' experiences in community participatory design projects using a qualitative approach. The study intends to capture a holistic view of the student's learning context and explore how those things influence their learning experiences.

Finally, this study will contribute to a deeper understanding of the pivotal role that community participation plays in enriching the educational journey of aspiring interior designers. The current approach in interior design pedagogy prioritizes "learning by doing" to enrich students' practical experience and foster heightened engagement. This pedagogical method is designed to not only enhance critical thinking, problem-solving, and creativity but also to provide students with hands-on learning opportunities that encourage active participation and application of theoretical knowledge in real-world scenarios.

2. Background

The domain of interior design education has witnessed a growing recognition of the critical role of experiential learning and community engagement in fostering the holistic development of students. In contrast to traditional pedagogical methods, which heavily rely on theoretical and classroom-based instruction, contemporary approaches prioritize real-world application and interaction with diverse user groups [2]. Within this context, community participatory design processes have emerged as a dynamic framework that empowers students to engage in collaborative problem-solving with community members,

thereby addressing authentic design challenges. This immersive approach not only enriches students' learning experiences but also equips them with the practical skills and awareness essential for their future professional identity.

Participating in these experiential learning opportunities equips students with the essential skills required for professional practice, such as the development of critical thinking and problem-solving abilities tailored to address complex societal issues [2].

Community participatory design has gained recognition as a transformative educational strategy within interior design programs. This approach involves students engaging directly with community stakeholders to collaboratively address local needs and aspirations through design projects. By working closely with diverse community members, students not only improve their practical skills in spatial planning and material selection but also develop empathy and cultural competence [1].

3. Literature Review

The literature review predominantly focuses on examining and synthesizing existing theories and studies about the interior design process, community participatory design process, and the learning experiences associated with these processes. Several factors, including definitions, perceptions, and affective and analytical parameters, influence the learning experience. This literature review chapter aims to establish a theoretical foundation for the research, identifying gaps and setting the context for the study.

3.1 Interior Design Education as a Dynamic Discourse

The field of interior design education is a multifaceted and ever-evolving discourse that encompasses a wide range of theoretical, practical, and pedagogical considerations. At its core, interior design education aims to equip students with the knowledge, skills, and critical thinking abilities required to create functional, aesthetically pleasing, and environmentally sustainable interior spaces [3]. As a discipline, interior design shares common ground with areas such as architecture, art history, and environmental psychology, each of which contributes to the rich tapestry of interior design education.

3.2 Interior Design Process as an Intellectual Engagement

The interior design process is a systematic and creative approach to improving the functionality, aesthetic appeal, and overall environment of interior spaces [3].

This process included several stages: initial consultation, concept development, design planning, implementation, and evaluation [3].

3.3 Community Participatory Design Process

The community participatory design process typically consists of several stages that lead to the collaborative development of built environments in collaboration with local communities [1].

The idea of 'community' refers to a group whose members have common interests interacting within a certain geographical area. A community evolves through human interaction, which gradually transforms into a common way of life determined by common patterns of behavior [4]. The role of communities in fostering social capital is significant. Social capital refers to the networks, norms, and social trust that facilitate coordination and cooperation for mutual benefit [5].

3.4 Learn By Doing Approach

The concept of learning experience has garnered significant attention in educational research and practice, reflecting its importance in shaping individuals' knowledge, skills, and personal development [6].

The main parameters of the learning experience include the cognitive parameter, affective parameter, environment parameter, instruction parameter, and learning characteristics parameter [7].

Table 36.1 Learning experience of main 5 parameters and their sub-parameters [7]

Parameter	Sub Parameter
Cognitive parameter	- Attention - Memory - Cognition - Problem–solving skill
Affective parameter	- Motivation - Engagement - Emotion - Attitudes
Environment parameter	- Physical setting - Collaborate - Technically tools
Instruction parameter	- Lectures - Group work. - Hands-on activities
Learning characteristics parameter	- Interest - Learning styles

4. Methodology

This research was conducted in five phases. In phase one, a background study was carried out to establish the research problem as well as the aims and objectives of the study.

In the second phase, a comprehensive literature review was conducted to identify the key parameters of the learning experiences and through those identified theories, a theoretical framework was created.

Accordingly, a systematic questionnaire survey was developed based on the criteria identified in the literature review learning experience parameters.

This research uses a qualitative approach to evaluate the learning experiences of interior design students engaged in community participatory interior design processes. The methodology is structured around a comparative case study of two projects: a community-based interior design project and a studio-based university library design project. This comparison will highlight differences and similarities in learning outcomes between the two approaches.

4.1 Case Study Descriptions

Case 01; This case study involves a community participatory interior design project focusing on the design of a factory and outlet for a community-based initiative. This project was chosen because its collaborative nature required students to engage directly with community stakeholders, understand their needs, and incorporate these insights into their planning process.

Case 02; This case study investigates a studio-based interior design project focused on the redesign of the NSBM Green University library. The project represents a more traditional educational setting where students work within the confines of a controlled academic environment. The studio-based approach allows for a structured exploration of instructor-led design principles with minimal outside input. This case was chosen to provide a baseline for comparison against the community participatory interior design project, highlighting differences in learning experiences.

4.2 Data Collection and Data Analysis

The data collection process for this research on the evaluation of students' learning experiences of interior design in community participation planning processes uses a qualitative approach mainly using questionnaires.

The data analysis method is used to analyze the overall impact of positive results. In this area calculate, and evaluate the overall learning experiences' 16 parameters impact comparison between both community participatory interior design process and studio based interior design process.

According to the ICDAT scale method, each can be answered specific scale number

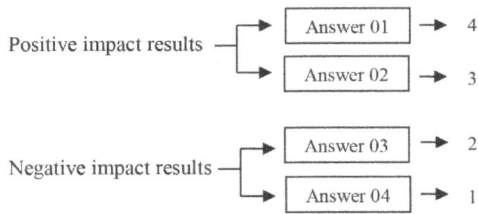

Positive impact results — Answer 01 → 4
Answer 02 → 3

Negative impact results — Answer 03 → 2
Answer 04 → 1

Fig. 36.1 Named answers and each answer to give ICDAT weight scale

The formula for calculating the impact weightage of results,

$$= \text{Number of students} \times \frac{\text{Impact of each answers' weight scale}}{} \quad (1)$$

5. Results and Discussion

This area systematically analyzed the learning experiences of interior design students through a comprehensive questionnaire survey focusing on community participatory-based and studio-based interior design processes. Each learning experience parameter was examined to determine how these educational approaches impact students. And below bar graph shows all the positive impact results of each 16 parameters in percentage.

The questionnaire survey was based on four areas: Section A (General Information), Section B (Community Participatory Interior Design Project), Section C (Studio-Based Interior Design Project), and Section D (Comparative Analysis). The survey consisted of 38 questions, with responses collected from 64 participants.

Section A: The data for this study covered four main areas: age, gender, year of study, and prior experience in design projects. According to the results, most participants (62) were between 20-25 years of age, indicating a primarily young group. The gender distribution shows higher female engagement in interior design programs. All participants were in their 2nd year of study, ensuring a consistent level of study across the sample. In addition, all 64 participants had 1–2 years of prior experience with design projects, providing a uniform basis for evaluating the impact of the participatory design process on their learning experiences.

Section B & C: Survey data from Parts B and C compare interior design students' learning experiences between participatory design processes and studio-based design projects. This comparison is based on 16 parameters obtained from a questionnaire survey. The community participatory interior design process shows significant positive results percentage across all the 15 parameters,

while the studio-based interior design process yields less percentage get positive impact results in 15 parameters in the analysis survey of the gathered results. One parameter was getting an equal positive impact result percentage in both processes (getting 62% positive impact results for the "interest" learning experience parameter).

Section D: According to the below 2 pie charts collected results the significant impact of the community participatory interior design process in promoting student engagement and enhancing learning experiences, emphasizing their effectiveness in interior design education.

5.1 The Impact Weightage of Learning Experience Parameters

This area calculates and evaluates the overall learning experiences' 16 parameters impact weightage comparison between both community participatory and studio-based interior design processes. According to the ICDAT scale and "Fig. 36.1." & "(1)".

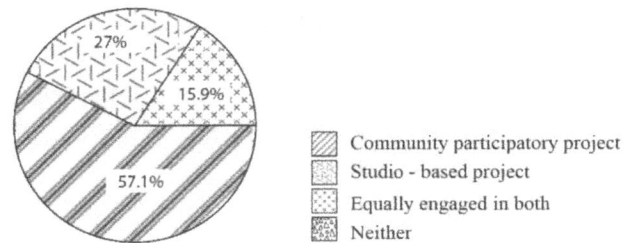

Pie Chart. 1 Student engagement

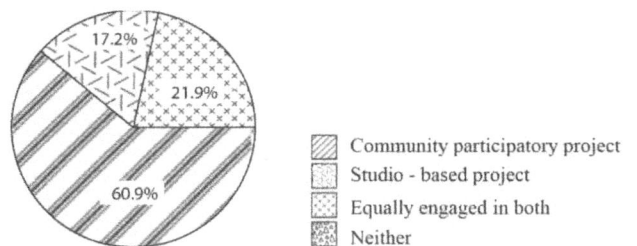

Pie Chart. 2 Learning experiences

Fig. 36.2 Results of the impact of community participatory interior design process in student engagement and learning experiences: Pie Chart 1 & Pie Chart 2

According "Table 36.2, Table 36.3, Table 36.4" and overall, 16 learning experience parameters the community participatory interior design process appears to have provided a more positive and beneficial learning experience for interior design students, showing higher positive affect and lower negative affect loads compared to the studio-based interior design process.

Table 36.2   Questionnaire survey 16 questions

Q. No.	Sub parameter	Question
01	Attention	How would you rate your level of focus during the community project activities?
02	Memory	How well did you retain the information learned during the community project?
03	Cognition	Did the community project challenge your ability to understand complex design concepts?
04	Problem–solving skill	How did the community project impact your problem-solving abilities?
05	Motivation	How motivated were you to contribute to the community project?
06	Engagement	How actively involved were you in the community project activities?
07	Emotion	How did your emotional response affect your participation in the community project?
08	Attitudes	How did engaging with the community influence your attitude toward the design process?
09	Physical setting	How would you rate the physical setting of the community project workspace?
10	Collaborate	How effective was the collaboration with community members in the design process?
11	Technically tools	How well were technological tools integrated into the community project?
12	Lectures	How helpful were the lectures related to the community project?
13	Group works.	How effective was the group work during the community project?
14	Hands-on activities	How beneficial were the hands-on activities in the community project?
15	Interest	How interested were you in the community project?
16	Learning styles	How well did the community project cater to your learning style?

Table 36.3   Community participatory interior design process learning experience overall impacts weightage

Q. No.	Impact weightage			
	Answer 01	Answer 02	Answer 03	Answer 04
01	37x4 = 148	27x3 = 81	0x2 = 0	0x1 = 0
02	38x4 = 152	26x3 = 78	0x2 = 0	0x1 = 0
03	34x4 = 136	30x3 = 90	3x2 = 6	0x1 = 0
04	28x4 = 112	35x3 = 105	1x2 = 2	0x1 = 0
05	38x4 = 152	25x3 = 75	1x2 = 2	0x1 = 0
06	48x4 = 192	16x3 = 48	0x2 = 0	0x1 = 1
07	33x4 = 132	31x3 = 93	0x2 = 0	0x1 = 0
08	29x4 = 116	31x3 = 93	3x2 = 6	1x1 = 1
09	22x4 = 88	35x3 = 105	5x2 = 10	2x1 = 2
10	35x4 = 140	26x3 = 78	3x2 = 6	0x1 = 0
11	20x4 = 80	40x3 = 120	4x2 = 8	0x1 = 0
12	41x4 = 164	22x3 = 66	1x2 = 2	0x1 = 0
13	40x4 = 160	23x3 = 69	1x2 = 2	0x1 = 0
14	33x4 = 132	28x3 = 84	3x2 = 6	0x1 = 0
15	40x4 = 160	23x3 = 69	0x2 = 0	1x1 = 1
16	33x4 = 132	30x3 = 90	1x2 = 2	0x1 = 0
Total	**2196**	**1344**	**52**	**5**

Positive impact of results = 3540   Negative impact of results = 57

Table 36.4   Studio-based interior design process learning experience overall impact weightage

Q. No.	Impact weightage			
	Answer 01	Answer 02	Answer 03	Answer 04
01	18x4 = 72	40x3 = 120	5x2 = 10	1x2 = 2
02	17x4 = 68	42x3 = 126	5x2 = 10	0x2 = 0
03	25x4 = 100	35x3 = 105	2x2 = 4	2x2 = 4
04	14x4 = 56	41x3 = 123	9x2 = 18	0x2 = 0
05	23x4 = 92	35x3 = 105	5x2 = 10	1x2 = 2
06	26x4 = 104	31x3 = 93	7x2 = 14	0x2 = 0
07	15x4 = 60	44x3 = 132	5x2 = 10	0x2 = 0
08	19x4 = 76	34x3 = 102	10x2 = 20	1x2 = 2
09	13x4 = 52	43x3 = 123	7x2 = 14	1x2 = 2
10	25x4 = 100	30x3 = 90	9x2 = 18	0x2 = 0
11	19x4 = 76	41x3 = 132	4x2 = 8	0x2 = 0
12	31x4 = 124	31x3 = 93	2x2 = 4	0x2 = 0
13	22x4 = 88	35x3 = 105	4x2 = 8	3x2 = 6
14	17x4 = 68	44x3 = 132	3x2 = 6	0x2 = 0
15	15x4 = 60	40x3 = 120	9x2 = 18	0x2 = 0
16	18x4 = 72	38x3 = 114	8x2 = 16	0x2 = 0
Total	**1268**	**1815**	**188**	**18**

Positive impact of results = 3083   Negative impact of results = 206

6. Conclusion

This study aimed to evaluate the learning experience of interior design students in a community participatory design process compared to a studio-based interior design project. The literature review first explored existing studies on interior design education, learning experiences, community participatory design processes, and studio-based learning approaches. It provided a theoretical framework for understanding the potential parameters to perform this evaluation. Understanding how these two educational approaches affect various learning parameters, attention, memory, cognition, problem-solving skills, motivation, engagement, emotions, attitudes, physical settings, collaboration, technology tools, lectures, group work, lectures, hands-on activities, interests, and learning styles.

A systematic questionnaire survey for qualitative research methodology assessed various learning experience parameters and compared the two types of projects. According to the results collected, parametric comparisons revealed that community participation projects excelled in all aspects. Overall positive impact weights were significantly higher for the community participatory design process (3540) compared to the studio-based process (3083). According to these findings the value of community participatory design processes in interior design education, highlighting their effectiveness in improving student learning experiences. This research supports the integration of the community participatory design process into the curriculum to better prepare students for real-world design challenges.

Acknowledgment

I would like to acknowledge the lecturers of the Design Department of NSBM Green University for giving their utmost support and knowledge to make this research successful. Also, I would like to thank the design students of the 22.1 &22.2 batches in the Department of Design Studies, NSBM Green University for their participation.

REFERENCES

1. Henry. Sanoff, *Community participation methods in design and planning*. Wiley, 2000.
2. A. M. Salama, "Spatial Design Education New Directions for Pedagogy in Architecture and Beyond," 2015.
3. Christine M. Piotrowski, *Professional Practice for Interior Designers.*, Third edition. 2001.
4. M. G. Barry Wellman, *Virtual Communities as Communities.* 1999.
5. M. Harraka, "Bowling Alone: The Collapse and Revival of American Community, by Robert D. Putnam," *Journal of Catholic Education*, vol. 6, no. 2, Dec. 2002, doi: 10.15365/joce.0602122013.
6. D. W. Livingstone, "Exploring the Icebergs of Adult Learning: Findings of the," 1999. [Online]. Available: http://nall.oise.utoronto.ca.
7. M. K. Khalil and I. A. Elkhider, "Best Practices Applying learning theories and instructional design models for effective instruction Khalil MK, Elkhider IA. Applying learning theories and instructional design models for effective instruction," *Adv Physiol Educ*, vol. 40, pp. 147–156, 2016, doi: 10.1152/advan.00138.2015.-Faculty.

Note: All the figures and tables (except Table 36.1) in this chapter were made by the authors.

Transformative Applied Research in Computing, Engineering, Science and Technology – Dr. Damayanthi Dahanayake et al. (eds)
© 2024 Taylor & Francis Group, London, ISBN 978-1-041-01782-0

37

Effect of Agricultural Sector (Non-Plantation) Determinants on Gross Domestic Production in Sri Lanka

A.P. Silva*

Department of Management,
Faculty of Management, NSBM Green University,
Sri Lanka

Abstract

Sri Lanka is an agriculture-based country and Food Production (FD), Forestry (FO), Fishery (FI) and Livestock (LS) are the major agricultural (non-plantation) determinants which contributes to the Gross Domestic Production (GDP) growth. Over the years the contribution of each sector has been varied and the study aims to identify which areas contributes to the GDP the most and which sectors require more policy and support to increase contribution to the country's economy. Based on secondary information obtained from Central Bank annual reports, a statistical analysis has been carried out to understand the correlation between each variable towards GDP. It has been identified that forestry and fishery are two top contributing determinants for the GDP and FP and LS needs more emphasis on the sectors to make the stronger sectors in the agriculture arena contributing substantially to the GDP of Sri Lanka.

Keywords

Agricultural determinants, GDP, Sri Lanka

1. Introduction

Sri Lankan is known for majorly depending on agriculture for the growth of the economy as well as the societal aspects. Agriculture sector supports the country's economy by contributing to the Gross Domestic Product (GDP) by 11% [1] and employing approximately 25% of the country's labor force in 2022 [2]. As per the [3] agriculture sector plays a significant role in establishing food security and bringing in around 24% of export income of the country by 2022. Agriculture sector in Sri Lanka is well known for providing employment and alleviating poverty[4] and supporting many small-scale industries as well as large domestic and multinational companies [5]. Thereby it is of paramount importance to elaborate the role of agriculture in supporting the economic framework of Sri Lanka and identify how each determinant contribute towards the economic growth of the country.

Sri Lankan agriculture sector is mainly made up of non-plantation crops (including paddy) [6] plantation crops, tea production [7] fruits, nuts and vegetables, coconut

---

*Corresponding author: prabha.s@nsbm.ac.lk

DOI: 10.1201/9781003616368-37

cultivation [3] and livestock and fisheries [8]. In a nutshell Sri Lanka has quite the diverse portfolio in terms of agriculture sector accommodating a variety of produce due to the country's unique weather patterns and ideal geographical setting [7]. According to the National Land Use Policy of Sri Lanka the total land area of the country is 6,552,500 hectares (ha) and 2,605,647 ha are used for agricultural purposes by 2022 [9].

Agriculture is known to be one of the substantial economic forces in Sri Lanka [6] and about 70% of the country's population depend on the agricultural livelihoods [7]. Given the contribution of the sector towards the country's wellbeing in many areas, agriculture is widely recognized in the country for the historic as well as cultural significance as well [10]. Therefore, it is identified as the backbone of the country. In a universal approach agriculture has been identified as a major driver of many nations in terms of economic development [11], food security [12], poverty reduction [13], environmental sustainability [14] and health and wellbeing [15] hence the study of the discipline has come up as important.

Given the significance of agriculture for the economic development of a nation, the study focusses on analyzing the determinants of agricultural sector to the growth and development of Sri Lankan economy between the year 2003 and 2023 utilizing the simple regression analysis for the promotion of export capacity.

2. Literature Review

2.1 Contribution of Agriculture to the Sri Lankan Economy

In Sri Lanka, agriculture sector has been a major driving force creating up to 25.5% of the livelihoods in the country and empowering the economic framework [16]. Along with the securing of the livelihoods in the country agriculture sector has the capacity to make up 11% of the country's GDP [1] with the agriculture sector determinants such as food production, forestry, fishery and livestock [16]. Not only the plantation and non-plantation produce but also the provision of raw materials for the growing industries and the positive link between the growth of the agricultural production and trade openness suggest that trade liberalization agrees with the economic development in Sri Lanka in the point of view of agricultural contribution [6]. It has been identified that agricultural exports are making up around 21% of the foreign earnings of Sri Lanka [16] and during the post trade liberalization period has paved the way for the export agriculture sector to bring in substantial amounts of foreign exchange [3]. For more than 2000 years agriculture has been a powerhouse for

Sri Lanka entwined with the country's natural resources [17,18]. Therefore it has been identified that Sri Lankan economy is substantially backed by the agriculture sector [1,3] because of its unmatchable capacities within the nation's boundaries.

2.2 Diverse Agricultural Exports of Sri Lanka

In terms of export crops coming under plantation agriculture, Sri Lanka's top product is Ceylon tea, and as in 2022 the worth of total exportation is USD 1.29 billion placing Sri Lanka as the third largest tea exporter in the world [3]. In global context, Sri Lanka accounts for approximately 16-18% of the global exports in terms of tea itself [3]. In other crops, coconuts, rubber and processed rubber along with rubber based products make up a substantial amount of the total agricultural exports [19]. In 2022, Sri Lanka exported used rubber tires worth of USD 455 million and became the biggest exporter in the world in the respective product category [20]. There is a notable portion of spices, fruits and vegetable in the export basket of Sri Lanka [3].

2.3 Challenges Faced by the Agriculture Sector in Sri Lanka

Despite of the significant contribution of agriculture towards Sri Lankan economy there have been major turndowns along the way such as small scale farmers struggling to access financial resources, inadequate infrastructure, climatic challenges, economic crisis and policy failures hindering the performance of agriculture sector as a whole [21]. But along the way many ventures have been implemented to ensure the sector stability by both government and nongovernmental organizations such as rehabilitation of irrigation infrastructure, technology demonstrations, development of infrastructure under the Agriculture Sector Modernization Project (2016), e-agriculture strategy (introducing ICT and digital technologies for the improvement of agriculture) [22], comprehensive frameworks introduced by the Sri Lanka National Agriculture Policy [6], promoting value addition processes, transportation methods to minimize pre and post-harvest losses, strengthening supply chains and encouraging private sector participation [22].

2.4 Impact of Agricultural Determinants on Economic Growth

Plantation crops have proven to have a significant impact on GDP of Sri Lanka [3]. Through the literature it has been identified that, non-plantation determinants of agriculture sector have a significant impact as well towards the economic development of the country when considering the period between 1987 to 2019 [16]. As per a similar study conducted to understand the impact of agricultural determinants on economic growth of Nigeria [23], the study has been conducted via a quantitative analysis of variables utilizing the Ordinary Least Square (OLS) econometric statistical technique. The data for this study were obtained from secondary sources, such as Central Bank of Nigeria (CBN), Statistical Bulletin and the Central Bank of Nigeria Annual Report and Statement of Accounts etc. The current study explores the latest information on the Sri Lankan context to fill the gap for unavailability of data up-to 2022. Data and Variables

3. Data and Variables

3.1 Study Period and Sample

The study is conducted through a quantitative analysis of variables with the Ordinary Least Square (OLS) econometric statistical technique using dependent and independent variables from 19 years (2003-2022). These determinants are identified as the economic activities under Agriculture, Forestry and Fishing category (Non-plantation) in the Central Bank Reports (2003, 2022) [24]. Along with these details, GDP was also tracked to understand the relationship between variables. The research data are extracted from secondary sources namely, Central Bank Report of Sri Lanka and other literature.

3.2 Dependent Variable

Gross Domestic Production (GDP) of Sri Lanka, used as an indicator of economic growth [16].

3.3 Independent Variables

The study uses four major independent variables. Food Production (FD), Forestry (FO), Fishery (FI) and Livestock (LS), – [16].

4. Methodology and Model Specifications

Based on the empirical tests and analysis of the secondary data used in this study, several tests were conducted to assess the stationarity of the dataset: the Augmented Dickey-Fuller (ADF) test, the Kwiatkowski-Philips-Schmidt-Shin (KPSS) test, and the Phillips-Perron (PP) test. Additionally, the Ordinary Least Squares (OLS) method and the Breusch-Godfrey serial correlation LM test were performed to evaluate the stationarity of the data, with the econometric equation being estimated to test the hypothesis.

4.1 Model Specifications

The model will be estimated using the ordinary least squares (OLS) method. Data analysis will be conducted using the appropriate tools, guided by economic theory, to address the issues of spurious correlation often found in non-stationary time series data.

$$Y_t = C_0 + C_1 FD_1 + C_2 FO_1 + C_3 FI_1 + C_4 LS_1 + U_1 \quad (1)$$

Where, Y_t, FD_1, FO_1, FI_1, LS_1, stand for Gross Domestic Production, Food Production, Forestry, Fishery and Livestock respectively and C_0, C_1, C_2, C_3, C_4 are the constants in respective order. U_1 stands for the Error Term.

4.2 Apriori Expectations and Justification of the Variables in the Models

Economic theories suggest that an increase in key agricultural sector determinants—such as food, forestry, fishery, and livestock—can boost a country's gross domestic product (GDP). Simply put, enhancing these agricultural determinants is expected to positively impact GDP, thereby driving overall economic growth. The anticipated signs of the regression coefficients in the equation are: C1, C2, C3, C4 > 0.

5. Empirical Results

5.1 Hypothesis Testing

Interpretation: The summary of Hypothesis testing based on P-values and the statistical significance is indicated in the Table 37.1, given above.

Table 37.1 Interpretation of hypothesis testing

Independent Variable	Coefficient	P-Value	Hypothesis Interpretation	Null Hypothesis
FD	12.3712	0.000	There is a statistically significant positive correlation between Fishery Development and GDP	Rejected
FO	60.9868	0.055	There is a statistically marginally significant positive correlation between Food Production and GDP.	Not rejected
FI	15.9154	0.354	There is no statistically significant correlation between Forestry Investment and GDP.	Not rejected
LS	-4.8405	0.572	There is no statistically significant correlation between the Livestock Sector and GDP.	Rejected

Source: Author's compilation

5.2 ADF, PP and KPSS Root Test

Based on the ADF and PP tests, the p-values are high in GDP, FO and FI therefore it indicates that the null hypothesis of the variables (non-stationarity) cannot be rejected whereas for FD null hypothesis of the variable is rejected at the 5% significance level indicating stationarity. But the KPSS test for GDP, FD, FO, and FI, the null hypothesis of stationarity is rejected. For LS, the null hypothesis of stationarity cannot be rejected (Table 37.1).

5.3 Unit Root Tests

Three standard tests for unit root were utilized to test the order of integration of the selected variables. They are Augmented Dickey-Fuller (ADF), Philips-Perron (PP) and Kwiatkowski-Philips-Schmidt-Shim (KPSS). The stationary test in terms of the time series is required to overcome the issue of spurious regression.

Table 37.2 elaborates the results of the ADF, PP and KPSS unit root test which indicates the level of stationarity of the data to be taken into consideration. In the tests conducted, constant without trend and constant with trend is considered.

Table 37.2 ADF, PP and KPSS unit root test

Variable	ADF Statistic	ADF P – Value	PP Statistic	PP P- Value	KPSS Statistic	KPSS P- Value
GDP	3.7270	1.0000	3.7270	1.0000	0.7092	0.0127
FD	-3.1800	0.0212	-3.100	0.0212	0.6430	0.0187
FO	12.4966	1.0000	12.4966	1.0000	0.5331	0.0342
FI	-1.1015	0.7145	-1.1015	0.7145	0.7020	0.0134
LS	-2.7569	0.0647	-2.7569	0.0647	0.3669	0.0914

Source: Author's compilation

5.4 Ordinary Least Square Regression

The test results the following regression equation,

$$GDP = \beta_0 + \beta_1 FD + \beta_2 FO + \beta_3 FI + \beta_4 LS \quad (2)$$

Where, β_0, β_2, β_2, β_3 and β_4 stand for Intercept (constant term), Coefficient for Fishery Development (FD), Coefficient for Food Production (FO), Coefficient for Forestry Investment (FI) and Coefficient for Livestock Sector (LS) respectively.

$$GDP = -3\,167\,000 + 12.371\,FD + 60.987\,FO + 15.915\,FI - 4.841\,LS \quad (3)$$

Considering the R squared value to test the goodness of the model fit, the value obtained for this OLS regression is, 0.965 which implies that 96.5% of the dependent variable's (log transformed GDP) variability is explained in by the independent variables (log transformed FD, FO, FI and LS). Since the R squared values is high it elaborates that there is a strong relationship between the independent variables and the dependent variable and the model fits the data well. In terms of the adjusted R-squared value, it is indicated as 0.954 which brings into light that the 95.4% of the variability in the dependent variable is explained by the independent variables, after adjusting for the number of predictors.

5.5 Breusch-Godfrey Serial Correlation LM Test

According to the Breusch-Godfrey Serial Correlation LM Test, the R-squared value is 1.5336 and the Chi squared value is 0.3666 which indicates an insignificant value. This could conclude the fact that this estimated model is free of autocorrelation.

6. Conclusion

The study focusses on the agricultural sector determinants (non-plantation), to the productivity of the economic growth in terms of the GDP of the country. Promoting major agricultural determinants such as are Food Production, Forestry, Fishery and Livestock could enhance the GDP of Sri Lanka, the findings elaborate that Livestock and Food Production needs more attention to be further developed and to contribute to the economy of the country and enhance the GDP. There should be better opportunities for other determinants as well for contribution of GDP by focusing on value addition and improving export opportunities for the Forestry and Fisheries. Policy recommendations should be there to improve the infrastructure, marketplace and private sector integration for the betterment of each field. For future research both plantation and non-plantation production information as well as annual growth of GDP could be considered. This was a cross sectional study therefore longitudinal studies could be recommended for future research avenues.

REFERENCES

1. M.S. Somarthne, and M. U. K. Jayasinghe, "An analysis of role of agriculture in economic development in Sri lanka (1970-2003),"Wayamba University of Sri Lanka, vol. 1, pp. 129–136, November 2005.

2. Department of Census and Statistics, "Sri Lanka Labour Force Statistics-Quarterly Bulletin, First Quarter 2022," statistics.gov.lk. http://www.statistics.gov.lk/Resource/en/LabourForce/Bulletins/LFS_Q1_Bulletin_2022.pdf (Accessed June 28 2024).

3. Sri Lanka Export Development Board, "Fruit and Vegetable - Agriculture Quality Standards in Sri Lanka.

2023,"srilankabusiness.com. https://www.srilankabusiness. com/fruits-and-vegetables/quality-standards.html (Accessed June 28 2024).

4. K. Karunagoda, "Changes in labour market and domestic agriculture," Sri Lankan Journal of Agricultural Economics, vol. 6, pp. 82–97, August 2004.

5. N. Dissanayaka and M. Thibbotuwana. "Sri Lanka's Agri-Food Trade: Structure, Opportunities, Challenges & Impacts Of Covid-19," The US Government's Global Hunger and Food Security Initiative, pp. 27–38, August 2021.

6. Ministry of Agriculture and Plantation and Industries, "Agriculture Sector Modernization Project," agrimin. gov.lk. https://www.agrimin.gov.lk/web/index.php/home-1/12-project/841-agriculture-sector-modernization-project (Accessed June 28 2024).

7. L.N. Ranathunga, W. M. D. I. S. Wijemanna, M. G. S. Sathsara, and R. G. B. K. Gamage, "Agriculture in Sri Lanka: The Current Snapshot." International Journal of Environment, Agriculture and Biotechnology, vol.3, pp. 118–125, August 2018.

8. International Trade Administration,"Sri Lanka – Agriculture Sector," trade.gov.lk. https://www.trade.gov/country-commercial-guides/sri-lanka-agricultural-sector (Accessed June 28 2024).

9. Department of Land Use Policy Planning. 2022, "National Land Policy of Sri Lanka," lupd.gov.lk. https://luppd.gov. lk/images/content_image/downloads/pdf/national_land_use_policy.pdf (Accessed June 28 2024).

10. M.K.L. Irangani and Yoshiharu Shiratake. "Indigenous techniques used in rice cultivation in Sri Lanka: An analysis from an agricultural history perspective," Indian Journal of Traditional Knowledge, vol. 4, pp. 638–650, September 2013.

11. U. Jayasinghe-Mudalige, "Role of Food and Agriculture Sector in Economic Development of Sri Lanka: Do We Stand Right in the Process of Structural Transformation?," Journal of Food and Agriculture, vol. 1, pp. 1–12, April 2010.

12. S.M.P. Senanayake and S. P. Premaratne, "Role of agriculture in improving the food and nutrition security in Sri Lanka," Sri Lanka Journal of Advanced Social Studies, vol.4, pp. 103–130, January 2014.

13. W. Abeysekara, C. S. Mendis, M. Siriwardana, and S. Meng, "Economic consequences of climate change impacts on the agricultural sector of South Asia: A case study of Sri Lanka," Economic Analysis and Policy, vol. 77, pp. 435–450, March 2023.

14. M. Munasinghe, Y. Deraniyagala, N. Dassanayake, and H. Karunarathna. "Economic, social and environmental impacts and overall sustainability of the tea sector in Sri Lanka," Sustainable Production and Consumption, vol. 12, pp. 155–169, July 2017.

15. B. Thoradeniya, U. Pinto, and B. Maheshwari, "Perspectives on impacts of water quality on agriculture and community well-being—a key informant study from Sri Lanka," Environmental Science and Pollution Research, vol. 3, pp. 2047–2061, June 2017.

16. P. Anusha and S. Vijesandiran, "An empirical analysis of the effect of agricultural sector determinants on economic growth in Sri Lanka," Business and Economic Research, vol. 12, pp. 155–167, December 2022.

17. International Reference Center for Community Water Supply and Sanitation, "Heritage in Natural Resource Management," ircwash.org. https://www.ircwash.org/sites/default/files/822-LK91-8684.pdf (Accessed June 28 2024).

18. P. B. Camisani, "Sri Lanka: a political ecology of socio-environmental conflicts and development projects," Sustainability Science, vol. 13, pp. 693–707, April 2018.

19. K. Karunagoda, P. Samaratunga, R. Sharma, and J. Weerahewa. "Sri Lankan Agricultural trade policy issues," Food and Agricultural Organization, vol. 1, pp. 5–15, 2011.

20. Observatory of Economic Complexity, " Used Rubber Tires in Sri Lanka," oec.world.en. https://oec.world/en/profile/bilateral-product/used-rubber-tires/reporter/lka (Accessed June 28 2024).

21. World Food Programme, "Food crisis in Sri Lanka likely to worsen amid poor agricultural production, price spikes and ongoing economic crisis, FAO and WFP warn," wfp. org. https://www.wfp.org/news/food-crisis-sri-lanka-likely-worsen-amid-poor-agricultural-production-price-spikes-and-ongoing (Accessed June 28 2024).

22. T.M.R. Dissanayake and N. K. Jain, "Status of post harvest technology of agricultural crops in Sri Lanka," Agricultural Mechanization in Asia, Africa & Latin America, vol. 41, pp. 16–23, August 2010.

23. O. O. Oluwatoyese and A. Shri Dewi, "Effect of agricultural sector determinants on economic growth," Australian Journal of Basic and Applied Sciences, vol. 8, pp. 68–72, 2017.

24. Central Bank of Sri Lanka, Annual Report, Colombo: Central Bank of Sri Lanka, 2003–2022.

Transformative Applied Research in Computing, Engineering, Science and Technology – Dr. Damayanthi Dahanayake et al. (eds)
© 2024 Taylor & Francis Group, London, ISBN 978-1-041-01782-0

38

Microbial-Derived Nanoparticles, A Sustainable Approach to Advanced Food Packaging—A Review

H.V. Athukorala and M.S.N. Samaranayake*
Department of Biomedical Science,
NSBM Green University,
Sri Lanka

Abstract

Microbial-derived nanoparticles (MDNPs) present a transformative approach to advanced food packaging, offering eco-friendly, durable, and biodegradable solutions. Synthesized by bacteria, fungi, and algae, these nanoparticles possess unique properties, including high surface area, biocompatibility, and inherent antimicrobial activity. This review explores the synthesis methods, properties, and applications of MDNPs in food packaging. Biological approaches for MDNP synthesis are explored, with a focus on the benefits of biological methods in terms of cost-effectiveness and environmental friendliness. The diverse properties of MDNPs, such as size, morphology, optical properties, composition, stability, and surface charge, make them highly desirable for various packaging applications. MDNPs enhance active packaging by scavenging oxygen, absorbing ethylene, and releasing antimicrobial agents, thereby extending shelf life and maintaining food quality. Intelligent packaging systems utilizing nanosensors provide real-time monitoring of freshness and condition. Despite their potential, the integration of MDNPs faces challenges, including safety concerns, regulatory compliance, production scalability, and consumer acceptance. Addressing these issues through comprehensive safety studies, regulatory standard development, and public education is essential. Future research should focus on scalable production methods, smart packaging technologies, and sustainable materials to fully realize the benefits of MDNPs. This review underscores the promise of MDNPs in revolutionizing food packaging, enhancing food safety, and promoting sustainability.

Keywords

Antimicrobial activity, Eco-friendly materials, Food packaging, Food safety, Microbial-derived nanoparticles

1. Introduction

Food packaging plays an important role in guaranteeing the quality and safety of food, as well as expanding its shelf-life. It allows food produced in one region to be transported to consumers in distant areas, ensuring global food availability [1]. Traditional packaging materials primarily serve to protect food from external environmental factors

---

*Corresponding author: sharini.s@nsbm.ac.lk

DOI: 10.1201/9781003616368-38

and facilitate handling. Nevertheless, the food business has seen significant advancements in packaging technology throughout the last several decades, influenced by changing customer tastes and industrial requirements. These innovations have resulted in packaging with enhanced protective features compared to traditional methods [2].

Advanced packaging technologies preserve food quality and safety and address modern challenges like food waste, supply chain efficiency, and environmental sustainability. These developments aim to prolong the period in which perishable foods may be stored without spoiling, decrease the occurrence of spoilage and contamination, and integrate smart features to monitor and manage the conditions of food [3]. Nanotechnology plays a crucial role in developing advanced food packaging by introducing materials with novel properties and functionalities unattainable with conventional materials [4]. Out of all the nanomaterials, microbial-derived nanoparticles (MDNPs) have shown tremendous potential. MDNPs are produced via the biosynthesis process by microorganisms that consist of bacteria, fungi, and algal species. The biologically synthesized nanoparticles possess distinct characteristics, including a significant surface area, biocompatibility, and inherent antibacterial properties, making them very appealing for food packaging [5].

The production of MDNPs is an eco-friendly process that reduces the need for harmful chemical synthesis and allows for the creation of nanoparticles with customized properties for specific food packaging uses. Integrating MDNPs into packaging materials enables active packaging, which interacts with food and its environment to extend shelf life and maintain quality. This includes releasing antimicrobial agents, absorbing oxygen, or incorporating sensors to monitor food conditions [6]. Therefore, MDNPs offer advanced solutions for food packaging, enhancing food safety, extending shelf life, and promoting environmental sustainability. This review explores current research on MDNPs, their production methods, applications, and potential future developments in the domain of food packaging.

2. Microbial Sources for Nanoparticles

Nanoparticles can be synthesized using a diverse range of microbial entities, including algae, bacteria, and fungi. Numerous studies have demonstrated both single-celled and multi-celled microbes can create inorganic nanomaterials [7].

2.1 Bacteria

Bacteria are extensively studied for nanoparticle synthesis due to their rapid growth and diversity [8]. In nature,

bacteria often encounter extreme environmental conditions, necessitating effective defense mechanisms. One key aspect of their survival is managing high concentrations of metallic ions. Bacteria achieve this through strategies such as efflux systems, redox state alterations, extracellular complex formation, and intracellular metal precipitation, to facilitate the creation of metallic nanoparticles. Bacteria synthesize nanoparticles via bio reduction, where enzymes reduce metal ions, and biosorption, where metal ions bind to the cell surface and are reduced. Some bacteria also produce proteins to stabilize nanoparticles [9]. *Klebsiella pneumoniae*, *Actinobacter* sp., *Lactobacillus* spp., *Corynebacterium* sp., *Escherichia coli*, *Bacillus cereus*, and *Pseudomonas* sp. are among the common bacterial species employed for nanoparticle manufacturing [7]. These bacterial species have shown the synthesis of AgNPs, AuNPs, CdNPs and TeNPs [9]. However, the main drawback of using bacteria is their slower synthesis rate and limited size range of nanoparticles in comparison to other techniques [8].

2.2 Fungi

The Fungi are advantageous for producing metallic nanoparticles due to their strong affinity for binding, ability to accumulate metals inside their cells, and considerable intake of metals into their intracellular structures. Fungi grow rapidly, are easy to handle, and can withstand harsh environmental conditions, making them ideal for nanoparticle synthesis [8]. Several fungi, such as *Aspergillus* sp., *Fusarium* sp., and *Penicillium* sp., have been reported for their ability to biosynthesize silver (Ag) and gold (Au) nanoparticles [7]. Other species, like *Verticillium* sp., *Cladosporium cladosporioides*, and *Trichoderma asperellum*, also demonstrate nanoparticle production capabilities [5]. *Volvariella volvacea* extract has been used to create gold, silver, and silver-gold nanoparticles. Similarly, *Penicillium fellutanum* found in coastal mangrove silt has been shown to synthesize AgNPs by using $AgNO_3$ as the substrate [8].

2.3 Algae

Algae, as aquatic microorganisms, have shown their ability to gather heavy metals and generate metallic nanoparticles via biological processes. One specific example is the marine alga *Sargassum wightii*, which has been shown to produce gold (Au), silver (Ag), and gold/silver bimetallic nanoparticles outside of its cells [10]. Furthermore, it has been shown that the green alga *Spirogyra insignis* and the red alga *Chondrus crispus* are capable of producing gold (Au) and silver (Ag) nanoparticles [7].

3. Synthesis of Microbial-Derived Nanoparticles

3.1 Method of Synthesis

Biological methods for synthesizing nanoparticles involve the use of biomolecules, microorganisms, and plants [11]. Unlike physical and chemical methods, which can contribute to environmental pollution through the release of toxic components and heat dissipation, biological methods are straightforward, cost-effective, efficient, and capable of achieving higher nanoparticle concentrations [8].

Microorganisms synthesize metal nanoparticles for two main reasons. First, to protect themselves from the toxicity of heavy metals, which disrupt metal enzyme function and generate reactive oxygen species. They detoxify metals through mechanisms like cell exclusion, vacuolar sequestration, and enzymatic redox processes, leading to the precipitation of metals as minerals or retention as ions. Second, some bacteria use metal ions as electron acceptors to gain energy [12]. Nanoparticles are biosynthesized when microorganisms absorb target ions from their environment and convert them into elemental metals through enzymatic processes. Depending on where the nanoparticles form, this process is categorized as either intracellular or extracellular synthesis [9]. The intracellular method involves transporting ions into microbial cells, where enzymes facilitate nanoparticle formation. In contrast, extracellular synthesis traps metal ions on the cell surface, reducing them through enzymatic activity [13].

3.2 Mechanism of nanoparticle formation

The formation of nanoparticles from biological entities involves three main phases [6]:

Activation Phase: Metal salts are converted into metal ions at specific temperatures and pH levels. These metal ions are then reduced to form metal atoms, which subsequently self-assemble or nucleate [14].

Growth Phase: During the growth phase, a process known as Ostwald ripening takes place, including heterogeneous nucleation and growth, and tiny nanoparticles are incorporated to create larger particles. This process enhances the thermodynamic stability of the nanoparticles [8].

Termination Phase: The physical shape of the nanoparticles is formed in the final stage of the procedure; capping and stabilization help to attain their stability. Biological capping agents act as growth terminators, preventing the nanoparticles from agglomerating and enhancing their stability [6].

4. Properties of Microbial-Derived Nanoparticles

4.1 Physical Properties

The major physical properties of MDNPs include size, morphology, surface area, and optical properties [12]. The biosynthesis process enables fine-tuned adjustment of MDNP dimensions and geometry, which typically range from 1 to 100 nanometers. Various morphologies of MDNPs include cubic, triangular, rod-like, and spherical shapes [9].

Research has shown that the shape, size, and surface area of nanoparticles affect their antimicrobial activity. Nanoparticles of smaller size, which have a greater ratio of surface area to volume, have increased antimicrobial efficiency. For instance, a study demonstrated that spherical and triangular shapes of AgNPs derived from biological methods show the highest antimicrobial activity [15]. MDNPs, such as those made from silver and gold, possess unique optical properties, including surface plasmon resonance (SPR). These properties are useful in active and smart packaging applications, such as sensors for detecting food spoilage or contamination [16].

4.2 Chemical Properties

The chemical properties of MDNPs include surface charge, composition, and stability. The bactericidal activity of MDNPs is significantly influenced by their surface charge. In research conducted by Abbaszadegan et al. (2015), the antibacterial effectiveness of synthesized AgNPs was examined against gram-positive bacteria (*Staphylococcus aureus, Streptococcus pyogenes, Streptococcus mutans*) and gram-negative bacteria (*E. coli, Proteus vulgaris*). Positively charged AgNPs showed the highest antimicrobial efficacy, neutral AgNPs exhibited moderate activity, and negatively charged AgNPs had the least antibacterial effect. The chemical composition of MDNPs varies depending on the microorganism and the synthesis process, contributing to their stability, reactivity, and antimicrobial properties [5]. For example, the capsular exopolysaccharides (EPS) of *Lactobacillus* bacteria are mainly made up of monosaccharides or disaccharides. A study has shown that nanoparticles derived from *Lactobacillus* bacteria containing disaccharides show enhanced antibacterial activity due to their smaller size [18].

4.3 Functional Properties

The functional properties of MDNPs are diverse and depend on the microbial entity used for their synthesis. These properties include antimicrobial activity, biocompatibility, and the ability to act as carriers for active substances [19].

The different functional properties exhibited by nanoparticles synthesized by various microbial entities are highlighted in Table 38.1.

5. Applications of Nanoparticles in Food Packaging

5.1 Active Food Packaging

Active and intelligent packaging systems enhance food safety, quality, and the consumer experience by integrating advanced technologies, such as incorporating nanoparticles into packaging materials [22]. Active packaging systems enriched with nanofillers, including nanoparticles derived from microorganisms, offer significant benefits for food preservation. Nanoparticles with biocidal properties such as AgNPs, AuNPs, TiNPs, ZnNPs and CuNPs remove oxygen, resulting in an oxygen-depleted atmosphere within the packaging [23]. This extends the lifespan of oxygen-sensitive food items, including snacks, cereals, and dried fruits. Moreover, they efficiently assimilate ethylene gas, accelerating the maturation process in some fruits and vegetables [3]. In addition, nanoparticles in active packaging materials enable the intentional diffusion of antimicrobial agents or natural preservatives into packed items, ensuring the preservation of the quality and safety of poultry, fresh meat, and seafood [24].

Research studies have demonstrated the efficacy of various nanoparticles in active food packaging, offering antimicrobial protection for different food products. AgNPs have been used to extend the shelf life of chicken meat by inhibiting *S. aureus* and *Salmonella Typhimurium*. Selenium-silver nanoparticles (Se-AgNPs) provide antimicrobial activity against *E. coli* and *S. aureus* in kiwi fruits. AuNPs are effective in banana packaging against *E. coli*, while TiO_2 NPs protect soft white cheese by targeting *S. aureus* and *E. coli*. Zn-MgO nanoparticles are utilized in smoked salmon to combat *Listeria monocytogenes*, and TiO_2 NPs are also applied in packaging for cheese, nuts, and cereals, offering antimicrobial protection against *S. aureus* and *E. coli* [21], [25], [26].

5.2 Intelligent Food Packaging Systems

Smart food packaging methods provide a multitude of advantages. Utilizing nanosensors and nanotags, freshness indicators provide immediate updates on the freshness of food by changing color or showing freshness levels for consumers to evaluate. Integrated nanosensors, including nanoparticles derived from microorganisms, also monitor temperature conditions throughout storage and transportation [27]. Some types of nano sensors used for tracking and reporting food status include active tags, anti-counterfeiting tags, time-temperature indicators (TTIs), microbial spoilage sensors, physical shock indicators, leakage sensors, allergen sensors, microbial growth sensors, pathogen sensors, contaminant sensors, and radio frequency identification (RFID) [4].

5.3 Food Safety and Preservation

When used in food packaging, microbe-derived nanoparticles (MDNPs), especially those with antibacterial characteristics, significantly improve food safety and quality. Incorporating MDNPs in this manner enhances food safety and extends the shelf life of several foods [6].

Research studies have highlighted the use of MDNPs in food packaging. One example involved developing a silver nanoparticle-coated paper for storing tomatoes. These nanoparticles were synthesized using bacteriocins produced by *Lactobacillus pentosus*, *Lactobacillus crustorum*, and *Lactobacillus spicheri*, demonstrating antimicrobial activity against *S. aureus* and *B. cereus* while maintaining the tomatoes' freshness and firmness for 10 days at room temperature (18-20°C) [28]. In another study, a composite of acidocin derived from *Lactobacillus acidophilus* and silver nanoparticles from *Aspergillus brasiliensis* was applied to eggshells, showing antibacterial activity against *S. aureus* and *B. cereus*, and extending the eggs' shelf life [29]. Also, a study demonstrated the incorporation of AgNPs derived from *T. viride* into sodium alginate as a film coating for carrots and pears, resulting in extended shelf life for these food items [21].

To illustrate the diverse applications of microbial-derived nanoparticles in the food industry, Table II summarizes different types of nanoparticles, their microbial sources, and their specific applications.

6. Advantages of Using Microbial-Derived Nanoparticles

The food industry is rapidly expanding due to the heightened demand for preservation and safety. Current techniques focus on extending shelf life while maintaining nutritional value and texture. However, the potential toxicity of certain preservatives and packaging materials necessitates eco-friendly alternatives [30]. Biologically produced nanoparticles are expected to become more uniform in size and structure, improving their reproducibility. This will facilitate easier assessment and management of potential environmental and health risks associated with their use [13]. Nanoparticles (NPs) synthesized by microorganisms (bacteria, yeast, fungi) offer a solution, with their green synthesis customizable through controlled environmental conditions [5].

Incorporating bio-based nanomaterials into packaging improves eco-friendliness, durability, low waste, biodegradation, and biocompatibility [6]. Bio-based packaging refers to biodegradable films designed to control moisture transfer and gas exchange in food products, enhancing safety and preserving nutritional and sensory quality [32]. Unlike conventional packaging produced from fossil fuels, bio-based packaging is made from renewable sources and can be recycled or incinerated to generate energy upon disposal. The key feature of biodegradable packaging films with MDNPs is their ability to decompose readily through the action of living organisms [33].

Sustainable packaging materials that include MDNPs are specially designed to be easily recycled or composted, resulting in a decrease in waste and the advancement of a circular economy. MDNPs enhance the robustness and longevity of these substances, enabling the use of lighter packaging that requires less raw materials and uses less energy during transit [30]. As a consequence, this leads to reduced carbon emissions and improved resource conservation [24].

Green synthesis of nanoparticles is preferred in smart packaging over traditional physicochemical methods due to its eco-friendliness, cleanliness, safety, cost-effectiveness, simplicity, and efficiency, ensuring high productivity and purity. Moreover, it operates without requiring high

Table 38.1 Different functional properties exhibited by the NPS synthesized by various microbial entities [5]

Microbial Entities	Type of Nanoparticle	Functional property	References
Brown marine algae	Ag NPs	*E. coli* and *S. aureus* (Antibacterial activity)	[6]
Aeromonas hydrophila (bacterium)	ZnO NPs	Bacteria (*Pseudomonas aeruginosa*) and fungi (*A. flavus*) (Antimicrobial activity)	[6]
Aspergillus flavus (fungus)	TiO$_2$ NPs	Effective against *S. aureus*	[20]
Arthrospira platensis (Cyanobacterium)	ZnO NPs	Antioxidant properties and barrier properties	[5]
Trichoderma viride (fungus)	Ag NPs	*S. aureus* and *E. coli* (Antibacterial activity)	[21]
Bacillus subtilis (bacterium)	TiO$_2$ NPs	Photocatalytic property	[5]

pressure or temperature, further enhancing its appeal [27]. This method is economical as it avoids the use of toxic and hazardous substances, as well as expensive external reducing, stabilizing, or capping agents [6].

By adopting MDNPs in food packaging, the industry can meet consumer demands for safer and more sustainable options while maintaining the integrity and quality of food products. This approach not only addresses environmental concerns but also provides functional benefits, making it a promising solution for the future of food packaging [5].

7. Challenges and Limitations

The incorporation of microbial-derived nanoparticles (MDNPs) in food packaging presents several challenges and limitations, including safety and regulatory issues, production scalability, and consumer acceptance.

7.1 Safety and Regulation

Nanoparticles, particularly those with distinctive attributes, generate suspicions about their toxicity and food safety implications. Comprehensive assessments of toxicity and risk are necessary to guarantee the secure use of MDNPs in food packaging [34]. It is crucial to navigate worldwide regulatory standards when authorities assess the safety of nanomaterials used in food-related applications. Packaging manufacturers must adhere to established guidelines and minimize the risk of nanoparticle migration or leaching into food. Creating and verifying analytical methods to detect any migration or leaching is important for ensuring safety [27].

7.2 Production Scalability

Scaling up the production of MDNPs to meet industrial demands poses significant challenges. Ensuring consistent quality, reproducibility, and functionality of these nanoparticles for smart packaging applications requires overcoming hurdles in synthesis, purification, and integration into packaging materials [6]. Additionally, smart packaging tools need to operate across a wide range of temperatures, humidity levels, light exposure, and gas concentrations. They require fast response times and high throughput for real-time and online identification. Designing these devices for high sensitivity and reversibility in their functions adds to the complexity [34].

7.3 Consumer Acceptance

It is crucial to educate people to establish confidence and promote the adoption of packaging that utilizes nanoparticles. Transparent labeling and efficient communication of advantages and safety precautions help ease concerns and enhance acceptance [24]. Addressing consumer concerns about the potential risks and highlighting the environmental and functional benefits of MDNPs in packaging can foster greater acceptance and trust [27].

8. Future Prospects and Research Directions

A major obstacle to integrating microbial-derived nanoparticles (MDNPs) into food packaging is a lack of research and assessments on their safety and health effects. Concerns about the potential migration of nanoparticles from packaging materials into food items need further examination [34]. Despite advancements in intelligent and enhanced packaging systems, their widespread market adoption remains limited due to increased costs and varying levels of acceptance among dealers and brand owners [4]. To address these difficulties, it is crucial to create safety protocols and preventive measures for developing packaging materials that are based on nanotechnology, environmentally friendly, sustainable, and economically viable for the food sector.

Table 38.2 Different microbial-derived nanoparticles and their applications in the food industry [5]

Microbes	Type of Nanoparticle	Application	References
Bacillus subtilis	Titanium oxide	Food packaging	[35]
Staphylococcus aureus	Ag NP	Food packaging Food preservation	[5]
Aeromonas hydrophila	ZnO	Food preservation	[5]
Streptomyces griseoruber	Au NP	Food preservation Food packaging	[36]
Arthrospira platensis	ZnO	Food additives	[37]
Colpomenia sinuosa	Fe_3O_4	Food safety	[38]
Neurospora crassa	AuNP	Biosensor Food preservation	[5]
Rhizopus oryzae	MgO	Micronutrient Food safety	[5]

Public acceptance also hinges on effectively addressing these safety concerns [6]. With the growing population and the increasing importance of food security and sustainability, the development of smart, web-linked biogenic nano-packaging holds great promise. However, further research is needed to fully realize and implement this advanced technology.

9. Conclusion

Microbial-derived nanoparticles (MDNPs) represent a transformative approach to eco-friendly, durable, and biodegradable food packaging. Synthesized by microorganisms like bacteria, fungi, and algae, MDNPs possess unique properties such as antimicrobial and antioxidant activity, high surface area, stability, and photocatalytic functions, making them ideal for food packaging.

MDNPs play a crucial role in active and intelligent packaging. Active packaging extends shelf life by removing oxygen and releasing antimicrobials, while intelligent packaging uses nanosensors to monitor freshness and food safety in real-time. Despite their potential, challenges like safety concerns, regulatory compliance, scalability, and consumer acceptance must be addressed. Comprehensive risk assessments and global regulatory frameworks are essential for the safe use of MDNPs.

Future research should focus on scalable production methods, smart packaging technologies, and sustainable, recyclable materials. With continued innovation, MDNPs can revolutionize food packaging, enhancing food safety, extending shelf life, and promoting sustainability.

REFERENCES

1. R. Priyadarshi, S. M. Kim, and J. W. Rhim, "Pectin/pullulan blend films for food packaging: Effect of blending ratio," *Food Chem*, vol. 347, Jun. 2021.
2. R. V Wagh, R. Priyadarshi, and J.-W. Rhim, "Novel Bacteriophage-Based Food Packaging: An Innovative Food Safety Approach," 2023.
3. P. Desai and P. P. Desai, "Advanced Food Packaging Technology Article in," *International Journal of Environmental Engineering*, 2023.
4. P. J. Babu, "Nanotechnology mediated intelligent and improved food packaging," *International Nano Letters*, vol. 12, no. 1, pp. 1–14, Jul. 2021.
5. Y. Muralidaran *et al.*, "Distinctive applicative potential of microbial nanoparticles in food technology: A comprehensive understanding," in *Microbial Nanotechnology: Advances in Agriculture, Industry and Health Sectors*, Walter de Gruyter GmbH, pp. 187–210, 2022.
6. S. Shende *et al.*, "Synthesis of copper nanomaterials by microbes and their use in sustainable agriculture," *Microbial Nanotechnology*, pp.256–287, May 2020.
7. M. Shah, D. Fawcett, S. Sharma, S. K. Tripathy, and G. E. J. Poinern, "Green synthesis of metallic nanoparticles via biological entities," 2015.
8. P. Ahuja, E. Rami, A. Singh, and D. Pathak, "Green synthesis of silver nanoparticles and their potenial biological applications," in *Nanotechnology and in Silico Tools: Natural Remedies and Drug Discovery*, Elsevier, pp. 97–115, 2023.

9. X. Li, H. Xu, Z. S. Chen, and G. Chen, "Biosynthesis of nanoparticles by microorganisms and their applications," 2011.

10. K. Govindaraju, V. Kiruthiga, V. G. Kumar, and G. Singaravelu, "Extracellular synthesis of silver nanoparticles by a marine alga, Sargassum wightii grevilli and their Antibacterial effects," in *Journal of Nanoscience and Nanotechnology*, pp. 5497–5501, Sep. 2009.

11. S. M. Mousavi *et al.*, "Green synthesis of silver nanoparticles toward bio and medical applications: review study," Nov. 12, 2018.

12. Y. Kato and M. Suzuki, "Synthesis of metal nanoparticles by microorganisms," *Crystals (Basel)*, vol. 10, no. 7, pp. 1–20, Jul. 2020.

13. N. Pantidos, "Biological Synthesis of Metallic Nanoparticles by Bacteria, Fungi and Plants," *J Nanomed Nanotechnol*, vol. 05, no. 05, 2014.

14. L. S. Alqarni, M. D. Alghamdi, A. A. Alshahrani, and A. M. Nassar, "Green Nanotechnology: Recent Research on Bioresource-Based Nanoparticle Synthesis and Applications," 2022.

15. I. Zorraquín-Peña, C. Cueva, B. Bartolomé, and M. V. Moreno-Arribas, "Silver nanoparticles against foodborne bacteria. Effects at intestinal level and health limitations," Jan. 01, 2020.

16. R. Pandey *et al.*, "The Fascinating World of Silver Nanoparticles: Exploring Synthesis, Characterization, and their Crucial Role in Shaping Nanotechnology," *Journal of Chemical Health Risks*, 2023.

17. A. Abbaszadegan *et al.*, "The effect of charge at the surface of silver nanoparticles on antimicrobial activity against gram-positive and gram-negative bacteria: A preliminary study," *J Nanomater*, vol. 2015, 2015.

18. I. Garmasheva, N. Kovalenko, S. Voychuk, A. Ostapchuk, O. Livins'ka, and L. Oleschenko, "Lactobacillus species mediated synthesis of silver nanoparticles and their antibacterial activity against opportunistic pathogens in vitro," *BioImpacts*, vol. 6, no. 4, pp. 219–223, 2016.

19. S. Mishra and B. Bhimrao, "Use of Nanotechnology and Nanoscience in Food Packaging," 2014.

20. G. Rajakumar *et al.*, "Fungus-mediated biosynthesis and characterization of TiO 2 nanoparticles and their activity against pathogenic bacteria," *Spectrochim Acta A Mol Biomol Spectrosc*, vol. 91, pp. 23–29, Jun. 2012.

21. A. Mohammed Fayaz, K. Balaji, M. Girilal, P. T. Kalaichelvan, and R. Venkatesan, "Mycobased synthesis of silver nanoparticles and their incorporation into sodium alginate films for vegetable and fruit preservation," *J Agric Food Chem*, vol. 57, no. 14, pp. 6246–6252, Jul. 2009.

22. X. Zhou, X. Zhou, L. Zhou, M. Jia, and Y. Xiong, "Nanofillers in Novel Food Packaging Systems and Their Toxicity Issues," *Foods*, vol. 13, no. 13, p. 2014, Jun. 2024.

23. N. Angelescu, D. Grigorescu, and D. N. Ungureanu, "Silver Nanoparticles in Food Bio Packaging. A Short Review," *Scientific Bulletin of Valahia University - Materials and Mechanics*, vol. 20, no. 22, pp. 30–34, Apr. 2024.

24. E. Pavlenko *et al.*, "Enhancing food packaging with nanofillers: properties, applications, and innovations," *Potravinarstvo Slovak Journal of Food Sciences*, vol. 18, pp. 139–156, 2024.

25. P. Vizzini, E. Beltrame, V. Zanet, J. Vidic, and M. Manzano, "Development and evaluation of qpcr detection method and zn-mgo/alginate active packaging for controlling listeria monocytogenes contamination in cold-smoked salmon," *Foods*, vol. 9, no. 10, Oct. 2020.

26. N. Omerović *et al.*, "Antimicrobial nanoparticles and biodegradable polymer composites for active food packaging applications," *Compr Rev Food Sci Food Saf*, vol. 20, no. 3, pp. 2428–2454, May 2021.

27. M. Primožič, Ž. Knez, and M. Leitgeb, "(Bio) nanotechnology in food science—food packaging," Feb. 01, 2021.

28. S. Sharma, N. Sharma, and N. Kaushal, "Utilization of novel bacteriocin synthesized silver naoparticles(AgNPs) for their application in antimicrobial packaging for preservation of tomato fruit," *Frontiers in Sustainable Food Systems*, vol. 7, Feb. 2023.

29. A. B. Abeer Mohammed, M. A. Al-Saman, and A. A. Tayel, "Antibacterial activity of fusion from biosynthesized acidocin/silver nanoparticles and its application for eggshell decontamination," *J Basic Microbiol*, vol. 57, no. 9, pp. 744–751, Sep. 2017.

30. A. I. Osman *et al.*, "Synthesis of green nanoparticles for energy, biomedical, environmental, agricultural, and food applications: A review," Apr. 01, 2024.

31. S. Shende *et al.*, "Synthesis of copper nanomaterials by microbes and their use in sustainable agriculture," *Microbial Nanotechnology*, pp.256-287, May 2020.

32. A. Dirpan, A. F. Ainani, and M. Djalal, "A Review on Biopolymer-Based Biodegradable Film for Food Packaging: Trends over the Last Decade and Future Research," Jul. 01, 2023.

33. M. Z. Al Mahmud, M. H. Mobarak, and N. Hossain, "Emerging trends in biomaterials for sustainable food packaging: A comprehensive review," Jan. 15, 2024.

34. R. Biswas, M. Alam, A. Sarkar, M. I. Haque, M. M. Hasan, and M. Hoque, "Application of nanotechnology in food: processing, preservation, packaging and safety assessment," Nov. 01, 2022.

35. N. K. Kaushik *et al.*, "Evaluation of antiplasmodial activity of medicinal plants from North Indian Buchpora and South Indian Eastern Ghats," *Malar J*, vol. 14, no. 1, 2015.

36. V. R. Ranjitha and V. R. Rai, "Actinomycetes mediated synthesis of gold nanoparticles from the culture supernatant of Streptomyces griseoruber with special reference to catalytic activity," *3 Biotech*, vol. 7, no. 5, Oct. 2017.

37. E. F. El-Belely *et al.*, "Green Synthesis of Zinc Oxide Nanoparticles (ZnO-NPs) Using Arthrospira platensis (Class: Cyanophyceae) and Evaluation of their Biomedical Activities," 2021.

38. D. M. S. A. Salem, M. M. Ismail, and M. A. Aly-Eldeen, "Biogenic synthesis and antimicrobial potency of iron oxide (Fe3O4) nanoparticles using algae harvested from the Mediterranean Sea, Egypt," *Egypt J Aquat Res*, vol. 45, no. 3, pp. 197–204, Sep. 2019.

Transformative Applied Research in Computing, Engineering, Science and Technology – Dr. Damayanthi Dahanayake et al. (eds)
© 2024 Taylor & Francis Group, London, ISBN 978-1-041-01782-0

39

Benchmarking Tea Quality— A Comparative Evaluation of Key Chemical Properties in Tea

L.S.D. Perera, D. Dahanayake*
Department of Life Sciences,
Faculty of Science, NSBM Green University,
Sri Lanka

Abstract

Throughout history, tea has been a beloved beverage for many people. Tea has been linked for centuries with the ability to "preserve the mind" and "purify the body." People drink tea regularly across the world, selecting between black, green, or oolong tea based on their preferences. The phrase "tea polyphenols" refers to the polyphenols found in tea, which have been demonstrated to have positive effects on lipid metabolism control, antioxidant and anti-inflammatory properties, as well as cancer prevention. According to customer preferences, there are various types of tea available in the market. The current study aimed to evaluate and compare antioxidant activity, moisture content, and caffeine content in six major black tea types available in the market, namely, Flavored Tea Base, English Breakfast, English Afternoon, Earl Grey, Premium Tea, and Ceylon Supreme. The antioxidant activity, moisture content, and caffeine content were measured using the 2,2-diphenyl-1-picrylhydrazyl (DPPH) method, ISO 3720 method, and the Dichloromethane method with modifications, respectively. The results obtained revealed that Ceylon Supreme has the strongest antioxidant activity (125.44+/-46.81 mg/100 mL). The moisture content of all tea samples was below 9.50%, which is under the specific limit for black tea. The caffeine content of six tea types varied between (2.36+/-0.13%) to (3.75+/-0.95%). This combined analysis helps in making informed choices based on both caffeine sensitivity and desired health benefits from antioxidants.

Keywords

Black tea, Antioxidant activity, Caffeine, Polyphenol

1. Introduction

Tea is the most affordable and widely used beverage worldwide, the second only to water [1]. Green tea, oolong tea, and black tea are major forms of tea that are manufactured from tender flushes of *Camellia sinensis* [2]. Tea is consumed by people of all ages and socioeconomic backgrounds [1]. Over 3 billion cups of tea are drunk every day worldwide[1]. The tea plant is believed to have originated in southwest China, and the tradition of drinking

*Corresponding author: damayanthi.d@nsbm.ac.lk

DOI: 10.1201/9781003616368-39

tea infusions is also thought to have started there thousands of years ago [4]. About 20% and 78% of tea consumed globally are made up of green and black tea, respectively, with oolong tea making up the remaining 2% [5]. In terms of regional preferences, black tea dominates the market in Western nations, while green, white, and oolong tea are popular in China and Japan [5]. Green tea is unfermented with minimal oxidation [6]. Oolong and black tea can experience partial to full oxidation, respectively, which darkens the color of the leaves and the resulting brew [4].

It has been established that tea beverages contain chemo-preventive properties[7].Consumption of tea is also linked with anti-inflammatory effects, cardioprotective effects, antiviral properties, improvement of cognitive function, and prevention of neurodegenerative disorders [8].

Sri Lankan tea, also known as "Ceylon Tea" for decades, is noted for its high-quality black tea [2]. Sri Lanka has the third-largest tea cultivation area behind China and India [9]. Currently, Sri Lanka leads in tea export revenue, value-added tea exports, and orthodox tea production[9]. Sri Lanka's largest tea export destinations are the Commonwealth of Independent States, the Middle East, North America, Turkey, Ukraine, Japan, and China [9].

The goal of the present study is to compare the antioxidant activity, moisture content, and caffeine content of main black tea types available in market namely, Flavored tea base, Earl Grey, English Breakfast, English Afternoon, Premium tea, and Ceylon Supreme using the 2,2-diphenyl-1-picrylhydrazyl (DPPH) method, ISO 3720 method, and the dichloromethane method with modifications, respectively.

2. Antioxidant Activity in Tea

Polyphenols, the primary components of tea, account for 20–35% of its dry weight and catechin is the most common kind of polyphenol, accounting for 60–80% of the polyphenols found in tea [10]. Numerous research conducted in the last few years have shown that tea polyphenols have potent antioxidant properties [10].

Polyphenols are a major kind of antioxidants found in tea [11]. Catechin, epicatechin, epicatechin gallate, epigallocatechin, epigallocatechin-3-gallate, and gallocatechin are the main types of catechins found in tea [12]. Among them, epigallocatechin-3-gallate is the most potent variety [11]. These polyphenols are found in black tea at smaller concentrations, where they are partially converted into complex condensation products such as theaflavins and thearubigins by the polyphenol oxidase-driven enzymatic fermentation process [13].

The typical antioxidant test is based on scavenging the DPPH (2,2 Diphenyl-1-picryl-hydrazyl) free radical [14]. DPPH is a stable free radical with one nitrogen bridge atom's valence electron unpaired [14]. For assessing antioxidant activity in various plant extracts, food products, biological samples, synthetic compounds, and cosmetic and personal care products the most used method is DPPH free radical assay which is known as ISO 14502-1:2005.

3. Caffeine in Tea

Caffeine is an alkaloid that belongs to the methylxanthines family [15]. Methylxanthines are naturally occurring compounds and caffeine is the most powerful xanthine named as 1,3,7-tri methylxanthine [16]. Caffeine is a white color powder at room temperature that is odorless and has a slightly bitter taste [17]. Coffee, tea, colas, and chocolates are rich in caffeine [18]. Depending on the product type, preparation methods, and serving size, there are differences in the caffeine content of food items [18].

In recent years caffeine has gained popularity in the culinary and pharmaceutical industries for its pharmacological characteristics [19]. Caffeine use should be closely monitored since excessive amounts of the stimulant can create several physiological problems [20].

Determination of caffeine using the UV-visible Spectrophotometric method which is known as ISO 20481:2008 is accurate and cost-effective and has a straightforward process [20].

4. Materials and Methods

Six major tea types that have high customer preferences were selected for the study. For each tea type, samples from three different batches were collected randomly. The selected tea types were as follows, Flavored Tea Base, English Breakfast, English Afternoon, Earl Grey, Premium Tea, and Ceylon Supreme.

All the chemicals were purchased from Sigma Aldrich as follows; DPPH, absolute ethanol, and dichloromethane.

4.1 Antioxidant Activity

The antioxidant activity of each tea sample was determined by the DPPH free radical scavenging assay.

4.2 Preparation of 2,2-diphenyl-1-picrylhydrazyl (DPPH) Solution

DPPH (4 mg) was weighed and dissolved in absolute ethanol (30.0 mL) in a 50 mL volumetric flask and topped up to the mark with absolute ethanol and maintained in a dark condition. The fresh DPPH solution was prepared daily.

4.3 Preparation of Ascorbic Acid Standard Series

Ascorbic acid (0.01 g) was weighed into a 100 mL volumetric flask, dissolved in distilled water, diluted to the mark, and mixed well. From the freshly prepared ascorbic acid stock solution (0.1 g/L), four dilutions were prepared by transferring 1.00 mL, 3.00 mL, 5.00 mL, and 7.00 mL of the stock solution into separate 100 mL volumetric flasks. Each flask was then diluted to the mark with distilled water to obtain a standard series of solutions, respectively.

4.4 Preparation of Tea Brew Samples

Each tea sample (2.0 g) was weighed and brewed with 200 mL of boiling water for 5 minutes. From each brewed sample 20.00 mL was pipetted into 100 mL volumetric flask and made-up volume to the mark with distilled water.

4.5 Preparation of Dilutions from Tea Brew Samples

The composition of the tea samples was not similar, because they came from different processing methods and different production batches. Thus, dilution may change among batches for the same tea type.

A series of dilutions was performed on samples from batch numbers 1 through 8, using volumes of 1.0 mL, 2.0 mL, 3.0 mL, and 4.0 mL. For samples from batch numbers 9 through 18, a different dilution series was applied, with volumes of 0.5 mL, 0.75 mL, 1.0 mL, and 2.0 mL. Each sample was measured into a 100 mL volumetric flask separately and diluted up to the mark with distilled water. Prepared dilution series were used for the assay. For each batch, a duplicate analysis was performed.

4.6 Determination of Antioxidant Activity

Ascorbic acid standard series was taken and pipetted out each ascorbic acid (2.00 mL) into four test tubes separately. Then DPPH solution (2.00 mL) was added into the same four test tubes. At the same time, the blank sample was prepared by adding 2.00 mL of distilled water and 2.00 mL of absolute ethanol. The control sample was prepared by adding 2.00 mL of distilled water and 2.00 mL of DPPH solution. All test tubes were mixed thoroughly with a vortex mixer and then kept in a dark place for 15 minutes. Then the samples were transferred into glass cuvettes and measured the absorbance at 517 nm using a UV-spectrophotometer (Thermo Scientific, Genesys 10s). The above procedure was repeated to all the dilution series prepared from tea samples. The antioxidant activity was calculated based on the ascorbic acid standard curve.

Antioxidant activity (AOA) was calculated using the following equation.

$$AOA = Ap \times \frac{100^a}{Sp} \times \frac{100^b}{20} \times \frac{100}{1000} \qquad (1)$$

Ap = Ascorbic acid ppm

Sp = sample ppm

100^a = final dilution

100^b = first dilution

20 = volume of brewed tea sample (20 ml)

5. Determination of Caffeine Content

5.1 Preparation of Tea Brew Samples

Each tea sample (1.0 g) was weighed and brewed with boiling water (100 mL) for 5 minutes. Then the tea brew was transferred into a beaker. The residue tea sample was brewed with another 100 mL of boiling water for 5 minutes and transferred to the same beaker. The extracted tea brew was transferred into a 200 mL volumetric flask. The prepared tea brew (10.00 mL) was transferred to a 50 mL volumetric flask and made up the volume with distilled water to obtain a diluted tea brew sample.

5.2 Determination of Moisture Content of Tea Samples

The moisture content of tea samples was measured according to the guidelines of ISO 7513:1990. The tea sample (5.0 g) was measured and dried in the oven at 103 ± 2 °C for six hours. Then dried sample weight was measured using an analytical balance. Duplicate analysis was performed.

Moisture content (MC) was obtained from the following equation.

$$MC = \frac{(E + S) - F}{S} \times 100\% \qquad (2)$$

E = Weight of empty petri dish (g)

S = Weight of initial sample (g)

F = Weight of dried sample with the petri dish (g)

5.3 Determination of Caffeine Content

A diluted tea brew sample (50.00 mL) was added into a clean separating funnel followed by dichloromethane (25.00 mL). The separating funnel was shaken vigorously and allowed to stand for 15 minutes. The dichloromethane layer was drained into a conical flask. The aqueous layer was again mixed with dichloromethane (25.00 mL) and extracted two times following the same procedure and the final caffeine extract in dichloromethane was 75 mL. The absorbance of the extract was measured at 260 nm wavelength using a UV-spectrophotometer (Thermo Scientific, Genesys 10s).

Caffeine content (CC) was calculated according to the following equation.

$$Cc = \frac{Cc}{1000} \times 5 \times 200 \times \frac{100}{w} \times \frac{100}{(100 - MC)} \times 10^{-3} \quad (3)$$

Cc = caffeine concentration (mg/L)

W = exact weight that was taken to prepare the brew (g)

MC = Moisture content (%)

6. Results

6.1 Antioxidant Activity

Table 39.1 represents the antioxidant activity of various tea types across multiple batches. The antioxidant activity was recorded in mg per 100 mL. Each tea type is listed with its batch numbers and corresponding antioxidant activity values. Additionally, the average antioxidant activity for each type of tea is also calculated using one-way ANOVA using Minitab software.

Table 39.1 Antioxidant activity of tea type

Tea Type	Batch No	Average Antioxidant Activity (Mg/ 100 Ml)	The Average Antioxidant Activity of A Tea Type (Mg/ 100 Ml)
Flavored Tea Base	01	69.55	78.12 ± 7.61
	02	80.72	
	03	84.10	
English Breakfast	04	82.71	82.72 ± 3.91
	05	86.64	
	06	78.82	
Premium Tea	07	135.11	121.55 ± 14.73
	08	105.88	
	09	123.65	
English Afternoon	10	78.66	96.80 ± 16.50
	11	100.83	
	12	110.91	
Earl Grey	13	94.15	102.37 ± 11.17
	14	115.09	
	15	97.86	
Ceylon Supreme	16	95.81	125.44 ± 46.81
	17	179.41	
	18	101.10	

6.2 Caffeine Content

Table 39.2 represents the caffeine content across various batches of different tea types. Each tea type is listed with its batch numbers, corresponding moisture content, and caffeine content. Additionally, the average caffeine content for each tea type was calculated using one-way ANOVA using Minitab software.

Table 39.2 Caffeine content of tea type

Tea Type	Batch No	Moisture Content (%)	Average Caffeine Content (%)	The Average Caffeine Content in A Tea Type(%)
Flavored Tea Base	01	8.63	2.51	2.36 ± 0.13%
	02	7.21	2.31	
	03	7.32	2.26	
English Breakfast	04	5.72	4.28	3.67 ± 0.53%
	05	6.63	3.35	
	06	7.84	3.39	
Premium Tea	07	5.22	3.15	3.04 ± 0.09%
	08	7.31	2.98	
	09	5.31	3.00	
English Afternoon	10	5.10	2.75	3.22 ± 0.41%
	11	8.20	3.38	
	12	8.04	3.52	
Earl Grey	13	6.83	2.74	3.75 ± 0.95%
	14	7.24	4.62	
	15	7.92	3.90	
Ceylon Supreme	16	7.11	2.91	3.35 ± 0.43%
	17	7.32	3.77	
	18	7.22	3.38	

7. Discussion

According to the results, Ceylon Supreme has the highest average antioxidant activity, with premium tea showing consistently high values across batches. flavored tea base has the lowest average antioxidant activity, though it does show an increasing trend across the batches. Ceylon Supreme tea shows the highest variability, especially due to the extreme value in batch seventeen. Among other tea types, English Breakfast tea shows the most consistency in antioxidant activity, Earl Grey tea exhibits the highest average caffeine content but is also high in variability. Ceylon Supreme tea shows a high and consistent caffeine content with minimal variability. This variability among the same tea type can happen due to the mixing of tea from different types of tea plantations. Each batch number given above indicated different tea samples for each tea type. Therefore, each tea sample did not contain the same tea from the same plantations.

In summary, the Flavored tea base offers low and consistent caffeine content along with moderate antioxidant activity. This makes it suitable for consumers looking for mild stimulation without high caffeine intake. English Breakfast tea provides a moderately high caffeine content and relatively high antioxidant activity. It is ideal for those who are seeking a significant energy boost with the added antioxidant activity, making it a good choice for a morning tea. Premium tea stands out with its moderate and consistent caffeine content combined with the highest average antioxidant activity. This tea is excellent for those who are looking to maximize their antioxidant intake while maintaining a balanced level of caffeine. English Afternoon tea has a moderate caffeine content with some variability and high antioxidant activity. It is suitable for those who are seeking a balanced caffeine intake and significant antioxidant benefits, making it a good choice for afternoon consumption. Earl Grey tea has the highest average caffeine content with significant variability and high antioxidant activity. It is ideal for those who enjoy a strong, stimulating tea with considerable health benefits from antioxidants but, the variability requires careful selection based on individual caffeine tolerance. Ceylon Supreme tea offers a relatively high and consistent caffeine content along with the highest variability in antioxidant activity. This tea is excellent for those who are looking for a reliable caffeine boost and significant antioxidant benefits, though batch-to-batch variations in antioxidant levels should be considered.

According to the previous research conducted the caffeine content of black tea was 2.27% - 3.86% [19]. There were no significant differences between the caffeine content among the tested teas.

The temperature of the water used for brewing and the brewing duration may have an impact on the determination of antioxidant activity and caffeine content of tea samples [20].

By understanding and leveraging the above data, both tea producers and tea consumers can make better decisions to optimize their tea experience in terms of both enjoyment and health benefits.

8. Conclusion

For tea types like Ceylon Supreme, further investigations are needed to understand the reason behind the variability in antioxidant activity among production batches and it may be necessary to ensure consistent quality of the product. It should be beneficial for tea producers to implement more standardized processing methods to minimize batch-to-batch variability, particularly for high-demand products with health claims linked with antioxidant content and caffeine content.

Tea consumers may also have an idea about storage and brewing techniques to gain the best health benefits from consuming a cup of tea.

In conclusion, the practical direction for future study on tea types might lie in areas to understand the specific compounds contributing to antioxidant content and caffeine content in different tea types how these compounds interact with other components in tea, and how different environmental conditions impact on antioxidant content and caffeine content in tea plants.

REFERENCES

1. A. Hicks, "Current status and future development of global tea production and tea products," Au J, vol. 12, no. November 2008, pp. 251–264, 2009.
2. Jayawardhane, Madushanka, K. M. Mewan, S. Jayasinghe, N. Karunajeewa, and Edirisinghe, "Determination of Quality Characteristics in Different Green Tea Products Available in Sri Lankan Supermarkets," 6th Symp. Plant. Crop Res., no. January 2017, pp. 57–68, 2016, [Online]. Available: https://www.researchgate.net/publication/312194646_Determination_of_Quality_Characteristics_in_Different_Green_Tea_Products_Available_in_Sri_Lankan_Supermarkets/link/5875a0cf08ae329d622063a3/download.
3. A. Gramza-Michałowska, "Caffeine in tea Camellia sinensis - Content, absorption, benefits and risks of consumption," J. Nutr. Heal. Aging, vol. 18, no. 2, pp. 143–149, 2014, doi: 10.1007/s12603-013-0404-1.
4. T. Tanaka and Y. Matsuo, "Production Mechanisms of Black Tea Polyphenols," Chem. Pharm. Bull., vol. 68, no. 12, pp. 1131–1142, 2020, doi: 10.1248/cpb.c20-00295.
5. S. Li, C. Y. Lo, M. H. Pan, C. S. Lai, and C. T. Ho, "Black tea: Chemical analysis and stability," Food Funct., vol. 4, no. 1, pp. 10–18, 2013, doi: 10.1039/c2fo30093a.
6. S. Ahmed and J. R. Stepp, "Green Tea: The Plants, Processing, Manufacturing and Production," Tea Heal. Dis. Prev., no. January, pp. 19–31, 2013, doi: 10.1016/B978-0-12-384937-3.00002-1.
7. T. C. Janet, W. K. John, K. Thomas, M. O. Kelvin, and W. N. Francis, "Effect of Seasons on Theanine Levels in Different Kenyan Commercially Released Tea Cultivars and Its Variation in Different Parts of the Tea Shoot," Food Nutr. Sci., vol. 06, no. 15, pp. 1450–1459, 2015, doi: 10.4236/fns.2015.615149.
8. J. Kochman, K. Jakubczyk, J. Antoniewicz, H. Mruk, and K. Janda, "Health Benefits and Chemical Composition of Matcha Green Tea: A Review," Molecules, vol. 26, no. 1, 2020, doi: 10.3390/molecules26010085.
9. S. Lanka, "INSTITUTE OF DEVELOPING ECONOMIES IDE DISCUSSION PAPER No . 642 Effects of Standards

on Tea Exports from Developing Countries : Comparison of China," no. 642, 2017.

10. T. Tong, Y. J. Liu, J. Kang, C. M. Zhang, and S. G. Kang, "Antioxidant activity and main chemical components of a novel fermented tea," Molecules, vol. 24, no. 16, pp. 1–14, 2019, doi: 10.3390/molecules24162917.

11. R. Balasooriya, M. Kooragoda, and P. Jayawardhane, "Comparative analysis on physical and chemical characteristics of commercially manufactured/ processed green tea in Sri Lanka," Int. J. Food Sci. Nutr. www. foodsciencejournal.com, vol. 4, no. July, pp. 43–47, 2019, doi: 10.13140/RG.2.2.11002.85441.

12. M. Franks, P. Lawrence, A. Abbaspourrad, and R. Dando, "The influence of water composition on flavor and nutrient extraction in green and black tea," Nutrients, vol. 11, no. 1, 2019, doi: 10.3390/nu11010080.

13. I. Peluso and M. Serafini, "Antioxidants from black and green tea: from dietary modulation of oxidative stress to pharmacological mechanisms," Br. J. Pharmacol., vol. 174, no. 11, pp. 1195–1208, 2017, doi: 10.1111/bph.13649.

14. O. P. Sharma and T. K. Bhat, "DPPH antioxidant assay revisited," Food Chem., vol. 113, no. 4, pp. 1202–1205, 2009, doi: 10.1016/j.foodchem.2008.08.008.

15. G. Çalışkan, K. U. Üniversitesi, N. Dirim, A. Akdogan, and G. Üniversitesi, "Mathematical Modeling on Thin Layer Microwave Drying of Corn Husk and Investigation of Powder Properties Mathematical Modeling on Thin Layer Microwave Drying of Corn Husk and Investigation of Powder Properties View project Determination Of Antimicrobial A," no. September 2018, 2017, [Online]. Available: https://www.researchgate.net/publication/323144765.

16. T. Atomssa and A. V. Gholap, "Characterization of caffeine and determination of caffeine in tea leaves using uv-visible spectrometer," African J. Pure Appl. Chem., vol. 5, no. 1, pp. 1–8, 2011, [Online]. Available:

Note: All the tables in this chapter were made by the authors.

Transformative Applied Research in Computing, Engineering, Science and Technology – Dr. Damayanthi Dahanayake et al. (eds)
© 2024 Taylor & Francis Group, London, ISBN 978-1-041-01782-0

40

Ensuring Authenticity in Green Tea— A Review of Common Adulterants and Detection Methods

Thilakarathna L.M.P.H, Rabindrakumar M.S.K*

Department of Biomedical Science,
Faculty of Science, NSBM Green University,
Sri Lanka

Abstract

The increasing recognition of green tea's health and therapeutic benefits among consumers has significantly boosted its global market demand. However, this heightened demand has also paved the way for compromising the quality and effectiveness of green tea through adulteration, aimed at maximizing profit. Various studies have reported common adulterants such as chicory, acetamiprid, cashew, sibutramine, sugar, and glucose syrup mixed with green tea. Adulteration not only misleads consumers but can also pose health risks by undermining the benefits that make green tea so popular. Hence, it is crucial to identify and understand these adulterants. Chromatography, spectroscopy, DNA barcoding, and Electronic Sensing Platforms (ESPs) are some techniques used to identify these adulterants in green tea. To sustain consumer trust and enhance transparency in the tea market, it is crucial to comprehend the impact of common adulterants in green tea and the methods used to detect them. This literature review offers a thorough overview of the various green tea adulterants and the sophisticated techniques employed to identify them. By understanding these aspects, stakeholders in the tea industry can take informed steps to combat adulteration, thereby preserving the integrity of green tea and safeguarding consumer health.

Keywords

Adulteration, Camellia sinensis, Green tea, Identification techniques, Tea

1. Introduction

Tea is a widely consumed beverage globally which only being second to water, especially in Asian countries [1]. It is a main commercial crop that originated in Southeast China and is grown in many tropical and subtropical countries including about 30 countries worldwide [2]. The two varieties of tea: are China tea (*Camellia sinensis* var. *sinensis*) and Assam tea (*Camellia assamica* var. *assamica*) [2]. Tea comes in different types based on the fermentation process. They are black, green, oolong, yellow, and white [3]. Black tea is a fully fermented traditional form of tea, while green tea is made from dried leaves of *Camellia sinensis* without any fermentation. Oolong tea undergoes

*Corresponding author: miruna.r@nsbm.ac.lk

DOI: 10.1201/9781003616368-40

a light fermentation process. White and yellow tea, which undergo light processing of steaming and drying are named after the respective color of the hair on the bud and younger leaves under the surface [3], [4].

Green tea is an unfermented tea derived from the *Camellia sinensis* plant and has been consumed for centuries due to its perceived health benefits and cultural significance. It is rich in nutrients which are responsible for its health benefits [4], [5]. According to a recent report, there is a growing demand in the global market due to increased recognition of green tea's health and therapeutic benefits among consumers [6]. Although the global supply chain of various teas has experienced sudden disturbance due to the COVID-19 outbreak, green tea sales continued to increase during and after the pandemic. However, the global popularity of green tea has led to increased instances of adulteration, threatening its quality and integrity. Reducing the quality of food by altering its composition intentionally or unintentionally is known as food adulteration [7].

In the green tea industry, adulteration mostly involves the intentional addition of inferior materials to green tea. This practice is frequently motivated by supply chain complications or economic considerations, normally to gain higher profits [8], [9]. Some adulterants that are added to green tea are chicory [3], acetamiprid [8], cashew [9], sibutramine [10], and sugar and glucose syrup [11]. These adulterations lead to various health problems. To preserve the quality and gain the most possible health and therapeutic advantages, it is crucial to understand and recognize green tea adulterations [9], [10]. Therefore, this literature review explores the different types of green tea adulteration as well as the techniques for identifying them. We conducted a comprehensive search of scientific databases, Google Scholar, and PubMed for academic journals to gather information on green tea adulteration and identification techniques. This literature survey included recent studies and methodologies published within the last decade to ensure relevance and accuracy.

2. Green Tea and its Composition

Fresh leaves of *Camellia sinensis* var. *sinensis* plant are typically dried and steamed to produce green tea [4], [5]. The particle size and color of green tea can vary, ranging from dusty to leafy and from greenish to brown, respectively. Brewed tea can range in color from golden yellow to dark brown, and black. The quality of green tea is determined by a variety of factors including soil, harvesting season, regions of origin, and environmental conditions [12]–[14]. Green tea is mostly consumed in countries such as China, Morocco, Korea, and Japan [15].

It is also commonly used in traditional medicines like Ayurveda, Unani, and Homeopathy [4].

The main components present in green tea are polyphenols such as catechins, thearubigins, and theaflavins which contribute to green tea's antioxidant properties [2]. The major component of total polyphenols is catechins, making up about 10-20% of dry green tea leaves [4]. Catechins are responsible for the high flavonoid content that gives green tea its bitter taste [12]. The four major types of catechins found in green tea are (-)-epicatechin (EC), (-)-epicatechin gallate (ECG), (-)-epigallocatechin (EGC), and (-)-epigallocatechin gallate (EGCG) [16], [17]. EGCG constitutes approximately 50-80% of total catechins and is predominantly found in green tea rather than in black tea and oolong tea [18].

Green tea is rich in essential components. It contains 15-20% proteins, and approximately 7% amino acids including tryptophan, glutamic acid, arginine, theanine, and others. It also includes 5-7% carbohydrates such as glucose, sucrose, cellulose, fructose, and pectin. Additionally, it contains 5% minerals and trace elements such as magnesium, calcium, iron, chromium, copper, and others. Green tea also provides approximately 3% xanthine bases such as theophylline, caffeine, and trace amounts of lipids, volatile compounds, sterols, pigments, and vitamins (B, C, E) [4], [16], [19]–[21]. In addition, the bioactive compounds found in green tea include linalool, hexanal, and geraniol, as well as saponins, theobromine, kaempferol, quercetin, and myricetin [22], [23].

3. Benefits of Green Tea Consumption

Green tea consumption provides numerous health benefits because of its antioxidant, anti-diabetic, anti-obesity, and anti-carcinogenic properties as well as its positive effects on skin and oral health. Polyphenols, specifically catechins, can neutralize reactive nitrogen and oxygen species and enhance the activity of detoxifying enzymes. Additionally, catechins can chelate metal ions during redox reactions [24]. Tang et al. revealed green tea is effective in better glucose tolerance, reducing high blood glucose levels, and restoring normal liver in the experiment performed using diabetic mice [25]. A cohort study on individuals consuming 3 cups of green tea showed increased antioxidant levels, which could have a positive impact on diabetes regulation [26]. Fluoride contained in green tea contributes to oral health by preventing tooth decay, curing dental problems, and inhibiting microbial growth in the mouth [20], [27]. After being consumed, catechins and their metabolites can be detected in skin tissues, suggesting that they can directly provide protective effects at the location of UV exposure. Additionally, green tea catechins may aid in shielding skin cells from UV-induced DNA damage, potentially enhancing skin health and reducing inflammation resulting from UV exposure [28]. Evidence indicates that the catechins and caffeine in green tea promote fat oxidation and energy utilization by increasing thermogenesis, as well as inhibiting some enzymes involved in lipid metabolism, which assists in weight loss [29]. EGCG reduces cancer risk by inhibiting pathways and enzymes, leading to cell apoptosis in various organs, including the skin, lungs, liver, esophagus, prostate, kidney, stomach, and oral cavity [24], [27].

4. Green Tea Adulterations

Throughout the cultivation process of green tea, pesticides are commonly utilized to safeguard tea plants from diseases, weeds, and pests. Neonicotinoid insecticides, such as acetamiprid, are used at different stages of cultivation [21]. Acetamiprid is commonly used in agricultural fields, including tea plantations, to paralyze or kill sucking insects such as aphids, thrips, and whiteflies that can damage tea plants. It has low toxicity to mammals and high insecticidal activity. However, the accumulation of residues in the environment and the leaves of green tea from extensive use can lead to unintended adulteration of green tea leaves, potentially posing health risks for humans and non-target organisms [8]. Acetamiprid demonstrates high transfer rates during green tea brewing, necessitating extended intervals between treatment and harvest to ensure residue levels remain below the maximum residual limit [30].

Roasted green tea is a very popular tea that is known for its high antioxidant activity and potential health benefits. However, some producers add sugar and glucose syrup to enhance the taste and appearance [11]. This adulteration can be harmful to diabetic patients and individuals with high blood sugar levels, who may consume green tea believing it has anti-diabetic properties. Further, it tends to cause health problems such as heart disease, dental caries, and obesity. Furthermore, adulteration with glucose syrup and sugar can increase moisture absorption which leads to bacterial growth, making it difficult to preserve the tea for extended periods [31].

Chicory is one of the common adulterants included in green tea that enhances its aroma. It originates from Europe and is cultivated worldwide, including in Northern Africa, Mid-Asia, Australia, and Eastern USA [32]. Chicory has sedative effects that can impair the normal functions of the central nervous system [33], [34] and can also cause oral and respiratory symptoms through allergic reactions [3].

Cashew (*Anticardium occidental L.*) nut husk is a common plant-derived material used to adulterate tea. This practice is particularly prevalent in Asian countries and is done to increase profits. The inclusion of cashew nut husk in tea can pose serious health risks as it contains allergenic substances that can cause intoxications, allergic reactions, and other life-threatening side effects [9].

Sibutramine (Sibutramine hydrochloride monohydrate) is commonly added to mixed herbal tea, green coffee, and green tea to aid in weight loss. It is an oral anorexiant and a centrally acting serotonin-norepinephrine reuptake inhibitor (SNRI) used to treat obesity. However, research has demonstrated that sibutramine intake increases the risk of heart attacks and strokes. The percentage of adulteration in the samples varied with the amount of sibutramine added. This analysis found that the adulteration quantities ranged from 0.375 mg to 12 mg of sibutramine per sample [10].

5. Techniques Used in the Identification of Green Tea Adulterations

Given the recent increase in adulteration incidents, it is crucial to develop accessible analytical methods for assessing the authenticity of tea and detecting and quantifying fraud. Chemical analysis involves chromatographic techniques, spectroscopic methods, molecular detections, and sensory evaluations to identify green tea adulterations [11], [35].

Pons et al. utilized chromatographic techniques, High-Performance Liquid Chromatography – Ultraviolet (HPLC-UV), and (High-Performance Liquid Chromatography - Fluorescence Detection (HPLC-FLD), in combination with chemometrics to identify chicory in green tea. These techniques can identify chicory in green tea, with specific patterns obtained at 280 nm and 280 nm/350 nm, respectively [33].

Furthermore, Lagiotis et al. utilized Bar-HRM or High-Resolution Melting analysis with a plant DNA barcoding marker to identify and measure the amount of cashew in adulterated tea [9]. These chromatographic and molecular methods may be accurate and sensitive, but they are complex and time-consuming, requiring expertise to handle. Sensory evaluations are not ideal for detecting adulterants due to limitations in objectivity and reproducibility. Expert tea tasters are susceptible to being influenced by psychological and physiological factors, which hinders the reliability of the evaluations [35].

In the modern world, researchers prefer to use simple, fast, cost-effective, and non-destructive analytical methods instead of complex methods for food analysis. Near-infrared Spectroscopy (NIRS) is a such analytical method used to measure the antioxidant potential of green tea [36] and distinguish green tea based on grades, varieties, and regions of origin [37]. Attenuated Total Reflection Fourier Transform Near Infrared spectroscopy (ATR-FTNIR) was used to detect sibutramine in green tea within a range of 0.375 to 12 mg per 1.75 g of green tea [10]. Furthermore, a study showed the effectiveness of a smartphone-based micro NIRS in qualitatively and quantitatively analyzing green tea adulterants [35]. Surface-enhanced Raman Scattering (SERS) is an exceptionally sensitive spectroscopy method utilized for biosensing. In a recent study by H. Li et al., a simple and fast biosensor relying on unmodified gold nanoparticles was employed for the colorimetric detection of acetamiprid in adulterated green tea. Though it is sensitive and easy to use, it is relatively expensive and requires lengthy sample preparations [8].

Recently, advanced techniques such as Electronic Sensing Platforms (ESPs) have been developed to evaluate the organoleptic attributes, making them essential in modern tea industries. Common ESPs include the electronic tongue (e-tongue), electronic nose (e-nose), and electronic eye (e-eye) [38]. A study conducted in the Chinese market revealed that an e-tongue using pattern recognition could successfully detect fake green tea, eliminating the need for sensory evaluation [39]. Additionally, artificial colorimetric nose and tongue were utilized to analyze Chinese green teas based on their regions of origin and grades, emphasizing the importance of flavor in evaluating teas [40]. ESPs offer certain advantages, yet they also come with limitations that need to be considered. One limitation of e-noses is the operation of Metal Oxide Semiconductor (MOS) sensors at high temperatures (150 – 400 °C), leading to increased energy consumption and requiring an extended heating time before measurements can be taken [38]. The limited response to charged species in solutions by potentiometric sensors in e-tongues, as well as the short lifespan of sensor materials, are some limitations present in e-tongues [41], [42]. The performance of e-eye systems can be greatly impacted by environmental conditions, such as lighting, which can affect both image quality and processing time [41]. Notably, there is limited research on using ESPs to quantify adulterants in green tea.

6. Conclusion

In conclusion, green tea's remarkable health benefits are mostly due to its polyphenol content, especially catechins. The adulteration of green tea poses a significant challenge to consumers' health, manufacturers, and regulating bodies, compromising the quality, safety, and authenticity of the product. Thus, the analysis of green tea adulteration is crucial to fully realize the potential health benefits of green tea. So, a multidisciplinary approach including chromatographic techniques, spectroscopic methods, and DNA barcoding is essential for effectively combating green tea adulteration. Advanced techniques such as Electronic Sensing Platforms (ESPs) have emerged in the modern tea industry to discover the organoleptic attributes of tea, but research on the quantification of adulterants using ESPs is limited.

REFERENCES

1. K. Shadrack, A. Faraj, K. Alex, N. Kenneth, and K. Wallace, "Anti-thrombotic effects of Camellia sinensis (Tea): A systematic review," no. May, pp. 29–33, 2019.

2. J. Omidi and S. Abdolmohammadi, "Green Tea (<i>Camellia Sinensis</i>) Ordinary Beverages or Medicinal Beverages: A Review," *Int. J. Bioorganic Chem.*, vol. 4, no. 2, p. 98, 2019, doi: 10.11648/j.ijbc.20190402.13.

3. M. Vilà, A. Bedmar, J. Saurina, O. Núñez, and S. Sentellas, "High-Throughput Flow Injection Analysis–Mass Spectrometry (FIA-MS) Fingerprinting for the Authentication of Tea Application to the Detection of Teas Adulterated with Chicory," *Foods*, vol. 11, no. 14, pp. 1–16, 2022, doi: 10.3390/foods11142153.

4. H. Vishnoi, R. Bodla, R. Kant, and R. B. Bodla, "Green Tea (Camellia Sinensis) and Its Antioxidant Property: a Review," *Artic. Int. J. Pharm. Sci. Res.*, vol. 9, no. 5, p. 1723, 2018, doi: 10.13040/IJPSR.0975-8232.9(5).1723-36.

5. W. C. Reygaert, "An update on the health benefits of green tea," *Beverages*, vol. 3, no. 1, pp. 9–12, 2017, doi: 10.3390/beverages3010006.

6. M. Nazir, S. Arif, R. S. Khan, W. Nazir, N. Khalid, and S. Maqsood, "Opportunities and challenges for functional and medicinal beverages: Current and future trends," *Trends Food Sci. Technol.*, vol. 88, no. May 2018, pp. 513–526, 2019, doi: 10.1016/j.tifs.2019.04.011.

7. S. Bansal, A. Singh, M. Mangal, A. K. Mangal, and S. Kumar, *Food adulteration: Sources, health risks, and detection methods*, vol. 57, no. 6. 2017.

8. H. Li, W. Hu, M. M. Hasan, Z. Zhenzhu, and Q. Chen, "A facile and sensitive SERS-based biosensor for colormetric detection of acetamiprid in green tea based on unmodified gold nanoparticles," *J. Food Meas. Charact.*, vol. 13, no. 1, pp. 259–268, 2019, doi: 10.1007/s11694-018-9940-z.

9. G. Lagiotis, E. Stavridou, I. Bosmali, M. Osathanunkul, N. Haider, and P. Madesis, "Detection and quantification of cashew in commercial tea products using High Resolution Melting (HRM) analysis," *J. Food Sci.*, vol. 85, no. 6, pp. 1629–1634, 2020, doi: 10.1111/1750-3841.15138.

10. N. Cebi, M. T. Yilmaz, and O. Sagdic, "A rapid ATR-FTIR spectroscopic method for detection of sibutramine adulteration in tea and coffee based on hierarchical cluster and principal component analyses," *Food Chem.*, vol. 229, pp. 517–526, 2017, doi: 10.1016/j.foodchem.2017.02.072.

11. L. Luqing, W. Lingdong, N. Jingming, and Z. Zhengzhu, "Detection and quantification of sugar and glucose syrup in

roasted green tea using near infrared spectroscopy," *J. Near Infrared Spectrosc.*, vol. 23, no. 5, pp. 317–325, 2015, doi: 10.1255/jnirs.1178.

12. Jayawardhane, Madushanka, K. M. Mewan, S. Jayasinghe, N. Karunajeewa, and Edirisinghe, "Determination of Quality Characteristics in Different Green Tea Products Available in Sri Lankan Supermarkets," *6th Symp. Plant. Crop Res.*, no. November, pp. 57–68, 2016, [Online]. Available: https://www.researchgate.net/publication/312194646_Determination_of_Quality_Characteristics_in_Different_Green_Tea_Products_Available_in_Sri_Lankan_Supermarkets/link/5875a0cf08ae329d622063a3/download.

13. K. M. Mewan, P. Jayawardhane, R. Balasooriya, and M. Kooragoda, "Comparative analysis on physical and chemical characteristics of commercially manufactured/processed green tea in Sri Lanka," vol. 4, no. July, pp. 43–47, 2019, doi: 10.13140/RG.2.2.11002.85441.

14. S. Kaushal, P. Nayi, D. Rahadian, and H.-H. Chen, "Applications of Electronic Nose Coupled with Statistical and Intelligent Pattern Recognition Techniques for Monitoring Tea Quality: A Review," *Agriculture*, vol. 12, no. 9, p. 1359, 2022, doi: 10.3390/agriculture12091359.

15. M. Saeed *et al.*, "Green tea (Camellia sinensis) and L-theanine: Medicinal values and beneficial applications in humans—A comprehensive review," *Biomed. Pharmacother.*, vol. 95, no. September, pp. 1260–1275, 2017, doi: 10.1016/j.biopha.2017.09.024.

16. M. M. Aboulwafa *et al.*, "Authentication and discrimination of green tea samples using UV–vis, FTIR and HPLC techniques coupled with chemometrics analysis," *J. Pharm. Biomed. Anal.*, vol. 164, pp. 653–658, 2019, doi: 10.1016/j.jpba.2018.11.036.

17. T. Atomssa and A. V Gholap, "Characterization and determination of catechins in green tea leaves using UV-visible spectrometer," vol. 7, no. 08795, pp. 22–31, 2015, doi: 10.5897/JETR2014.0527.

18. K. W. Lange, K. M. Lange, and Y. Nakamura, "Green tea, epigallocatechin gallate and the prevention of Alzheimer's disease: Clinical evidence," *Food Sci. Hum. Wellness*, vol. 11, no. 4, pp. 765–770, 2022, doi: 10.1016/j.fshw.2022.03.002.

19. G. Polianna de Brito, F. Laura dos Santos, D. Isabella Andreoni, and F. Adaliene Versiani Matos, "Effects of Phytotherapeutic Administration of Green Tea (Camellia sinensis) as a Treatment for Obesity: A Systematic Review of Clinical and Experimental Studies," *J. Nutr. Med. Diet Care*, vol. 8, no. 1, 2022, doi: 10.23937/2572-3278/1510057.

20. R. Rehman and M. Khalid, "Fluoride contents analysis of tea infusion, mouthwash and tooth paste samples of Pakistan using ion selective electrode," *Asian J. Chem.*, vol. 27, no. 8, pp. 2847–2850, 2015, doi: 10.14233/ajchem.2015.18243.

21. Y. Ikenaka *et al.*, "Contamination by neonicotinoid insecticides and their metabolites in Sri Lankan black tea leaves and Japanese green tea leaves," *Toxicol. Reports*, vol. 5, no. February, pp. 744–749, 2018, doi: 10.1016/j.toxrep.2018.06.008.

22. C. T. Scoparo, L. M. de Souza, N. Dartora, G. L. Sassaki, P. A. J. Gorin, and M. Iacomini, "Analysis of Camellia sinensis green and black teas via ultra high performance liquid chromatography assisted by liquid-liquid partition and two-dimensional liquid chromatography (size exclusion×reversed phase)," *J. Chromatogr. A*, vol. 1222, pp. 29–37, 2012, doi: 10.1016/j.chroma.2011.11.038.

23. M. Kato and T. Shibamoto, "Variation of major volatile constituents in various green teas from southeast Asia," *J. Agric. Food Chem.*, vol. 49, no. 3, pp. 1394–1396, 2001, doi: 10.1021/jf001321x.

24. C. Musial, A. Kuban-Jankowska, and M. Gorska-Ponikowska, "Beneficial Properties of Green Tea Catechins," *Int. J. Mol. Sci.*, 2020.

25. W. Tang, S. Li, Y. Liu, M. T. Huang, and C. T. Ho, "Anti-diabetic activity of chemically profiled green tea and black tea extracts in a type 2 diabetes mice model via different mechanisms," *J. Funct. Foods*, vol. 5, no. 4, pp. 1784–1793, 2013, doi: 10.1016/j.jff.2013.08.007.

26. N. A. Toolsee *et al.*, "Effectiveness of green tea in a randomized human cohort: Relevance to diabetes and its complications," *Biomed Res. Int.*, vol. 2013, 2013, doi: 10.1155/2013/412379.

27. D. Anand Gupta, D. John Bhaskar, K. Gupta, B. Karim, A. Jain, and D. Ranjan Dalai, "Green tea: A review on its natural anti-oxidant therapy and cariostatic benefits," *Issues Biol. Sci. Pharm. Res.*, vol. 2, no. 1, pp. 8–012, 2014, [Online]. Available: http://www.journalissues.org/IBSPR/.

28. K. A. Clarke *et al.*, "Green tea catechins and their metabolites in human skin before and after exposure to ultraviolet radiation," *J. Nutr. Biochem.*, vol. 27, pp. 203–210, 2016, doi: 10.1016/j.jnutbio.2015.09.001.

29. D. Türközü and N. A. Tek, "A minireview of effects of green tea on energy expenditure," *Crit. Rev. Food Sci. Nutr.*, vol. 57, no. 2, pp. 254–258, 2017, doi: 10.1080/10408398.2014.986672.

30. R. Y. Hou *et al.*, "Comparison of the dissipation behaviour of three neonicotinoid insecticides in tea," *Food Addit. Contam. - Part A*, vol. 30, no. 10, pp. 1761–1769, 2013, doi: 10.1080/19440049.2013.820356.

31. H. Wang *et al.*, "Simultaneous determination of fructose, glucose and sucrose by solid phase extraction-liquid chromatography-tandem mass spectrometry and its application to source and adulteration analysis of sucrose in tea," *J. Food Compos. Anal.*, vol. 96, no. June 2020, p. 103730, 2021, doi: 10.1016/j.jfca.2020.103730.

32. J. Perović *et al.*, "Chicory (Cichorium intybus L.) as a food ingredient – Nutritional composition, bioactivity, safety, and health claims: A review," *Food Chem.*, vol. 336, no. February 2020, p. 127676, 2021, doi: 10.1016/j.foodchem.2020.127676.

33. J. Pons, À. Bedmar, N. Núñez, J. Saurina, and O. Núñez, "Tea and chicory extract characterization, classification and authentication by non-targeted HPLC-UV-FLD fingerprinting and chemometrics," *Foods*, vol. 10, no. 12, 2021, doi: 10.3390/foods10122935.

34. A. Deb Pal and T. Das, "Analysis of adulteration in black tea," *Int. J. Biol. Res.*, vol. 3, no. 1, pp. 253–257, 2018, [Online]. Available: www.biologyjournal.in.

35. L. Luquing *et al.*, *Potential of smartphone-coupled micro NIR spectroscopy for quality control of green tea*, vol. 247. Elsevier B.V., 2021.

36. Z. Guo *et al.*, "Simultaneous quantification of active constituents and antioxidant capability of green tea using NIR spectroscopy coupled with swarm intelligence algorithm," *Lwt*, vol. 129, no. April, p. 109510, 2020, doi: 10.1016/j.lwt.2020.109510.

37. P. Liu *et al.*, "A novel strategy of near-infrared spectroscopy dimensionality reduction for discrimination of grades, varieties and origins of green tea," *Vib. Spectrosc.*, vol. 105, p. 102984, 2019, doi: 10.1016/j.vibspec.2019.102984.

38. S. M. T. Gharibzahedi, F. J. Barba, J. Zhou, M. Wang, and Z. Altintas, "Electronic Sensor Technologies in Monitoring Quality of Tea: A Review," *Biosensors*, vol. 12, no. 5, 2022, doi: 10.3390/bios12050356.

39. Y. Li, J. Lei, and D. Liang, "Identification of fake green tea by sensory assessment and electronic tongue," *Food Sci. Technol. Res.*, vol. 21, no. 2, pp. 207–212, 2015, doi: 10.3136/fstr.21.207.

40. D. Huo, Y. Wu, M. Yang, H. Fa, X. Luo, and C. Hou, "Discrimination of Chinese green tea according to varieties and grade levels using artificial nose and tongue based on colorimetric sensor arrays," *Food Chem.*, vol. 145, pp. 639–645, 2014, doi: 10.1016/j.foodchem.2013.07.142.

41. M. Xu, J. Wang, and L. Zhu, "The qualitative and quantitative assessment of tea quality based on E-nose, E-tongue and E-eye combined with chemometrics," *Food Chem.*, vol. 289, no. March, pp. 482–489, 2019, doi: 10.1016/j.foodchem.2019.03.080.

42. M. Xu, J. Wang, and S. Gu, "Rapid identification of tea quality by E-nose and computer vision combining with a synergetic data fusion strategy," *J. Food Eng.*, vol. 241, pp. 10–17, 2019, doi: 10.1016/j.jfoodeng.2018.07.020.

Transformative Applied Research in Computing, Engineering, Science and Technology – Dr. Damayanthi Dahanayake et al. (eds)
© 2024 Taylor & Francis Group, London, ISBN 978-1-041-01782-0

41

Navigating the Obesity-Breast Cancer Nexus—Epidemiology, Mechanistic Insights, Tumour Characteristics and Clinical Outcomes

M A U Samarasiri
Department of Life Sciences, NSBM Green University,
Sri Lanka

K T Madhurangi
Divisional Hospital, Maligawatte,
Colombo 10, Sri Lanka

K A K P Perera*
Department of Life Sciences, NSBM Green University,
Sri Lanka

Abstract

Breast Cancer (BC) represents the dysregulated proliferation of the breast cells, primarily originating in the ductal and lobular regions. This narrative review delves into the epidemiology, mechanistic insights, tumor biology, molecular types and clinical outcomes of BC in obese and overweight women. Epidemiological data suggests a significant increase in BC incidence among obese women, also correlating with poor prognosis, large tumors and more aggressive tumor subtypes. Significant differences in tumor features between these groups compared to their normal counterparts suggest potential molecular intricacies that impact treatment efficacy and disease progression. Additionally, menopausal status modifies the obesity–BC relationship, with postmenopausal obese facing higher BC risks. Insulin growth factor (IGF) signaling, sex hormone alternation, adipocyte and adipokine effects and leptin and its receptor expression are linked with obesity, which subsequently leads to the worse outcomes of breast cancers. Moving forward, tailored inventions, including weight management and behavioral programs, are needed to mitigate the obesity-related BC risk. Current findings emphasize the necessity for personalized treatment plans that address the myriad issues faced by these patients. This review calls for comprehensive, longitudinal studies to validate the current findings and support the development of personalized treatments.

Keywords

Breast cancer, Tumour characteristics, Clinical outcomes

*Corresponding author: kushani.p@nsbm.ac.lk

DOI: 10.1201/9781003616368-41

1. Introduction

1.1 Overview of BC

Breast cancers represent uncontrolled growth of the breast. Most cases originate either in the ductal and lobular region of the breast, in which the organization begins from ductal hyperproliferation and can progress into benign and metastatic carcinomas due to factors that are found to be carcinogenic [1-3]. Breast cancers are classified according to the specific location within the breast that is affected. Non-invasive BC is when the spreading of cancerous cells is restricted to areas within the breast and does not extend into surrounding tissues. The ductal carcinoma in-situ (DCIS) and lobular carcinoma in situ (LCIS) are the two forms of non-invasive breast cancers. Invasive BCs are characterized by the invasion of adjacent stroma, especially surrounding adipose tissues, and two types of invasive breast carcinomas are infiltrating lobular (ILC) and infiltrating ductal carcinomas (IDC). Respectively, DCIS and ILC have been identified as the most prevalent non-invasive and invasive BC types [1]. Factors such as age, alcohol consumption, obesity, genetic mutations, family and reproductive history of BC [4], use of hormone replacement therapy (HRT) have been implicated in the risk of developing BC [5]. According to the WHO criteria, those who have a Body Mass Index (BMI) between 25-29.9 kg/m^2 and $\geq$30 kgm^2 respectively are defined as overweight and obese.

Primary factors leading to obesity are lack of physical activity, inadequate exercise, and a high-calorie diet [6, 7].The early identification of BC has significantly decreased mortality rates. Mammography, a common screening method has been demonstrated to effectively aid in lowering mortality associated with BCs [2, 8].

1.2 Epidemiology of BCs and Obesity

In 2022, it accounted for 2.3 million BC diagnosed women and 67000 deaths globally [9]. Since the year 2000, BC has been the prominent type of cancer across all demographics in Sri Lanka [10]. Cancer incidence data gathered from 2005 to 2009 in Sri Lanka, reveals that BC has become the leading cause of cancer-related death for women. Each year, approximately 3000 women are diagnosed with BC [3]. The age-standardized incidence of BC in Sri Lanka has increased from 17.3 per hundred thousand in 2001 to 24.7 per hundred thousand in 2010, reflecting an increase of 1.4 times. The highest incidence were among women aged 50-54, with the increasing trend higher among those older than 50 years [11].According to the World Obesity Federation, it is estimated that 20 out of 100 people will be obese by the next five years [12]. The incidence of BC

and obesity have shown a noticeable increase over the past several decades. Obesity has been identified as a risk factor for BC in several scientific studies [14, 15].

Besides the fact that evidence has failed to be conclusive, there are also conflicting results [16-19] on how BMI correlates with other features of BC, such as Human Epidermal Growth Factor (HER2) receptor status [16-19]. Furthermore, exposure to ultraviolet radiation and demographic characteristics like race could influence in prediction of cancer progression [13, 20].

This narrative review delves into the epidemiology, mechanistic insights, tumor biology, molecular types and clinical outcomes of BCs in women who are overweight and obese.

2. Understanding Biological Pathways Connecting Obesity to BC

The intricate connection between obesity and BC is woven through four primary mechanisms: insulin and insulin growth factors (IGF) signalling pathway, sex hormone alteration, the effect of adipocytes and adipokines, and expression of leptin and its receptors.

2.1 Insulin and IGF

Obesity leads to elevated insulin and IGF-1 levels, both associated with BC development. IGF-1 promotes malignant cancer traits by activating PI3K/Akt and MAPK signalling pathways, which enhance cell survival proliferation and angiogenesis. Hyperinsulinemia is an independent BC risk factor, in part by increasing the bioavailability of IGF-1 through the reduced level of IGF binding proteins. Additionally, insulin directly stimulates cancer cell growth by binding to the insulin receptors and cross-activating the IGF-1 receptor. This signalling cascade fosters tumorigenesis by promoting cellular growth and inhibiting apoptosis. Targeting IGF-1 and its receptors can benefit specific BC subtypes that are particularly sensitive to insulin and IGF-1-driven proliferation [21, 22].

2.2 Sex Hormone Alteration

In postmenopausal women, increased blood estrogen level is linked with an elevated risk of hormone-sensitive BC. Estrogens act as tumor promoters by activating the gene transcription involved in cell proliferation such as cyclin and growth factors. This leads to increased cell division and tumor growth. Estrogen can also stimulate the PI3K/Akt and MAPK pathways which can subsequently upregulate survival signals and increase resistance to apoptosis. Adipose tissues act as the primary estrogen provider in postmenopausal women. Agents that interfere with estrogen pathways, such as selective estrogen receptor modulators and aromatase inhibitors, show therapeutic potential in BC treatment [23, 24].

2.3 Effect of Adipocytes and Adipokines

Adipose tissue significantly influences BC development and progression, serving as a key player in the disease's dynamics. [22, 26, 27]. The synthetic capacity of estrogen in adipose tissues with the catalytic activity aromatase enzyme increases the local estrogen level, subsequently leading to adverse consequences on BC [13]. In obese women, overnutrition-induced energy imbalance contributes to excessive inflammatory mediator expression. Chronic inflammation in obesity is mainly caused by the proinflammatory phenotype of adipose tissue, characterized by adipocyte hypertrophy and dysregulated adipokine synthesis. Obesity-related inflammation leads to greater BC risk and poor prognosis, associated with increased levels of IGF-1 and insulin levels [20-22, 28, 29].

2.4 Leptin and Its Receptor Expression

Leptin is a hormone synthesized by fatty tissues. Obese women have higher adipose tissue mass, and a higher leptin level is present in their bodies [21,25]. It interacts with various signaling molecules, such as Estrogen Receptor alpha (ER α), growth factors, and inflammatory factors, to promote tumor initiation, progression, and metastasis. It is known to be that notch signaling which is a fundamental pathway that regulates cell differentiation and apoptosis, cytokines such as interleukin-6, chemokines such as CXCL12 and glycoproteins involved in bone remodeling like Osteopontin which is cumulatively called as Leptin-NILCO signaling increases leptin receptor expression, activating cancer stem cells [30]. Additionally, leptin drives epithelial-mesenchymal transition, enhancing tumor invasion, motility, and resistance to therapies influences BC through multiple signaling pathways, including PI3K [31,32], MAPK [32,33] and JAK/STAT. The STAT3 protein, upregulated by the JAK2/STAT3 pathway, induces cell proliferation. The MAPK pathway stimulates transcription factors involved in cell division, while the PI3K pathway alters cellular attributes associated with obesity and leptin. Leptin also promotes cell movement, aggressiveness, and replication, with studies showing increased BC risk in obesity models [22, 25].

Understanding these pathways and linking points of obesity/ overweight status impacts the obesity in BC manifestation and helps to develop target therapies against BC cells.

3. Tumor Characteristics

3.1 Tumor Biology

The complex association between obesity and the characteristics of BC implies more than one biological mechanism and clinical endpoint. Researchers have extensively studied tumour size, grade, hormone receptor status, aggressiveness, and histological and molecular subtypes of BC. A direct relation between obesity and tumour aggressiveness in BC patients has been observed [13]. Widschwendter et al. and Luis et al. demonstrated that obesity leads to poorly differentiated, large tumours compared to non-obese women, with a tendency for lower overall survival. Not only that but an increased nodal involvement has also been noticed in obese females [13, 34].

3.2 Molecular Types and Expression of Biochemical Markers

Moreover, researchers have made an effort to identify how different BMI categories affect different molecular subtypes of BC (luminal A, luminal B, HER 2 and basal cancers) in patients using the HER2 overexpression test [35]. However, it is indicated that there is no significant relation between molecular subtypes and BMI, which can be detected via statistical analysis in pre- and post-menopausal women. The most frequently found molecular subtype of BC in obese premenopausal groups is Estrogen receptor (ER+) or Progesterone receptor positive (PR+) cancers [35-37].

Panteliomon et al. and Gioseffi et al. have revealed that aggressive cancer subtypes such as HER 2 positive and cancers which are negative for ER, PR and HER 2 receptors (triple negative) are also prevalent in obese patients. Additionally, they found that elevated leptin levels in obese individuals are linked to the aggressive nature of these cancer types [38, 39]. Moreover, Gioseffi et al. have established the relationship between obesity, central adiposity, and hypoglycemia with more advanced tumor stages and lymph node involvement [40]. They emphasized that obese women have an 18% higher likelihood of BC recurrence within 5 years compared to their normal counterparts [39].

4. Menopausal Status and Effect of BC Risk

Menopausal status has modified the correlation between obesity and BC [41, 42]. Studies consistently demonstrate an increased risk in post-menopausal obese women and the protective effect of obesity in premenopausal obese women against the occurrence of BCs [42-44]. However, a clinical trial done by Anderson and Neuhouser et al. contradicted this notion, reporting a 59% and 70% higher risk of invasive BC, respectively in overweight and obese premenopausal women compared to their normal-weight counterparts [42].

It was found that class I (BMI 30-34.9) and class II (BMI 35-39.9) obesity categories have a 52% and 86% respectively increased breast cancer risk compared to individuals with normal BMI in a randomized clinical trial done in the United States by Neuhouser et al. [45]. Studies like the Nurses' Health Project [44] and the European Prospective Investigation into Cancer Project confirm the link between increased body weight in postmenopausal women and the heightened risk of ER-positive BC [46]. Although the relationship between obesity and BC risk in premenopausal women shows mixed results, a meta-analysis reveals that obese premenopausal women have a higher likelihood of developing triple-negative and inflammatory BC, regardless of their menopausal and estrogen receptor status [47].

On the other hand, it is suggested that obese premenopausal women with ER+/PR+ cases have shown an inverse relationship with BCs suggesting that obese premenopausal women have a lower risk of developing breast cancers. In contrast, most obese postmenopausal women are likely to have ER+/PR+ cases, which raises the developing risk of BC. This is indicative of a positive relationship between BC and obese post-menopausal status [42,43,48, 49]. Older obese women are frequently associated with cancers that are positive for both Estrogen and progesterone receptors [42,50,51].

It was known that the BC risk and obesity association is modified by hormone replacement therapies (HRT) in post-menopausal women. Evidence is found that HRT users beyond five years have an identified risk for BC in post-menopausal women compared to non-HRT users. [52-54]. However, evidence has pointed out that neither ethnicity nor short-term use of HRT has significantly modified the overall risk of BC in postmenopausal women [45].Furthermore, Table 01 summarizes key findings that could be extracted from the retrospective and clinical trial studies conducted between 2012 and 2022.

5. Clinical Presentation and BC Diagnosis in Obese / Overweight Women

Evidence provided from the studies is not strong enough to prove that the symptoms and signs of BC in obese are distinct from their normal counterparts, including features such as the presence of a lump or mass, skin changes such as dimpling puckering or redness, nipple changes (nipple retraction, discharges in nipple or changes in appearance and pain) [49]. But dense breast tissues in obese women can obscure tumors, making them harder to identify [49].

Obesity impacts BC screening and treatment. Mammography, the most widely used technique for detecting BC, is influenced by BMI. Obese women who are less likely to adhere to screening guidelines such as annual or biennial screening experience higher rates of false-positive mammograms [55-58]. As BCs are not homogeneous, genetic microarray technologies can identify subtypes with gene expression profiles, aggressiveness, and treatment response. However, the microarray technique is expensive and not practical in clinical settings. Immunohistochemistry, HER2 gene amplification tests by qPCR and detection of copy number variation by FISH can be incorporated to obtain a reliable and cost-effective method. MRI is not frequently used in clinical settings [59].

6. Prognosis and Survival

Literature indicates that women with BC who are overweight or obese have poor disease prognosis and a higher likelihood of BC recurrence [61]. Overweight or obese premenopausal women might have a slight advantage from the recurrence of the cancer from a distant site (distance relapse) within 5 years compared to their normal, underweight counterparts. Postmenopausal women with a lower BMI tend to have better long-term outcomes in terms of avoiding distant relapse [62]. Overweight and obese women have a higher hazard ratio for recurrence-free survival, overall survival, and BC-specific survival as compared to normal-weight ones. The negative impact of a higher BMI on survival outcomes was significant only for ER-positive patients; it was insignificant in the ER-negative or HER-positive groups [48].

7. Common Comorbidities and Complications of BC in Obese/ Overweight Women

As overweight and obesity conditions are connected with excessive fat accumulation, it can cause a wide spectrum of comorbidities, including type II diabetes mellitus, hypertension and cardiovascular disease [63]. Survival of diabetic women with BC has been demonstrated to be poorer compared with non-diabetic women, possibly because of the interplay between hyperglycemia and insulin resistance and the progression of neoplastic disease [61]. Cardiovascular diseases may further complicate cancer treatment and increase the likelihood of treatment-related morbidity and mortality. Breast cancer treatment, especially chemotherapy radiation and target therapies can lead to cardiovascular complications damaging heart muscles, causing inflammation in blood vessels which increases heart failure. Shanghai BC Survival Study has reported that hypertension, chronic gastritis, diabetes mellitus chronic bronchitis/ asthma, coronary heart disease, and stroke are common comorbidities included in their study which may further complicate cancer treatment and increase the risk of treatment-related morbidity and mortality [64].

8. Treatments, Responses and Challenges

A patient's BMI significantly influences the efficacy of BC treatments. Chemotherapy dosing, often based on body surface area, may not be optimal for obese patients, leading to subtherapeutic dosing or increased toxicity. Nephropathy and cardiotoxicity, like chemotherapy-mediated complications, are common in obese women, necessitating dose reductions that compromise treatment effectiveness [65, 66].

Hormone therapy targeting estrogen receptor-positive BCs may be less effective in obese women due to altered hormone metabolism and increased estrogen production by adipose tissue [67]. Targeted therapies, such as those for HER2-positive cancers, may also have variable efficacy due to obesity-related factors. Obesity complicates the surgical management of BC, with higher rates of surgical site infections, poor wound healing, and lymphedema observed in obese women [68]. These complications can delay adjuvant treatments like chemotherapy or radiation therapy, potentially compromising overall treatment outcomes. Additionally, delivering radiation therapy can be technically challenging in obese patients due to difficulties in achieving optimal positioning and dosing, affecting treatment efficacy [69].

to obesity-related factors. Obesity complicates the surgical management of BC, with higher rates of surgical site infections, poor wound healing, and lymphedema observed in obese women [68]. These complications can delay adjuvant treatments like chemotherapy or radiation therapy, potentially compromising overall treatment outcomes. Additionally, delivering radiation therapy can be technically challenging in obese patients due to difficulties in achieving optimal positioning and dosing, affecting treatment efficacy [69].

9. Concluding Remarks

Obesity also correlates with worse BC outcomes. These include higher mortality rates, more distant recurrences, and an increased risk of secondary malignancies. It impacts metastasis, detection, and treatment of BC. Research indicated a link between obesity and higher Tumor Node Metastasis (TNM) stages and more lymph node involvement at diagnosis. These links may stem from challenges in diagnosing BC or less adherence of mammography screening among obese women. Furthermore, obesity is connected to a poor response to treatment, potentially due to dose-limiting toxicities and the tendency for obese patients to be undertreated.

Behavioral interventions, weight control, and community programs can be incorporated to reduce the incidence of obesity, which can ameliorate increasing BCs. Regular exercise and stress management techniques can improve health-related quality of life (HRQOL). However, few programs promote both physical activity and mindfulness for these survivors. Community-based wellness workshops aim to foster healthy lifestyles, improve HRQOL and possibly reduce mortality. These workshops align with public health initiatives, like the Institute of Medicine's report advocating for healthy behaviors in cancer survivors [70]. As evidence grows linking physical activity and stress reduction to better outcomes, tailored educational programs are needed for diverse, underserved BC survivors to address their unique health beliefs and barriers. Sustained weight loss may require long-term lifestyle changes lasting more than a year. A cognitive-behavioral weight management programs that emphasize increased physical activity and dietary changes can result in substantial weight reduction, improved body composition, blood, and lipid profiles in overweight and obese BC survivors. These changes may reduce cardiovascular disease risk and enhance health-related life quality of patient.

Additional studies and comprehensive reviews are needed to validate the connection between obesity and BC development, treatment outcomes, and the spread of the disease focusing on the molecular pathways and inflammatory markers, hormonal regulations physical activity and lifestyle interventions to reduce the cancer risk in obese patients etc. The strengths of the current studies include their significant sample sizes and use of robust statistical analysis, which together provide valuable insights into the effect of obesity on BC outcomes. Some limitations include heterogeneity of study populations, variations in defining or measuring obesity, and confounding factors concerning treatment variations and comorbidities. Most studies are observational, hence unable to be used to infer causality.

Table 41.1 Summary of studies conducted on BCs and obese/ overweight women with the findings from 2000 – 2023

Country & Published Year	Type of Study	Study Conducted Year/ Year Range	Characteristics of cases		Measured parameters	Findings/ Results
			Sample Size	Stratification		
Portugal 2022 [13]	Retrospective study	2012 - 2016	2246 Women	Categorized based on BMI • Normal (BMI < 25) • Overweight (BMI = 25 – 30) • Obese (BMI > 30)	**Demographic information:** Age (< 50 and ≥ 50 years), family history **Tumor Features:** Topographic localization, histological type, receptor status of tumors, laterality, **Clinical Outcomes:** Overall survival, tumor stage & differentiation grade, bilaterality of breast tumor	**Obese Patients:** • Larger tumours • More poorly differentiated tumors • Lower overall survival (Not statistically significant) **Overweight Patients** • Higher proportion of bilateral breast • Less distant metastasis • Non-significant association - Topographic localization and laterality
United States 2012 [60]	Retrospective study	2000 - 2008	1352 Women with BC 76% -nonobese 24% - obese	Patients have been categorized based on BMI • Nonobese (BMI < 30) • Obese (BMI ≥ 30).	**Demographic information:** Age at the presentation of tumor **Tumor Features:** Tumor size, Lymph node metastasis, HER2 Positivity, Multifocality and tumor palpability **Clinical Outcomes:** Reconstruction after mastectomy, survival data	**Obese patients** • More commonly found in the over 50-year cohort (90%) compared to the non-obese patients • More frequently diagnosed via imaging as opposed to being an incidental finding than their nonobese counterparts (67% vs. 56%) • Larger tumours on average (1.7 cm vs 1.4cm) • Incidence of lymph node metastasis ↑ • Incidence of HER2 positivity ↓ (16% obese vs 22% non-obese) and multifocality Following mastectomy, less likely to undergo reconstruction.
United States 2015 [45]	Women's Health Initiative (WHI) Randomized Clinical Trials	Women were enrolled from 1993 to 1998 with 13 years of follow up	67,142 postmenopausal women (aged 50 -79 years) 3388 of BC	Patients have been categorized based on BMI	**Demographic information:** Age, height, weight, family history, personal habit (smoking, physical activity) **Tumor Features:** Hormone receptor status, stage, grade, tumor size, nodal involvement **Clinical Outcomes:** Incidence and mortality of BC Annual or biennial mammograms	**Overweight and obese postmenopausal women** • Significant ↑ risk for invasive BC in ER+ cases • 1.58 times higher invasive BC risk in women with a BMI > 35.0 compared to average weight **Obese had presented** • Poor prognosis • Large tumours • Nodal involvement • Poorly differentiated tumours (strong association in women with a BMI> 35.0) • Mortality ↑ • HRT and ethnicity – no effect on obesity–BC association

Country & Published Year	Type of Study	Study Conducted Year/ Year Range	Characteristics of cases		Measured parameters	Findings/ Results
			Sample Size	Stratification		
United States 2012 [42]	Clinical Trials	Prevention trial - 4.1 years Study of Tamoxifen and Raloxifene – 6.4 years	Not specified	BMI categories • Normal weight (BMI <25.0) • Overweight (25.0 to <30.0) • Obese grade 1 (30.0 to <35.0); grade 2+,3 (≥35.0). Menopausal state (pre and postmenopausal)	**Demographic information** BMI, Height and weight **Tumor Features:** Expression of ER and PR	**In pre and postmenopausal women** • Positive association between BMI and the incidence of invasive BC risk • Overweight and obese premenopausal women carried a higher risk of BC compared to normal-weight premenopausal women. • BMI and BC risk are differently affected by menopausal status and BMI categories **Premenopausal women** In ER+/PR+ cases, BMI and risk are inversely associated. ER-/PR- cases – less strong inverse association Post-menopausal women The positive association between BMI and risk of BC.
European women population 2013 [41]	Observational cohort study	January 1999 to December 2009	2148 patients (Premenopausal – 592 and postmenopausal 1556)	Patients have been categorized based on BMI • nonobese (BMI < 30) • obese (BMI ≥ 30).	**Tumor features (Histopathological):** Tumor size, nuclear grade, Expression of ER and PR HER-2/neu Histological subtypes, Ki-67 index, Lymphatic/vascular invasion axillary nodes involvement Incidence of different subtypes Distance and local recurrence of tumors	**The overweight and obese women (both pre-and post-menopausal categories)** • Larger tumours (more than 40% of obese and overweight present with breast cancers above 2 cm diameter) • ↑ Metastatic axillary nodes • Tumor vascular invasion – frequently observed • Postmenopausal women with BMI > 25 had a higher percentage of ER+ tumours • No association with the tumour nuclear grade, HER 2 overexpression, Ki 67 or lymphatic invasion **Premenopausal women** • No statistically significant differences in hormonal-positive tumour incidence rates among premenopausal women of varying BMI. **Postmenopausal Women** • BMI >25 - present with worse distant recurrence-free survival compared to lean counterpart
United State 2013[48]	Retrospective Study	1996 - 2005	6342 Patients (stage I-III BC)	BMI categories Normal (BMI < 25) • Overweight (BMI = 25 – 30) • Obese (BMI > 30)	**Demographic information** Age (< 50 and ≥ 50), race (White, African American and other) **Survival Outcomes** Recurrence-free survival (RFS), Overall Survival (OS), Breast Cancer Specific Survival (BCSS) **Other** Stage grade, ER/PR status, treatment received (Chemotherapy and endocrine therapy	**Overweight and obese women** • The higher hazard ratio for RFS, OS, and BCSS in comparison to normal weight counterpart The negative impact of a higher BMI on survival outcomes was significant only for ER-positive patients; it was insignificant in the ER-negative or HER-positive groups.

Source: Authors

Future research should determine the specific biological pathways involved in the link between obesity and BC. Longitudinal studies need to be performed where definitions of obesity and related definitions have been defined uniformly, and comprehensive information regarding treatment regimens and comorbidities must be documented. Interventional studies regarding weight management strategies and their results on BC outcomes are also essential.

10. Disclosure

No potential conflicts of interest regarding the publication of this review article.

REFERENCES

1. G. N. Sharma, R. Dave, J. Sanadya, and P. Sharma, "Various types and management of breast cancer: an overview," Journal of advanced pharmaceutical technology & research, vol. 1, no. 2, pp. 109–126, 2010.
2. Y.-S. Sun et al., "Risk factors and preventions of breast cancer," International journal of biological sciences, vol. 13, no. 11, p. 1387, 2017.
3. D. T. Wijeratne et al., "Demographic, tumour, and treatment characteristics of female patients with breast cancer in Sri Lanka; results from a hospital-based cancer registry," BMC cancer, vol. 21, pp. 1–8, 2021.
4. E. R. Schuur and J. P. DeAndrade, "Breast cancer: molecular mechanisms, diagnosis, and treatment," International Manual of Oncology Practice: (iMOP)-Principles of Medical Oncology, pp. 155–200, 2015.
5. C. G. o. H. F. i. B. Cancer, "Menarche, menopause, and breast cancer risk: individual participant meta-analysis, including 118 964 women with breast cancer from 117 epidemiological studies," The lancet oncology, vol. 13, no. 11, pp. 1141–1151, 2012.
6. C. L. Gray, L. C. Messer, K. M. Rappazzo, J. S. Jagai, S. C. Grabich, and D. T. Lobdell, "The association between physical inactivity and obesity is modified by five domains of environmental quality in US adults: A cross-sectional study," PloS one, vol. 13, no. 8, p. e0203301, 2018.
7. T. Kazmi et al., "Relationship between physical inactivity and obesity in the Urban Slums of Lahore," Cureus, vol. 14, no. 4, 2022.
8. C. E. DeSantis, S. A. Fedewa, A. Goding Sauer, J. L. Kramer, R. A. Smith, and A. Jemal, "Breast cancer statistics, 2015: Convergence of incidence rates between black and white women," CA: a cancer journal for clinicians, vol. 66, no. 1, pp. 31–42, 2016.
9. W. H. Organization. (2024). Breast Cancer. Available: https://www.who.int/news-room/fact-sheets/detail/breast-cancer
10. H. Peiris, L. Mudduwa, N. Thalagala, and K. Jayatilaka, "Do breast cancer risk factors affect the survival of breast cancer patients in Southern Sri Lanka?," Asian Pacific Journal of Cancer Prevention: APJCP, vol. 18, no. 1, p. 69, 2017.
11. A. Fernando, U. Jayarajah, S. Prabashani, E. A. Fernando, and S. A. Seneviratne, "Incidence trends and patterns of breast cancer in Sri Lanka: an analysis of the national cancer database," BMC cancer, vol. 18, pp. 1–6, 2018.
12. W. O. Federation, "World Obesity Atlas 2023.," 2023.
13. C. Luís et al., "A retrospective study in tumour characteristics and clinical outcomes of overweight and obese women with breast cancer," (in eng), Breast Cancer Res Treat, vol. 198, no. 1, pp. 89–101, Feb 2023.
14. M. P. Cleary and M. E. Grossmann, "Obesity and breast cancer: the estrogen connection," Endocrinology, vol. 150, no. 6, pp. 2537–2542, 2009.
15. M. Shirdarreh and R. C. Pezo, "Impact of obesity on clinical outcomes in hormone receptor-positive breast cancer: a systematic review," Breast Cancer, vol. 28, pp. 755–764, 2021.
16. E. M. de Dueñas et al., "Prospective evaluation of the conversion rate in the receptor status between primary breast cancer and metastasis: results from the GEICAM 2009-03 ConvertHER study," (in eng), Breast Cancer Res Treat, vol. 143, no. 3, pp. 507–15, Feb 2014.
17. R. T. Fortner et al., "Parity, breastfeeding, and breast cancer risk by hormone receptor status and molecular phenotype: results from the Nurses' Health Studies," (in eng), Breast Cancer Res, vol. 21, no. 1, p. 40, Mar 12 2019.
18. D. Leithner et al., "Radiomic signatures with contrast-enhanced magnetic resonance imaging for the assessment of breast cancer receptor status and molecular subtypes: initial results," (in eng), Breast Cancer Res, vol. 21, no. 1, p. 106, Sep 12 2019.
19. Y. Liu et al., "Obesity and survival in the neoadjuvant breast cancer setting: Role of tumor subtype and race," Journal of Clinical Oncology, vol. 35, 2017.
20. Y. M. Coyle, "The effect of environment on breast cancer risk," Breast cancer research and treatment, vol. 84, pp. 273–288, 2004.
21. A. M. Blaszczak, A. Jalilvand, and W. A. Hsueh, "Adipocytes, innate immunity and obesity: A mini-review," Frontiers in immunology, vol. 12, p. 650768, 2021.
22. R. Kolb and W. Zhang, "Obesity and breast cancer: a case of inflamed adipose tissue," Cancers, vol. 12, no. 6, p. 1686, 2020.
23. T. Key, P. Appleby, I. Barnes, and G. Reeves, "Endogenous sex hormones and breast cancer in postmenopausal women: reanalysis of nine prospective studies," (in eng), J Natl Cancer Inst, vol. 94, no. 8, pp. 606–16, Apr 17 2002.
24. M. A. KH, S. Ekanayake, and K. Samarasinghe, "Serum sex hormone levels and hormone receptor status in identifying breast cancer risk in women," (in eng), Indian J Cancer, vol. 58, no. 4, pp. 525–531, Oct-Dec 2021.
25. M. F. Atoum, F. Alzoughool, and H. Al-Hourani, "Linkage between obesity leptin and breast cancer," Breast Cancer: Basic and Clinical Research, vol. 14, p. 1178223419898458, 2020.

26. A. Booth, A. Magnuson, J. Fouts, and M. Foster, "Adipose tissue, obesity and adipokines: role in cancer promotion," (in eng), Horm Mol Biol Clin Investig, vol. 21, no. 1, pp. 57–74, Jan 2015.

27. J. W. Kim, J. H. Kim, and Y. J. Lee, "The Role of Adipokines in Tumor Progression and Its Association with Obesity," Biomedicines, vol. 12, no. 1, p. 97, 2024.

28. J. Becaria Coquet et al., "Diet Quality, Obesity and Breast Cancer Risk: An Epidemiologic Study in Córdoba, Argentina," (in eng), Nutr Cancer, vol. 72, no. 6, pp. 1026–1035, 2020.

29. J. P. M. Milambo, M. J. Kotze, E. P. Rajiv, J. M. Akudugu, and T. L. Jacques, "Meta-regression analysis of the effect of lifestyle interventions on mediators of inflammation in postmenopausal breast cancer women with cardiovascular risk factors," 2019.

30. C. C. Lipsey, A. Harbuzariu, R. W. Robey, L. M. Huff, M. M. Gottesman, and R. R. Gonzalez-Perez, "Leptin Signaling Affects Survival and Chemoresistance of Estrogen Receptor Negative Breast Cancer," (in eng), Int J Mol Sci, vol. 21, no. 11, May 27 2020.

31. M. Olea-Flores, J. C. Juárez-Cruz, M. A. Mendoza-Catalán, T. Padilla-Benavides, and N. Navarro-Tito, "Signaling Pathways Induced by Leptin during Epithelial-Mesenchymal Transition in Breast Cancer," (in eng), Int J Mol Sci, vol. 19, no. 11, Nov 6 2018.

32. F. Sánchez-Jiménez, A. Pérez-Pérez, L. De la Cruz-Merino, and V. Sánchez-Margalet, "Obesity and breast cancer: role of leptin," Frontiers in oncology, vol. 9, p. 596, 2019.

33. M. Mullen and R. R. Gonzalez-Perez, "Leptin-Induced JAK/STAT Signaling and Cancer Growth," (in eng), Vaccines (Basel), vol. 4, no. 3, Jul 26 2016.

34. P. Widschwendter et al., "The influence of obesity on survival in early, high-risk breast cancer: results from the randomized SUCCESS A trial," Breast Cancer Research, vol. 17, pp. 1–11, 2015.

35. N. Biglia et al., "Body mass index (BMI) and breast cancer: impact on tumor histopatologic features, cancer subtypes and recurrence rate in pre and postmenopausal women," Gynecological Endocrinology, vol. 29, no. 3, pp. 263–267, 2013.

36. S. Tubtimhin, S. Promthet, K. Suwanrungruang, and P. Supaattagorn, "Molecular Subtypes and Prognostic Factors among Premenopausal and Postmenopausal Thai Women with Invasive Breast Cancer: 15 Years Follow-up Data," (in eng), Asian Pac J Cancer Prev, vol. 19, no. 11, pp. 3167–3174, Nov 29 2018.

37. F. Ntirenganya, J. D. Twagirumukiza, G. Bucyibaruta, B. Rugwizangoga, and S. Rulisa, "Premenopausal Breast Cancer Risk Factors and Associations with Molecular Subtypes: A Case-Control Study," (in eng), Int J Breast Cancer, vol. 2021, p. 5560559, 2021.

38. I. Pantelimon et al., "Aspects Regarding the Influence of Obesity on the Molecular Characteristics of Breast Tumors," (in eng), Cureus, vol. 14, no. 7, p. e26952, Jul 2022.

39. C. Gioseffi, P. d. C. Padilha, G. V. Chaves, L. C. d. Oliveira, and W. A. F. Peres, "Body Weight, Central Adiposity, and Fasting Hyperglycemia Are Associated with Tumor Characteristics in a Brazilian Cohort of Women with Breast Cancer," Nutrients, vol. 14, no. 22, p. 4926, 2022.

40. C. Gioseffi, P. C. Padilha, G. V. Chaves, L. C. Oliveira, and W. A. F. Peres, "Body Weight, Central Adiposity, and Fasting Hyperglycemia Are Associated with Tumor Characteristics in a Brazilian Cohort of Women with Breast Cancer," (in eng), Nutrients, vol. 14, no. 22, Nov 21 2022.

41. N. Biglia et al., "Body mass index (BMI) and breast cancer: impact on tumor histopathologic features, cancer subtypes and recurrence rate in pre and postmenopausal women," (in eng), Gynecol Endocrinol, vol. 29, no. 3, pp. 263–7, Mar 2013.

42. G. L. Anderson and M. L. Neuhouser, "Obesity and the risk for premenopausal and postmenopausal breast cancer," (in eng), Cancer Prev Res (Phila), vol. 5, no. 4, pp. 515–21, Apr 2012.

43. A. Amadou et al., "Overweight, obesity and risk of premenopausal breast cancer according to ethnicity: a systematic review and dose-response meta-analysis," (in eng), Obes Rev, vol. 14, no. 8, pp. 665–78, Aug 2013.

44. S. E. Hankinson et al., "Reproductive factors and family history of breast cancer in relation to plasma estrogen and prolactin levels in postmenopausal women in the Nurses' Health Study (United States)," (in eng), Cancer Causes Control, vol. 6, no. 3, pp. 217–24, May 1995.

45. M. L. Neuhouser et al., "Overweight, Obesity, and Postmenopausal Invasive Breast Cancer Risk: A Secondary Analysis of the Women's Health Initiative Randomized Clinical Trials," (in eng), JAMA Oncol, vol. 1, no. 5, pp. 611–21, Aug 2015.

46. M. Ellingjord-Dale et al., "Long-term weight change and risk of breast cancer in the European Prospective Investigation into Cancer and Nutrition (EPIC) study," (in eng), Int J Epidemiol, vol. 50, no. 6, pp. 1914–1926, Jan 6 2022.

47. C. E. Taylor et al., "Obesity and triple negative breast cancer diagnosis among premenopausal women," Journal of Clinical Oncology, 2023.

48. S. Jiralerspong, E. S. Kim, W. Dong, L. Feng, G. N. Hortobagyi, and S. H. Giordano, "Obesity, diabetes, and survival outcomes in a large cohort of early-stage breast cancer patients," (in eng), Ann Oncol, vol. 24, no. 10, pp. 2506–2514, Oct 2013.

49. N. M. Ayoub, R. J. Yaghan, N. M. Abdo, Matalka, II, L. M. Akhu-Zaheya, and A. H. Al-Mohtaseb, "Impact of Obesity on Clinicopathologic Characteristics and Disease Prognosis in Pre- and Postmenopausal Breast Cancer Patients: A Retrospective Institutional Study," (in eng), J Obes, vol. 2019, p. 3820759, 2019.

50. M. F. Munsell, B. L. Sprague, D. A. Berry, G. Chisholm, and A. Trentham-Dietz, "Body mass index and breast cancer risk according to postmenopausal estrogen-progestin use and hormone receptor status," (in eng), Epidemiol Rev, vol. 36, no. 1, pp. 114–36, 2014.

51. P. Berstad et al., "A case-control study of body mass index and breast cancer risk in white and African-American

women," (in eng), Cancer Epidemiol Biomarkers Prev, vol. 19, no. 6, pp. 1532–44, Jun 2010.

52. N. M. Iyengar et al., "Association of Body Fat and Risk of Breast Cancer in Postmenopausal Women With Normal Body Mass Index: A Secondary Analysis of a Randomized Clinical Trial and Observational Study," (in eng), JAMA Oncol, vol. 5, no. 2, pp. 155–163, Feb 1 2019.

53. S. A. Norman et al., "Combined effect of oral contraceptive use and hormone replacement therapy on breast cancer risk in postmenopausal women," (in eng), Cancer Causes Control, vol. 14, no. 10, pp. 933–43, Dec 2003.

54. "ACOG committee opinion. Risk of breast cancer with estrogen-progestin replacement therapy," (in eng), Int J Gynaecol Obstet, vol. 76, no. 3, pp. 333–5, Mar 2002.

55. R. C. Miles, C. D. Lehman, S. F. Mercaldo, R. M. Tamimi, B. N. Dontchos, and A. K. Narayan, "Obesity and breast cancer screening: Cross-sectional survey results from the behavioral risk factor surveillance system," (in eng), Cancer, vol. 125, no. 23, pp. 4158–4163, Dec 1 2019.

56. B. Miller et al., "Diabetes, Obesity, and Inflammation: Impact on Clinical and Radiographic Features of Breast Cancer," (in eng), Int J Mol Sci, vol. 22, no. 5, Mar 9 2021.

57. J. Soon et al., "The financial implications of investigating false-positive and true-positive mammograms in a national breast cancer screening program," (in eng), Aust Health Rev, vol. 47, no. 2, pp. 159–164, Apr 2023.

58. K. McBride, S. Munasinghe, S. Sperendei, and A. Page, Impact of BMI on breast screening participation: a data linkage study. Eur J Public Health. 2022 Oct 25;32(Suppl 3):ckac131.213. doi: 10.1093/eurpub/ckac131.213. eCollection 2022 Oct.

59. M. Meghavath, R. Gorantla, and A. R. Danaboyina, "Augmenting breast cancer diagnosis: Incorporating MRI for the assessment of major molecular subtypes," Indian Journal of Breast Imaging, 2023.

60. D. J. Haakinson et al., "The impact of obesity on breast cancer: a retrospective review," (in eng), Ann Surg Oncol, vol. 19, no. 9, pp. 3012–8, Sep 2012.

61. D. S. M. Chan et al., "Body mass index and survival in women with breast cancer-systematic literature review and meta-analysis of 82 follow-up studies," (in eng), Ann Oncol, vol. 25, no. 10, pp. 1901–1914, Oct 2014.

62. L. K. Helyer, M. Varnic, L. W. Le, W. Leong, and D. McCready, "Obesity is a risk factor for developing postoperative lymphedema in breast cancer patients," (in eng), Breast J, vol. 16, no. 1, pp. 48–54, Jan-Feb 2010.

63. D. P. Guh, W. Zhang, N. Bansback, Z. Amarsi, C. L. Birmingham, and A. H. Anis, "The incidence of co-morbidities related to obesity and overweight: A systematic review and meta-analysis," BMC Public Health, vol. 9, no. 1, p. 88, 2009/03/25 2009.

64. S. Nechuta et al., "Comorbidities and breast cancer survival: a report from the Shanghai Breast Cancer Survival Study," (in eng), Breast Cancer Res Treat, vol. 139, no. 1, pp. 227–35, May 2013.

65. D. P. Guh, W. Zhang, N. Bansback, Z. Amarsi, C. L. Birmingham, and A. H. Anis, "The incidence of co-morbidities related to obesity and overweight: a systematic review and meta-analysis," BMC public health, vol. 9, pp. 1–20, 2009.

66. K. H. Ross, K. Gogineni, P. D. Subhedar, J. Y. Lin, and L. E. McCullough, "Obesity and cancer treatment efficacy: Existing challenges and opportunities," Cancer, vol. 125, no. 10, pp. 1588–1592, 2019.

67. M. Shirdarreh and R. C. Pezo, "Impact of obesity on clinical outcomes in hormone receptor-positive breast cancer: a systematic review," (in eng), Breast Cancer, vol. 28, no. 3, pp. 755–764, May 2021.

68. A. Lee, C. Larck, and D. C. Moore, "Impact of obesity on safety outcomes and treatment modifications with ado-trastuzumab emtansine in breast cancer patients," (in eng), J Oncol Pharm Pract, vol. 28, no. 1, pp. 49–54, Jan 2022.

69. M. S. Moran and A. Y. Ho, "Radiation Therapy for Low-Risk Breast Cancer: Whole, Partial, or None?," (in eng), J Clin Oncol, vol. 40, no. 36, pp. 4166–4172, Dec 20 2022.

70. D. Spector, C. Battaglini, A. Alsobrooks, J. Owen, and D. Groff, "Do breast cancer survivors increase their physical activity and enhance their health-related quality of life after attending community-based wellness workshops?," (in eng), J Cancer Educ, vol. 27, no. 2, pp. 353–61, Jun 2012.

Transformative Applied Research in Computing, Engineering, Science and Technology – Dr. Damayanthi Dahanayake et al. (eds)
© 2024 Taylor & Francis Group, London, ISBN 978-1-041-01782-0

42

A Novel Hybrid Cooling Approach Through Airflow Optimization for Power Electronic Circuits

I. D. K. Ilesinghe, and M.P.I.G. Wijedasa*

Department of Electrical,
Electronics and Systems Engineering, NSBM Green University,
Sri Lanka

Abstract

Use of reliable cooling methods for power electronic circuits affects their performance and durability. Traditional cooling methods have some limitations for cooling and most of the available literature do not present cooling methods combining active and passive cooling methods. This paper presents a novel hybrid cooling technique that optimizes airflow to enhance the cooling efficiency of power electronic circuits. This technique integrates thermoelectric coolers (TECs) as the active cooling method with other traditional active cooling methods of cooling fan and air blowers, and heat sinks as the traditional passive cooling method. The proposed approach achieved reliable thermal management. The combination of these cooling techniques not only mitigates heat accumulation but also ensures a more uniform airflow distribution across the circuit components. Experimental results demonstrated the effectiveness of this hybrid cooling method in reducing thermal resistance and improving the overall reliability of power electronic circuits. The findings suggested that this airflow-optimized hybrid cooling method can be a valuable solution for advanced thermal management in power electronics.

Keywords

Cooling techniques, Hybrid cooling methods, Power electronic circuit cooling, Thermoelectric coolers (TECs)

1. Introduction

Electronic circuits used in industrial and domestic devices present high efficiency and proper control. These electronic circuits minimize the space and helps to decrease the sizes of the products [1]. Manufacturers design most of the electronic components using semiconductors. Integrated circuits, Metal Oxide Semiconductor Field Effect Transistors (MOSFETs), Insulated Gate Bipolar Transistors (IGBTs) are common examples of semiconductor materials used in electronic circuits. These semiconductor components generate heat during operation due to the electrical resistance of the materials and the energy they consumed. This generated heat mainly affect to the efficiency of the semiconductor components [2].

*Corresponding author: imesha.w@nsbm.ac.lk

DOI: 10.1201/9781003616368-42

Power electronic circuits used to deal with high currents and high voltages. Power inverters, power converters are common examples for power electronic circuits. IGBT is a power semiconductor device that combines the insulated gate input of a MOSFET with the low resistance of a bipolar transistor. IGBTs can switch in very high frequency, and it can provide high current flow through the component. When switching the IGBTs in very high frequency, it causes passing of high range of currents through them which increases their temperature rapidly. This heat enhancement causes to decrease the transistor performance and sometimes it damages the component [3].

Heat sinks are mostly used to dissipate heat from electronic circuits. It is a passive cooling method, because it does not use external power to operate. It uses the heat convection method to transfer the heat from heat elements to the outside [4].

Thermoelectric coolers (TECs) are used as an active cooler in this study. It consists of two ceramic plates with an array of p-type and n-type semiconductor couples in between. These couples are electrically connected in series and thermally in parallel. When a positive DC voltage is applied to the device, electrons move from the p-type to the n-type semiconductor, causing one surface to cool and the other surface to heat up. The heat absorption rate depends on the number of thermoelectric couples and the applied current [5].

Thus, this paper presents a novel cooling technique which combines active cooling and passive cooling techniques through the utilization of TECs and Heat sinks respectively. Section II in this paper presents the literature review followed by a detailed methodology in section III. Then, the developed model and the results are presented in sections IV. Finally, Section V presents the conclusion of this study.

2. Literature Review

The increasing need for miniaturization and expanded power density in power electronic circuits have intensified the challenge of thermal management. Efficient operation hinges on maintaining component temperatures within a safe range to prevent performance degradation and premature failure [6]. Power electronic circuits typically operate under $120°C$, with critical components reaching even higher temperatures [7].

2.1 Limitation of Traditional Cooling Techniques

Passive Cooling Methods

Passive cooling methods, such as heat sinks [8] are based on natural convection to dissipate heat. This operation involves the transfer of heat from a hot surface to the surrounding air without the assistance of any external power. The cooling capacity of passive methods is not sufficient for high-power electronic circuits. The rate of natural convection is limited by several factors [9]. (i) Temperature Gradient: The difference in temperature between the heat source and the ambient air drives natural convection. In high heat dispassion, this gradient may not be sufficient to dissipate the large amounts of heat. (ii) Airflow: Passive cooling depends on the natural airflow. It does not provide an appropriate heat exchange from heat sink. (iii) Surface Area: While increasing the surface area of a heat sink can enhance heat dissipation, it is not a practical scenario with size of electronic components.

Active Cooling Methods

Use of external power to enhance heat dissipation has made active cooling suitable for heat dissipation in mass heat generations. Common active cooling methods are cooling fans and air blowers. Other than that, thermoelectric coolers (TECs) also used as an active cooling method [8].

Thermoelectric coolers (TECs) can use as a cooling or a heating element. There are two ceramic plates inside it. Between these two ceramic plates, there is an array of p-type and n-type semiconductor junctions. The arrangement of these components is thermally parallel and electrically series. When a positive DC voltage supply provided to n-type semiconductor, electron pass from p-type semiconductor to n-type semiconductor causing heat reduction on cooled side and heating up the hot side. That device can be used to provide cold air flow to the cooling pad cooler surface using convection methods [10].

2.2 Hybrid Cooling Techniques

Hybrid cooling combines passive and active methods to increase the benefits of both. This concept can significantly enhance the thermal management of power electronic circuits by using active cooling methods to supplement passive heat dissipation [3].

2.3 Circuit Airflow Optimization

Airflow management is the most important factor for efficient thermal regulation. Optimizing airflow ensures uniform temperature exchange, decrease hotspots, and enhances overall cooling performance [1].

Inspiration from existing cooling technologies and product designs, this research strives to develop and implement a highly efficient and effective cooling solution specifically tailored for the unique thermal challenges of modern power electronic circuits.

3. Methodology

Analysing power electronic circuit heat generations and conducting experiments and simulations with thermoelectric coolers (TECs) to find a suitable path for combined active and passive cooling method is the methodology followed in this study. First, heat-generating components in the power electronic circuit such as IGBTs, MOSFETs, and other semiconductors were identified and data about heating power was gathered. Then, using MATLAB software, a physical structure of the cooling device was simulated. MATLAB model was used to collect data about the thermoelectric cooler cooling performance. Also, through an experiment, tested the heat sinks with thermoelectric coolers.

3.1 Power Dissipation in Electronic Circuits

The total power dissipation from the power electronic circuit can be calculated using (1) below.

$$P_D = V_{DS} \cdot I_D \tag{1}$$

Where, P_D, V_{DS}, and I_D denote power dissipation, drain-source voltage and drain current respectively. Then, the junction temperatures of transistors can be calculated using (2) below.

$$T_J = T_A + P_D \cdot R_{\theta JA} \tag{2}$$

Where, T_J, T_A and $R_{\theta JA}$ denote junction temperature, ambient temperature and thermal resistance from junction to ambient respectively. Then, heat dissipation from the transistors can be calculated using (3) below.

$$P_D = \frac{T_J - T_A}{R_{\theta th}} \tag{3}$$

MATLAB Simulink model on MathWorks was used to calculate the heat dissipation from transistor (Fig. 42.1). Provided the ambient temperature, heat sink temperature, and junction temperature, this model uses (3) to output the heat dissipation from the transistor.

3.2 Thermoelectric Cooler Software Simulation

MATLAB Simulink model of thermoelectric cooler was used to simulate the variation of Coefficient of Performance (COP) with input current, Cooling Power (QC) with input current and input current with temperature difference between the hot side and cold side. The thermoelectric MATLAB Simulink model is shown in Fig. 42.2.

3.3 Thermoelectric Cooler Experimental Analysis

A setup was designed to analyze the physical characteristics and practicalities of thermoelectric coolers as shown in

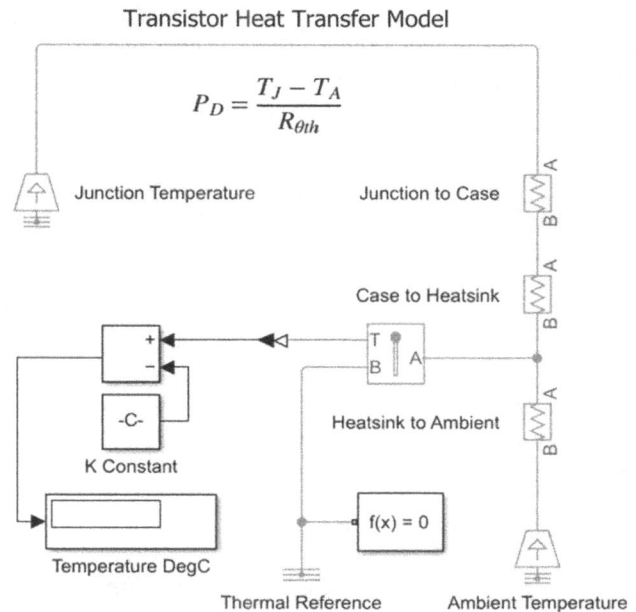

Fig. 42.1 Transistor heat transfer model

Source: MATLAB simulink

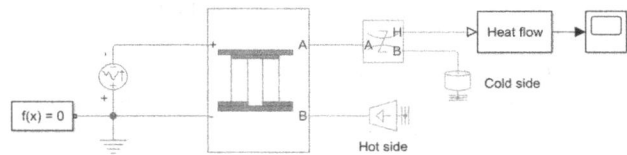

Fig. 42.2 Thermoelectric cooler model

Source: MATLAB Simulink

Fig. 42.3. TEC-12706 thermoelectric cooler, two W1209 temperature controllers, one room temperature meter, one cooling fan and several kinds of heat sinks were used to build the setup.

Fig. 42.3 Thermoelectric cooler testing setup

Source: Authors

24V 10A switch mode power supply (SMPS) was used to power up the setup and a current and voltage control buck convertor and LM2596 buck convertor were used to drop the voltage and control the currents. Current control method was used to control the thermoelectric cooler.

Two heat sinks were attached to the two surfaces of thermoelectric cooler which act as the heat absorbing sink and the heat dissipation sink. The cooling fan was used to help to dissipate the heat from heated side heat sink which will increase the thermoelectric cooling performance. Heat side temperature, cold side temperature, voltage and current measurements were taken using this set up at 5 minutes time period which was used to find the relationship between temperature difference and the power consumption. The setup was used in an ambient temperature of 27.1°C.

4. Modelling and Results

4.1 Thermoelectric Cooler Software Simulation and Experimental Analysis Results

The variation of Coefficient of Performance (COP) with input current, Cooling Power (QC) with input current and input current with temperature difference between the hot side and cold side were obtained from the software simulation of Thermoelectric cooler as shown in Fig. 42.4, Fig. 42.5 and Fig. 42.6 respectively. According to these graphs, it was observed that, when the input current increases, COP reduces whereas cooling power reaches a maximum value and then reduces. Thus, it can be concluded that, in order to have a high COP with low cooling power, it is desirable to maintain the input current at a low value. But, from Fig. 42.6, it was observed that in order to reduce the temperature by a high value, it is required to have a high input current.

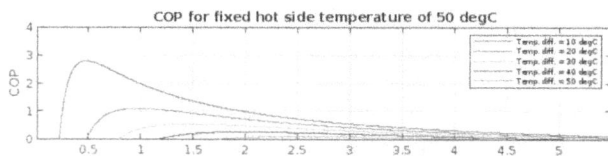

Fig. 42.4 Variation of COP with input current

Source: MATLAB simulink

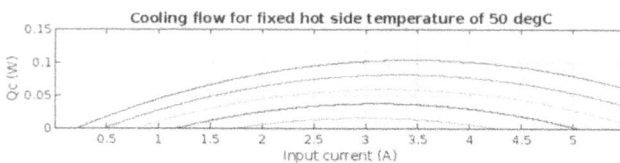

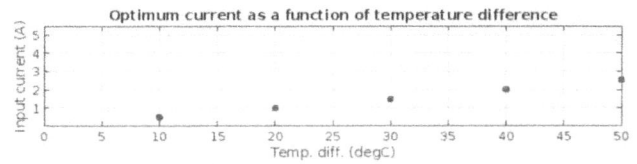

Fig. 42.5 Variation of cooling power with input current

Source: MATLAB simulink

Fig. 42.6 Variation of input current with Temperature difference

Source: MATLAB simulink

Table 42.1 Data measured from the experimental setup

Time	Heat Side (°C)	Cold Side (°C)	Voltage (V)	Current (A)	Power (W)
07:10	27.1	27.1	12.00	0.00	0.0000
07:15	30.5	6.6	4.24	1.22	5.1728
07:20	30.6	6.3	4.79	1.31	6.2749
07:25	31.3	4.3	8.73	2.67	23.3091
07:30	34.9	-0.5	10.40	3.39	35.2560
07:35	35.1	-0.6	11.70	3.45	40.3650
07:40	35.1	-0.7	11.80	3.49	41.1820

Source: Authors

Table 42.1 presents the predicted date from the experimental analysis. According to that, when the source current increases, the temperature difference increases and when the current was controlled, the voltage was maintained automatically related to the power usage.

4.2 Comparison between MATLAB Simulation and Physical Simulation Setup

Figure 42.7 and Fig. 42.8 show the MATLAB simulation results and experimental results of the thermoelectric cooler. The MATLAB simulation results show a linear variation, whereas the experimental results show a non-linear variation between input current and temperature difference.

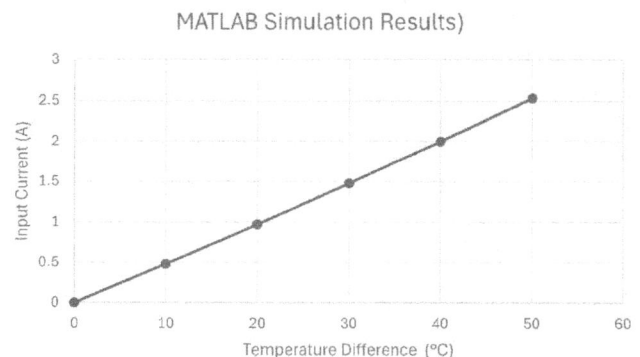

Fig. 42.7 MATLAB simulation results

Source: Authors

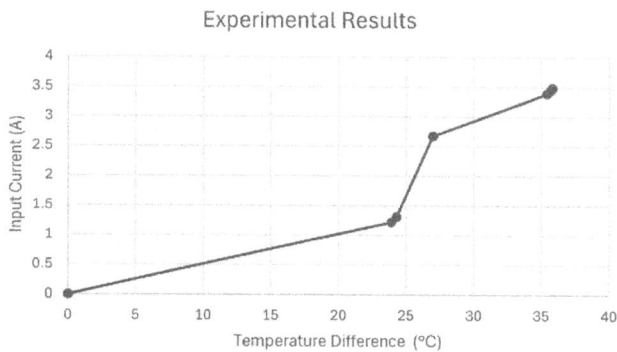

Fig. 42.8   Experimental results

Source: Authors

4.3 Prototype Design

A novel mechanism was developed to combine active and passive cooling methods together and additionally, thermoelectric cooler was used to increase the performance of cooling design. Thermoelectric cooler was used to cool the directed air to the electronic circuits. An air-cooling chamber was used to absorb heat from the inlet air and direct the cooled air to the electronic circuits.

SolidWorks software was used to model the prototype design. The developed model is shown in Fig. 42.9. A large opening was used to intake the air and a small air outlet was used to output air which was inspired by the intercooler turbo housing design to design the long radius air chamber.

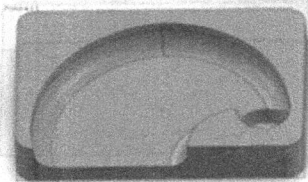

Fig. 42.9   Air chamber solidworks design

Source: Authors

This long radius bend is used to get mass air flow into the chamber, and it contributes to time lagging to cool the inlet air flow. A 4020 DC air blower was used to direct the air into the electronic circuit.

Fully assembled prototype design is shown in Fig. 42.10 which consists of thermoelectric cooler with heat sinks and a fan.

4.4 Airflow Simulations

Airflow simulation was done by Solidworks flow simulations. The intake air temperature was assigned as 27°C and the simulation resulted in 14°C air outlet temperature.

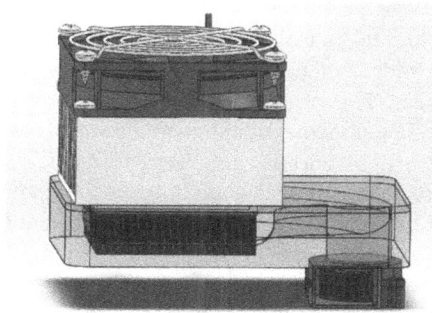

Fig. 42.10   Fully assembled solidworks design

Source: Authors

4.5 Prototype Fabrication

The prototype was physically fabricated using SolidWorks drawings. Regiform was used to fabricate the long radius air chamber (Fig. 42.11).

Fig. 42.11   Fabricated prototype

Source: Authors

4.6 Monitoring and Controlling of the Overall Process

The current control method was used to control the thermoelectric cooler as the controller must control the input current of the thermoelectric cooler. It was observed that, in thermoelectric cooler testing, thermoelectric cooler decreases their performance when it is running continuously. Thus, the control process must need a thermoelectric device switching process as well.

5. Conclusion

This paper presented a novel cooling technique for power electronic circuits with airflow optimization. By combining both active and passive cooling methods, it was aimed to increase the efficiency and reliability of power electronic device. The approach was utilizing a combination of heat sinks for passive cooling and thermoelectric coolers (TECs) for active cooling. The experimental results demonstrated that this hybrid cooling system effectively decreases the operating temperature of the power electronic circuits by 13°C. The heat sinks used in the analysis provided efficient thermal management through convection, while the TECs offered precise temperature control by using the Peltier effect. This dual approach ensured that the power electronic components maintained optimal performance even under high current and high frequency operation conditions. The proposed cooling technique offers a significant improvement in thermal management for power electronic circuits, potentially extending the lifespan of semiconductor devices and enhancing the performance of power inverters and converters. Future research could explore further optimizations and the application of this cooling technique to other types of electronic circuits and devices.

REFERENCES

1. A. R. Dhumal, A. P. Kulkarni, and N. H. Ambhore, "A comprehensive review on thermal management of electronic devices," Dec. 01, 2023, *Institute for Ionics*. doi: 10.1186/s44147-023-00309-2.

2. T. Islam, U. I. Aziz, R. Karmaker, and U. Ibn Aziz, "Enhancement of Electronic Chip Cooling Efficiency: A CFD Approach," 2024. [Online]. Available: https://www.researchgate.net/publication/380604640

3. T. Yong, W. Bo, and Q. Pang, "Thermal Breakdown Failure Mechanisms of IGBT Chips," in *IOP Conference Series: Earth and Environmental Science*, Institute of Physics Publishing, Jan. 2019. doi: 10.1088/1755-1315/223/1/012024.

4. O. V. Soloveva, S. A. Solovev, and R. Z. Shakurova, "Numerical Study of the Thermal and Hydraulic Characteristics of Plate-Fin Heat Sinks," *Processes*, vol. 12, no. 4, Apr. 2024, doi: 10.3390/pr12040744.

5. N. H. Ranchagoda, M. N. Akram, C. P. K. Vithanage, and N. D. Jayasundere, "Implementation of an External Intelligent Cooling System for Laptops using TECs," IEEE, 2016.

6. M. Mahesh, K. Vinoth Kumar, M. Abebe, L. Udayakumar, and M. Mathankumar, "A review on enabling technologies for high power density power electronic applications," in *Materials Today: Proceedings*, Elsevier Ltd, 2020, pp. 3888–3892. doi: 10.1016/j.matpr.2021.02.340.

7. J. Galins, A. Laizans, and A. Galins, "Review of cooling solutions for compact electronic devices," in *Research for Rural Development*, Jelgava : Latvia University of Agriculture, 2019, pp. 201–208. doi: 10.22616/rrd.25.2019.030.

8. I. Oropeza-Perez and P. A. Østergaard, "Active and passive cooling methods for dwellings: A review," 2018, *Elsevier Ltd*. doi: 10.1016/j.rser.2017.09.059.

9. F. J. R. Gil and A. D. Mejia, "Thermal finite element analysis of complex heat sinks using open source tools and high performance computing," 2023.

10. T. Ming, L. Liu, P. Zhang, Y. Yan, and Y. Wu, "The Transient Cooling Performance of a Compact Thin-Film Thermoelectric Cooler with Horizontal Structure," *Energies (Basel)*, vol. 16, no. 24, Dec. 2023, doi: 10.3390/en16248109.

Transformative Applied Research in Computing, Engineering, Science and Technology – Dr. Damayanthi Dahanayake et al. (eds)
© 2024 Taylor & Francis Group, London, ISBN 978-1-041-01782-0

43

A Review of the Therapeutic Potential of *Gymnema Sylvestre* in Diabetes Management

J.D. Wandana and D. Dahanayake*

Department of Life Sciences, NSBM Green University,
Sri Lanka

Abstract

This One of the biggest worldwide health concerns today is diabetes mellitus (DM), a chronic metabolic disease marked by elevated blood sugar levels. As standard medications often come with high costs, dosage intolerance, and adverse effects, research has shown more interest in moving to natural remedies due to the safer and more affordable alternatives, addressing these significant concerns. Natural products are gaining recognition for their effectiveness and minimal side effects, making them a favorable option for diabetes management. This review explores *Gymnema sylvestre's* therapeutic potential in the treatment of diabetes. *Gymnema sylvestre*, also known as Gurmar, is a plant that has anti-diabetic properties since it contains bioactive components like gymnemic acid and gymnemasaponins. *Gymnema sylvestre* exhibits potential as a natural and comprehensive method of managing diabetes through mechanisms that include inhibition of sugar absorption, stimulation of insulin secretion, alpha- glucosidase inhibitory activity, alpha-amylase inhibitory activity and reduction of fat accumulation. These actions collectively aid in controlling blood glucose levels and improving metabolic health. According to recent research, when taken as directed, *Gymnema sylvestre* can significantly improve metabolic indicators and lower blood sugar levels with no adverse toxicity. On the other hand, side effects such as hypoglycemia and muscular atrophy could result from high dosages. *Gymnema sylvestre* presents a natural and supplemental approach to managing diabetes, given its possible benefits over traditional medications. To validate its therapeutic potential and incorporate it into standard diabetic treatment protocols, further research and clinical trials are recommended. With its potential benefits beyond traditional therapies, *Gymnema sylvestre* emerges as a promising supplementary therapy in addressing the challenge of diabetes.

Keywords

Antidiabetic, Gymnema sylvestre, Gymnemic acids, Hypoglycemia, Triterpenoid saponins

1. Introduction

One of the current most pressing worldwide health emergencies is emerging as diabetes, according to a report published in the International Diabetes Federation's (IDF) [1]. It indicates a steady increase in the prevalence of diabetes, from 537 million people in 2021 with the projection of 643 million by 2030 and 783 million by

*Corresponding author: damayanthi.d@nsbm.ac.lk

DOI: 10.1201/9781003616368-43

2045. Furthermore, diabetes affects individuals across all age groups, with an increasing number of children and adolescents diagnosed each year [1].

Diabetes mellitus (DM), commonly known as diabetes, is a group of metabolic disorders characterized by high blood sugar levels over a prolonged period. The condition arises when the body either cannot produce sufficient insulin or fails to use the insulin it produces effectively [2]. Hyperglycaemia, hyperlipidaemia, and oxidative stress are all hallmarks of diabetes, which can further result in chronic conditions that impair the kidneys, blood vessels, eyes, and nerves, among other organs [2]. However, these serious complications can be postponed or eliminated, if diabetes is properly managed. Diabetes can currently be treated with insulin and a variety of oral anti-diabetic medications, ranging from glinides, biguanides, α-glucosidase inhibitors, and sulfonylureas [3].

Nonetheless, these treatments become ineffective due to concerns with lifestyle adjustments, such as patient discontent, inadequate control of diabetic risk factors, etc [4]. So, there is high need for the researchers to focus on new, safe, and affordable treatments for the management of diabetes due to the prevailing high cost and dosage intolerance and adverse effects of standard medication [5].

Since ancient times, naturopathic medicine has been investigated and used. Today, herbal remedies gain popularity for their potential health benefits compared to commercially available medications [6]. The medicinal properties of ethnobotanical groups have attracted interest due to their diverse antihyperglycemic effects [7]. Many kinds of plants that are rich in phenolics, flavonoids, coumarins, terpenoids, and other bioactive components have demonstrated a decrease in blood glucose levels [6].

Gymnema sylvestre has long been used in traditional Ayurvedic medicine for its ability to lower blood sugar levels, and recent scientific studies have confirmed its potent anti-diabetic properties [8].The key bioactive components of the plant, especially gymnemic acids, have been reported to inhibit glucose absorption in the intestines, suppress sugar craving, and stimulate insulin secretion [9].This herb has gained increasing attention in diabetes research for its potential to complement conventional treatments. It not only improves glycaemic control but may also mitigate complications associated with diabetes [10].

Given these promising findings, this literature review aims to explore the significant role of Gymnema sylvestre, a rare herb commonly known as "Gurmar," in diabetes management. This review focuses on current knowledge regarding the plant's phytochemical composition, its mechanism of action, and clinical efficacy as an antidiabetic

medicinal plant. Through an exploration of these areas, the review illuminates Gymnema sylvestre's potential as a useful complementary therapy in the ongoing battle against diabetes.

2. Types of Diabetes Mellitus

Diabetes is categorized into multiple forms based on aetiology, pathophysiology, and clinical presentation. This helps with research, prognosis prediction, treatment decisions, and patient empowerment. The four main types of diabetes are type 1 diabetes mellitus (T1DM), type 2 diabetes mellitus (T2DM), gestational diabetes mellitus (GDM), and secondary diabetes mellitus, which arises due to specific underlying conditions such as pancreatic disease, hormonal disorders, or medication use [11].

T1DM also called as insulin-dependent diabetes mellitus is a chronic autoimmune disease described by the loss of pancreatic β-cells that produce insulin resulting in hyperglycaemia [1]. T1DM is a complex and diverse condition with a genetic susceptibility that leads to atypical immune reactions in response to unclear environmental attacks on pancreatic islets [1].

Diabetes mellitus also known as non-insulin-dependent diabetes mellitus is a prolonged metabolic disorder marked by high blood glucose levels [12]. Type 2 diabetes mellitus (T2DM) is one of the most prevalent metabolic disorders globally, accounting for approximately 90-95% of all diabetes mellitus cases [11]. Over time, chronic hyperglycaemia leads to damage in various organs, including the blood vessels, heart, eyes, kidneys, and nerves [11]. This damage occurs through mechanisms such as oxidative stress, endothelial dysfunction, and the formation of advanced glycation end-products (AGEs), which thicken blood vessel walls and reduce blood flow. These processes increase the risk of complications like diabetic retinopathy, nephropathy, neuropathy, heart disease, and stroke [13].

The two primary factors that work together to predominantly induce its development are inadequate insulin production and insulin resistance, where insulin-sensitive tissues fail to respond properly to insulin, reducing glucose uptake [14]. This insulin resistance plays a crucial role in the onset of T2DM, leading to compensatory overproduction of insulin by the pancreas [11]. However, over time, this mechanism becomes ineffective, resulting in hyperglycaemia as insulin secretion is no longer able to maintain glucose homeostasis [12]. Various environmental and genetic factors, including obesity, sedentary lifestyles, genetics, dyslipidaemia, hypertension, and prior gestational diabetes mellitus (GDM), contribute to the development of insulin resistance and T2DM [11, 15].

According to the American Diabetes Association, diabetes mellitus of any type or degree diagnosed during pregnancy, usually in the 2nd or 3rd trimester, is referred to as gestational diabetes mellitus, or GDM [16]. GDM usually disappears completely after childbirth or the end of a pregnancy, in contrast to preexisting diabetes [11]. Obesity, history of previous GDM, glycosuria, family history, ethnicity, and hypertension are risk factors for developing gestational diabetes mellitus during pregnancy [17].

3. Gymnema Sylvestre

Gymnema sylvestre, commonly known as the "sugar destroyer" or "Gurmar," is a woody climbing plant from the Asclepiadaceae family, native to the tropical regions of Central and southern India, Sri Lanka, Africa, and Australia, Malaysia, and Japan [18].

Among the traditionally used Ayurvedic medicine, *Gymnema sylvestre* has gained attention not only for its purported anti-diabetic properties, but also for its anti-inflammatory activity, antibiotic, and antimicrobial activity. *Gymnema sylvestre* is called as; Periploca of woods in English, Gurmar in Hindi, and Mas bedda in Sinhala [19].

3.1 Botanical Information about Gymnema Sylvestre

Gymnema sylvestre is a green perennial woody climber herb with a slow growth. This plant has a distinct smell, and the leaves have a mildly bitter and astringent flavour. The length of the leaves is 2–6 cm, and their breadth is 1–4 cm (Fig. 43.1). The little blossoms are yellow in colour [18].

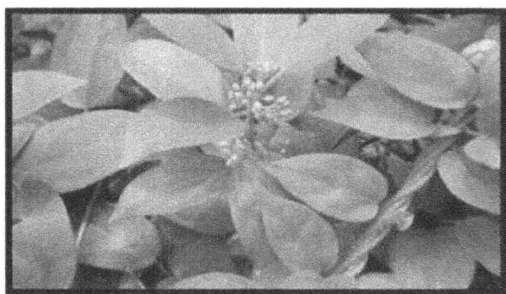

Fig. 43.1 Fresh leaves of *Gymnema sylvestre*. [41]

3.2 Traditional Uses of Gymnema Sylvestre

The ancient medical book Shushruta, describes *Gymnema sylvestre* as a treatment for urinary disorders and glycosuria [1]. This herb has remarkable antidiabetic properties and is used in homeopathic, ayurveda, and folk medicine systems. Traditionally inflammations, snakebite, family planning, asthma, and vision issues are all being treated with it [21].

Additionally, this herb is prescribed in Ayurveda for the treatment of Asthma, bronchitis, amenorrhea, conjunctivitis, dyspepsia, constipation, hepatitis, haemorrhoids, diabetes, inflammation, renal and vesicle calculi, cardiopathy, and leukoderma [20].

3.3 Phytochemistry of Gymnema Sylvestre
Antidiabetic Compounds

Gymnema sylvestre has a variety of secondary metabolites. Chromatographic analysis of Gymnema sylvestre stems revealed the presence of many chemical substances with potential medicinal use, including stigmasterol and triterpenoid saponin [22]. This stigmasterol is a type of sterol that includes many important properties like antidiabetic, anticancer, hypoglycaemic, anti-hypercholesteraemic and antioxidant activities. In addition, multiple studies have proven the anti-tumour, anti-fungal, hepatoprotective, and antidiabetic properties of triterpenoid saponins [23].

The leaves contain anthraquinones, and their derivatives, alkaloids-conduritol, gymnamine, cardiac glycosides, oleanane saponins, and dammarane saponins which are the two types of saponins in the leaves [24]. The major chemical constituents of *Gymnema sylvestre* are gymnemic acid (Fig. 43.2) and gymnemasaponins classified under oleanane saponins. Gymnemic acid and related compounds were identified in over ten different varieties [25]. According to [26], leaves possess about 0.0050 - 0.012% of gymnemic acid. However, a study carried out in India reveals that the concentration of gymnemic acid varies depending on the organ of the plant. They reported that the shoot tip has the highest amount of gymnemic acid (54.29 mg·g-1 DW) [27]. Gymnemagenin and gymnestrogenin are two examples of the aglycone saponins that make up Gymnema saponins [28]. Gymnemasides (I–VII) [Fig. 43.4] are a class of dammarane saponins [10].

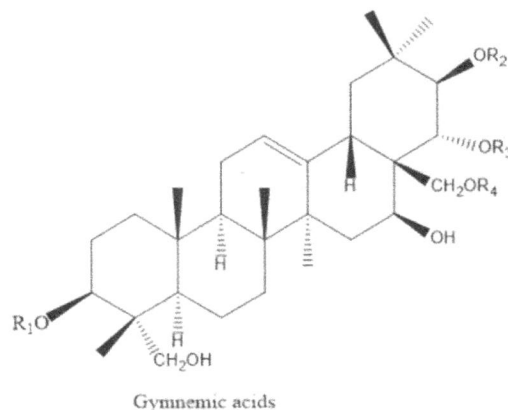

Gymnemic acids

Fig. 43.2 Basic structure of gymnemic acid [42]

These compounds are believed for its anti-diabetic properties, impacting insulin secretion, glucose absorption, and utilization [29]. Besides, the leaves contain lupeol, anthraquinone derivatives, β amyrin, stigmasterol, alkaloids, pentriacontane, α and β chlorophyll, resin, tartaric acid, trimethylamine which contain therapeutical potentials [2].

Bioactive and Antioxidant

Gymnema sylvestre contains a variety of bioactive compounds, many of which possess antioxidants properties. These compounds include flavonoids, tannins, alkaloids, phenols, cinnamic acid, butyric acid, folic acid, ascorbic acid, and tartaric acid [8]. Studies has indicated that extracts from *Gymnema sylvestre* exhibit significant antioxidant properties that could provide therapeutic advantages in the control of diabetes, thereby preventing organ damage linked to the condition [32].

3.4 Mechanism of Action of Gymnema Sylvestre for Antidiabetic Activity

Gymnema sylvestre, has garnered significant attention for its potential in managing diabetes mellitus. Its antidiabetic properties are attributed to a spectrum of mechanisms, each playing a role in its overall therapeutic effectiveness [33].

Inhibition of Sugar Absorption

Gymnemic acids, bioactive compounds found abundantly in *Gymnema sylvestre* and is a mixture of at least 17 distinct saponins, plays a key role in inhibiting the intestinal absorption of dietary sugars [34]. Gymnemic acids competitively bind to sugar receptors in the intestines, blocking the absorption of dietary sugars into the circulation because of their structural similarity to glucose molecules [6]. The mechanism, as shown in study [6], elucidated by resulting in a notable reduction in postprandial blood glucose levels [6].

Stimulation of Insulin Secretion

Add Apart from inhibiting sugar absorption, Gymnemic acids also contribute to insulin secretion. Studies have shown that Gymnema sylvestre may have a role in stimulating the β-cell regeneration and insulin secretion [35]. A research study of leaf and callus methanolic extract of Gymnema sylvestre revealed anti-diabetic benefits through beta-cell

regeneration [35]. In this study, alloxan was injected into the Wistar rats which caused the rats to develop diabetes, and they were tested with administration of Gymnema sylvestre leaf and callus extracts. The study discovered the gymnemic acids present in Gymnema sylvestre leaf and callus extracts have increased the beta- cell regeneration in these treated rats, also presenting potential therapeutic drugs for insulin-dependent diabetes mellitus [35].

Furthermore, the peptide Gurmarin, extracted from the leaf of Gymnema sylvestre, alters taste buds' capacity to differentiate between bitter and sweetness. Insulin secretion and release are triggered by this alteration of incretin activity, which leads to Gymnema sylvestre 's antidiabetic effects [6].

α-Glucosidase Inhibitory Activity

The in vitro investigation demonstrated that the Gymnema sylvestre extract shown considerable inhibitory activity against α-glucosidase [36]. With an IC50 value of 68.70 ± 1.22 μg/mL, the extract inhibited the enzyme by 50% at this concentration, suggesting its potential in hindering carbohydrate breakdown. When compared with Acarbose, a known α-glucosidase inhibitor, Gymnema sylvestre was slightly less effective. Nevertheless, the findings suggest the Gymnema sylvestre extracts has the antidiabetic potential in interfering of the breakdown of carbohydrates [36].

A rapid screening and identification process using affinity ultrafiltration and liquid chromatography-mass spectrometry (UF-HPLC-MS) identified nine compounds with elevated enrichment factors (EFs) as α-glucosidase inhibitors from Gymnema sylvestre. According to the structure-activity interactions, the study shows the glycosylation can reduce the sapogenins antisweat effect. Additionally, they reveal that, because of the synergistic actions of other components in Gymnema sylvestre like alkaloids and flavonoids also have the potential to act as effective α-glucosidase inhibitors [35].

α-amylase Inhibitory Activity

Following the α-glucosidase inhibition, gymnemic acid, isolated from *Gymnema sylvestre* leaves, also showed notable inhibitory activity on α-amylase (Fig. 43.3), an

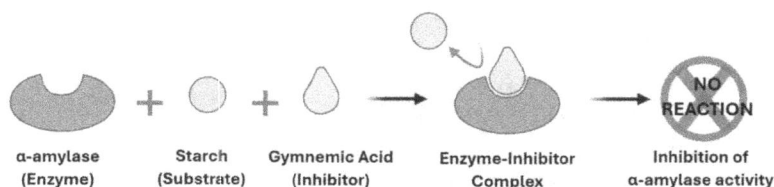

α-amylase (Enzyme) + Starch (Substrate) + Gymnemic Acid (Inhibitor) → Enzyme-Inhibitor Complex → NO REACTION Inhibition of α-amylase activity

Fig. 43.3 α-amylase inhibition activity of *Gymnema sylvestre*

Source: Created by the author using the reference source: [43]

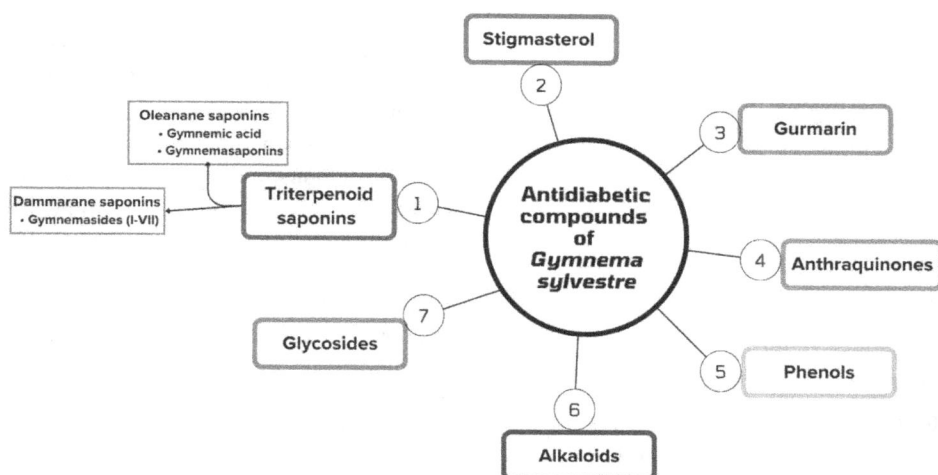

Fig. 43.4 Antidiabetic constituents of *Gymnema sylvestre*

Source: Created by the author using the reference source: [43]

enzyme responsible for the breaking down of starch into simpler sugars [36]. In a study conducted through in vitro assays, gymnemic acid showed 17.49% inhibition at a concentration of 5 mg/mL and 14.23% at 10 mg/mL [36]. This indicates that gymnemic acid could delay the breakdown of complex carbohydrates, thereby reducing the rate of glucose absorption.

Although *Gymnema sylvestre* exhibited lower inhibitory activity compared to Acarbose, which showed 48.21% inhibitory activity at 1 mg/mL, the findings suggest that it may act as a natural alternative for inhibiting α-amylase activity [36]. This action help mitigate the glycemic response after meals high in carbohydrates, further highlighting its antidiabetic potential. Moreover, the presence of additional bioactive compounds, such as steroids and glycosides, may contribute to the overall inhibitory effect, indicating a possible synergistic action that enhances the therapeutic valve of *Gymnema sylvestre* [36].

Reduction of Fat Accumulation

Beyond its antidiabetic effects, *Gymnema sylvestre* demonstrates potential in reducing fat accumulation and improving metabolic parameters, offering additional benefits for diabetes management[10] *G. sylvestre* extracts have been used to treat diabetes and obesity in humans and animals [33].

One such study was investigating the obesity control method without the rebound effect of gymnemate, a compound extracted from *Gymnema sylvestre*, on Otsuka Long-Evans Tokushima Fatty rats (OLETF), a genetic rat model exhibiting multifactor syndrome including hyperlipidaemia, hyperglycaemia and increased body weight. After a 3-week

treatment period of the administration of a water-based extract of *Gymnema sylvestre* via diet to the Male 4 weeks old OLETF rats, the findings indicate that the body weight, serum triglycerides, total cholesterol, and LDL+VLDL cholesterol levels have significantly reduced. In summary, gymnemate supplementation aided in weight loss by lowering hyperlipidaemia, and there was no withdrawal rebound [37].

According to Preuss et al., the combination of *Gymnema sylvestre* extract (HCA+GSE) and hydroxycitric acid (HCA-SX), an active component extracted out of the rind of the Indian fruit Garcinia cambogia, led to significantly lower body weight gain, BMI, and improved metabolic parameters related to diabetes management [3]. In a study conducted in India for 8 weeks by taking 60 moderately obese (ages 21–50, BMI >26kg/m2) randomized, double-blind, placebo-controlled human patients who were administered 60% HCA (which includes 2800 mg d−1) along with 400 mg of G. sylvestre extract (HCA+GSE) at the end of 4 and 8 weeks, respectively, encountered a reduction in body weight of about 2.35 and 4.53 kg in the HCA group, and about 2.74 and 5.69 kg in the HCA+GSE group [3].

Additionally, HCA+GSE combination led to a 44.3% decrease in serum leptin levels, indicating improved control of adipose tissue and fat metabolism. This combined alsoresulted in significant decreases in LDL levels (19.1%) and triglycerides (20.2%) [38].

The results indicate that the combination of HCA and G. sylvestre extract plays an important part in reducing fat accumulation and enhancing metabolic parameters, highlighting a potential mechanism of action for *Gymnema sylvestre* in its antidiabetic activity, although the study does not specifically isolate the effects of *G. sylvestre* extract alone [38].

Correction of Metabolic Derangements

Gymnema sylvestre exerts corrective actions on various metabolic abnormalities associated with diabetes, including insulin resistance and dysregulated enzyme activity. Through its multifaceted effects on glucose metabolism and insulin sensitivity, Gymnema helps restore metabolic equilibrium and ameliorate diabetic pathology [38].

3.5 Toxicity of Gymnema Sylvestre

Studies on the toxicity of *Gymnema sylvestre* extract indicate that, when used at recommended dosages, it is harmless. But excessive sweating, hypoglycaemia, weakness, shakiness, and muscle dystrophy can occur if it is used in high doses [19]. A study conducted in Japan revealed that administering of 0.01, 0.10 and 1.00% of *Gymnema sylvestre* extract basal powder (GS) including in the diet of Wistar rats showed that there were no toxic effects, and no mortality throughout the experiment of 52 weeks. They concluded that no observable effect level was 1.00% when male rats were given up to 504 mg/kg/day of GS, and female rats were given up to 563 mg/kg/day of GS [39]. A clinical case was reported by a 60-year-old patient who has shown toxic hepatitis or drug-induced liver injury due to the consumption of GS for treating diabetes [40]. Thus, data and reports for confirming the safety of GS are not available.

4. Future Directions

Comprehensive clinical trials are required to confirm the long-term safety and effectiveness of *Gymnema sylvestre* (GS) for treating diabetes across diverse populations. To optimize GS's benefits and reduce any potential risks, it is important to investigate the best effective dose and delivery techniques. Significantly, as excessive doses of GS may be harmful to these organs, research should concentrate on reducing negative effects on the liver and kidneys. Investigating the usage of GS in combination with the anti-diabetic drugs that are currently on the market may provide novel treatment approaches with enhanced safety profiles. In conclusion, the investigation of genetic variables that impact individual reactions to GS could result in personalized diabetic therapies, ensuring patients' safety and effectiveness.

5. Conclusion

The literature reviewed underscores the significant potential of *Gymnema sylvestre* as a therapeutic agent in diabetes management. With its rich array of bioactive compounds and multifaceted mechanisms of action, *Gymnema sylvestre* offers a holistic approach to addressing the complexities of diabetes. From inhibiting sugar absorption to stimulating insulin secretion and reducing fat accumulation, this herbal remedy demonstrates promising anti-diabetic properties. However, further research is warranted to fully elucidate its molecular mechanisms and establish standardized doses for long-term use. Nevertheless, *Gymnema sylvestre* emerges as a valuable addition to the range of therapeutic options of diabetes therapies, providing a natural and complementary alternative to conventional treatments. Its potential in improving patient outcomes and reducing the global burden of diabetes merits continued exploration and clinical investigation.

REFERENCES

1. D. J. Magliano, E. J. Boyko, and I. D. F. D. Atlas, "What is diabetes?," in IDF DIABETES ATLAS [Internet]. 10th edition, International Diabetes Federation, 2021.

2. A. K. Jugran, S. Rawat, H. P. Devkota, I. D. Bhatt, and R. S. Rawal, "Diabetes and plant-derived natural products: From ethnopharmacological approaches to their potential for modern drug discovery and development," Jan. 01, 2021, John Wiley and Sons Ltd. doi: 10.1002/ptr.6821.

3. L. V K, "Pharma Science Monitor An International Journal Of Pharmaceutical Sciences Gymnema Sylvestre: A Comprehensive Review," vol. 3, no. 4, 2012, [Online]. Available: www.pharmasm.com

4. N. G. Forouhi, J. Luan, S. Hennings, and N. J. Wareham, "Incidence of type 2 diabetes in England and its association with baseline impaired fasting glucose: the Ely study 1990–2000," Diabetic Medicine, vol. 24, no. 2, pp. 200–207, 2007.

5. S. Devangan, B. Varghese, E. Johny, S. Gurram, and R. Adela, "The effect of Gymnema sylvestre supplementation on glycemic control in type 2 diabetes patients: A systematic review and meta-analysis," Dec. 01, 2021, John Wiley and Sons Ltd. doi: 10.1002/ptr.7265.

6. P. Tiwari, B. N. Mishra, and N. S. Sangwan, "Phytochemical and Pharmacological Properties of Gymnema sylvestre: An Important Medicinal Plant," Biomed Res Int, vol. 2014, p. 830285, 2014, doi: 10.1155/2014/830285.

7. J. K. Grover, S. Yadav, and V. Vats, "Medicinal plants of India with anti-diabetic potential," J Ethnopharmacol, vol. 81, no. 1, pp. 81–100, 2002.

8. S. Laha and S. Paul, "Gymnema sylvestre (Gurmar): A potent herb with anti-diabetic and antioxidant potential," Apr. 01, 2019, EManuscript Technologies. doi: 10.5530/pj.2019.11.33.

9. G. S. Thakur, R. Sharma, B. S. Sanodiya, M. Pandey, G. B. K. S. Prasad, and P. S. Bisen, "Gymnema sylvestre: An alternative therapeutic agent for management of diabetes," J Appl Pharm Sci, vol. 2, no. 12, pp. 1–6, Dec. 2012, doi: 10.7324/JAPS.2012.21201.

10. K. Yoshikawa, S. Arihara, K. Matsuurat, and T. Miyase~, "Dammarane Saponins From Gymnema Sylvestre," 1992.

11. M. Z. Banday, A. S. Sameer, and S. Nissar, "Pathophysiology of diabetes: An overview," Avicenna J Med, vol. 10, no. 04, pp. 174–188, Oct. 2020, doi: 10.4103/ajm.ajm_53_20.

12. U. Galicia-Garcia et al., "Pathophysiology of type 2 diabetes mellitus," Sep. 01, 2020, MDPI AG. doi: 10.3390/ijms21176275.

13. W. T. Cade, "Diabetes-Related Microvascular and Macrovascular Diseases in the Physical Therapy Setting Diabetes Special Issue," 2008. [Online]. Available: www.ptjournal.org

14. M. Roden and G. I. Shulman, "The integrative biology of type 2 diabetes," Dec. 05, 2019, Nature Research. doi: 10.1038/s41586-019-1797-8.

15. W. Y. Fujimoto, "The Importance of Insulin Resistance in the Pathogenesis of Type 2 Diabetes Mellitus," 2000.

16. S. Ta, "Diagnosis and classification of diabetes mellitus," Diabetes Care, vol. 37, no. 1, pp. 81–90, 2014.

17. L. Yuen, "Gestational diabetes mellitus: Challenges for different ethnic groups," World J Diabetes, vol. 6, no. 8, p. 1024, 2015, doi: 10.4239/wjd.v6.i8.1024.

18. C. Sharma, "Gymnema Sylvestre (Gurmar): A Review." [Online]. Available: https://www.researchgate.net/publication/267408796

19. P. Tiwari, B. N. Mishra, and N. S. Sangwan, "Phytochemical and pharmacological properties of Gymnema sylvestre: An important medicinal plant," 2014. doi: 10.1155/2014/830285.

20. N. Pankaj, V. Kumar Gupta, and A. Vikash, "A REVIEW Article in," International Journal of Pharmacognosy and Phytochemical Research, vol. 10, no. 7, pp. 356–361, 2023, doi: 10.13040/IJPSR.0975-8232.IJP.10(7).356-61.

21. P. Kanetkar, R. Singhal, and M. Kamat, "Serial Review Gymnema sylvestre: A Memoir," 2007.

22. Y. Liu et al., "Chemical constituents from the stems of Gymnema sylvestre," Chin J Nat Med, vol. 12, no. 4, pp. 300–304, 2014, doi: 10.1016/S1875-5364(14)60059-5.

23. J. Chaudhary, A. Jain, N. Kaur, and L. Kishore, "Stigmasterol: A Comprehensive Review," Article in International Journal of Pharmaceutical Sciences and Research, vol. 2, no. 9, 2011, [Online]. Available: https://www.researchgate.net/publication/264420218

24. M. R. Patel, "Pharmacognostic And Phytochemical Valuation Of Gymnema Sylvestre Leaf.," World J Pharm Pharm Sci, pp. 1532–1538, Jul. 2017, doi: 10.20959/wjpps20177-9574.

25. R. Suttisri, I.-S. Lee, and A. D. Kinghorn, "Plant-derived triterpenoid sweetness inhibitors," J Ethnopharmacol, vol. 47, no. 1, pp. 9–26, 1995.

26. N. Murakami, T. Murakami, M. Kadoya, H. Matsuda, J. Yamahara, And M. Yoshikawa, "New Hypoglycemic Constituents In" Gymnemic Acid" Form Gymnema Sylvestre," Chem Pharm Bull (Tokyo), vol. 44, no. 2, pp. 469–471, 1996.

27. S. H. Manohar, P. M. Naik, N. Praveen, and H. N. Murthy, "Distribution of gymnemic acid in various organs of Gymnema sylvestre," J For Res (Harbin), vol. 20, no. 3, pp. 268–270, 2009, doi: 10.1007/s11676-009-0046-7.

28. G. S. Rao and J. E. Sinsheimer, "Constituents from Gymnema sylvestre leaves VIII: Isolation, chemistry, and derivatives of gymnemagenin and gymnestrogenin," J Pharm Sci, vol. 60, no. 2, pp. 190–193, 1971, doi: 10.1002/jps.2600600205.

29. M. S. Mariappan Senthilkumar, "Phytochemical screening and antibacterial activity of Gymnema sylvestre R. Br. Ex Schult.," 2015.

30. M. Senthilkumar, "phytochemical screening and antibacterial activity of Gymnema Sylvestre R.BR. Ex Schult," Int J Pharm Sci Res, vol. 6, no. 6, p. 2496, 2015, doi: 10.13040/IJPSR.0975-8232.6(6).2496-03.

31. V. Gunasekaran, S. Srinivasan, S. Sudha Rani, and C. Velvizhi Gunasekaran, "Potential antioxidant and antimicrobial activity of Gymnema sylvestre related to diabetes," Journal of Medicinal Plants Studies, vol. 7, no. 2, pp. 5–11, 2019, [Online]. Available: https://www.researchgate.net/publication/331732815

32. R. Pothuraju, R. K. Sharma, J. Chagalamarri, S. Jangra, and P. Kumar Kavadi, "A systematic review of Gymnema sylvestre in obesity and diabetes management," Mar. 30, 2014. doi: 10.1002/jsfa.6458.

33. N. P. Sahu, S. B. Mahato, S. K. Sarkar'~, and G. Poddart, "Triterpenoid Saponins From Gymnema Sylvestre," 1996.

34. A. B. A. Ahmed, A. S. Rao, and M. V. Rao, "In vitro callus and in vivo leaf extract of Gymnema sylvestre stimulate β-cells regeneration and anti-diabetic activity in Wistar rats," Phytomedicine, vol. 17, no. 13, pp. 1033–1039, Nov. 2010, doi: 10.1016/j.phymed.2010.03.019.

35. G. Chen and M. Guo, "Rapid screening for α-glucosidase inhibitors from Gymnema sylvestre by affinity ultrafiltration-hplc-ms," Front Pharmacol, vol. 8, no. APR, Apr. 2017, doi: 10.3389/fphar.2017.00228.

36. Vijayalakshmi A, "In vitro assay of alpha amylase inhibitory activity of gymnemic acid isolated from Gymnema Sylvestre leaves." [Online]. Available: https://www.researchgate.net/publication/316367027

37. H. Luo, A. Kashiwagi, T. Shibahara, and K. Yamada, "Decreased bodyweight without rebound and regulated lipoprotein metabolism by gymnemate in genetic multifactor syndrome animal," Mol Cell Biochem, vol. 299, no. 1–2, pp. 93–98, May 2007, doi: 10.1007/s11010-005-9049-7.

38. H. G. Preuss, D. Bagchi, M. Bagchi, C. V. S. Rao, D. K. Dey, and S. Satyanarayana, "Effects of a natural extract of (-)-hydroxycitric acid (HCA-SX) and a combination of HCA-SX plus niacin-bound chromium and Gymnema sylvestre extract on weight loss."

39. K. Baskaran, B. Kizar Ahamath, K. Radha Shanmugasundaram, and E. Shanmugasundaram, "Antidiaretic effect of a leaf extract from gymnema sylvestre in non-insulin-dependent diabetes mellitus patients," 1990.

40. Y. Ogawa et al., "Gymnema sylvestre leaf extract: a 52-week dietary toxicity study in Wistar rats," Shokuhin Eiseigaku Zasshi, vol. 45, no. 1, pp. 8–18, 2004.

41. A. Shiyovich, I. Sztarkier, and L. Nesher, "Toxic hepatitis induced by gymnema sylvestre, a natural remedy for type 2 diabetes mellitus," American Journal of the Medical Sciences, vol. 340, no. 6, pp. 514–517, 2010, doi: 10.1097/MAJ.0b013e3181f41168.

42. L. Kishore, "Role of Gymnema sylvestre as Alternative Medicine," Journal of Homeopathy & Ayurvedic Medicine, vol. 03, no. 04, 2015, doi: 10.4172/2167-1206.1000172.

43. K. B. Triveni, V. K. Lakshmi, S. Shashidhara, and S. Anitha, "Gymnema Sylvestre: a comprehensive review.," Pharma Science Monitor, vol. 3, no. 4, 2012.

Transformative Applied Research in Computing, Engineering, Science and Technology – Dr. Damayanthi Dahanayake et al. (eds)
© 2024 Taylor & Francis Group, London, ISBN 978-1-041-01782-0

44

Exploring the Relationship Between Heat Stress, Dehydration, and Chronic Kidney Disease of Unknown Etiology

E. M.T.P. Ekanayaka and D. Dahanayake*

Department of Life Sciences, NSBM Green University,
Sri Lanka

Abstract

Chronic Kidney Disease of unknown etiology (CKDu) is a disease that causes irreversible kidney damage which is identifiable by its gradual development, irreversibility, and asymptomatic status until late stages. Notably, CKDu does not occur due to hypertension, diabetes, or other known risk factors linked to other renal disorders. While CKDu and CKD have commonalities, they differ due to specific etiological causes. CKDu has been observed worldwide, most notably among agricultural groups. In Sri Lanka, CKDu is common among farmers and proceeds through four stages, affecting both society and individuals. This study investigates the effects of heat stress and dehydration on the course of CKDu. Prolonged exposure to extreme temperatures and a lack of water, which are frequent among agricultural workers, worsen the condition. These conditions lead to repeated dehydration episodes, causing hyperosmolarity and activation of damaging physiological pathways, including vasopressin-induced vasoconstriction. The resultant hypoxia, tubulointerstitial damage, inflammation, and fibrosis contribute to CKDu's development. Additionally, heat stress and severe physical labor can lead to subclinical and clinical rhabdomyolysis, releasing myoglobin and other intracellular substances that further damage the kidneys. Hyperuricosuria, resulting from dehydration and increased blood osmolarity, leads to crystallization and additional renal injury. Understanding the role of heat stress and dehydration in CKDu is crucial for developing targeted prevention and management strategies to mitigate the disease's impact on vulnerable populations.

Keywords

CKDu (Chronic Kidney Disease of unknown etiology), Dehydration, Heat stress, Renal diseases

1. Introduction

Chronic Kidney Disease of unknown etiology (CKDu) is a growing health concern impacting agricultural laborers, particularly in tropical and subtropical countries [1]. CKDu predominantly affects impoverished male agricultural laborers in underdeveloped countries, with wealthier countries being immune owing to global trade considerations [2]. It was first found in Balkan nations in the 1960s and then detected in Central America before

---

*Corresponding author: damayanthi.d@nsbm.ac.lk

DOI: 10.1201/9781003616368-44

being discovered among rice producers in Sri Lanka's North Central Province (NCP) in the mid-1990s, and over the next several decades, CKDu expanded to adjacent agricultural districts, with the highest frequency among residents aged 30-60 in the particular area [3]. CKDu has become a global problem, notably among young male agricultural laborers in Mesoamerica, South Asia, Central America, and Eastern Europe [1,4]. The geographical clustering of cases indicates that environmental and occupational variables are important. These laborers frequently work in difficult conditions, including high temperatures, and dehydration which are thought to have a role in the disease's development.

CKDu is a noncommunicable occupational disease that causes a gradual decline of kidney function in the absence of CKD risk factors such as hypertension, glomerulonephritis, and diabetes, with diagnosis only possible in the late stages when kidneys are no longer function in the required efficiency [2]. CKDu patients have symptoms such as shortness of breath, decreased appetite, weight loss, sleep disturbance, excessive tiredness, and nausea [5]. This illness strikes people during their productive years, which are aged 30-60, and creates enormous public health and economic issues.

Environmental variables that may cause CKDu include heavy metal exposure, pesticide usage, dehydrating working conditions, nutritional status, hereditary vulnerability, high-ground fluoride levels, and the use of poor-quality aluminum cookware. Recent investigation suggests that high temperatures, heat stress, insufficient water intake which cause dehydration, intense physical effort, and exposure to contaminated water and agricultural fields also may contribute to CKDu [2,6,7]. Heat stress and dehydration are detected as one of the main hypothetical reasons for CKDu, as they can directly impact the kidneys.

Sri Lanka experiences some of the highest average temperatures globally, ranging from 27 °C to 2 °C year-round [8]. Temperature increases are particularly during the main harvest seasons, with a greater rise from March to July than from August to February by 1 °C to 2 °C [9]. This heightened heat exposure significantly affects farmers and other outdoor workers, who are exposed to both heat stress and dehydration in CKDu-endemic regions. The country's northern areas are identified as hotspots for extreme temperatures and that area also includes North Central province and some regions of Eastern, Northern, and North Western which are hotspots for CKDu condition [5,9].

This review aims to investigate the complex interaction between CKDu and heat stress, focusing on the role of heat stress and dehydration as CKDu risk-associated factors because understanding the link between heat stress, and dehydration on CKDu is critical for addressing public health concerns raised by CKDu in vulnerable communities.

2. Clinical Characteristics and Histopathological Findings in CKDu

The clinical characteristics of CKDu include proteinuria and deranged renal function. Clinically, CKDu is similar to chronic kidney disease (CKD) which is caused by other factors including vascular diseases, hypertension, obstructive uropathy, and diabetic mellitus [10]. Increased excretion of alpha-1 microglobulin in the urine has been observed in CKDu patients, leading to its potential use as a biomarker for screening purposes. However, it is important to note that the excretion of alpha-1 microglobulin is not specific to CKDu alone [11,12].

CKDu is closely associated with tubulointerstitial disease. Multiple histopathological abnormalities were reported in undetectable CKDu patients such as varying degrees of interstitial fibrosis, proteinuria, glomerulosclerosis, interstitial inflammation, and tubular atrophy [13]. Interestingly, asymptomatic proteinuric patients often exhibit interstitial fibrosis without inflammation. Glomerular alterations in these patients include glomerular sclerosis, enlargement of glomerular ischemic obsolescence wrinkled and collapsed glomerular tufts, and relatively uncommon, focal segmental glomerulosclerosis. Additionally, tubulointerstitial inflammation, characterized mainly by mononuclear infiltrate, is observed. Understanding these pathological features is crucial for diagnosing and managing CKDu effectively [13, 14].

3. Heat Stress and Dehydration

Heat stress is defined as the net heat load that workers experience as a result of metabolic heat generation, while dehydration occurs when the body loses more water than it replaces. It might be caused by a failure to replenish obligated water losses [15]. The resting core temperature of healthy individuals varies within an extremely restricted range between 36.5 °C - 37.5 °C, while the inner tissues of the thorax and head hold 36 °C - 38 °C resting temperature [16]. Outdoor workers and farmers, especially in CKDu endemic regions which included the North Central province as well as sections of nearby provinces thus Giribawa, Nikawewa, and Nickaweratiya in the North Western province, Dehiattakandiya in the Eastern province and Giradurukotte in the Uva province that are frequently exposed to high temperatures. As a result, they often experience deep body temperature elevations reaching 38 °C - 40 °C which increases their risk of heat stress and dehydration that initiates or worsens CKDu conditions [14,17].

Those conditions may occur due to several factors such as prolonged exposure to high temperatures, particularly when working outdoors under direct sunlight, and low water-consuming levels. Non-breathable clothing can also hinder the body's ability to cool down through sweat evaporation, and high humidity levels [18]. However, as heat exposure reaches a human tolerance level (38°C) and exceeds that level, the risk of heat-related disorders rises [19]. Mild symptoms include skin rashes, muscular cramps, dizziness, headaches, nausea, fatigue, and weakness while severe symptoms encompass confusion, irrational behavior, poor coordination, fainting, vomiting, convulsions, cellular death of organs, and loss of consciousness [20].

4. Mechanisms Linked to Heat Stress and Dehydration

The pathways connecting heat stress and dehydration to CKDu are complex and include various physiological system impacts that cause damage or increase already presented damage to kidneys. The Fig. 44.1 illustrates the key effects of heat stress and dehydration on the body, particularly their impact on kidney health and the kidney damage that can cause CKDu condition with prolonged affection.

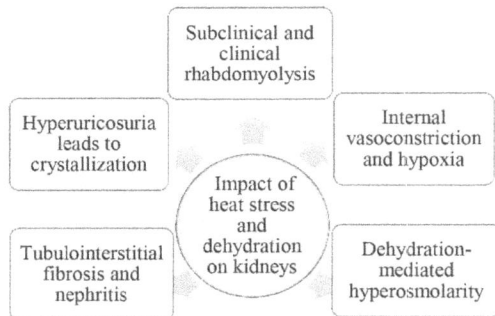

Fig. 44.1 Renal health conditions that occur due to heat stress & dehydration

Source: Authors

4.1 Tubulointerstitial Disease with Fibrosis and Tubulointerstitial Nephritis (Inflammation of Renal Tissues)

Experimental investigations in mice have revealed that daily exposure to dehydration and heat continuously can lead to chronic tubulointerstitial disease that is characterized by inflammation and fibrosis [21]. Notably, providing rehydration intermittently throughout the day, rather than only at the end, significantly mitigates renal injury, even when the total amount of water consumed is the same. This finding is particularly relevant to field

workers who typically rehydrate only during lunch and at the end of their shifts. The underlying mechanism involves the development of hyperosmolarity, which activates the antidiuretic hormone (ADH) also known as vasopressin and aldose reductase/fructokinase pathway. Specifically, recurrent dehydration triggers aldose reductase activity in the proximal tubule, which converts glucose to fructose. This fructose is then metabolized by fructokinase, resulting in the production of oxidants that cause localized tubular damage [22].

4.2 Dehydration-Mediated Hyperosmolarity

Dehydration-induced hyperosmolarity induces the posterior pituitary gland to produce ADH [21]. ADH maintains the equilibrium of fluids by increasing water reabsorption in the kidneys, which decreases urine output and contributes to bodily fluid equilibrium. This hormone conserves water and protects the body against dehydration-related problems [21, 23].

Hyperosmolarity can contribute to CKDu via a variety of processes. Dehydration can decrease glomerular filtration rate and impair renal blood flow, causing kidney damage and malfunction over time. Furthermore, dehydration can promote the creation of kidney stones due to crystallization which may create obstruction in the urinary tract and harm the kidneys. Also, dehydration can cause electrolyte imbalances and the buildup of toxins in the body, further impairing renal function and potentially contributing to the development or progression of CKDu [24].

4.3 Internal Vasoconstriction and Hypoxia Caused by Heat Stress and Dehydration

Heat stress causes internal vasoconstriction, a condition in which blood vessels contract in reaction to increased body temperatures, and this restricts blood flow to muscles and organs, potentially restricting oxygen delivery and nutrition availability to kidneys which results in hypoxia. Hypoxia, in turn, reduces kidney function by decreasing renal blood flow and disrupting fluid and electrolyte balance [25]. The combination of dehydration and heat stress causes these effects, raising the risk of kidney damage. As a result, the kidneys become more vulnerable to harm, because their capacity to filter waste and maintain homeostasis is impaired [21].

4.4 Subclinical and Clinical Rhabdomyolysis in the Kidney Caused by Heat Stress and Dehydration

Rhabdomyolysis, both subclinical and clinical, can result from the combination of heat stress and severe physical labor, which causes muscle tissue disintegration and causes myoglobin and other intracellular substances to enter the circulation, potentially damaging the kidneys [21, 26]. Rhabdomyolysis-induced acute renal damage is specially a concern in CKDu conditions. Strenuous work under heat stress exacerbates the problem, making rhabdomyolysis a major risk factor for CKDu. The continuous strain on the kidneys from these repeated injuries contributes to the progression of CKDu [26].

4.5 Hyperuricosuria which Leads to Crystallization

The 'chronic recurring dehydration' theory proposes that participating in physical activity in hot surroundings without enough hydration causes increased blood osmolarity and subclinical muscle damage. This damage causes the release of purines, which increases xanthine oxidoreductase (XOR) activity and uric acid (UA) synthesis, contributing to Hyperuricemia which leads to Hyperuricosuria condition. This UA crate crystal accumulation within renal tubules resulting in tubular damage, a major contributor to the development of CKDu which causes crystallization [28]. Crystalluria condition was frequently observed among farmers in CKDu endemic areas, suggesting emphasizing the importance of maintaining appropriate hydration levels to avoid kidney disease development [28].

5. Safety Measures to Avoid Dehydration and Heat Stress

Staying hydrated is crucial in preventing dehydration which leads to kidney damage, especially in people exposed to heat stress. Promoting regular water intake and electrolyte replenishment can greatly prevent dehydration-induced kidney damage.

Workplace safety measures, such as providing shaded areas, adequate ventilation, and regular breaks in hot situations, are critical in preventing heat-related kidney injury [2]. Furthermore, ensuring that individuals are physically prepared for heavy labor in hot temperatures through regular monitoring of kidney function in persons subjected to heat stress, suitable training and conditioning programs can aid in the early diagnosis of kidney injury, allowing for timely medical intervention and avoiding acute kidney injury from progressing into CKDu. Also, individuals at high risk of kidney impairment owing to heat stress and dehydration may require medical treatments such as the use of protective medicines such as allopurinol and sodium bicarbonate, as directed by healthcare specialists [29].

Furthermore, a well-balanced diet high in antioxidants and anti-inflammatory foods can help reduce oxidative stress and inflammation in the kidneys. Limiting the intake of purine-rich foods is critical to avoid hyperuricemia, which can worsen kidney injury [27]. Implementing educational and training programs to improve knowledge of hydration, heat stress, and early indicators of dehydration can help people take proactive actions to maintain their kidney health [2].

6. Conclusion

CKDu continues to be an enormous danger to public health, particularly within agricultural communities across the world. Multiple mechanisms were hypothesized to be the cause of renal damage reason to CKDu such as tubulointerstitial disease with fibrosis or nephritis, dehydration-mediated hyperosmolarity induces vasopressin, internal vasoconstriction, hypoxia, crystallization, subclinical and clinical rhabdomyolysis in the kidney.

Several explanations have been proposed, and studies carried out in Sri Lanka including heat stress, dehydration, alcohol intake, metals and trace elements, exposure to agrochemicals, polluted water and agricultural land usage, intake of heavy metal-contaminated food, and smoking even though the specific causes of CKDu are unknown. The most attention was going to hypotheses such as agrochemicals, metals, trace elements, and hard water while heat stress and dehydration were not studied sharply. Therefore, further research is essential to determine the relationship between dehydration, heat stress and CKDu in tropical countries including Sri Lanka due to the higher impact of heat from the sun throughout the whole year. In order to comprehend how heat stress and dehydration contribute to the development of CKDu, it is necessary to examine various occupational settings where workers experience dehydration and heat stress with other variety of environmental and physical conditions. This thorough approach will assist in identifying unique risk variables and informing effective preventative efforts suited to each occupational group.

REFERENCES

1. K. B. Jayasekara *et al.*, "Relevance of heat stress and dehydration to chronic kidney disease (CKDu) in Sri Lanka," *Preventive Medicine Reports*, vol. 15, p. 100928, Sep. 2019, doi: https://doi.org/10.1016/j.pmedr.2019.100928.
2. W. V. D. Priyadarshani, A. F. D. de Namor, and S. R. P. Silva, "Rising of a global silent killer: critical analysis of chronic kidney disease of uncertain aetiology (CKDu) worldwide and mitigation steps," *Environmental Geochemistry and Health*, Sep. 2022, doi: https://doi.org/10.1007/s10653-022-01373-y.

3. A. Chattopadhyay, S. Podder, S. Agarwal, and S. Bhattacharya, "Fluoride-induced histopathology and synthesis of stress protein in liver and kidney of mice," *Archives of Toxicology*, vol. 85, no. 4, pp. 327–335, Sep. 2010, doi: https://doi.org/10.1007/s00204-010-0588-7.

4. V. M. Weaver, J. J. Fadrowski, and B. G. Jaar, "Global dimensions of chronic kidney disease of unknown etiology (CKDu): a modern era environmental and/or occupational nephropathy?," *BMC Nephrology*, vol. 16, no. 1, Aug. 2015, doi: https://doi.org/10.1186/s12882-015-0105-6.

5. H. M. Abeywickrama *et al.*, "Quality of Life and Symptom Burden among Chronic Kidney Disease of Uncertain Etiology (CKDu) Patients in Girandurukotte, Sri Lanka," *International Journal of Environmental Research and Public Health*, vol. 17, no. 11, p. 4041, Jun. 2020, doi: https://doi.org/10.3390/ijerph17114041.

6. N. Jayatilake, S. Mendis, P. Maheepala, and F. R. Mehta, "Chronic kidney disease of uncertain aetiology: prevalence and causative factors in a developing country," *BMC Nephrology*, vol. 14, no. 1, Aug. 2013, doi: https://doi.org/10.1186/1471-2369-14-180.

7. K. E. Levine *et al.*, "Quest to identify geochemical risk factors associated with chronic kidney disease of unknown etiology (CKDu) in an endemic region of Sri Lanka—a multimedia laboratory analysis of biological, food, and environmental samples," *Environmental Monitoring and Assessment*, vol. 188, no. 10, Sep. 2016, doi: https://doi.org/10.1007/s10661-016-5524-8.

8. S. Nanayakkara and L. Chandrasiri, "Heat-related public health impacts based on the WBGT index in Colombo, Sri Lanka", [Online]. Available: http://www.bom.gov.au

9. "Sri Lanka climate risk country profile," 2021. Available: https://climateknowledgeportal.worldbank.org/sites/default/files/2021-05/15507-WB_Sri%20Lanka%20Country%20Profile-WEB.pdf

10. L. C and K. N, "Identification of Social and Occupational Risk Factors Associated with CKDu (Chronic Kidney Disease of Unknown Etiology) Patients Living in an Agricultural Community in Kebithigollewa, Sri Lanka," *International Journal of Nephrology and Kidney Failure*, vol. 7, no. 4, 2021, doi: https://doi.org/10.16966/2380-5498.217.

11. C. Jayasumana, S. Gunatilake, and P. Senanayake, "Glyphosate, Hard Water and Nephrotoxic Metals: Are They the Culprits Behind the Epidemic of Chronic Kidney Disease of Unknown Etiology in Sri Lanka?," *International Journal of Environmental Research and Public Health*, vol. 11, no. 2, pp. 2125–2147, Feb. 2014, doi: https://doi.org/10.3390/ijerph110202125.

12. S. Nanayakkara *et al.*, "Evidence of tubular damage in the very early stage of chronic kidney disease of uncertain etiology in the North Central Province of Sri Lanka: a cross-sectional study," *Environmental Health and Preventive Medicine*, vol. 17, no. 2, pp. 109–117, Jun. 2011, doi: https://doi.org/10.1007/s12199-011-0224-z.

13. S. Wijetunge, N. V. I. Ratnatunga, T. D. J. Abeysekera, A. W. M. Wazil, and M. Selvarajah, "Endemic chronic kidney disease of unknown etiology in Sri Lanka: Correlation of pathology with clinical stages," *Indian Journal of Nephrology*, vol. 25, no. 5, p. 274, 2015, doi: https://doi.org/10.4103/0971-4065.145095.

14. S. Rajapakse, M. C. Shivanthan, and M. Selvarajah, "Chronic kidney disease of unknown etiology in Sri Lanka," *International Journal of Occupational and Environmental Health*, vol. 22, no. 3, pp. 259–264, Jul. 2016, doi: https://doi.org/10.1080/10773525.2016.1203097.

15. K. Taylor, A. K. Tripathi, and E. B. Jones, "Adult Dehydration," *StatPearls*, 2022

16. C. L. Chapman, B. D. Johnson, M. D. Parker, D. Hostler, R. R. Pryor, and Z. Schlader, "Kidney physiology and pathophysiology during heat stress and the modification by exercise, dehydration, heat acclimation and aging," *Temperature*, vol. 8, no. 2, pp. 108–159, Oct. 2020, doi: https://doi.org/10.1080/23328940.2020.1826841.

17. M. N. Cramer, D. Gagnon, O. Laitano, and C. G. Crandall, "Human temperature regulation under heat stress in health, disease, and injury," *Physiological Reviews*, vol. 102, no. 4, pp. 1907–1989, Oct. 2022, doi: https://doi.org/10.1152/physrev.00047.2021.

18. P. Boonruksa, T. Maturachon, P. Kongtip, and S. Woskie, "Heat Stress, Physiological Response, and Heat-Related Symptoms among Thai Sugarcane Workers," *International Journal of Environmental Research and Public Health*, vol. 17, no. 17, p. 6363, Sep. 2020, doi: https://doi.org/10.3390/ijerph17176363.

19. G. Howard D. and K. Risto, *Industrial Ventilation Design Guidebook*. Elsevier, 2020. doi: https://doi.org/10.1016/c2017-0-04103-4.

20. S. Carter, E. Oppermann, E. Field, and M. Brearley, "The impact of perceived heat stress symptoms on work-related tasks and social factors: A cross-sectional survey of Australia's Monsoonal North," *Appl Ergon*, vol. 82, 2020, doi: 10.1016/j.apergo.2019.102918.

21. P. M. C. S. De Silva *et al.*, "Occupational heat exposure alone may not explain chronic kidney disease of uncertain aetiology (CKDu) in Sri Lanka," *The Journal of Climate Change and Health*, p. 100143, Jun. 2022, doi: https://doi.org/10.1016/j.joclim.2022.100143.

22. J. Glaser *et al.*, "Climate Change and the Emergent Epidemic of CKD from Heat Stress in Rural Communities: The Case for Heat Stress Nephropathy," *Clinical Journal of the American Society of Nephrology*, vol. 11, no. 8, pp. 1472–1483, May 2016, doi: https://doi.org/10.2215/cjn.13841215.

23. C. Wenneberg, "Physiology, Vasopressin," *StatPearls*, vol. 12, no. 1, 2022.

24. N. Bouby, S. Bachmann, D. Bichet, and L. Bankir, "Effect of water intake on the progression of chronic renal failure in the 5/6 nephrectomized rat," *American Journal of Physiology-Renal Physiology*, vol. 258, no. 4, pp. F973–F979, Apr. 1990, doi: https://doi.org/10.1152/ajprenal.1990.258.4.f973.

25. A. P. Akerman, M. Tipton, C. T. Minson, and J. D. Cotter, "Heat stress and dehydration in adapting for performance: Good, bad, both, or neither?," *Temperature*, vol. 3, no. 3, pp. 412–436, Jul. 2016, doi: https://doi.org/10.1080/23328940.2016.1216255.

26. T. Komada *et al.*, "Role of NLRP3 Inflammasomes for Rhabdomyolysis-induced Acute Kidney Injury," *Scientific Reports*, vol. 5, no. 1, Jun. 2015, doi: https://doi.org/10.1038/srep10901.

27. H. W. Korsmo, U. S. Ekperikpe, and I. S. Daehn, "Emerging Roles of Xanthine Oxidoreductase in Chronic Kidney Disease," *Antioxidants*, vol. 13, no. 6, p. 712, Jun. 2024, doi: https://doi.org/10.3390/antiox13060712.

28. J. Crowe, M. Nilsson, T. Kjellstrom, and C. Wesseling, "Heat-Related Symptoms in Sugarcane Harvesters," 2015.

29. Dinesha Himali Sudusinghe, Y. Aggarwal, C. Laing, and M. Harber, "Prevention and Treatment of Acute Kidney Injury," *Springer eBooks*, pp. 197–226, Jan. 2022, doi: https://doi.org/10.1007/978-3-030-76419-7_10.

Transformative Applied Research in Computing, Engineering, Science and Technology – Dr. Damayanthi Dahanayake et al. (eds)
© 2024 Taylor & Francis Group, London, ISBN 978-1-041-01782-0

45

Exploring the Benefits of Natural Plant Compounds in Hair Oils—A Mini Review

I.G.E.P. Jayasinghe and D. Dahanayake*

Department of Biomedical Science, NSBM Green University,
Sri Lanka

Abstract

In today's global landscape, there is a heightened focus on hair care as individuals recognize the significance of maintaining healthy and lustrous hair. The nutritional needs of hair have garnered attention not only in Sri Lanka but also worldwide, reflecting the integral role of hair health in personal grooming and self-esteem. Traditional Indian medicine has long extolled the virtues of herbal remedies in supporting scalp health and addressing various hair concerns. Herbal-based hair oils, enriched with bioactive ingredients sourced from medicinal herbs such as coconut oil, keekiridiya, amla, savandara, aloe vera, curry leaves, hibiscus, fenugreek, black cumin, and onion, have emerged as favored formulations for preventing hair problems and promoting robust hair growth. This review underscores the importance of these essential constituents, providing a comprehensive overview of their historical significance and potential health benefits in the context of herbal hair oils. With their diverse pharmacological properties, including antibacterial, anti-inflammatory, antioxidant, and hair-growth-promoting effects, these herbal ingredients work synergistically to fortify hair shafts, nourish hair follicles, and provide essential moisture for scalp health. Furthermore, the formulation of herbal hair oils considers the complex structure of human hair and the dynamic nature of hair follicles, ensuring optimal delivery of bioactive components to the intended sites. In conclusion, herbal-based hair oils offer a natural, safe, and effective solution for maintaining optimal scalp and hair conditions, thereby enhancing both the health and aesthetic appeal of hair.

Keywords

Herbal hair oil, Healthy hair, Skin, Penetration, Natural compounds

1. Introduction

Hair is made up of keratinized protein strands that emerge from dermal follicles and influence a person's overall appearance. Hair strength, condition, and texture can all affect one's physical appearance. Targeted therapies are frequently necessary for common hair-related issues such as trichoptilosis (split ends), canities (graying of the hair), seborrheic dermatitis (dandruff), and alopecia (hair loss). Alopecia is a common illness that can afflict people of

*Corresponding author: damayanthi.d@nsbm.ac.lk

DOI: 10.1201/9781003616368-45

various racial and gender identities. The hair care industry has created solutions containing bioactive components to address these issues and try to mitigate them. Certain herbal and botanical therapies have long been known to support hair health and growth in traditional Indian medicine, or Ayurveda. Based on these principles, herbal hair oils are formulated to tackle conditions such as alopecia, split ends, and other hair-related disorders [1]. These oils are made from plants and include bioactive substances that improve the health of the scalp and encourage hair development. These plants' bioactive ingredients have antibacterial, anti-inflammatory, and antioxidant properties that support the upkeep of healthy scalp and hair. These medicinal plants can be added to hair oils for a natural, scientifically supported way to promote the health of the scalp and hair [2]. Herbal hair oils are frequently used to treat a range of hair-related issues, encourage hair growth, keep the scalp hydrated, and improve the sheen of hair. These oils are full of vital elements that help to maintain healthy hair growth by controlling the activity of sebaceous glands. The need for hair oils has grown as living standards have increased. These oils are more appealing to consumers since they frequently have natural smells and tints made from plant extracts [3].

2. Hair and Delivery Mechanisms

Human hair on the scalp is made by the body and has a complicated inside structure as shown in Fig. 45.1. It usually grows about 90 cm long in grown-ups and is 20 to 180 μm wide. Hair has different layers: the cortex, medulla, and cuticle, which are all held together by a special cell membrane. The cuticle is the outside layer and has flat, overlapping cells that are 6-7 μm apart, like scales. The very top part of the cuticle is the epicuticle, a thin layer of lipo-protein about 10-14 nm thickness [4]. Under that is a

layer rich in cysteine, then the exocuticle, which has a lot of cysteine and can be different thicknesses, and finally the endocuticle, which has less cysteine and is about the same thickness. The main part of the hair is cortex and has cells shaped like spindles that line up along the hair's length. Cortical cells are categorized into ortho cortex, paracortex, and mesocortex, and their distribution influences the hair fiber's curvature [5]. In straight hair, the ortho and paracortices are generally symmetrically distributed, whereas, in curly hair, they are asymmetrically distributed [6]. Keratin, the primary protein in many cortical cells, imparts structural stability and defines the characteristics of the hair [4].

The way substances work when applied to the skin is affected by the shape, density, and health of hair follicles. The hair follicle cycle, which is made up of the anagen (growth), catagen (regression), and telogen (resting) phases, as shown as in Fig. 45.2 [8]. During their existence, hair follicles go through regular growth cycles. The key changes that take place during these cycles are the development of new hair shafts (HS), the shedding of existing hair, and modifications to the morphology and structure of the dermal papillae at the base of the follicles. More vascularization in the anagen phase improves blood flow to the follicle, promoting cellular development and active hair growth. Follicle regression and growth stoppage are caused by a reduction in blood flow as the follicle enters the catagen and telogen phases. The immunological privilege of the follicle is modulated by this cyclical activity, which may result in inflammatory reactions during catagen and telogen and immune evasion during anagen. Apoptosis, keratinocyte proliferation, hair shaft production, and follicular regeneration are all regulated by phase-dependent gene expression within the follicle

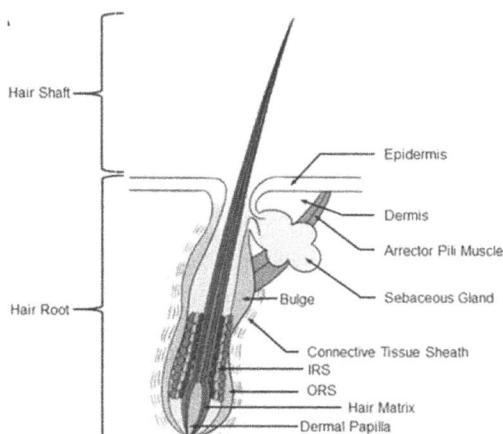

Fig. 45.1 The cross section of hair follicle [5]

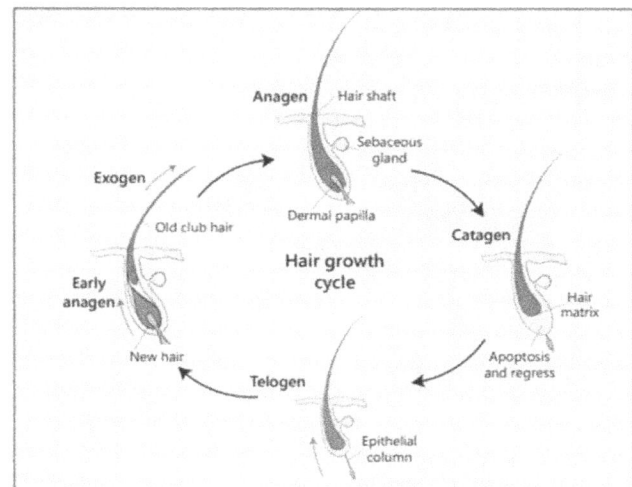

Fig. 45.2 Hair growth cycle [7]

[7]. When making ways to deliver medicine through the skin, we need to consider how hair follicles change. Hair follicles can be either open or closed. Open follicles allow skin application and absorption of ingredients, oil flow, and hair growth, while closed follicles are blocked by dry oil, dead skin cells, and other debris, stopping absorption and oil flow. The absorbance of a substances depends on the size and the hair follicles count [9].

The complex nature and intricate mechanisms of hair follicles makes penetration through the follicular pathway as a complex process. Encapsulation of a drug in particulate carriers significantly decreases transdermal transmission, because the particles are preferentially retained in the follicular orifices and tend to penetrate the orifices of hair follicles [10]. The drug penetration through the skin can take place following two primary routes: the trans-epidermal pathway and the follicular penetration pathway. As shown in Fig. 45.3, molecules travel through the stratums corneum, a mechanically intricate, stratified, multicellular barrier, in the trans epidermal pathway [6]. There are two pathways of follicular pathway: the intra-cellular pathway and extra-cellular pathway. The intra-cellular route involves the passage of molecules across corneocytes, terminally differentiated keratinocytes, which can allow molecules such as hydrophilic or polar solutes to pass across the skin. The inter-cellular pathway involves the diffusion of molecules over a lipid matrix located between cells as well as the transport of lipophilic or non-polar solutes. Also, molecules pass through the sweat glands and hair follicles in the follicular penetration pathway [11]. These nutritional molecules enter the blood circulation through these pathways and provide nourishment to the hair and scalp. Due to their restricted blood supply, nutrients intended for hair follicles are frequently less efficient [8]. The skin's vasculature, composed of plexus and post-capillary venules, provides glucose and oxygen to the follicle bases. This network promotes hair development by encouraging dermal papillae stem cells and facilitating their rapid production during the anagen phase [7]. The vascular niche governs hair physiology from the embryonic stage onwards. The proper establishment of capillary beds and angiogenesis is necessary for hair growth. Blood arteries join stem cells during development stages of the hair cycle, from which covering the bulge area. Proteins located in the upper bulge region stimulate vasculature growth and angiogenesis [12].

3. Important Compounds and Actions

Hair oil contains a variety of components, including essential nutrients that promote hair health and growth. Coconut oil is the primary carrier for optimal absorption and penetration into the scalp and hair shaft, due to its ability to penetrate the hair shaft and soothe the scalp, making it effective for treating scalp and hair loss. The principal fatty acid in coconut oil, lauric acid, enhances hair health and is readily distributed. Lauric acid and monolaurin are valuable additions to hair oil formulation because they have strong antibacterial effect against gram-positive bacteria, fungi, and viruses [13]. Additionally, *Aloe barbadensis miller, Phyllanthus emblica, Trigonella foenum-graecum, Hibiscus rosa-sinensis* like herbal plants include essential nutrients such as vitamins B, C, E, and D, and minerals such as zinc, iron, sulfur, and selenium are essential for preserving cellular turnover and the hair follicular cycle. Deficiencies in these nutrients can lead to hair loss, as they are vital for normal cell growth and function. Flavonoids provide antioxidant activity, protecting hair follicles from free radical damage and potentially reducing hair loss and thinning. Therefore, a comprehensive hair oil should include these nutrients and bioactive compounds to enhance hair health and prevent losing hair [14].

4. Oil Ingreadients

4.1 Coconut Oil - (Cocos Nucifera)

Its rich content of lauric acid and other fatty acids (caprylic acid C -8:0 (8%), capric acid, C-10:0,(7%), lauric acid C-12:0, (49%), myristic acid C-14:0(8%), palmitic acid C-16:0 (8%), stearic acid C-18:0 (2%), oleic acid C-18:1 (6%) and 2% of C-18:2 linoleic acid) allows it to penetrate the hair shaft, reducing water absorption and limiting [15]. Coconut oil exhibits antifungal properties, promotes the growth of beneficial bacteria, reduces scalp flaking, and may aid in repairing the skin barrier [16]. Nevertheless, with its proven effectiveness in promoting healthy hair and scalp, coconut oil remains a natural and beneficial option for those seeking to improve their hair care regimen [2, 17].

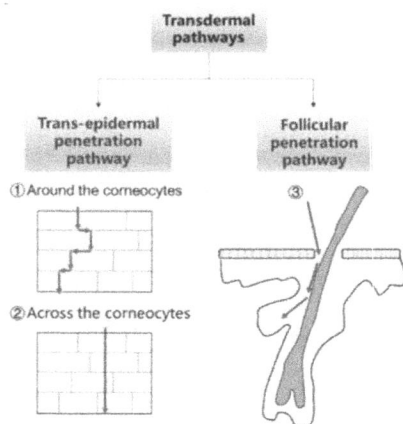

Fig. 45.3 Transdermal pathways for penetration [11]

4.2 Keekiridiya (Eclipta Alba)

Eclipta alba, commonly found in tropical and subtropical regions worldwide. Extracts from *Eclipta alba,* when ingested or applied topically, have been traditionally associated with the blackening of hair due to its rich phyto-constituents, including alkaloids, coumestans, glycosides, flavonoids, triterpenoids, and Polyacetylenesare coumestan derivatives like wedololactone(1.6%), demethylwedelolactone, desmethyl-wedelolactone-7glucoside and other constituents are ecliptal, β-amyrin, luteolin-7-O-glucoside, hentriacontanol, heptacosanol, stigmasterol [18]. Wedelolactone, stigmasterol, and various glucosides are among the identified compounds in its leaves, roots, and aerial parts [1]. *Eclipta alba* stands out as a versatile botanical for scalp and hair health. In ayurvedic hair care formulations, *Eclipta alba* is renowned for its ability to promote hair growth, imparting a soft and shiny appearance to the hair while preventing scalp dryness and itchiness [3]. Its role extends beyond aesthetics, offering nourishment and soothing effects to both hair and body. With its extensive array of bioactive compounds, *Eclipta alba* demonstrates antioxidant, antimicrobial, and hair growth-promoting properties, making it a valuable ingredient in hair care products aimed at preventing hair loss, stimulating hair growth, and restoring hair health [19].

4.3 Nelli (Emblica)

Commonly known as Indian Gooseberry or Amla, is revered for its rich content of: alkaloids (Phyllantidine, phyllostine), vitamin C, Gallot annis (5%), carbohydrates (14%), pectin, minerals, phenolic acid, gallic acid, ellagic acid, phloemic acid, embolic, amino acid (alanine, aspartic acid, glutamic acid, lysine, proline), tannins, and minerals like phosphorus, iron, and calcium, which not only nourish the hair but also contribute to its darkening. This emblica is celebrated for its multifaceted benefits in hair care, including strengthening hair follicles, combating dandruff, and promoting healthy hair growth. With its anti-inflammatory properties, amla soothes the scalp and prevents premature greying, making it a popular choice in traditional hair care remedies [3]. Its chemical constituents, such as alkaloids, gallotannins, and various acids, further enhance its efficacy in maintaining scalp health and stimulating hair growth. Whether used in herbal hair oils or consumed internally, Amla continues to be a cornerstone in hair care formulations, offering a natural and comprehensive approach to achieving strong, lustrous hair [2 ,20 ,21].

4.4 Savandara (Vetiveria Zizanioides)

Vetiveria zizanioides, commonly known as vetiver, possesses remarkable properties beneficial for hair health.

Its essential oil exhibits potent antifungal, antimicrobial, and antioxidant activities. Derived from the aromatic roots of the vetiver plant, vetiver oil is renowned for its ability to promote hair growth by stimulating blood circulation to the scalp, nourishing hair follicles, and reducing scalp irritation. It contains sesquiterpenes that enhance blood flow, delivering essential nutrients and oxygen to the hair follicles for healthy growth [22]. Additionally, vetiver oil's anti-inflammatory properties help reduce scalp inflammation, which can contribute to hair loss [3]. Moreover, vetiver oil strengthens hair roots, which nourish and fortify the hair shaft, making it resilient to breakage. Its astringent properties tighten the hair follicles. Additionally, vetiver oil conditions the hair, moisturizing and softening it for improved manageability and styling. Vetiver oil is rich in chemical components such as vetiverol, vetiverone, and khusimo vetiverol, benzoic acid, furfurol, α-vetivone, β-vetivone, α- and β-vetispirene, terpenes[22,23].

4.5 Aloe Vera (Aloe Barbadensis Miller)

Aloe vera acts as a potent conditioner, imparting smoothness and shine to the hair while fostering growth, relieving scalp itchiness, reducing dandruff, and enhancing overall hair health [3]. Its effectiveness stems from a rich array of active components, including vitamins (A, C, E, B12, folic acid), enzymes (such as bradykinase), minerals (calcium, magnesium, zinc), sugars (glucose, fructose, polysaccharides), anthraquinones, fatty acids (cholesterol, campesterol, β-sisosterol and lupeol), hormones (auxins, gibberellins), and other essential amino acids and compounds like salicylic acid and lignin. These constituents contribute to its antioxidant, anti-inflammatory, antibacterial, and cleansing properties, making aloe vera a versatile and beneficial ingredient for hair care and scalp health [2].

4.6 Curry Leaves (Murraya Koenigii)

Curry leaves, scientifically known as *Murraya koenigii*, are packed with essential nutrients beneficial for hair health. They contain significant amounts of vitamin A (beta-carotene), calcium, potent ingredients. Vitamin C, and fiber, making them a potent ingredient for promoting hair growth and preventing hair loss and thinning. Additionally, curry leaves are rich in proteins, crucial for the development and strength of hair, as hair itself is composed of protein [21]. The amino acid content in curry leaves further enhances the hair fiber's strength, contributing to healthier and stronger hair. Moreover, these leaves are known for their ability to prevent hair greying and effectively treat damaged hair, adding bounce to limp hair, strengthening thin hair shafts, and addressing issues like hair fall and dandruff [2].

4.7 Hibiscus (Hibiscus Rosa-Sinensis)

Hibiscus (*Hibiscus rosa-sinensis*), characterized by its large, trumpet-shaped flowers. It is commonly found throughout the tropics and is often grown as a house plant worldwide [3]. The dried flower of *Hibiscus rosa sinensis*, is utilized for various hair care purposes. Hibiscus leaves are rich in flavonoids, alkaloids, glycosides, tannins, and steroids/terpenoids and known for their potent hair-strengthening properties [17,21]. Ethanol extracts of hibiscus leaves have been found to contain active constituents such as flavonoids and tannins, which contribute to their ability to promote hair growth and treat scalp conditions like dandruff and itchiness. In vivo testing with animals has demonstrated that ethanol extracts of hibiscus leaves can effectively stimulate hair growth, with optimum concentrations of 10% extract exhibiting remarkable results. Overall, hibiscus is valued for its ability to prevent hair loss, prevent premature greying, thicken hair, add volume, and treat dandruff, making it a popular choice in natural hair care remedies [1,2].

4.8 Uluhal (Trigonella Foenum-Graecum)

Fenugreek, also known as Methi seed, stands out as one of the most effective home remedies for preventing hair loss and promoting hair regrowth. Derived from the dried seeds of *Trigonella foenum graceum* or fenugreek offers a range of benefits for hair health. It aids in repairing damaged hair follicles and controlling scalp inflammation, resulting in shinier and softer hair. Fenugreek seed extract is rich in micronutrients such as B-vitamins, antioxidants, and trace elements [17]. This leguminous herb, native to Southern Europe, Western Asia, and the mediterranean region, contains various active ingredients including saponins, trigonelline alkaloids, flavonoids, vitamins, and fiber. While the exact mechanism by which fenugreek promotes hair growth is not fully understood, it is believed to enhance the blood supply to hair follicles and regulate the synthesis of dihydrotestosterone (DHT), a hormone associated with hair loss. By binding to genetically predisposed hair follicles, DHT can lead to progressive miniaturization and eventual hair loss. Fenugreek's ability to interact with DHT synthesis underscores its potential as a natural remedy for combating hair loss and supporting overall hair health [2,21].

4.9 Kaluduru (Nigella Sativa)

Nigella sativa, commonly known as black cumin, is an annual flowering plant native to the mediterranean countries, Pakistan, and India. This plant contains key pharmacologically active components such as thymoquinone (TQ), dithymoquinone (DTQ), thymohydroquinone (THQ), and thymol (THY). These compounds exhibit anti-inflammatory properties by inhibiting nuclear factor kappa B (NF-kB) activation, and prostaglandin D2 (PGD2) synthesis. *Nigella sattva's* ability to inhibit NF-kB and PGD2 activation and synthesis can potentially regulate the hair cycle, promoting the growth and preservation of healthy hair [24]. Black seed oil extracted from *Nigella sativa* seeds has been used for centuries in various treatments due to its antibacterial, antifungal, anti-inflammatory, and antioxidant properties. Advocates of black seed oil for hair care claim that it can treat dandruff, moisturize the scalp, soothe inflammation, and promote hair regrowth in thinning areas [17].

4.10 Onion (Allium Cepa)

The onion, scientifically known as *Allium cepa*, is rich in phenolics, flavonoids, and sulfur compounds, onions boast a range of health benefits. These properties make onions effective in treating various scalp issues, such as dandruff and infections, while also inhibiting hair thinning and slowing down premature greying [2]. The antibacterial properties of onions combat scalp infections, while the sulfur content enhances blood circulation to the hair follicles, promoting hair growth and controlling hair loss. Additionally, the sulfur in onion juice aids in the production of essential collagen, which further stimulates hair growth. Moreover, the antioxidants found in onions, such as flavonoids, help protect the hair follicles from damage caused by free radicals, potentially reducing hair thinning and loss. Overall, onions serve as a natural remedy for maintaining healthy hair and scalp, nourishing dry or brittle hair, and supporting hair regrowth [3].

5. Conclusion

Herbal-based hair oils have garnered significant attention due to their diverse array of ingredients, each packed with bioactive compounds essential for promoting scalp health and addressing various hair concerns. Ingredients such as coconut oil, keekiridiya, amla, savandara, aloe vera, curry leaves, hibiscus, fenugreek, black cumin, and onion. These compounds exhibit potent anti-inflammatory, antibacterial, and antioxidant properties, alongside actions that stimulate hair growth. By nourishing hair follicles, strengthening hair shafts, and providing essential moisture for scalp health, herbal-based hair oils present a natural and scientifically backed solution for maintaining optimal hair conditions. Their comprehensive approach to hair care ensures not only the improvement of hair health but also enhancement in appearance, making them a preferred choice for individuals seeking safe and effective hair care remedies.

REFERENCES

1. B. R. Kuber, Ch. Lavanya, Ch. N. Haritha, S. Preethi, and G. Rosa, "Preparation and evaluation of poly herbal hair oil," Journal of Drug Delivery and Therapeutics, vol. 9, no. 1, pp. 68–73, Jan. 2019.

2. P. S. Banerjee, M. Sharma, and R. Kumar Nema, "Preparation, evaluation and hair growth stimulating activity of herbal hair oil," 2009. J Chem Pharm Res, 1(1), 261–7.

3. K. G. Suman, B. Kumar, and S. Mukopadayay, "Herbal hair oil," Int J Health Sci (Qassim), pp. 13449–13465, Jun. 2022.

4. F. C. Yang, Y. Zhang, and M. C. Rheinstädter, "The structure of people's hair," PeerJ, vol. 2014, no. 1, 2014.

5. M. Grymowicz et al., "Hormonal effects on hair follicles," Int J Mol Sci, vol. 21, no. 15, pp. 1–13, Aug. 2020.

6. Y. Gu, Q. Bian, Y. Zhou, Q. Huang, and J. Gao, "Hair follicle-targeting drug delivery strategies for the management of hair follicle-associated disorders," May 01, 2022, Shenyang Pharmaceutical University.

7. X. Lin, L. Zhu, and J. He, "Morphogenesis, Growth Cycle and Molecular Regulation of Hair Follicles," May 12, 2022, Frontiers Media S.A. doi: 10.3389/fcell.2022.899095.

8. K. S. Houschyar et al., "Molecular Mechanisms of Hair Growth and Regeneration: Current Understanding and Novel Paradigms," Jul. 01, 2020, S. Karger AG. doi: 10.1159/000506155.

9. A. Patzelt and J. Lademann, "Drug delivery to hair follicles," Jun. 2013. doi: 10.1517/17425247.2013.776038.

10. Y. Gu, Q. Bian, Y. Zhou, Q. Huang, and J. Gao, "Hair follicle-targeting drug delivery strategies for the management of hair follicle-associated disorders," May 01, 2022, Shenyang Pharmaceutical University. doi: 10.1016/j.ajps.2022.04.003.

11. A. Z. Alkilani, M. T. C. McCrudden, and R. F. Donnelly, "Transdermal drug delivery: Innovative pharmaceutical developments based on disruption of the barrier properties of the stratum corneum," Oct. 22, 2015, MDPI AG. doi: 10.3390/pharmaceutics7040438.

12. S. Salim and K. Kamalasanan, "Controlled drug delivery for alopecia: A review," Sep. 10, 2020, Elsevier B.V. doi: 10.1016/j.jconrel.2020.06.019.

13. F. M. Dayrit, "The Properties of Lauric Acid and Their Significance in Coconut Oil," J Am Oil Chem Soc, vol. 92, no. 1, pp. 1–15, Jan. 2015, doi: 10.1007/s11746-014-2562-7.

14. H. M. Almohanna Azhar A Ahmed John P Tsatalis Antonella Tosti, H. M. Almohanna, A. A. Ahmed, J. P. Tsatalis Á A Tosti, and A. Tosti, "The Role of Vitamins and Minerals in Hair Loss: A Review", doi: 10.6084/m9.figshare.7398692.

15. S. Nur, A. Haninah, S. M. Fauzi, N. Bajiru, and A. Husain, "HaniAisya Hair Oil MALAYSIA *Corresponding Author Designation," Multidisciplinary Applied Research and Innovation, vol. 3, no. 4, pp. 161–168, 2022, doi: 10.30880/mari.2022.03.04.023.

16. A. Rahman Mat Amin, R. Abu Bakar, and R. Jaafar, "The effectiveness of coconut oil mixed with herbs to promote hair growth," 2014. [Online]. Available: www.ijeee.in

17. R. Tiwari, G. Tiwari, A. Yadav, and V. Ramachandran, "Development and Evaluation of Herbal Hair Serum: A traditional way to Improve Hair Quality," Open Dermatol J, vol. 15, no. 1, pp. 52–58, Jan. 2022, doi: 10.2174/18743722011150100052.

18. C. S. Lee, J. A. Kang, G. Y. Kim, and G. R. Kim, "A study on the effect of eclipta prostrata extract and mts on the improvement of scalp health and prevention of hair loss for workers in their 20s and 30s," Medico-Legal Update, vol. 20, no. 1, pp. 1850–1856, Jan. 2020, doi: 10.37506/v20/i1/2020/mlu/194573.

19. Sumanta Mondal, "p38," Asian Journal of Pharmacy and Pharmacology 2016; 2(5): 121–127, 2016.

20. P. K. Jain, "Evaluating Hair Growth Activity of Herbal Hair Oil," 2016. [Online]. Available: https://www.researchgate.net/publication/301553424

21. A. A. Joshi and P. M. Dyawarkonda, "Formulation and evaluation of polyherbal hair oil."

22. U. R. M. Arpana Ashokrao Durge*1, "1529-Article Text-1578-1-10-20220715," Durge et al., J Adv Sci Res, 2021; ICITNAS: 01–06, 2021.

23. M. Nazrul and I. Bhuiyan, Essential oil in roots of Vetiveria zizanioides. 2008. [Online]. Available: https://www.researchgate.net/publication/244478796

24. H. Verma, S. P. Sudhir, V. O. Deshmukh, and H. N. Verma, "Nigella sativa seed, a novel beauty care ingredient: A review," Article in International Journal of Pharmaceutical Sciences and Research, vol. 7, no. 8, p. 3185, 2016, doi: 10.13040/IJPSR.0975-8232.7(8).3185–96.

Transformative Applied Research in Computing, Engineering, Science and Technology – Dr. Damayanthi Dahanayake et al. (eds)
© 2024 Taylor & Francis Group, London, ISBN 978-1-041-01782-0

46

Multimodal Stock Price Prediction— Integrating Machine Learning, Reinforcement Learning, and Sentiment Analysis of News Headlines

Shemeen Fernando*

Independent Researcher, Colombo,
Sri Lanka

Rasika Ranaweera

Faculty of Postgraduate Studies, NSBM Green University,
Sri Lanka

Abstract

The stock market plays a critical role within the broader financial market by providing a venue for trading company stocks at mutually agreed prices among market participants. Understanding fluctuations in market parameters is crucial for investors, and this research addresses this by proposing a stock price prediction system that utilizes machine learning, reinforcement learning, and sentiment analysis through NLP of news headlines. The goal is to reduce trading risks and increase profits compared to traditional statistical methods and simplistic time series forecasting techniques. The proposed system offers advantages by leveraging advanced machine learning models to analyze vast datasets more effectively. Machine learning and deep reinforcement learning are used to forecast market trends and generate buy and sell signals. The proposed ensemble model combines LSTM networks, ARIMA, and a reinforcement learning agent, with the LSTM model incorporating sentiment analysis of daily stock news. Each model makes individual predictions, which are then combined into a final forecast through a weighted average based on each model's accuracy. The accuracy is assessed by comparing predicted prices with actual prices over multiple weeks of testing conducted over a seven-day period. This study illustrates how integrating advanced technologies can help understand and navigate the complexities of the stock market.

Keywords

Stock prediction, Reinforcement learning (RL), Long short-term memory (LSTM), Autoregressive integrated moving average (ARIMA), Natural language processing (NLP)

1. Introduction

The stock market is regarded as a crucial element of a country's economy, offering one of the largest investment opportunities for businesses and investors. For investors, it can be an opportune time to purchase new stocks and earn dividends through the company's shareholder programs. Additionally, investors can engage in trading within the

*Corresponding author: fdoshemeen61@gmail.com

DOI: 10.1201/9781003616368-46

stock market. Although investing in the stock market carries risks, a disciplined approach can lead to substantial profits. Before purchasing stocks of a specific company, investors typically evaluate the company to make informed decisions about potentially risky investments. This evaluation involves analyzing the company's historical performance and consulting financial news sources, among other factors. Given the vast amount of data to consider, investors may struggle with thorough analysis. Therefore, an automated decision support system is necessary to assist in making informed investment decisions.

This research focuses on developing an automated stock price prediction system by harnessing the capabilities of information technology and machine learning techniques. Recent advancements in algorithmic trading, such as high-frequency trading algorithms and machine learning-based predictive analytics, have intensified the pursuit of effective prediction models. The aim of this study is to fill the gaps in existing research by integrating sentiment analysis from online news sources like Alphavantage into the automated prediction system. The primary objective is to develop a reliable and precise model that not only improves decision-making but also mitigates the challenges associated with emotional biases that traders encounter in manual predictions.

In the financial industry, predicting financial data, specifically stock prices, has long been an interesting topic [1]. Among the various methods employed for stock market prediction, statistical and econometric methods that analyze past market movements have been the most widely adopted [2]. Numerous studies have demonstrated that machine learning models often outperform classical forecasting techniques [3, 4]. Incorporating sentiment analysis has been shown to enhance prediction accuracy by capturing market sentiment that traditional methods might overlook, thus providing a more nuanced view of potential price movements. This has led to widespread use of automated trading systems and an increasing demand for higher yields, driving researchers and practitioners to continuously develop and seek better models for forecasting stock prices. Consequently, the fields of finance and computational intelligence are consistently inundated with new implementations and publications.

2. Literature Review

This measurement and others are deliberate, using specifications that anticipate your paper as one part of the entire proceedings, and not as an independent document. Please do not revise any of the current designations. Stock market researchers have employed various techniques,

including reinforcement learning and machine learning, to mine historical data, news articles, and social media posts for creating prediction models. Research on stock prediction has utilized historical data [5, 6, 7], social media data [8, 9], and news data [10, 11, 12] to forecast the stock market using machine learning algorithms. Various predictive models have been proposed, each leveraging different types of data to enhance prediction accuracy. Ultimately, these systems offer valuable insights to investors, aiding decisions to buy, sell, or hold stocks.

Researchers have also implemented methods, including deep learning [12] and regression analysis [13], to analyze historical stock prices. Historical data is often used in technical analysis to predict future trends [10]. However, external influences, such as unexpected social media events and financial news, can also impact stock prices [12, 14]. Predicting financial data's complexity stems from this uncertainty, with elements like traders' expectations, economic conditions, and political developments making accurate forecasting a challenge. A recent study carried out by Vijh et al. (2020) noted that stock markets are inherently unpredictable and dynamic [3]. Historically, researchers relied on past stock prices for predictions before the rise of social media and financial news. Accurate forecasting can significantly influence traders' buy or sell decisions. With advancements in deep learning, stock price prediction has become a prominent research area, though the task remains complex and time-consuming due to the stock market's characteristics [15].

Mehta et al. (2021) proposed fundamental approaches for stock price prediction, focusing on sentiment analysis models. They utilized classification techniques and integrated news content, social media data, and historical stock data. Their findings indicated that polarity detection could determine news sentiment, influencing stock prices [16]. Other studies show a correlation between news articles and stock price movements [14].

Nelson et al. (2017) applied the LSTM model with multiple stock analysis indicators and found it outperformed traditional models and there has been extensive research in stock market prediction and LSTM applications [17, 18]. Mehta et al. (2021) found that combining sentiment analysis with historical stock prices enhances prediction accuracy, aiding informed decisions [16]. Kordonis et al. (2016) explored the influence of Twitter sentiment on stock prices, while Porshnev et al. (2013) analyzed 755 million tweets, concluding that incorporating Twitter data did not significantly improve prediction accuracy, with the highest accuracy at 64.10% for the Dow Jones Industrial Average [19, 20]. Although numerous studies have integrated sentiment analysis in stock prediction, gaps remain in comprehensive approaches that synergize multiple data sources with advanced machine learning techniques, potentially enhancing prediction accuracy and providing more robust tools for investors.

3. Methodology

The automated stock price prediction system was developed by carefully selecting technologies based on an extensive literature review. LSTM networks were chosen for their ability to identify patterns in time-series data and incorporate sentiment analysis of stock news headlines. The ARIMA model complemented this by effectively predicting stationary time-series data. Additionally, Q-Learning, a reinforcement learning technique, was selected due to its effectiveness in making sequential decisions based on the exploration-exploitation trade-off, which is crucial for optimizing trading strategies. The methodology included several key steps: identifying trends and predicting daily closing prices for AAPL, MSFT, and ORCL; collecting historical stock prices from the Yahoo Finance API for a time range of 1.5 years and news data from the Alphavantage API covering the same period; and preprocessing data to handle missing values and outliers. Real-time data collection, user interface development, model evaluation, continuous optimization, and user support ensured a robust and reliable prediction system. This comprehensive approach aimed not only at accurate predictions but also at providing a practical tool for informed trading strategies.

3.1 LSTM Model

LSTM, a type of recurrent neural network, excels in capturing long-term dependencies in sequential data, making it ideal for stock price prediction. To build the LSTM model, historical stock prices and news sentiment data are processed, cleaned, and merged. The preprocessing steps involve handling missing values through imputation techniques and removing outliers using statistical methods. Using Keras, a stacked LSTM model with dropout layers is defined, taking scaled inputs of closing prices, trading volumes, and sentiment scores. The model is trained to predict future closing prices based on these features, and both the trained model and MinMaxScaler instances are saved for future use.

3.2 ARIMA Model

ARIMA is a popular statistical method for time series forecasting that model's sequential data like stock prices by combining autoregressive (AR), differencing (I), and moving average (MA) components. The parameters (p, d, q) adjust the model to fit various data types, where

'p' represents the number of lag observations included in the model (autoregressive part), 'd' is the number of times that the raw observations are differenced (to make the series stationary), and 'q' is the size of the moving average window. For example, parameter tuning can be conducted using techniques like the Akaike Information Criterion (AIC) or Bayesian Information Criterion (BIC) to determine the optimal values. In this study, it uses an automated grid search approach for hyperparameter tuning and these ARIMA models are used to predict stock prices for multiple ticker symbols. The process involves preprocessing historical stock data, training ARIMA models for each ticker symbol based on the tuned parameters, and saving the models for future use.

3.3 RL Agent

Reinforcement Learning (RL) agents in stock price prediction learn optimal trading strategies from historical data through trial and error, unlike traditional methods. This study implements a Q-learning-based RL agent for multiple stock symbols by setting up a custom gym-like environment for each, defining the state space to include features such as current stock price, moving averages, and sentiment scores. The agents are trained with historical data, with careful tuning of the learning rate, discount factor, and exploration probability to balance exploration and exploitation effectively. After training, the models are saved, allowing for tailored trading strategies for each stock while efficiently managing resources during the process.

This method develops tailored trading strategies for each stock, efficiently managing resources during the process.

3.4 Sentiment Analysis

Sentiment analysis is crucial in stock price prediction, offering insights into the collective sentiment surrounding stocks or financial assets [19]. By automatically gauging sentiment from news articles or social media posts, it determines if the sentiment is positive, negative, or neutral. In the current study, sentiment analysis utilizes a lexicon-based approach, assessing news article sentiment related to specific stocks by identifying keywords such as "rising," "bullish," or "buy" for positive sentiment, and "falling," "bearish," or "sell" for negative sentiment. This helps classify the articles into categories based on their potential impact on stock prices, providing a clearer understanding of market sentiment.

3.5 Ensemble Model

The ensemble model combines predictions from LSTM, ARIMA, and RL models using a weighted average method, where weights are based on the Root Mean Square Error

(RMSE) of each model. Models with lower RMSE receive higher weights, integrating insights from all three models to enhance prediction accuracy and reliability, as shown in Table 46.1. RMSE is crucial for evaluating model accuracy, measuring the average error magnitude between predicted and actual stock prices. Lower RMSE values indicate higher accuracy, while higher values suggest less reliability. The weights for each model were calculated using the steps outlined below, ensuring an optimized predictive approach.

Step 1: First, compute the inverse of each model's RMSE value to obtain preliminary weights.

Step 2: Next, sum these preliminary weights to get the total weight.

Step 3: Finally, determine the final weights for each model by dividing each preliminary weight by the total weight.

Table 46.1 Weight distribution of models

Stock Symbol	Model	RMSE	Weight
AAPL	ARIMA	2.95	0.476
	LSTM	3.39	0.417
	RL Agent	13.39	0.106
MSFT	ARIMA	5.40	0.439
	LSTM	6.63	0.358
	RL Agent	11.73	0.203
ORCL	ARIMA	1.83	0.505
	LSTM	2.24	0.381
	RL Agent	8.20	0.113

This method ensures that models with lower RMSE values, which indicate higher accuracy, are given greater influence in the ensemble prediction.

4. Methodology

Hyperparameter tuning is crucial for improving the predictive accuracy of LSTM models in stock price forecasting. Key hyperparameters such as the number of units per layer and dropout rates are optimized using methods like grid search, random search, or Bayesian optimization. In this study, a RandomSearch tuner was used to enhance the LSTM model's performance by capturing complex stock price patterns and reducing overfitting. Similarly, ARIMA models require tuning of parameters (p, d, q) for accurate predictions and with the optimal values found to be AAPL = (0, 1, 0), MSFT = (1, 1, 1), and ORCL = (1, 0, 0) The parameters include the number of lag observations (p), the degree of differencing (d), and the order of the moving average (q). Historical stock price data from Yahoo Finance was used to test different parameter combinations, with the best configuration minimizing the root mean squared error (RMSE). For the reinforcement learning (RL) model, tuning focused on the learning rate, discount factor, and exploration probability. The RL agent's performance, measured by metrics like Mean Squared Error (MSE) and RMSE, was optimized through various hyperparameter combinations. After 200 episodes, the best settings were identified, enhancing the agent's adaptability in the dynamic stock market environment.

5. Evaluation and Results

The accuracy and reliability of the predictive models are rigorously evaluated over a 7-day period for multiple weeks. Each day, the models predict stock prices based on user inputs, and these predictions are compared to the actual prices the next day. Accuracy is measured by calculating the percentage of correctly predicted prices, with daily results averaged over the week to assess overall performance. This approach captures real-world stock price fluctuations and provides a robust measure of model effectiveness. Each model (ARIMA, LSTM, and RL) is tested individually, alongside an ensemble model that combines their predictions. The testing involves forecasting prices for AAPL, MSFT, and ORCL over seven days, with accuracy calculated as a percentage reflecting prediction alignment with actual prices. This process, detailed in Table 46.2 and using a specified equation, offers valuable insights into the models' reliability and effectiveness, enhancing the credibility and practical relevance of the research findings.

$$Accuracy\ Percentage = 100 - [(|Actual\ Price - Predicted\ Price| / Actual\ Price) * 100] \quad (1)$$

Table 46.2 Accuracy test results summary

Stock Symbol	Model	Average Accuracy
AAPL	ARIMA	98.04%
	LSTM	97.83%
	RL Agent	94.28%
	Ensemble	97.46%
MSTF	ARIMA	98.15%
	LSTM	94.65%
	RL Agent	91.39%
	Ensemble	96.74%
ORCL	ARIMA	97.89%
	LSTM	97.53%
	RL Agent	73.65%
	Ensemble	97.17%

The preliminary findings indicate that ARIMA performs better in short-term predictions due to its ability to model stationary time series effectively. However, for long-term forecasting, it struggles to capture complex trends, where the LSTM model, designed to identify sequential patterns, excels. The RL agent underperforms, largely due to limitations in the training process, including restricted resources and inadequate data. Despite these challenges, the ensemble model combines the strengths of each model, achieving a collective accuracy exceeding 97%. While not offering a definitive investment strategy, this ensemble approach underscores the potential of machine learning in improving stock market predictions and advancing financial market analysis.

5.1 Findings during the Development Process

One major obstacle in the project's development was the early models' reliance on training data, leading to overly linear predictions that failed to capture the complex, nonlinear nature of stock price movements. This overfitting occurred because the models were too tailored to the training data, limiting their ability to generalize to new data. To address this, techniques such as dropout layers in LSTM, cross-validation, and regularization were implemented to prevent overfitting and improve the models' ability to generalize patterns. These changes resulted in more accurate, dynamic predictions. Future work will focus on acquiring larger datasets, improving computational resources, and fine-tuning hyperparameters to further enhance prediction accuracy and model robustness. Figures 46.1 and 46.2 illustrate predicted 'AAPL' stock prices before and after resolving the dependency issue.

5.2 Findings dur Limitations and Future Work

The project faced significant challenges, including blocked access to Twitter data and limited historical news articles from the Alphavantage API, which reduced analysis depth from 10 years to 1.5 years. Training the RL agent was also constrained by limited computational power, requiring training in manageable batches. These issues highlighted the need for adaptability and problem-solving in real-world research. As the system evolves and collects more data, its ability to provide reliable stock price predictions will improve. Integrating real-time data and expanding historical datasets will enhance its adaptability to market dynamics, making it a valuable tool for investors and an educational resource for stock market prediction.

6. Conclusion

This research contributes to existing knowledge by developing advanced stock price forecasting models using LSTM, ARIMA, and RL agents, enhanced with news sentiment analysis. The ensemble model, combined with a user-friendly interface, improves prediction accuracy and practical utility for investors (Figs. 46.3, 46.4, and 46.5). Figure 46.3 shows the application's homepage, Figure 46.4 displays real-time stock price fluctuations as a dashboard in candlestick graphs, and Fig. 46.5 illustrates AAPL stock closing price predictions for a 20-day period. The integration of machine learning, reinforcement learning,

Fig. 46.1 Predictions before solving the dependency issue

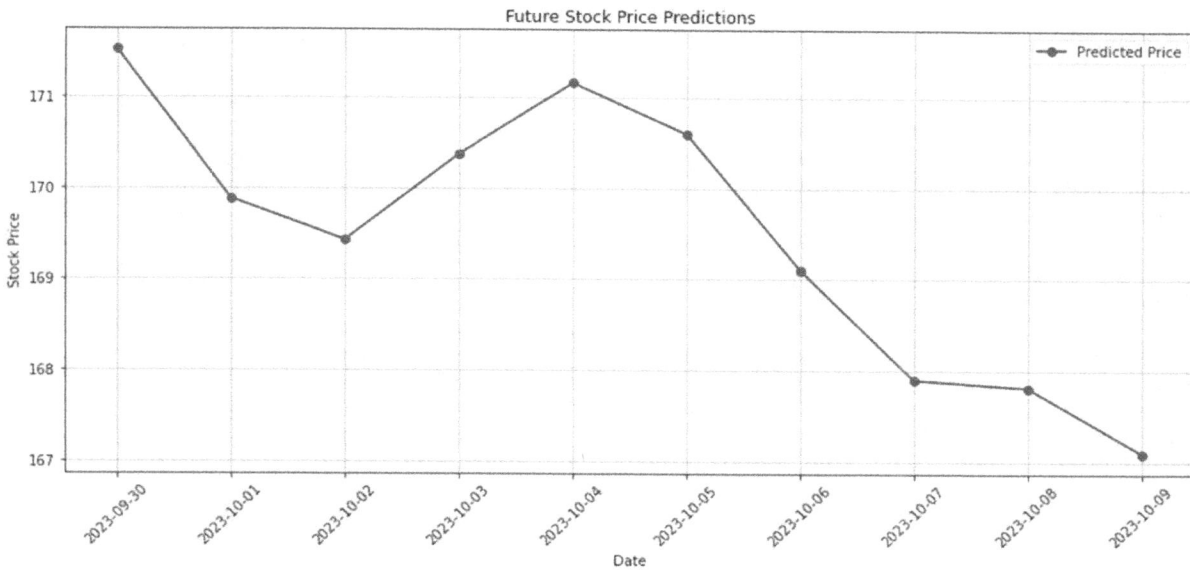

Fig. 46.2   Predictions after solving the dependency issue

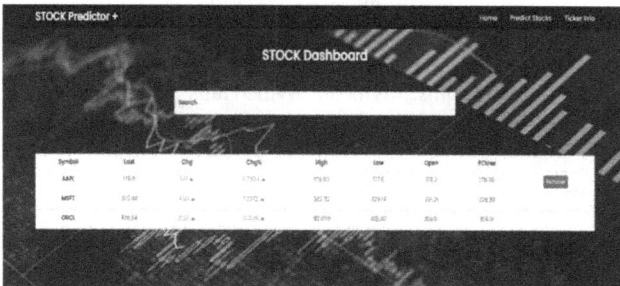

Fig. 46.3   Home page of the application

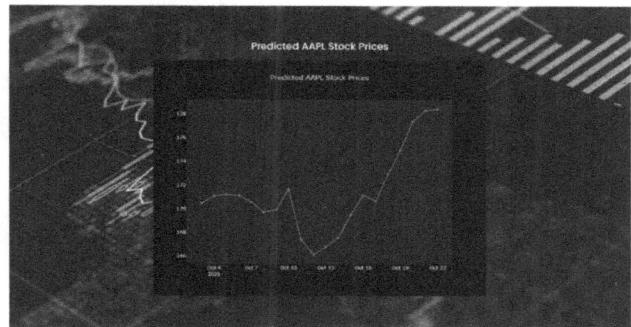

Fig. 46.5   Dashboard for predicted stock prices

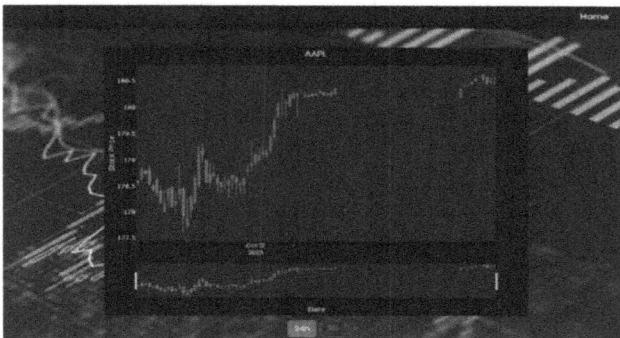

Fig. 46.4   Dashboard for real-time stocks

and NLP techniques enhances existing methodologies, offering a practical tool for informed decision-making. Future enhancements, including real-time updates, broader stock range, and enriched data, will further improve the system's reliability and adaptability in dynamic financial markets.

REFERENCES

1. O.B. Sezer, M.U. Gudelek, A.M. Ozbayoglu, "Financial Time Series Forecasting with Deep Learning: A Systematic Literature Review: 2005–2019," 2019. [Online]. Available: http://arxiv.org/abs/1911.13288.
2. Eunsuk Chong, Chulwoo Han, Frank C. Park, "Deep learning networks for stock market analysis and prediction: Methodology, data representations, and case studies," *Expert Systems with Applications,* vol. 83, pp. 187–205, 2017.
3. Mehar Vijh, Deeksha Chandola, Vinay Anand Tikkiwal, Arun Kumar, "Stock Closing Price Prediction using Machine Learning Techniques," *Procedia Computer Science,* vol. 167, pp. 599–606, 2020.
4. Mahla Nikou, Gholamreza Mansourfar, Jamshid Bagherzadeh, "Stock price prediction using DEEP learning algorithm and its comparison with machine learning algorithms," *Intelligent Systems in Accounting, Finance and Management,* vol. 26, pp. 164–174, 2019.

5. Lin Chen, Zhilin Qiao, Minggang Wang, Chao Wang, Ruijin Du, Harry Eugene Stanley, "Which Artificial Intelligence Algorithm Better Predicts the Chinese Stock Market?," *IEEE Access,* vol. 6, pp. 48625–48633, 2018.

6. Osman Hegazy, Omar Soliman, Mustafa Abdul Salam, "A Machine Learning Model for Stock Market Prediction," *International Journal of Computer Science and Telecommunications,* vol. 4, pp. 17–23, 12 2013.

7. Yunus Yetis, Halid Kaplan, Mo Jamshidi, "Stock market prediction by using artificial neural network," in *2014 World Automation Congress (WAC),* Waikoloa, HI, USA, 2014.

8. Siddhaling Urolagin, "Text Mining of Tweet for Sentiment Classification and Association with Stock Prices," in *International Conference on Computer and Applications (ICCA),* 2017.

9. Pranjal Chakraborty, Ummay Sani Pria, Md. Rashad Al Hasan Rony, Mahbub Alam Majumdar, "Predicting stock movement using sentiment analysis of Twitter feed," in *6th International Conference on Informatics, Electronics and Vision & 7th International Symposium in Computational Medical and Health Technology (ICIEV-ISCMHT),* 2017.

10. Dang Lien Minh, Abolghasem Sadeghi-Niaraki, Huynh Duc Huy, Kyungbok Min, Hyeonjoon Moon, "Deep Learning Approach for Short-Term Stock Trends Prediction Based on Two-Stream Gated Recurrent Unit Network," *IEEE Access,* vol. 6, pp. 55392–55404, 2018.

11. Weiling Chen, Chai Kiat Yeo, Chiew Tong Lau, Bu Sung Lee, "A study on real-time low-quality content detection on Twitter from the users' perspective," *PLOS ONE,* vol. 12, pp. 1–22, 2017.

12. Qing Li, Tiejun Wang, Ping Li, Ling Liu, Qixu Gong, Yuanzhu Peter Chen, "The effect of news and public mood on stock movements," *Information Sciences,* vol. 278, pp. 826–840, 2014.

13. Seungwoo Jeon, Bonghee Hong, Victor Chang, "Pattern graph tracking-based stock price prediction using big data," *Future Generation Computer Systems,* vol. 80, pp. 171–187.

14. Saloni Mohan, Sahitya Mullapudi, Sudheer Sammeta, Parag Vijayvergia, D. Anastasiu, "Stock Price Prediction Using News Sentiment Analysis," in *Fifth International Conference on Big Data Computing Service and Applications (BigDataService),* San Francisco East Bay, 2019.

15. Wei Liang, Songyou Xie, Dafang Zhang, Xiong Li, Kuan-ching Li, "A Mutual Security Authentication Method for RFID-PUF Circuit Based on Deep Learning," *ACM Transactions on Internet Technology (TOIT),* vol. 22, pp. 1–20, 2021.

16. Pooja Mehta, Sharnil Pandya, Ketan V. Kotecha, "Harvesting social media sentiment analysis to enhance stock market prediction using deep learning," *PeerJ Computer Science,* vol. 7, 2021.

17. David M. Q. Nelson, Adriano C. M. Pereira, Renato A. de Oliveira, "Stock market's price movement prediction with LSTM neural networks," in *International Joint Conference on Neural Networks (IJCNN),* Anchorage, AK, USA, 2017.

18. Achyut Ghosh, Soumik Bose, Giridhar Maji, Narayan Debnath, Soumya Sen, "Stock Price Prediction Using LSTM on Indian Share Market," in *32nd International Conference on Computer Applications in Industry and Engineering,* San Diego, 2019.

19. John Kordonis, Symeon Symeonidis, Avi Arampatzis, "Stock Price Forecasting via Sentiment Analysis on Twitter," in *20th Pan-Hellenic Conference on Informatics,* Patras, Greece, 2016.

20. Alexander Porshnev, Ilya Redkin, Alexey Shevchenko, "Machine Learning in Prediction of Stock Market Indicators Based on Historical Data and Data from Twitter Sentiment Analysis," in *International Conference on Data Mining Workshops,* 2013.

Note: All the figures and tables in this chapter were made by the authors.

Transformative Applied Research in Computing, Engineering, Science and Technology – Dr. Damayanthi Dahanayake et al. (eds)

47

Unraveling Thalassemia's Genetic Code— A Molecular Diagnostic Approach

K.A.D.E. Kahandawala*, Madhavi Hewadikaram

Department of Biomedical Science, NSBM Green University,
Sri Lanka

Abstract

Thalassemia is an inherited blood disorder characterized by reduced expression of one of the two globin chains in the hemoglobin molecule. There are two types of thalassemia: alpha and beta, based on the fact which part of the hemoglobin molecule is affected. Prenatal and postnatal molecular diagnosis, as well as genetic counseling, is becoming increasingly crucial for the prevention and treatment of the disease. Molecular diagnosis of thalassemia involves various techniques to detect the mutations or deletions in the alpha or beta globin genes that cause the disorder. These methods have revolutionized the accurate detection and classification of thalassemia mutations, enabling precise clinical management and early intervention. Gap-PCR, Reverse dot blot analysis, multiplex ligation-dependent probe amplification (MLPA), Single-tube Multiplex Amplification Refractory Mutation System Polymerase Chain Reaction (ARMS-PCR), and Next-generation and Third generation sequencing are some of these approaches. Each method has its advantages and limitations, and the choice is based on the method's availability, cost, and accuracy. This literature review provides an extensive examination of the various molecular diagnostic techniques utilized in thalassemia detection and explores how Next-Generation Sequencing (NGS) and Third-Generation Sequencing transform thalassemia diagnostics. Continued advancements in these techniques hold promise for further refining thalassemia diagnostics, ultimately leading to better disease management and a positive impact on global healthcare.

Keywords

Molecular diagnosis, Next-generation sequencing, Thalassemia, Third-generation sequencing

1. Introduction

The primary component of red blood cells (RBCs), hemoglobin (Hb), plays a role in providing oxygen to all human tissues. Adult hemoglobin (Hb A) is a tetrameric protein made up of two alpha (α) and two beta (β) globin chains, each with an area containing the heam group for binding oxygen [1]. Thalassemia is a heterogeneous set of inherited anemias caused by a decrease or absence of production of one or more normal globin chains in hemoglobin [2], [3]. Thalassemia is the most frequent monogenic disorder throughout the world. The Middle

*Corresponding author: kadekahandawala@students.nsbm.ac.lk

DOI: 10.1201/9781003616368-47

East, the Mediterranean nations, North and Central Africa, and southeastern as well as southern Asia all have higher rates of thalassemia [4].

The α-like and β-like genes, which code for the α and β chains of hemoglobin, are located on chromosomes 16 and 11, respectively [5]. Individuals inherit two α -globin genes, one each on chromosome 16, and two β -globin genes, one each on chromosome 11.

Thalassemia is characterized as α- or β-thalassemia based on the defective globin chain and underlying molecular abnormalities. Reduced synthesis of globin genes will result in α+ and β+ thalassemia, while absent synthesis of globin genes will result in α0 and β0 thalassemia. Approximately 1–5% of the world's population is thought to carry a hereditary thalassemia mutation, making it the most prevalent recessive disorder[6].

β-thalassemia major is the most common type of thalassemia, accounting for 73.9% of all cases [7]. According to global estimates, around 50,000 new individuals are born each year with a severe form of thalassemia. Nearly 80% of these births happen in developing countries. It is estimated that roughly 1.5% of the global population (80 to 90 million people) are carriers of β-thalassemia, with over 60,000 symptomatic individuals born each year [8].

Alpha thalassemia is most common in Southeast Asia, although it also occurs in the Mediterranean, the Middle East, India, and Sub-Saharan Africa, with carrier rates ranging from 15% to 30%. Alpha-thalassemia affects about 5% of the world's population [9]. Clinically, thalassemia is divided into three groups: (a) thalassemia major, which identifies individuals who have been dependent on blood transfusions and have severe anemia; (b) thalassemia minor, which often refers to persons who are carriers but have no clinical symptoms. (c) thalassemia intermedia, which is defined as patients with phenotypes varying in severity from mild to severe anemia with thalassemia-like bone changes [2].

Since there is no defined cure for thalassemia, the major measures of the thalassemia control approach are carrier screening and prenatal diagnosis for high-risk families [10]. Molecular diagnosis methods of thalassemia are techniques that can identify the specific mutations that cause thalassemia in a person's DNA, and help to diagnose thalassemia, determine its severity, and provide genetic counseling for patients and their families.

2. Molecular Basis of Alpha and Beta-Thalassemia

Alpha-thalassemia (α-thalassemia) involves HBA1 and HBA2 genes [11]. It includes types caused by gene deletions and other mutations. Defects typically result from deletions of one or both α-globin genes. A healthy person has four α-globin genes, two from each parent. In 95% of cases, either or both of the α-genes on chromosome 16 are deleted, reducing α-globin chain production. Some cases are due to point mutations, causing severe symptoms [12]. In fetuses, defective α-chain formation causes excess γ-chains resulting in Hb Bart's, while in adults, excess β-chains form Hb H [13]. The most serious type is Hb Bart's, with severity depending on the number of missing alleles.

Besides deletions, there are non-deletional types of α-thalassemia. Point mutations and minor deletions or insertions affecting gene expression are more common than complete gene deletions. Some non-deletion variants of α+ thalassemia can cause a more severe reduction in α-globin production than single-gene deletions [14].

β-thalassemia is an inherited condition caused by over 200 known mutations or deletions in the β-globin gene (HbB) on chromosome 11, resulting in either no or deficient β-globin production[15], [16].

Mutations leading to β-thalassemia include splice site mutations and nonsense mutations. Splice-site mutations result in abnormal transcripts and lower functional β -globin levels [17], while nonsense mutations introduce an early stop codon, producing incomplete or nonfunctional proteins [18], [19]. Having one defective or missing β gene causes mild symptoms (β-thalassemia minor). Two defective or missing genes lead to moderate (thalassemia intermedia) to severe symptoms (β thalassemia major or Cooley's anemia [20]. This type of thalassemia is the most common type found in Sri Lanka [21].

3. Conventional Molecular Techniques for Thalassemia Diagnosis

One of the prominent conventional methods is allele-specific PCR (ARMS PCR), which identifies specific mutations in globin genes by using primers to differentiate between normal and mutant alleles [22], [11]. Moatter et al. have reported that ARMS PCR is a beneficial method in the prenatal diagnosis of thalassemia, and it showed a higher success rate in mutation detection[23]. However according to [22], this method can only be used for identifying known mutations.

Dot-blot analysis; denatured DNA fragments are attached to a membrane and hybridized with allele-specific probes, identifying mutations associated with both α and β-thalassemia [6]. This method can be used to identify mutations associated with both α- and β-thalassemia.

Additionally, gap-PCR, a conventional technique, was employed to detect large deletions or insertions in the globin gene clusters [27]. According to Lin et al. stated that this method is the most commonly used method to identify the deleted regions associated with α- thalassemia, but it is not suitable for large-scale deletion screening [28].

Another method used to find deletions and duplications in the globin gene sequences was Multiplex Ligation-dependent Probe Amplification (MLPA) [29]. Basha et al. have stated that the MLPA method can detect α- globin gene deletions, including uncommon variations that may be missed by the usual Gap-PCR method. However, Lee et al. have expressed that this method has a low frequency of detecting point mutations [25], [26]. Table 47.1 summarizes the advantages and limitations of some of these conventional methods used in thalassemia diagnosis.

Table 47.1 Advantages and limitations of techniques used to diagnose thalassemia

Diagnostic Methods	Advantages	Limitations
Dot Blot Analysis [6], [24]	To detect point mutations and small deletions	Complicated processing Limited ability to process many samples
Gap-PCR [24]	Rapid diagnosis of α-thalassemias, sensitive method to detect common deletions; especially for α-thalassemia	Not suitable for large-scale screening
ARMS-PCR [22], [23]	High specificity and sensitivity, Rapid method that can be used to detect thalassemia genes	It can only be used to detect known mutations.
MLPA[25], [26]	Large chromosomal areas can be covered for deletion analysis.	Cannot detect point mutations and has a low-resolution

4. Role of Next-Generation Sequencing in Thalassemia Diagnosis

NGS expands sequencing capacity from a few hundred to several thousand base pairs in a single examination. NGS is based on massively parallel sequencing of clonally amplified DNA molecules [30]. It minimizes false negatives and false positives compared to traditional methods and simultaneously analyzes multiple genes in a single run, saving time and resources. The NGS workflow consists of several key steps: DNA extraction from patient samples, library preparation, sequencing, and finally, bioinformatics analysis [31] (as shown in Fig. 47.1).

It finds differences linked with thalassemia mutations by comparing the patient's DNA to a reference genome like insertions and deletions (indels) [32].

It detects a wide range of thalassemia-causing mutations, including complex and rare variants. This technology can be used for whole genome sequencing, whole exome sequencing, prenatal diagnosis, carrier screening, epigenetic analysis, and specifically targeted gene sequencing [33], [34].

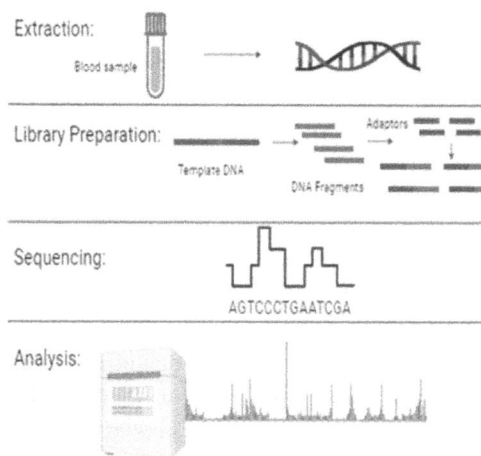

Fig. 47.1 The next-generation sequencing work flow

4.1 Noninvasive Prenatal Diagnosis (NIPD) of Thalassemia

Non-invasive prenatal diagnosis (NIPD) with next-generation sequencing (NGS) is a significant improvement in prenatal care, especially for discovering genetic abnormalities like thalassemia. This approach uses NGS to examine cell-free fetal DNA (cffDNA) in maternal blood, resulting in a complete genetic profile of the fetus [35].

NGS with NIPD provides numerous major benefits. It detects a broad range of genetic abnormalities with acceptable sensitivity and specificity, providing accurate and comprehensive information about the fetal genome. NGS-based NIPD can be conducted early in pregnancy, allowing for earlier decision-making and possible treatment options [36]. Erlich et al. have reported that nine out of ten reports were accurate in the NIPD method [32]. The accuracy of this method was again proved in studies conducted by Jiang et al. by diagnosing the fetal status of 12/13 families correctly [15].

4.2 Targeted Sequencing for Mutation Detection

It has been proven that NGS has a higher diagnostic rate with this targeted approach compared to traditional diagnosis methods [37]. Adekile et al. have proved a higher diagnostic rate of NGS (29.4%) when compared to the traditional diagnostic method (27.7%)[38].

This strategy is designed to focus exclusively on the regions of the genome known to be associated with thalassemia mutations, and it specifically targets the areas containing thalassemia-related genes, such as HBB, HBA1, and HBA2. This can reveal changes such as single nucleotide alterations, minor insertions, or deletions in the coding areas of hemoglobin genes in thalassemia [39].

4.3 Whole-Exome Sequencing (WES)

Whole-exome sequencing (WES) is a pioneering approach within the NGS toolkit, providing an entire overview of the human genome's protein-coding regions [40]. While targeted sequencing homes in specific regions; WES delves into the entire exome, enabling the discovery of novel mutations that might not have been captured by conventional approaches [30].

For example, a study conducted by Spring et al. has shown how the NGS method re-diagnosed thalassemia carriers as thalassemia intermedia using a whole exome sequencing approach [41]. WES is all about capturing the exome, the portion of the genome that encodes proteins. In this process, mRNA is typically reverse-transcribed into cDNA, which is then enriched for exonic sequences through targeted enrichment techniques. These cDNA fragments, representing the exons, are then sequenced using high-throughput sequencing platforms, generating vast numbers of short DNA sequences that can be analyzed to detect genetic variants [42], [43].

4.4 Carrier Screening

Carrier screening is an important component of thalassemia management and prevention because it addresses the genetic component of the condition by identifying individuals who are at risk of transmitting thalassemia-associated mutations [44]. Individuals who possess one normal and one altered gene (carrier status) in the context of an autosomal recessive condition such as thalassemia remain clinically unaffected but can convey the altered gene to their offspring[45] (as shown in Fig. 47.2).

NGS plays a critical role in carrier screening. For instance [46] was able to find an additional 35 carriers that were missed by traditional molecular genotyping techniques. He et al. have also compared the action of NGS for carrier screening over the diagnosis method [47]. NGS was also able to detect a higher carrier rate (49.5%) when compared to traditional methods.

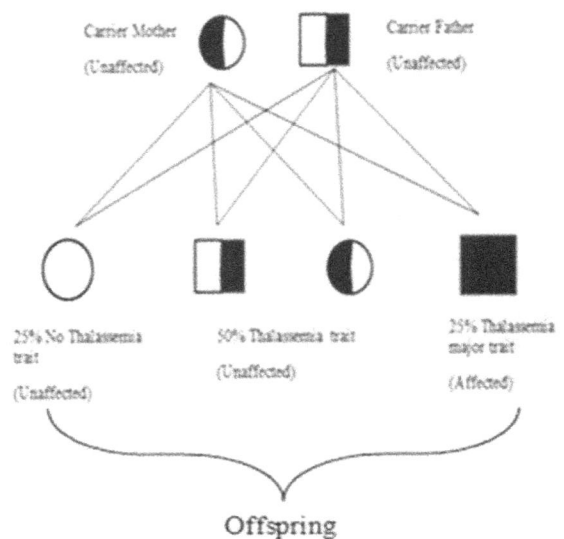

Fig. 47.2   The inheritance of thalassemia

5. Third-Generation Sequencing

Third-generation sequencing (TGS) is another latest method for thalassemia genetic testing [48]. Unlike NGS, which relies on short-read sequencing technologies, third-generation sequencing technologies enable the generation of long reads, thereby providing valuable insights into complex genomic variations, such as those often encountered in thalassemia [48]–[50].

Long-read sequencing reads DNA in longer segments, allowing it to screen larger genetic changes in thalassemia. It contributes to understanding the complexities of compound heterozygous mutations, which are common in thalassemia patients [51]. This approach enables for accurate assessment of whether mutations occur on the same allele, distinct alleles, or in cis or trans configurations [48], [52].

TGS technologies primarily consist of single-molecule real-time (SMRT) and nanopore sequencing. Pacific Biosciences (PacBio) invented the first TGS technology, SMRT sequencing, which was introduced in 2010. SMRT sequencing detects nucleotide binding while the DNA polymerase moves along a single DNA molecule, resulting in long reads with great precision and low error rates of up to tens of kilobases [53]. Oxford Nanopore Technologies (ONT) introduced nanopore sequencing in 2014, allowing for the determination of changes in DNA or RNA molecules traveling through a nanopore, resulting in novel sequencing technology. This method also generates lengthy reads with an average length of tens of kilobases [54].

Table 47.2 Example studies of thalassemia using NGS and TGS

Method	Application	Reference	Year	Findings
NGS	Noninvasive prenatal diagnosis	[32]	2022	NGS reported 9/10 correct fetal diagnosis with one inconclusive result
		[15]	2021	NGS correctly determined the fetal status of 12/13 families with thalassemia
	Whole exome sequencing	[41]	2017	NGS method re-diagnosed thalassemia carrier as thalassemia intermedia
	Target sequencing	[38]	2020	NGS has a higher diagnostic rate (29.4%) when compared with traditional diagnostic method(27.7%).
	Carrier screening	[46]	2017	NGS found an additional 35 carriers who were missed by traditional molecular genotyping techniques
		[47]	2017	NGS can detect a higher carrier rate (49.5%) when compared to traditional methods (22%)
TGS	Carrier screening	[56]	2021	TGS found 33 HBA/HBB mutations not identified by conventional methods.
		[60]	2022	Able to detect the HBB gene mutations of the carrier couples accurately.
	To identify rare variants	[55]	2023	TGS was able to yield a 7.14% increment in rare α- and β- globin gene variations associated with thalassemia compared with traditional methods.
		[61]	2022	TGS was able to identify 10 rare thalassemia variants
		[62]	2023	TGS identified additional variants in eight subjects that were not detected by conventional method.

Applying TGS technology will help in analyzing genomic structural variations, such as deletions, duplications, and inversions, which may be associated with thalassemia, detection of known and unknown mutations, and also for thalassemia carrier screening [55]. For instance, Liang et al. have confirmed the results about carriers, which were obtained by conventional methods (GAP-PCR, Dot Blot analysis) with no false negative or no false positive [56]. Single-molecule real-time sequencing was used by Wu et al. to analyze the genetic material of three β-thalassemia mutation carrier couples in the 7.7 kb and 7.4 kb HBB gene regions[50]. They were able to precisely identify the HBB gene alterations in all three couples. Zhuang et al. have reported how TGS became successful in identifying rare variants of thalassemia [48]. According to that TGS was able to yield a 7.14% increment in rare α- and β- globin gene variations associated with thalassemia compared with traditional methods (Gap –PCR)(Table 47.2).

6. Clinical Implications and Future Perspectives

Molecular genetic testing is useful in detecting individuals who have thalassemia traits that can lead to negative results in their offspring. Molecular diagnosis can aid in the identification of the exact mutation causing the disease [57]. It can also assist in identifying patients who are thalassemia carriers [25]. Stem cell transplantation has the potential to be an effective treatment for thalassemia [58].

CRISPR/Cas9 gene editing is a more powerful and efficient emerging technology that can effectively correct genes causing mutations when compared to previous gene therapy methods. The CRISPR/Cas9 approach has the potential to modify the genomes of β-thalassemia patients, offering hope for treatment[59].

7. Conclusion

Next-generation sequencing and third-generation sequencing were recently utilized to screen for thalassemia. It improves the precision of DNA analysis and enhances understanding of the genotype-phenotype correlation. NGS and TGS allow for less DNA usage and sample multiplexing, resulting in increased throughput. While exciting progress has been made in thalassemia diagnostics, some areas need further study. The cost of implementing NGS and Third-Generation Sequencing can be high, restricting their widespread acceptance, particularly in resource-limited settings.

Understanding how genetics, splicing patterns, and epigenetics work together requires more research to reveal their full roles in thalassemia. By addressing these gaps, strengthening thalassemia diagnostics can make a way for personalized treatments based on genetic information.

REFERENCES

1. G. [1] U. Hoeger, J. Robin, and H. Editors, Subcellular Biochemistry 94 Vertebrate and Invertebrate Respiratory Proteins, Lipoproteins and other Body Fluid Proteins. 2020.

2. X. Gu and Y. Zeng, "A review of the molecular diagnosis of thalassemia," Hematology, vol. 7, no. 4, pp. 203–209, 2002.

3. D. E. Sabath and C. M. E. Sam, "Molecular Diagnosis of Thalassemias and Hemoglobinopathies An ACLPS Critical Review," pp. 6–15, 2017.

4. R. Colah, A. Gorakshakar, and A. Nadkarni, "Global burden, distribution and prevention of β-thalassemias and hemoglobin e disorders," Expert Rev. Hematol., vol. 3, no. 1, pp. 103–117, 2010.

5. D. R. Higgs, "The molecular basis of α-thalassemia," Cold Spring Harb. Perspect. Med., vol. 3, no. 1, 2013.

6. V. Brancaleoni, E. Di Pierro, I. Motta, and M. D. Cappellini, "Laboratory diagnosis of thalassemia," Int. J. Lab. Hematol., vol. 38, pp. 32–40, 2016.

7. K. A. Kadhim, K. H. Baldawi, and F. H. Lami, "Prevalence, Incidence, Trend, and Complications of Thalassemia in Iraq," Hemoglobin, vol. 41, no. 3, pp. 164–168, 2017.

8. R. Jha and S. Jha, "Beta thalassemia - a review," J. Pathol. Nepal, vol. 4, no. 8, pp. 663–671, 2014.

9. H. Akhavan-Niaki et al., "Hematologic features of alpha thalassemia carriers.," Int. J. Mol. Cell. Med., vol. 1, no. 3, pp. 162–7, 2012.

10. H. W. Goonasekera, C. S. Paththinige, and V. H. W. Dissanayake, "Population screening for hemoglobinopathies," Annu. Rev. Genomics Hum. Genet., vol. 19, no. May, pp. 355–380, 2018.

11. D. Vijian, W. S. Wan Ab Rahman, K. T. Ponnuraj, Z. Zulkafli, and N. H. Mohd Noor, "Molecular detection of alpha thalassemia: A review of prevalent techniques," Medeni. Med. J., vol. 36, no. 3, pp. 257–269, 2021.

12. D. Vijian, W. S. Wan Ab Rahman, K. T. Ponnuraj, and Z. Zulkafli, "Clinical and Haematological Parameters of Commonly Reported Non-deletional α-thalassaemia Mutations in Southeast Asia: A Review," Malaysian J. Med. Heal. Sci., vol. 18, no. 5, pp. 190–199, 2022.

13. H. Tamary and O. Dgany, "Alpha-Thalassemia Summary Genetic counseling," Gene Rev., pp. 2–3, 2020.

14. L. P. W. Goh, E. T. J. Chong, and P. C. Lee, "Prevalence of alpha(α)-thalassemia in Southeast Asia (2010–2020): A meta-analysis involving 83,674 subjects," Int. J. Environ. Res. Public Health, vol. 17, no. 20, pp. 1–11, 2020.

15. F. Jiang et al., "Noninvasive prenatal testing for β -thalassemia by targeted nanopore sequencing combined with relative haplotype dosage (RHDO): a feasibility study," Sci. Rep., pp. 1–9, 2021.

16. S. He et al., "Molecular Characterization of α- and β-Thalassaemia Among Children From 1 to 10 Years of Age in Guangxi, A Multi-Ethnic Region in Southern China," Front. Pediatr., vol. 9, no. August, pp. 1–6, 2021.

17. J. Y. Chin et al., "Correction of a splice-site mutation in the beta-globin gene stimulated by triplex-forming peptide nucleic acids," Proc. Natl. Acad. Sci. U. S. A., vol. 105, no. 36, pp. 13514–13519, 2008.

18. K. R. Katsumura et al., "The Molecular Basis of β -Thalassemia The Molecular Basis of b -Thalassemia," 2014.

19. P. Ropero, A. Villegas, J. M. Nieto, F. A. González, and R. Martínez, "Novel nonsense mutation in the α 1-globin gene [HBA1 : C . 49A > T . is responsible for non-deletion α -thalassemia," Clin. Biochem., no. October, pp. 0–1, 2018.

20. S. Ali et al., "Current status of beta-thalassemia and its treatment strategies," Mol. Genet. Genomic Med., vol. 9, no. 12, pp. 1–14, 2021.

21. A. P. Premawardhana et al., "A nationwide survey of hospital-based thalassemia patients and standards of care and a preliminary assessment of the national prevention program in Sri Lanka," PLoS One, vol. 14, no. 8, pp. 1–11, 2019.

22. X. Yang et al., "Non-invasive prenatal diagnosis of thalassemia through multiplex PCR, target capture and next-generation sequencing," Mol. Med. Rep., vol. 22, no. 2, pp. 1547–1557, 2020.

23. T. Moatter, S. Ghani, T. Kausar, J. A. Pal, and M. Aban, "Prenatal screening for β-thalassemia major reveals new and rare mutations in the Pakistani population," Int. J. Hematol., vol. 95, no. 4, pp. 394–398, 2012.

24. M. Lin et al., "Development and evaluation of a reverse dot blot assay for the simultaneous detection of common alpha and beta thalassemia in Chinese," Blood Cells, Mol. Dis., vol. 48, no. 2, pp. 86–90, 2012.

25. J. S. Lee, S. I. Cho, S. S. Park, and M. W. Seong, "Molecular basis and diagnosis of thalassemia," Blood Res., vol. 56, no. April, pp. 39–43, 2021.

26. B. Basha, F. Mularo, and J. R. Cook, "Design, Validation, and Clinical Implementation of a Gap-Polymerase Chain Reaction Method for α-Thalassemia Genotyping Using Capillary Electrophoresis," Hemoglobin, vol. 41, no. 2, pp. 124–130, 2017.

27. T. Munkongdee et al., "Rapid diagnosis of α-thalassemia by melting curve analysis," J. Mol. Diagnostics, vol. 12, no. 3, pp. 354–358, 2010.

28. M. Lin et al., "Blood Cells , Molecules , and Diseases Development and evaluation of a reverse dot blot assay for the simultaneous detection of common alpha and beta thalassemia in Chinese," Blood Cells, Mol. Dis., vol. 48, no. 2, pp. 86–90, 2012.

29. S. Luo et al., "Detection of four rare thalassemia variants using Single-molecule realtime sequencing," Front. Genet., vol. 13, no. September, pp. 1–13, 2022.

30. V. Rizzuto et al., "Usefulness of NGS for Diagnosis of Dominant Beta-Thalassemia and Unstable Hemoglobinopathies in Five Clinical Cases," Front. Physiol., vol. 12, no. February, pp. 1–9, 2021.

31. T. Munkongdee, P. Chen, P. Winichagoon, S. Fucharoen, and K. Paiboonsukwong, "Update in Laboratory Diagnosis of Thalassemia," Front. Mol. Biosci., vol. 7, no. May, pp. 1–12, 2020.

32. H. A. Erlich et al., "Noninvasive Prenatal Test for β-Thalassemia and Sickle Cell Disease Using Probe Capture Enrichment and Next-Generation Sequencing of DNA in Maternal Plasma," J. Appl. Lab. Med., vol. 7, no. 2, pp. 515–531, 2022.

33. R. Russo, R. Marra, B. E. Rosato, A. Iolascon, and I. Andolfo, "Genetics and Genomics Approaches for Diagnosis and Research Into Hereditary Anemias," Front. Physiol., vol. 11, no. December, pp. 1–11, 2020.

34. F. Jiang et al., "Utilization of multiple genetic methods for prenatal diagnosis of rare thalassemia variants," Front. Genet., vol. 14, no. July, pp. 1–13, 2023.

35. I. Hudecova and R. W. K. Chiu, "SC," Best Pract. Res. Clin. Obstet. Gynaecol., 2016.

36. T. E. Madgett, "First Trimester Noninvasive Prenatal Diagnosis of Maternally Inherited Beta-Thalassemia Mutations," Clin. Chem., vol. 68, no. 8, pp. 1002–1004, 2022.

37. A. Nishiyama, T. Niihori, H. Warita, and R. Izumi, "Neurobiology of Aging Comprehensive targeted next-generation sequencing in Japanese familial amyotrophic lateral sclerosis," Neurobiol. Aging, 2017.

38. A. Adekile, N. A. Jeradi, and M. Fernandez, "The Diagnosis of HbS Genotypes and Identification of β -Thalassemia Mutations in Patients with Hbs β -," Blood, vol. 136, p. 38, 2020.

39. D. M. Toledo and K. A. Lafferty, "Clinical Perspective on Use of Long-Read Sequencing in Prenatal Diagnosis of Thalassemia," Clin. Chem., vol. 69, no. 3, pp. 211–212, 2023.

40. J. Majewski, J. Schwartzentruber, E. Lalonde, A. Montpetit, and N. Jabado, "What can exome sequencing do for you ?," 2011.

41. C. Spring, "Downloaded from molecularcasestudies.cshlp. org on July 2, 2017 - Published by Cold Spring Harbor Laboratory Press".

42. R. H. Zulkeflee, R. Bahar, M. Abdullah, M. A. R. Mohd Radzi, A. Md Fauzi, and R. Hassan, "Application of Targeted Next-Generation Sequencing for the Investigation of Thalassemia in a Developing Country: A Single Center Experience," Diagnostics, vol. 13, no. 8, 2023.

43. A. Achour, T. T. Koopmann, F. Baas, and C. L. Harteveld, "The Evolving Role of Next-Generation Sequencing in Screening and Diagnosis of Hemoglobinopathies," Front. Physiol., vol. 12, no. July, pp. 1–6, 2021.

44. R. Huang et al., "Back-to-Back Comparison of Third-Generation Sequencing and Next-Generation Sequencing in Carrier Screening of Thalassemia," Arch. Pathol. Lab. Med., 2023.

45. C. Mensah and S. Sheth, "Optimal strat e gies for car rier screen ing and pre na tal diag no sis of α - and β - thal as se mia," pp. 607–613.

46. X. Shang et al., "Rapid Targeted Next-Generation Sequencing Platform for Molecular Screening and Clinical Genotyping in Subjects with Hemoglobinopathies," EBioMedicine, vol. 23, pp. 150–159, 2017.

47. J. He et al., "Next-generation sequencing improves thalassemia carrier screening among premarital adults in a high prevalence population: The Dai nationality, China," Genet. Med., vol. 19, no. 9, pp. 1022–1031, 2017.

48. J. Zhuang et al., "Third-Generation Sequencing as a New Comprehensive Technology for Identifying Rare α- and β-Globin Gene Variants in Thalassemia Alleles in the Chinese Population," Arch. Pathol. Lab. Med., vol. 147, no. 2, pp. 208–214, 2023.

49. C. Peng et al., "Analysis of rare thalassemia genetic variants based on third-generation sequencing," Sci. Rep., vol. 12, no. 1, pp. 1–9, 2022.

50. H. Wu et al., "Long-read sequencing on the SMRT platform enables efficient haplotype linkage analysis in preimplantation genetic testing for β-thalassemia," J. Assist. Reprod. Genet., pp. 739–746, 2022.

51. S. Ardui, A. Ameur, J. R. Vermeesch, and M. S. Hestand, "Single molecule real-time (SMRT) sequencing comes of age: Applications and utilities for medical diagnostics," Nucleic Acids Res., vol. 46, no. 5, pp. 2159–2168, 2018.

52. S. Liu, H. Wang, D. Leigh, D. S. Cram, L. Wang, and Y. Yao, "Third-generation sequencing : any future opportunities for PGT ?," pp. 357–364, 2021.

53. L. Zhan, C. Gui, W. Wei, J. Liu, and B. Gui, "Third generation sequencing transforms the way of the screening and diagnosis of thalassemia: a mini-review," Front. Pediatr., vol. 11, no. July, 2023.

54. S. Hassan et al., "Next-Generation Sequencing (NGS) and Third-Generation Sequencing (TGS) for the Diagnosis of Thalassemia," Diagnostics, vol. 13, no. 3, 2023.

55. J. Zhuang et al., "Third-Generation Sequencing as a New Comprehensive Technology for Identifying Rare a- and b-Globin Gene Variants in Thalassemia Alleles in the Chinese Population," Arch. Pathol. Lab. Med., vol. 147, no. 2, pp. 208–214, 2023.

56. Q. Liang et al., "A More Universal Approach to Comprehensive Analysis of Thalassemia Alleles (CATSA)," J. Mol. Diagnostics, vol. 23, no. 9, pp. 1195–1204, 2021.

57. D. E. Sabath and C. M. E. Sam, "Molecular Diagnosis of Thalassemias and Hemoglobinopathies An ACLPS Critical Review," pp. 1–10, 2017.

58. M. Kleanthous, "Thalassemia and its relevance to personalized medicine," pp. 141–153, 2008.

59. A. Finotti and R. Gambari, "Combined approaches for increasing fetal hemoglobin (HbF) and de novo production of adult hemoglobin (HbA) in erythroid cells from β-thalassemia patients: treatment with HbF inducers and CRISPR-Cas9 based genome editing," Front. Genome Ed., vol. 5, no. July, pp. 1–13, 2023.

60. H. Wu et al., "Long-read sequencing on the SMRT platform enables efficient haplotype linkage analysis in preimplantation genetic testing for β-thalassemia," J. Assist. Reprod. Genet., vol. 39, no. 3, pp. 739–746, 2022.

61. C. Peng et al., "Analysis of rare thalassemia genetic variants based on third - generation sequencing," pp. 1–9, 2022.

62. Q. Liu et al., "Identification of rare thalassemia variants using third-generation sequencing," Front. Genet., vol. 13, no. January, pp. 1–9, 2023.

63. Y. Yorozu, M. Hirano, K. Oka, and Y. Tagawa, "Electron spectroscopy studies on magneto-optical media and plastic substrate interface," IEEE Transl. J. Magn. Japan, vol. 2, pp. 740–741, August 1987 [Digests 9th Annual Conf. Magnetics Japan, p. 301, 1982].

64. M. Young, The Technical Writer's Handbook. Mill Valley, CA: University Science, 1989.

Note: All the figures and tables in this chapter were made by the authors.

For Product Safety Concerns and Information please contact our EU
representative GPSR@taylorandfrancis.com
Taylor & Francis Verlag GmbH, Kaufingerstraße 24, 80331 München, Germany

www.ingramcontent.com/pod-product-compliance
Lightning Source LLC
Chambersburg PA
CBHW081046220326
41598CB00038B/7005